BOOK OF THE DEAD

C000253741

THE COMPLETE HISTORY OF
ZOMBIE CINEMA

UPDATED AND FULLY REVISED

JAMIE RUSSELL

BOOK OF THE DEAD

THE COMPLETE HISTORY OF
ZOMBIE CINEMA

BOOK OF THE DEAD
THE COMPLETE HISTORY OF ZOMBIE CINEMA

ISBN: 9781781169254

Published by
Titan Books
A division of Titan Publishing Group Ltd.
144 Southwark Street
London
SE1 0UP
United Kingdom

First edition: October 2014
2 4 6 8 10 9 7 5 3 1

Printed in the USA.

TM & © 2014 Jamie Russell. All Rights Reserved.

Front cover images copyright George Romero/Shutterstock.

Interior images courtesy of Corbis (p. 10 and p. 212), Frisson Film, Getty Images
(p. 23), H2ZZ Productions, the Hulton-Deutsch Collection, Hydro Films, the Kobal
Collection, MVD Entertainment Group, Off World Films & Bleeding Edge Films Ltd,
and Transcendental Graphics.

Did you enjoy this book? We love to hear from our readers. Please e-mail us at:
readerfeedback@titanemail.com or write to Reader Feedback at the above address.

To receive advance information, news, competitions, and exclusive offers online,
please sign up for the Titan newsletter on our website: **www.titanbooks.com**

No part of this publication may be reproduced, stored in a retrieval system, or
transmitted, in any form or by any means without the prior written permission of the
publisher, nor be otherwise circulated in any form of binding or cover other than that
in which it is published and without a similar condition being imposed on the
subsequent purchaser.

A CIP catalogue record for this title is available from the British Library.

BOOK OF THE DEAD

THE COMPLETE HISTORY OF ZOMBIE CINEMA

JAMIE RUSSELL

TITANBOOKS

ACKNOWLEDGEMENTS

The original crew: FAB Press, Paul Brown, Nigel Burrell, Ingo Ebeling, Daniel Etherington, Jamie Graham, Julian Grainger, Adele Hartely, Brian Holmes, Alan Jones, Sam McKinlay, Marc Morris, David Oakes, Alan Simpson, Ling Eileen Teo and David Whittaker.

The second edition team: Adam Newell, Laura Price and Simon Ward at Titan; my agent Andrew Mills; and the inspirational Nev Pierce, a true friend.

Zombie scholars: a long list that includes Kyle William Bishop, Arnold T. Blumberg, Peter Dendle, David Flint, Glenn Kay, Sarah Juliet Lauro, Shawn McIntosh, Kim Paffenroth, Keith J. Rainville, Gary D. Rhodes, Tony Williams and many others. On a personal note, I have come to realise that this book would never have been written if I hadn't picked up a copy of Kim Newman's seminal *Nightmare Movies* sometime around 1988 and read it obsessively until the pages came unglued. Thank you, Kim.

Filmmakers: Everyone who's ever made a zombie movie and contributed to this book's filmography; the generous John Landis; and, of course, the Don of the Dead himself: George A. Romero.

Family: My mother, father and stepmother; the Whitehouses; the McDonalds; and the Groombridges. Finally, my eternal love and gratitude goes to my wife Louise and our daughters Isobel and Alice, who have put up with me and the rest of the living dead for far too long.

CONTENTS

WOW, WHAT JUST HAPPENED?

Back in 2000, when I started researching the first edition of *Book of the Dead*, nobody really cared about zombies. They were the great unwashed of horror cinema, low-rent and disreputable. "Who wants to read a book about zombie movies?" people would ask when they found out what I was working on. It seemed I was writing for a niche audience, a handful of horror fans like myself who found zombies strangely compelling.

By the time the original edition of *Book of the Dead* was published by FAB Press in October 2005, things were already changing. Zombies were undergoing a huge renaissance thanks, in part, to *Resident Evil*, *Shaun of the Dead* and the *Dawn of the Dead* remake. It was a renaissance that went on and on, as *Book of the Dead* went through reprint after reprint. Almost a decade later, Z-culture is now a phenomenon, spanning movies, novels, comics and videogames. We're all zombies now.

Initially, I turned down requests to update *Book of the Dead*. I thought I'd said everything I wanted to say about zombies. But as the zombie boom grew it became clear that this wasn't just a popularity spike. An evolution was happening in the very fabric of what the zombie represents.

Writing this introduction in January 2014, not long after *World War Z*'s release on DVD, it feels like the time is right to reassess zombie cinema. This edition updates the original text in a few minor ways and inserts a couple of missing films – for instance, the forgotten 1960s British Nazi zombie movie *The Frozen Dead* (1966). It also adds an entirely new section focussing the boom in living dead cinema that has occurred since *Land of the Dead*'s release back in 2005. With more zombie films released in the period 2005 to 2013 than were in the original edition of this book, there is definitely enough to talk about.

In keeping with the zombie's own evolution, *Book of the Dead* now has an exciting new home at Titan Books. I'm grateful to Adam Newell for originally championing the update there, as well as Laura Price and Simon Ward for guiding it towards the edition you hold in your hands. I'm also indebted to my friend Nev Pierce for reading and commenting on early drafts.

The original *Book of the Dead* was written at a time when zombie scholarship was in its infancy. Since then there's been a huge explosion of interest in zombies, offering exciting new perspectives on why we're fascinated by the dead that walk. As ever, I remain convinced that Peter Dendle's exhaustive and pioneering two-volume work *The Zombie Movie Encyclopaedia* is the towering achievement of Z scholarship – and it's been a resource I've repeatedly turned to while writing this new update.

Many thanks to all those filmmakers who agreed to talk about their movies with me, or supply stills and screeners. I'm also grateful to all the zombie fans I've chatted with over the last few years, whether in person or via email, Facebook or Twitter. Their enthusiasm and insight into zombie culture has been inspiring and incredibly useful in helping me see why the living dead remain so popular.

Finally, a very special thanks to my family and friends. Their love and support has not only helped me survive endless zombies, but also my own very personal horror show after I had surgery to remove a spinal-cord tumour in 2012. Thank you.

With that, there's nothing left to do but invite you to read on. To those who have been with this book since the first edition, thank you and welcome back. To everyone else: I sincerely hope, in the nicest possible way, that this book gives you nightmares…

DEAD MEN WALKING

In his wide-ranging study of the Western world's fascination with horror, James B. Twitchell is strangely dismissive of the living dead. "The zombie myth seems flawed by its lack of complexity," he claims. "The zombie is really a mummy in street clothes with no love life and a big appetite. Both are automatons; neither is cunning nor heroic. They simply lumber about (Karloff called it 'my little walk'), shuffling their feet like dateless high school students before the prom. As opposed to the vampire, who is crafty, circumspect and erotic, these two cousins are subhuman slugs."

If that wasn't harsh enough, Twitchell goes on to brand the zombie "an utter cretin, a vampire with a lobotomy" before delivering a final, stinging *coup de grace* that would send any self-respecting ghoul rushing back to the graveyard: "This is what has tended to make [all the films following *I Walked with a Zombie* (1943)] little more than vehicles of graphic violence, full of people (usually men) poking each other and then occasionally eating them. The zombie is so shallow [...] even Abbott and Costello refused to meet with him."[1] Ouch!

Few horror movie monsters are as maligned as the zombie. While vampires, werewolves and even serial killers command respect, the zombie is never treated as anything other than a buffoon who stumbles around on the margins of horror cinema messily decaying. There are no aristocrats, blue bloods or celebrities among zombies, no big-name stars or instantly recognizable faces, just low-rent, anonymous monsters who usually can't talk, can barely walk and spend most of their energy trying to hold their decomposing bodies together.

Zombies are the great unwashed of horror cinema, soulless creatures that wander around without personality or purpose – a grotesque parody of the end that awaits us all. For all their lack of finesse or style, though, the living dead have been a constant presence in horror films since the 1930s, with a filmography that includes many critically acclaimed and popular films: *White Zombie* (1932), *I Walked with a Zombie* (1943), *Invasion of the Body Snatchers* (1956), *Night of the Living Dead* (1968), *Dawn of the Dead* (1978), *The Beyond* (orig. *L'aldilà*, 1981), *Dellamorte Dellamore* (1993), *28 Days Later* (2002) and *Shaun of the Dead* (2004).

So why hasn't the zombie ever been treated seriously until recently? Partly it's because the living dead lack an established literary heritage. Dracula, Frankenstein's monster, Dr Jekyll and Mr. Hyde and even the Wolf Man can boast a lineage that stretches back to Gothic fiction, European folklore and ancient legends. In contrast, the zombie is the most modern of monsters, a twentieth-century interloper whose first fully fledged appearance in the English-speaking world dates back to the publication of *The Magic Island*, William Seabrook's groundbreaking study of Haiti, in 1929.

Without the force of history behind it the zombie became a forlorn figure, cast aside by most movie fans as a second-rate villain with none of the instantly recognizable legitimacy – or celebrity – of Count Dracula or Frankenstein's monster. It's no wonder, then, that zombies have never made the cover of *Empire* magazine, are rarely seen at the Oscars and don't get invited to appear on many talk shows. Boris Karloff may have become famous for his turn as Frankenstein's monster, but no one has ever become famous playing one of the living dead. Even Bela Lugosi, a horror actor not known for being choosy about his roles, always played the zombie master and never one of the walking corpses.

Given the lowly status of its monstrous stars, it is not surprising that the zombie movie remained on the cultural margins for so long. Rejected by the academy – scholarly studies of horror movies generally prefer to discuss vampires, werewolves and even serial killers before the living dead – these films were consigned to the graveyard of popular culture, and the zombie itself was traditionally *persona non grata* with everyone except those horror fans who like their movies raw and bloody.

What has always troubled critics and mainstream audiences about the zombie is its frequent appearance in such terrible films. There's simply no way of getting around the fact that the zombie, more than any other horror monster, has an appalling track record in terms of quality control. Whether starring in Poverty Row-era trash, Italian rip-offs or homemade shot-on-video shockers, the living dead are often found lurking in movies that are low on stars, short on cash and often hurried into the cinematic equivalent of a shotgun wedding.

Yet just because some of these outings fall far below the standard set by mainstream A-list Hollywood doesn't mean that they're not worthy of serious attention. Indeed, it is often the very marginality of these zombie movies that makes them so fascinating. The aim of this book is to chart the history of the zombie in the West and, in particular, its development as a horror-movie icon. I hope to trace the historical and cultural shifts that brought the zombie out of Africa and into the horror film industries of America and Europe via the Caribbean.[2] Why did the zombie first come to the attention of the American public in the late 1920s? Why has it had a constant screen presence ever since? What does our fascination with – and frequent hatred of – the zombie tell us about ourselves? And why did zombies suddenly burst into the mainstream in 2005?

The monsters that dominate any particular culture or period offer an unusual insight into the specific fears and anxieties that characterise that historical moment. As horror theorist Judith Halberstam argues, "monsters are meaning machines" whose existence gives us insight into the anxieties of the culture that produced them.[3] After all, the very word "monster" has etymological roots that can be traced back to the Latin *monstrare*, meaning: to show, to display, to de*monstrate*.[4]

Since it's such a recent addition to the Western world's pantheon of bogeymen, the zombie is a monster whose cultural significance isn't shrouded by centuries of over-familiarity. Entering American – and then European – popular culture in the late 1920s at the height of the United States' geopolitical interest in Haiti, the zombie was appropriated from Afro-Caribbean culture for a wide variety of different ends.

Ultimately, the zombie is a symbol of mankind's most primitive anxiety: the fear of death. Full of a morbid sense of the body's limitations and frailties, the zombie myth is closely bound to our troubled relationship with our own bodies. That's enough to make it significantly different from the vampire legend and from those stories of the dead returning to life as ghastly apparitions or demons, which is why films about the "resurrected" – such as *City of the Dead* (aka *Horror Hotel*, 1960) and *Baron Blood* (1972) – are absent from this book's filmography. Put simply, the zombie is a corpse reanimated through some form of magic or mad science that returns to "life" without regaining any of its former personality.

In the many ways it has been deployed in Western popular culture, however, the zombie has slowly been transformed. It has come to signify something much more complex that just the fear of death. Growing out of a wide range of cultural anxieties – from American imperialism to domestic racial tensions, Depression-era fears about unemployment, Cold War paranoia about brainwashing, post-1960s political disenfranchisement and AIDS-era body horror – the zombie has become, as we will see, a potent symbol of the apocalypse. It's a monster whose appearance always threatens to challenge mankind's faith in the order of the universe.

Forever poised in the space between the traditional Western understandings of white/black, civilised/savage and life/death, the zombie is a harbinger of doom. Its very existence hints at the possibility of a world that cannot be contained within the limits of human understanding, a world in which these binary oppositions no longer stand fixed. Trampling over our cherished certainties, the zombie is, above all else, a symbol of our ordered universe turned upside down as death becomes life and life becomes death. In the chapters that follow, this book hopes to explain the allure of such a catastrophic occurrence, placing the development of the zombie in its socio-historical context in an attempt to understand why it is that, even after all these years, we are still so fascinated with the dead that walk.

CHAPTER ONE

CARIBBEAN TERRORS

I. TRACKING THE WALKING DEAD

It was in 1889 in the pages of *Harpers Magazine* that the zombie made its debut appearance in the English-speaking world, in a short article by journalist and amateur anthropologist Lafcadio Hearn entitled "The Country of the Comers-Back". Although the term "zombie" was first recorded in *The Oxford English Dictionary* in 1819, and was frequently heard mentioned by slaves in America's Deep South in the latter part of the 18th century, it was Hearn's article that became the first widely circulated report of the existence of the living dead.[5]

A Greek by birth, Hearn emigrated to the United States in 1869. He travelled out to the island of Martinique in 1887 to study the local customs and folklore for a series of popular articles on life in the Caribbean. Among the many stories and legends he came across on his travels around the island there was one in particular that fascinated him: the story of the *corps cadavres* or "walking dead". Wherever he went, the islanders talked in hushed tones about the disaster that would befall anyone unlucky enough to encounter one of the horrific beings known as zombies. Whenever Hearn asked them to explain what these creatures were and where they came from, his questions were greeted with tightly sealed lips. No one, it seemed, was willing to enlighten him about the *corps cadavres* and he could only speculate about the link between these mysterious monsters and the island's nickname of "*le pays de revenants*" (the country of the comers-back).

Even when Hearn did find people who were willing to speak to him about the *corps cadavres*, the contradictory anecdotes, vague stories and superstitious mumblings he encountered proved more confusing than illuminating. His journey through the mountainous region near Calebasse was typical of his experience. Spending the night in the home of a local family, Hearn decided to question them about island superstition. As supper was being cleared away, the traveller asked his host's eldest daughter to tell him what she knew of the zombie. Replying in French – the language stamped on the island's populace by years of colonial rule – the young girl gave him an answer that was as vague as it was intriguing: "*Zombi? Mais ça fais dèsodè lanuitt, zombi!*" ("Zombie? It is something that causes disorder in the night.").

Perplexed, Hearn tried asking the girl's mother for her views on the subject. The old woman gave him a longer, though no more illuminating, explanation: "When you pass along the high road at night, and you see a great fire, and the more you walk to get to it the more it moves away, it is the zombie that makes that... Or if a horse with three legs passes you: that is a zombie." Warming to the topic, her daughter chimed in with some additional information: "Or again, if I were to see a dog that high [she held her hand about five feet above the floor] coming into our house at night, I would scream: *Mi Zombi!*"[6]

Unable to get to the bottom of the mystery surrounding the *corps cadavres*, Hearn returned to America with little to offer *Harpers Magazine* other than a colourful account of his travels. Even though his mention of the zombie was enough to ensure that he would go down as one of the first white Westerners to popularise the notion of the walking dead, it would be left to a very different writer to bring the zombie to the world's attention. In 1928 the American adventurer William

Seabrook arrived in Haiti, the so-called "voodoo capital" of the Caribbean. Like Martinique, St Croix and most of the Lesser Antilles, Haiti was dominated by zombie legends, and so it wasn't long before Seabrook's curiosity was piqued by stories of the walking dead. However, unlike Hearn, Seabrook wasn't the kind of man to be fobbed off with tales of three-legged horses. Researching Haiti's superstitions for a full-length book on the island's voodoo culture, he was determined to get to the bottom of the mystery of the zombie.

Born in Westminster, Maryland on 22 February 1887 – coincidentally, the same year that Hearn first visited Martinique – Seabrook studied at the University of Geneva before graduating into a career as a journalist, foreign correspondent and daring adventurer. A veteran of the First World War (he was gassed at Verdun in 1916 and cited for the *Croix de Guerre*), he went on to become a peripheral member of the "Lost Generation" of American writers and artists who congregated in 1920s Paris – a group that included such luminaries as Gertrude Stein, William Faulkner and Ernest Hemingway.

Seabrook's reputation rested on his non-fiction work. His first book, the wonderfully titled *Adventures in Arabia: Among the Bedouins, Druses, Whirling Dervishes & Yezidee Devil Worshipers*, was published to great acclaim in 1928. Seabrook's crisp prose, coupled with his unquenchable desire to sample every unusual aspect of the cultures that he

The American author William Seabrook (1886–1945), *c.*1930.

visited, paved the way for a series of autobiographical travelogues about his adventures in Haiti (*The Magic Island*, 1929) and Africa (*Jungle Ways*, 1931; *The White Monk of Timbuktu*, 1934), as well as a candid account of his treatment for alcoholism (*Asylum*, 1935) and a book on the occult (*Witchcraft: Its Power in the World Today*, 1940).

His willingness to throw himself into his research in the hope of finding material that would entertain, shock and horrify his readers was one of the more distinctive features of his work. It was also the source of his reputation as a daring – and rather unusual – adventurer. At first sight, no one would have ever guessed that this short and unimposing man was anything out of the ordinary. Arriving in Haiti's bustling capital of Port-au-Prince in 1928, Seabrook was hardly conspicuous, even as a white man. Haiti had fallen under American rule in 1915 and the island was awash with white soldiers, bankers, clerks and businessmen. With his well-groomed moustache, cleft chin and narrow, intense blue eyes, Seabrook looked like just another white-collar American drawn to the so-called "Black Republic" of Haiti in the hope of combining exotic adventure with financial reward.[7] A rare photograph of the author in *The Magic Island* shows a stern yet vaguely comical figure; khaki shirt sleeves rolled up to the elbow to let his pale arms catch the glare of the Caribbean sun, gallopers and riding boots recalling the stereotype of the 1920s white explorer. All that is missing, perhaps somewhere off camera, is a pith helmet.

In reality, though, Seabrook was anything but ordinary. From his friendship with the notorious occultist Aleister Crowley to his penchant for bizarre sexual encounters, he cultivated a reputation that owed more to the ideals of artistic bohemianism than adventuring. His sexual peccadilloes were the stuff of legend. According to one infamous rumour, he travelled everywhere – whether through the jungles of Africa or the deserts of Arabia – with a suitcase full of whips and chains. It was a story that was given added credence after one of his bohemian circle, the photographer Man Ray, recounted how Seabrook had asked him to watch over his apartment one afternoon. Man Ray arrived to find a young girl "nude except for a soiled loincloth, with her hands behind her back chained to the post [of the staircase] with a padlock."[8] The astonished photographer was given specific instructions not to untie her, since she was being paid handsomely for her services.

Such enthusiasm for the bizarre spilled over into Seabrook's writing. This was an author who was ready to gamble life and limb to bring back sensational stories of exotic native cultures that his readers would be unlikely to ever see for themselves. His thirst for the unusual – and his belief in writing only about what he'd experienced first-hand – led him into a series of hair-raising adventures in Arabia, Haiti and Africa. Indeed, he was so scrupulous about the necessity of subjective experience that he refused to write about cannibalism for his book *Jungle Ways* until he'd actually tasted human flesh. Having missed the chance to sup with cannibals while in the heart of Africa, Seabrook paid a Paris hospital orderly to secure him a pound of flesh from the body of a workman killed in a traffic accident.

With his prize neatly tucked away in a surgical napkin, he rushed over to a friend's apartment and convinced his cook to roast, broil and stew pieces of the meat, telling her that it was "a kind of wild goat that no one had ever eaten before." Then, as he sampled the human dish, he made notes. It tasted, he later said, like pork, except that it needed more seasoning.[9]

Quite how much truth there was in these fantastic stories, only Seabrook knows. But whatever the extent of their veracity, they proved one thing: he was someone who knew how to transform the ordinary into the sensational. It was a talent that would inform his work on Haitian voodoo and, in particular, the zombie. Attracted to the occult, the unusual and the just plain weird, Seabrook proved to be the perfect person to uncover the stories of Haiti's voodoo lore. Not for him a vague article in the pages of *Harpers Magazine*; his work would reach a far more receptive audience, eager to know the truth about the walking dead.

II. THE ORIGINS OF THE ZOMBIE

As Seabrook tells the story in his book *The Magic Island*, it was a Haitian farmer called Polynice who first introduced him to some real-life zombies. During the course of his research into the island's voodoo superstitions, Seabrook had already established far more about the *corps cadavres* than Hearn had ever dreamt of. Travelling the length and breadth of Haiti, interviewing as many islanders as possible, taking part in voodoo rites and hoarding as much information about the mysteries of the island's superstitions as he could lay his hands on, Seabrook had become quite an expert on voodoo lore by the time he encountered Polynice.

For the Haitians who Seabrook talked to, the zombie was a powerful symbol of fear, misery and doom. It was also an integral part of the religious beliefs that dominated the island. The origins of Caribbean *voudoun* can be traced to the moment when the first slaves were transported from Africa into the West Indies. Within fifty years of arriving on the island that would later become known as Haiti, the first European settlers had wiped out the indigenous population through a combination of brutal violence and deadly disease. In an attempt to bolster the declining number of natives – and keep the lucrative production of sugar cane running smoothly – hundreds of thousands of slaves were shipped across the ocean from West Africa. As a result of this interference in the island's population, Haiti's indigenous culture was irrevocably altered as the native Indians were systematically replaced by a population of around 70,000 whites and mulattoes who dominated a slave force of half a million Africans.

In the close cultural confines of the island, the slaves' religious beliefs gradually transformed into a complex hybrid of African animism and Roman Catholicism that eventually became known to Westerners as "voodoo". Despite various attempts to outlaw these heathen practices during the Spanish and French rule of Haiti, voodoo flourished and strengthened in the face of adversity.

One of the central concepts in most voodoo ceremonies is the idea of possession by the gods. During these ceremonies, music and dance are used to encourage a trance-like state that will enable a god to descend and take control of one of the assembled worshippers. In order for a person to be possessed in this way, their essential soul has to be removed from their body. According to the tenets of the voodoo faith, a person is comprised of two souls, the *gros-bon-ange* (literally, the big good angel) and the *ti-bon-ange* (the little good angel). The first of these is an individual's life force, the second is everything that defines them as *them*. For a god to take possession of a worshipper, the second of these two souls has to be cast out of the body. The spirit of the god then takes over the empty shell of flesh. Later, when the god departs, the person's *ti-bon-ange* returns to the body. In voodoo, much as in Christianity, the soul and the body are considered separate entities and thus one can exist without the other.

The very real danger – and it is here that the concept of the zombie begins – is that if a person's soul can be separated from their body during a voodoo rite, an unscrupulous sorcerer might make this kind of separation occur outside of these closely managed ceremonies. According to zombie legend, such necromancy usually occurred after the sorcerer brought about the victim's "death" through a combination of magic and potions. After the unlucky victim had mysteriously fallen ill and apparently died, the sorcerer captured their essential soul and, on the eve of the burial, opened up their grave and removed the body. The sorcerer could then bring this corpse back to "life" as an obedient, mindless slave that could be put to work on some distant part of the island where it was unlikely to be recognised.

Since the existence of zombies was considered common knowledge in Haiti, the families of the newly dead did their best to prevent the bodies of loved ones from being reanimated. If they were wealthy, they'd bury the body in a proper tomb that was solid enough to deter intruders; if they were poor, the corpse was interned beneath heavy masonry. Often the family would post a guard at the graveside to watch over the site until the body had had time to decompose. Alternatively, the corpse might be buried near a busy street or crossroads. In more extreme circumstances, the corpse was "killed" again – shot through the head or injected with poison – to prevent the body being of any use to grave robbers.

If such precautions weren't followed, there was no doubting the potential horror of what could happen: the body of the dead loved one might rise from the grave as a zombie. As the origins of the word indicate, it was a horrifying prospect. Linguists have claimed that the etymological root of "zombi" might be derived from any (or all) of the following: the French *ombres* (shadows); the West Indian *jumbie* (ghost); the African Bonda *zumbi* and Kongo *nzambi* (dead spirit). It may also have derived from the word *zemis*, a term used by Haiti's indigenous Arawak Indians to describe the soul of a dead person.

For most Haitians, the predominant fear was not of being attacked by zombies, but of *becoming* one. The best horror stories have always been those that tap into their audience's daily fears. The success of the Caribbean zombie as a figure of superstition was because it did exactly that. For a population whose ancestors had been captured, shackled and shipped out of Africa to the far-off islands of the Caribbean, dominated by vicious slave masters and forced to work for nothing more than the bare minimum of food to keep them strong enough to live another day, the zombie symbolised the ultimate horror. Instead of an escape into paradise, death might just be the beginning of an eternity of work under a different master, the voodoo sorcerer. Nothing, for a nation that had been born into slavery and had only just succeeded in throwing off the imperial shackles of its European oppressors, could be more terrifying.

As biologist and anthropologist Wade Davis writes, "Zombis [sic] do not speak, cannot fend for themselves, do not even know their names. Their fate is enslavement. Yet given the availability of cheap labour, there would seem to be no economic incentive to create a force of indentured service. Rather, given the colonial history, the concept of enslavement implies that the peasant fears, and the zombi [sic] suffers, a fate that is literally worse than death – the loss of physical liberty that is slavery, and the sacrifice of personal autonomy implied by the loss of identity."[10]

Seabrook already had a fair sense of most of this when he sat down to talk to Polynice, since his research into the island's voodoo culture had been exhaustive to say the least. As he later wrote in *The Magic Island*, he knew that the zombie was supposed to be "a soulless human corpse, still dead, but taken from the grave and endowed by sorcery with a mechanical semblance of life – it is a dead body which is made to walk and act and move as if it were alive."[11] Yet he had no idea of quite how seriously the islanders took these stories of the walking dead.

During the course of his conversation with the farmer, Seabrook quizzed him about all manner of mythical creatures, from vampires to werewolves to ghosts. Polynice scoffed loudly at each of these monsters, claiming that they were nothing more than old wives' tales. But when Seabrook enquired about the legend of the zombie, the farmer's tone changed and he became deeply serious, warning his newfound friend that the zombie was more than just a legend. "They exist to an extent you whites do not dream of," he told Seabrook in hushed tones.[12] "At this very moment in the moonlight, there are *zombies* working on this island, less than two hours ride from my own habitation [...] If you will ride with me tomorrow night, yes, I will show you dead men working in the canefields."[13] Before he fulfilled this promise, this farmer recounted to Seabrook what would become the first proper zombie story to be published in the West.

In 1918 the Haitian sugarcane crop was larger than usual. Concerned that this bumper harvest would be too much for the regular workforce to cope with, the Haitian-American Sugar Company (HASCO) offered bonuses to farmers to help them bring in the crop. Desperate for the money that was being offered, poverty-stricken Haitians of all ages streamed into the HASCO plantations. One man, who some of the farmers knew as Ti Joseph of Colombier, arrived with a ragged-looking group of men and women. The other farmers realised immediately that these blank-faced creatures were zombies, yet the white bosses of HASCO didn't care who or what they were, as long as they were good workers.

Camping out on the edge of the plantation, Ti Joseph and his wife Croyance kept the zombies away from the rest of the workforce, partly because the creatures were terrified of the noise of the sugar factory but also out of fear that someone might recognise them as dead friends or relatives. Even at mealtimes the zombies were kept apart as Croyance fed them a special *bouillie* (stew) that she carefully prepared without seasoning since

salt was the one thing that could free a zombie from the sorcerer's control.

The living dead workforce toiled in the sun-baked fields for several weeks until the annual *Fête Dieu* holiday when HASCO granted its employees a short break so that they could attend the island's many celebrations. Ti Joseph decided to keep the zombies billeted in the cane fields to avoid any suspicious questioning, but since he was eager not to miss out on the festivities he told his wife to watch over them while he travelled into Port-au-Prince to join the carnival. Angry at being left to babysit the living dead slaves, Croyance decided to ignore her husband's instructions and took the zombies into a nearby town to watch the local processions.

Feeling sorry for her forlorn-looking charges, Croyance bought them some candy from a roadside stall, little realising that the candy had been made with salted nuts. As soon as the group tasted the candy they began to awaken, slowly becoming aware of their surroundings as the salt broke Ti Joseph's magical hold over them. Moving off with a single purpose, they shuffled towards their home village in the nearby mountains, ignoring Croyance's frantic attempts to stop them.

As the zombies returned home, their terrified relatives came out of their houses to watch in appalled silence as these former loved ones limped through the village towards the cemetery where they had been buried. Collapsing onto their empty graves, the zombies fell still as death took hold of them again. The next day, the outraged relatives hired a band of assassins to waylay the unsuspecting Ti Joseph as he travelled back to the cane fields from Port-au-Prince. The sorcerer was beheaded and his body was left to rot by the roadside.

After listening to this lurid story, Seabrook realised that he had found the perfect centrepiece for his book on Haitian voodoo. Eager to replicate his previous work on Arabia and Africa, the author was convinced that the occult practices of the island – with their enticing mix of sex, living death and witchcraft – would be the blueprint for an immediate bestseller. Excited, he asked Polynice to show him the dead men working in the cane fields.

A few days later Polynice led the white adventurer deep inland. It was mid-afternoon when they reached their destination. The glare of the sun made the fields shimmer in a heat haze as Polynice pointed out four distant figures working in the middle of a plantation. After riding on ahead to ask the man in charge of the zombies if he would consent to letting a white traveller see them, Polynice eventually beckoned his friend over to take a look. Ever curious, Seabrook went up to each of the three zombie workers and stared deep into their eyes. It was, according to his account in *The Magic Island*, a truly shocking encounter.

"My first impression of the three supposed *zombies*, who continued dumbly at work, was that there was something about them unnatural and strange. They were plodding like brutes, like automatons," Seabrook recounts. "The eyes were the worst. It was not my imagination. They were in truth like the eyes of a dead man, not blind, but staring, unfocused, unseeing. The whole face, for that matter, was bad enough. It was vacant, as if there was nothing behind it. It seemed not only expressionless, but incapable of expression. I had seen so much previously in Haiti that was outside ordinary normal experience that for the flash of a second I had a sickening almost panicky lapse in which I thought, or rather felt, 'Great God, maybe this stuff is really true and, if it is true, it is rather awful, for it upsets everything.' By 'everything' I meant the natural fixed laws and processes on which all modern human thought and actions are based."[14]

As the first documented meeting between a white man and a zombie, Seabrook's description is an important starting point in any attempt to understand the West's fascination with the living dead. Explicitly describing the zombie as an affront to both science and reason, Seabrook claims they upset all of mankind's certain certainties. Brought back from beyond the grave to perform some servile labour, the zombie appears to be an automaton whose existence challenges not only "all modern human thought" but also the "natural fixed laws and processes on which all modern human thought and actions are based". Defying Western science's understanding of the realities of life and death, the zombie was – for Seabrook at least – a powerful symbol of a world turned upside down. If the zombie was more than just a legend, then perhaps death might not be the end after all. One can understand why Seabrook's first response was "a sickening almost panicky lapse". What he had just seen was an affront to science, religion and common sense.

Yet, for all his professions of fear and surprise Seabrook was quick to explain this encounter with the living dead in scientifically acceptable terms. Staring into the blank eyes of the zombies, the adventurer decided that these weren't the dead brought back to life, but simply members of Haiti's underclass – mentally challenged unfortunates who were being exploited under the guise of some ancient superstition. They were nothing more than "poor, ordinary human beings, idiots, forced to toil in the fields".[15] Their blank expressions weren't proof of some black magic, but just their dumb misery and confusion as they were exploited as cheap labour.

Continuing his research in the months that followed this historic confrontation, Seabrook realised that there might also be another explanation for the ubiquitous zombie legends that dominated Haiti and much of the rest of the Caribbean. Consulting various medical experts on the island, the adventurer uncovered an explanation for the living dead phenomenon that, he believed, might stand up to the scrutiny of medical science. Discussing the zombie with a Haitian doctor in Port-au-Prince, Seabrook realised that these living dead corpses might be nothing more than drugged sleepwalkers whose appearance of "death" had been manufactured through the use of some kind of toxic substances.

The official Haitian *Code Pénal* hinted at exactly this, with a specific paragraph (article 249) referring to dubious practices that might make the living appear dead. "Also shall be qualified as attempted murder the employment which may be made against any person of substances which, without causing actual death, produce a lethargic coma more or less prolonged. If, after the administering of such substances, the person had been buried, the act shall be considered murder no matter what result follows."[16]

No matter what result follows. Even – Seabrook guessed – if the body of the alleged murder victim was later found harvesting sugar-cane crops in a distant plantation.

It wouldn't be until the 1980s that such suspicions would be fully investigated by Western scientists (something discussed in chapter seven). Perhaps if the riddle of the living dead had been solved sooner, the zombie would never have taken root in the imagination of the Western world. Without offering a full and proper explanation of the mystery surrounding the living dead, Seabrook's *The Magic Island* unleashed the *corps cadavres* on an audience that was all too eager to believe that the dead could really walk.

III. THE ZOMBIE IN THE WEST

On its publication in America in 1929, *The Magic Island* was warmly received, quickly becoming the best-selling travel book of the year. It was instantly hailed by the critics, with the *New York Evening Post* calling it "the most thrilling book of exploration that we have ever read".[17] It once again proved Seabrook's knack for writing popular and accessible travelogues that combined personal recollections with amateur anthropology. Much of the book's success was the result of fortuitous timing. It hit the shelves just as the American public's interest in Haiti reached a considerable peak. In order to understand the reasons why Haiti, Seabrook and, ultimately, the zombie had such an impact on American popular culture, it is necessary to outline the history of America's fraught involvement with the Caribbean island itself.

By the early 1800s, Haiti had forcibly freed itself from the yoke of French colonial rule and become an independent state. The island's chequered colonial past and its unusual independent status gave it a powerful hold over the imagination of the white world. As Seabrook explained in his introduction to *The Magic Island*, Haiti shared many histories, from the "wrecked mansions of 16th-century French colonials who had imported slaves from Africa and made Haiti the richest colony in the Western Hemisphere," to the scenes of the "white massacres when the blacks rose with fire and sword".[18] But the greatest lure of all, for both the author and his readership, was the natives' inherent savagery: "Only the jungle mountains remained, dark and mysterious; and, from their slopes came presently far out across the water the steady boom of Voodoo drums."[19]

After a series of bloody slave revolts led by François Dominique Toussaint Louverture and Jean-Jacques Dessalines at the end of the 18th century, Haiti became the second black nation in the Western hemisphere to gain independence from its white rulers. The slaves successfully fought off a 40,000-strong invasion force dispatched by Napoleon Bonaparte to retake the island and formally declared their independence in 1804. As Dessalines's angry inaugural speech proved, it was a hard-won victory that none of the former slaves were likely to forget: "We will write this Act of Independence using a white man's skull as an inkwell, his skin as parchment and a bayonet as a pen."[20]

Victory came at a price, though. The country was left in ruins, the economy was on the verge of bankruptcy and, as the following decades would painfully prove, the revolutionaries had little idea of how to run the island. Having thrown off its colonial oppressors, this "Black Republic" was effectively isolated by the international community, particularly by those states that had vested interests in the Caribbean. Fearing that Haiti might set an example that other colonies would eagerly follow, the European powers did their best to hamper the new nation's development.

By the end of the 19th century, the situation had progressed from bad to worse. The island began to feel pressurised by America's growing interest in securing its Caribbean "backyard" in order to keep careful control of the Panama Canal. After the Spanish-American War of 1898, in which US-funded Cuban revolutionaries led an uprising against Spanish rule, America's presence in the Caribbean grew exponentially, with at least thirty military interventions in the region from 1900–1930.

As the internal stability of Haiti worsened, with seven different regimes rising and quickly falling during the years 1908–1915, America's interest in the island's internal politics grew increasingly ominous. Spurred on by concerns about maintaining stability in the region – and using the fact that Haiti had defaulted on a $21 million debt it owed America's banks as a none-too-subtle pretext – US military intervention became a foregone conclusion.

In July 1915, America became directly involved

in the island's affairs when Admiral Caperton of the gunboat *USS Washington* arrived in the harbour of Port-au-Prince. Already aware of the wave of domestic unrest that was plaguing the newly instated government of President Guillaume Sam, the United States had sent the *Washington* to observe the situation.

As Admiral Caperton would later testify to a Senate inquiry into the reasons for the gunboat's intervention, the crew of the *Washington* "observed" more than they'd bargained for. "I was about a mile off and I saw much confusion, people in the streets, and apparently there was a procession, as if they were dragging something through the city, and I afterwards found out, from officers whom I sent ashore that this was the body of President Guillaume Sam, which had been mutilated, the arms cut off, the head cut off, and stuck on poles, and the torso drawn with ropes through the city."[21]

Under the guise of protecting American and European interests on the island, Admiral Caperton ordered a Marine taskforce ashore to secure Port-au-Prince, and then sent an anxious cable to Washington requesting reinforcements. It was an action that would drastically alter American foreign policy in the region. In previous years, America's intervention in Haiti's turbulent politics had been restricted to diplomatic wrangling, but as the first Marines landed on the island, two decades of American military occupation began.[22]

Officially the American intervention was supposed to be limited to protecting American, British and French holdings on the island as well as, in the words of ex-Secretary of State Robert Lansing, "terminat[ing] the appalling conditions prevalent in Haiti for decades".[23] However, there were other – less altruistic – reasons for America's interest in the island's affairs. In Washington, the predominant concern was that a foreign power might take advantage of the political unrest in Haiti and intervene with a military taskforce. To prevent a nation like Germany from turning Haiti into a military base strategically placed on the United States' doorstep, President Wilson committed additional troops to Caperton's taskforce in an attempt to quell the rebels and restore order.

For ordinary Haitians, the American occupation was not only an insult to their country's sovereignty but also an attack on their individual freedom. The American-Haitian treaty, signed shortly after the Marines took control of Port-au-Prince, promised to improve the island's basic amenities such as sanitation, roads and schooling. In reality, these philanthropic aims were thwarted by the suspicious relationship that existed between the two nations. Outbreaks of revolutionary violence and banditry throughout 1918–1919 reminded the occupying forces that their presence was far from welcome, while American attempts to improve the island's infrastructure relied on forced labour policies which antagonised local Haitians. Ruthlessly upheld by the local police, such infringements of the islanders' civil liberties led many press-ganged Haitians to wonder if the arrival of the Americans was really nothing more than a return to the days of colonial rule.

From the moment the first American troops landed, tensions ran high. As reports of atrocities carried out by American Marines began to circulate, popular opinion on the island began to turn against the occupation. The all-white Marine taskforce had little time for the natives or the Caribbean.

As one American Marine put it, "It hurt. It stunk. Fairyland had turned into a pigsty. More than that we were not welcome. We could feel it as distinctly as we could smell the rot along the gutters... In the streets were piles of evil-smelling offal. The stench hung over everything. Piles of mango seeds were heaped in the middle of the highway, sour smelling. It was not merely that these, mingled with banana peels and other garbage, were rotting – the whole prospect was filthy."[24]

The troops' hatred of the islanders extended to Haiti's light-skinned, racially mixed elite despite the fact that they were generally better educated than their black brothers: "No matter how much veneer and polish a Haitian may have," wrote one American officer, "he is absolutely savage under the skin and under strain reverts to type".[25] It was an explicitly racist attitude that bred only fear and resentment among Haiti's social and political leaders. "The Americans have taught us many things," explained Ernest Chauvet, owner of the island's *Le Nouvelliste* newspaper, to Seabrook. "Among other things they have taught us is that we are niggers. You see, we really didn't know that before. We thought we were Negroes."[26]

As long as the occupation continued, the

tension between the islanders and the Americans increased. The streets of Port-au-Prince were awash with drunken off-duty soldiers, prostitutes began to openly ply their trade, saloons and dance halls sprang up everywhere and the Americans began to introduce Jim Crow laws, making provisions for segregated residential areas, hotels and even Catholic masses. "In as many ways as they could manage, the Americans were remaking Haiti in their own image," explains historian Elizabeth Abbott.[27]

Published at the height of America's involvement in Haiti, Seabrook's book tapped into the American public's thirst for information about the exotic island that had unexpectedly fallen under their control. "To Americans in particular, Haiti was like having a little bit of Africa next door," says Wade Davis. "Something dark, and foreboding, sensual and terribly naughty."[28] And it wasn't just Seabrook who set the cash-tills ringing. After the success of The Magic Island, publishers began falling over themselves to commission increasingly lurid accounts of the island's voodoo culture.

Although The Magic Island was relatively restrained in its sensationalism, other books were less so. The titles of John Huston Craige's books Black Bagdad: The Arabian Nights Adventures of a Marine Captain in Haiti (sic, 1933) and Cannibal Cousins (1934) tell their own story about the racial prejudice underpinning such projects. As well as books, several films also followed: Voodoo Land (1932), a short about Haitian superstition and Voodo (sic, 1933), a documentary about a Marine sergeant who claimed to have spent three years as a local native king.

This interest in Haiti's exotic voodoo rites – and the allegations of cannibalism and savagery that accompanied it – was more than just a sensational marketing ploy. It was also a rather crude attempt to attempt to justify the American occupation of the island, since, as Davis reflects, "any country where such abominations took place could find its salvation only through military occupation".[29] Sensationalism and propaganda went hand in hand. The zombie played an important role in this, since it was a monster whose alleged existence could be cited as proof of Haitian savagery, occultism and perhaps even Satanism.

The first sign of Seabrook's influence and the zombie's arrival in American popular culture was to be found in 1930s horror fiction. Before The Magic Island, the zombie had never appeared in any literary works in either Europe or America, for while tales of the dead returning to life were not unheard of (Edgar Allen Poe's stories gave enough examples of this alone), the Caribbean zombie – the dead body that doesn't simply return to "life", but is reanimated into living death – was something altogether new and different.

By the early 1930s the situation had radically altered, as the success of The Magic Island turned the zombie into a recognizable horror monster. Henry S. Whitehead, Archdeacon to the Virgin Islands from 1921 to 1929, was one of the first writers to tackle the subject of the zombie in his short story "Jumbee" (1930) about undead goings on in St Croix. The following year, Garnett Weston published "Salt Is Not For Slaves" in the August issue of Ghost Stories magazine (under the pseudonym G. W. Hutter). More short stories followed, including August Derleth's "The House in the Magnolias" in the July issue of Strange Tales magazine in 1932. Derleth, who would later become a pivotal figure in the history of horror publishing after founding the legendary Arkham House, was sufficiently in touch with shifts in the contemporary horror scene to realise that the zombie was ready to leave its Caribbean homeland. Setting his story in New Orleans, he brought the walking dead firmly onto American soil, highlighting the close cultural ties between the Caribbean and the voodoo superstitions to be found among the black population in the American South.

The growing popularity of the zombie was enough to suggest that its cultural usefulness extended beyond the crude propaganda of the Haiti occupation. This ancient symbol of Haitian fears about slavery, work and the resurrection of the body after death had clearly tapped into some deep-seated American anxiety. The military occupation of Haiti and Seabrook's voodoo research brought the living dead into American culture in the guise of popular travelogues and pulp-fiction horror stories. Yet it would be a very different medium that would firmly ensconce the zombie in the West. As the craze for stories about Haiti and voodoo superstitions reached a crescendo, it was Hollywood – the nation's dream factory – that turned the zombie into an American nightmare.

CHAPTER TWO

THE ZOMBIE GOES TO HOLLYWOOD

I. HORROR HITS THE STAGE

From the well-trodden boards of The Strand to the bright lights of Broadway, horror dominated the theatre stage on both sides of the Atlantic in the 1920s. The trend began in earnest in the aftermath of the First World War with productions like *The Bat* (1920), *The Monster* (1920) and the hugely influential *The Cat and the Canary* (1922), before reaching its apotheosis in Horace Liveright's box office juggernaut *Dracula* (1927). Liveright's stage production – with its staggering $2 million gross – proved what canny theatre producers had known for several years: the public had an insatiable appetite for chills, thrills and buckets of blood.

Whether this horror lust was simply a passing fad or some cultural pressure valve releasing the pent up anxieties of the war and its aftermath – the on-stage death and destruction safely repackaging the all-too-real horrors of the European trenches in a manageable form – wasn't certain. But it didn't pass unnoticed that in Weimar Germany the war-scarred nation's home-grown cinema had begun to harness the still-new medium of film to produce some terrifying visions: *Das Cabinet des Dr Caligari* (*The Cabinet of Dr Caligari*, 1919), *Der Golem, Wie er in die Welt Kam* (*The Golem*, 1920) and *Nosferatu – eine Symphonie des Grauens* (*Nosferatu*, 1922).

The success of Liveright's *Dracula* play and the popularity of German horror films in American cinemas encouraged a new generation of movie producers to try and cash in on the horror trend with their own frightfests. In films like *The Phantom of the Opera* (1925) and *London After Midnight* (1927), Hollywood studios began to toy with the idea of making pictures that would utterly terrify their audiences. As a new decade began, two film properties emerged that would set the standard for American horror: Tod Browning's *Dracula* (1931) and James Whale's *Frankenstein* (1931).

It was into this world that Seabrook's *The Magic Island* was released. The author would no doubt have seen little relation between his voodoo research and the horror stage-plays, but America's entertainment industry was far more imaginative in recognising the potential of his work. By the time *Dracula* and *Frankenstein* had been produced in both the theatre and the cinema, the amount of sure-fire material available to scriptwriters was rapidly dwindling, and it was clear that in order to capitalise on the trend for horror pictures some new property was needed.

Given such circumstances the announcement of *Zombie*, a new stage production for 1932, probably shouldn't have been surprising. For Kenneth Webb, a theatre writer and producer, the zombie was everything he needed. Not only was it a fresh concept that would scare jaded audiences, but it also didn't require lengthy copyright negotiations. Liveright had been forced to barter with the Stoker estate for several years to secure permission for his stage production of *Dracula*, but Webb gleefully realised that he could filch Seabrook's zombie chapter and dramatise it without paying a single cent, since it was reputedly based on fact.

Webb, whose previous experience as a playwright included such throwaway productions as *One of the Family* (1925) and the revue *Who Cares?* (1930), kept the concept as simple and accessible as possible with a three-act story about a pair of American plantation owners, Jack and Sylvia Clayton, and their adventures on Haiti. After Jack dies from a mysterious illness, the plantation's Haitian overseer, Pedro, reanimates his corpse in a cunning attempt to take control of the estate. Confronted by this walking corpse, Sylvia enlists the help of two brainiac Americans – Dr Paul Thurlow and Professor Wallace – to solve the mystery surrounding his death.

Despite its novelty value, *Zombie* was a pretty meagre production. With all three acts set in "The Living Room of a Bungalow in the Mountains of Haiti" and some supporting roles for a couple of "Haitian Labourers" (played first by white actors in blackface and then, in an attempt to gain some extra publicity, a pair of Haitian immigrants) it was obvious that this was one horror play that lacked the necessary fright factor. Although Jack ended up – in the words of one reviewer – "stalking about the place and scaring the daylights out of everybody" and a later scene cooked up a whole army of living dead extras, *Zombie* didn't come

White Zombie (1932).

close to replicating the success of Liveright's *Dracula*.[30] Not even the surprise ending in which the real zombie master turns out to be Professor Wallace could make up for the play's dreary lack of imagination and faintly ludicrous feel.

In his seminal study *White Zombie: Anatomy of a Horror Film* scholar Gary D. Rhodes charts the history of Webb's production in detail and notes that this self-proclaimed "Play of the Tropics" received generally poor notices. The suspicion among most reviewers was that it was more likely to elicit hilarity rather than horror, and the press gleefully recounted reports of audiences sniggering in the aisles. The *Herald Tribune*'s scathing review was indicative of the disdainful reaction: "Happily, Mr Webb hasn't even the skill to make himself be taken seriously by ingenuous judges of book-of-the-month-clubs."[31]

Opening in New York's Biltmore theatre on 10 February 1932, *Zombie* closed after just twenty performances. Webb relocated to Chicago, opening the play at the Adelphi Theatre on 13 March 1932. It remained there for two months, moved to a couple of smaller theatres in the city, then suddenly closed for good.

However disastrous this production was, *Zombie* secured a place in the history books by helping to pave the way for the film that would make the living dead truly famous, Victor and Edward Halperin's *White Zombie* (1932). Intrigued by Webb's stage-play, the Halperins decided that there might well be money to be made from bringing the dead back to life.

II. CULTURAL ANXIETIES: HAITI, THE DEPRESSION AND RACE

Publication of *The Magic Island* may have brought the walking dead into American popular culture, but the book's impact was rather limited. For those

who hadn't read Seabrook's book or seen Webb's short-lived play, the zombie was still *persona non grata*. Dracula, Frankenstein, the Hunchback of

Notre Dame and the double act of Jekyll and Hyde had a cultural cachet that meant they were instantly recognizable to millions of cinemagoers, but the zombie was something of a cultural upstart, an interloper from the Caribbean that no one really knew anything about.

According to Rhodes, Webb had hoped that *Zombie* might generate interest in Hollywood much as the stage version of *Dracula* had done before it. After its initial run in New York and Chicago, *Zombie* went on the road heading westwards to Hollywood with the aim of being noticed by movie producers. In the end, though, it was zombies not *Zombie* that piqued the interest of the movie world – and, in particular, that of independent filmmakers Victor and Edward Halperin, a director and producer team.

By January 1932, the trade press was reporting that the Halperins were in pre-production on "Zombie" which, despite its title, officially had nothing to do with Webb's Broadway play. Although historians have claimed that Webb tried to sue the filmmakers, Rhodes reveals that there is no legal evidence to suggest that Webb ever brought a lawsuit against the Halperins. However, as he notes, the fact that the movie's title changed to *White Zombie* before it was shot may well hint that complaints were made out of court. Either way, it's very probable that *Zombie* was an influence on some level. As Rhodes puts it: "Whatever the actual influence of Webb's *Zombie* on the decision to produce a zombie film in general, the play's preproduction hype may have helped the Halperins justify audience interest in cinematic zombies to themselves or to potential investors."

The Halperins commissioned screenwriter Garnett Weston to write a treatment for what would become the zombie's big-screen debut. Weston was the perfect choice. The author of the Seabrook-inspired short story "Salt Is Not For Slaves" (published in 1931), Weston fully understood what made the walking dead tick. He soon delivered a treatment and later a script for his new employers.

As an independent production put together without the clout or protection of a big-name Hollywood studio, *White Zombie* was always destined to be something of a risky venture. No doubt that was why the brothers decided to insure themselves by finding a recognizable star to ensure

some degree of box office return on their investment. Fortunately, they were in luck. Bela Lugosi, straight from the set of *Dracula*, agreed to take the role of zombie master Murder Legendre. Best of all, Lugosi wasn't just interested, he was desperate for the part – although, in truth, it was an enthusiasm that had more to do with his precarious financial situation than his love of the material.

Despite his considerable talent, Lugosi was down on his luck by the time the Halperins approached him in 1932. The Hungarian-born actor had arrived in New York in 1920 when he was 46 years old. He'd taken a series of forgettable dramatic parts before landing the title role in Horace Liveright's *Dracula* stage-play in 1927. It should have been his breakthrough performance, and in many ways it was, but it didn't do much to rescue his ailing finances. While Liveright raked in the dollars, Lugosi found that his slice of the box office takings were considerably less than the star of a smash-hit stage production might have hoped. The contract had been weighted against him, and in his rush to sign he hadn't negotiated a particularly good deal.

When Universal began to cast their cinematic production of the same story, Lugosi was convinced that his problems were finally over. The Count was, after all, a role he'd made his own. Who else would be able to portray the Transylvanian aristocrat better than himself? Universal weren't convinced, though. Decidedly lukewarm about hiring this Hungarian thespian, they invited him in for an audition and were pleasantly surprised. In the negotiations that ensued, the actor badly tipped his hand, letting Universal see just how desperate he was for the part. Safe in the knowledge that his back was against the wall, they hired him for $500 a week for seven weeks' work.

After *Dracula* set the box office alight, Universal began to wonder if Lugosi's mesmerising acting style and inimitable Hungarian accent might be the traits of a new star player. Deciding to groom him into the new Lon Chaney, the studio offered Lugosi a role in the upcoming film adaptation of Mary Shelley's novel *Frankenstein*. First he was asked to play the eponymous mad scientist and then, in keeping with Chaney's reputation as the man of a thousand faces, the role of the monster itself. Lugosi got as far as having the test make-up applied before declining the part, famously claiming: "I'm an actor, not a scarecrow!" It was a disastrous decision. In his place, Universal hired a young unknown British actor named Boris Karloff to play the monster. The rest is horror movie history.

When the Halperins approached Lugosi, he was ready to accept whatever acting work he could find. *White Zombie* didn't do much to improve his contract rates. The Halperins hired him for around $800 a week for just 11 days work. It might have been a step up from his *Dracula* salary, but Lugosi obviously hadn't learnt from his earlier mistakes. He was taken to the Beverly Hills cleaners once again as *White Zombie* grossed an unexpected $8 million at the box office. It was a staggering amount for an independently produced movie – with an original budget of just $62,500 – to recoup.

Regardless of this terrible salary, Lugosi was definitely the star of the picture. None of the other actors, with the possible exception of the heroine Madge Bellamy, were well-known performers. Bellamy had been a successful actress back in the silent era, but she had been struggling to reassert herself in the brave new world of the "talkies" (and judging by her childlike voice, it was obvious why). *White Zombie* helped keep her career alive for a few more years – perhaps because her role was largely a non-speaking one – until she was arrested for shooting her two-timing millionaire boyfriend in 1943. Christened "Pistol Packing Madge" by the papers, who were eager to play up this tale of violence and pre-marital sex, it proved to be her last great role. She put a brave face on the whole story, later claiming: "I only winged him, which was all I meant to do. Believe me, I'm a crack shot."[32] In retrospect, it seems significant that this fiery young woman would be cinema's first victim of zombification.

Taking *The Magic Island* as its starting point, Weston's screenplay for *White Zombie* was a cleverly packaged piece of sensationalism, sex and the living dead. It begins with a scene set at a dark Haitian crossroads that could have been lifted straight out of Seabrook. An American couple, Neil (John Harron) and Madeleine (Bellamy), arrive in a horse-drawn carriage and discover a voodoo ceremony in full sway. Asking their black driver to explain what's happening, the terrified couple learn that they're witnessing a special burial designed to deter those "who steal dead bodies".

A little further down the track, the Americans receive their second fright of the evening as the driver pulls up to ask directions from a caped figure standing by the roadside. Ignoring the driver's questions, the ominous stranger stares at Madeleine, seemingly transfixed by her. Suddenly, the driver spies several figures shuffling down the hillside towards them. "Zombies!" he cries, whipping the horses onwards in a terrified frenzy. As the carriage plunges forwards, the stranger clutches Madeleine's scarf, almost strangling her until she frees it from around her neck.

After this creepy opening, things spiral out of control. Neil and Madeleine discover that their Haitian benefactor, a fellow American named Beaumont (Robert Frazer), is not as altruistic as he appears. Desperately in love with Madeleine, Beaumont is determined to have her for himself, and when she refuses his advances he hires the help of Murder Legendre (Lugosi), the man from the crossroads. A European plantation owner who has discovered the secrets of voodoo, Legendre is employed to zombify Madeleine on the eve of her marriage.

At Neil and Madeleine's wedding, Beaumont's plan goes into action. Armed with a secret potion from Legendre, Beaumont poisons the new bride. Later that night, Legendre and his zombies steal her body from the crypt and spirit her away to the sorcerer's clifftop retreat (known locally as "The Land of the Living Dead") where she's reanimated as a zombie. But Beaumont quickly becomes bored with how unresponsive his zombie bride is and tries to convince Legendre to return her to normal. Already peeved by Beaumont's snobbish attitude towards him, Legendre spikes his employer's drink with poison and terminates their business agreement once and for all.

His victory is short-lived, though, as Neil and a local Christian missionary named Dr Bruner (Joseph Cawthorne) storm his castle to do battle with his zombie slaves. In the ensuing fight, Legendre orders Madeleine to kill her husband, but she resists his command and tries to throw herself off the cliffs instead. After battling the zombies – who prove impervious to bullets – the heroes manage to save the day. Dr Bruner knocks Legendre unconscious, severing his control over the zombies, who career off the cliff like lemmings. Then, as Legendre comes round, Beaumont staggers out of the castle. He grapples with his poisoner and the two men fall over the precipice onto the rocks below. Neil and Dr Bruner tend to Madeleine who, it transpires, was only drugged and never actually dead.

For most cinemagoers in 1932, this shocking story of love and necrophilia was their first encounter with the living dead. Taking the bare bones of Seabrook's research – the Haitian setting, the sugarcane fields and voodoo trappings – as its starting point, Weston's screenplay ushered the zombie into cinema history. It didn't matter that the critics hated the film; audiences loved the dark and moody setting, Lugosi's voodoo sorcerer and, of course, the zombies.[33]

Keenly aware that few cinemagoers had read *The Magic Island*, the publicity department at distributors United Artists blitzed America with an aggressive marketing campaign. Not only did they play up the veracity of the events depicted in the film – "The story of *White Zombie* is based upon personal observation in Haiti by American writers and research workers and, fantastic as it sounds, its entire substance is based on fact"[34] – but they also arranged a sensational series of promotional events. By the time the film opened on 29 July 1932, the living dead had finally arrived as a 20th-century monster.

"When *White Zombie* was ushered into the Rivoli Theater in New York, all Broadway was startled by the sudden appearance of nine zombies on a boardwalk erected above the marquee of the theatre," claimed *The 1933 Film Daily Year Book of Motion Pictures*.

The film's aggressive and inventive PR campaign stunned audiences. "Thousands packed the sidewalks and gasped with amazement as the nine figures, faithfully garbed and made-up to simulate actual members of the *White Zombie* cast, went through a series of thrilling dramatic sequences [...] The doll-like figures of the girls were dressed in white flowing robes and the men looked as if they had been dug up from the ground with wooden splints on their legs and battered facial expressions." Meanwhile, loudspeakers played the film's sound-effects records, which included "the screeching of vultures, the grinding of the sugar mill and the beating of the tom toms and other nerve wracking sounds."[35] One can only imagine what nightmares passersby suffered when the lights went out that evening.

The monsters of *White Zombie* truly deserved the name "walking dead". Madeleine may have been simply drugged into zombification, but the rest of the ghouls were the real deal: ghastly corpses reanimated without souls. With make-up by Carl Axcelle and Jack Pierce from Universal (the latter had been responsible for transforming Boris Karloff into Frankenstein's monster the previous year), the zombies were memorable creations. Shuffling slowly but purposefully through the shadowed scenery, they even managed to survive being upstaged by Lugosi's hammy villain. But what really ensured their success was the way in which they tapped into fears that resonated well beyond the walls of the movie theatres.

The American horror boom of the 1930s was, as so many film historians have pointed out, intimately tied to the economic bust of 29 October 1929 when the Wall Street crash wiped millions of dollars off US share prices in the space of just a few hours. If the international effects of the dollar's sudden collapse were spectacular, the domestic upheaval it produced was devastating. Millions of ordinary Americans found themselves unemployed and queuing in the breadlines as their savings and investments were wiped out overnight. The Roaring Twenties had roared themselves hoarse and the economic hangover that followed would bring nothing but misery and destitution.

Drawing a link between the economic downturn and the sudden dominance of horror pictures hardly requires a great leap of the imagination. By 1929 horror was on the nation's streets as well as its screens. As the *Washington Post*'s critic Nelson B. Bell presciently noted in February 1932, just five months before *White Zombie* took the country by storm. "Many are without employment, many are employed only by virtue of having accepted drastic curtailment of income, many lead their lives in a state of constant dread of the disaster that may overtake them at any minute. This is a state of mind that creates a vast receptivity for misfortunes more poignant than our own."[36]

That the zombie should burst into American popular culture at precisely this moment hardly seems surprising. In Haiti, the zombie had always encapsulated fears of enslavement and the terrifying loss of individual freedom that the slave trade had imposed on generations of displaced Africans. In 1930s America, the zombie and the stock-market crash segued neatly together, expressing the powerlessness that so many felt as they suffered under an unstable economy that reduced princes to paupers, bank managers to bums and whole families to beggars. The zombie – a dead worker resurrected as a slave into a hellish afterlife of endless toil – was the perfect monster for the age.

White Zombie capitalised on exactly this, its vision of a living dead workforce neatly tapping into the American public's fears. The scene in Legendre's sugar mill, where all the workers are mindless zombies, must have seemed like a startlingly grim vision of hell and an ironic inversion of every American's hopes of employment through the Depression. At a time when the greatest fear was losing one's job – unemployment had reached almost 25 per cent – here was a film that transformed work itself into horror.

View of a breadline during the Great Depression in New York City, 1931.

The zombies who operate the sugar mill are human beings who have become expendable automatons. Even when one of their number plummets into the mill they continue working, crunching his body in the machinery (one can only imagine the impact that the startling sound of his death must have had on audiences who were still getting used to the aural effects of the "talkies"). It's a pivotal moment that highlights the film's wider resonance: for Americans who had seen the crushing forces of capitalism at work, the scene must have seemed particularly poignant. "They work faithfully and they're not afraid of long hours," Legendre says menacingly, offering Beaumont some worker zombies for his own plantation. Here was the dark side of capitalist economics – which so many had seen from the breadline – laid bare.

From this perspective, it's easy to see why *White Zombie* became such a commercial success. The zombie's arrival was perfectly timed. It wasn't just Madge Bellamy who had to suffer the indignity of being zombified. Everyone faced the awful possibility of joining the shuffling, blank-faced down-and-outs waiting in line for bread and soup, an economic zombification of terrifying proportions. "Millions already knew they were no longer in control of their lives; the economic strings were being pulled by faceless, frightening forces," explains film historian David J. Skal. "If the force had a face, it was likely to be that of zombie-master Bela Lugosi, commanding you mesmerically."[37]

Whether or not the Halperins were aware of the film's intimate relation to America's economic collapse isn't certain. They were clearly savvy enough to recognise the movie's other appeals, though. "A weird love story, the strangest in 2,000 years. A zombie bride whose soul and heart were dead, performing every wish of he who had her by his magic," exclaimed the lurid lobby posters. As if such necrophiliac sensationalism wasn't enough to get the punters through the door, other posters had Lugosi's eyes focussing on a nude woman with the tagline "He brought her back to life … and made her his slave." The hints of morbid sexual perversity in both the publicity material and the movie itself are quite blatant, suggesting that at least one of the film's pleasures lay in the way its erotically charged script played with the taboos surrounding sex and death.

Trapped between her husband, her kidnapper and the zombie master who controls her, Madeleine is compromised three times over. As Weston's screenplay turns her into the stereotypical male fantasy – a completely compliant and subservient woman – *White Zombie* addresses some very contemporary fears about women's independence, fears that were surfacing in a wide range of 1930s films, from *Svengali* (1931) to *Mad Love* (1935) and even *The Bride of Frankenstein* (1935). In each of these films, heroines find their autonomy compromised by evil male villains. The answer to *White Zombie*'s tagline – "What does a man want in a woman, is it her body or her soul?" – was readily apparent in Legendre's wanton willingness to keep Madeleine zombified and take his pleasure. Unlike Beaumont – who loses his nerve too soon, crying, "I thought that beauty alone would satisfy me. But the soul is gone. I can't bear those empty staring eyes" – Legendre is far beyond such worries. As Lugosi's magnificently evil smirk testifies, he's the kind of man who doesn't need the object of his affections to be anything more than that, an object.

It's no accident that the dreamlike quality of *White Zombie*'s evocative cinematography and its long stretches of eerie silence are punctuated by what is probably the film's most famous image, the close-up of Lugosi's eyes. Zombification – whether it's turning men into slaves or women into sex objects – is closely linked with themes of powerlessness and the loss of personal autonomy. Lugosi's eyes, first seen hovering above the road like doom-laden twin moons, are not only a symbol of Legendre's voodoo power, but also his ability to bend others to his will. When Lugosi stares straight into the camera lens – breaking the first rule of cinematic realism which states that the actors must never acknowledge the camera's existence – Legendre's gaze suggests that he even has the power to hypnotise the audience itself. At one point, shortly after Madeleine's "death", he emphasises his power over the filmic medium by walking straight towards us as if he were about to come out of the screen. The result is spectacularly unsettling. We are transformed from passive spectators into potential victims as the security of the darkened auditorium is threatened by his looming figure. In a film that bases its horror on the collapse of boundaries, specifically those between life and death, and work and slavery, this tampering with the cinema's own boundary line is extremely effective.

As a comment on America's relationship with Haiti, *White Zombie* is equally intriguing. By the time of the film's release in 1932 the occupation of the island was entering its final stages, but the American public's interest in the island was at its height. Popular books about Haiti's heady mix of exoticism and the supernatural were joined by a sudden rash of Hollywood films that took voodoo as their starting point: *Drums O' Voodoo* (1934), *Chloe: Love is Calling You* (1934), *Ouanga* (1935) and *The Devil's Daughter* (1939). Without Seabrook's research or the box office success of *White Zombie*, it's unlikely that any of these pictures would have ever seen the light of day.

On the most basic level, the story of a white American woman kidnapped by natives appealed to the popular belief that the Caribbean was ruled by primitive desires. By ignoring the reality of Haiti's former independence prior to the American occupation of 1915–1934, the film argues that the island's culture is only a few steps removed from outright savagery. When Neil suggests that they contact the local police about Madeleine's missing corpse, Dr Bruner carefully spells out his lack of faith in the island's indigenous law enforcement: "Neil my boy, you don't know these islands. The native authorities are afraid to meddle." How much more strongly could the filmmakers have expressed their support for American intervention on an island where, as Bruner claims, "we may encounter sins that even the devil himself would be ashamed of"?

The American occupation of Haiti is never mentioned during the proceedings, however, making it the film's silent subtext. While tracking down Madeleine, Bruner and Neil rely on their own resources and there is no suggestion of enlisting the help of any American authorities. True enough, contemporary audiences wouldn't have needed to be told why an American boy like Neil was working in the Port-au-Prince bank – yet there's no denying the fact that the film is spectacularly coy about the realities of the American presence.

For Tony Williams, whose essay "*White Zombie* Haitian Horror" is the most illuminating exploration of the film's relation to its contemporary American audiences' concerns, "the film has much to say about US imperialism then." His sustained analysis of the film's themes and symbolism leads him to suggest that *White Zombie* is "an important example of the disguised and suppressed radical critique the horror genre can often manifest."[38] This is a horror film that works both as cheap entertainment and as a fascinating insight into America's relationship to Haiti during the occupation – even though it never even acknowledges the occupation's reality.

Neil is a fairly representative member of the various American clerks and personnel who travelled out to the island to oversee Haiti's bureaucratic and economic infrastructure, and his view of the Caribbean is in keeping with America's imperialism; he describes the region to Madeleine as "*our* West Indies." In contrast, Beaumont is rather more complex. A flamboyant entrepreneur, the plantation owner may hold an American passport, but he's quite obviously a European at heart. His impressive mansion, expensive clothes and ostentatious manners mark him out as something of a dandy, as does his pusillanimous failure to see his scheme through to its dastardly conclusion.

What the interplay between Neil, Beaumont and Legendre sets up is a neat parallel of Haiti's contested status, with Madeleine standing in for the island itself as she's torn between these three men. As Williams puts it, "[Madeline] personally experiences what has happened to Haiti, moving from the freedom of life to the slavery of death [...] In her zombie state, she loses all will power and thus echoes Haiti's plight deprived of government and Constitution."[39]

Beaumont's European manners and apparent willingness to go native by enlisting voodoo to ensnare the object of his affections are clearly not meant to win our sympathy. Yet, it's Legendre himself who is the film's real European and hence its real villain. His licentious habits, evil smirk and slightly camp mannerisms signal that he's the most dangerous threat to both Madeleine *and* the stability of the island itself.

The film's plot revolves around a conflict over Madeleine/Haiti in which the American hero Neil, aligned with the forces of Christian moral rectitude (Dr Bruner, the missionary), must fight off the dangerous solicitations of Beaumont and Legendre, the representatives of European colonialism that once dominated the Caribbean. Building on American fears that Haiti might fall back under European influence – the occupation had, after all, begun in response to fears that Germany might invade the island – *White Zombie* dramatises the conflict between America and Europe over Haiti's independent status.

But where do the zombies fit into all of this? It's no accident that the film's six main zombies comprise a cross-section of Haitian society. As the evil European, Legendre has zombified the island's key representatives. The scene in which he boasts about his conquest to Beaumont is wonderfully staged, with Lugosi capturing Legendre's self-congratulatory flamboyance with a characteristic flourish: "In their lifetimes, they were my enemies: Ledot, the witchdoctor, once my master; his secrets I tortured out of him. Von Gelder, the swine, swollen with riches. He fought against my spells right to the last; he even yet tries to struggle and fight. Ricard, once Minister of the Interior; Scalpiere, Brigand Chief; Marque; and this is Chauvin, the high executioner. He almost executed me. I took them, just as we will take this one [Madeleine]." Clearly disturbed by this carnival of lost souls, Beaumont asks what will happen if they ever regain their independence. Legendre's answer suggests both his own coming doom and American fears of releasing its grip over the Caribbean: "They will tear me to pieces."

Similarly, the scene in Legendre's sugar mill emphasises his association with Europe's colonial past. His zombie workers are segregated in exactly the same way as they would have been during the French rule of Haiti, with the Negroes performing the manual labour and the mulattoes acting as supervisors. If Legendre is supposed to represent the decadent Europeans who enslaved the Haitian population, then Neil is obviously a symbol of America's guardianship of the island (no wonder he's clad in a brilliant white suit). Teaming up with Bruner, Neil's heroic pursuit of Legendre promises to restore order to the island through the civilising influence of a combination of American might and Christian guidance. Bruner's desire to have "every witchdoctor in Haiti shaking in his sandals" makes this apparent enough. Civilising the natives – and eradicating the subversive influence of Europe – is a definite priority.

In his book *White Zombie: Anatomy of a Horror Film*, Rhodes chronicles the film's genesis and release in fascinating detail. He also highlights how the American and British press books for the movie played up this racial dimension in a series of startlingly crass ways. One suggestion was to "hire several negroes to sit in front of your theatre and beat a steady tattoo on tom-toms. Attire them in tropical garments and every once in a while have them cut loose with a couple of blood-curdling yells."[40]

Even more indicative of the racial tension that

worked its way through the film was the following suggestion to drum up business: "Here's a ballyhoo that will actually bring pounds into your box office. Arrange for a parade of zombies through the main streets of your city, the men following a girl in white." To ensure the maximum impact, the British press book advised, the zombies' faces "should be stolid, staring, gaping with empty eyes. They should walk with a mechanical, deathlike precision, looking neither to the left nor the right and not returning the gazes of the interested onlookers." On their backs the ghouls would bear cards reading "I'm a Zombie". Meanwhile, the girl dressed in flowing white robes would bear a sign reading "White Zombie" with "the emphasis on the word White". The final piece of advice was to "tip off newspaper offices that 'Black Magic' is being practised on the streets of your city."[41]

Three years after *White Zombie*, such racial themes resurfaced in George Terwilliger's *Ouanga* (1934), a lurid tale of Caribbean voodoo and zombies that has slipped into obscurity since its low-key release. Fredi Washington stars as Clelie, a mulatto plantation owner on the Haitian-esque Paradise Island who falls in love with her American neighbour Adam (Philip Brandon). Furious at being rebuffed by him, Clelie flies into a terrifying rage, crying "Don't draw away from me as though I were a black wench in your fields!" Adam, though, is resolute; they can never be anything more than friends: "The barrier of blood that's between us can't be over come… You belong with your kind." Angry at Adam's brusque treatment and jealous of his obvious interest in New York party girl Eve (Marie Paxton), Clelie uses her voodoo powers to get even. She sends Eve a death charm – the ouanga of the title – then dispatches a pair of burly black zombies to abduct her rival when she falls into a coma.

Clelie intends to sacrifice Eve to the voodoo gods but is stopped by her black servant LeStrange (confusingly played by white actor Sheldon Leonard). Desperately in love with Clelie himself, LeStrange is convinced that her refusal to acknowledge his affection is simply a result of her confused racial identity. He's determined to make her see the error of her ways in pursuing a white man – "Your white skin doesn't change what's inside you! You're black! You belong to us. To me!" – but she loathes everything that he represents:

"I hate you, you black scum!"

Exaggerating the sensational treatment of voodoo in *White Zombie*, *Ouanga* plays up the supposed savagery of the Caribbean. Styling the light-skinned Clelie as a black sorceress intent on breaking up the relationship between this white Adam and Eve, *Ouanga* presents its racially confused heroine as the satanic snake in the Caribbean paradise. Her desire for a white man is, the film argues, totally unacceptable.

As a reaction to America's imperialist adventures in the Caribbean, *Ouanga* is fascinating. Clelie not only represents white fears about miscegenation (her light skin allows her to "pass" in white society), but also about the state of Haiti itself. Imagining the island as a hotbed of native superstition, savagery and occultism, *Ouanga* suggests that the black population's belief that they can govern themselves is dangerously mistaken. The scenes of dozens of native extras entranced by the power of Clelie's voodoo ceremony and swaying in unison like brainwashed automatons makes the film's unsubtle subtext quite clear: Paradise Island/Haiti needs white American rule to bring it back from the brink of social, political and spiritual disaster.

Even the film's well-documented production history seems to have been cooked up to bolster exactly this assessment. Much was made of the run of bad luck that reportedly hampered the film. According to film historian Bryan Senn, the cast and crew suffered a series of accidents after an over-eager prop master decided to steal various voodoo paraphernalia from a market in Port-au-Prince. On the first day of the shoot, cast and crewmembers were attacked by a swarm of hornets. A few days later, a barracuda attacked a key-grip while he was standing in the surf; he died in hospital from massive blood loss. Then a make-up man succumbed to yellow fever and an assistant soundman broke his neck in a fall. Finally, actor Sheldon Leonard had the extremely painful experience of falling into a patch of barbed cactus quills that had to be cut, one by one, out of his backside. Regardless of whether they were true or false, such stories had an important role in bolstering American discourses about Haitian savagery and occultism.[42]

The transparent pro-American ideological politics of *Ouanga* and *White Zombie* did little to save these cheap outings from a critical mauling. The

The Walking Dead (1936).

remarked: 'The whole thing has me confused; I just can't understand it.' That was, as briefly as can be expressed, the legend for posterity of 'White Zombie.' Charity – still the greatest of the trilogy – suggests that the sentence be allowed to stand as comment. To go on would lead only to a description of why the eagle screamed, and that would prove very little, indeed, in the orderly scheme of life. There was, in short no great reason. Nor was there, to be candid, much reason for 'White Zombie.' The screen shuddering slightly can go on; it can forget, it can be a zombie, too."[43]

Audiences didn't seem to care what the critics said, though. Although the torturous distribution history of *Ouanga* meant that most American cinemagoers didn't see the film until the 1940s, *White Zombie* became an instant box office success.[44] Whether it was Lugosi's central performance, the evocative cinematography or the topical subtext that made *White Zombie* such an overnight sensation is difficult to say for certain. One thing is clear, though: the history books may show that the Americans occupied Haiti between 1915 and 1934, but in the year of 1932 the island's zombie-culture invaded the American imagination.

sarcastic review of *White Zombie* in *The New York Times* was typical of that film's dismissive notices.

"Necromancers waved their sinister hands from the screen of the Rivoli yesterday and tried to hypnotise blondes into killing their boyfriends. A legion of individuals, with deceased minds but alert bodies, threw butlers into subterranean streams. Eagles screamed and vultures carried on a terrific caterwauling all around a mountainous castle. And half way through the picture that inspired all these things an actor wistfully

III. THE ZOMBIES ARE REVOLTING

Although the success of *White Zombie* was undeniable, few of the major studios were interested in pursuing the living dead. Widely regarded as little more than a box office fluke, *White Zombie* didn't encourage any established filmmakers to turn their hand to movies about the walking corpses or the Caribbean. Most of the Hollywood establishment regarded the zombie as little more than a ragged upstart, a one-hit wonder that was vaguely downmarket. Unconvinced that there was money to be made from seeing the dead walk, the big studios turned their backs on the zombie, and the monster's long-running association with low-budget, critically dismissed films began in earnest.

Since the zombie lacked a well-established literary base, those screenwriters who did decide to tackle the living dead frequently took liberties with the legend, displaying an irreverence that would have been unthinkable towards respected contemporary properties such as *Dracula* or *Frankenstein*. Forced to play the part of the eternal poor relation (and with no copyrights and few vested interests to protect it), the zombie was pushed from pillar to post by writers who had little idea what to do with it.

Hot on the heels of Lugosi's *White Zombie*, his chief rival Boris Karloff appeared in three zombie-styled chillers during the decade, all of which dropped the Caribbean focus of the Halperins' outing. In British horror movie *The Ghoul* (1933),

Karloff played an Egyptologist whose knowledge of ancient burial rights allows him to return from the dead. Sadly, his doubting manservant hasn't carried out his instructions properly, leaving Karloff to return as a half-dead, half-alive ghoul in what was little more than an echo of his star turn in *The Mummy* (1932). In *The Walking Dead* (1936) Karloff played a man wrongly executed for a crime he didn't commit and then brought back to "life" as a shuffling zombie who takes revenge on the gangsters who framed him. Meanwhile in *The Man They Could Not Hang* (1939), he starred as a crazed scientist experimenting with artificial hearts, who's hanged for murder after the accidental death of one of his test subjects. Needless to say, he doesn't stay dead for long.

Produced under the respective banners of Gaumont, Warner Bros. and Columbia, *The Ghoul*, *The Walking Dead* and *The Man They Could Not Hang* illustrate the extent to which the major studios were only interested in the zombie when it was completely stripped of its Caribbean heritage.[45] Uninterested in the racial anxieties inherent within films like *White Zombie*, Karloff's movies turned the living dead into just another bogeyman.

As interest in Haiti and the Caribbean waned and the first rumblings of war in Europe began to be heard, the focus of the United States' foreign policy moved further afield. It's not surprising then that the next film to feature the zombie – and use the word in its title – would have little to do with Karloff's insipid outings. Released in 1936, *Revolt of the Zombies* was conceived as an unofficial sequel to *White Zombie*. Produced and directed by the Halperin brothers in a vain attempt to cash-in on that earlier movie's success, *Revolt* may have completely divorced itself from the Caribbean, yet it succeeded in linking the zombie with a very different kind of American foreign policy.

Breaking their collaboration with Bela Lugosi and screenwriter Garnett Weston, the Halperins brought in a cast of fresh faces along with two new scriptwriters, Howard Higgin and Rollo Lloyd. The results of these changes were rather disappointing. As Weston went off to a lucrative career scripting Bulldog Drummond adventures, the new writers struggled to come up with a plausible reworking of the genre. Lacking Weston's intimate knowledge of both the zombie myth and Seabrook's voodoo research, Higgin and Lloyd's script rehashed many of the elements of *White Zombie*, while failing to match the earlier film's powerful impact. At times, the similarities between the two properties bordered on the ludicrous, with a love-triangle plot that explicitly echoed that between Neil, Madeleine and Beaumont in the earlier film. Adding to the feeling of déjà vu, the Halperins also recycled the distinctive footage of Lugosi's mesmerising eyes. Originality, it seems, was difficult to come by.

The plot broke with Seabrook and *White Zombie* by relocating the action from the Caribbean to the Far East. During the height of the First World War, Armand Louque (Dean Jagger) discovers that Cambodian priests are in possession of a devastating mind-control technique that allows them to turn ordinary soldiers into zombie warriors completely impervious to pain, bullets and the bitter misery of the trenches. Believing that these "tireless, fearless human machines" could turn the tide of the war in the Allies' favour, Armand approaches General Duval

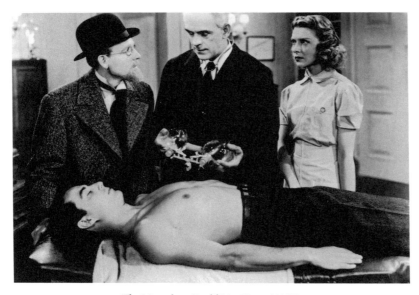

The Man they Could Not Hang (1939).

(George Cleveland), who is unimpressed by his findings until he sees the Cambodian zombies in action. They storm a German trench under the telepathic control of the priest, slaughtering everyone who gets in their way and shrugging off enemy fire.

Terrified that this power should reside in Cambodian hands – and explicitly concerned that it might bring about the "destruction of the *white* race" – General Duval imprisons the priest then sets out with Armand and various Allied officers to Angkor, where they plan to destroy all trace of this super-weapon. But one of the group, the distinctly Russian-looking Colonel Mazovia (Roy D'Arcy), has other plans. He wants to use this telepathic power for his own ends. Killing the priest and stealing the map that shows where the secret of the mind-control technique is hidden, Mazovia travels out to Cambodia with a very different agenda.

During their adventures in the jungle, Armand falls in love with General Duval's daughter Claire (Dorothy Stone), but after a brief engagement she dumps him for his friend Grayson (Robert Noland). Furious at being slighted, Armand feels powerless to intervene until he unexpectedly discovers the secret of the zombie mind-control technique himself. Killing Mazovia to prevent any unwelcome interference in his plan, Armand then binds the whole of Cambodia to his will and turns its citizens into his own private zombie army.

Still desperately in love with Claire, Armand blackmails her into seeing him. She sweet-talks him into proving his love by releasing the Cambodian populace from his grip. The film ends with Armand being killed by his former slaves who are – quite understandably – rather annoyed about having been zombified. The Cambodians storm Armand's palatial mansion and take their revenge, while the rest of the cast bemoan the dangers of one man having too much power.

In comparison with *White Zombie*, *Revolt* is strictly second-rate. Where the first film built up both atmosphere and mood to create a nightmarish mix of death and desire, *Revolt* is more likely to send audiences to sleep with its hackneyed acting and languorous pace: one ten-minute chase sequence follows Armand as he silently pursues a Cambodian monk through a back-projected jungle swamp, with both actors doing their best to "wade" through the non-existent water.

Originally, the Halperins had planned to open the film in AD 839 with a sequence showing the Cambodian city of Angkor being built by zombie slaves. In the end, budgetary restrictions scuppered the plan and hampered the rest of the project itself. Combining truly awful back-projection of Cambodian temples with unconvincing attempts to show a whole nation under the sway of one man's mental power, *Revolt* never escapes the dreary limitations of its cheap and slapdash roots. The original posters boasted that the film contained 500,000 zombies, but the true number is probably about fifteen.

Yet for all its explicit cribbing from its predecessor, the film remains an important milestone in the development of the genre. In contrast to the small-scale terrors of *White Zombie*, *Revolt* was the first film to appreciate the fact that one potential avenue for the living dead's development was in linking the image of the zombie to the masses. With its cast of "Cambodian" extras and a flawed but ambitious attempt to depict a whole nation of zombies, *Revolt* established what in later years would become a genre staple: the zombie apocalypse in which the living are terrorised not by one or two walking dead, but a whole army of them.

One reason why *Revolt*'s influence took so long to take effect was undoubtedly because of the film's central red herring of making its "zombies" into brainwashed victims of Armand's telepathic control. Instead of reanimated corpses, these Cambodian supersoldiers are living subjects whose zombification is mental rather than physical. For contemporary critics, this offhand reworking of zombie lore was simply too much. Writing in the *New York Times*, critic Frank S. Nugent reprimanded the Halperins for their misguided attempts to change the central tenets of the zombie myth. "The zombies, the revolting zombies, are revolting at the Rialto this week and we don't blame them. Even a zombie has his rights and we loyal necrophiles will fight to the last mandrake root to protect them. Under any code of fair practice, a zombie is entitled to be authentically dead but revived horrendously by some sorcerer to do his evil bidding"

The problem with *Revolt of the Zombies* for Nugent was it played fast and loose with the myth. "To suggest, as 'Revolt of the Zombies' does, that our blank-faced, glazed-eyed heroes are merely under the hypnotic spell of a handsome chap who found a synthetic zombie formula in a Cambodian temple is to discredit an honourable profession. And to hint that they are not really zombies at all, but sleepwalkers or something, is to imperil the very foundations of a grand spook legend. No wonder the zombies revolted, turned on their love-forlorn master and shot him down: he was their conjur' man and he done them wrong."[46]

It wasn't just the reviewers who were unhappy with the Halperins' attempts to style these "robot soldiers" as zombies. Amusement Securities Corporation, the company who'd purchased the redistribution rights for *White Zombie*, took the filmmakers to court protesting that a second Halperin film with the word "zombie" in the title constituted unfair competition. The Halperins, well used to such legal wrangling, agreed to rename it *Revolt of the Demons* until an appeal hearing later overturned the case and the film reverted to its original title.

If nothing else, such incidents prove just how firmly established in American popular culture the zombie was by the mid-1930s. But they also underestimate the film's chief innovation, for by tampering with the voodoo basis of the zombie mythology, *Revolt* opened up the genre's scope in quite unexpected ways that, in time, would have a significant impact on the zombie movie.

Although *White Zombie* and *Ouanga* played with American anxieties surrounding the Depression and the occupation of Haiti, *Revolt* confronts a very different set of concerns. It's no accident that the film's "robot soldiers" owe a considerable debt to the sleepwalking murderer of Robert Wiene's classic of German Expressionism *Das Cabinet des Dr Caligari* (*The Cabinet of Dr Caligari*, 1919). In that earlier film, the sleepwalking Cesare (Conrad Veidt) became a suggestive symbol of the way in which Germany's populace had been brainwashed into the bloody madness of the First World War. In *Revolt*, the image of the sleepwalking (zombified) mass is closely bound to similar concerns, including the growing re-emergence of German military aggression.

With its First World War setting, *Revolt* seems determined to force a link between the zombie army and the tensions of the world stage in the mid-1930s. As National Socialism restructured German society for its own world-conquering ends,

the similarities between *Revolt*'s vision of a whole nation held under the hypnotic spell of a single dictator and events in Europe were readily apparent. Given this, Armand's vocal attempts to justify his actions by using the sub-Nietzschean chatter of his friend Grayson seem particularly pointed. Grayson's off-hand talk about taking what one wants could have been lifted verbatim from *Mein Kampf*: "If you want anything, ride roughshod over everything... Be ruthless, forget all sentiment. Get to your objective, take it and hold it."

Significantly, *Revolt of the Zombies* wasn't the only film from the period to draw links between the zombie and the impending war. In France, a very different kind of film was toying with zombie iconography in a similar attempt to underscore the relationship between the living dead and the bloody insanity of 20th-century conflict. While placing Abel Gance's arty anti-war film *J'Accuse* (1937) beside *Revolt of the Zombies* may seem like an affront to the terrible beauty of Gance's vision, there are undeniable similarities between the two films in terms of their use of the zombie to mirror fears about the impending European hostilities.

An extended remake of his silent 1919 short of the same name, Gance's 1937 version of *J'Accuse* is an indictment of the 20th century's ongoing war lust, in which shell-shocked First World War soldier and poet Jean Diaz (Victor Francen) tries to warn the world not to repeat the mistakes of 1914–1918. The only survivor of a platoon that is massacred in the trenches, Diaz becomes a pacifist and invents a form of unbreakable "steel" glass that he hopes might put an end to war. The military want to use this invention as a weapon and so, in a delirious reaction to their pigheaded stupidity, Diaz orders the dead of the First World War from their graves to march across the country and remind the living of their past folly. It's a startling sequence that owes a great debt to the traditions of the horror genre. Gance's controversial decision to use real members of the *Union de Gueules Cassées*, who get to display their horrific wounds alongside made-up extras, gives it an added resonance. Released to a Europe on the brink of another round of slaughter, *J'Accuse* stands as one of history's most poignant productions – a cinematic warning cry that no one heeded.

CHAPTER THREE

DOWN AND OUT ON POVERTY ROW

I. HORROR COMEDY ON BLACK ISLAND

Throughout the 1930s, the predominant characteristic of zombie movies was their low-budget origins. Lacking the sponsorship of the major horror-producing studios, the living dead never achieved the same status as the other critically and popularly acclaimed monster movies of the period.[47] This marginal position remained part of the genre's limitation during the 1940s as well, for as the 1930s horror boom came to an end, the living dead slipped out of the limelight into the slums of Hollywood's Poverty Row studios.

Before being eased out of the mainstream, the zombie did have its first and (for many, many years) last shot at the big time as Paramount released the horror farce *The Ghost Breakers* (1940) with a cast that included Bob Hope, Paulette Goddard and Anthony Quinn. Envisioned as a sequel to the successful comic partnership of Hope and Goddard in the previous year's horror comedy *The Cat and the Canary*, *The Ghost Breakers* transported the voodoo-zombie thematics of *White Zombie* and other 1930s Caribbean pictures to Havana, where American beauty Mary Carter (Goddard) inherits a reputedly haunted Cuban castle on Black Island.

Although she doesn't know it, Carter's castle stands over a lucrative silver vein. Various bad guys are planning on snaffling the mine out from under her nose by playing up the castle's reputation as a haunted house and scaring her off.

Fortunately she has the help of radio celebrity Larry Lawrence (Hope) and his black valet (Willie Best), two comic cowards who solve the riddle of the castle while fending off the unwelcome attentions of the island's chief residents: Mother Zombie (Virginia Brissac) and her living dead son, The Zombie (Noble Johnson).

As a horror comedy, *The Ghost Breakers* succeeds because of the sublime comic partnership of Hope and Willie Best. Competing over who can be the most cowardly, this well-matched duo play up the movie's chills with their hammy comic mugging. Stumbling over one another to get out of harm's way, tripping over each other's feet and generally jumping at the sight of their own shadows, their wide-eyed expressions of terror are hilariously funny. As they creep around the haunted castle, the sparklingly polished gags shine through, with Hope getting all the best lines: "If a couple of fellas come running down the stairs in a few minutes, let the first one go – that'll be me."

As far as the film's horror content goes, it's Johnson's zombie who steals the show. A shuffling, ragged monster with a misshapen head and wrinkled, decomposing skin, the zombie is far scarier than the rest of the film's alleged shocks – rubber bats on strings, cobwebbed skeletons, hidden passageways and gun-toting bad guys – put together. Johnson (who once played the African chief in *King Kong*) transforms the zombie into

The Ghost Breakers's real threat. The scene in which he chases the terrified Goddard through the spooky house is quite possibly the only unsettling moment in the film.

The Ghost Breakers is significant because its monster is the first cinematic member of the walking dead who actually looks *dead*. During the 1930s, American horror movies simply dressed their zombies in rags and slapped on some cadaverously pale make-up. In comparison, the zombie in *The Ghost Breakers* appears to have spent the last few decades decomposing in the castle grounds.

Repeatedly upstaging Johnson's monster with humour, though, the film walks a thin line between comic effectiveness and horror bankruptcy. As Hope arrives in the Caribbean, he's given the requisite lesson in living dead mythology. "A zombie has no will of its own. You see them sometimes walking around blindly, following orders, not knowing what they do, not caring," someone explains. To which Hope deadpans: "You mean like Democrats?" Later, in a blatant disregard for all conventions, the zombie dresses up in a suit of armour and tries to bump off our blundering heroes with a spiked mace. It's an unlikely proposition that not even Hope's "quick, get the can-opener" quip can paper over.

Such comedy may have taken the bite out of the film's chills, yet it did little to disguise *The Ghost Breakers*'s reactionary racial politics. Poised between the first and second cycle of zombie films, the picture marked the beginning of a trend that would thread its way throughout the period. Pitting a white hero and his black manservant against the forces of the living dead, *The Ghost Breakers* signalled a shift away from the Haiti-dominated voodoo films of the 1930s by setting its action in Cuba, a land far less foreign to the United States than Haiti. Yet like those earlier films, *The Ghost Breakers* is obsessed with issues of race. It certainly seems significant that the castle is located on *Black* Island, was built by "Cuba's greatest slave trader" and is haunted by "those lost souls who were starved and murdered in the castle dungeons". Nor does it come as any surprise to learn that the zombie and his mother are black.

The equation of the zombie with America's racial Others was something that would become a permanent feature in the zombie films of the 1940s, as issues of race and imperialism intertwined. As the promotional posters for *The Ghost Breakers* made clear, the zombie could serve as a potent symbol of white America's anxieties over its African-American populace. "Step right up Paulette and meet the Spooks," Bob Hope says to a seated Paulette Goddard on one of the original publicity posters. Willie Best stands behind her, while above them hover the spectral figures of two misshapen black zombies. The link between "spooks" and African-Americans becomes transparent as Goddard is invited to meet both the African-American Willie Best and the non-Caucasian zombies. That "spook" was a slang term of racial abuse in 1940s America simply adds grist to the dubious pun. Given this, the fact that *The Ghost Breakers* was the first American zombie movie to employ a black actor to play its monster seems more than coincidental.

In the films that followed *The Ghost Breakers* – particularly *King of the Zombies* (1941) and *Revenge of the Zombies* (1943) – the relationship between the comic antics of the black servant and the films' zombies became a recurrent theme. The black servant was made to mimic, mirror or even replace the living dead as the films' chief source of anxiety. This racial dynamic eventually reached its zenith in Jacques Tourneur's *I Walked with a Zombie* (1943), a gothic horror tale set in the Caribbean. Exaggerating white anxiety over racial difference to hysterical proportions, *I Walked with a Zombie* equated the living dead not only with the primitive but also with the total collapse of truth, reason and meaning.

II. THE POVERTY ROW YEARS

The *Ghost Breakers* marked the end of the big studios' obsession with the horror film. The boom that had begun in the early 1930s ground to an abrupt halt as America and the rest of the world found itself coming to terms with the realities of war once again. While horror-movie production never stopped – with its European backdrop Universal's *Wolf Man* series proved unexpectedly popular during the Second World War – there was a significant shift within the industry as the genre was slowly marginalised, eventually taking up residence in Hollywood's Poverty Row studios.

Unlike Universal or MGM, the studios grouped together under the Poverty Row banner were small independent companies. They coexisted in the gaps between the "A" and "B" picture productions of the major studios on the one hand and the twilight world of "exploitation" films, with their sensationalist warnings about sex hygiene, crime and drugs, on the other.[48] Founded during the Depression, Poverty Row companies like Republic, Grand National, Mascot, PRC and Monogram managed to survive in the overcrowded movie marketplace by churning out exceedingly cheap productions. Specialising in one-horse Westerns, action films (usually involving lots of inexpensive fist-fights and foot chases) and horror movies, these were hand-to-mouth operations interested only in making enough profit to keep them in business for another week.

Monogram was one of the first of these independent studios, founded shortly after the 1929 stock market crash by Midwesterner W. Ray Johnston. Using second-rate talent on both sides of the camera, there was little room for art, originality or risks. In the early 1940s, the average Monogram picture made a profit of just $1,932 and twelve cents in change. As Tom Weaver points out in his excellent history of Poverty Row horror, it was a "minuscule dividend that left little room for tinkering and fine tuning."[49]

The success of the big-studio horror pictures of the 1930s convinced the Poverty Row players to try their hand at the chiller market. Picking up where Universal left off – though without a fraction of the budget of films like *Dracula* – the studios produced scores of cheap movies that promised to curdle the blood, but in reality were often only terrifying in terms of how truly awful they were. The years from 1940 to 1946 were a golden age in the world of hackneyed scares and Z-grade schlock horror, with casts that frequently included talented but hard-up actors like Lugosi, John Carradine, George Zucco, Glenn Strange and Lionel Atwill.

There are few apologists for the Poverty Row horror films of the period, and even the biggest Lugosi fan will admit that these nickel-and-dime productions did little to enhance his floundering career. Yet, in spite of their very obvious failings, Monogram's pictures always found an audience, because, as Tom Weaver explains, they usually had at least a hint of a good idea behind them. "The unfortunate part about the Monogram horror films is that in some ways, a number of them came awfully close to being halfway decent; all they needed was a bit more production and a good writer to fiddle with the scripts and the dialogue. Monogram's horror scripts were notoriously bad, but somewhere in them – buried in incoherent dialogue and goofy plot twists – were often ideas that had a good bit of unrealised potential."[50] With such tiny profits at stake, however, there was little inclination to "fiddle" with the niceties of plot, dialogue or character.

The horror pictures of this period range from PRC's *The Devil Bat* (1941) and *The Mad Monster* (1942) to Republic's *The Lady and the Monster* (1944) and *The Vampire's Ghost* (1945). Unlike its rivals, Monogram's chiller movies were usually horror-lite affairs in which Bela Lugosi would wade through a supposedly scary, but actually rather mediocre, script. Trading on Lugosi's reputation as the master of horror, Monogram's scriptwriters did their best to ensure that there was actually very little scary content (and therefore little expense) other than the presence of the man who had once played Dracula. Crippled by budget restrictions often even worse than many of its equally cash-starved competitors, Monogram's films rarely even stretched to a half-decent monster.

A quick comparison of the PRC and Republic titles listed above with those of Monogram's catalogue is telling. Movies such as *Invisible Ghost* (1941), *The Corpse Vanishes* (1942), *Ghosts on the Loose* (1943) and *Spook Busters* (1946) reveal the extent of the studio's budgetary constraints. While the other Poverty Row studios may have been cheap, they could usually scrounge together a few dollars to invest in a monster of some description. Monogram, however, relied on invisible ghosts and vanished corpses – budget-saving devices around which Lugosi had to conjure up some semblance of horror.

One monster that Monogram could always

afford was the zombie. All the living dead films that came out of the Poverty Row studios bore the Monogram stamp: *King of the Zombies* (1941), *Bowery At Midnight* (1942), *Revenge of the Zombies* (1943) and *Voodoo Man* (1944).[51] They were all, without exception, dreadful.

Monogram's filmmakers repeatedly returned to the zombie because the living dead required little in the way of special effects. A hard-pressed director could churn out a relatively effective zombie film without having to spend more than a handful of dollars on make-up and wardrobe; the casting director wouldn't have to search out skilled professionals to play the film's living dead roles; and the zombie actors' fees would be negligible since, as horror-movie historian Denis Gifford points out, the union-scale payment for non-speaking parts was considerably lower.[52]

Unfortunately for the genre, Monogram's involvement with the zombie merely confirmed the suspicions of the Hollywood mainstream. The major studios became convinced that the zombie was a cheap, low-rent monster that was more of an embarrassment than a worthy successor to the chills of *Dracula* or *Frankenstein*. It was a prejudice that would shape the genre's development over the next two decades.

The first Poverty Row production to employ the zombie was an unabashed cash-in on the success of *The Ghost Breakers* entitled *King of the Zombies*, which ripped-off the white hero/black

valet pairing of Hope and Best. Directed by Jean Yarbrough, *King of the Zombies* was originally conceived as one of Monogram's many Lugosi vehicles, but after he dropped out – and an ambitious attempt to sign up Peter Lorre fell flat – the role of the mad scientist went to Henry Victor. Victor had played the strongman in Tod Browning's *Freaks* a decade before, and by the 1940s his German upbringing and distinctive accent kept him typecast in Nazi roles.

King of the Zombies begins as Bill (John Archer), his black valet Jeff (Mantan Moreland) and their pilot Mac (Dick Purcell) crash land their plane on a mysterious Caribbean island during the Second World War. Discovering a nearby mansion owned by Austrian scientist Dr Sangre (Henry Victor), the trio gradually realise that all is not well on the island. Sangre has taken an American admiral captive and is trying to interrogate him using voodoo magic. Eager to allay his new guests' suspicions, Sangre attempts to hypnotise Jeff and Mac, but his plans fall apart as Jeff blows the whistle on his cellar full of zombies.

It wasn't just the mix of horror and comedy that *King of the Zombies* owed to *The Ghost Breakers*. It also replayed much of the earlier film's racial subtext. In copying the white investigator/black manservant pairing of Hope and Willie Best, though, *King* significantly changed the formula. Hope's cowardice and Willie Best's scared bumbling are combined in the character of Jeff, while white hero Bill is transformed into a brave but bland everyman, whose role is significantly diminished. It was a subtle shift that made the film's racial politics far more transparent. What *King of the Zombies* illustrates is the manner in which the zombie movie of the 1940s lost interest in the American-Caribbean and became, instead, an oblique commentary on domestic relations between whites and African-Americans.

Significantly, this shift occurred in a period that had become particularly self-conscious about the role of black actors in American cinema. As film historian Donald Bogle suggests in his book *Toms,*

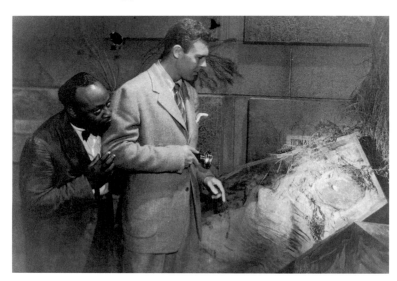

King of the Zombies (1941).

Coons, Mulattoes, Mammies and Bucks: An Interpretative History of Blacks in American Film, the 1930s were "the Age of the Negro Servant" since "no other period could boast of more black faces carrying mops and pails or lifting pots and pans than the Depression years. In the movies, as in the streets, it was a time when the only people without job worries were the maids, the butlers, the bootblacks, the bus boys, the elevator men, the cooks and the custodians."[53]

Relishing the visibility that mainstream Hollywood cinema was offering them, black performers made the most of their limited parts, turning their cooks, butlers and maids into larger-than-life characters who challenged African-American stereotypes, even as they were forced to play up to them.

By the 1940s, however, the situation was changing. Black commentators were becoming increasingly critical of such strategies of visibility, claiming that its oppositional potential was, at best, deeply flawed. Meanwhile, white audiences were becoming bored with the constant stream of dark-skinned comic characters that Hollywood's screenwriters were churning out. One such stereotype – the "coon" – was a staple of the period. Most famously represented by actor Stepin Fetchit (his stage-name was significantly servile – "step and fetch it"), the "coon" was usually a black male servant who was pathologically lazy, greedy and prone to getting ideas above his station.

By the 1940s, such representations of black masculinity were on the wane, but it was Willie Best and Mantan Moreland who squeezed the dregs out of the stereotype. It was a role that Moreland made his trademark in the Monogram zombie pictures and elsewhere. Moreland, as Bogle explains, "added a perverse twist to the tradition. Generally, Mantan was always there *until* his white friend needed him. Then he took off for the hills. He was a fantastic cowardly lion with an uncanny command of stagecraft. In those films in which he was terr'fied of de ghosts, Moreland displayed an arsenal of gestures and grimaces that actors had traditionally used to steal scenes and develop characters. He was notorious for his perfectly timed double takes. No other actor could widen his eyes like Moreland. Nor could any other manage his trick of appearing to run without actually moving at all. He always looked as if he were about to trip over his own feet as he tried to make a hasty departure."[54]

Although played for laughs, the role of the "coon" spoke volumes about white America's racial stereotyping. The audience's reaction to him was necessarily double-edged. On one hand his laziness, cowardice and greed were used for comic effect; at the same time, these qualities were generally reviled. The "coon" was thus simultaneously both the comic star and the comic villain, playing a role that invited guffaws and censure in equal measure.

In *King*, Moreland's "coon" act is intimately bound up with the film's zombies. As the lazy black servant who doesn't know his place, Jeff is zombified by Sangre in a manner that suggests that his predicament is more than just the outcome of the necessities of plot. By zombifying Jeff, Sangre puts this bumptious Negro in his place, offering (white) audiences not only a comic adventure in which Jeff joins the "fugitives from the undertaker" but also a blatant piece of wish fulfilment as the "coon" gets taught the error of his ways. *King* may end with Sangre's plot exposed and Jeff returned to normal, but the (white) audience's enjoyment of his transformation from "coon" to zombie is, without doubt, the film's chief focus.

In the scenes leading up to Jeff's zombification, the antagonism between Jeff and Sangre is spectacularly pointed. We already know that Jeff's behaviour regularly steps outside the normal limits of what a black manservant ought to be able to get away with; Bill and Mac's exasperated expressions tell us that his laziness, cheekiness and outright incompetence is a nuisance to them both. Yet the general sense is that he's tolerated by them in much the same way as a badly behaved puppy dog might be.

Sangre has less patience with the servant's uppity behaviour. As Jeff tries to join the three white men in a glass of brandy (Sangre pointedly pulls the tray out of his reach) and badgers their host about the sleeping arrangements ("Excuse me doctor, but didn't you forget something? What about me?"), it's clear that the Austrian scientist doesn't agree with Bill's indulgent attitude towards his valet. Refusing to let Jeff sleep upstairs because it "might set a bad example for the other servants", Sangre puts Jeff in his place by sending him down to the basement. Jeff's mournful complaints – "The idea of me doing skulduggery in the kitchen; why that ain't no business for a man who's used to resorting with big shots" – suggests just how unused to such treatment he is. In the basement, Jeff meets two of Sangre's servants: Samantha the maid (Marguerite Whitten) and Tahama the cook (Madame Sul-Te-Wan). He also encounters the household zombies: a ragged group of ghouls brought back from the dead to work as slaves. When Jeff tries to tell his boss what's lurking downstairs, the idea is ridiculed and Sangre claims these supposed "zombies" are actually just his servants.

Eager to take his revenge on the ever-troublesome Jeff, Sangre then hypnotises him into thinking he's a zombie, pointedly commanding: "Get over there where you belong." It's a sequence that's shot through with humour: "Move over boys, I'm one of the gang now," Moreland wisecracks as he joins the ranks of the undead. By the next scene, Jeff has fulfilled the promise of the film's title, becoming (quite literally) the king of the zombies and drilling his undead cohorts as if on parade: "Company! Halt!"

For all the supposed comedy of these scenes, there's an underlying seriousness to the horseplay. The transformation of Jeff into a "zombie" may appear to be a subplot, but it's actually the main focus (significantly, when Mac is hypnotised into thinking he's a zombie he's shunted to the sidelines until the film's final moments). By turning Jeff into a zombie, Sangre takes his revenge on the character's cheeky arrogance, effectively punishing the "coon" for his wayward behaviour and failure to know his place.

The effect of this is twofold: the audience (both white and black) get to enjoy Jeff's comic misdemeanours, his slighting of authority and his barefaced cheek. Yet his zombification also acts as a punishment that the (white) audience can simultaneously enjoy before the film closes with the defeat of the Nazi scientist and the return of Bill, the white hero, to centre stage. The film has it both ways. It presents the African-American Jeff as dangerously arrogant *and* comically incompetent; as dangerously autonomous *and* as naturally passive (the fact that Sangre's real zombies are presented as lazy, dim-witted and constantly hanging around the kitchen waiting for food obviously has more to do with white-led representations of African-Americans than

conventions of zombie lore). In other words, *King* raises the spectre of growing African-American autonomy in 1940s America, only to undercut it by turning its black hero into a zombie and having him serve the needs of his white masters in thwarting their common enemy.

Race not only dominated the film's subtext, but also the publicity material. Describing director Jean Yarbrough as a man of "tact and discretion", the film's press book recounted a story that allegedly occurred during the shoot. Preparing for a scene in which Dick Purcell, Joan Woodbury and Moreland stumble across a zombie, Yarbrough reportedly told his cast, "Now when you see this 'dead man' rise from the coffin, recoil and blanch with fear – you know, turn pale". Moreland, described in the press book as "a gentleman of colour from Alabama", is said to have replied: "Mistah Yarbrough, that is a little difficult for me." Yarbrough thought things over and said, "Okay Mantan – you just sort of blanch darkly."[55]

While this story might appear to be nothing more than an innocuous piece of press book trivia, its racial dimension is telling. Not only does it underscore the film's obsession with race, but it also puts Moreland in his place once again as a cheeky "gentleman of colour from Alabama" whose disruptive potential (interrupting the white director; trying to make things more difficult than they are) is circumvented by the quick-thinking Yarbrough. It was a joke that someone at Monogram obviously thought was particularly amusing since it also occurs in the film itself when, in a suitably scary moment, Jeff mutters: "If it was in me I sure would be pale now."

By Monogram's standards, *King of the Zombies* was an unexpectedly successful venture. Audiences enjoyed the comedy and – though it's difficult to believe today – some even found the horror elements frightening. *The Monthly Film Bulletin* claimed, "except for those who enjoy an eerie and gruesome film, this is a most unpleasant one of its type, full of voodooism, black magic, graveyards and walking dead."[56] What was even more surprising was the fact that by some strange quirk of showbiz fate, *King of the Zombies* was nominated for an Academy Award for Best Score – the first, and most definitely last, time that a Monogram horror movie made it to the Oscars. Competing against films like *Citizen Kane* and *Dr*

Jekyll and Mr Hyde, Edward J. Kay's score didn't have much hope of winning. Quite how any soundtrack containing the lyrics "Eddie loves those cocoa beans / Zombies! / I like cocoa, I like cocoa" could ever have been nominated in the first place has yet to be explained. Perhaps if the planned sequence in which the zombies gave a rendition of a musical number called "The Gravedigger's Song" had gone ahead an Oscar might have become a reality. Instead, the award went to Bernard Herrmann's infinitely more deserving score for *The Devil and Daniel Webster*.

With *King of the Zombies* achieving such unexpected success, a sequel was put into production and released in 1943. Co-written by *King* scribe Edmond Kelso, *Revenge of the Zombies* saw the return of Mantan Moreland in a film that was more of a remake than a sequel. Although boasting slightly better production values than its predecessor, *Revenge* proved far less memorable. Its storyline was lifted almost verbatim from *King* and jazzed up for Second World War audiences with an explicitly Nazi villain named Max von Altermann (John Carradine) who clicks his heels, speaks fluent German and commands a platoon of goose-stepping zombies.

Hiding out in his laboratory, von Altermann is creating a race of zombie supersoldiers to help his beloved Fatherland win the war: "I am prepared to supply my country with a new army, numbering as many thousands as are required," he brags. The chief advantage of these soldiers is that they're already dead and so can't be killed on the battlefield: "Against an army of zombies, no armies could stand. Why, even blown to bits – undaunted by fire and gas – zombies would fight on so long as the brain cells which receive and execute commands still remained intact."

Budgetary constraints meant that audiences never got to see this formidable army in action. Instead, *Revenge* managed to muster a handful of assorted male extras to stumble bare-chested around von Altermann's basement lab. None of these domesticated zombies look capable of taking over the world and, if von Altermann's zombified wife is anything to go by, they don't even seem to be particularly obedient. Playing up the Nazi theme and struggling under a hefty dollop of wartime propaganda, *Revenge* dispenses with the racial subtext of *King*, giving Mantan Moreland far less

screen time and focussing instead on some crass Jerry-bashing.

The other zombie-themed Monogram films of the 1940s had little to recommend them either. Two vehicles for Bela Lugosi – *Bowery At Midnight* (1942) and *Voodoo Man* (1944) – put the poverty squarely into Poverty Row, with shockingly terrible scripts and laughable living dead extras. Proving that Monogram's interest in the zombie was only ever the result of financial necessity, both *Bowery* and *Voodoo Man* brought the still-youthful genre to a new low.

In *Bowery At Midnight*, Monogram attempted to revive the zombie-gangster movie that had begun with Karloff's *The Walking Dead*. Lugosi, whose career slide had led him to embark on a permanent cycle of public appearances as Dracula and quick acting jobs on Poverty Row, played a dual role. By day he's Professor Brenner, an acclaimed psychologist and upstanding member of the community; but by night he's Karl Wagner, a villainous criminal who uses a Manhattan soup kitchen called the Bowery Friendly Mission as a front for his crime syndicate.

For most of its sixty-minute running time, *Bowery* is distinctly lacking in any horror content whatsoever. As the ridiculously intricate plot unfolds, Lugosi switches back and forth between his roles, performing a few cold-blooded (but resolutely bloodless) murders and generally trying to evade arrest. The film's zombies only arrive in the final reel as we discover that the drug-addled Bowery janitor Doc (Lew Kelly) has been reviving the dead bodies of Wagner/Brenner's victims and keeping them locked away in a secret room in the basement. As Wagner tries to hide from the police in the soup kitchen, Doc decides he's had enough of his double-crossing employer and so unleashes the zombies. Eager for revenge, the living dead tear Wagner to pieces. Bloodlessly and off-screen of course.

Implicitly expanding on the link made between the living dead and the unemployed during the Depression, *Bowery*'s down-at-heel setting is the perfect location for the American zombie. Putting the living dead in a soup kitchen populated by New York's bums and petty thieves, the film belatedly proves the monsters' symbolic ties to the poor, dispossessed and unemployed. No wonder the Poverty Row studios loved the zombie so much – here was a monster that summed up their own feelings of being low-rent, mass-produced and only one step away from complete destitution.

Lugosi's next zombie outing for the Monogram stable proved little better. *Voodoo Man* caught the luckless actor just as he finished a stage-production of *Arsenic and Old Lace* and teamed him up with George Zucco and John Carradine in a witless story that was even more ridiculous than *Bowery*. Anyone who had the misfortune of seeing director William Beaudine's earlier film *The Living Ghost* (1942) – another cheap and flatly boring Monogram production about a banker who's turned into a catatonic killer – knew pretty much what to expect. Everyone else was caught off guard by the truly terrible plotting.

Mad old Dr Marlowe (Lugosi) kidnaps lone female motorists with the help of gas station attendant Nicholas (Zucco) and moronic handyman Toby (Carradine). He's hoping to use voodoo magic to transfer their minds into the body of his zombified wife Evelyn (Ellen Hall) who's been dead for the last twenty years. A succession of failures has left Marlowe's rickety old house full of former abductees who've been turned into zombies – and rather pretty ones at that. Since none of these girls' temperaments match that of his wife, the experiments keep failing adding yet more lasses to the collection of zombies in the basement. Keeping an eye over the braindead ladies is Carradine's half-wit handyman, who spends most of his time gawping at them: "Gosh – you've got pretty hair."

The triple bill of Poverty Row horror stalwarts Lugosi, Carradine and Zucco didn't offer three times the chills as hoped, just three times the ridiculousness. Of the trio, Lugosi just about escaped with what remained of his dignity, while Carradine made a complete fool of himself by pulling stupid faces from underneath a silly haircut. Zucco fared the worst of the three as he was forced to don a "voodoo" costume comprised of a feather headdress, a bone necklace and star-spangled cape and intone solemn prayers to the god Ramboona.

"It has been obvious for some time that if Bela 'The Mad Doctor' Lugosi, John 'The Mad Scientist' Carradine and George 'The Mad Man' Zucco kept it up long enough they would be reduced to utter absurdity," wrote the *New York Post*'s reviewer. "Now the obvious has come to pass. They kept it up."[57] Worse still, it was patently obvious that the zombie plot was actually little more than an excuse for Monogram to parade a selection of its starlets for the gratification of the (male) audience. As Peter Dendle succinctly puts it, "Marlowe's experiments amount to a veritable machine for female objectification, with women going in one end and women's bodies coming out the other."[58]

Voodoo Man signalled the beginning of the end for Monogram's horror output. Although there were rumours of another Mantan Moreland movie – *When Zombies Walked* – nobody's heart was in it anymore. The reviewer at the *New York Daily News* got it right when he summed up *Voodoo Man* by commenting that the film wasn't merely content "to portray zombies; it gives the impression of having been made by them."[59] Harsh words, but in respect of so much of Monogram's living dead films, it was unquestionably true.

III. VAL LEWTON: A TOUCH OF CLASS

RKO Pictures may have been in a totally different league than the cheapskates at Monogram but in the 1940s the studio was plagued by financial difficulties. Still feeling the balance sheet pinch after young buck Orson Welles crippled the studio with his expensive commercial flops *Citizen Kane* and *The Magnificent Ambersons*, RKO was in desperate need of new ideas to rescue it from its growing stream of creditors. So, the RKO horror unit was set up in 1942 with just one aim in mind: profits.

The horror unit's remit was to make sensational chillers on a tight $150,000 budget per film. In comparison with the Poverty Row studios, this was blockbuster funding, although in mainstream Hollywood terms it amounted to little more than small change. The only artistic input the studio heads had over the productions was the list of titles – *The Leopard Man*, *The Body Snatcher*, *Bedlam* – that they issued in expectation of some suitably exploitative pictures. Heading the unit was producer Val Lewton, poached from MGM.

According to Lewton's own self-deprecating (and probably apocryphal) account, he'd been headhunted by RKO because someone had told them that he was the author of several "horrible novels". Mishearing their informant, the RKO executive thought Lewton was a horror novelist and offered him the job. For Lewton, a well-educated, impeccably mannered Russian immigrant, horror films were the last things he wanted to be involved with. Completely uninterested in the genre, he even dismissed the monsters of Universal's classic horror movies as a collection of

I Walked With a Zombie (1943).

"mask-like faces, hardly human, with gnashing teeth and hair standing on end."[60]

Despite his qualms, Lewton was smart enough to realise that heading up the horror unit might be his best chance to show Hollywood what he could do. Giving up his job as David O. Selznick's story editor at MGM, he accepted RKO's offer and set about twisting the unit's remit so that it suited his own agenda. "They may think I'm going to do the usual chiller stuff which will make a quick profit, be laughed at and forgotten," he told his friends. "But I'm going to make the kind of suspense movies I like."[61]

Over the next four years, Lewton produced nine low-budget films at RKO: *Cat People* (1942), *I Walked with a Zombie* (1943), *The Seventh Victim* (1943), *The Leopard Man* (1943), *The Ghost Ship* (1943), *The Curse of the Cat People* (1944), *Isle of the Dead* (1945), *The Body Snatcher* (1945), and *Bedlam* (1946). All of them were invariably *not* what the RKO studio executives had expected. Instead of Universal style creature features, Lewton delivered remarkably restrained, hauntingly poetic movies. It was highbrow horror, not bargain basement shocks.

The RKO executives realised that they were getting far less than they'd bargained for as soon as the unit's first production *Cat People* was unveiled in 1942. The studio wanted a schlock horror tale about subhuman cat creatures. What they got was

an understated psychological thriller about a woman who believes she'll turn into a panther if she has sex with her husband. Replacing sensationalism with a set of low-key chills, *Cat People* should have spelt the premature end of Lewton's career as a producer. Except that audiences flocked to see the picture, making it a huge success.

In *I Walked with a Zombie*, Lewton tried to replicate much the same blend of psychological horror, hysteria and eerie atmosphere. Teaming up with director Jacques Tourneur, the producer returned to the zombie's Haitian roots. Lyrical, creepy and thoroughly unsettling, *I Walked with a Zombie* single-handedly thrust the living dead into the canon of critically acclaimed cinema. By exploring the thematic and symbolic potential of the zombie, Lewton rescued the living dead from the purgatory of Poverty Row once and for all.

The RKO executives had taken the title "I Walked With a Zombie" from an *American Weekly* article by Inez Wallace. Although it was an uninspired piece of journalism, Wallace's article was significant – at least in terms of the zombie's cultural standing – because it returned to the voodoo-fixated anthropology of Seabrook's work. Cribbing almost all of his material from *The Magic Island*, Wallace shamelessly recycled that earlier book's catalogue of voodoo history, anecdotes about the living dead, references to Article 249 of the Haitian penal code and descriptions of zombies as (rather inevitably), "dead men working in the cane fields." Passing itself off as a first-person confession about walking with zombies, Wallace's article was little more than a blatantly sensational piece of pulp anthropology that owed as much to movies like *Ouanga* or *White Zombie* as it did to serious research. To anyone familiar with Seabrook's book it was obvious that Wallace had never even set eyes on a zombie, let alone walked with one.

The article inadvertently ended up establishing a rather strange opposition between its attempts to convince the reader that the zombie was a reality and Wallace's own ignorance and lack of firsthand knowledge of the subject he was writing about. While it's clear that this oscillation between fact and fiction, truth and ignorance, the real and the imagined is an unfortunate (and unplanned) result of Wallace's limitations as a writer, the article actually ends without having kept the promise implied in its title. The author doesn't walk with zombies. What's more, he fails to offer any evidence of their existence other than a collection of second-hand stories which we're asked to believe are true because they come from "the lips of white men and women whose word I can not doubt."[62] For all its claims to offer first-hand reportage about the existence of the living dead, Wallace's article ends without having proved (or disproved) anything. The zombie remains a completely unknowable figure.

As far as the moneymen at RKO were concerned it was the perfect title for the kind of gutsy, lurid horror movie they were after. What Lewton took from Wallace was more than just the article's title, though. The finished film mimics Wallace's uncertainty and hesitation, absorbing the inherent paradoxes between the clash of knowledge and ignorance found in the article. Taking this as its starting point, *I Walked With a Zombie* interrogates the limits of truth and, in a spectacularly breathtaking move, elevates the zombie into an image of entropy, confusion and empirical impotence. It gave the living dead a seriousness that few cinemagoers of the period – jaded by Monogram's inane efforts – were expecting.

During pre-production for *I Walked with a Zombie*, Lewton told his staff to gather as much information about voodoo as possible. "We were all plunged into research of Haitian voodoo, every

book on the subject Val could find," recalls Ardel Wray, one of the younger members of the horror unit.[63] It was a period of study that left Lewton immensely dissatisfied with the script that had been turned in by Universal scribe Curt Siodmak. The nervous studio executives had foisted the screenwriter on him in the hope that some of Siodmak's pulp style – his previous projects included *The Wolf Man* (1941) – might rub off on Lewton. It didn't. Over the following weeks, the producer and his team put the original draft through multiple rewrites, transforming the story into a Caribbean-set version of *Jane Eyre* and completely changing its focus.

The filmed script opens with a long shot of two figures walking along a deserted beach as the voiceover narration from Betsy (Frances Dee) starts: "I walked with a zombie [laughs]. It does seem an odd thing to say. If anyone had said that to me a year ago I'm not sure I'd have known what a zombie was. I might have had some notion that it was strange or frightening, even a little funny. It all began in such an ordinary way…"

Initially, this opening appears to be the first half of a fairly conventional framing narrative. The couple on-screen don't mean anything to us – the figures are too far away for us to make out who they are – and the rather silly confessional tone, complete with its embarrassed attempt to dismiss the word "zombie," punctures any expectations we might have had about the title's promise. The first audiences to see the film at a special preview in the Hawaii Theatre in Hollywood in 1943 reportedly "tittered" at this opening line though by the end of the film they were "much impressed".[64] Perhaps they would have laughed even louder if they had noticed that the wording of the traditional disclaimer had been altered: "The characters and events depicted in this photoplay are fictional. Any similarity to actual persons living, dead or *possessed* is purely co-incidental."

This opening has set up certain expectations that are deliberately left unfulfilled. First of all, the framing narrative doesn't actually "frame" since the story ends without a return to Betsy's voiceover (an unspecified narrator delivers the film's sombre concluding lines). By the time the credits roll, we realise that the couple walking along the beach at the beginning are in fact Betsy and the main zombie, Carrefour. However, nothing in the film explains when, where or how such a stroll along the sand could have come about. What's more, the film never answers the question of what a zombie actually is – nor what it means to walk with one. Few cinematic openings promise so much and yet deliver so little.

The story of *I Walked with a Zombie* focuses on Betsy, a young nurse who travels out to the island of San Sebastian to take care of Jessica (Christine Gordon), the invalid wife of American plantation owner Paul Holland (Tom Conway). When she arrives on the island, Betsy slowly learns the story of Jessica's illness. According to the locals, Jessica has been turned into a zombie, but the Holland family doctor claims this is nonsense and that she is simply suffering from the irreversible effects of a rare tropical fever that burnt out portions of her spinal cord and left her "a sleepwalker who can never be awakened."

As Betsy settles into her new job, she begins to fall in love with Jessica's husband, Paul. She's also courted by Paul's half brother, Wesley Rand (James Ellison). The more she enquires into the circumstances of Jessica's illness, the more she learns about the Holland family, including the local rumour – turned into a calypso song that Wesley and Jessica had an affair and were planning to run away together before she fell ill.

Desperate to help Jessica, even though she's actually deeply in love with the invalid's husband, Betsy asks the doctor to try an experimental treatment she's heard about. It doesn't work and so, in an act of desperation, Betsy leads Jessica out to the island's houmfort (voodoo church), where she hopes to find some alternative cure for her condition. Taking Jessica through the cane fields and surviving an encounter with Carrefour, the local zombie, Betsy is shocked to learn that the houmfort is run by Mrs Rand (Edith Barrett), the mother of Wesley and Paul. It transpires that she's been dabbling in voodoo in order to win the islanders' trust and give them access to Western medicine.

Jessica's appearance at the houmfort causes a commotion among the islanders who – for reasons that are never explained – want to keep this white zombie for themselves. After Betsy takes Jessica back home to Fort Holland, one of the local voodoo sorcerers sends Carrefour to abduct her. When that fails, he casts a spell over Wesley. Later,

when Wesley hears that Jessica is to be sent to an asylum on the mainland in the hope of calming the locals, he decides to take matters into his own hands. He leads the sleepwalking Jessica down to the beach and kills her and then himself. Was he bewitched or simply wracked with guilt and desperation?

Released in 1943, *I Walked with a Zombie* was quite unlike any other film that had previously featured the living dead. Abandoning the more straightforward horror aims of films like *White Zombie* and contemporary Poverty Row chillers, Lewton's picture returned to the zombie's voodoo origins. Completely ignoring every living dead film that had gone before it, Lewton built up a heady mix: repressed sexuality, a philosophical meditation on the limits of knowledge, and a visual style that bordered on the poetic in its beautiful play of light and shadow.

The two zombies in Lewton's film – Jessica and Carrefour – mark a break with previous cinematic interpretations of the walking dead in that they are resolutely passive figures. Although they never attack anyone, they're still terrifying creations. Trading visceral shocks for a more cerebral set of terrors, *I Walked with a Zombie* succeeds by challenging our cherished certainties about the world we live in and our place in it. Wallace's article was unable to prove or disprove the existence of the zombie; Lewton's film turns such uncertainty into the stuff of nightmares.

The predominant theme of the film is mis-seeing. Drawing on the Gothic literary tradition, *I Walked with a Zombie*'s heroine is a naïve nurse who is, as Paul Holland points out, so "afraid of the dark" that she mistakes everything she sees for something else. Nothing in the film is what it seems: a puff pastry brioche looks like a huge meal but is just a thin shell of pastry full of air; the island's jungle drums sound threatening, but are actually nothing more than "San Sebastian's version of the factory whistle." As Paul Holland gruffly tells Betsy during the sea crossing to the island, "everything seems beautiful because you don't understand."

It's not only Betsy who proves to be an unreliable judge of appearances, though. No one is fully able to explain Jessica's condition: the doctor thinks it's the result of a tropical fever, Paul thinks he may have driven her mad and Mrs Rand thinks that she unconsciously placed a voodoo curse on her. The myriad explanations for both Jessica's illness and the island's voodoo rites eventually end up cancelling each other out.

The impossibility of any of these characters (or us) ever finding the truth about the mysteries that surround them is repeatedly worked into the film's visual framework. Tourneur shrouds his characters and locations in a darkness that's as impenetrable as the confusion that envelops the film's textual meaning. He sets up a delicate play of light and shadow that obscures as much as it reveals and makes everything appear different from what it actually is.

Betsy's nocturnal explorations in the fort's tower, where she discovers the sleepwalking Jessica, are a prime example of this skilful intersection of form and content. Her confusion (has she really heard a woman crying?) is matched by the camera's slow, disorientating glide up the spiral stone staircase and by the subtle lighting, which ensures that each frame is filled with more darkness than light. Every aspect of the film is pervaded by "uncertainty, ambiguity, [and] the reversal of expectations," according to film historian Robin Wood. "The shadows and half-lights of the film's haunting atmospheric quality are in fact but the expression of its moral and spiritual world, in which nothing is fixed or certain, nothing is as it seems; a world subtly dominated by the subconscious, a world of shadows in which we can do no more than cautiously and hesitantly grope."[65]

By employing a variety of distancing devices, the filmmakers underline the manner in which the questions raised by the action of *I Walked with a Zombie* cannot be reduced to simple yes/no, true/false, real/unreal answers. The gaps in the film's narrative (including the inexplicable opening shot of Betsy and Carrefour walking together), the lack of a conventional musical soundtrack and the film's steadfast refusal to explain the central conundrum of whether the zombie is real or not, leave us completely at a loss to account for what we have witnessed. Are these events supernatural in origin, or are they perfectly explicable in rational terms? Sidestepping such questions, the film ultimately reaches a point where it gives up the struggle to explain, and surrenders instead to what Chris Fujiwara calls, "a mute acceptance of the inexplicable".[66] Like Betsy's investigations, our own detective work fails to deliver any answers

since the world of the film refuses to fit itself into any pattern we can recognise.

As many critics have pointed out, *I Walked with a Zombie*'s hesitation over issues of truth and knowledge owes more to the literary genre of the fantastic than the conventions of the Hollywood horror movie. In the seminal theory of the fantastic advanced by Bulgarian literary critic Tzvetan Todorov, this particular mode is said to be characterised by a hesitation about whether the story's phantoms or apparitions are real or imagined, a hesitation that reduces the reader's sense of certainty in the veracity of events described. As Todorov argues, in the fantastic the worlds of the real and the imagined are so closely intertwined that they're impossible to separate – and so they co-exist together.[67]

In *I Walked with a Zombie*, it's the living dead who embody this sense of hesitation and the attack on the forces of reason, certainty and knowledge that it brings about. Picking up on the unique position of the zombie as a monster that is always caught in a liminal state somewhere between life and death, science and magic, reason and unreason, *I Walked with a Zombie* builds on the ambiguity that lies at the heart of Wallace's article. It transforms its two zombies into powerful symbols of uncertainty, disorder and chaos. Because it refuses to offer an explanation of the events it depicts, *I Walked with a Zombie* demands to be read as an unsettling text – one that challenges our assumptions about the world as an ordered and knowable realm. As such, the film raises surprisingly philosophical questions about the limits of knowledge. It employs the figure of the zombie – a monster that cannot be satisfactorily explained in terms of either magic or science – as the central image of this uncertainty.

The first meeting between Betsy and the island's native zombie, Carrefour (Darby Jones) emphasises exactly this hesitation. The filmmakers present the encounter between nurse and peasant, white woman and black man, as the first step on a journey into the realm of the unknowable. Leading Jessica through the dark canefields, armed only with a flashlight, Betsy comes face to face with Carrefour, a gigantic, bare-chested zombie who guards the path to the voodoo houmfort. Illuminating his lithe, towering body with her flashlight, Betsy stares into his cold dead eyes – but finds no answers, only more questions.

It's a meeting that reverses our expectations. Betsy has been warned that she'll only be able to pass this guardian of the crossroads if she carries a voodoo charm. Since she loses the charm on her journey through the canefields, we expect Carrefour to attack her, but he remains resolutely passive. So who is this silent figure? Is he alive or dead? A zombie? Or just a native who's trying to scare her? Nothing in the film answers these questions. When Carrefour later invades Fort Holland – the family's home and the island's last bastion of white authority – we expect violence. But he grinds to a halt like a naughty child as soon as Mrs Rand calls his name. Later, when Wesley kills Jessica on the beach, Carrefour follows him to the water's edge, but doesn't intervene. In the final scene he helps the fishermen carry the couple's dead bodies – and none of the islanders seem the least bit perturbed by his presence. Without any explanation of who or what he is, Carrefour remains completely unknowable.

Like the voodoo films of the 1930s and the Mantan Moreland zombie movies at Monogram, *I Walked with a Zombie* centres on a clash between the world of white American colonialism and native superstition. Yet unlike those other films, *I Walked With a Zombie* elevates this cultural clash to a central position the narrative. In doing so, Lewton and Tourneur's film skilfully plays with the zombie's status as a monster that's caught between two opposing states of life and death, body and soul, science and magic. The film deconstructs these opposites, turning the living dead into a metaphor of the limits of (white, Western) knowledge.

Whereas earlier zombie films had explicitly used the living dead to suggest the primitive Otherness of the Caribbean and its black populace, *I Walked With a Zombie* turns the focus back on the white world itself. The zombies in Lewton's film are terrifying not because they're the symbols of some primitive culture, but because their existence can't be explained. If First World science can't explain Third World superstition then perhaps white Westerners' belief in their superiority is simply self-delusion. Offering questions but no answers, the empirical puzzle of *I Walked with a Zombie* proved that the living dead had a career far beyond the skids of Poverty Row, for here was a monster that had a rich, yet relatively untapped, symbolic potential.[68]

Sadly, it was a potential that would remain untapped for years to come. In response to the success of Lewton's *I Walked with a Zombie*, RKO produced an unofficial comedy sequel, *Zombies on Broadway* (1945). Having absolutely nothing to do with Lewton and Tourneur's sublime masterpiece except for the use of the word zombie in its title, this riotous (read risible) outing starred the studio's answer to Abbott and Costello, Wally Brown and Alan Carney.

Poaching actors Darby Jones and Sir Lancelot from *I Walked with a Zombie*, the story centres on the attempts of incompetent press agents Jerry and Mike (Brown and Carney), who have to come up with a suitable promotion for the newly opened "Zombie Hut" nightclub or face a painful dressing down from the ex-con manager Ace (Sheldon Leonard, once seen in *Ouanga*). Escaping to the Caribbean, the boys encounter fruity scientist Dr Renault (Bela Lugosi), a zombie (Darby Jones), various empty graves and voodoo ceremonies.

Even by Abbot and Costello's uninspired standards, Carney and Brown were a painfully unfunny comic partnership. What few laughs there are involve Carney getting turned into a ping pong ball eyed automaton and Lugosi battling a cheeky monkey. As a result, this horror comedy survives only on the "scary" moments, which director Gordon Douglas sets-up reasonably well. Lugosi's intermittent appearances leave most of the chills in the capable hands of Jones who once again proves himself the black & white era's most majestic and terrifying zombie. But for the most part, *Zombies on Broadway* proves two things: firstly, that the zombie concept had become so familiar by 1945 that it could effortlessly provide the basis for such mainstream entertainment and secondly, that the major studios were still finding it impossible to do anything interesting with this particular monster.

By the time the inaccurately titled *Valley of the Zombies* was released in 1946, there seemed little doubt that the potential of the zombie was still eluding filmmakers. This voodoo chiller about an undertaker (Ian Keith) who discovers the secret of immortality in the eponymous valley of the zombies had less to do with the living dead than a bloodsucking vampire.[69] It seemed that the zombie was destined to spend many more years on the margins.

CHAPTER FOUR

ATOMIC INTERLUDE

I. SCI-FI HORRORS

As the shadow of the mushroom cloud fell across the globe, the American horror movie experienced a sudden and unexpected period of change. In a world where scientific progress had given man the power to split the atom and destroy the planet several times over, the terrors of yesterday no longer seemed frightening. Vampires, werewolves, ghosts and zombies were now out-dated; superstition was replaced with science and a new kind of monster was born. It was a modern, nuclear-powered breed against which the old mumbo jumbo of crucifixes, silver bullets and holy water wouldn't be much use.

In movies like *The Beast from 20,000 Fathoms* (1953), *Attack of the 50 Foot Woman* (1958) and *The Monster that Challenged the World* (1957), horror and science fiction began to merge. The Cold War interplay of anti-Communism, nuclear anxiety and fears about extra-terrestrial invasion mutated both genres into something more suited to the period. As a result, horror became science-fictional and science-fiction became horrific, producing a new pantheon of monsters engineered for the specific concerns of the atomic age. Giant ants, spiders, crabs, or dinosaurs suggested the disastrous possibilities of tampering with Nature; alien invaders became inextricably linked with America's anti-Communist anxieties; and apocalyptic sci-fi captured the all-too real possibility of a nuclear holocaust. It was no accident that Universal's original 1930s creature features were sold to the newly emerging television market during the period; they were old-fashioned monsters, small screen terrors from a more innocent age.

According to cultural theorist Mark Jancovich, one of the key shifts that occurred in 1950s sci-fi/horror was a change of emphasis "away from a reliance on Gothic horror and towards a preoccupation with the modern world."[70] As a result of this seismic upheaval in the realm of film nightmares, the "threats which distinguish 1950s horror do not come from the past or even from the action of a lone individual, but are associated with the processes of social development and modernisation."[71]

Part of the reason for this radical change was the momentous array of cultural upheavals that was shaping the West in the wake of the Cold War standoff. But it was also brought about by the huge advances in mass capitalism that were set into motion by the post-war consumer boom – especially the transformation of the social and economic realm through Fordist practices of labour regulation. As America entered a new age of atomic energy, consumerist plenty and Cold War paranoia, Hollywood's sci-fi/horror genre promised to sweep aside the old traditions and deliver monsters that were terrifyingly modern.

This shift threatened to return the zombie to the cultural graveyard once and for all. Indeed, the 1950s proved to be the worst decade for the production of films about the living dead with only a handful of – often not particularly memorable – zombie films being produced during these years: *Scared Stiff* (1952), *Creature with the Atom Brain* (1955), *Invasion of the Body Snatchers* (1956), *Teenage Zombies* (1957), *Voodoo Island* (1957), *Womaneater* (1957), *Zombies of Mora Tau* (1957), *Quatermass 2* (1957), *The Unknown Terror*

(1957), *Plan 9 from Outer Space* (1958) and *Invisible Invaders* (1959).

Hindsight is a wonderful thing, though. Looking back, it's clear that the 1950s proved to be a transitional period in the zombie movie's history. While many of the decade's living dead movies were shoddy, trite or just plain boring, they marked a decisive change in the genre's dynamics. It's in these films that the issues of voodoo, race and colonial anxiety were supplanted by fears of invasion of brainwashing and mass apocalypse. Taking the living dead out of the Caribbean and placing them firmly in the realm of atomic America, this handful of films initiated the dawn of the dead and paved the way for George Romero's landmark *Night of the Living Dead* (1968).

II. VOODOO'S LAST GASPS

Such exciting changes didn't happen overnight. Still haunted by the spectre of *Zombies on Broadway*, one of the first films of the 1950s to return to the living dead was little more than a rather blatant – and painfully unfunny – remake of *The Ghost Breakers*, which replaced Bob Hope and Willie Best's interracial partnership with the whitebread comedy of Dean Martin and Jerry Lewis (the latter taking Best's role).

Abbot and Costello may have had enough sense not to joke around with anyone other than Dracula, Frankenstein or the Wolf Man, but in the search for quick gags, the screenwriters of *Scared Stiff* (the title itself a dreadful pun) weren't so prudent. Stealing the director, the plot and the Cuban setting wholesale from *The Ghost Breakers*, *Scared Stiff* may have been one of the biggest grossing movies of 1953 but it didn't have the imagination to come up with a frightening villain – the zombie barely gets a look in and lacks the menacing presence of Noble Johnson's ghoul in the earlier film. That all helped make its title seem spectacularly redundant.

In terms of redundant titles, however, few films could compete with Fred C. Bannon's *Zombies of the Stratosphere* (1952), a story about a group of evil Martians conspiring to knock the Earth out of its orbit so that their home planet can take its place. Conceived as a twelve-part serial sequel to the director's *Radar Men from the Moon* – released earlier that same year – *Zombies of the Stratosphere* is notable for starring a young Leonard "Mr. Spock" Nimoy but little else.

Featuring jetpack footage lifted from Bannon's earlier *King of the Rocket Men* (1949), laughable spaceships, and a robot that looked like a hand-me-down from the previous decade, and *absolutely no zombies whatsoever*, Bannon's film should have been sued for misleading advertising. The extra-terrestrials are referred to as "zombies" – simply because they're human. All it really does is make an already incomprehensible plot even more confusing.

Chopped down into a seventy-minute feature film in 1958, and released under the equally misleading title of *Satan's Satellites*, the *Zombies of the Stratosphere* serial suggested that the living dead would have to adapt quickly to the decade's obsession with science fiction if they wanted to survive in any recognizable shape or form.

Not every horror filmmaker was far-sighted enough to realise the necessity of such changes. The year 1957 proved a bumper one for voodoo-themed zombie films: *Voodoo Island*, *Womaneater* and *Zombies of Mora Tau*. These three low-budget efforts offered audiences an uninspired and largely unwelcome alternative to the sci-fi trappings of standard B-movie fare. They had a spectacularly short screen life, going up against Universal's creature feature *The Deadly Mantis*, Roger Corman's extra-terrestrial *Not Of This Earth*, and the atomic-anxieties of *The 27th Day* (all 1957).

These films' stale reliance on voodoo and the supernatural was evident to everyone involved in them. For Aubrey Schenck, producer of the Boris Karloff vehicle *Voodoo Island*, the film proved to be an obvious flop: "I only have memories of *good* pictures," he told an interviewer when asked about the project in 1996. "That [film] was a lost cause. But, hell, you take a chance. With Karloff's name we thought we had a good chance, but it didn't work out. I'm not proud of that picture."[72] If horror fans couldn't be suckered into a picture that had Karloff as top billing, the writing was clearly on the wall for the supernatural scares of yesteryear.

Shot on location on the Pacific island of Kauai, *Voodoo Island* had little to recommend it other than its exotic locale. Investigator Philip Knight (Karloff) is hired by the owner of an American hotel chain to investigate an island in the South Pacific that is reportedly cursed. A crew of engineers and architects who were sent out to the island to draw up plans for a new hotel complex have disappeared. The only surviving member of the group has returned home to America as a zombie and is unable to do anything except stare straight ahead with wide, bulging eyes.

At first, Knight and his research assistant Sarah Adams (Beverly Tyler) believe it's all nothing more than a canny publicity stunt to promote the island's new hotel. On setting out to the tropical paradise they begin to think differently, though, as the expedition runs into a series of mishaps all of which appear to be directly linked to the voodoo death charm that's discovered on the deck of their boat. After man-eating plants, voodoo-dolls and a group of natives who have been chased out of their homes by the ever-encroaching world of white industrialisation have taken their toll on the expedition, Knight concedes that there might be some truth in the zombie myth after all.

The clash between white, Western science and native superstition is the focus of *Voodoo Island's* narrative, suggesting that its terrors are closely bound to colonial anxieties. However, screenwriter Richard Landau, who had earlier co-written the first *Quatermass* adaptation for Hammer, also links these fears into the film's sexual politics. It is Adams, Knight's pretty young assistant, who bears the brunt of much of this. Described by rakish ship's captain Gunn (Rhodes Reason) as being a "push button control system," who is only one step away from becoming a "machine," Adams is explicitly styled as the film's second zombie: "[Are you] so crammed full of facts and figures, names, dates and places, reports, typing up Knight's lectures that you've no room left inside to be like a woman?" Gunn demands of her, with characteristic tact.

Gunn has clearly fallen for the secretary, but he's perturbed by her apparent lack of emotion and her overtly scientific outlook on life. He's already reeling from the fact that Winter (Jean Engstrom), the group's other female member, rejected his advances. An older, more sexually confident woman, Winter is no stranger to the pleasures of the flesh – stripping off to bathe in a jungle pool and generally vamping her way across the island. Armed with all the frostiness that her name suggests, she's also immune to Gunn's charms. This leads him to suspect that she may be a lesbian with the hots for Adams!

Both of these women prove more threatening to Gunn than anything on the island, even the zombies. Adams is a woman who possesses the cold calculating mind of a man; Winter is a woman who refuses heterosexuality. No wonder Gunn – with his phallic, masculine name – feels under siege. He prevails, of course, conquering the island and the women with aplomb. Adams is turned into a "real" woman, swapping the masculine world of facts and figures in favour of a life of settled domesticity. Meanwhile, Winter proves to be beyond salvation; she is eaten by the jungle's carnivorous plants, that look like botanical versions of the *vagina dentata*. Clearly it is only by containing the feminine that the threat of the island – and its inhabitants' ability to turn white men into passive, feminised zombies – can be overcome.

At least the presence of a major star guaranteed *Voodoo Island* some slight box office return. Other projects were less fortunate. *The Unknown Terror* (1957) only had former Bulldog Drummond John Howard and another calypso singing role for Sir Lancelot (*I Walked with a Zombie, Zombies on Broadway*) to recommend it. Somewhere south of the border, a team of Americans search for a missing explorer amid hostile locals, rumours of a cave called "La cueva de la muerte", and a secretive scientist Dr Ramsay (Gerald Milton) researching antibiotics.

Warning the team that the drum-pounding local Indians are restless, Dr Ramsay doesn't tell them the truth: the cave hides a special kind of fungus that grows so quickly – "like binary fission" – that you can see it reproducing with the naked eye. He also doesn't tell them that he's been dispatching a few unlucky locals into the cave. Down in the darkness, they've become fungus-covered, long-haired ghouls who look like they've been dunked in a bubble bath.

Nightmare flora and fauna also made an appearance in the British production *Womaneater* where another far-from sane scientist (George Coulouris) tries to resurrect the dead with the help of some dubious botanical chemistry that he's picked up from an Amazon shaman… as you do. *Womaneater* featured some strange scenes of women being fed to a shaggy carnivorous plant (clearly a trend had been set by *Voodoo Island*), but not much to satisfy zombie fans' appetites. It may well be the missing link between *Little Shop of Horrors* and *The Evil Dead*'s groping tree branches.

On the basis of these flops, it was clear to even the most enthusiastic producers that horror in general and the zombie movie in particular had out-grown the voodoo-focussed films of the 1930s and 1940s. If it wasn't atomic and didn't glow in the dark, it wasn't going to sell. Even the most imaginative voodoo thriller of 1957 – *Zombies of Mora Tau*, released in the UK as *The Dead That Walk* – couldn't overcome the fact that audiences weren't interested in any expeditions that didn't involve rocket ships or nuclear power.

Set in West Africa, *Zombies of Mora Tau* marked not only a return to the zombie's voodoo roots, but also a clever relocation of voodoo itself, tracing the religion back from the Caribbean to its West African origins. The screenplay's inventiveness didn't stop there: with its underwater ghouls and a radical reworking of the basic zombie myth, Edward L. Cahn's film promised so much. More in fact than it could actually deliver. *Zombies of Mora Tau* may have been better than producer Sam Katzman's first zombie film – the lamentable *Voodoo Man* (1944) – but it wasn't by a very wide margin. It was hampered by being set in an unspecified African locale that's strangely devoid of any Africans and crippled by strained acting, atrocious dialogue and a perfunctory script.

Young colonial girl Jan Peters (Autumn Russell) returns to her great-grandmother's house on the coast of Africa after finishing her schooling abroad. She's not the only arrival in the tiny coastal village: a team of treasure hunters have dropped anchor in the hope of finding the wreck of the 19th-century ship the *Susan B*. According to legend, the *Susan B* sank in 1894 after its European crew stole a collection of diamonds from a local native tribe. The treasure, it is rumoured, is somewhere at the bottom of the ocean.

"They're dead I tell you. They have no morality, no free will. They'll kill anyone who comes for the diamonds," warns Granny Peters (Marjorie Eaton) as she regales the treasure hunters with tales about the zombies who guard the wreck. She claims that the tribe's witchdoctor turned the *Susan B*'s crew into living dead slaves who've been forced to spend eternity guarding the diamonds from greedy treasure hunters.

Naturally, the American expedition led by Captain Harrison (Joel Ashley), his floozy wife Mona (Allison Hayes) and young buck diver Jeff (Gregg Palmer) don't believe a word of it. Not even Granny Peters's talk of the Spanish, Portuguese and British treasure hunters who previously dived to their doom can sway them – nor can the old woman's claim that her husband is among the ship's zombified crew.

When Jeff's first dive to the wreck unleashes aquatic zombies, he begins to have second thoughts about the expedition. Harrison, however, is too greedy to care and it's only after his wife is infected by the ghouls that his resolve begins to waver. Even then, his desire for the diamonds is difficult to dampen and Jeff has to save the day by casting the troublesome gems back into the ocean. As they sink without trace, the zombies crumble to dust.

Zombies of Mora Tau was a modest genre entry, but its influence on future productions was more significant than might have been predicted. The film's walking (and swimming) dead are fairly unconvincing: dressed in assorted nautical costumes and draped with the odd strand of seaweed, they lumber after the principal characters, strangling anyone they can get their hands on. Still, they're decidedly creepy, prefiguring the mass zombie apocalypse that would later become a genre staple. Unlike their predecessors, these living dead attack *en masse*; towards the end of the film they storm the treasure hunters' ship and pound on the doors of the barricaded cabin. They're the first cinematic ghouls to be capable of turning their victims into zombies as well, which makes Cahn's film an important milestone in the zombie's on-screen evolution.

At the heart of *Zombies of Mora Tau* is a story about colonial anxiety as the pillaging of West Africa by white Europeans leads to a reversal of the colonial mission. Here it's the natives who subdue and enslave the colonial invaders using voodoo witchcraft. Revolving around issues of contamination, *Zombies of Mora Tau*'s chief horror stems from the fact that the characters are unable to contain the zombie threat. Just as the white crew of the *Susan B* were unable to dominate the natives, so the new adventurers find themselves at the mercy of zombies who constantly cross the boundaries of life and death, land and sea, inside and outside.

Given such fears, it's no surprise that Mona, the film's blatantly "bad" woman, should be zombified.

The response of her male counterparts is to imprison her within a perimeter of burning candles (logically, these watery zombies are afraid of fire). In this vision of the world, the failure to keep a tight reign over the Other – whether it be racial or sexual – has disastrous consequences. It is only when the diamonds are cast into the sea that the repressed can be contained as the sign of white, colonial guilt is dispersed by the cleansing waters.

III. THE MASS DESTRUCTION OF MEN'S MINDS

In his book *An Illustrated History of the Horror Film*, critic and historian Carlos Clarens cast his eye over the films of the 1950s and argued that "the ultimate horror in science fiction is neither death nor destruction but dehumanisation, a state in which emotional life is suspended, in which the individual is deprived of judgment." The most successful sci-fi films, he decided, were those that tapped into "collective anxieties about the loss of individual identity, subliminal mind-bending, or downright scientific/political brainwashing (not by accident the trend began to manifest itself after the Korean War and the well publicised reports coming out of it of brainwashing techniques)."

He cannily drew a comparison between this modern horror and a much older brand of zombie scares. "The automatoned slaves of modern times look perfectly efficient in their new painless state. From this aspect they are like the zombies of old – only we never bothered to wonder if zombies were happy in their trance. Zombies, like vampires, seemed so incontrovertibly different; the human counterfeits of [...] *Invasion of the Body Snatchers* are those we love, our family and friends. The zombies are now among us, and we cannot tell them and the girl next door apart any more."[73]

While many sci-fi/horror films of the 1950s were dominated by anxieties about the Bomb, there was also another equally fraught Cold War discourse threading its way through the films of the period. Fears about communist subversion, stoked by the mass hysteria surrounding the witch hunts led by Senator Joseph McCarthy and the House Un-American Activities Committee (HUAC), were a

recurrent theme and in the sci-fi/horror films being produced by the Hollywood studios, invasion narratives proliferated. Martians were a particularly useful metaphor for communist infiltration and invasion. Where else would the Reds come from but the "red planet"?

Not all invasions were military ones, though. Films like *Invaders from Mars* (1953), *It Came from Outer Space* (1953) and *I Married a Monster from Outer Space* (1958) suggested that the alien threat might be less visible, and therefore more dangerous, than the arrival of conspicuous flying saucers. If it was possible for aliens to take over family, friends and loved ones without them appearing significantly different, then we would have to be eternally vigilant. Like those fifth columnist "Reds under the bed" that Senator McCarthy had whipped America into a paranoid frenzy over, the aliens might already be here among us, subverting the course of democracy and capitalism from the inside.

While reactionary commentators were concerned that America was going to be overrun by Commies determined on enslaving the populace, leftwing voices warned that conservative consumer culture was threatening to enslave ordinary citizens in a very different way. As Mark Jancovich claims, the 1950s were equally characterised by "deep-seated anxiety about social, political, economic and cultural developments which led many to argue that America was becoming an increasingly homogenous, conformist and totalitarian society; that the basis of individuality was being eroded and that the possibility of resistance was disappearing."[74] Sociologist William Whyte summed up such fears in his warnings about the rise of the Organisation Man, a living dead worker whose place in the economy was guaranteed "only in exchange for his soul". It seemed that, for many, capitalism was just as capable of producing zombified slaves as extra-terrestrial Communism.[75] Ditching the supernatural, voodoo-related connotations of the walking dead, several films deployed the image of the zombie slave as a metaphor for these Cold War fears about co-option and the loss of individuality.

Concerns about thought control reached hysterical proportions during the decade. Journalist Edward Hunter first coined the word "brainwashing" in a *Miami Daily News* article in 1950. A literal translation of the Chinese "*hsi-nao*" ("to wash the mind"), the concept of brainwashing came to have a special resonance for the American public after the Korean War, when it was alleged that the Communists had coerced American POWs into signing statements denouncing the conflict and America's involvement in it. Dubbed "Manchurian Candidates" after the publication of Richard Condon's 1959 novel, these POWs had apparently been brainwashed by sophisticated psychological techniques involving solitary confinement, sleep deprivation and coercive interrogation techniques.

For the American authorities, and the CIA in particular, the news that the Reds were employing such new-fangled tactics was a major concern. The CIA had been researching their own mind-control techniques, with little success, since the end of the Second World War in top secret projects BLUEBIRD, ARTICHOKE and, later, MK-ULTRA. Eager to answer the question of whether or not it was possible to, in the words of one classified brief, "get control of an individual to the point where he will do our bidding against his will and even such fundamental laws of nature as self-preservation," the CIA commissioned research into special interrogation techniques and the use of psychoactive drugs as varied as magic mushrooms, nitrous oxide, and LSD25.[76]

Some commentators have suggested that the CIA may have played up this alleged brainwashing to increase funding for their often-questionable research into mind-control techniques: Edward Hunter, the journalist who first brought "brainwashing" to the American public's attention, was a CIA operative; more suspiciously, no British or Turkish POWs were reported to have suffered the same treatment in Korea as American servicemen. Whatever the truth, there's no doubting the impact that the *idea* of brainwashing had on the American public. Stories about mind-control and mental slavery cropped up everywhere, mirroring the public's paranoid fears.

The zombie was the perfect monster to encapsulate such anxieties about the loss of individuality, political subversion and brainwashing. Several films – including *Creature with the Atom Brain* (1955), *Invasion of the Body Snatchers* (1956), *Teenage Zombies* (1957), *Quatermass 2* (1957), *Plan 9 From Outer Space* (1958), and *Invisible Invaders* (1959) – presented a modern version of the zombie myth. They swept aside the racial concerns of earlier films in favour of updating the living dead to Cold War America.

In Jerry Warren's schlock drive-in movie *Teenage Zombies*, the links between zombies, insidious mental control and communism are so clearly spelled out that even the most inattentive audience could grasp them. When a bunch of Beatnik kids find a secret laboratory on a deserted island, they uncover a communist plot to take over the United States by contaminating the nation's water supply with a chemical agent designed to turn the American public into mindless zombie slaves. According to vampy Russian scientist Dr Myra (Katherine Victor), it's a more effective and less destructive strategy than dropping the Bomb. "With half the people on Earth in this condition we'd have the epitome of civilisation," she smirks as she introduces the kids to her zombie henchman (named, rather too appropriately, Ivan). Suddenly communist science, not voodoo, was capable of creating zombies.

In Don Siegel's *Invasion of the Body Snatchers*, the links between zombification and communist subversion proved less obvious but far more effective. Based on Jack Finney's best-selling novel of the same name, *Invasion of the Body Snatchers* posits the invasion of the Earth by extra-terrestrial seedpods that are able to grow into exact replicas of any humans they come into contact with. It begins in a small American town where the seedpods replace the local inhabitants with replicas, killing the originals while they sleep. Since the alien replicas look, talk, walk and act like us, it's almost impossible to tell the copies from the original. The only thing that identifies the invaders is their zombie-like lack of emotion.

In *Invasion of the Body Snatchers*, zombification isn't even remotely linked to ideas of the supernatural, voodoo or magic. This is a crisis of individual autonomy that is perfectly suited to Cold War fears of co-option: "Tomorrow you'll be one of us," threaten the invaders as they capture Miles (Kevin McCarthy) and Becky (Dana Wynter). They're promising a new order, a society without pain and misery. Apparently it's nirvana, but for our hero, it's nothing short of the end of the world, the end of mankind and the end of all vestiges of difference.

This is an apocalypse in which zombification occurs on a massive scale. The threat posed by the Body Snatchers isn't confined to just one or two individuals. It's one that's gone beyond individuals, beyond families, beyond the small-town where it starts. It's threatening to engulf the whole of America and perhaps even the world. For the first time since *Revolt of the Zombies* (1936), the idea of the zombie was linked to a global apocalypse. Hardly surprising, then, that the film's most famous sequence occurs when Miles and Becky realise that they're the only two humans left in town. Chased through the streets by a mob of body-snatched townsfolk, they're among the first cinematic characters to experience the terror of being pursued by a zombie horde.

Such fears were not just American in origin. In the UK, Hammer also tapped into this fascination with body snatching and zombification. Reworking popular British radio and television serials for the screen, Hammer's first horror picture was an adaptation of Nigel Kneale's 1953 BBC serial *The Quatermass Experiment*. Playing up its status as the first British film to be awarded the newly created "X" certificate, Hammer's big screen adaptation was entitled *The Quatermass Xperiment* (1955). It became an instant hit in the UK as its horrific tale of an astronaut returning to Earth as a monster caught the public's imagination. The studio was canny enough to realise that a sequel was needed and released *Quatermass 2* in 1957, with American actor Brian Donlevy reprising his role as the eponymous professor.

Reworking the central theme of *Invasion of the Body Snatchers*, *Quatermass 2* toyed with the same fears of mass brainwashing and zombification in a story about the invasion of the Earth by tiny meteorites that carry an alien parasite. As the meteorites land they crack open, releasing a gas that turns any nearby humans into slaves compelled to work on the invaders' behalf.

After spotting the arrival of this stream of meteorites, Quatermass eventually discovers the aliens' secret facility and realises that they are attempting to recalibrate the Earth's atmosphere to make it suitable for them to breathe. His attempt to blow the whistle on these intergalactic carpetbaggers is hampered by the fact that they've already turned key members of the UK police force, government and military into their slaves.

With its vision of fifth columnists infiltrating Britain's military industrial complex, *Quatermass 2* voices the same kind of paranoid fears about external influence that were established in *Invasion of the Body Snatchers*. The Cold War tone – emphasised by the coalition of American and British heroes – takes the premise far beyond Siegel's film, further emphasising the underlying links between the invasion and ideas of disease and contagion. The gas released from the meteors leaves plague-like black burns on the skin and allows the alien parasite to take control of the host's body, turning the human victims into creatures that Quatermass explicitly describes as "zombies". In case we're still in any doubt about the dangers or the scope of this infiltration, Quatermass goes on to explain that it produces "an invasion of [the] nervous system. Something is implanted ... an instinct, a blind compulsion to act for them." The very real threat is a global apocalypse in which the invaders effect "the mass destruction of men's minds" – robbing us of our individuality and creating a conformist society of mindless slaves.

While *Quatermass 2*, *Invasion of the Body Snatchers* and *Teenage Zombies* used the living dead to work through Cold War fears about subversion, invasion and brainwashing, a small group of other films approached the atomic age from a very different perspective. As we've seen, the movies that link the zombie with brainwashing rarely kept to the zombie's origins as a living corpse, preferring instead to update the idea of "zombification" as a mental rather than physical state. But at least three American movies of the period weren't so shy about making sure that their living dead were actually *dead*. In *Creature with the Atom Brain* (1955), *Plan 9 From Outer Space* (1958) and *Invisible Invaders* (1959), the zombie remained a corpse, albeit an atomic one.

All three of these films are strictly Z-grade fare. Director Edward L. Cahn's *Creature* and *Invisible Invaders* are vaguely competent low-budget efforts, while Ed Wood Jr.'s *Plan 9* is widely regarded as the worst film ever made. However, the way in which they conflate the atomic age with stories of dead men walking is curiously suggestive of the reason why the zombie largely fell out of favour during the 1950s.

Filmed either side of Cahn's *Zombies of Mora Tau*, *Creature with the Atom Brain* and *Invisible Invaders* diverge remarkably from that old-fashioned voodoo tale, focussing instead on two typical Cold War concerns: nuclear energy and extra-terrestrial invasion. Following the adventures of a gangster (Michael Granger) and his scientist sidekick (Gregory Gaye), *Creature with the Atom Brain* features a gaggle of radioactive zombies. They are reanimated as radio-controlled automatons dispatched to kill their creators' underworld rivals.

Scripted by Curt Siodmak – the screenwriter who produced the first draft of *I Walked with a Zombie* – *Creature* is pure nuclear schlock complete with plenty of sci-fi gizmos: clunking radiation suits, chirruping Geiger counters and a bizarre wind tunnel contraption that the villains have to clamber through before using their radioactive material. For all its high-tech trappings, though, the film is blatantly sceptical of the benefits of atomic power. Its nuclear scientist is an ex-Nazi and it repeatedly emphasises the dangers of radiation sickness and exposure.

Perhaps that explains why the film is so fascinated with the bodies of its zombies. In the final reel showdown between the local police department and the zombie army, Cahn delights in the chaos, letting the bullet-scarred faces of his zombies loom menacingly into the camera lens. Other scenes focus on the corporeality of these radioactive living dead, whose foreheads boast nasty looking brain surgery scars.

Meanwhile, in *Creature with the Atom Brain*'s subplot, the crusading Dr Walker (Richard Denning) takes time out from his pursuit of the nuclear corpses to keep his cute little daughter

from discovering the realities of death. He makes up a cock and bull story about why her favourite copper, Captain Harris (S. John Launer), won't be coming to visit her anymore (he's actually been turned into a zombie). The importance of this silly aside is pretty transparent: this is a movie about the fear of death in the nuclear age.

In Cahn's third zombie film, *Invisible Invaders*, this theme is developed further. Invading extra-terrestrials plans to take over the bodies of the dead and use them as shock troops in the battle to destroy humanity. The invasion is tinged with nuclear anxiety: the extra-terrestrials claim that our newfound atomic ability has become too much of a threat to the rest of the galaxy. Fortunately, a lone band of scientists and military personnel (including Philip Tonge and John Agar) eventually stop them by using high frequency sound waves. But not before Cahn conjures up the image of an army of corpses – dressed as white-collar professionals – rising up around the globe to suppress the living. It's an idea that's played out again in *Plan 9 from Outer Space* where the extraterrestrials spend most of their time in a graveyard, recruiting new foot soldiers for their zombie army.

What's so intriguing about these three films is the way in which they link their walking corpses with Cold War concerns about nuclear power and invading aliens. Fixated by the idea of a global apocalypse dominated by a mass of dead bodies, they make explicit, however unwittingly, the realities of a nuclear war: a mountain of corpses. It's something that few other horror/sci-fi movies of the period – with their campy bug-eyed monsters, flying saucers and mutant creatures – were able or willing to confront.

In retrospect, one wonders whether the general disappearance of the zombies during the 1950s – and their later return in the 1960s – was a result of this uncomfortable association between the zombie and death. In a period when death itself was transformed from being personal and individual into an event of global apocalypse, movies about the dead rising up against the living fell out of favour. Facing up to the realities of mass death and destruction – even through the distorted lens of zombie-themed science fiction – was something that few people living in the shadow of the Bomb were willing to do.

CHAPTER FIVE

BRINGING IT ALL BACK HOME

I. KEEPING IT IN THE FAMILY

The landmark horror film of 1960 may not have involved zombies, but it did feature the mummified corpse of a mommy. After all the bug-eyed monsters that dominated the cinema screens of the 1950s, Alfred Hitchcock's *Psycho* took horror into the heart of the American family with a sadistic audacity that made it an instant success. The film was one of the first expressions of a new kind of horror – a terror which came from "within" rather than from "without," a terror that was already among us, lurking somewhere out on the back roads of America in places as innocuous as the Bates Motel.

While the previous decade's scary movies had taught audiences to watch the skies, *Psycho* warned them to watch their neighbours. If the shy motel clerk turned out to be a schizophrenic transvestite with a penchant for putting mom's kitchen knives to anti-social uses, who could you trust? Your family? Your neighbours? The person sitting next to you in the darkened movie theatre? That Norman Bates seemed so ordinary was what made him so terrifying. He hadn't been turned into a murdering psychopath by alien invaders, communist infiltrators or atomic explosions, but because of his seemingly ordinary American upbringing. Here was a horror that was internal, that was part of our society, that was part of *us*.

Bringing horror into the home, collapsing the boundaries between the ordinary and the monstrous, and locating the family as the site of terror, the post-*Psycho* horror film frequently asks us to recognise the terrors that are all around us. "What distinguishes contemporary horror films from a more traditional stage in the genre is that the threat emerges much closer to home," explains film critic Lianne McLarty. "The threat is located in the commonplace and the body is a site/sight of graphic images of invasion and transformation."[77] It is a vision of the horrific in which "the monster is not simply *among* us, but possibly *is* us."[78]

In the previous chapter we saw that this shift from the horror of Them to the horror of Us was something that was already well underway in the zombie-themed movies of the 1950s. Abandoning the racial anxieties of earlier zombie films, these pictures blurred the line between the living and the living dead. As the small town American setting and doppelgänger scenario of *Invasion of the Body Snatchers* suggested, the monsters might not be readily identifiable as bug-eyed aliens. Much worse – they might look like our friends and neighbours. In many ways, the zombie was perfectly suited to this paranoid fear of the horror within since the living dead looked so ordinary: they looked like us; heck, they once *were* us.

After the string of zombie-themed box office debacles that dominated the 1950s, though, most Hollywood producers wanted nothing more to do with walking corpses. As a result, the early half of the 1960s saw the zombie flourish in various other national cinemas outside America, from Britain to Mexico to Italy. What proved so provocative about these admittedly scrappy international efforts was the way in which they styled the zombie as a symbol of this kind of internal, familial horror.

II. STIFF UPPER LIPS AND THE WALKING DEAD

Harold Macmillan in Number Ten, The Beatles singing "I Want To Hold Your Hand", The Profumo Affair hitting the headlines. Britain in the early 1960s seemed like a rather unlikely location for the rebirth of zombie cinema. Yet it was on these shores that four low-budget horror films were shot: *Doctor Blood's Coffin* (1960), *The Earth Dies Screaming* (1964), *The Frozen Dead* (1966) and *The Plague of the Zombies* (1966). Together they helped bring the moribund genre back from the grave.

Doctor Blood's Coffin dusted off the Frankenstein myth with a grisly story about a young surgeon named, rather appropriately, Dr Blood (Kieron Moore). After completing his medical studies in Vienna, Blood returns to his home village in Cornwall full of grandiose ideas about reviving the dead through heart transplant surgery. His father, the village doctor, hopes he'll settle down into a career as a general practitioner not realising that Peter has little time for the Hippocratic Oath. Systemically murdering the locals after paralysing them with curare and delving around in their insides, young Dr Blood continues his harebrained schemes to revive the dead. He's such a cad he even romances Linda Parker (Hazel Court), the pretty young widow who works as a nurse in his father's surgery, while secretly planning to bring her husband back from the dead.

Funded by United Artists, helmed by Canadian television director Sidney J. Furie and photographed by Stephen Dade (with a young Nicolas Roeg acting as camera operator), *Doctor Blood's Coffin* is very different from the Gothic horror tradition of the Hammer studios. Updating the mad scientist story to the 1960s with impressive efficiency, it's a clinical little movie full of visceral shocks and a lone zombie who sadly only appears well into the film's final reel. But it's also an interesting example of the kind of familial horror that was beginning to become fashionable during the period.

Returning to his home village after years abroad, Peter is a classic example of the interloper whose arrival disturbs the established order. Upsetting his father's routine, his surgery and the extended family of the village, he's full of the arrogance of youth. Furie takes pains to ensure that the dangers of his monomaniacal obsession are understood, styling him as a sadistic killer with little sympathy for those he considers beneath his social station. Yet, no matter how evil he is, he's also a part of the community that he's preying on.

The film's zombie is central to this familial dynamic. As Peter reanimates the decomposed body of Linda's dead husband Steve, *Doctor Blood's Coffin* eventually turns into a hysterical psychosexual drama in which Linda is forced to confront the lumbering remains of the man who she once loved: "You haven't brought Steve Parker back to life," she screeches in a blind panic as Blood invites her to meet the decomposed body of his first successful transplant subject, "this is something from hell!" Romancing the widow, Blood has already made her feel guilty about being unfaithful to her dead husband's memory; then he brings the corpse back to life just for good measure. It's hardly surprising that the zombie's reaction isn't to hug his long lost wife but lunge at her in a murderous, inarticulate rage.

Centring on the age-old fear of coming face to face with the dead, *Doctor Blood's Coffin* neatly illustrates the classic Freudian belief that fears about the dead returning to life stem from the living's guilty consciences. In *Totem and Taboo*, Freud claims that the terror of confronting a dead relative is always the result of the "unconscious hostility" that the living project onto the dead, making "the dead man into an enemy".[79] Expanding on this in his essay "The Uncanny," Freud suggests that this fear of the dead is tied to the assumption that "the deceased becomes the enemy of his survivor and wants to carry him off to share his new life with him."[80] As Linda Parker's experience suggests, the return of the dead signifies not only our own fear of death but also our fear of the dead themselves – those who we loved, but were unable to save from the inevitable end. Given such psychological stakes, it makes sense that cinema's zombies are always so bad tempered. Their return to life is always tied up with our guilty assumption that they're here to punish us for our misdemeanours and transgressions.

Such provincial and familial horrors were given a slightly different but equally telling spin in Terence Fisher's *The Earth Dies Screaming* (1964), a sci-fi movie that relocates the premise of *Invasion of the Body Snatchers* and *Invisible Invaders* to the Home Counties with all the production values of an early episode of *Doctor Who*. After an extraterrestrial gas attack wipes out most of the earth's population, a band of survivors group together in an English country hotel. Robot invaders amble through the streets reactivating the dead to use as "mindless slaves, worse than animals" while the survivors bicker about how to respond to the threat. Unlike *Quatermass 2*, which crisscrossed up and down the country as the aliens began to take over the planet, *The Earth Dies Screaming* limits itself to just a handful of locations. The result of this budgetary penny pinching proves unexpectedly unsettling as the film is forced to focus on the ordinary, the local and the familiar.

The Earth Dies Screaming was actually the first film in a loose trilogy of invasion narratives directed by Terence Fisher and was followed by *Island of Terror* (1966) and *Night of the Big Heat* (1967). While unrelated in terms of plot or character, these three films share the same provincial viewpoint. As critic Peter Hutchings explains, the alien invasion is always "represented on a much smaller scale, often in terms of the domestic and the familial, and played out in isolated settings."[81] Rather than focussing on the attempts of the nation to pull together, each film in Fisher's trilogy centres on a small group of survivors.

The Earth Dies Screaming is more interested in the interpersonal dynamics of the group than the invaders. The scariest moments in the film are the unexpected return of friends and family members such as Violet (Vanda Godsell) and Quinn (Dennis Price) who have been and resurrected as zombified slaves. Being invaded by alien robots is one thing, but watching as the dead bodies of husbands, wives and friends are brought back to life is enough to test the stiffness of any English gentleman's upper lip.

In *The Frozen Dead* (1966), directed by Herbert J. Leder, the invaders aren't aliens but Nazis. Years after the Second World War, German scientist Dr Norberg (Dana Andrews) is hiding away in an English castle, perfecting his "instant freeze" techniques to bring frozen corpses back to life. Over 1,500 of the Nazi Party elite were apparently put into suspended animation at the end of the war and hidden away in caves in Germany, France and even Egypt. They're waiting for the moment when Norberg succeeds so they can bring about the Fourth Reich.

Unfortunately, Norberg's costly experiments have so far been disastrous. Seven out of eight revived soldiers have survived, but they are all basket cases. "To revive a body is one thing," he explains to his financial backers. "I've done that. But reviving a brain so that it functions normally that's another – still unsolved – problem." The defrosted corpses amble about in their Nazi uniforms like lobotomy victims: one constantly bounces an imaginary ball, another repeatedly combs his hair. The most dangerous is the doctor's own brother (played by Edward Fox, yes *that* Edward Fox) who exhibits a desire to strangle anyone who gets too close. Even in this Nazi zombie movie, the family remains a site of horror.

Less fun than it sounds *The Frozen Dead* lumbers through murder and outré mad scientist experiments on a wall of severed arms and the decapitated blue head of a pretty friend of Norberg's niece. Despite the implicit promise of Nazi ghouls rampaging through the English countryside, the zombies don't get much of a look in. It makes *The Frozen Dead* a forgotten footnote in both the Nazi zombie cycle and 1960s British cinema.

While *Doctor Blood's Coffin*, *The Earth Dies Screaming* and *The Frozen Dead* were low-budget attempts to cash-in on the success of the British horror market that had been revived by Hammer, their appeal was distinctly limited. Rather inevitably, it was an entry from the venerable studio itself that would become the most influential British zombie film of the decade. Director John Gilling's *The Plague of the Zombies* (1966) may not be one of Hammer's best-known films but it's an accomplished piece of living dead cinema nonetheless. Breaking with the zombie's American history it's set in 19th-century Cornwall where a country squire is zombifying the local villagers and using them as cheap labour in his tin mine.

Given this distinctly British setting, it's ironic that the production's original treatment owed a fair deal to *The Magic Island*. First announced in 1963 as *The Zombie*, the story was supposed to open in 19th-century Haiti with a young English squire playing cards in a disreputable gambling den. After being caught cheating, the squire is chased out into the jungle. Escaping his pursuers, he stumbles across a native voodoo ceremony and learns the secrets of zombification.

On returning to Cornwall, the squire discovers that he has inherited his late father's estate and replaces the staff with Haitian servants from the Caribbean. Not long after this, the village is blighted by a dreadful and unexplained plague that the locals believe – in a plot development ripe for the kind of racial subtext so many American zombie movies of the 1930s and 1940s possessed – is being spread by the Haitian servants. In actual fact, the squire and his servants are killing off the villagers, using their knowledge of voodoo spells and potions to resurrect them as zombie slaves.[82]

Beset by pre-production problems, *The Zombie* fell by the wayside as Hammer concentrated on other projects. In 1965, the treatment was rediscovered, dusted off and given a thorough revision by screenwriter Peter Bryan. It was then shot back-to-back with *The Reptile* (1966) by director John Gilling.

During the course of this redevelopment, the racial focus of the original outline was exchanged

The Plague of the Zombies (1966).

for some very different concerns. The filmed version of *The Plague of the Zombies* opens with a voodoo ceremony in which white-robed priests perform some unspecified, but clearly nefarious, ritual. Strangely, the setting isn't the Caribbean but a dank English mineshaft. The film then cuts to London where Sir James Forbes (André Morrell) receives a letter from Dr Peter Thompson (Brook Williams), a general practitioner in a tiny Cornish village. Thompson's letter is a muddled plea for help; his patients are dying from a mysterious illness and he needs his old teacher's help.

Arriving in Cornwall a few days later, Sir James and his daughter Sylvia (Diane Clare) find the village in uproar. The terrified locals believe that the new doctor is responsible for the "plague" that is killing their loved ones. Meanwhile, the thuggish young friends of the local squire terrorise the village. Riding through the streets on horseback during a foxhunt, they carelessly charge through the funeral procession of the plague's latest victim. Sir James and Sylvia look on in horror as the coffin is overturned and a grotesquely contorted corpse is tipped onto the road.

After meeting Thompson and his wife Alice (Jacqueline Pearce), Sir James begins to investigate the plague's origins. Ironically, the next victim is Alice, who falls ill with a fever and then wanders out onto the moors. There Sylvia sees her being attacked by a strange-looking man. Alerting the local police, Sir James and Thompson head off to the moors; there they find Alice's body and a drunken mourner from the funeral who takes the blame for her murder. Suspecting far fouler play, Sir James orders the grave of the plague's most recent victim exhumed – and discovers an empty coffin. After Alice's burial, Sir James and Thompson keep watch over the cemetery and see Alice return to life as a zombie. Horrified, Sir James decapitates her with a spade.

Guessing that Squire Hamilton (John Carson) is dabbling in voodoo, Sir James confronts him. He realises that the squire has been killing the villagers and resurrecting them as zombie slaves to work in his tin mine. After putting a spell on Sylvia, the squire tries to sacrifice her in a voodoo ceremony. But Sir James and Thompson storm the mine to save her. In the fracas, the mine is set on fire, the zombies attack the squire and his henchmen, and our heroes escape as the shaft collapses.

While it would have been exciting to see what Hammer might have made of *The Zombie*'s Haitian setting, Gilling's film is refreshingly original. Abandoning the traditional racial elements of American zombie films and relocating the action to the mannered social hierarchies of 19th-century England, the director built on Britain's Gothic heritage: the film borrows liberally from Bram Stoker's *Dracula* and Sir Arthur Conan Doyle's Sherlock Holmes novels, in particular *The Hound of the Baskervilles*.

In keeping with so many of Hammer's films, it's class rather than race that dominates *The Plague of the Zombies*. Uniting Dr Thompson and Sir James against Squire Hamilton, the film sets its bourgeois heroes against the aristocracy in a bid to save the village proletariat. It's a template that could have been lifted straight from Hammer's many *Dracula* adaptations, in which the aristocratic vampire is hunted down and destroyed by a coalition of middle class vampire hunters led by Van Helsing. What's so important about this class theme, however, is the way in which it is intimately tied to the kind of family based horror that was dominating the films of the period. Squire Hamilton's abuse of his position brings horror into both the extended family of the village and, more importantly, Dr Thompson's own home.

Revolving around a series of paternal relationships – Sir James and Thompson (mentor/ student), Thompson and the villagers (doctor/ patients), Squire Hamilton and the villagers (aristocrat/peasants) – *The Plague of the Zombies* focuses on the way in which this Cornish village is ruined by its abusive and manipulative feudal overlord. Instead of caring for those in his charge,

the young squire breaks the relationship between the peasantry and the bourgeoisie, upsetting the hierarchical community of the village and plunging its populace into a state of fear, disease and ruin. Exploiting his charges by turning them into zombie slaves, Squire Hamilton is the bad father whose law is corrupt. His overthrow is an act of social reorganisation that says as much about the post-war Labour government's desire to limit the overreaching power of the aristocracy than anything concerning 19th-century Cornwall.

The scene in which Thompson and Sir James encounter the zombified Alice is pivotal to the film's play of familial horror. Coming out of her coffin and walking towards the camera with a slow step and voracious smirk, Alice is transformed from dowdy housewife to lascivious zombie. As Thompson and Sir James recoil from this image of feminine sexual appetite, it's clear that their disgust has more to do with Alice's sexual transformation than her physical reanimation. Much like Lucy's sexualised transformation from virgin to vampire in Stoker's *Dracula*, Alice is an affront to the primacy of male sexual authority. She is dealt with accordingly as Sir James – the good father – lops her head off with a spade.

Clearly, the squire's voodoo dabbling has not only wrecked the extended community of the village but also Thompson's own family, forcing him to confront his wife's repressed sexuality. The film's most memorable moment is a dream sequence in which Thompson watches ragged corpses claw their way out of the ground in the village graveyard. Here the doctor realises the full extent of the squire's destructive power: this reckless aristocrat has even turned the villagers' ancestral family ties into a site of horror.

Taking the zombie out of the Caribbean and placing it in the provincial world of the British countryside, *Doctor Blood's Coffin*, *The Earth Dies Screaming* and *The Plague of the Zombies* pursue much the same ends. In each, the horror represented by the zombie is local, familial and personal; in each, the chief focus is not on confronting racial difference but the Otherness that lies within the family unit itself. It is a confrontation in which all that was *famil*-iar is transformed into something unrecognizable and horrifying.

III. SOUTH OF THE BORDER

Britain wasn't the only country to have recognised the zombie genre's appeal after Hollywood lost interest in the walking dead. A sudden rash of Mexican movies began with *The Curse of the Doll People* (orig. *Muñecos infernales*, 1960) and flourished into a micro-genre of enchilada-flavoured zombie horrors throughout the 1960s. Directed by Benito Alazraki, *Curse of the Doll People* returned to Haitian soil. Its story followed some unlucky tourists who are cursed by a voodoo priest after they inadvertently witness a secret occult ceremony. They don't realise how much trouble they're in until they're picked off one by one by the "doll people" of the title – murderous animated dolls controlled by the sorcerer's chief zombie, Sabud.

From this inauspicious start, Alazraki tried his hand at more living dead cinema by creating the first in a series of zombie movies starring masked wrestler El Santo (aka Rudolfo Guzmán Huerta), who became a popular icon in Mexican cinema during the 1960s. He fought a wide variety of traditional horror personalities – including Dracula and Frankenstein's monster, as well as assorted demons, werewolves and vampires – in a long-running series of comic book adventures that were the mainstay of Mexico's floundering national cinema during the period.

In *Invasion of the Zombies* (orig. *El Santo contra los zombies*, 1961), the first of several Mexican wrestling/zombie mash-ups, the masker wrestler fights an evil mastermind sending radio-controlled zombies on a crime spree across Mexico. Despite talk of Haitian voodoo, the zombies are actually more like high-tech automatons and are kitted out with special belts that let their master use them as his goons. They wander about slowly, robbing jewelley stores with blow torches, tossing the odd hand grenade and shrugging off the police's bullets. Dressed in tunics and leggings, they don't look dead – just a bit mindless.

Santo, who's never seen without his mask and cape even outside the ring, tracks them down – fighting them in an orphanage dormitory while terrified kids look on – before eventually meeting their hooded master in his underground lair. Although they're dead, these zombies know a few good lucha libre grappling holds.

Santo fought more Mexican zombies with his tag team partner Blue Demon in *Santo and Blue Demon Against the Monsters* (orig. *Santo y Blue Demon contra los monstruos*, 1968), *Santo and Blue Demon in The Land of the Dead* (orig. *El mundo de los muertos*; aka *The Land of the Dead*, 1969). He even made it out to Haiti in *Santo vs. Black Magic* (orig. *Santo contra la magia negra*, 1972). Padded out with footage of the island and its customs, it had the silver masked wrestler battling a voodoo priestess (Sasha Montenegro). She has an army of zombies including some striking, Haitian ghouls. Again, they don't seem especially living dead – one even abseils into Santo's room to drop a snake on his chest while he sleeps! The exotic locales – all sunlit beaches and frenzied voodoo ceremonies – make it feel like a cheapo Mexican zombie James Bond movie. *Live and Let Die* with ghouls and masked wrestlers.

Other Mexican productions followed Santo's lead. By the far best of the bunch was *Dr Satan vs. Black Magic* (orig. *El Dr Satán y la magia negra*, 1967), a high camp horror romp featuring a magician named Dr Satan (Joaquín Cordero). When he isn't busy battling his archenemy Black Magic (Noe Murayama), Dr Satan proves he's a real swinger by hanging out with zombie girls dressed in miniskirts and boob-enhancing sweaters. In *Invasion of the Dead* (orig. *La invasión de los muertos*, 1972) Santo's tag partner Blue Demon battled living dead enemies who were able to drive cars and fly helicopters. It's not half as much fun as it sounds.

More interesting was the cycle of Mexican "momias" movies, based on the real-life, naturally preserved, corpses found in a cemetery in Guanajuato in the 19th century ("Las Momias de Guanajuato"). They appealed to Mexico's morbid fascination with death and also, after they were housed in a creepy museum, to the international tourist trade. Despite being called "mummies" they owe little to the Egyptian or Aztec mummy traditions – instead, they're unbandaged corpses persevered in a state of semi-decay.

El Santo first encountered them, alongside his friends Mil Máscaras and Blue Demon, in *The Mummies of Guanajuato* (orig., *Las momias de Guanajuato*, 1970). Opening with a tourist friendly trawl through the city and its museum, the film has a century-old wrestler – the towering Satan – coming back from the dead and attacking a midget tour guide before leading his ghouls into the city.

It turns out that Satan is one of a special group of ghouls whose bodies have been perfectly preserved from the neck down – although their rotten, decomposed faces are another matter entirely. He's come back to find El Santo, the modern day ancestor of the hero who put him in the ground a hundred years earlier and he's brought a few more momias back from the grave with him.

With his latex mask and wispy hair, Satan certainly looks the part of a zombie. The rest of his ghoulish compadres are also kitted out with latex masks and make a striking comparison with the fresh-faced, radio-controlled automatons of *Invasion of the Zombies* almost a decade earlier. They're also formidable lucha libre opponents and things look bleak for our heroes in the climactic graveyard tag-team rumble until El Santo breaks out the flamethrower pistols he conveniently keeps in his convertible's glovebox.

Critic Keith J. Rainville has argued that the Mexican momias movies are often unfairly overlooked by zombie fans and scholars confused by the semantics of their name. "Filming a zombie movie in the catacombs of Guanajuato was as natural as shooting a Western in Monument Valley," he writes in reference to *The Mummies of Guanajuato* in his book *Zombi Mexicano*. "But the mystery of why this film has been denied recognition in zombie fan circles goes no deeper than its title. 'Guanajuato' is just too damn hard to pronounce, and *mummies aren't zombies, right?*"[83]

Semantic confusion aside, las momias returned in several more Mexican films alongside wrestlers like Blue Demon, Blue Angel and Superzán. The best of these were *Theft of the Mummies of Guanajauto* (orig. *El robo de las momias de Guanajuato*, 1971) in which a magician and a scientist call the famed mummies from their tombs

to work in a radioactive mine; and *Castle of the Mummies of Guanajuato* (orig. *El castillo de las momias de Guanajuato*, 1973) where another mad scientist uses the mummies to kidnap and torture innocents so that he has a fresh supply of "terrified" blood. Tying their scantily clad victims upside down in a torture chamber cave and inflicting pain with racks and hot irons, these ghouls are unusually sadistic.[84] The whole film has a curious S&M vibe that sits uneasily with the sheer silliness of its midgets, masked wrestlers and kiddie supporting players.

What's notable about all these Mexican zombie efforts though – whether momias or muertos – is how little interest they have in their zombies as dead men walking. They're villains and bad guys, nothing much more than hammy fodder for the garishly masked luchadores to grapple and throw and punch out. The ontological horror of them as dead things that still live never really registers at all. If Mexican wrestlers are a south of the border answer to Adam West era Batman – all BIFF! POW! WHAM! – then their zombie antagonists are the Jokers of the zombie world. They're always ready to rumble but their stiff, outstretched arms, dodgy latex appliances, midget supervisors and lack of cannibal threat make them more comical than scary – like rejects from a Saturday morning kids' TV show.

Other international productions took their zombie horrors more seriously. One of the most thoroughly European films of the period was *Dr Orloff's Monster* (orig. *El secreto del Dr Orloff*; aka *Brides of Dr Jekyll, Dr Jekyll's Mistresses*, 1964), a Spanish production shot by infamous exploitation film director Jesús "Jess" Franco. Fusing pretentious artiness, technical incompetence and sleazy exploitation, Franco became a legend in cult European horror circles and made (literally) hundreds of movies before his death in 2013. His films may be a strange mix of the inept, the ridiculous and the just plain boring, but they're always good fun.

No stranger to the zombie's curious charms, Franco's living dead films include the surreal family drama *A Virgin Among the Living Dead* (orig. *Une vierge chez les morts vivants*, 1971); a so-brief-it-remains-uncredited stint on *Zombie Lake* (orig. *Le lac des morts vivants*, 1980) – he vanished during preproduction and was replaced by a bewildered

Jean Rollin; another Nazi zombie outing – *Oasis of the Zombies* (orig. *La tumba de los muertos vivientes*, 1982) and the over-sexed, Canaries-shot *Mansion of the Living Dead* (orig. *La mansión de los muertos vivientes*, 1982).

However, it's Franco's first zombie film *Dr Orloff's Monster* that's probably his best. It was loosely styled as a sequel to Franco's first major production, *The Awful Dr Orlof* (orig. *Gritos en la noche*, 1961), which starred Howard Vernon as a scientist terrorising young girls with the help of a blind, bug-eyed zombie-esque automaton called Morpho (Ricardo Valle). In *Dr Orloff's Monster*, Franco upped the stakes with a similar tale of perversity and Euroschlock that paid far more attention to the existential angst of being dead – with a ghoul who was explicitly styled as a zombie.

The film opens with Austrian college student Melissa (Agnès Spaak) travelling out to her aunt and uncle's run-down castle to spend the Christmas holidays. Uncle Conrad (Marcelo Arroita-Jáuregui) is a secretive and quite obviously insane scientist who has inherited some innovative research into "ultrasonics" from one of his late colleagues – the Dr Orloff of the title. Using this new-fangled technology Conrad – or Dr Jekyll as he's more infamously known – manages to reanimate the dead. His first test subject is his dead brother, and Melissa's father, Andros (Hugo Blanco). Jekyll murdered Andros several years earlier, after discovering that he was having a torrid affair with his wife. Melissa is totally ignorant of the circumstances surrounding her father's death and his unexpected return to life. She also doesn't know about her uncle's penchant for using his new zombie slave to murder the local good time girls – a foolish indiscretion that eventually leads the police straight to his door.

Kicking off with a surreal montage of shots involving Jekyll, his wife and Andros, *Dr Orloff's Monster* is chiefly memorable because of Franco's consistent attempts to fashion this cheap zombie film into high art. Employing regular bursts of eye-catching editing and unusual camera angles, Franco desperately tries to disguise the fact that this is actually little more than a risqué exploitation movie. The fact that the zombie spends most of his time pursuing strippers and streetwalkers gives the game away, though.

In keeping with Franco's pretentious artiness, Hugo Blanco proves to be one of cinema's most refined ghouls – a black-suited cadaver whose face is horrendously scarred and whose hands are always clad in leather gloves. He actually looks as though he'd be happier sitting in a Parisian Left Bank café sipping espresso and reading Sartre than stuck in this cheap B-movie. A few years later, Franco would return to this chic style for his espionage movie *Attack of the Robots* (orig. *Cartes sur table*, 1966) featuring robotic assassins dressed in similar black suits and turtleneck jumpers.

When Andros finally escapes Jekyll's control and disappears into the night, the police ask Melissa to help them find him before he kills again. How she'll be able to find him better than anyone else isn't explained, but it does allow Franco to set up some *faux*-pathos as daughter lures zombified father to his doom. He dies with a supposedly poignant "*pourquoi?*" on his lips.

Films like *Dr Orloff's Monster* helped European cinema discover the living dead's potential. In Italy, a couple of movies featuring zombies added to the growing sense that the time of these ghouls was coming. During the 1960s, Italy's home-grown cinema developed the "peplum", a cycle of movies named after the tunics that dominated the wardrobes of these sword and sandal epics. By 1964, the peplum boom was running short on ideas and one filmmaker, Guiseppe Vari spiced up the genre with a battalion of living dead soldiers in his magical epic *War of the Zombies* (orig. *Roma contro Roma*, 1964).

The film centred on an evil sorcerer (John Barrymore) who raises an army of zombies – the corpses of an ambushed detachment of Legionnaires. Determined to force the Roman Empire to its knees, Barrymore's sets "Rome against Rome" as the literal translation of the film's Italian title suggests. Only briefly toying with the psychological horror of soldiers fighting their dead comrades, *War of the Zombies* proved more interested in putting together a rousing climactic battle sequence in which ghostly zombie soldiers fought living infantry. It was ethereal and operatic and it proved the quip that old soldiers never die – they just go to hell to regroup.

Few other Italian productions of the period could offer anything quite as spectacular. Massimo Pupillo's *Terror-Creatures from the Grave* (orig. *Cinque tombe per un medium*, 1965) told the story of a medium who returns to life after being killed by his adulterous wife (Barbara Steele). Despite a number of gruesome set pieces including a wheelchair bound protagonist rolling himself onto a sword blade and various amputated limbs coming to life, *Terror Creatures from the Grave* suffered from an abundance of Gothic atmosphere that was all build up and no climax, leaving it distinctly lacking in any "terror".

Perhaps the most important European film of the decade was an Italian-American co-production directed by Ubaldo Ragona and Sidney Salkow called *The Last Man on Earth* (orig. *L'ultimo uomo della terra*, 1964). The film secured a Stateside release thanks to the intercession of American International Pictures (AIP), who were encouraged by the presence of their favourite actor Vincent Price in the lead role. Adapted from American author Richard Matheson's classic vampire apocalypse novel, *I Am Legend* (1954), *The Last Man on Earth* proved far more influential in America than its bilingual production history might have suggested. Although it is ostensibly a vampire movie, its bloodsucking ghouls had a significant impact on Romero's zombie cinema.

The Last Man of the title is Robert Morgan (Price), a scientist caught up in a global plague that wipes out the entire human race and leaves just a handful of vampires in its place. Through some strange quirk of fate, Morgan is the only human survivor. Desperate to drink his blood, the half-witted, lumbering vampires congregate around his barricaded house every night moaning, "Come out Robert!" in a vain attempt to entice him from his fortified abode.

Since the vampires can only come out after sunset, Morgan is free to roam the empty city streets by day, searching for fellow survivors and supplies while killing as many of the sleeping ghouls as he can before night falls again. Each morning he loads up his car and drives out to the still-burning plague pit that lies on the city's outskirts to dump his most recent kills into the flames. It's a hellish existence and as Price's cracked voiceover threatens to spill over into outright hysteria, we begin to appreciate the horror of Morgan's dreadful loneliness as the only uninfected human being left alive.

The Last Man On Earth (1964).

With its urban locale (shot in Rome for Los Angeles), deserted streets and mounds of corpses, *The Last Man on Earth* is directly related to the atomic anxieties that dominated the previous decade. Yet, there's more to this tale than simply a presaging of nuclear doom. Morgan's situation is made all the more terrifying because he is forced to confront ghoulish creatures who were once his neighbours. His chief antagonist is Ben (Giacomo Rossi-Stuart) a former friend and colleague who was also the only scientist to guess that the plague was turning its victims into vampires. In a flashback we see that Morgan dismissed Ben's far-fetched – but ultimately accurate – theory out of hand in a moment of arrogance that only helped hasten the apocalypse. As a constant reminder of Morgan's own culpability and failure, Ben is more than just another ghoul; which is why Morgan projects all his impotent anger onto him: "When I find him, I'll drive a stake though him just like all the others," he promises with grim determination.

Confronting past friends and neighbours is admittedly difficult, but the greatest horror is coming face to face with relatives and loved ones. The scene in which Morgan encounters his dead wife is as unsettling as any in the film. Refusing to believe that his wife would return to harm him, Morgan decides not to incinerate her body in the plague pit and buries her in the backyard instead. No sooner has she been laid to rest than she's back from the grave, eager to drink his blood. He's left with the unenviable responsibility of dispatching her reanimated corpse again with a stake. It's a disturbing sequence that underlines the ways in which the apocalypse of *The Last Man on Earth* is one that's played out in the local community and (quite literally) Morgan's own backyard. In the process, the benign world of American suburbia is turned into a nightmarish realm of abject horror.

What makes *The Last Man on Earth* so important in the development of the zombie genre's obsession with family based horror is its attempt to challenge the line between Us and Them. While searching the city streets, Morgan discovers that he's not the only person to have survived the plague. In addition to the lumbering, imbecilic vampires, there's also a small section of the populace who have managed to retain their higher mental functions. Forced to spend all day in the shadows, these infected survivors have set up an alternative post-apocalyptic society, a new order in which Morgan's immunity to the plague is seen as an aberration rather than a stroke of luck.

During his daylight raids on the sleeping vampires – a series of which we see in a short montage where Price bursts into apartments armed with a hammer and stake – Morgan has been inadvertently killing members of this new order, mistaking them for ghouls when they're actually something else: a new breed of humanity. As the film draws to a close, these survivors hunt Morgan down. They're convinced that *he* is the real monster of this post-apocalyptic world.

"You're a legend in this city," explains Ruth (Franca Bettoia) the infected girl sent to assassinate him. "Living by day instead of night, leaving as evidence of your existence bloodless

corpses – many of the people you destroyed were still alive." Inverting the vampire dynamic so that it's Morgan who seems abnormal, the film erodes the line between "Them" (the monsters) and "Us" (humanity).

In the final sequence, Morgan is chased into a church by an army of black-uniformed, machine gun-carrying vampire soldiers. "Freaks! All of you!" he screams as they open fire, "I'm a man, the last man!" His bullet-strewn body collapses on the church altar with pointed symbolism, yet Morgan's potential role as the messiah is significantly undermined. This version of *The Last Man on Earth* turns him into a scapegoat as he becomes messiah and monster simultaneously. The result is a film that challenges us to reassess where the Self and the Other begin and end.[85]

Whatever the film's faults – and there are many, chief among them being the miscasting of Price, whose velvety voice and occasional flashes of camp humour leave us waiting for a punch line that never comes – *The Last Man on Earth* is an intelligent slice of apocalyptic sci-fi/horror. In its willingness to envision the end of the world, it overturns all sense of the heroic, the good and the true with a bleak nihilism rarely seen in the films of the period. Significantly, this downbeat attempt to challenge all notions of selfhood, truth and value was something that Romero would shape into the genre's seminal masterpiece, the *Citizen Kane* of zombie cinema, *Night of the Living Dead* (1968).

IV. BACK ON AMERICAN SOIL: *NIGHT OF THE LIVING DEAD*

Shunted out into Europe, Mexico and Great Britain, the living dead were in exile from both the country that had invented them and the land that had turned them into cinematic terrors. In America, the zombie had become a poor relation, ignored by the mainstream and trampled over by the exploitation circuit. For most of the 1960s, American zombie productions struggled to reestablish themselves. Devoid of their Caribbean racial dynamic and cut adrift by the atomic influence of the previous decade, the majority of American zombie films during this period were marginal genre entries that had little to offer

anyone except perhaps the most undiscerning horror fans.

Even after three decades of screen history, it seemed that some American filmmakers still didn't know what a zombie was. Many films played fast and loose with living dead mythology. *The Cape Canaveral Monsters* (1960) had aliens taking over the bodies of a couple killed in a car crash (the goofy joke being that their bodies are slowly falling apart). *The Horror of Party Beach* (1963) touted a bunch of radioactive sea monsters as zombies. *Orgy of the Dead* (1965) presented its ghouls as damned female souls who spend their time doing stripteases in glorious "Sexicolor".

Needless to say, such dreadful drive-in movies were strange enough to guarantee an audience of curiosity seekers. The most bizarre American film of the decade was surely *The Incredibly Strange Creatures Who Stopped Living and Became Mixed Up Zombies!!?* (1963). The "creatures" of the title are the unwitting victims of a funfair gypsy fortune-teller (Brett O'Hara) and her sister (Erina Enyo) who douse their punters with acid, brainwash them with a swirling, psychedelic spinning wheel, and keep them locked up in a cage at the back of their tent. Sadly, the zombies play second fiddle to the film's crazy mixed-up hero Jerry (played by director Ray Dennis Steckler), who is hypnotised into becoming a murderer by the gypsy woman. Not even Steckler's desperate overacting can stop him being upstaged by the film's abundant catalogue of strippers, girlie show dancers and musical revues – all of which are shown in mind-numbing and distinctly unerotic detail in the hope of padding out the flimsy script.

The hypnotised victims theme got a different spin in Agentina's *The Deadly Organ* (orig. *Placer sangriento*, aka *Feast of Flesh*, 1965) in which a masked "Love Drug" killer turns girls into zombie sex slaves using heroin and some groovy organ music. Released in the US in 1967 with an English dub chock full of swinging 1960s slang ("This place is a drag. I'm splitting, ciao!"), it luridly played on fears that the burgeoning drugs 'n' sex counter culture was turning the youth of the day into blank-eyed "zombies".

Such silliness was only surpassed in two mad scientist movies: *Monstrosity* (1963) and *The Astro Zombies* (1967). In the former, director Joseph Mascelli (cameraman on *The Incredibly Strange Creatures*) took audiences on a crazed journey into the heart of atomic medicine with the story of a doctor (Frank Gerstle) who's trying to implant the brain of his aging employer (Marjorie Eaton, the old grandma from *Zombies of Mora Tau*) into a fresh young body. Seeing as all he's produced to date are a girl with the brain of a cat who now has a taste for mice and a man who thinks he's a dog, things don't look too promising. The added complication is that if the brains are too far deteriorated, the subject becomes a zombie. Whether that is better or worse than being a cat woman is never made clear.

In *The Astro-Zombies*, another mad scientist (John Carradine, natch) attempts to create a Frankenstein style "Quasi-Man". Rather than the superhuman all-purpose man-machine expected, the fruit of his labour turns out to be a solar-powered zombie with an electrically driven synthetic heart, a stainless steel mesh stomach, a plastic pancreas and the brain of a psychopath (since that was the only one available at the time!). He quickly goes on the rampage – as any self-respecting psycho-monster would in such dire circumstances. Decked out in a cheap joke store skull mask, this "Astro Zombie" marks the nadir of 1960s ghouls. Still, there's much fun to be had in watching writer-director-producer Ted V. Mikels plumb the depths of stupidity. The zombie's habit of recharging his solar-powered batteries by clamping flashlights against his forehead during nocturnal excursions offers some unintentional hilarity, as does the script's choice collection of atrocious dire-logue: "When a man doesn't know the difference between an experiment on an Air Force officer and a cadaver, I think it's time to drop him from the team."

If trash films like *The Incredibly Strange Creatures Who Stopped Living and Became Mixed Up Zombies!!?* or *The Astro-Zombies* had continued unchecked, it's quite possible that the zombie genre might have completely disappeared. Fortunately, in deepest Pennsylvania, one low-budget filmmaker was about to change the course of the zombie movie forever by bringing to fruition the themes of family horror, the apocalypse and the living dead that so many movies had touched on yet failed to turn into cinematic gold. The result was a film that pushed the envelope of modern horror in a manner that perhaps no other movie since *Psycho* had done.

When *Night of the Living Dead* was released on 2 October 1968, the response to it was immediate, incensed and utterly hysterical. Typical of the moral outrage that accompanied George A. Romero's debut film was the original review in the pages of *Variety*: "Until the Supreme Court establishes clear-cut guidelines for the pornography of violence, *Night of the Living Dead* will serve nicely as an outer-limit definition by example. In a mere 90 minutes this horror film (pun intended) casts serious aspersions on the integrity and social responsibility of its Pittsburgh-based makers, distributor Walter Reade, the film industry as a whole and [exhibitors] who book [the picture], as well as raising doubts about the future of the regional cinema movement and about the moral health of filmgoers who cheerfully opt for this unrelieved orgy of sadism."

The reviewer wasn't finished there and continued: "No brutalising stone is left unturned: crowbars gash holes in the heads of the 'living dead,' people are shot in the head or through the body (blood gushing from their back), bodies are burned, monsters are shown eating entrails." There was still one more put down to come. "On no level is the unrelieved grossness of *Night of the Living Dead* disguised by a feeble attempt at art or significance."[86]

With provocatively sensational notices like this, it's hardly surprising that Romero's low-budget horror film would become a license to print money. Inspired by such damning reviews, thousands of patrons rushed to the movie's limited showings turning it into an overnight smash hit. Contrary to what *Variety* might have thought, it seemed that there was a large section of the public who would "cheerfully opt for this unrelieved orgy of sadism" if given half a chance.

Although few critics were able to see it at the time, there was far more to *Night of the Living Dead* than just its visceral impact. *Psycho* might have recalibrated the focus of modern horror, but it was Romero who widened its scope. Taking the family based terror of Hitchcock's masterpiece as his starting point, the Pittsburgh director moulded it into a wide-ranging critique of contemporary America marked by unrelenting nihilism, graphic violence and visceral scenes of a world turned completely upside-down. This was a film that dragged American horror kicking and screaming into the modern age.

It took audiences completely by surprise. Film critic Roger Ebert was so concerned about the disastrous effect *Night of the Living Dead* might have on young minds that he penned a potent warning to parents in the pages of *Reader's Digest*. He was prompted, he explained, by his own experience of sitting through a matinee performance of the film surrounded by wailing nine-year-olds whose parents had left them at what they'd assumed was just another silly monster movie.

"The kids in the audience were stunned. There was almost complete silence. The movie had long ago stopped being delightfully scary, and had become unexpectedly terrifying. A little girl across the aisle from me, maybe nine years old, was sitting very still in her seat and crying. I don't think the younger kids really knew what hit them. They'd seen horror movies before, but this was something else. This was ghouls eating people – you could actually see what they were eating. This was little girls killing their mothers. This was being set on fire. Worst of all, nobody got out alive – even the hero got killed. I felt real terror in the neighbourhood theatre. I saw kids who had no resources they could draw on to protect themselves from the dread and fear they felt."[87]

No one was more surprised by the movie's phenomenal success than the filmmakers themselves. Romero and his producers Karl Hardman and Russell Streiner (who both appear in front of the camera playing Cooper and Johnny respectively) had originally wanted to make a non-horror art-house movie. Fortunately for genre fans, they were deterred from this lofty aim and realised that their best chance of seeing some return on the $114,000 budget they'd scraped together would be to make an exploitation movie.

Funding the project out of their own pockets and enlisting the help of local sponsors, the filmmakers decided that their subject matter would have to be dictated by the realities of the financial constraints they faced. With little money for make-up, costumes or special effects, they opted to build the story around the cheapest monster they could come up with – the zombie.

Night of the Living Dead begins on a deserted stretch of highway in the Pennsylvania countryside. It's the late evening and Johnny (Streiner) and his sister Barbara (Judith O'Dea) are driving along the isolated road to a nearby cemetery where the couple are planning on paying their respects at their father's grave. Cranky and irritable, Johnny's angry about having to drive so far and doesn't see the point in this empty ritual of honouring the dead. Bored, he begins to taunt Barbara. Once they reach the cemetery, he tries to scare her by pretending that the elderly man they see walking between the gravestones is a ghoul. It's a cruel joke – but it turns out to be unexpectedly true as the approaching stranger attacks Barbara and, in the ensuing scuffle, kills Johnny. So begins *Night of the Living Dead*'s assault on its audience.

Escaping to an isolated farmhouse further down the road, Barbara hides until the arrival of Ben (Duane Jones), who comes into the house to take shelter. After killing a few of the ghouls massing outside, Ben starts to barricade the doors and windows while the terrified girl looks on helplessly. Once the commotion subsides, a group of people emerge from the cellar: two sappy young kids Tom (Keith Wayne) and Judy (Judith Ridley); an arrogant but cowardly businessman named Harry Cooper (Karl Hardman); his wife Helen (Marilyn Eastman); and their daughter Karen (Kyra Schon), who has fallen sick after being bitten by one of the ghouls.

The fact that they stayed hidden downstairs while he fought for his life doesn't do much to endear them to Ben. Almost immediately, an argument breaks out between Ben and Cooper over who's in charge and whether or not the group ought to hide downstairs in the cellar (Cooper's plan) or fortify the house (Ben's plan). As the characters bicker about the best course of action, the television news reports the outbreak of "murders being committed in the Eastern third of the nation". At first, citizens are advised to stay in their homes; later they're told to make their way to the nearest rescue station where the National Guard will protect them.

After discovering the keys to the petrol pump outside, Ben suggests that they make a run for safety using the truck. In the course of the escape attempt, though, everything goes wrong. The truck catches fire and then explodes, killing Tom and Judy whose barbecued remains are eaten by the ghouls. Cooper tries to lock Ben out of the house, but he manages to get back inside and, in the ensuing struggle, the spineless businessman is shot. Barbara, who's been catatonic for most of the proceedings, pulls herself together and helps Ben fight off the advancing zombies. But she is eventually dragged out of the front door by her brother Johnny who's come back from the dead.

Down in the cellar, the Coopers' daughter has died from the bite she received and joined the ranks of the living dead. She kills her mother with a garden trowel, then emerges from the cellar and attacks Ben. Realising that he has no other option, Ben barricades himself inside the cellar and shoots Harry and Helen Cooper in the head as they return to life. When morning finally dawns, the zombies

have dispersed. A posse of policemen and militia approach the farmhouse and as Ben, the only survivor of the night, emerges from the cellar he's shot in the head by the rednecks. The film closes with a montage of still images showing Ben's body being dragged out of the house on meat hooks and tossed onto a bonfire of zombie corpses.

For the average audience in 1968, the visceral horror of *Night of the Living Dead* packed quite a punch. While blood-soaked special effects had been enlivening drive-in horror movies for a few years before Romero's debut – particularly in the outrageous gore of films like Herschell Gordon Lewis's *Blood Feast* (1963) and *Two Thousand Maniacs!* (1964) – the Pittsburgh director's take on the "meat" movie was completely different. Lewis and his imitators offered lashings of gore simply for its own sake, with scenes of dismemberment and mutilation framed by plots that were perfunctory at best, incoherent at worst. Romero displayed a far lighter touch, only pushing the boundaries of good taste in a handful of *Night of the Living Dead*'s scenes and, what's more, doing it in black & white cinematography. Intriguingly, this restraint helped increase rather than diminish the film's impact, foregrounding the one thing that's always the inevitable focus of any zombie movie, the human body itself.

Under Romero's direction, the corporeal was made decidedly *real*. From the half-eaten skull of the farmhouse's owner that's discovered on the first floor landing, to the numerous scenes in which zombie foreheads are bashed by tire irons and grasping hands are cut down to size by kitchen knives, Romero never lets us forget that this is a film about the body. Or, to be more accurate, the horror of the body. Refusing to skirt the issue of the zombie's physicality – both in its monstrous form as a reanimated corpse and in its newly threatening form as a flesh-eating creature – Romero brought an uncompromising realism to the genre. He also added a previously unheard of dimension to the zombie myth: cannibalism.

Before *Night of the Living Dead*, zombies had been content to scare, strangle or bludgeon their victims. Romero upped the ante by giving them a taste for warm, human flesh. As a result, the scene in which the barbecued remains of Tom and Judy are eaten by ghouls became the film's most influential moment. Although the crew jokingly dubbed this sequence "The Last Supper", there was nothing comical about its execution. Romero shipped in real animal entrails from a Pittsburgh butcher in order to achieve the right degree of authenticity, and then found extras who were willing to chomp greedily on pig hearts and sheep intestines. It was gory, it was distressing and it was innovative enough to dominate the genre's development forever. From that moment onwards cinematic zombies would almost always be flesh-eaters.

Such uncompromising commitment to realism characterises the film. The grainy cinematography – bolstered by TV footage of anxious news anchormen and bewildered Washington officials – gives the film a *cinema verité* look. It suggests that these events aren't part of some *super*natural horror, but something altogether more ordinary. Indeed, even the film's newsreaders find themselves at a loss when trying to describe these "unidentified assassins" since they're so "ordinary looking" that "there is no really authentic way for us to say who or what to look for or guard yourself against." Tellingly, Romero refrains from calling his monsters "zombies" at any point in the film.

This ordinariness is the key to the film's horror. As Gregory Waller has suggested, Romero's ghouls aren't conventional horror movie monsters. Rather *Night of the Living Dead* is a film that sets out to "redefine the monstrous – thereby redefining the role of the hero and the victim as well – and situate horror in the everyday world of America."[88] The zombies of *Night of the Living Dead* are not really monsters at all. Instead, they're "our fellow citizens who, with no leader and no motive beside hunger, have returned to feed on us."[89] They are simply, as Romero is so fond of saying, "the neighbours".[90]

By excising both the supernatural and the magical connotations of the zombie's voodoo origins, *Night of the Living Dead* foregrounds its horror in the real world as it is transformed from safe to horrific by an inexplicable shift in the natural order. Much like Hitchcock's *The Birds* (1963), a film that was an apparent influence on Romero, the action centres on a situation that

Night of the Living Dead (1968).

challenges our understanding of the fundamental dynamics of the universe. As birds group together to attack humans or dead bodies return to feed off the living, the whole basis of civilisation – and man's sense of mastery over his environment – is instantly altered.

What makes Romero's apocalyptic vision so utterly unsettling is the nihilism that informs it. The rising up of the dead against the living is presented as a sustained attack on every truth, value and comfort that civilisation holds dear. It is a revolution, claims Gregory Waller, in which "we are given no secure basis for dealing with the escalating horrors."[91] All objective standards of truth and value are swept aside, trampled beneath the feet of the living dead as they march on the nation's cities. Every vestige of authority, every convention of heroism, is overturned by Romero's script.

In many respects, it is the living's failure to cooperate and put aside their petty differences that invites the chaos. Fascinated by how quickly the social order can crumble – a theme he would return to in the next two instalments of his living dead series, *Dawn of the Dead* (1978) and *Day of the Dead* (1985), as well as in his biological warfare thriller *The Crazies* (1973) – Romero shows us that it's the territorial bickering of the living that's the real threat to civilisation. The problem of the dead returning to life actually seems quite containable if only Ben and Cooper – and on a much larger scale the infighting authorities in

Washington – could stop arguing for long enough to formulate a plan of action. For Romero, this is the way the world ends: not with a bang, but with a series of whimpering arguments that invite a chaotic collapse of the social order into arguments, fistfights and dispassionate news reports.

As anarchy prevails, even the comforts of conventional horror movie wisdom falter. Authority is one of the first casualties of the upheaval swiftly followed – on a more local level – by the collapse of the American family. The TV news reports show harassed Washington officials rushing between meetings, and Romero himself appears as an exasperated reporter fruitlessly trying to ascertain the facts of the situation from the politicians. It's clear that the government is unable to help those caught in the midst of the crisis. What's more, the implicit suggestion is that it may well have been the military industrial complex that caused the catastrophe in the first place. Talk about the dangerously high levels of radiation returning to Earth with a crashed "Venus probe" hint at where the blame may lie.

If the politicians and military can't help us, who should we look to? The answer seems to be no one. The police and militia are little more than trigger-happy rednecks. Even the film's ostensible hero, the resourceful Ben, is rather suspect. His assertion that the cellar is a "death trap" is proved hopelessly wrong and his cold-blooded killing of the cowardly Cooper – however understandable – is hardly admirable, or heroic.

The family fares little better. As Johnny and Barbara's opening argument about their visit to their father's grave illustrates, familial ties have already collapsed, long before the dead start walking. The Coopers' traditional nuclear family can't offer any hope either. Mother and father both hate each other and their daughter ends up turning on them when she becomes one of the zombies, hacking her mother to death with a garden trowel in a scene that's an eerie but poignant echo of *Psycho*'s shower murder.

The redefinition of the monstrous that Romero undertakes eventually comes to challenge our understanding of the line between Self and Other. "They're us and we're them," claims Barbara in the 1990 remake of *Night of the Living Dead* (written, though not directed, by Romero). It's a throwaway line that's actually deeply significant in respect of Romero's original 1968 film. By challenging the distinction between the living and the dead, the normal and the monstrous, *Night of the Living Dead* brings terror into the American home, hearth and family. One of the most memorable moments is when the zombified Johnny – who was killed in the film's opening reel – returns from the dead to drag his sister out of the house. It encapsulates the predominant terrors of the post-*Invasion of the Body Snatchers* zombie movie; namely, that the individual may be co-opted into the mass. It also pinpoints the way in which *Night of the Living Dead* locates its terror in the familiar and ordinary rather than the alien and extraordinary.

The visceral scenes of flesh-eating that appalled contemporary commentators are also typical of this thematic clash between the Self and the Other. Making the body into the site of Otherness, *Night of the Living Dead* offers a vision of the world in which our own flesh is made to seem strange, disgusting and gross. The cannibalism that Romero adds to the zombie mythology wasn't simply a spectacular ploy to drum up controversy and boost ticket sales. It is central to the film's provocative vision of individuals being consumed/subsumed into the larger group. Romero takes the paranoid fears of *Invasion of the Body Snatchers* – in particular its vision of the mass as a terrifyingly homogenous entity – and multiples them several times over.

What exactly do the ghouls represent? For critic Linda Badley, the zombie horde is like some "ambulatory mass grave" and thus both a reminder of the inevitability of death and an affront to our belief in its finality.[92] For Robin Wood, Romero's vision of the living dead as a relentless, unswerving group enacts a return of the repressed in which our fear of dead family members – and even the dead of Vietnam – leads us to imagine them taking their revenge on the living. Wood's Freudian reading of the horror film in general suggests that, "the true subject of the horror genre is the struggle for recognition of all that our society *represses* or *oppresses*".[93] Thus for Wood, the monster can be understood as a projection of our secret desires that comes to haunt us in a very literal fashion, returning from the graveyard of the unconscious. From the perspective of this psychoanalytic reading of the horror genre, there is a reason why the characters of zombie movies spend most of their time barricading themselves away inside houses, cellars and attics. They are terrified of coming face to face with a repressed horror that they previously refused to acknowledge.

Vietnam lurks in every frame of Romero's film. Hitting cinemas at the height of the war, as race riots, peace demonstrations and the angry outbursts of a youthful counterculture raged through America, Romero's debut pulled no punches in its representation of a nation falling apart on every level. Echoes of the conflict itself are everywhere in the film: the search and destroy missions are carried out by the local militia under the insistent thud-thud-thud of helicopter rotor blades; the men on the ground tackle the ghouls with gung-ho enthusiasm; the TV news reports are dominated by an anxious discourse of contagion and containment. The sheriff's matter-of-fact response to the return of the dead sounds like an extension of the detached "professionalism" that dominated the official descriptions of the war in Vietnam: "Shoot 'em in the head… beat 'em or burn 'em, they go up pretty easy … they're dead, they're all messed up." The living dead enemy even possesses a linguistic echo of the one in South East Asia: "ghoul" is only a few letters removed from "gook". It's hardly surprising, then, that at least one contemporary commentator made the link with the war explicit by suggesting that if Lyndon B. Johnson had seen it he might never "have permitted the napalming of the Vietnamese."[94]

Aligning itself in direct opposition to the dominant American patriarchal order of family, community, police and military, *Night of the Living Dead* suggests that the whole of society is rotten to the core. It's this maggot ridden, flesh-eating putridity that's crawled back from the grave to jab a decomposing finger of blame at us all, much like the dead of Abel Gance's *J'Accuse* (1937). No accident, then, that the film opens with a young couple visiting the grave of their dead father: this is a world completely lacking in patriarchal authority.

The extent of Romero's critique of the forces of law, order and authority is underscored in the film's conclusion. As Ben emerges from the cellar, having survived the long, dark night of the living dead, he's shot in the head by the sheriff's posse who believes he's "one of *them*". Have the rednecks made a genuine error and mistaken him for a zombie? Or do they think that, as an African-American, Ben is

simply a different kind of *them*? The film ends without answering the question, but perhaps it doesn't matter. Romero has already convinced us that the world has gone to hell, giving Ben's death all the terrifying, but inevitable, logic of a bad dream. As the film closes, with a series of stills showing his body being tossed onto a bonfire, the parallels with 1960s newsreel footage of everything from Vietnam to the Watts race riots are obvious.

If *Psycho* set the trend for placing horror in the family, Romero develops Hitchcock's strategy through his use of the zombie. In *Night of the Living Dead*, family horror is everywhere. The Coopers are faced with their zombified daughter ("It's Mommy," Helen vainly whispers as her murderous daughter approaches, armed with a garden trowel). Barbara has to confront her dead brother. Ben is forced to watch as former members of the farmhouse community return from the dead. More than anything else, *Night of the Living Dead* suggests that the nationwide family of America itself is a site of horror. There is no longer any simple way to tell the monsters from the normal people.

Central to these strategies is the zombie itself. Romero's breathtaking rejuvenation of the genre centres on his total break with the past. Ignoring the voodoo mythology of the living dead that had been thriving since the 1930s, *Night of the Living Dead* takes its energy from films like *Invasion of the Body Snatchers* and *The Last Man on Earth*. These aren't voodoo zombies, but reanimated corpses functioning without emotion or malice. Their only desire is to feed on the living in order to sate their incessant hunger. By forcing audiences to sit up and recognise the zombie for what it really was – a cadaver – Romero challenged our understandings of the monstrous and our long-held beliefs about the finality of death. Turning the death of the body into his film's main focus, he asked audiences to confront the horror that lay within them, the Otherness of their own flesh. It was a vision that finally gave the zombie film a credibility it had previously lacked. By collapsing the boundaries between the normal and the monstrous, living and dead, Romero signalled a new stage in the zombie's development. Filmmakers no longer had to hide behind half-baked plots and silly special effects. Instead they could approach serious issues with a grim, apocalyptic nihilism that was shocking and exhilarating in equal measure.

CHAPTER SIX

DAWN OF THE DEAD

I. ROMERO'S CHILDREN

Night of the Living Dead was a watershed movie. It played for years after its initial release, screened at drive-ins, grindhouses, film clubs and even dormitory walls (courtesy of Super 8 projectors).[95] It established the "midnight movie" trend – late-night film screenings which privileged cult, low-budget horror films – and it reminded American filmmakers that exploitation cinema could be socially progressive, radical, and even revolutionary. Dragging the horror movie kicking and screaming into the post-1968 world, its subdued, black & white visuals and unrelenting violence left audiences in no doubt that the acid-tinged optimism of the hippie era was coming to an end.

Romero's bleak focus on the destruction of the present order spoke volumes about the cataclysmic shifts in American consciousness that had occurred since the assassination of President Kennedy in 1963. Imagining an apocalyptic catastrophe of such epic proportions that all hope of social regeneration becomes impossible, Romero took his audience on a journey into America's heart of darkness. As the war in Vietnam spiralled out of control and the counterculture's idealistic dreamers awoke to an acid hangover that included the Manson murders, the violence at the Altamont rock concert and the shamefaced truth of the Watergate scandal, Romero's nihilism seemed perfectly in tune with the times.

Perhaps that explains why the films that followed in the wake of *Night of the Living Dead* took the disillusionment and rude awakening of the acid generation as their starting point. For Alan Ormsby and Benjamin "Bob" Clark, *Night of the Living Dead* was certainly an inspiration. After graduating from the University of Miami, the two young budding filmmakers were encouraged by the box office success of Romero's film into making their own foray into the world of low-budget horror with two productions: the horror comedy *Children Shouldn't Play with Dead Things* (1972) and the far more ambitious *Deathdream* (aka *The Night Andy Came Home, Dead of Night*, 1972). What distinguishes both of these movies is their savage satirical bent. *Children Shouldn't Play with Dead Things* begins as a spoof of *Night of the Living Dead* then proceeds to rip the heart out of the 1960s counterculture as a group of obnoxious hippies unwittingly unleash some zombies.[96] *Deathdream* combines the vengeful tongue-in-cheek logic of the E.C. horror comics of the 1950s with a surprisingly powerful anti-Establishment thrust and a story about a Vietnam veteran who returns to America as a flesh-eating ghoul.

Both films turned out to be successful enough to launch Clark and Ormsby's respective film careers. Indeed, *Children Shouldn't Play With Dead Things* proved such a hit on the drive-in circuit that the pair found themselves in the enviable position of being able to convince their financial backers to give them five times that film's budget for *Deathdream*. Following their second collaboration, Clark went on to enjoy a successful career as a director with films like the ground-breaking slasher picture *Black Christmas* (1974) and the phenomenally successful teen comedy *Porky's* (1981). Meanwhile Ormsby stayed in the horror genre long enough to write and direct *Deranged* (1974), based on the Ed Gein case, and script Paul Schrader's *Cat People* remake in 1982.

Filmed over 11 nights in 1972 for the minuscule

sum of $50,000 *Children Shouldn't Play With Dead Things* follows a theatre troupe of hippies as they travel out to a Florida burial island for a midnight adventure. Their leader is the self-styled "Uncle Alan" (Ormsby) a bitchy megalomaniac with a nasty tongue and a penchant for loud clothes. The rest of the group are an assorted ragbag of 1960s acid casualties and stoner drama queens who have reluctantly agreed to the trip in order to stay in their employer's good books. Like the kids of *The Texas Chain Saw Massacre* (1974), they're dumb, brash and completely unsympathetic characters.

Alan claims that he's planning to perform a magic ritual that will wake the dead from their graves. But the troupe guesses that he's simply trying to scare them senseless. It's a suspicion that's confirmed when the first two "ghouls" to come back from the grave are nothing more than a couple of Alan's friends caked in suitably pallid make-up. Alan's not content with a successful prank, though. He really does want to raise the dead and instructs the group to carry a freshly exhumed corpse (dubbed "Orville") into the house of the island's caretaker. After a series of false starts, the magic incantation actually works and the dead rise from their graves to lay siege to the isolated house.

Structured as a horror comedy, with the zombies only arriving in the last half hour of the film, *Children* rarely rises above the level of a spoof. Yet at least it's a spoof with bite. Setting their sights squarely on the disillusionment of the early 1970s, Clark and Ormsby's aim is to expose the rotten core of the hippie dream of peace, love and community. Alan and his cohorts are living proof of how and where the counterculture failed to deliver on its idealistic vision of a better society. Dominated by power games, sexism, bitchy backstabbing and sadistic threats, the theatre troupe appears to be as corrupt and unpleasant as the established order it's supposed to be an alternative to. As the group's idle chatter about weird cults and mass murderers suggests, this is a world in which hippie idealism has already turned sour.

Underlying this scathingly satirical take on the bankruptcy of the counterculture is a dark despair that finds its fullest expression in Alan himself. Far from believing in traditional flower power values, the villainous anti-hero espouses a disturbed and disturbing vision of the empty pointlessness of existence: "The dead are losers. If anybody hasn't earned the right for respect, it's the dead… Man is a machine that manufactures manure."

Alan positively revels in his appreciation of a world without truth or value, describing his handsome leading man as "a slab of meat I hired to dress my stage" and praying to Satan with a mock-seriousness that suggests he can't even find enough faith to take the Antichrist seriously. He thrives on making his audience face up to the dreary emptiness not only of life, but also of death. "That's all you are old buddy – clay, mud," he tells the dead Orville in a moment of outright nastiness. Much to the chagrin of his fellow hippies, he then threatens to feed the corpse's rotting flesh to the dogs and use his bones as soup ladles and Christmas decorations.

Glibly riffing on the transitory nature of physical existence, Alan faces up to the realities of a world in which God is absent. After his nihilistic pronouncements, the return of the dead seems to have an inexorable logic. Rather than a sign of some higher power at work the ghouls are styled as machines that have malfunctioned, dead flesh that has forgotten to die and is continuing to move around in a parody of the living's pointless and expendable existence.

That Alan isn't ready to deal with such emptiness on anything other than his own terms is the film's chief source of blackly comic *schadenfreude*. Instead of embracing the ghouls as proof of his solipsistic beliefs, Alan desperately does everything in his power to save his own hunk of flesh, culminating in an outrageous scene that fans of the film fondly remember as typical of its dark pessimism. Chased onto the staircase by the marauding zombies, Alan tries to save himself by pushing death-obsessed hippie chick Anya (Anya Ormsby, the actor's real-life wife) into the path of the pursuing horde. As she tumbles into their grasp the action momentarily pauses as everyone – including the zombies – is stunned by Alan's despicable cowardice. Naturally, Alan eventually gets his just desserts as Orville comes back from the dead and eats him. In this world it's Death, not God or Satan, who will always have the last laugh.

The vengeful tradition of E.C. Comics was also an inspiration in Clark and Ormsby's next film, *Deathdream* (1972). If *Children Shouldn't Play with Dead Things* frequently seems rather reactionary in its gleeful attack on the spirit of the 1960s counterculture, *Deathdream* redresses the balance by using the zombie to take a broad swipe at the Establishment instead. The story of a killed-in-action G.I. who returns home from Vietnam as a blood-slurping zombie, *Deathdream* was remarkably bold. It was one of the first horror films to deal with the subject of the Vietnam War at a time when Hollywood considered the conflict box office poison. Proving that marginal productions can often be unexpectedly radical in ways that the mainstream can never manage, *Deathdream* joined a small band of grindhouse movies – including cheap beat 'em ups featuring troubled veterans such as *Billy Jack* and *Chrome and Hot Leather* (both 1971) – that were willing to deal with the impact of the war on their own terms.

Deathdream has all the hallmarks of a Vietnam veteran movie. The opening scenes take place in some dark "in country" location, where tracers and explosions light up the sky as a gun battle rages in the jungle. The film then cuts to America, where the family of G.I. Andy Brooks (Richard Backus) are concerned that they haven't heard from him for several weeks. While his father and sister are secretly convinced that he's dead, his mother hysterically refuses to face reality and makes a desperate monkey's paw wish for his safe return. And return he does.

There's a slight problem though: Andy's *different*. He doesn't talk much, sits in his room all day in his rocking chair, wears dark glasses even when it's night, and seems to be totally devoid of any human warmth or emotion. It turns out he's a blood-drinking zombie who has to chomp on human flesh to keep his rapidly deteriorating body from falling apart. After a series of unexplained murders are reported in the local newspapers, his father begins to suspect that this Andy isn't the same all-American boy who was shipped out to the 'Nam. When Andy strangles the family dog in front of the neighbourhood kids, it's clear that something is very, very wrong.

Unlike the Vietnam-themed horror of the much later *House* (1985) – a jokey tale in which a veteran-turned-novelist is haunted by the zombified remains of a fellow G.I. – *Deathdream* doesn't let the laughs outweigh the potential seriousness of the set-up. Taking their cue from Romero's socially conscious stance in *Night of the Living Dead*, the filmmakers use the zombified return of Andy as a savagely bitter commentary on America's war against Communism, capturing the disillusionment of the period in quite unexpected ways.

Deathdream's effectiveness stems from the simplicity of its central idea. When Andy returns home from the horror of the war in South East Asia as a blood-drinking ghoul, Andy's atrocities back on American soil are little different in scope than those he may have committed while acting in the service of his country. Bringing the war back home with him, Andy's murderous impulses prove impossible for anyone around him to comprehend. "Why would a soldier want to do that?" naively asks a local waitress on hearing that the police are looking for a Vietnam veteran in connection with the recent murders. It's a deliciously ironic line matched only by Andy's glib attempts to style his ghoulish needs as commensurable with his community's willingness to ship him off to Vietnam in the first place: "I died for you, Doc. Now why shouldn't you return the favour?"

Such satirical intent makes *Deathdream* a fitting companion piece to *Children Shouldn't Play with Dead Things*. Taken together, these two films comprise a quite remarkable attack on both ends of the political spectrum – the counterculture and the military industrial complex – of 1970s America. Clearly, *Night of the Living Dead* had done more than just revitalise the zombie as a credible monster. It had also radicalised the low-budget American horror movie, reinstating the marginal genre's potential for putting forward oppositional critiques of the prevailing social order.

Not all of the films that followed *Night of the Living Dead* proved as successful in delineating the disillusionment that followed in the wake of the 1960s. Several zombie-themed horror movies – including *Let's Scare Jessica to Death* (1971), *Garden of the Dead* (1972), *Messiah of Evil* (1972), Romero's own *The Crazies* (1973), *Shivers* (1975) and *Blue Sunshine* (1977) – tried to imitate Romero's blend of nihilistic despair and political radicalism. Yet, the results were rarely inspired (the exception to the rule is David Cronenberg's *Shivers*, which proved to be one of the most subversive, misanthropic movies of the decade). What's fascinating about these 1970s films is the way in which they insist on overturning the ideals of the flower power generation. Forming a backlash

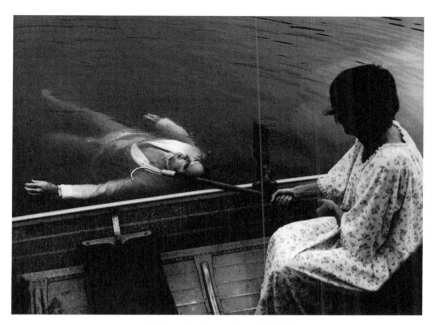

Let's Scare Jessica to Death (1971).

against the utopian hippie dream, these films toy with fears about the dangers of mind-altering drugs and rampant sexuality, while also displaying a stark mistrust of the strangeness of other people.

In Jeff Lieberman's demented *Blue Sunshine* (1977), ex-hippies are turned into raving homicidal maniacs as a delayed side effect of a batch of bad acid – the Blue Sunshine of the title – that they sampled during the years of turning on, tuning in and dropping out. Having already abandoned their tie-dyed flares to become upstanding members of the community, these bankers, lawyers and doctors suddenly lose all their hair. They then become psychotic zombie anti-hippies who go on the rampage, murdering everyone they can lay their hands on.

Such chemical anxiety is also to be found in John Hayes's dire romp *Garden of the Dead* (1972) in which hillbilly prisoners get high on formaldehyde fumes.[97] After being shot to bits by the guards during an escape attempt, the stoned convicts are buried in formaldehyde-soaked shallow graves. Pretty soon they're back on their feet seeking revenge. It was an idea that would later be replayed in *Toxic Zombies* (aka *Bloodeaters*, 1979) in which a field of marijuana is sprayed with experimental herbicides turning the local rednecks into bloodthirsty cannibal maniacs. Meanwhile, in

Romero's *The Crazies* (1973), a bio-chemical weapons spill turns ordinary American citizens into demented killers. On the basis of these films, it seemed that horror filmmakers had come to the conclusion that the drugs didn't work.

The most disturbing of this cycle of movies was one of the first, John Hancock's *Let's Scare Jessica To Death* (1971). After possibly taking one too many tabs of LSD, hippie heroine Jessica (Zohra Lampert) loses her marbles and becomes convinced that the spirit of a dead Victorian girl is haunting her. As a muted expression of acid anxiety, *Let's Scare Jessica To Death* is a profoundly creepy and effective little film. Far from embracing the idealism of the previous decade, Hancock exposes the fear and loathing underpinning it by focussing on Jessica's mental disorientation. She's convinced that the local townsfolk are zombies out to get her (they all bear the same strange scar on their faces) and slowly begins to believe that the drifter hippie who's sharing her house is a vampire. Instead of the hippie dream of community, Hancock hints at a world ruled by Jean-Paul Sartre's famous dictum "*L'enfer c'est autres*" (hell is other people). The sour-faced locals even scratch the word "love" off the side of the hippies' flower power hearse.[98]

In many respects, Sartre's misanthropic disgust is the perfect index of the concerns of the zombie movie after *Night of the Living Dead*. These films are dominated by storylines in which our friends, neighbours and families reveal their threatening Otherness by becoming flesh-eating ghouls whose only aim is to make us become part of their horrific group. In the low-budget, but ambitiously arty, *Messiah of Evil* (aka *Dead People*, 1972), this sentiment is taken to its logical conclusion as the heroine Arletty (Marianna Hill) searches for her missing father. Ending up in a strange town that's one part David Lynch to two parts H.P. Lovecraft, Arletty discovers that the local populace is comprised of zombies, who roam the streets late at night looking for fresh victims. While the film's hundred-year-old Satanic plot proves difficult to follow even with extended bursts of voiceover narration, there's no mistaking the point of the surreal episodes in which the living dead prove that they really are – to borrow Romero's term – "the neighbours". The standout scenes are those in which the inhabitants of the deserted town of Point Dune unexpectedly appear in the most banal settings. The ghouls interrupt a late-night trip to the supermarket by feeding themselves from the meat counter and, in the film's most memorable sequence, they slowly occupy the empty seats around an unsuspecting girl (Joy Bang) as she sits engrossed in a movie in the local cinema.

Other filmmakers made even more of the zombie's potential as a metaphor for the collapse of the hippie dream. In David Cronenberg's shocking debut *Shivers* (1975), hell is not only other people but also the body itself. It takes place in a hi-tech middleclass apartment block besieged by a parasite that unleashes the unbridled sexual desire of anyone infected by it. Pretty soon these phallic, turd-like creatures have turned the uptight bourgeoisie of the building into rapacious, sex-frenzied maniacs.

Shivers opens like a commercial as still shots of des-res apartment block Starliner Towers are overlaid with an estate agent's patter: "All our apartments come fully equipped with the most modern brand name electrical appliances. And cable TV is standard too." Something's not quite right, though. The pictures of this tower block paradise look bleached and soulless, like a relative of the cavernous shopping mall of Romero's later *Dawn of the Dead* or, better yet, the tower block in J.G. Ballard's novel *High-Rise* published the same year. The soft-spoken sales pitch sounds creepy rather than enticing. You know something's wrong even if you can't quite put your finger on what exactly it is.

What's actually happened is that crazed scientist Dr Hobbes (Fred Doederlein) has been experimenting with a new form of laboratory-bred parasite. Ostensibly the creatures have been created to replace damaged organs; introduced into the body, they are supposed to take over the functions of the liver or kidneys. In actual fact, though, their purpose is more sinister: the parasites have an aphrodisiac quality that reduces their hosts to slavering, horny maniacs. Eager to strip away the veneer of civilisation and reveal man's basest desire, Hobbes has sown the seeds of a sexual apocalypse. He has used the apartment block's most promiscuous resident as a kind of Thyphoid Mary. The zombies he ends up creating don't want to eat you, but bang your brains out.

Shivers is a kinky film – part softcore skin flick, part gloopy horror movie – and it flashes plenty of flesh in its quest to keep the grindhouse crowd happy: cute, doe-eyed nurse Lynn Lowry does an impromptu striptease; scream queen Barbara Steele tries some girl-on-girl tonsil tennis with busty co-star Susan Petrie; every woman wears nipple hugging sweaters; and, for the neglected ladies in the audience, actor Allan Migicovsky bares his hairy medallion man chest as parasites wriggle around inside his stomach. Yet, the titillation serves only to fuel the horror.

Made in the gap between the 1960s love in and AIDS era fear and loathing, *Shivers* was definitely ahead of its time with zombie-esque ghouls whose exists satirises the ethos behind the Free Love generation's belief in better living through orgasmic pleasure. As the parasites spread through the building, they turn Starliner Towers into a mass orgy which resident doc Roger St Luc (Paul Hampton) is unable to contain. Bankers, insurance agents and accountants become horny rapists. Fathers cop off with their daughters. Old women drool with desire ("I'm hungry! I'm hungry for love!"). Little girls are turned into knowing Lolitas and the disgusting parasites crawl out of the plughole to literally enter Barbara Steele as she lies in the bathtub.

"The very purpose was to show the unshowable, to speak the unspeakable," Cronenberg explained years later.[99] The willingness to unleash the forbidden is what gives *Shivers* its raw power. It's a radical, restless piece of agitprop disguised as exploitation – an angry young man's film, consumed by its hatred of the established order. Cronenberg made it while living penniless in the real-life apartment building that served as his principal location surrounded by the very white-collar professionals he loathed – a kind of bilious method directing. The resulting film comes with a subversive, misanthropic edge. It may not, strictly speaking, feature zombies. But it takes Romero's nihilism and runs with it, presenting an ambiguous sexual apocalypse that demands to be read as liberatory (Cronenberg celebrating the zombies' reduction of mankind to their primal instincts) and simultaneously terrified (as Cronenberg's obvious distaste for the flesh shines through). It's one of those remarkable works of art that manages to occupy two contradictory positions at once: a radical/reactionary masterpiece in which the world ends not with a bang, but with a whimpering, moaning, venereal orgasm. Perverse to the last, it closes with the zombies heading into Toronto to turn the world into a mindless, polymorphous orgy. Is it the end, or a new beginning? Cronenberg's not telling.

While these varied productions tried to ape Romero's success, the Pittsburgh director was desperately trying to do much the same thing himself after having been knocked back by two total flops. Convinced that he was destined to make arthouse cinema in the tradition of Rohmer or Bergman rather than drive-in horror flicks, Romero followed up the success of *Night of the Living Dead* with a romantic drama *There's Always Vanilla* (1972) that left critics and audiences completely bored. He then decided to play it safe, returning to the genre that loved him. The proto-feminist psychological horror movie *Jack's Wife* (aka *Season of the Witch*, 1972) about a suburban housewife who dabbles in the occult was the result. It was quickly followed by *The Crazies* (1973). Although neither movie found the same audience as *Night of the Living Dead*, *The Crazies* succeeded in reconfiguring Romero's zombie apocalypse without actually featuring any zombies. It's a significant film, though, since it paved the way for Romero's *Dawn of the Dead* five years later.

After a secret bio-chemical weapon codenamed Trixie is accidentally released into the water supply of a small town in Pennsylvania, the local inhabitants turn into homicidal maniacs. The army move in and declare martial law but the town erupts into an orgy of violence as little old ladies attack soldiers with knitting needles, an amorous father almost commits incest with his daughter, and a variety of rednecks (some crazy, some just plain angry) go on the rampage. Building on the hysteria he dissected so expertly in *Night of the Living Dead*, *The Crazies* saw Romero refining his exploitation-cinema-as-social-critique approach.

Here the catastrophe is nothing if not proof of the Establishment's boneheaded stupidity and its willingness to sacrifice citizens in order to escape censure.

Romero's satire is startlingly effective. Blurring the line between the trigger-happy soldiers, the homicidal "crazies" and the angry townsfolk, the filmmaker asks us to question who the real crazies are. The fact that nobody at the Pentagon bothered to commission an antidote to "Trixie" before pulling the plug on the project is typical of Romero's cynical take on the military-industrial complex's bureaucratic incompetence. Indeed, the military is so inherently stupid that it allows two opportunities to contain the outbreak – in the shape of a specially designed vaccine and a valuably immune citizen – to be thrown away. If that's sanity, the film seems to be saying, who knows where madness starts.

As the military infringe the civil liberties of the townsfolk by imposing martial law and beating, harassing and pistol-whipping anyone who objects, it's clear that Romero has lost none of his anti-Establishment fervour, nor his despair at the sheer stupidity of the human race. The film makes veiled, but striking, references to the Vietnam War. A local priest immolates himself in the manner of the Buddhist monks who doused themselves in petrol; the military can't tell the "crazies" (read communist guerrillas) from innocent civilians; and there are implicit parallels between the biochemical weapons-spill and the use of Agent Orange on the jungle canopies (and civilian populations) of South East Asia. Romero's central conceit – that the real crazies may be those in charge – makes for sobering viewing.

With such hard-hitting politics, it's unsurprising that *The Crazies* failed to find its audience. Yet much of the reason for its failure at the box office actually had more to do with distributor Lee Hessel than its dark edge. Hessel tried to style this low-budget horror as a big-budget blockbuster, erecting a huge billboard in Times Square and hiring some out of work actors to wander around the New York theatre district in white bio warfare suits. The result was a total bomb. "About four people showed up," recalls Romero.[100]

II. THE GHOULS CAN'T HELP IT

Horror fans have always had a cruelly intimate knowledge of the law of diminishing returns. Few genres require the triumph of hope over experience quite as often as horror cinema does: for every brilliant shocker like *The Exorcist* there's an *Exorcist: The Beginning*. For every groundbreaking *Nightmare on Elm Street* there's a cash-in *Freddy Vs. Jason*. Blood may drip, but money talks.

Night of the Living Dead certainly produced more than its fair share of cash-ins. most of these showed so little imagination that they threatened to bore zombies back to death. Nazi zombies, kiddie zombies even zombie mimes all fought to succeed Romero's masterpiece in the years following its release. It made for a bumper crop of movies that have since slid into (mostly) deserved obscurity.

William Castle's *Shanks* (1974) is a case in point. An ingenious attempt to take the zombie into new territory, it fell flat on its face as dodgy production values and ropey acting took their toll. Proving that not all of the decade's films about the living dead were obsessed with the end of the hippie dream, *Shanks* was one of a clutch of zombie productions that was allegedly more interested in entertainment than social commentary.

In his first starring role in a feature film, legendary mime artist Marcel Marceau plays Shanks, a mute puppeteer who takes a job as an assistant to a local scientist (also played by Marceau). The boffin is attempting to reanimate dead animals using electrical currents. Following his employer's unexpected demise, Shanks takes over his work and replaces dead animals with dead people. With three corpses under his control, he plays puppet master and takes his new family out on shopping sprees before eventually putting them to far less innocent uses. A fairy tale blend of fantasy and horror, *Shanks* used Marceau's mime expertise to choreograph the jerking movements of the zombies as they're charged with electrical current. Uncertain what to do with such an oddity, Paramount quickly pulled it from cinemas – then watched in perplexed horror as it went on to pick up an Oscar nomination for Best Score a few months later.

Academy Award nods stayed well away from most of the other American zombie outings of the decade. In 1971, director Del Tenney followed up *The Horror of Party Beach* with *I Eat Your Skin*, a laughable voodoo-esque tale about a playboy novelist (William Joyce) who heads out to the Caribbean to research his latest thriller. Once there he gets mixed up with a scientist who's creating an army of zombies. While it sounds like the kind of production that harks back to the Poverty Row chillers of the 1940s, its pedigree actually dated back to 1964 when it was originally shot under the title *Zombies* then shelved for reasons obvious to anyone who has had the misfortune of sitting through it. Dusted off and re-titled in 1971, it was then released on a double bill with David E. Durston's equally disposable hippie-Satanists-on-LSD thriller *I Drink Your Blood*.

"Meet Sugar Hill and her zombie hit men. Devil woman with voodoo powers to raise the dead, she's supernatural," promised the posters for Paul Maslansky's *Sugar Hill* (1974). Taking the living dead out of Haiti and into the urban sprawl of the American ghetto, *Sugar Hill* cleverly blended badass blaxploitation attitude with plenty of zombies and voodoo trappings familiar from Bond movie *Live and Let Die* (1973).

After gangsters kill her fiancé, Sugar Hill (Marki Bey) makes a pact with a voodoo god (Don Pedro Colley) to secure her vengeance. Pretty soon, she's terrorising the criminals with a band of zombies: glassy-eyed former slaves, covered in cobwebs and shackled in irons. Despite brilliantly combining the zombie's Caribbean heritage with the blaxploitation boom, *Sugar Hill* failed to do anything particularly interesting with its premise.

At least *Sugar Hill*'s ghouls were more interesting than the dull zombie stalking a crew of horror filmmakers around a stately home in Paul Harrison's irritating *The House of Seven Corpses* (1973). Raised from the grave after an actress reads from the Tibetan Book of the Dead, he only manages to get in a couple of good kills right before the credits roll. Meanwhile, the unfriendly reanimated stiff in

Ron Honthaner's *The House on Skull Mountain* (1974) was barely on-screen for more than a few minutes before heading back to the graveyard. Resurrected by her voodoo practising butler, Pauline (Mary J. Todd McKenzie) returns to find her will in dispute and decides to end the arguments by simply killing her scheming servant.

American audiences had it bad, but Britain wasn't doing much better. There were only four notable British zombie productions keeping ghouls in work during the 1970s: Fred Burnley's sombre love story *Neither the Sea Nor the Sand* (1972), Tom Parkinson's forgotten *Disciple of Death* (1972), Amicus's UK/US co-production *Tales from the Crypt* (1972) and Hammer's UK/ Hong Kong outing *The Legend of the 7 Golden Vampires* (1973). Burnley's film was little more than a genre oddity: a terribly depressing story about a married woman (Susan Hampshire) whose lover dies during a beach lovemaking session then comes back from the grave as a zombie. Played absolutely straight by all concerned it's a drab little British affair that's more interested in its central romance than its lighthouse keeper turned zombified lover (played by Michael Petrovitch). His return from beyond the grave comes with little horror and little explanation.

In *Disciple of Death*, meanwhile, little known BBC radio star Mike Raven set out to corner the horror market as the new Christopher Lee with a "blood-curdling" tale of Satanic worship and virgin sacrifices in 18th-century Cornwall. After Hammer lost interest in the script (co-written by Raven under a pseudonym), the ambitious thesp stumped up some of his own cash to cover the £50,000 budget. Playing a demon brought back from hell by some spilt blood, Raven goes in search of a virgin bride (chief candidate being Marguerite Hardiman) while surrounding himself with pallid female zombies. Christopher Lee had little to fear.

Fortunately, British horror studios Hammer and Amicus were on hand to deliver some more conventional pleasures in their two living dead movies released around the same time. Styled as Dracula Goes To China, director Roy Ward Baker's *The Legend of the 7 Golden Vampires* updated the bloodsucking legend to the Far East. Teaming Chinese martial artists with Van Helsing (Peter Cushing), his son Leyland (Robin Stewart) and Norwegian pinup Julie Ege as the film's token love

interest, it was pretty obvious that Hammer wanted to capitalise on the kung fu craze of the early 1970s. That the aging British studio managed to make the Shaw Brothers' chopsocky antics seem vaguely ridiculous summed up its ailing fortunes. It came as no surprise that this turned out to be Hammer's penultimate horror film.

The film's reputation wasn't much helped by the appearance of John Forbes-Robertson as Count Dracula. Stepping in after Christopher Lee finally said fangs-for-the-memories and decided against another outing as the toothsome aristocrat, Forbes-Robertson delivered a terribly camp performance as the Count. Over-indulging himself in the make-up trailer, he played Dracula as a hammy old queen caked in rouge. In such circumstances, the zombies were probably glad to play only a minor role. Much as in the old Santo movies, the film's green-faced fugitives from the undertaker are little more than punching bags rolled out for the extended fight sequences.

The Legend of the 7 Golden Vampires was Cushing's penultimate movie role for Hammer. Although the venerable genre star made his name as vampire hunter Van Helsing in the studio's inimitable Dracula films, he wasn't always the good guy. In Amicus's portmanteau horror collection *Tales from the Crypt*, based on the American E.C. comic book of the same name, he appeared as a zombie in the third section of the film entitled "Poetic Justice".

It told the story of a suburban estate agent (Robin Phillips) who's keen to get rid of his down-at-heel neighbour Mr. Grimsdyke (Cushing), because he believes he is lowering the tone of the street. When the kindly old man refuses to move on voluntarily, he receives a sack-load of poison pen Valentine cards that are so nasty he hangs himself. One year later, Grimsdyke returns from the dead as an eyeless, decomposing zombie to take his revenge; the startling make-up effects came courtesy of Roy Ashton who had previously worked on Hammer's *The Plague of the Zombies*. The story ends as the estate agent's mutilated body is discovered next to a Valentine's card with a verse written in blood: "You were mean and cruel right from the start. Now you really have no…" The letter unfolds to reveals the bully's bloody and still beating heart.[101]

The film's other zombie segment "Wish You

Were Here" is a tired variation on "The Monkey's Paw". Still, it's nasty enough in the savagely funny manner of the E.C. Comics tradition to be entertaining. When Enid (Barbara Murray) gets her hands on a Chinese curio that will allegedly grant her three wishes, she thinks she's solved her crooked husband's cash flow problems once and for all.

Her first wish is for lots of money and after her husband (Richard Greene) dies in a car accident she receives a hefty lump sum from his life insurance. Horrified, she uses her second wish to bring him back to how he was before the crash – only to discover that he died from a heart attack just before the car went off the road. With one wish left, she asks that he be given eternal life. A great idea with just one flaw: the undertaker has already treated her husband's remains. He returns to life screaming in agony as an embalmed corpse. Enid cracks and tries to dispatch him with a sword yet there's one more twist to come: his body stays alive even when it's hacked into itty bitty pieces…

Tales from the Crypt was successful enough to spawn a sequel, *The Vault of Horror* (1973) directed by Roy Ward Baker. Sadly, its five segments dispensed with the zombies of the previous film although it was canny enough to resurrect the dead in its framing story's twist ending. That gave Ashton's cadaverous make-up some more, very welcome, screen time. E.C. Comics weren't happy with the finished result and called time on the series.

Peter Cushing didn't return for *The Vault of Horror* but he did make a guest star appearance in one of the most underrated American zombie films of the decade, *Shock Waves* (1976). Directed by Ken Wiederhorn, who would later go on to helm *Return of the Living Dead Part II* (1988), it updated the minor but notable tradition of Nazi zombies – a theme that had first found currency in the 1940s with John Carradine's plans for world domination in *Revenge of the Zombies*. *Shock Waves* follows a group of American holidaymakers led by Brooke Adams, whose trip to the tropics goes disastrously wrong when they land on an island guarded by former Nazi officer Peter Cushing (looking thin and rather ill by this point in his career). He warns them against staying but they ignore his advice and end up falling victim to a squad of SS zombies.

According to the film's backstory, these living dead are the result of a series of macabre experiments that the Nazis conducted on homicidal maniacs during the Second World War. The SS had hoped to engineer a race of supersoldiers who could man U-boats without the usual human requirements of food and oxygen. After the German high command lost control of these deranged aquatic soldiers, Cushing's officer sank their submarine off the coast of the island. He has been keeping watch over them ever since. Surfacing from their watery graves after being awakened by strange atmospheric conditions, the Nazi zombies proceed to pick off the holidaymakers one by one with all the ruthless efficiency one would expect from a corps of genetically engineered SS stormtroopers.

Rich in atmosphere and complete with a cast of corpses dressed in Nazi uniforms – a truly disturbing sight in itself – *Shock Waves* is a moody genre piece with some brilliant shots of the ghouls moving through the murky depths. Unfortunately it never manages to flesh out its distinctive zombie scares with anything solid, hastening its slide into undeserved obscurity.

Jumping ahead of ourselves slightly, *Shock Waves* initiated a short-lived trend for Nazi zombies during the beginning of the 1980s, all of which were of considerably lesser quality. These included the atrocious American entry *Night of the Zombies* (aka *Gamma 693*, 1981) and two dubious European efforts: Jean Rollin's *Zombie Lake* (orig. *Le lac des morts vivants*, 1980) and Jess Franco's *Oasis of the Zombies* (orig. *La tumba de los muertos vivientes*, 1982).[102]

Night of the Zombies focuses on a Second World War gas dubbed "Gamma 693" that's being tracked by a CIA agent (porno stud Jamie Gillis) who's eager to stop it from falling into the wrong hands. American and German zombie soldiers are protecting the canisters containing the stockpiled gas; they were exposed to it during the war and are now planning to use it to take over the world. A truly awful piece of cinematic trash full of terrible acting, wonky camerawork and ridiculous zombies who appear to be caked in flour, it's the kind of film that's achieved a near mythic status among cult movie fans.

On the scale of artistic worthlessness, *Zombie Lake* and *Oasis of the Zombies* only rank a few notches higher but they're both more fun in a perverse kind of fashion. Produced and distributed by legendary purveyors of Z-grade trash cinema, Eurociné, these two European Nazi-zombie movies are chiefly remembered because of their troubled production histories.

Director Jess Franco disappeared just before shooting started on *Zombie Lake*. Unable to find the legendary hack, Eurociné hired a bemused Jean Rollin to take over the production at the midnight hour.

"Well Jess Franco just didn't turn up," recalled Rollin years later. "It was the day before shooting and nobody knew where he was. No trace of him, nothing. I was about to go on holiday when the phone rang. It was the production company, Eurociné, who asked if I was interested in shooting a film for them. I said: "Why not? When do you need me?" and they replied "You start tomorrow." I didn't read the script, I knew nothing about the film except it was about zombies and the producer explained to me each morning what I was supposed to shoot. I never took this film seriously."

It certainly gave Rollin a story he could dine out on. But it also made him question the thinking of the production company itself. "Eurociné is a really weird company. I am not really 100 per cent sure what they are doing. I mean, I believe they think films like *Zombie Lake* are good horror films! They live on another planet!"[103]

Given the circumstances, Rollin did the best he could with the story about a bunch of German soldiers who're executed by the French Resistance and dumped in a village lake. Arising to attack nude bathers the Nazi zombies cause plenty of havoc, yet Rollin is more interested in following one of the dead soldiers as he clambers out of the lake to visit his daughter. Padded out with lots of naked female flesh, a handful of algae-covered zombies and an off-kilter electronic score, *Zombie Lake* is extremely trashy but occasionally fun.

The same wasn't true of the company's next living dead outing, *Oasis of the Zombies*. It was helmed by Jess Franco, who managed not to disappear during pre-production this time round. The resulting mess turned out to be bad enough to make most horror fans wish that Franco had never returned from his mystery trip. The story was lame: teenagers head into the African desert in search of some lost Nazi gold only to fall foul of the zombified remains of the soldiers who were guarding it. But it was Franco's direction that really sank the proceedings. Over-indulging his customary penchant for pointless zooms, nonsensical editing and crummy shock sequences, Franco rendered the finished product almost completely unwatchable. The film marked the end of the short-lived Nazi zombie cycle for many years, until it was revived in the 2000s.

Other cycles were equally brief, in particular the rather curious trend for kiddie zombie movies that was encouraged by mommy-killing zombie young Karen in *Night of the Living Dead*. The nipper in Robert Voskanian's creepy *The Child* (1976) may not have been a zombie, but she's able to make the dead rise from their graves using her ESP-powers. In the true tradition of the zombie movie, things quickly turn nasty as Rosalie (Rosalie Cole) realises that she can use the ghouls to kill anyone who upsets her.

From *The Child*, things snowballed. A pair of zombie ankle biters attacked characters in *Dawn of the Dead* (1978) and got hammered by an M16 assault rifle locked on full auto in the process – a taboo-shattering moment that left UK censors feeling rather queasy. Then a whole band of nippers turned to the dark side in Max Kalmanowicz's *The Children* (1980) in which a school bus is exposed to a radioactive leak. Although they survive the accident, the children are turned into atomic zombies with a penchant for murder most foul. Meanwhile, in *The Boneyard* (1990) zombie children are discovered feasting on brains in a rundown mortuary. Grubby little demon-urchins with Neanderthal social skills, they're possibly the screen's most memorable kiddie ghouls. It's just a shame that director James Cummins decided to upstage them by unleashing a giant zombie poodle on the cast... Whatever was he thinking?

III. DESTRUCTIVE TENDENCIES

Returning to the 1970s, the true successor to Romero's crown wasn't an American, but a European. In 1974, Spanish director Jorge Grau released *The Living Dead at Manchester Morgue* (orig. *No profanar el sueño de los muertos*) a UK-shot living dead outing that followed directly in the footsteps of Romero's masterpiece. Escaping from his native Spain – which was under the influence of General Franco's fascist regime – into the wet and windy English countryside, Grau delivered one of the finest zombie movies of the 1970s. It was a film that bridged the gap between Romero's *Night of the Living Dead* and his later *Dawn of the Dead* (1978), reaffirming the savage nihilism of the first while prefiguring the comic book "splatter" of the second.

The nightmare of Grau's zombie apocalypse begins in a smog-filled Manchester where antique dealer George (Ray Lovelock) is preparing for a weekend holiday in the Lake District.[104] By all accounts he can't escape soon enough: the city is a dark, grey place where commuters hurry through the streets with makeshift facemasks to protect themselves from the fumes; a bowler-hatted gent surreptitiously swallows a handful of suspect-looking pills; a dead sparrow rots in the gutter; and a busty female streaker – two fingers held aloft in the traditional peace sign – jogs through the traffic jams attracting little attention from the jaded motorists. Clearly, the hippie dream has given way to pollution, ennui and the beginning of the strike-filled, unemployment-soaring 1970s.

Out in the rolling green fields of the Lake District, George meets Edna (Christine Galbo) at a petrol station after she accidentally backs into his motorcycle.[105] Since his bike needs to be repaired, George makes her give him a lift to Windermere. Along the way they stop at a farm to ask for directions and George witnesses a demonstration of an experimental pest-killing device that's being field-tested by Ministry of Agriculture scientists. Using ultrasonic emissions to drive insects into a frenzy in which they attack each other, the machine is already being hailed as an alternative to chemical pesticides. George is unconvinced, arguing that it's simply another tool in man's quest to destroy the natural world.

Heading back to the car, George finds Edna screaming in terror after being attacked by a creepy man (Fernando Hilbeck) who apparently bears an uncanny resemblance to a local tramp who died a few weeks earlier. Confused, George takes his shaken companion to her sister's house but as they arrive, they realise that something strange is afoot. Edna's sister Katie (Jeannine Mestre) has just been attacked by the same tramp – who murdered her husband and then vanished.

When the police arrive on the scene it quickly becomes apparent that they don't believe the story. Bluff copper Sergeant McCormick (Arthur Kennedy) doesn't have much time for all their wild talk of dead people rising from the grave and suspects that the three of them are personally responsible for the murder. Even after one of his police constables is killed by zombies, Sgt McCormick refuses to believe the story. Instead he decides that our heroes must be Satanists.

On the run from the police, Edna and George try to piece the mystery together. They eventually find themselves back in the field where the pesticide machine is still running. "Not even DDT was this effective when it first came out," remarks one of the technicians. However, George has begun to suspect that it may have some unexpected side-effects. Unable to convince a local hospital surgeon to take action against the testing, he vandalises the machine. But it's not enough to save the day as the recently dead have already begun to rise from their graves.

Bigoted Sergeant McCormick proves to be part of the problem, not the solution. He gruffly dismisses George's hysterical talk of zombies and belittles his hippie appearance: "You're all the same the lot of you with your long hair and faggot clothes, drugs, sex and every sort of filth." As a result, the chance to avert the coming apocalypse is lost. At the hospital George rescues Edna from a horde of the living dead who were waiting to be shipped out to the Manchester morgue, then is shot in the head by McCormick who arrives too late to see the proof that the dead really are walking. "I wish the dead could come back to life you bastard," he tells George's corpse, "because then I could kill you again." In the film's closing scenes, the newly repaired pest machine brings George back from the grave to take an ironic revenge on the fascist policeman.

With its insistent ecological message ("We are poisoned by a progress which doesn't consider the consequences," explained Grau when asked to account for the film's politics[106]) and its cynical presentation of the authorities as stupid, ineffectual and downright reactionary, *The Living Dead at Manchester Morgue* clearly owes a considerable debt to Romero. Yet, it's a captivating film in its own right, offering an unforgettably bleak vision " of entropy and decay. From the opening shots of a polluted, smog-filled Manchester to the rural, grey locations (comprised entirely of gloomy riversides, cluttered farmhouses, ramshackle churches and rundown hospitals), the action takes place in a country – perhaps even a world – that's already half-dead itself.

Of all the characters we meet, only George seems to have any radical passion. The rest of the cast are washed-out automatons desperately grasping at anything they can find – from opiates to fascist brutality – to numb themselves against the bleak reality that surrounds them. Even the zombies seem listless, as if equally weighed down by this world's sagging lack of energy.

Challenging all conventional values of authority, heroism and religious faith, *The Living Dead at Manchester Morgue* takes place in a world in which humanity has lost its way and has nothing left to believe in. The radio news reports discuss the possibility of an impending environmental catastrophe. But the government announces that such "ecological problems are exaggerated". The sign outside the cemetery proclaims "This is God's acre, let nothing defile it." But it's already awash with zombies. Not even the hospital surgeon can help. When George takes him out to see the pest machine, he claims his hands are tied: "You can't get the government to act on much more serious concrete facts these days. Imagine what success we'd have getting anyone to act on a mere hypothesis. I'm afraid they'd laugh at us."

None of the traditional institutions – from the church to the state to the scientific establishment – are able to offer any guidance. Their authority has already collapsed, even before the zombies arrive. It's something Grau makes desperately apparent in his depiction of the Manchester police force in general and Sergeant McCormick in particular. The blinkered, reactionary conservatism of the forces of law and order seems to be the only thing that's propping up the rotten system. McCormick's cantankerous nastiness (wonderfully played by Arthur Kennedy) eventually makes us desire rather than fear the liberatory destruction that the zombies represent.

The first stirrings of this occur in the hospital as George tries to rescue Edna from the ghouls who've emerged from the basement mortuary. Battling the living dead, George manages to pull Edna out into the corridor. But as he embraces her, he suddenly recoils in horror as he realises that she's already a zombie. Pushing her backwards into a room that's on fire, he watches the flames engulf her.

On paper, this scene sounds fairly uninteresting. Yet, the way it is filmed gives it a curious undertow. Grau cuts to a point of view shot from George's perspective and we watch as Edna bursts into flames. She reaches out one hand to the camera plaintively, whimpering in fear. There's a certain ambiguity to the scene. It's as if Edna were actually still alive and begging George to save her. It's only momentary but its effect is to make us sympathise, for the first time in the film, with the living dead.

In a way this brief scene serves as a prologue for the final shift of allegiance that Grau forces us to experience as George returns from the dead and kills McCormick. It's a crowd-pleasing moment in which our zombified hero takes revenge on the film's real villain. It's also a scene that once again asks us to align ourselves with the zombies since everyone we've rooted for (George, Edna and Katie) are no longer among the living. The underlying sentiment is that in a world this rotten the retributive force that the zombies represent deserves to be unleashed.

The deliberate destruction of the present social order in favour of apocalyptic chaos is something that the post-*Night of the Living Dead* zombie film is frequently fascinated by. Presenting us with a revolution in which the dead rise up against the living, films like *Night of the Living Dead*, *The Living Dead at Manchester Morgue*, *Deathdream* and *Children Shouldn't Play with Dead Things* flout every cherished value and symbol of authority. They deliver a progressive fantasy about the overthrow of a dominant order that is inherently corrupt and reactionary. Most fascinating of all, however, is the way in which the old order is overturned without *anything* being offered in its place. Calling for the destruction of the present order without advancing any plans for social renewal or regeneration, filmmakers like Romero, Grau and Clark offer a nihilistic howl of destructive rage that cannot be assuaged. These films are progressive without ever progressing to anything in particular – as if the filmmakers are wary of creating an alternative order that's as flawed and corrupt as the one it replaces.

In the eyes of some producers, the public's desire to embrace the apocalypse promised to garner sizeable box office returns. That was certainly what French producer Claude Guedj believed when he hired director Jean Rollin to helm the Gallic zombie apocalypse movie *The Grapes of Death* (*Les raisins de la mort*, aka *Pesticide* 1978). Keen to cash-in on the big-budget American disaster movies of the period, Guedj and Rollin decided to use that template for a horror movie – since the towering infernos and sinking cruise liners of Hollywood were well beyond the reach of their limited budget. After watching a range of films – including *The Poseidon Adventure* (1972) and *Earthquake* (1974) – Rollin came to the conclusion that these destructive blockbusters all followed a similar pattern. "We took *The Poseidon Adventure* and reduced it to a diagram to see how it was built: basically, it was a group of people moving from a place to another and stopped on their way – for various reasons – every four minutes. We took that construction. But as, obviously, we didn't have the money to make a catastrophe film we decided to shift to the fantastic."[107] Grafting this template onto a zombie movie in the vein of *Night of the Living Dead* was a simple but inspired decision.

For Rollin, the project was a change of pace from his usual obsessions. Making his reputation in France in the late-1960s with the infamous *Le viol du vampire* (*The Rape of the Vampire*, 1968), the director was more used to dealing with the undead rather than their living dead counterparts. On its first release in France in 1968, *The Rape of the Vampire* caused a sensation. The project had begun life as a short film produced to accompany screenings of PRC's Poverty Row chiller *Dead Men Walk* (1943) in late-1960s Paris. A distributor friend of Rollin's had secured the rights to the old George Zucco vampire picture but at just an hour's running time it was considered too short to play alone. Rollin was hired to shoot additional footage to bolster the black & white production, and the result was a film that became the director's most infamous "Rollinade".

The Rape of the Vampire's deliriously crazed and nonsensical narrative created a public outcry. It broke the conventions of cinematic storytelling in a manner that shocked and dismayed most contemporary cinemagoers. Critics walked out in disgust, audiences splattered the screen with garbage and several of the cast and crew denounced the film, claiming that they had had no idea that the finished project would turn out the way it did.

A decade later, Rollin had established himself as a director obsessed with the undead in a series of films that included *La vampire nue* (*The Naked Vampire*, 1969), *Le frisson des vampires* (*Shiver of the Vampire*, 1970), *Requiem pour un vampire* (*Requiem for a Vampire*, 1971) and several other characteristically bizarre genre entries. When the opportunity arose, he was willing to stray into alternative areas of filmmaking including pornography and the zombie film. His other forays into living dead territory were the rather risible *Zombie Lake* (1980) and *La morte vivante* (*The Living Dead Girl*, 1982). The latter is a mournful tale in the tradition of the director's immensely personal vampire efforts, in which a young girl (Françoise Blanchard) is resurrected from the dead after toxic chemicals are spilled in the family crypt beneath her château.

In *The Grapes of Death*, though, Rollin offered something very different: a straight-ahead horror movie with little room for his customary bursts of lyricism. Deciding to base this disaster-horror movie on some form of contaminated consumer product, Rollin suggested to his co-screenwriters Christian Meunier and Jean-Pierre Bouyxou that they choose one of two typically French delights: wine or tobacco. In the finished script, a batch of wine contaminated by a defective pesticide is turning vineyard workers in rural France into crazed "zombies". Although not actually dead, those who drink the wine begin to rot from the inside out. The condition that leads to increasingly erratic and violent behaviour towards the uninfected.

Elizabeth (Marie-Georges Pascal) is travelling by rail through the French countryside on her way to visit relatives when she first realises that something's amiss. It's October and the out-of-season train is spookily deserted. Suddenly a hideously disfigured man bursts into Elizabeth's carriage and, crazed with bloodlust, kills her travelling companion. He then chases our heroine through the train until she pulls the emergency cord and escapes into the empty, dusky countryside.

What follows is – as Rollin planned – a series of chases, escapes and yet more chases that runs on a continuous cycle of short bursts with only the briefest of lulls in between each set piece. It's a narrative structure that denies the audience any sense of safety or pause, a juggernaut of events that throws near-hysterical Elizabeth from frying pan to fire and back again with an insistence that borders on the sadistic. Interspersed among these chase sequences are bouts of explosive violence that are rendered all the more shocking because they interrupt the film's hypnotic rhythm. These sudden and often totally unexpected moments range from a young girl's evisceration with a pitchfork, to a crazed local who batters his bloodied, gooey forehead against a car window, and – in the film's most infamous scene – the frenzied decapitation of a blind girl carried out with the aid of a decidedly blunt axe.

Deliberately distancing himself from his most obvious influence, Rollin claimed that his tactics were notably different from Romero's: "In *Night of the Living Dead*, claustrophobia is the dominant element; normal people are locked in and the dead are outside; in my film normal people would constantly move outside."[108] Just because the action takes place outside doesn't dilute the horror. Rather, Rollin's choice of location emphasises the desolate wasteland that accompanies the zombie apocalypse. Here, the wide, open spaces and dank, dark villages form a kind of reverse pastoral. It's a spectral environment that's more like some annexe of hell than any traditional image of the French countryside.

In reality, the location itself proved so inhospitable that the filmmakers ran into production difficulties. Filming in the deserted mountain region of Les Saivennes, Rollin's cast and crew found themselves at the mercy of the elements as temperatures dropped so low that the camera had to be housed in a special shelter to keep it filming at 24 frames per second. The fact that the director's favourite actress, porn star Brigitte Lahaie, willingly stripped off for a striking nude scene in such conditions remains an impressive testament to their long-running professional relationship (to say the least). Recalling the difficulties posed by the location, Rollin said: "I remember the scene in which Brigitte had to undress herself. There she was, naked, and supposed to deliver her lines, but when she opened her mouth, she literally couldn't speak because it was so cold."[109]

After a series of narrow escapes from the zombified locals, Elizabeth eventually encounters a pair of grumbling construction workers who have taken it upon themselves to eliminate the infected locals. It's at this point that the film's debt to *Night of the Living Dead*'s angry social commentary becomes clear. Elizabeth's gruff escorts have escaped the infection since they only drink beer (or, at a push, champagne). Their mean-spirited response to the outbreak marks them as villains rather than heroes; they take potshots at the crazed locals and treat the situation as an opportunity to do as they please. The Gallic cousins of Romero's redneck posse, they're hateful figures who positively revel in the chaos: "Wait till I tell my wife about this!"

Although it lacks the impact of *Night of the Living Dead*, *The Grapes of Death* is one of the best zombie films of the decade – a gloriously off-kilter shocker made by a director who understands (and subverts) the conventions of the genre. In one particularly playful scene, Rollin dupes the audience into expecting a zombie attack as he introduces a supporting character. Focusing first on a close-up of a woman's fumbling, outstretched hands, then on her shuffling feet, Rollin mimics the traditional framing of an attacking zombie. Then he cuts to a medium shot that reveals that this figure is nothing more than a blind girl desperately groping her way through the carnage.

It's an ironic moment that, when coupled with random bursts of the film's creepy electronic score and the disturbing violence, makes this an exceptional entry in the genre. Dogged by the kind of distribution problems that Rollin's films have frequently experienced – according to legend one German bootleg print of the film re-titled it *Torture Mill of the Raped Women* (!) – *The Grapes of Death* has never found the audience it deserves.[110]

It drifted instead into relative obscurity on the bootleg video market for over twenty years before DVD restored it to its rightful, if still somewhat marginal, glory.

IV. SEX, DEATH AND AMANDO DE OSSORIO'S TEMPLARS

While European films like *The Grapes of Death* and *The Living Dead at Manchester Morgue* carefully toyed with the social criticism of *Night of the Living Dead*, one Spanish director took Romero's nihilism and put it to very different uses. In the early 1970s, Amando de Ossorio began an influential series of films – *Tombs of the Blind Dead* (orig. *La noche del terror ciego*, 1971), *Return of the Blind Dead* (orig. *El ataque de los muertos sin ojos*, 1973), *Horror of the Zombies* (orig. *El buque maldito*, 1974) and *Night of the Seagulls* (orig. *La noche de los gaviotas*, 1975) – that reworked Romero's emphasis on the physicality of the body into a curious blend of sex, violence and death.

For Spanish horror cinema, de Ossorio's quartet of "Blind Dead" movies was something of a breath of fresh air. As the Franco regime gradually crumbled under the weight of the General's ill health and the public's increasingly vocal demands for liberalisation, the horror movie became one of the Spanish cinema industry's most cost-effective productions. The growing international demand for horror, together with the widening domestic market, meant that the genre was the easiest place for eager producers to make some fast cash. As a result, they began to export their home-grown productions around the globe often with additional scenes of sex and violence that had been cut from domestic prints.

The first person to benefit from the booming horror market was Spanish filmmaker Paul Naschy (aka Jacinto Molina) whose prolific career was largely spent recycling Universal and Hammer traditions with roles that included Dracula, Frankenstein and a wolfman called Waldemar Daninsky. During his time on both sides of the camera, Naschy inevitably turned his hand to the zombie movie. In director Carlos Aured's *Horror Rises from the Tomb* (orig. *El espanto surge de la tumba,* 1972) Naschy played an executed 15th-century warlock whose disembodied head wants revenge and raises a few zombies to do his bidding. In Leon Klimovsky's *Vengeance of the Zombies* (orig. *La rebelión de las muertas*, aka *Rebellion of the Dead Women*, 1972), he starred as an Indian fakir turning the pretty daughters of British ex-colonialists into ghouls. Meanwhile, in José Luis Merino's *Return of the Zombies* (orig. *La orgía de los muertos*, 1972), he played second fiddle to the main zombie plot as a hunchback halfwit who keeps a stack of corpses in an underground lair.

Naschy's films attracted wide audiences in the 1970s and have remained cult curiosities ever since. Yet his vision of horror was more camp than chilling. Other Spanish films like *Devil's Kiss* (orig. *La perversa caricia de Satán*, 1973) and the Spanish-American co-production *The Swamp of the Ravens* (orig. *El pantano de los cuervos*, 1974) tried to raise the zombie horror stakes with more atmospheric terrors. But it was writer-director Amando de Ossorio who really helped Spanish horror cinema catch up with the times (his Blind Dead films also helped pave the way for Grau's far gorier Spanish/Italian co-production *The Living Dead at Manchester Morgue*, which didn't receive a release in Spain until late 1975). Filming in Portugal, De Ossorio escaped Franco's moral watchdogs and countered Naschy's eminently unfrightening productions with his own impressively original take on the zombie genre.

The Blind Dead films were based on the writings of 19th-century Spanish author Gustavo Adolfo Bécquer, whose work frequently referred to the Knights Templars. The Templars were soldiers who fought in the Crusades during the twelfth and thirteenth centuries and amassed great wealth until King Philip IV of France, who was scared of their autonomy, disbanded the order.

In de Ossorio's version of the story, the Templars

return from the Crusades having swapped Christianity for the occult. Obsessed with the idea of achieving eternal life, they perform a series of blood-drinking rituals involving female virgins that they learned during their sojourn in the Middle East. Excommunicated by their former church and condemned to death, they're rounded up and hanged en masse. As they dangle from the tree branches, crows swoop down and peck out their eyes.[111]

However, their occult rituals pay dividends and they're returned to "life" as mummified zombies who emerge from their tombs at regular intervals to drink the blood of unsuspecting victims. Since they are now completely blind, they're forced to track their prey by sound alone.

Although de Ossorio was always rather modest about his contribution to the zombie genre – "I didn't set out to innovate, I just wanted to do something different," he told interviewers[112] – his zombies turned out to be the most original living dead monsters since Romero's flesh-eating ghouls. They were popular enough to spawn three sequels as well as making a brief appearance in John Gilling's *La Cruz del Diablo*, 1974 (lit. *The Cross of the Devil*) and be mooted as possible companions of Naschy's wolfman Waldemar Daninsky in a project entitled "El necronomicon de los templarios".[113] Although this rather risible plan came to nothing, Naschy went on to use the idea of blind zombies in *The People Who Own the Dark* (orig. *Último deseo*, 1976) a post-apocalyptic tale about a bunch of cynical survivors trapped in a country château by sightless peasants whose eyes have been burnt out by a nuclear blast.

What's so striking about the Blind Dead is the way in which they underline the zombie's role as an image of mortality. With their skeletal frames, mildewed cowls, tufts of beard and eyeless faces, de Ossorio's zombies look like distant relatives of the four horsemen of the apocalypse, the ferryman of the Styx, or even the Grim Reaper himself. Unsurprisingly, though, it was the scenes in which they emerge from their tombs and ride through the countryside on ghostly horses – as the soundtrack crescendos in a barrage of beating drums and chanting monks – that would become de Ossorio's instantly recognizable trademark. Still, there's more to the Blind Dead quartet than just a clever reworking of the zombie's appearance. These four films also try, with varying degrees of success, to

build up a thematic link between the zombies and the sex-obsessed narratives in which they appear.

During the 1970s, European horror cinema was deeply affected by the decade's booming pornography industry. As sex films crossed over into the mainstream, with outings like *Deep Throat* (1972) and *Emmanuelle* (1974) playing to packed houses, the horror genre underwent an important transformation. The line between horror and pornography became blurred. One seminal influence on this shift was the French *fantastique*. The *fantastique* is a mode that, as horror movie critics Cathal Tohill and Pete Tombs explain, is dominated by sex. "[In the *fantastique*] linear narrative and logic are always ignored [and] the pictorial, the excessive are the privileged factors," they write. "With logic and rationality out of the way, the repressed takes the centre stage, and it's hardly surprising that the other guiding factor inside the *fantastique* film is its predilection towards the erotic."[114]

Since many of the filmmakers involved in the sexploitation boom were writers and directors who were "renegades from the fantasy and horror cinema," it was only a matter of time before a crossover between the worlds of sexploitation and horror occurred.[115] Paving the way for such cross-genre fertilisation were films like Walerian Borowczyk's *The Beast* (orig. *La bête*, 1975), Rollin's vampire fantasies and Jess Franco's experiments with "horrotica" and "sexpressionism". By the late-1970s and early 1980s, directors like Franco, Rollin, Aristide Massaccesi and Andrea Bianchi frequently flitted between the worlds of hardcore pornography and "hard-gore" horror.

Although not the most sexually graphic zombie productions (as the next chapter will amply demonstrate), de Ossorio's Blind Dead films repeatedly foreground the issue of sexuality with an insistence that borders on the obsessive. In the first film of the series, *Tombs of the Blind Dead*, the opening sequence takes place at an outdoor swimming pool where old school friends Betty (Lone Fleming) and Virginia (María Elena Arpón) unexpectedly run into each other. Between the scantily clad leads and nubile extras wandering around in the background, the scene's undercurrent of eroticism is clear. The building sexual *frisson* is only complicated by the arrival of Virginia's

Tombs of the Blind Dead (1971).

flirtatious boyfriend Roger (César Burner), who eagerly invites Betty to join him and Virginia on a weekend camping trip. The glint in his eye suggests he's interested in erecting more than just tent poles.

For contemporary Spanish audiences, this must have seemed like a utopian glimpse of exactly the kind of sexually liberated, consumer/leisure paradise that Franco's repressive regime was denying them access to. As if to underline the truth of that, foreign prints of the film contain an additional soft-focus flashback sequence in which Betty recalls having a lesbian fumble with Virginia while they were both schoolgirls.

As the trio embark on their ill-fated camping trip, things quickly get out of hand. Jealous of Roger's flirtations with Betty, Virginia jumps off the train in the middle of the countryside, little realising that her friend is a lesbian who has no interest in Roger's macho advances. Deciding to camp overnight in a ruined monastery, Virginia pitches her tent and strips down to her underwear, at which point the gathering sexual tension reaches its climax.

In a different kind of horror film, the sight of this half-naked heroine might alert us to the impending arrival of a serial killer or rapist. Here, however, her scantily clad presence tempts the Templars out

of their tombs. Their protracted abuse of Virginia as they blindly chase her around the monastery and the orgy of blood drinking (shot off-screen) that follows is styled as a symbolic rape. In case we miss the significance of her name (*Virgin*-ia) or the way in which she is killed, the morgue attendants in the following scene make de Ossorio's point quite clear, complaining: "Young girls show too much these days."

Conflating sex and horror, de Ossorio seems intent on challenging our understanding of where the link between the two lies. In the uncut prints of the later Blind Dead films, he takes this even further. Flashback sequences detail the Templars' medieval revels in which young women are chained, whipped, stripped then forced to watch as their bare breasts are mutilated. Significantly, *Tombs of the Blind Dead* also includes a literal rape, as swarthy smuggler Pedro (José Thelman) tries to convert Betty to heterosexuality by force. In the later films in the series, rape becomes a narrative prerequisite with at least one of de Ossorio's pretty young hotpants or bikini-clad heroines being subjected to a sexual assault at some point in the story.

Although it would be easy to dismiss such moments of misogynist violence as nothing more than a questionable attempt to keep the attention of the film's (male) audiences, this catalogue of sexual abuse actually plays an integral role in the series' thematics. Made during the era of Franco's repressive regime, the Blind Dead films turn sex into the site of a clash between two very different generations: hard line fascists and youngsters who just want to have fun. As Nigel J. Burrell points out, *Tombs of the Blind Dead* can be read as an analogy of "the rising up of Old Spain against the permissive generation, the repressive fascism of the Franco regime [...] versus the youth of the day."[116]

While this reading is insightful, it's important to

note that de Ossorio's sexual vision doesn't really present death as a punishment for the joy of sex. Ultimately, there is no sexual pleasure in de Ossorio's universe, only violence, rape and thwarted desire. Unlike the teen horror movies of the 1980s, the Blind Dead films never present sex as a transgressive experience that needs to be punished. Rather, it's a violent business in which men bully and brutalise young women.

What the Blind Dead films offer is a replay of the dark nihilism of so many of the other zombie films of the period. Instead of concentrating on the corrupt social order of the present (something far too dangerous to do during Franco's rule), the series shifts its nihilism towards the presentation of the sexually active body. It's a pessimistic vision in which youth and beauty are always destroyed.

De Ossorio's decision to pit his heroines against the desiccated remains of the Templars is more than just a throwaway whim. In each of the four films – but especially in *Tombs of the Blind Dead* and *Horror of the Zombies* – the women outnumber the men. They're invariably young, pretty and shown in various states of undress. They are also the primary focus of the films' horror as the zombies chase and attack them. *Horror of the Zombies*, for instance, begins with an arresting display of female flesh during a bikini photo shoot. The rest of the story takes place on a mysterious 16th-century galleon where the Templars emerge from below decks and attack the assembled cast who've foolishly strayed aboard. Amid the mayhem, the girls are captured by the Blind Dead and dragged below as the grasping, skeletal hands of the Templars tear off their skimpy clothing. While Romero's ghouls were distinctly oral monsters who bit and chomped their victims' flesh, the Blind Dead are tactile. Each attack is styled as some kind of living dead gang rape as hands grope female flesh and sex becomes nothing more than a prelude, a "little death" that brings us ever closer to the final end.[117]

By concentrating on the nubile bodies of his female cast as they confront these cowled representations of Death himself, de Ossorio suggests that the flesh is simply a reminder of our own mortality. The younger and prettier it is, the more poignant the realisation of its eventual death, decay and destruction. As the Templars shuffle blindly and (incredibly) slowly towards their

victims, it's impossible not to see them as the literal embodiment of death's relentless and completely implacable approach. The fact that these lumbering blind ghouls always manage to catch their victims says less about the stupidity of the living than the inevitability of the end.

The exacting demands of the Spanish censors meant that de Ossorio was unable to mimic the gory set pieces of films like *The Living Dead at Manchester Morgue* or *The Grapes of Death*. Still, his quartet manages to demonstrate the body's inevitable fragmentation and destruction in quite novel ways. In *Tombs of the Blind Dead*, Betty's mannequin workshop is a metaphor for the kind of physical trauma that de Ossorio can't explicitly show on-screen. The sequence begins with a close-up of what appears to be a real (and troublingly empty) eye socket. At first it we think it must be one of the Blind Dead but then, in a startling moment, an eyeball appears swivelling wildly around the socket. At this point the camera pulls back to reveal that this potentially hideous image is actually nothing more than one of Betty's assistants assembling the head of a shop window dummy. The rest of the sequence frames Betty and Roger in the workshop where they are surrounded by half-assembled mannequins, plastic arms, legs, torsos and heads. The flickering light of a red neon sign outside the window bathes the whole scene in hellish hues. It's a prescient image of the dismemberment that awaits our heroes.

In a knowing homage to Romero, *Tombs of the Blind Dead* ends as the ghouls head into a nearby city on a train. As they pull into the station, the film's action dissolves into a montage of grainy stills similar to those that close *Night of the Living Dead*. Screams rise to a crescendo on the soundtrack and the film ends with a sick little joke: a title card bearing the legend "Fin" appears on-screen and the skeletal hand of one of the Templars drops across it.

It's a thrillingly bleak conclusion that turns the train into an apt image of the inevitability of death. Hurtling ever onwards, the living characters of de Ossorio's films are trapped on a fast track to doom. There's no turn offs, no reverse gear: death is the final destination. Instead of the savage satirical critiques offered by Romero, Grau and Rollin, de Ossorio gives us a quartet of films that ask us to acknowledge the inevitable *Fin* that awaits us all.

V. BY THE DAWN'S EARLY LIGHT

It's everywhere," mutters one of the characters in the opening half hour of *Dawn of the Dead* (1978). Spreading across America, the zombie plague of *Night of the Living Dead* has not stopped. At the end of that 1968 film, the authorities appeared to be in control of the situation as martial law was put into effect and "search and destroy" squads worked their way through the countryside. As *Dawn of the Dead* opens, it's apparent that the balance of power has radically changed.

Shot ten years after *Night of the Living Dead*, Romero's return to the genre that made his name was as exciting as it was expected. Unable to rediscover the success of his debut in films like *There's Always Vanilla*, *Jack's Wife* and *The Crazies*, the decision to return to the zombie had as much to do with economics as artistry. The result was *Dawn of the Dead*, a film that would have an irrevocable impact on the zombie's cinematic status. Indeed, it's almost impossible to overestimate the film's importance – particularly on the European horror market of the late 1970s and early 1980s. Rather than simply replaying the zombie apocalypse of *Night of the Living Dead* with a bigger budget and colour film stock, *Dawn of the Dead* took the concept in unexpected directions, reviving the zombie genre with comic panache just as it was threatening to become moribund.

The origins of the story can be traced back to the mid-1970s, when Romero was given a tour of a sprawling shopping mall in Monroeville, Pennsylvania by a business associate who had offices in the gigantic complex. Overawed by this cavernous temple to American consumerism, the filmmaker began to wonder what it would be like if the survivors of his apocalyptic scenario found themselves taking shelter there. "It centred around this couple – a guy and a pregnant woman – who were living up in this crawl space. He was like the hunter-gatherer, going down into the mall for supplies and food. They were really like cave people; they were naked all the time. I was really going out there, very heavy. It was too dark. It was really ugly."[118]

Convinced that this idea was simply too much for the sequel to handle – in terms of both tone and chronology – Romero decided to take a step back and come at the material from a different angle. He was eager not to play all his aces at once, realising that if *Dawn* began with the complete destruction of civilisation, there would be little chance of continuing the story in a third film. To compensate, Romero moved the action of *Dawn of the Dead* back to the catastrophe itself, focussing instead on the collapse of the social order that had only been hinted at obliquely in *Night of the Living Dead*. Although ten years had passed between the original movie and its sequel, Romero presented the action as if was occurring the morning after *Night of the Living Dead*. Despite the change in fashions and technology that had occurred in the intervening decade, this bold move worked surprisingly well and the join between the two films feels completely seamless.

The news that Romero was writing a new zombie script attracted lots of attention, some of it from rather exciting quarters. In Italy, producer Alfredo Cuomo received an incomplete draft of the sequel script in the hope that he might be willing to find European support for the film's projected $1.5million budget, which was more than thirteen times *Night of the Living Dead*'s $114,000 cost. Much to the delighted surprise of Romero, Cuomo passed on an Italian translation of the script to his friend Dario Argento, a legendary horror director whose films *Deep Red* (1975) and *Suspiria* (1977) Romero greatly admired. It was to prove a marriage made in heaven (or perhaps, given their respective interests, hell). Full of mutual respect for one another, Romero and Argento brokered a distribution deal that would allow Romero to pursue his ideas without interference from pusillanimous financial backers.

Selling Argento the foreign rights to the film in all non-English speaking territories except South America, Romero and his partners secured $750,000 of the film's budget upfront. Argento, who had come on board with his brother Claudio and producer Cuomo, had no input in the project apart from giving his blessing to the shoot. Once the editing process began Argento then cut his own European version of the film. It was eight minutes shorter than Romero's edit, a little lighter on the humour and bolstered by an extended score from Argento's favourite musicians Goblin.[119]

Dawn of the Dead starts with Fran (Gaylen Ross) jolting out of a bad dream into the waking nightmare of the zombie reality. The living dead have won the upper hand and the fabric of society is crumbling, not least of all in the chaotic Pittsburgh television station where Fran works. "We're blowing it ourselves," she whispers as ratings-hungry producers try to air a list of rescue stations that they know is already out of date in order to keep the viewers from switching channels. Fran's right: it's not the dead that are the problem; it's the living.

Outside the television station, martial law prevails. In a nearby ghetto, National Guardsmen, cops and SWAT storm a tenement building where the occupants are hiding the (living dead) corpses of their relatives. Chaos reigns supreme and in the ensuing gun battle, scores of Latinos and African-Americans are killed as the police attack with tear gas, shotguns and automatic weapons. One officer goes "ape-shit," indiscriminately blowing off heads while ranting about "niggers". The wrong door is opened and a horde of zombies pours out. A woman rushes into the arms of her dead husband, only for him to take a deep bite out of her shoulder. SWAT officers Peter (Ken Foree) and Roger (Scott H. Reiniger) make their way down into the cellar where the dead are being kept. In a gruesome sequence, the heroes shoot scores of the living corpses as they writhe about on the floor.

The constant refrain of *Dawn of the Dead* is "shoot 'em in the head!" and in the unmitigated chaos of the film's opening scenes, it's a mantra that seems terrifyingly perverse. The headshot may be the only way to "kill" the zombies once and for all, but it also symbolises everything that's wrong with the authorities' response to the crisis. "Shoot 'em in the head" is the policy of a world gone mad. It's also a policy that's doomed to failure since giving up the head (reason, logic, the intellect) can only encourage the body (emotion, desire, the flesh) to gain ascendancy. Judging by all the mindless corpses milling around, that's something that's already happening of its own accord.

Only the scientists seem to have kept their heads, but their cold rationality is too much for the rest of the populace to bear. "We must not be lulled by the concept that these are our family members or our friends," explains one. "They are *not*! They will *not* respond to such emotion." His demand that the ghouls be "exterminated on sight," only provokes anger and his suggestion that the living ought to start feeding the zombies is met with horror. The failure to face up to the grim reality of this changed world becomes more of a threat to the living's survival than the ghouls themselves.

This apocalypse of reason dominates the film. As Peter, Roger, Fran and her boyfriend Stephen (David Emge) escape Pittsburgh in a stolen helicopter, Romero paints this world as increasingly "headless": law and order has vanished; the television and radio signals have been switched off; no one is in control anymore. Landing at an abandoned out of town mall, the group secure the building by blocking the doors, then settle into a life of quiet domesticity as the world goes to hell. This supposedly idyllic existence quickly gives way to boredom, though. Their ennui is only broken by the arrival of a band of looters who break into the mall and open it up to the zombies once again. In the ensuing three-way battle between bikers, zombies and mall occupants only Peter and Fran survive. As the mall is completely overrun they fly off in the helicopter to face an uncertain future and potential oblivion.

The irrationality of this "headless" world is mirrored in the increasingly foolish antics of the living. Losing one's head becomes a recurring theme. Roger's whooping macho antics as the group secures the mall leads to his death as he compromises his SWAT team professionalism by getting off on the adrenalin rush of fighting the zombies. Bitten in the arm because of his carelessness, he's the group's first victim. Later Stephen follows his example: he fights the bikers in a ridiculously venal attempt to save the array of useless consumer goods that the mall houses ("This is ours, we took it"). Had Stephen restrained himself, the group could have survived. The upstairs hideaway would have kept them hidden from both zombies and bikers and the survivors might have been able to resecure the mall again once the looters departed. By trying to defend his "property" Stephen wrecks everything they've worked for and inadvertently leads the zombies to the upstairs den

Dawn of the Dead (1978).

after he becomes one of the living dead.

While the social critique of *Night of the Living Dead* was largely implicit, its sequel is somewhat heavy-handed in its satirical impact. "*Night* [*of the Living Dead*] reflected the time in which it was made and the anger around that time, the late 1960s," Romero later reflected, adding that his aim in *Dawn of the Dead* was to reflect the 1970s a bit more."[120] The finished film certainly captures the empty materialism of the "Me-generation" decade as consumer goods and gadgets have started to replace human relationships and community. As Stephen King suggests, the film's apocalyptic vision also captures the sense of decay and entropy that was working its way through American culture at the time of its production.

"As the oil runs out, as the Three Mile Island nuclear plant sprays radiation into the atmosphere like an atomic teakettle that someone forgot to take off the burner and as the dollar gradually becomes more and more transparent, Romero invites us into a crazed bedlam where zombies stagger up and down escalators, stare with dulled fascination at department store dummies wearing fur coats and try to eat perfume bottles. The movie's four protagonists at first segregate themselves from this world, and then, unknowingly become part of it. The only difference is that they're not dead. At least not yet..."[121]

Romero's decision to turn his zombies into mindless consumers is the perfect illustration of *Dawn of the Dead*'s cartoon satire. As the zombies roam the mall, drag themselves around the ice

rink and trundle through the empty shopping aisles to the sound of a Muzak style polka called "The Gonk," Romero leavens the apocalypse with slapstick buffoonery. He even stages a one-sided custard-pie throwing and soda-siphon squirting battle between the rampaging bikers and the living dead.[122]

Such comedy keeps *Dawn of the Dead* far lighter than its predecessor, but it doesn't blunt the edge of Romero's critique. While some viewers have complained that Romero's central conceit – the zombies are simply a different kind of late-capitalist consumer – is rather too obvious, that is arguably the whole point of the movie's underlying irony. Romero doesn't have a vision of how to save capitalist society; he's only interested in destroying the whole rotten structure itself. The mordant humour barely conceals the film's disgust at the shallow, zombified wasteland that is 1970s America.

Reading through and beyond the comedy, Barry Keith Grant has claimed that the serious intent of Romero's project means that for the filmmaker, "the zombie becomes as crucial a metaphor of social relations as the prostitute for Godard" as well as a tool for challenging "macho masculinism and conspicuous consumption".[123] Pointedly lampooning the faux utopian logic behind the consumerist boom of the 1970s, the middle section of *Dawn of the Dead* places its four protagonists inside the zombie-free, empty enclosure of the mall, gives them all they could ask for (cash, food, sports facilities, gadgets and unlimited leisure time) and then quietly watches as they descend into abject misery and self-loathing. Apparently, the zombies aren't the only ones who've lost their souls.

Yet the target of Romero's satire is more than just consumerism; it's the whole fabric of postmodern capitalist culture itself. As Robin Wood suggests, "the premise of *Dawn of the Dead* is that the social order (regarded in all Romero's films as obsolete and discredited) *can't* be restored".[124] In other words, what *Dawn of the Dead*'s narrative trajectory encompasses is a nihilism similar to that found in *Night of the Living Dead*, *The Living*

Dead at Manchester Morgue and *The Grapes of Death*. The zombie apocalypse is one in which everything our heroes had believed in crumbles into nothingness. As actress Gaylen Ross explains, the consumer goods in the mall are "only *symbols*. A pound of coffee from a store is not just a pound of coffee; it represents a way of being. In *Dawn of the Dead*, the symbols have lost their meaning. The film's characters have given it value only to realise that none of it *is* valuable anymore, because there's no longer any context for it."[125]

In this world the only thing that still seems certain is the vulnerability of the flesh. Hacking at the bodies of his characters and monsters with gleeful aplomb, Romero offers us a glimpse of a universe in which all spiritual values have been replaced by our awareness of the material realities of the corporeal and consumerism.

The film's special effects and make-up were created by Tom Savini, a former Vietnam combat photographer. His work on *Dawn of the Dead* catapulted him to instant genre fame as one of the industry's leading special effects artists. It was a reputation that he went on to cement by working on *Friday the 13th* (1980), *Maniac* (1980) and Romero's *Day of the Dead* (1985). Employing Savini's talent with fake blood and latex – not to mention his first hand experience of battlefield carnage – Romero shows us the body fragmented: heads are exploded by shotgun blasts, brains are scrambled by screwdrivers, chunks of flesh are bitten off the bone and helicopter rotor blades slice open the head of an advancing zombie. It's a vision that, in the true spirit of the grotesque, comes with as much humour as horror. In one particularly memorable moment, a foolish biker is pulled to pieces by zombies while he sits in a blood pressure reading machine. As the zombies drag him away, his dismembered arm is left in the machine's strap and the reading goes off the scale as his blood pressure plummets.

The comedy of such horrific scenes does little to reduce the impact of their gross violence. In fact, the comedy exaggerates the horror by making us even more aware of just how ridiculously vulnerable the flesh is. If Romero's aim really is to make us lose all faith in bodily integrity, then it's the comic impact of the gory special effects (what Romero dubbed the "splatter") that hammers the point home. The human body isn't just a hunk of flesh – it's a *ludicrous* hunk of flesh.[126]

It was this grimly funny willingness to expose the body's object status that caused the film to fall foul of the American censors. *Dawn of the Dead* was released in Italy in September 1978 under the alternative title *Zombi* in a 119-minute cut credited to Argento, who excised most of the humour giving the action a harder edge. It proved an immediate success. In America, it was another eight months before the film reached cinemas as a pitched battle with the Motion Picture Association of America (MPAA) began. The censors decreed that unless significant cuts were made to Romero's 127-minute edit of the film they would be forced to give it an X rating. This would be the commercial kiss of death since it would deny the film any possible chance of respectability, consigning it to the level of a hardcore porn movie (despite the fact that there wasn't a single sex scene in it) and imposing strict rules on how it could be advertised

In the months that followed, Romero and his producers decided to take a chance and release the film unrated. This was something that they were legally entitled to do, although received industry wisdom suggested that it might also be commercial suicide. In the end, the decision proved unbelievably lucrative. Released in New York in April 1979, this $1.5 million film became a sensation, taking over $900,000 in the city alone in just its first week of release.[127] It was a sign of things to come, as the film eventually took $55 million worldwide. Romero's return to the monster that had made his name was a staggering financial coup.

Best of all, the critics were upbeat, with a string of glowing reviews hailing the sequel as a masterpiece. Even Roger Ebert – who had been so worried by the original film's impact on the young – was impressed by Romero's vision of the end of the world. He declared it "The ultimate horror film!" and claimed it was "Brilliantly crafted, funny, droll, disgusting [...] a savagely satanic vision of America [...] How can I defend this depraved trash? I do not defend it. I praise it. Nobody said art had to be tasteful."[128] Naturally, there were dissenters. *Variety* dismissed the enterprise much as it had the original as "banal when not incoherent" and claimed "Romero professes no pretension to 'art' on his film's behalf."[129] *New York Times* reviewer Janet Maslin apparently left the preview theatre after just fifteen minutes. She peevishly remarked that in the years since *Night of the Living Dead* Romero had "discovered colour," adding, "perhaps horror movie buffs will see this as an improvement."[130] She clearly did not.

Using the horror genre to critique American culture, capitalism and the political status quo, *Dawn of the Dead* was distressing for more reasons than its gory scenes of bodily trauma. The assault on the body politic is equally – if not more – shocking. Perhaps this explains why the MPAA couldn't be mollified. One can only imagine what the puritanical censors made of the film's refusal to countenance the film's broad swipes at religious authority. Refusing to offer a cohesive theological explanation for the apocalypse, *Dawn of the Dead* gives us only two tantalisingly brief religious discussions as an alternative to the nihilistic pragmatism of the scientists.

The first of these comes from the lips of a one-legged Hispanic priest who rebukes Peter and Roger as they catch their breath after the tenement building slaughter that opens the film. "When the dead walk señores, we must stop the killing or lose the war," he warns them, subtly harking back to the zombie's Caribbean heritage and implicitly suggesting that Judgment Day may well be at hand. Later, as our heroes watch the zombies clamouring outside the mall, Peter recalls the superstitious mutterings of his Caribbean grandfather: "There's no more room in hell," he whispers, adding, "Something my granddaddy used to tell us. You know Macumba? Voodoo. Granddaddy used to be a priest in Trinidad. Used to tell us: 'When there's no more room in hell, the dead will walk the earth.'"

Romero is careful to ensure that the suggestion that the zombie apocalypse might be a divine punishment is left unresolved. In a world where neither science nor capitalism have answers, it's telling that religion doesn't fare any better. It offers no hope to these beleaguered characters as they struggle to make sense of a world turned upside down.

If that weren't enough of an affront to the censors, then the memorably bleak finale probably did little to endear the film to them either. With Roger and Stephen dead, the mall half-destroyed and the zombies everywhere again, Peter and Fran head up to the roof. Despairing, Peter contemplates suicide as Fran climbs into the helicopter. Then, in a sudden change of heart, he turns his single-shot pistol on an advancing zombie and then karate

chops his way to the helicopter. As zombies stumble over the roof, the surviving pair fly off into the horizon in a chopper that's low on fuel. Will it get them to safety? Is there any safety left? Resigned to their fate Fran and Peter share a wry smile, then the credits roll.

In many respects, it's an ambiguous conclusion. Will they survive? We don't know for certain. But if they do live long enough to reach another safe haven, Romero seems to be hinting at the possibility of a progressive new beginning for the human race as black man and (pregnant) white woman head off in hope of a fresh start. Perhaps they might even found some radical interracial utopia. As the only two characters who have managed to keep their heads throughout the proceeding action, it seems fair to say that Fran and Peter represent mankind's last, best hope.

For Robin Wood, writing shortly after the film's American release in 1979, *Dawn of the Dead* offers proof that the horror film is "currently the most important of all American genres [because it is] progressive, even in its overt nihilism."[131] Claiming that such horror films offer "the possibility of radical change and rebuilding," Wood cites *Dawn of the Dead* rather than *Night of the Living Dead* as a film whose characters are absolved from the value-structures of the past.[132]

Intriguingly, Romero claims that such a positive outcome wasn't his original intention. In the shooting script, the action ends with a spectacular double suicide. Escaping into the upper levels of the mall, Peter and Fran separate. Too exhausted and despairing to carry on, Peter puts a gun to his head while Fran starts the helicopter. Hearing the gunshot, though, she loses all interest in carrying on alone and steps up into the whirling rotor blades, decapitating herself. As the summation of the film's thematic obsession with losing one's head, this shocking sequence would have made a staggeringly evocative finale. According to Romero, it was replaced with the alternative, and more ambiguous, ending because the special effects sequence created for Fran's decapitation wasn't up to the standard that he wanted.[133] Eager not to end the movie with a piece of bad splatter, Romero instead decided to let his hero and heroine fly off towards a tenuous future. It may not possess the pessimism or shock that the planned conclusion would have delivered, but it carries its own grim logic all the same.

CHAPTER SEVEN

SPLATTER HORROR

I. THE ITALIANS ARE COMING!

The world wasn't prepared for Lucio Fulci's *Zombi 2*. Released in 1979 as a strictly unofficial sequel to Romero's *Dawn of the Dead* – which had been distributed throughout Continental Europe under the title *Zombi* – Fulci's gorefest took audiences completely by surprise. At first glance, it looked like just another "spaghetti" rip-off, but in reality it was something more: a bravura piece of exploitation filmmaking that was so successful it was rumoured to have out-grossed the very film it was unabashedly imitating.

By the 1980s, the Italian film industry had developed something of a reputation for shamelessly replicating other countries' films. Churning out cheap remakes, pastiches and even outright copies of any picture that achieved a healthy box office, unscrupulous Italian producers cared little about charges of plagiarism. The bigger the film, the more likely a rehash, which is why *Star Wars*, *Jaws* and *The Deer Hunter* were all reinvented spaghetti style.

Much of the credit for *Zombi 2*'s success belonged to make-up artist Gianetto De Rossi, who brought Fulci's gory vision to the screen with graphic chutzpah. His portfolio of torn jugulars, skewered eyeballs and clay-faced zombies ushered in a new kind of realism, nastier and more brutal than Tom Savini's blue-skinned living dead with their custard pie slapstick gore. It made what could have been a pale imitation of *Dawn of the Dead* into a visceral orgy of – as the UK release title called them – *Zombie Flesh-Eaters*.

Flesh-eating was nothing new for Italian audiences. Ever since the cannibal cycle of the 1970s, Italian cinema had been awash with scenes of evisceration and entrail-munching as the success of Umberto Lenzi's *Deep River Savages* (orig. *Il paese del sesso selvaggio*, 1972) launched a wave of anthropophagous outings. Showcasing bodily trauma in graphic detail, these films had a huge influence on *Zombi 2* and its many Italian imitators, not least of all because so many of the industry's make-up artists cut their teeth (so to speak) on them. De Rossi, for instance, went from *Zombi 2* to *Cannibal Apocalypse* (orig. *Apocalypse domani*, 1980), then back to Fulci's later zombie movies *The Beyond* (orig. *L'aldilá*, 1981) and *The House by the Cemetery* (aka *Quella villa accanto al cimitero*, 1981).

Following the example of these notorious cannibal films, Fulci set out to give gorehounds exactly what they wanted: scene after scene of outrageous special effects in which bodies are ripped to shreds. *Zombi 2* was a rollercoaster ride of graphic nastiness in which each new gore shot had to top the last in terms of visceral impact and inventiveness.

The film's prologue is a perfect example of this desire to deliver more blood, more gore and more flesh trauma than had ever been seen on-screen before. On the fictional Caribbean island of Matul, white doctor David Menard (Richard Johnson) stands watch over a corpse wrapped in a sheet and tied up with rope. As the body inevitably starts to twitch, he shoots it in the head, spattering the sheet with bright red blood.

Fulci then cuts to New York's harbour district, where an unidentified yacht sails towards the docks. A police launch intercepts the vessel, but as the officers board it, an overweight zombie bursts out of the downstairs cabin and goes on a bloody rampage. In the fight that ensues, one of the policemen has his jugular ripped open in a graphic close-up, sending spurts of claret flying in all directions. The other cop opens fire, repeatedly shooting the ghoul in its blubbery belly until it falls overboard into the water. All this is before the film has even properly started.

As the rest of *Zombi 2* unfolds there's no let up in the violence. Arriving on the Caribbean island heroine Anne (Tisa Farrow, Mia's sister) and reporter Peter West (Ian McCulloch) go in search of Anne's missing father. What they discover instead is an army of indigenous ghouls lurking in the shadows of the palm trees. Giving his characters and audience little time to catch their breath, Fulci unleashes a torrent of gory attacks as clay-faced native zombies chow down on the Western interlopers in graphic detail. Eyeballs are skewered, flesh is eaten, heads are bludgeoned with blunt instruments and – in an insane moment – an undersea zombie wrestles a bull shark.

We can blame Fulci for *Zombi 2*'s brooding atmosphere. Jungle drums beat a steady rhythm on the soundtrack, making each sun-drenched location ten times more terrifying than most horror movies' pitch-black corridors or deserted houses. Much of the credit for the violence, however, belongs to De Rossi's skill as a make-up artist and, as he modestly recalls, a little bit of luck.

"Although I'd done the make-up for *The Living Dead at Manchester Morgue*, nobody took any real notice until my work with Fulci," De Rossi later explained. "Lucio was a very strange person. Very cultured and artistic on one side, a sleazy bum on the other. *Zombi 2* was made for no money, so not only could I not afford to make latex appliances, but we also never knew what extras would be available to be the living dead as they were all homeless itinerants or hopeless winos. I just smeared clay on whoever's face was in front of me and, by accident, it turned out to be the perfect look for the film."[134] Fulci, according to horror movie legend, dubbed his living dead extras "walking flowerpots".

In *Zombi 2*, just as in almost all the Italian films that were rushed into production in its wake, the body is always the central focus of the horror. Many critics have been eager to read this as a perverse reflection of Italian Catholicism. Stephen Thrower, for instance, suggests that the Italian zombie movie is closely bound to Christian understandings of the flesh. "It's hardly surprising that Italy, a country under the desiccated thrall of Catholicism, should have produced the most dedicated and compulsive volume of zombie films. A zombie in Italian cinema carries an iconoclastic connotation. It is explosive; able to fragment realism by inferring the implacable presence of something supernatural yet stubbornly corporeal: and it is philosophical, beyond good and evil; parading the flesh *without* the much-vaunted spirit. For Christians the body is a mere waste product, excreted by the passage of the soul into heaven."[135] The Catholic fascination with the flesh certainly informs the mechanics behind this kind of philosophical-spiritual-religious questioning, which may well explain why Romero's original zombie films were succeeded by Spanish contributions such as de Ossorio's Blind Dead movies and Grau's *The Living Dead at Manchester Morgue*. Yet what's so interesting about the Italian zombie movie is the way in which it frequently refutes any possibility of spiritual transcendence whatsoever, focussing instead on the collapse of the body, the unravelling of narrative meaning and an extensive revision of the genre's inherent racial politics. This section and the two that follow it will address each of these issues (the body, narrative and race) separately, while the final part of this chapter will look at the ways in which American cinema tried to assimilate the impact of these bloody spaghetti horrors during the latter half of the decade.

The financial success of Fulci's *Zombi 2* was enough to convince ever-eager Italian producers to churn out similar living dead movies. An explosion of zombie films ensued as various pictures competed to dominate this niche market, with distributors often using a numerical suffix in a rather blatant attempt to cash-in on the public's eagerness for a sequel to *Zombi 2* (many of these were imposed after the films' release to increase video sales).[136] Unable to replicate *Zombi 2*'s shocking impact, these films were largely hamstrung by poor dubbing, cheap production values and some wild variations in the quality of the acting and direction.

The sheer range of films churned out during this period is staggering. There were vaguely competent but hugely enjoyable films like Umberto Lenzi's *Nightmare City* (orig. *Incubo sulla città contaminata*; aka *City of the Walking Dead*, 1980) and Andrea Bianchi's *The Nights of Terror* (orig. *Le notti del terrore*; aka *Burial Ground, Zombie 3*, 1980). Yet there were also truly atrocious schedule-fillers such as Bruno Mattei's *Zombie Creeping Flesh* (orig. *Virus, Apocalipsis caníbal*; aka *Night of the Zombies*, 1980). Claudio Lattanzi's *Killing Birds* (*Raptors*, 1988), Fulci's own *Zombi 3* (aka *Zombie Flesh-Eaters 2*, 1988) and Claudio Fragasso's *Zombie 4: After Death* (orig. *After Death (Oltre la morte*, 1990) and Frank Agrama's *Dawn of the Mummy* (1981) which, although often thought of as an Italian film, is actually an American production that employed a largely Italian crew.

Undoubtedly, the centrepiece of the Italian zombie cycle is Fulci's loose trilogy: *City of the Living Dead* (orig. *Paura nella città dei morti viventi*; aka *The Gates of Hell*, 1980), *The Beyond* (orig. *L'aldilà*, aka *Seven Doors of Death*, 1981) and *The House by the Cemetery* (orig. *Quella villa accanto al cimitero*, 1981). Going far beyond the simple charm of *Zombi 2*, these three films have a dark majesty quite unlike anything else in the genre, which is why they're discussed separately in the following section.

The other Italian directors working in this genre could only dream of achieving such an effect, offering outrageous splatter and little else. Yet the cumulative impact of this onslaught of spaghetti horror is spectacularly visceral and curiously intriguing. Taking the theme of bodily trauma that had become a genre staple in the hands of Romero, Grau, Rollin and de Ossorio as their starting point, these distinctly marginal exploitation movies offered horror audiences an array of gruesome shock set pieces. It was definitely a case of the gore the merrier. Existing in the gap between mainstream, non-horror productions and the increasingly comedy-focussed horror output of the major American studios, these refreshingly nasty movies enjoyed a success that was inextricably linked to their willingness to challenge the boundaries of good taste. Unsurprisingly, the more competitive the market became post-*Zombi 2*, the more sensational the driving force behind these films' violence became.

So what do the Italian zombie movies share with one another? The basic pattern of these films usually revolves around some kind of man-made disaster: the nuclear spill of *Nightmare City*, the biochemical viruses of *Zombie Creeping Flesh* and *Zombi 3*, or the experiments of the mad scientist in *Zombi Holocaust* (orig. *La regina dei cannibali*, aka *Dr Butcher, M.D.* 1980). Occasionally the cause is supernatural in origin, as in the Etruscan magic of *The Nights of Terror* or the voodoo of *Erotic Nights of the Living Dead* (orig. *Le notti erotiche dei morti viventi*, 1980) and *Porno Holocaust* (1980). Whatever triggers these films' zombie outbreaks, the majority of the action usually takes place in some Third World locale – frequently the Caribbean, but sometimes Africa or the Far East – as these movies stage a violent and bloody revolution in which the living dead rise up and threaten a global apocalypse *à la* Romero.

With a few exceptions, for example, Pupi Avati's sublimely creepy, but vaguely nonsensical, chiller *Zeder – Voices from the Beyond* (1983) and Lamberto Bava's insipid TV movie *Graveyard Disturbance* (orig. *Una notte nel cimitero*, 1987), most of the Italian zombie movies revolve around scenes of graphic violence. In these films, the body is presented as nothing more than a hunk of flesh, a machine that shows little or no sign of being connected to either the divine or the spiritual. Proving this are graphic scenes that have become infamous landmarks in the history of splatter cinema: the eyeball gouging of *Zombi 2*, the hand inserted so far into a victim's mouth that the eyeballs are pulled out of their sockets from the *inside* in *Zombie Creeping Flesh*, and scenes of breast-ripping in both *Nightmare City* and *The Nights of Terror*. Add to this all manner of zombie bites, bullet-ridden bodies, spilled entrails and Romero style exploding heads and it's easy to see why these Italian gore-fests frequently upset moral guardians and censors in their nihilistic treatment of the flesh as nothing more than a vessel on which to inscribe pain.

The other defining characteristic of these Italian outings is sex. Naturally, as exploitation movies, the necessity of having some bare female flesh on display is pretty obvious. However, rather than serving a purely titillating function, the nudity and sex in many of these films actually adds to their horror. Showing the female body in various states of undress and arousal adds an undeniable *frisson* to the zombie genre's inherent anxieties about the messy corporeality of the flesh. Creating a disturbing link between physical pleasure and physical pain these films frequently link sex with bodily trauma.

Bianchi's *The Nights of Terror* (1980) is a forthright example of this intersection of sex and death. It opens with bourgeois holidaymakers arriving at a lavish country mansion where they're due to spend the weekend. Modern cousins of the decadent revellers of Edgar Allen Poe's *The Masque of the Red Death*, they disappear into their rooms to indulge in some heavy petting as soon as they arrive. However, their naughty pleasures are constantly interrupted: first by the creepy young son of one of the couples, who insists on walking into their rooms while they're *in flagrante*; then later by a group of Etruscan zombies who have been accidentally brought to life by a local archaeology professor.

As the zombies attack the castle – rising up from their graves and arming themselves with pitchforks, scythes and a makeshift battering ram – the story's political undertone becomes clear enough. This is a revenge of the dead against the living in which the ragged, plebeian zombies overthrow the decadent, libertine bourgeoisie. What's more insistent than the issues of class warfare, however, is the sexual undercurrent.

Like so many of the directors of the Italian zombie cycle, Bianchi had had firsthand experience as a pornographer. Here, though he seems intent on making a porno-horror movie in which the scenes of sex and violence are played simultaneously rather than separately. The opening zombie attack takes place as two lovers enjoy a quick fumble in the château's grounds – "You look like just a whore. But I like that in a girl!" whispers the randy lothario as he pulls his young lass onto the grass – and it sets the tone for all that follows. As events unfold, Bianchi frequently cuts between sexual clinches and scenes of the zombies milling around. As in de Ossorio's Blind Dead films, there's no sexual pleasure in this world, chiefly because the interloping zombies always interrupt it. Sex again becomes a prelude to death.

The link between sex and death is exemplified in an infamous scene in *The Nights of Terror* where a slutty mother (Mariangela Giordano) attempts to suckle her son (Peter Bark) in the midst of the zombie apocalypse. This clumsy Oedipal moment is bizarre not simply because of its incestuous undercurrent (the boy is supposed to be a pre-teen and so is far too old to be breastfed), but also because of the strange presence of Bark, a strikingly odd looking actor who looks more like a midget version of horror director Dario Argento than a young child. As the zombified boy sinks his teeth into his mother's breast, he rips a huge chunk out of her bosom thereby linking sex and maternal nourishment with pain and death.

In other films, the collision between sex and death is even more remarkable. After the success of *Zombi 2*, Fulci's producer Fabrizio de Angelis went on to script and produce *Zombi Holocaust* with many of *Zombi 2*'s cast and crew. Lacking much in the way of technical or artistic competence, *Zombi Holocaust* (1980) is a mishmash of the cannibal and zombie cycles, but it's notable for its astounding catalogue of gore shots. On its US release the film was renamed *Doctor Butcher M.D.* – the M.D. apparently stands for "Medical Deviate" (sic) – capturing this movie's near-clinical obsession with sex and the flesh.

The plot is pretty perfunctory. A New York policeman, played by *Zombi 2*'s Ian McCulloch, investigating a spate of corpse mutilations follows the trail of murder all the way to the jungles of Southeast Asia. With the help of busty heroine Alexandra Delli Colli he discovers a cannibal-zombie cult presided over by a mad scientist (Donald O'Brien) who's intent on prolonging lifespan. All that really matters is the film's parade of sex and gore. If *Hustler* magazine merged with *Mortuary Management Monthly*, this might be the result. Lead actress Alexandra Delli Colli bares her breasts at inappropriate moments, while hospital cadavers are dissected for the benefit of the camera; McCulloch uses a boat's outboard motor to blend an attacking zombie's face to mush; various poor souls are impaled in bamboo traps, eaten alive and generally cut into shreds for the benefit of the audience. Getting off on the corporeality of the body, *Zombi Holocaust* features shots of hands delving into eviscerated bodies, reaching through incisions and gaping wounds in a desperate attempt to see what lies inside. By the end of the film's interminable running time, it seems as if bloody wounds and sexual orifices are on the verge of becoming interchangeable.

In the movies of Aristide Massaccesi (better known in the English-speaking world as Joe D'Amato), this kind of sleaze became integral to the splatter. His movies took zombie sex far beyond the bounds of good taste. In *Erotic Nights of the Living Dead* (1980) and its unofficial sequel *Porno Holocaust* (1980), Massaccesi created bizarre syntheses of pornography and horror. *Erotic Nights* allows bloodletting and orgasms to crossover as white holidaymakers find themselves on a Caribbean island where zombies roam the jungle and the beaches. Featuring lots of scenes of fellatio and cunnilingus – and in the film's most bizarre sequence a woman whose party trick involves opening a bottle of champagne with her vagina – *Erotic Nights* plays like a dated porno flick cut with bouts of zombie violence. With its grainy cinematography and drab Dominican Republic locations, the film proves a suitably depressing cinematic experience, possessing little eroticism but plenty of misanthropic – and corporeal – loathing.

What's so troubling about *Erotic Nights* is the way in which the sex and the horror merge. In one sequence Massaccesi cuts from a man enjoying the oral attentions of two young ladies to an external scene in which an unrelated character has his throat ripped open by a ragged zombie. Later moments cut from sexual encounters to close-ups of diseased and maggot-ridden zombie flesh, gouged-out eyeballs and decapitated bodies. In the film's most wince-inducing sequence our hero (George Eastman, aka Luigi Montefiori) lets the beautiful, naked native woman who's apparently controlling the zombies go down on him. He then watches in horror as she sinks her teeth into his penis and bites it clean off. It's the closest that this strand of "erotic" horror ever gets to a traditional money shot.

In Massaccesi's follow-up, the wonderfully titled *Porno Holocaust* – a riff on Ruggero Deodato's seminal Italian flesh-eating movie *Cannibal Holocaust* (1980) – things follow much the same course. Only this time there are more hardcore sequences and a zombie who isn't afraid of taking an active role in the sexual couplings. Wandering around his Caribbean island killing off white holidaymakers, *Porno Holocaust*'s black zombie brings the collision between sex and horror to an inevitably silly and undeniably racist conclusion as

he rapes the female members of the group with his monstrous phallus. One young lady is forced to perform fellatio until she chokes to death, while others are ripped apart by his huge girth.[137]

Sex and zombies have a curiously fertile history in exploitation cinema. The granddaddy of the "gore-nography" trend is undoubtedly Claude Pierson's little-seen *Naked Lovers* (orig. *Le fille á la fourrure*, 1977) in which aliens possess the bodies of the recently dead in order to experiment with sex with earthlings. Released in a hardcore print under the upfront English language title *Porno Zombies*, and a trimmed softcore print that usually circulated under the *Naked Lovers* title, it was a forerunner of Massaccesi's films.

After Massaccesi's explicit outings, the sex zombie really had nowhere left to go. Director Mario Siciliano did his best to set a new porno benchmark in *Erotic Orgasm* (orig. *Orgasmo esotico*, 1982), which again made the zombies active participants in the bedroom Olympics on display. This time however they proved more interested in getting off than eating anyone. Lesbian sex, threesomes, dildos and a zombified woman going down on her male partner padded out an incomprehensible plot about a black witch who turns horny lovers at an isolated villa into crazed sex fiends.

The trend continued under its own steam for decades to come. French softcore gore outing *The Revenge of the Living Dead Girls* (orig. *La revanche des mortes vivantes*, 1987) had a batch of toxic waste tainted milk turning girls into sexually ravenous zombies. Kelly Hughes's *La Cage Aux Zombies* (1995) was a gender-bending, cross-dressing spoof of cult gay French classic *La cage aux folles* (1978). Vidkid Timo's gay porno-horror movie *At Twilight Come the Flesheaters* (1998) was a hardcore sex flick that was also a very funny spoof of *Night of the Living Dead* (best line: "He's eating me while he fucks me!"). In more recent years, sexed up zombies have morphed into a whole little sub-strand of adult entertainment – which probably says much about how both zombies and porn have gone mainstream in the Internet age (more on that in the following chapters).

There was also a rather minor trend for softcore titillation that encompasses zombies and prostitutes. Spanish filmmaker Ignasi P. Ferré gave us the relatively bloodless but bizarre *Morbus*

(1982), which has a scene where zombies attack a couple of prostitutes who've taken a client into the woods to read him fairy stories (!); Hugh Gallagher's *Gore Whore* (1994) features a prostitute who is actually a zombie (as does Andrew Parkinson's far from salacious *Dead Creatures*, 2001). The nadir of this cycle is Jeff Centauri's deplorably misogynist *Zombie Ninja Gangbangers* (1998) in which a stripper and occasional hooker (Stephanie Beaton) is raped not once, but twice, by vomiting zombies. Ugh. It was something that would become even more prevalent in the mid-2000s, as we will see in the second half of this book.

The link between pornography and horror isn't as odd as it might at first seem. Both genres deal in the forbidden and the fleshy and both, as film theorist Carol J. Clover claims, are "body genres" that try to produce a physical reaction in their audiences (pleasurable arousal and/or pleasurable fear). What's more, both genres also deal with extreme images of the body, the kind of images that are usually kept hidden behind the locked doors of the bedroom or the morgue.

What makes the films of the Italian cycle so distinct from other sex zombie efforts is their insistence on creating a different kind of pornography in which the body's surface is ruptured, exposing its inner mechanics to the audience's gaze. It's a frightening confrontation with the body's materiality and its status as an object. While conventional hardcore pornography revels in this object status and finds pleasure in exposing the body's traditionally hidden zones (the genitals) to view, these zombie movies offer us something more horrific: a vision of the body's essential emptiness. Opening up the body for the camera, the Italian splatter movies try to show us what lies beneath the skin. Significantly, they discover nothing but a bloody mess of tubes and piping in which there is no indication of the divine. As a result, gore becomes a poor substitute for God.

While *Dawn of the Dead* took this splattery nihilism as the basis of a grim comedy of terrors in which the body's materiality made it a ludicrous hunk of meat, the Italian cycle finds nothing funny in it at all. Dark, depressingly grim and relentlessly nasty, these films seek to remind us that sex and death aren't laughing matters. Instead, they are proof of our status as little more than meat. As

characters hop from the bed to the grave and back with dismaying speed, this simple point becomes ever more transparent.

The curious thing about these Italian sex-splatter efforts is just how empty the films themselves are. As the initial rush of the transgressive pleasure offered by *Zombi Holocaust*, *The Nights of Terror*, *Erotic Nights of the Living Dead*, *Porno Holocaust* and *Erotic Orgasm* palls, boredom quickly sets in. These are one-note movies, resounding with the mournful but monotonous toll of the death-knell. But that, arguably, is their entire point. Making us recognise the gore that lies underneath our skin, these films ask us to confront the great unspoken truth of our existence: that we are, in material terms, nothing more than a collection of organs, blood and messy slop.

For feminist theorist Julia Kristeva, the fear of the body's internal reality – what she calls "abjection" – is closely tied to our understandings of ourselves as independent subjects.[138] For Kristeva, the sight of the bodily fluids and excrement are disturbing because they remind us of our own inevitable deaths and shatter our sense of the stability of our own egos. We try to hide or deny these horrid secretions because they are proof of our status as machines that will, one day, stop working. "A wound with blood and pus, or the sickly, acrid smell of sweat, of decay, does not signify death. In the presence of signified death – a flat encephalograph, for instance – I would understand, react, or accept. No, as in true theatre, without make-up or masks, refuse and corpses show me what I permanently thrust aside in order to live. These body fluids, this defilement, this shit are what life withstands, hardly and with difficulty, on the part of death. There, I am at the border of my condition as a living being."[139]

The most terrifying image in this respect, she goes on to argue, is the corpse. "Seen without God and outside of science, [the corpse] is the utmost of abjection. It is death infecting life." It is disturbing because it reminds us that one day we will be no longer ourselves. "If dung signifies the other side of the border, the place where I am not and which permits me to be, the corpse, the most sickening of wastes is a border that has encroached upon everything. It is no longer I who expel. 'I' is expelled."[140]

With this is mind, it's no wonder that censors,

mainstream moviegoers and film critics largely hated the Italian cycle. Shattering all the taboos about bodies and death, these films deliberately break the protective psychological barrier that our skin offers us and delve deep into the body. Their horror is both physical and psychological: a dizzyingly nihilistic refusal to find anything meaningful within us apart from the truth of our death.

Emerging at a moment in our history when the flesh was already under attack from the HIV/AIDS pandemic, the films of this period revolve around a desire to provoke their audiences by turning the body itself into a site of horror. Denying all our attempts to delude ourselves that the body is either the sign of our personal autonomy or proof of some divine wonder, these films drag us into a confrontation with the strangeness that lies within and the emptiness that lies without.

II. THE APOCALYPSE OF NARRATIVE: FULCI'S ZOMBIE TRILOGY

"I am the Italian cinema's last zombie!" proclaimed Lucio Fulci before his death in 1996. As the man responsible for launching a whole cycle of spaghetti living dead movies, it's a claim few would argue with. However, Fulci's reputation is based on much more than just his impressive rip-off of Romero. In his Gothic trilogy of *City of the Living Dead* (1980), *The Beyond* (1981) and *The House by the Cemetery* (1981) the director produced not only the finest work of his career but also three distinctive additions to the genre. Eschewing Romero's influence, these films strike a different path, combining the occult mythos of H.P. Lovecraft with the portentous tone of the biblical Book of Revelation. It was a brilliant change of focus, offering an alternative to the Italian cycle's obsession with the flesh and concentrating instead on fragmented storylines that challenge our understanding of the conventions of linear narrative.

Teaming up with his favourite screenwriter, Dardano Sacchetti, Fulci set out to create three radical, avant-garde gore movies. Infused with the skewered, irrational logic of a nightmare, each instalment in this unholy troika constitutes a quite remarkable viewing experience. "Fulci's Gothic films," explains Thrower, "use the supernatural as a means to subvert cause and effect, leading to situations where the very structures of the films seem to be under attack from the stories' otherworldly agents".[141]

It was something that Fulci himself was explicit about. "My idea was to make an *absolute* film, with all the horrors of our world," he told *Starburst* magazine after *The Beyond* was released. "It's a plotless film: a house, people, and dead men coming from The Beyond. There's no logic to it, just a succession of images [...] We tried in Italy to make films based on pure themes, without a plot, and *The Beyond* like [Dario Argento's] *Inferno*, refuses conventional and traditional structures.[142]

Such refusal is startling obvious to anyone who watches any of the three films. *City of the Living Dead* begins with Father Thomas (Fabrizio Jovine), a priest in the small American town of Dunwich, hanging himself from a tree in his church's graveyard. This act of suicidal despair triggers an apocalyptic rift in the spiritual world, opening one of the seven gateways to hell. Unless the gateway is shut before All Saint's Day, the dead will flood back into the world and evil will triumph.

At a séance in New York, Mary (Catriona MacColl) sees a horrific vision of the priest's suicide and apparently dies from shock. Investigating her death is reporter Peter Bell (Christopher George), who rescues the (actually catatonic) young woman from being buried alive. With the help of psychiatrist Gerry (Carlo De Mejo), Mary and Peter trace the vision back to the Dunwich priest's suicide and attempt to close the gateway before the Earth is overwhelmed by evil.

In synopsis, this opening sounds perfectly straightforward. The experience of watching it, however, is anything but. The first thirty minutes of *City of the Living Dead* are completely disorienting. Cutting back and forth between events in Dunwich and New York, Fulci casts us adrift in a story that's packed full of incident but little coherence. We flit from the priest's suicide to scenes of the dead returning to life. Then from a scene involving a

BOOK OF THE DEAD

young man, a dead baby and an inflatable sex doll to the office of a Dunwich psychiatrist. Then from a New York séance to spooky goings on in a Dunwich bar. Then back to New York where the reporter is trying to work out what's going on. Fulci bombards us with a dizzying vortex of characters, plot lines and information. There are so many conflicting narrative threads that we don't know which one to follow. Who is the hero of this film? Mary, the reporter, or the psychiatrist?

Even when the film's storyline begins to take on some semblance of shape – albeit with five major characters and two main story arcs – Fulci resists the temptation to appease the audience. Instead, he flits between exposition-heavy scenes and moments of outrageous violence as the zombified priest and his living dead hordes attack the residents of Dunwich. What Fulci gives us is a collage of images, some of which fit into the film's story arc, while others simply add to the overall atmosphere of apocalyptic doom. A shower of maggots appears out of nowhere; a boy's head comes into contact with an industrial drill; and a woman vomits up her intestines.

This willingness to privilege special effects set pieces over and above narrative conventions reaches a dizzying extreme in the second film in the trilogy, *The Beyond*. A startlingly bold attempt to make what Fulci called an "absolute" film that's devoid of plot, *The Beyond* is probably the finest film of the director's career. Fusing a Lovecraftian sense of a world dominated by forces that are beyond our ken with Gothic atmosphere and lots of apocalyptic chaos, *The Beyond*'s fractured story follows New Yorker Liza (MacColl again) as she inherits a rundown hotel in New Orleans.

Back in 1927, the hotel was the scene of a gruesome outbreak of mob violence when locals dragged one of the residents into the basement and crucified him for being a warlock. Liza doesn't know anything about this hidden history and so she is baffled when a series of bizarre occurrences interrupt the hotel renovations. A zombie attacks and kills the plumber (Giovanni De Nava) when he goes down into the cellar to fix a leaky pipe; a local architect (Michele Mirabella) is attacked by tarantulas in the town library; the housekeeper (Veronica Lazar) has her head impaled on a rusty nail, forcing one of her eyeballs out of its socket; and acid is poured over the face of the plumber's

wife (Laura De Marchi) when she visits his body in the local morgue.

While the film clearly has a perfunctory narrative goal – our heroes must defeat the zombies and close the portal to the Beyond – Fulci is distinctly uninterested in playing out this story in a conventional manner. As the apocalypse draws closer, the film fragments and distorts as narrative logic is sacrificed to its brooding, Gothic atmosphere and outbreaks of gory violence. Liza and hospital doctor John (David Warbeck) are left totally confused and, as the border between this world and "The Beyond" begins to blur, things only get worse: the conventions of cause and effect and all spatial and temporal logic are jettisoned. Zombies randomly appear and then vanish. Various supernatural events occur without explanation and, in the film's demented conclusion, geographical space itself collapses.

The final reel is simple, yet startling. Trapped in the hospital morgue by reanimated zombies, Liza and John eventually escape into the confines of the hospital's basement. When they get there, they find that they have been inexplicably transported back into the basement of the hotel, several miles away. While they're still trying to comprehend how this could have happened, the hotel basement morphs into The Beyond – a formless, white realm that stretches infinitely in all directions and is littered with corpses.

Is this hell? We don't know. But as John and Liza turn to face the camera, we see that their eyes have become blank and milky white like those of the film's zombies. "And you will face the Sea of Darkness," growls a portentous but resolutely nonsensical voiceover, "and all therein that may be explored". As the credits roll, all our questions about the nature of The Beyond and the fate of our two heroes and the rest of the world are left unanswered. Have we just witnessed the apocalypse? Maybe.

In *The House by the Cemetery*, Fulci turns his hand to a more intimate family horror story. It's the most conventional of the three films, but even its simple set-up is dominated by great jumps of narrative logic as university researcher Norman (Paolo Malco), his wife Lucy (MacColl, on her Fulci hat trick) and their son Bob (Giovanni Frezza) move into an isolated country house in Boston, New England.

As in *The Beyond*, the house proves cursed. It once belonged to the Freudstein family and, unbeknown to our heroes, the zombified remains of Dr Freudstein – a 19th-century scientist rumoured to have dabbled in several unethical practices – are lurking in the basement. He's somehow keeping himself alive by dismembering the bodies of the living and feasting on their flesh.

As the name Freudstein – with its unsubtle conflation of Freud and Frankenstein suggests – *The House by the Cemetery* is a monster movie psychodrama, in which the evil zombie's influence upsets the balance of the family and the house. Apart from the sheer ridiculousness involved in keeping a murderous zombie hidden in a small basement for almost ninety minutes, *The House by the Cemetery* makes other demands on the logic of cinematic realism. What are we to make, for instance, of the scene in which the neck of a decapitated shop window mannequin suddenly gushes blood? Or the fact that when Lucy finds her babysitter mopping up a huge bloodstain in the kitchen she doesn't think to ask her where it's come from? These scenes apparently make no sense at all leaving us to either condemn the script as amazingly incompetent or wonder if Fulci is trying to make us question our faith in the tenets of realism itself.

Perhaps a clue is to be found in the film's logic-defying conclusion. Having seen both his parents brutally killed by the monstrous Dr Freudstein, little Bob escapes from the house's basement. Except, paradoxically, he doesn't really escape at

The House By The Cemetery (1981).

all. The basement leads into a house, the very same house that he was in a moment ago, but populated by turn-of-the-century characters. We suddenly realise that he's been transported through a time warp back to the days when the Freudsteins' owned the house. It simultaneously makes perfect sense and absolutely no sense at all.

The House by the Cemetery and *The Beyond* both end leaving their protagonists trapped in a circular logic puzzle that offers them no escape. In comparison, *City of the Living Dead* does something rather different while offering what may well be the perfect image of Fulci's desire to fracture narrative structure. Emerging from the crypt where they've successfully battled the living dead and closed the gateway to hell, our heroes stand blinking in the sunlight. A child rushes towards them ostensibly to hug them. As he approaches, though, they recoil in fear and their faces contort in horror. Fulci doesn't show us what they've seen. Instead, he simply freezes the picture on the running child in mid-dash. As this still image hangs on-screen, it slowly cracks apart like a shattered pane of glass and falls to pieces, leaving nothing but an empty void in its place.

It's a deliberately unsatisfactory ending, leaving us uncertain what has happened. But it's in keeping with the trilogy's desire to create films in which, as Thrower suggests, the "overall dynamic is discontinuous, not progressive, fragmentary instead of explicatory."[143] Is Fulci acknowledging his desire to rupture and fragment the conventions of storytelling in this striking image? Quite possibly.

Typically, though, the director refused to explain it in such terms, claiming it was simply an accident – and adding an additional layer of confusion to the matter in the process. "Originally, the child ran towards the camera, and we cut to the two adults smiling to themselves," Fulci later recalled. "That was it, a happy ending. One day, I was in the editing room [with editor Vincenzo Tomassi] and we watched the footage of the adults who were arguing in the shot – they didn't get along. So we cut to the little boy running and cut back to the footage of them arguing. But in that shot, there was an aberration on the film where it looked like the image started to break up. Well, Tomassi said, "Why don't we use that?" So we did and now it's not so happy. Reviewers have written volumes on this ending, which was just basically a mistake saved by an ingenious idea. That's Tomassi."[144]

There's something rather perverse in Fulci's mockery of reviewers for interpreting this ending in so many ways. After all, it's the trilogy's refusal to offer an absolute, coherent textual meaning that encourages such (mis)interpretation in the first place!

Interestingly, one of the persistent images in Fulci's trilogy is that of the ruptured eyeball. It becomes an apt metaphor for the violence the filmmaker directs towards the conventions of cinematic storytelling – his desire to assault his audience's eyes. In these three films and in his earlier *Zombi 2*, Fulci proves to be fascinated with eyeballs. He frequently zooms into his actors' eyes and films them in close-ups reminiscent of the trademark shots in Sergio Leone's stylised spaghetti Westerns. However, unlike Leone, Fulci takes this ocular fascination to gruesome extremes and regularly places the eyeballs of his characters in distress.

Recalling the razorblade slicing an eyeball at the start of Buñuel's surrealist classic *Un chien andalou* (1928), Fulci's zombie films pierce, split and skewer the eye with sadistic glee. In *Zombi 2* a protracted and often censored scene shows actress Olga Karlatos's eyeball impaled on a splinter of wood as a zombie pulls her head through a broken doorframe. In graphic detail, Fulci shows us what happens when the soft globular tissue of the eye is pierced by sharp wood. A totally disgusting and deeply disturbing attack on one of the body's most vulnerable zones that particular gore shot has become an infamous landmark in horror movie history.

Such ocular trauma is replayed again and again in the trilogy: in *City of the Living Dead*, the zombie priest has the power to make his victims' eyes gush out blood. In *The Beyond*, various characters have their eyeballs attacked culminating in a baroque sequence in which a man's eyes are bitten by tarantulas. *The House by the Cemetery* skimps on the violence but proves itself fascinated with ways of *seeing* as it foregrounds Bob's child's-eye view of this world – and the next.

This eyeball horror is always closely linked to the trilogy's attack on narrative, as our own cinematic gaze is ruptured by Fulci's refusal to adhere to conventional storytelling. Violence against the eye becomes a metaphor for the loss of meaning that the zombie apocalypses of these films embody. Picking up on the nihilism of the post-*Night of the Living Dead* zombie movie, Fulci's trilogy offers a very different approach to the same theme. Here the apocalypse involves more than just the destruction of the flesh or social institutions – the body and the body politic. Fulci wants to destroy the body of the text as well.

In Fulci's zombie movies the End of Days isn't a Christian event. Rather he gives us an atheist's apocalypse. In the Bible, the end of the world in the Book of Revelation reaffirms God's existence as the material world is destroyed and we ushered into the next realm. Fulci, in contrast, leaves us suspended in a spiritual vacuum. His vision owes more to the Lovecraftian *Book of Eibon*, a fictional occult volume penned by *Weird Tales* writer Clark Ashton Smith, than Scripture. It's an end which offers no truth, no value, no hope. Talking about *The Beyond* as "a film without borders" Fulci underlined this nihilism and linked the movie to the avant-garde.[145]

"What I wanted to get across with that film was the idea that all of life is often really a terrible nightmare and that our only refuge is to remain in this world, but outside time," he later explained. "In the end, the two protagonists' eyes turn completely white and they find themselves in a desert where there's no light, no shade, no wind… no nothing. I believe, despite my being a Catholic, that they reached what many people imagine to be the Afterworld […] I'd like to emphasise that I wanted to make a completely Artaudian film out of an almost non-existent script by Sacchetti."[146]

As the reference to French theatre director and poet Antonin Artaud makes clear, Fulci viewed his trilogy as more than just a collection of cheap horror thrills. While all three films are undeniably motivated by the demands of exploitation cinema, they simultaneously offer something more ambitious. These three thrilling and innovative films want to do more than just make us jump. They want to question our faith in the ordered universe we've built up around ourselves. Hence what the trilogy most resembles in zombie movie history isn't Romero's satiric splatterfests, but the haunting world of *I Walked with a Zombie* with its probing questioning of the limits of knowledge.

This nihilism leads Fulci from Catholicism towards a vision of the world in which God is apparently absent. Presenting us with Biblical tableaux – several of the gory set pieces in *City of the Living Dead* and *The Beyond* reference the crucifixion and the stigmata – Fulci creates horror movies that deliberately subvert Christian certainty. In Fulci's zombie movies there is no God. The afterlife is an empty void populated by the living dead. There is no hope of paradise, only the *nothingness* of the Beyond.[147] In the unlikely event that God does exist, He can only lie somewhere beyond the Beyond.[148]

It's a startlingly nihilistic viewpoint for an Italian Catholic to adopt, an irony that Fulci himself was more than aware of. "I think each man chooses his own inner hell, corresponding to his hidden vices. So I am not afraid of hell, since hell is already in us. Curiously enough, I can't imagine a paradise exists, though I am a Catholic – but perhaps God has left me? – yet I have often envisaged hell, since we live in a society where hell can be perceived. Finally, I realise that paradise is indescribable. Imagination is much stronger when it is pressed by the terrors of hell."[149]

Ultimately, these films revolve around a questioning of faith. What does it mean to exist in a world of horror? "This may seem strange," Fulci later reflected, "but I am happier than somebody like Buñuel who says he is looking for God. I have found Him in others' misery, and my torment is greater [...] for I have realised that God is a God of suffering. I envy atheists, they don't have all these difficulties.[150] Faced with such questions, Fulci's characters find no answers. The world they move through is without transcendent meaning. Tellingly, every figure of paternal authority in the trilogy is useless. Psychiatrists, priests, journalists, doctors and academics prove to be useless in preventing the coming apocalypse. Indeed, it's a priest who opens the zombie disaster by hanging himself at the start of *City of the Living Dead*. Assaulted by writhing maggots, bloodthirsty bats and the emptiness of the Beyond, we find ourselves in a universe with no meaning, only horror.

Romero charted the destruction of American society. Fulci envisions the obliteration of faith. His world is one in which meaning has collapsed, the dead walk and there is nothing beyond this plane other than a limitless void. When John and Liza are turned blind at the end of *The Beyond* it makes perfect sense. "Their sight has no *raison d'être* any more in this lifeless world," explains the director.[151] It's a bleak vision of the empty meaninglessness of existence that recalls the words of philosophy's greatest nihilist Friedrich Nietzsche: "He who fights with monsters should look to it that he himself does not become a monster. And when you gaze long into an abyss the abyss also gazes into you."[152]

III. THE RETURN TO THE CARIBBEAN

Interviewed by *Fangoria* magazine at the time of *Zombi 2*'s release, Lucio Fulci explained what made his vision of the reanimated dead so different from that of his contemporaries. "I wanted to recapture the moody atmosphere of witchcraft and paganism that must have been prevalent when Europeans first settled in the Caribbean during the 1700s. That's when the concept of zombies – human slaves brought back from the dead – first became known to Western civilisation. Fright films such as *I Walked with a Zombie*, *Voodoo Island* and *The Walking Dead*

[aka *The Zombies of Mora Tau*] were in the back of my mind as I made this picture."[153]

While it's obvious that Fulci had much to gain from distancing himself from Romero's *Dawn of the Dead* – the Italian director did have a good case for arguing his originality. While Romero is largely uninterested in his ghouls' cultural heritage, *Zombi 2* is fascinated by the Caribbean origins of the monster. As his black zombies shuffle through sandy coastal villages flanked by palm trees and the crashing surf of the Caribbean Ocean, Fulci recreates a "moody atmosphere" that harks back to the supernatural chills of the films of the 1930s and 1940s.

It was something that the director apparently felt insanely passion about, even penning an angry letter to Dario Argento accusing him of trying to obscure the monster's cultural heritage. "When Argento wrote that *Dawn of the Dead* was his creation, I wrote him a letter listing twelve films which demonstrated that zombies were around even before Tourneur's day, before *I Walked with a Zombie*. Zombies belong to Haiti and Cuba, not to Dario Argento."[154]

By foregrounding the Caribbean, *Zombi 2* returns to issues of racial anxiety and imperialism that the previous three decades had largely ignored or reworked beyond all recognition. In many respects, Fulci's interest in the Caribbean needs to be understood in terms of the Italian cycle's European sensibilities. In *Zombi 2*, for instance, the corpses of maggot-eaten Spanish conquistadors claw their way out of the makeshift graves where they were buried centuries before. It serves as a powerful reminder of European colonial guilt, a guilt that the unexplained apocalypse of the movie seems to be some kind of punishment for.

As ragged black zombies stumble out of the jungle to attack the white heroes, *Zombi 2* sets up an a series of oppositions between white and / black, science and voodoo, civilisation and savagery that's more than familiar from the zombie films of the 1930s and 1940s.

Fulci wasn't the first Italian to use the horror film to address such racial issues. The cannibal cycle of the 1970s frequently depicted the clash between the First and Third Worlds, perhaps nowhere more strikingly than in Ruggero Deodato's *Cannibal Holocaust* (1980), in which white filmmakers goad a native South American tribe into committing the holocaust of the title; then find themselves on the dinner menu as a result. Focussing on the epitome of savagery – man eating man – the cannibal films may have predominantly relied on flesh-eating for sensational splatter, but they weren't blind to the ironic potential of dispossessed natives from the Third World eating invading whites.

Zombi 2 and the other living dead films that took their inspiration from the cannibal cycle, often imagined an apocalypse in which the Third World's dead rise up against white, Western civilisation in bloody revenge for centuries of imperial conquest. It's not just confined to the Caribbean. Other exotic backdrops include Southeast Asia (*Zombi Holocaust*); the Philippines (*Zombi 3*) it's the Philippines; and New Guinea in *Zombie Creeping Flesh*, a Spanish-Italian co-production in which an experimental plan to reduce global overpopulation turns the locals into zombies. The latter film wears its crude politics on its sleeve, featuring a laughably silly meeting at the United Nations (actually just a room with couple of desks), where a spokesman for the Third World berates the developed nations: "You have murdered my people. You have treated them like a crowd of human larvae, like insects, savage beasts, prehistoric animals! They are running from their children, their parents, their brothers, transformed into vile creatures that feast on human flesh!" It's risible stuff, but the overriding point becomes pretty clear as the virus makes the population of the Third World eat themselves in a kind of auto-anthropophagous genocide (!).

Such plotting gives some indication of the ludicrous over-simplicity of these films' treatment of race. At times, it borders on the purely offensive. The ghouls of *Zombi Holocaust, Zombie 4: After Death, Zombi 3* and Jess Franco's *Devil Hunter* (orig. *Il Sexo caníbal* , 1980) are styled as expendable fodder as much because of their skin colour as the fact that they're already dead. Aristide Massaccesi's zombie films are even cruder. The misshapen native zombie of *Porno Holocaust*, for instance, rapes and kills the film's white females with his monstrously huge phallus, suggesting that he's really little more than a demeaning stereotype of black virility run amok.

Rather interestingly, the Italian cycle's obsession with race prefigured a much wider return to the Caribbean that occurred during the 1980s. During this period, American zombie films also began to highlight the Caribbean origins of the monster once again, though for very different reasons than their Italian cousins. The most significant of these American returns was to be found, unsurprisingly, in Romero's *Day of the Dead* (1985), the director's third instalment in his living dead series.

Day of the Dead begins where *Dawn* left off, with the living dead apocalypse having taken over the whole planet. Every last vestige of the civilised world has been wiped out. As the film opens, a civilian-military team left over from the final days of the old order land their helicopter in a deserted Florida street in the vain hope of finding survivors.[155] They're greeted by living dead ghouls who spill out of shops and apartment complexes, hungry for food.

Years on from *Dawn*, time has taken its toll on the zombies who are now more gruesome monsters – dirty, decomposing and played less for laughs. The development of special effects techniques allows Savini to really push the gore to the limit, giving the film a bleak nastiness that's suitably chilling. The first zombie we see has had its lower jaw ripped off and its tongue flicks around wildly; later, a zombie with its abdomen cut open sits up, spilling its internal organs onto the floor in a bloody heap. In the finale, the film's chief villain is pulled apart by ghouls who rip off his limbs and head in what's become an iconic moment in zombie cinema. Despite the occasional flash of splat-stick humour – like the swivelling eyes in a freshly decapitated zombie head – the tone is darker, edgier and far more depressing than before.

Back at the team's base, an old mine shaft previously converted into a missile silo and government records depository, the divisions among the group quickly become apparent. Even with a corral full of zombie test subjects Sarah (Lori Cardille) and her fellow scientists Dr Logan (Richard Liberty) and Ted Fisher (John Amplas) haven't been able to work out what's causing the bodies of the dead to come back to life. The situation is slowly getting out of hand. Logan is beginning to look like a mad scientist – chopping up body after body in his search for answers, while trying to socialise his subjects into good behaviour. His star pupil in this respect is a zombie called Bub (Howard Sherman) who is beginning to display vague traces of memory and perhaps even humanity.

Meanwhile, the military arm of the group is fed up of waiting for results. Captain Rhodes (Joseph Pilato) is turning into a tin-pot dictator. The only thing that's keeping Rhodes and his men from deserting the compound and the scientists is the fact that they're unable to fly the helicopter. The group's pilot is civilian contractor John (Terry Alexander) who – along with communications engineer McDermott (Jarlath Conroy) – apparently has no interest in either the group's scientific mission or in helping the fascist bully boys led by Rhodes.

Having established this community of characters, *Day* proceeds to pull them apart as they bicker their way to oblivion. The film ends as the compound is overrun by the living dead who have been let into the camp by Sarah's boyfriend Miguel (Antone DiLeo) who goes insane after being bitten in the arm by a ghoul. As in *Night* and *Dawn*, it is the stupidity of the living that is the greatest threat, with the zombies simply capitalising on the petty squabbles. *Day* proves once and for all that the real horror in this world isn't the returning dead, but the inhumanity of the living and the inherent rottenness of contemporary society. While Logan socialises Bub into "good" behaviour, Rhodes and his soldiers slowly regress into barbarism. The apocalypse has destroyed the necessity for civilised behaviour and primitive anarchy beckons.

The only character who recognises and understands this is John. Cutting themselves off from the rest of the community, John and McDermott live deep within the mineshaft tunnels in a converted Winnebago they call "The Ritz". In John, Romero revives his zombie trilogy's dormant racial subtext. The third black hero in this set of films, John is clearly linked with Ben in *Night* and Peter in *Dawn*. But since he is explicitly West Indian, he's also tied to the Caribbean heritage of the zombie.

John represents a significant change of direction for Romero. In *Night of the Living Dead*, the filmmaker deliberately avoided mentioning voodoo, arbitrarily blaming the zombie apocalypse on radiation from space. In *Dawn*, the return of the dead is largely taken for granted by the main characters, who are more interested in working out how to survive than discovering what has caused the end of the world. The nearest we get to an explanation in that film are the vague remarks of the Puerto Rican priest in the tenement building and Peter's throwaway reference to voodoo in the "No more room in hell" speech. In *Day of the Dead*, however, Romero returns to the zombie's cultural heritage in the Caribbean and makes John the chief explicator of the apocalypse – something that his biblical name hints at.

Early films in the zombie genre – from *White Zombie* to *King of the Zombies* and *I Walked with a Zombie* – used the monster to play up the racial anxieties of the period. They styled the Caribbean as a terrifying realm that contained the seeds of the white world's destruction. Romero turns this innate racism on its head. John, a smart, witty and compassionate black hero, is a figure who offers hope and salvation. And the Caribbean itself becomes a potential utopia, a place where mankind might be able to start again. It's a theme that comes to a head as John delivers an impassioned monologue about how humanity might survive the zombies.

Surveying the silo and its stacks of government records, John lectures Sarah about the rottenness of pre-zombie America and the importance of the chance they've been given to start again afresh. This lengthy speech becomes the most poignant commentary in Romero's series:

JOHN

We don't believe in what you're doing, Sarah… You know what all they keep down here in this cave? Man, they've got the books and the records of the top five hundred companies, they got the defence budget here and they got the negatives of all your favourite movies, they got microfilm with tax returns and newspaper stories, they got immigration records and census reports and they've got official accounts of all the wars and plane crashes and volcanic eruptions and earthquakes and fires and floods and all the other disasters that interrupted the flow of things in the good old USA. Now, what does it matter Sarah, darling? All this filing and record keeping? Are we ever going to get a chance to see it all? This is a great big fourteen mile tombstone with an epitaph on it that nobody's gonna bother to read. And here you come with a whole new set of charts and graphs and records. What you gonna do? Bury them down here with all the other relics of *what once was*? And I'll tell you what else, you ain't never gonna figure it out. Just as they never figured out why the stars are where they are. It ain't mankind's job to figure that stuff out… So what you're doing is a waste of time, Sarah… and time is all we got left, you know.

SARAH

I'm doing the only thing that's left to do.

JOHN

(As a Caribbean style calypso plays on the soundtrack)

There's plenty to do, plenty to do. S'long as there's you and me and maybe some other people we could start over, start fresh. Get some babies… and teach them never to come over here and dig these records out.

A ghoul's moan interrupts the Caribbean calypso. The music switches to something electronic and darker.

JOHN (CONT'D)

You want to put some kinda explanation down here before you leave? Here's one as good as any you're likely to find – we've been punished by the creator. He visited a curse on us so we might get a look at what hell was like. Maybe He didn't want to see us blow ourselves up, put a big hole in His sky. Maybe He just wanted to show us He was still the boss man. Maybe He figured we was getting too big for our britches trying to figure his shit out.

If *Night* and *Dawn* exposed the rotten underbelly of 20th-century America, *Day* fantasises the possibility of an alternative – a new society born from the ashes of the rotten old one. Over the first three films of Romero's trilogy the story is one in which, as critic Sue Ellen Case points out, "the dead have eliminated the family unit, claimed commodity reification for their own in the shopping mall and defeated the military-industrial complex."[156] All that's left is the possibility of beginning again by ditching the signs and symbols of the old order and starting over from scratch. As Romero biographer Paul R. Gagne explains, "If the Monroeville shopping mall is a temple to the consumer society Romero pokes fun at in *Dawn*, then [the missile silo cave of *Day*] is its tomb."[157]

The trilogy ends with an upbeat scene that shows Sarah, John and McDermott safely ensconced on a (presumably) zombie-free island in the Caribbean. In Romero's hands, the zombie movie has come full circle, inverting its origins so that the Caribbean becomes a place of safety and civilisation while the American mainland is the site of primitive ghoulish cannibalism. Civilisation and savagery have exchanged places and the implicit suggestion is that what we once considered civilised was never actually civilised at all.

However, what John's speech also makes clear is the extent to which Romero has oversimplified the racial theme in his rush to perform this stunning *volte-face* of the genre's internal dynamics. With his thick patois, laid back manner and decision not to concern himself with issues that are beyond his understanding, John could be read as a facile racial stereotype of black masculinity. Even his speech, which Romero gives such an important place in the narrative, is affected by this as his talk of knowing one's place ("It ain't mankind's job to figure that stuff out") and transparent allusion to slavery ("Maybe He just wanted to show us He was still the bossman [...] We was getting too big for our britches") reinstates a hierarchical view of the world at precisely the same time as it is apparently trying to overturn it.

There's no doubt that Romero wants us to take this black man as the film's chief hero. Sarah may be *Day*'s main protagonist but she's too misguided to be completely heroic. Unfortunately, both the script and Terence Alexander's performance make John into little more than a rehash of a creaky old racial stereotype, a distant cousin of Mantan Moreland's obstinate "coon" who's happier fishing than fighting and has no interest in filling his head with things that are beyond his ken.

As in the earlier movies, Romero is keen to attack the prevailing order and expose its corruption. Asking the audience to delight in the destruction of a rotten world, Romero uses his living dead ghouls to elicit our sympathy for the cause. Enslaved by the military team, the zombies are invested with a new found humanity in *Day*. Logan tries to socialise his zombie captives by offering them meaty treats for good behaviour and claiming, "They are *us*, they are extensions of us. They are the same animal simply functioning less perfectly." Yet even his actions seem like those of a benevolent slave master or white missionary doing his best to educate the savages. His angry shouts when the zombies don't conform to the patterns of behaviour he desires are the demented ravings of a mad man.

In Bub, the zombie with a soul, Romero extends his zombie mythology into new territory. Bub becomes part of Romero's project to transform the zombies into the film's most sympathetic characters. Incarcerated by Rhodes, teased and insulted by the enlisted men and hacked up in grotesque Frankenstein experiments by Logan, the zombies are used and abused by the film's humans. Chained and bound and herded around like cattle, they're little more than slaves and, since Romero is keen to present the living as more dangerous than the living dead, we come to have a strange sympathy with their plight.[158]

Bub can remember bits and pieces of his past life including how to salute, how to fire gun and even how to read a Stephen King novel. Sherman's fantastic performance gives him a heart and – dare one say it? – soul that no other screen zombie has ever possessed. Listen closely to his apparently inarticulate grunts and various sentences can be heard, including a whisper of "I...ain't...finished..." when Logan turns off Bub's Walkman in mid-symphony. Like the ghouls drawn to the shopping mall in *Dawn*, Bub's blessed with faint stirrings of memory and, as a result, humanity. Could it be that the zombies are more than just dead bodies stumbling around without purpose or meaning?

Romero wasn't the only American filmmaker interested in returning to the Caribbean in the 1980s. Several directors, as diverse as Wes Craven and Steven Fierberg, all headed south. It's tempting to wonder how much this had to do with the island's internal troubles during the period.

By the mid-1980s, Haiti had become the poorest country in Latin America. The stagnating economy triggered widespread food riots and sporadic instances of political unrest that were brutally suppressed by the military and the secret police. The country that had once been the jewel in France's colonial crown – with an annual output that far exceeded any of its other colonies – was on the verge of economic and political bankruptcy because of the greed of its tyrannical rulers.

Chief among these was Françoise Duvalier, commonly known as "Papa Doc", who dominated the island's troubled history from the late-1950s until his death in 1971. The Duvalier regime was characterised by human rights abuses, widespread poverty and a culture of fear and intimidation fuelled by Papa Doc's secret police force, the infamous Ton Ton Macoute. His legacy was the slow destruction of the country. By 1970, over a million Haitians had fled the island to take up residence in other parts of the Caribbean, America and Europe. After Papa Doc's death in 1971, his son Jean-Claude Duvalier ("Baby Doc") took over. He proceeded to run the island's already troubled economy completely into the ground.

America watched the rapid deterioration of its

neighbour with a combination of fascination and contempt. In the early 1980s, Haiti had been explicitly blamed for the rise of AIDS, with some leading American health officials drawing links between the island and the spread of the disease in the US. According to these commentators, Haiti was the geographical facilitator for the spread of this so-called "African" disease from the Third World to the First – because of its alleged encouragement of sexual tourism among American homosexuals. In 1985, the Centers for Disease Control (CDC) eventually overturned this erroneous (as well as racist and homophobic) myth about the virus's origins. But it came too late to save Haiti's devastated tourist industry, which put further economic strain on the country.

"The damage done to Haiti's reputation recapitulated the old repulsion and horror that the West had felt for the 'Black Republic'," writes historian Brenda Gale Plummer, "and it was expressed in similar metaphors of isolation and quarantine."[159] America still viewed Haiti as a place of terror and savagery and, just as in previous decades, the US responded to the threat in no uncertain terms.

America played the role of international policeman, piling on diplomatic pressure and the threat of military violence as Haiti's decline continued under Baby Doc Duvalier. The United Nations initiated economic sanctions and American aid packages to the island were reduced or cancelled. By 1986 the failing Duvalier regime was overthrown and Baby Doc fled to Europe aboard an American military plane. He took the corpse of his father with him to prevent the looting mobs from molesting – or, it was rumoured, reanimating – it.

As the Duvalier regime fell, America became increasingly concerned about the growing refugee crisis that accompanied the island's political unrest. The American authorities were determined to stem the rising tide of immigrants. By the early

Day of the Dead (1985).

1990s, President Clinton's government was making explicit reference to the problems of immigration, human rights abuses on the island, and Haiti's alleged role as a shipment point for cocaine bound for the US.

In September 1994, Clinton sent a US-led intervention force to the island. "Operation Uphold Democracy" was launched to overthrow the military regime that had forced democratically elected president Jean-Bertrand Aristide and was authorised by the UN Security Council. Haiti, which had remained at the forefront of US foreign policy throughout the Reagan, Bush and Clinton years, was the country that America just couldn't forget.

If history seemed to be repeating itself, so too was America's culture industry. Just as Seabrook's *The Magic Island* had offered the American public a glimpse into Haitian voodoo in the 1930s, so a new book popularised a different take on the island's superstitions. *The Serpent and the Rainbow*, written by Harvard ethnobiologist Wade Davis and published in 1986, wasn't a Caribbean travelogue. Instead it was a factual (if occasionally sensational) account of Davis's experience on the island and his research into the so-called "zombie powder" that turned people into the living dead.

Davis had been sent to the Caribbean by an American biochemical firm that hoped that he might be able to uncover the mysteries of zombification. The practical applications of such a process, if it really existed, were clear enough. The drugs company hoped that the zombification formula might be used either as an anaesthetic or to develop a form of suspended animation for NASA astronauts undertaking long trips through space.

Eager to gain access to the closed and suspicious world of Haitian voodoo, the white explorer attended religious ceremonies and sorcerers' rites in an attempt to separate the biochemical realities of zombification from its mythical voodoo trappings. Beginning his adventure as a sceptical non-believer, Davis returned home to the US with a newfound appreciation of voodoo's place in Haitian society. He surmised that zombification did exist and was actually a form of capital punishment inflicted on the island's rural peasantry at the whim of the leaders of Haiti's many secret societies.

As a scientific study aimed at the lay reader, *The Serpent and the Rainbow* frequently merges factual reportage with adventure story elements. A comparison with Davis' more academic tome *Passage of Darkness: The Ethnobiology of the Haitian Zombie* (1988), illustrates the extent to which *The Serpent and the Rainbow* glosses over some rich scientific, historical and anthropological issues in the hope of keeping the story cracking along at a lively pace. This wasn't some academic lab experiment but a dangerous piece of fieldwork that blended anthropology and biochemistry with a significant degree of macho bravado. Mixing science with acts of daring, and social history with descriptions of moonlit visits to graveyards, *The Serpent and the Rainbow* was aimed squarely at the bestseller lists.

During the course of his research into Haiti's voodoo culture, Davis came to the conclusion that the active ingredient in the zombification potion used by the voodoo sorcerers wasn't magic, but a poison known to the Western world as "tetrodotoxin". Extracted from the pufferfish, tetrodotoxin can induce a paralysis that resembles death. The poison, as Davis explained, is powerful enough to induce "a state of profound paralysis, marked by complete immobility during which time the border between life and death is not at all certain, even to trained physicians. It became clear that the tetrodotoxin was capable of pharmacologically inducing a physical state that might actually allow an individual to be buried alive."[160]

In Japan anecdotal evidence had already suggested that gourmet diners who ate badly prepared pufferfish often experienced similar symptoms. Yet they never for a moment believed they'd been turned into zombies. Why was it, Davis wondered, that so many Haitians who had been drugged in this way thought they'd joined the ranks of the living dead? The answer seemed to lie in the island's voodoo culture. Poor education, lots of superstition and a lifetime's worth of socialisation into voodooism meant that the majority of the

islanders wholeheartedly believed that zombification was possible. The effects of the drug merely compounded this, leading Davis to conclude that "in the phantasmagoric cultural landscape of Haiti [the victim] had his own cultural expectation that he carried with him literally into and out of the grave."[161]

If *The Serpent and the Rainbow* was *The Magic Island* for the 1980s, filmmaker Wes Craven's movie adaptation of the book was the decade's answer to *White Zombie*. Released in 1987, at the height of America's interest in the Haitian crisis, the film starred Bill Pullman in the lead role of Dr Dennis Alan (a fictional substitute for Davis). Replacing any hint of scientific investigation with all-out adventure and a liberal dash of horror, Craven's film works brilliantly as a scary movie. Taking liberties with the source material and exaggerating its more sensational aspects, *The Serpent and the Rainbow* movie played directly into American fears about Haiti's impending collapse as the Duvalier regime crumbled.

Craven had previously forayed into the zombie genre in *Deadly Friend* (1986). It was a lacklustre tale about a teenage science prodigy who uses his expert knowledge of artificial intelligence to bring his girlfriend back from the dead by implanting a microchip in her brain. Ignored by most audiences, *Deadly Friend* turned out to be one of the few turkeys of Craven's high-profile transformation from disreputable director of grindhouse shockers like *Last House on the Left* (1972) to major Hollywood player.

In *The Serpent and the Rainbow*, Craven set his sights on the mainstream. He adds a political context to the story that skilfully taps into American anxieties of the period – and even recycles archive footage of the collapse of the Duvalier regime. He also creates a memorable villain for Dr Alan to battle against, Port-au-Prince secret police chief and voodoo sorcerer Peytraud (creepily played by Zakes Mokae). Much like Freddy Krueger in Craven's seminal slasher movie *A Nightmare on Elm Street* (1984), Peytraud possesses the disturbing ability to enter Dr Alan's dreams. Tapping into the way that voodoo is able to invest the everyday with a sinister undercurrent of magical menace, Craven blurs the line between reality and hallucination.

One of the film's scariest sequences is set in the

US when, during a dinner party, Alan is troubled by the phantom image of a hand emerging from his soup bowl. Before he can recover, his prim and proper hostess suddenly throws herself across the table to try and stab him with a steak knife. Voodoo has the power to erupt into the real world turning it into a waking nightmare.

Unsurprisingly, Craven also makes the most of the book's zombie-emphasis. Several scenes feature the living dead and there is a terrifying sequence in which Alan is drugged, paralyzed and buried alive in a coffin with only a tarantula for company.

However, in trying to deal with the political upheaval of mid-1980s Haiti that Davis had deliberately sidestepped in the book, Craven comes unstuck. The script's reliance on the confrontation between the forces of white America (Alan) and black Haiti (Peytraud) is so simplistic that it verges on parody. Whatever Craven's intention, *The Serpent and the Rainbow* plays into the hands of reactionary American discourses about Haitian "backwardness" with its depiction of the island as a savage and terrifying realm.

The film's most astute political observation actually comes from the mouth of its chief villain. As Peytraud prepares to kill his captured American adversary, he explains his view of US foreign policy: "This country lives on the edge, Dr Alan. One weakness in the wrong place and over it goes into slavery again. Just like with the French. The United States would like anarchy here, I'm sure. Well this isn't Grenada, Dr Alan. I'm here now."

Peytraud has a canny grasp of the strategic importance of this tiny island to the world's greatest superpower and his attempt to justify his methods using anti-imperialist rhetoric has some value. But, as a voodoo torture master with a comic book villain's flair for overkill, no one in the audience is unlikely to take his words with anything but a pinch of salt. America's fraught interest in Haiti's internal politics is arguably

more complicated than the movie's formulaic interplay of good vs evil can cope with. In the end, *The Serpent and the Rainbow* ends up styling America as a force for good in the region. Dr Alan becomes the island's white saviour – symbolically overthrowing an evil Haitian despot who tortures the populace and turns them into zombies. Future US president Bill Clinton would, one suspects, have retrospectively approved of Pullman's portrayal – much as he would see himself reflected in the actor's later presidential turn in *Independence Day*.

Released at the height of Haiti's internal turmoil, *The Serpent and the Rainbow* was just one of a series of voodoo-themed films that took advantage of the renewed interest in the region. Horror films like *Angel Heart* (1987) and *Voodoo Dolls* (1990) marked the return of Caribbean magic to cinema screens, while living dead movies like John N. Carter's *Zombie Island Massacre* (1984) and Steven Fierberg's *Voodoo Dawn* (1989) – managed to find a place for the zombie among their stories of black magic.

Putting a characteristically negative spin on the Caribbean, *Zombie Island Massacre* and *Voodoo Dawn* played up to America's willingness to delude itself about its interest in Haiti's political strife in simplistic ways. In *Zombie Island Massacre* American tourists in the Caribbean are murdered by what everyone assumes to be a zombie (but actually turns out to be warring drug dealers). In *Voodoo Dawn* an ex-Ton Ton Macoute torturer (Tony Todd) flees Haiti and arrives in America's Deep South. There he starts butchering the African-American locals in the hope of creating a patchwork zombie from their body parts. Both movies served much the same ideological role as *White Zombie* and *Ouanga* did decades before, suggesting that the Caribbean needed the guiding hand of Messrs. Reagan, Bush and Clinton to steer it from anarchy to democracy.

IV. SPLATTER HOUSE OF HORRORS

During the 1980s, more American zombie films went into production than at any time in the genre's brief history. In terms of quality, however,

many of these efforts dragged the already beleaguered genre to new lows. While the Italian cycle produced films that succeeded in delivering flashes of brilliance amidst stretches of technical and artistic incompetence, the new popularity of zombie movies in the 1980s signalled a return to the Poverty Row standards of the 1940s.

Lured by the promise of quick profits and low overheads, a host of fly-by-night independent companies and straight-to-video merchants churned out a succession of cheesy horror comedies, exploitation flicks and Z-grade schlock. It was a blatant attempt to cash-in on the ever-increasing demands of the VCR-dominated marketplace. And overnight it squandered what little credibility the zombie genre had established.

Naturally, it wasn't just zombie movies that were susceptible to this shoddy treatment. However, with the exception of the ubiquitous post-*Halloween* serial killer, the zombie appeared in far more of these cheap scare-fests than any other monster. As a result, the vast majority of the zombie's American appearances during the decade have entered the history books as some of the worst examples of modern horror cinema. Mixing ultra-cheap production values with teen-orientated comedy and occasional dashes of sexploitation films such as *The Alien Dead* (1980), *One Dark Night* (1982), *Bloodsuckers from Outer Space* (1984), *The Gore-Met Zombie Chef From Hell* (1986), *Neon Maniacs* (1986), *Redneck Zombies* (1987), *Zombie High* (1987), *Ghost Town* (1988), *Night Life* (1989) *Dead Men Don't Die* (1990) and *Space Zombie Bingo* (1993) ripped the guts out of the Italian cycle's subversive potential. These films replaced the spaghetti movies' extreme gore with lame horror comedy, inept scares, scantily clad babes and unconvincing special effects. And, sometimes, all of the above.

There were, of course exceptions to the rule. Two American outings that followed hot on the heels of *Dawn of the Dead* were John Carpenter's ghostly *The Fog* (1979) and Gary Sherman's less-famous, but perhaps more deserving, *Dead & Buried* (1981).

Carpenter's film reworked the classic return of the repressed set-up with a slick and stylish production and a host of nautical corpses strangely reminiscent of *The Zombies of Mora-Tau*. In *The Fog*, Carpenter focuses on Californian settlement Antonio Bay, where preparations for the town's hundredth anniversary reach a grisly end as a thick fog sweeps in off the sea and various residents are killed in a series of nasty ways. As local radio presenter Stevie (Adrienne Barbeau) eventually realises, the fog hides an army of zombies who've risen from their watery graves to take revenge on the town on the anniversary of their deaths. A hundred years earlier, a ship full of lepers was wrecked off the coast after the town's founding fathers' refused to let it dock – planning instead to steal its cargo of gold. Now the lepers have returned from their watery mass grave – armed with cutlasses, hooks and other nautical equipment – to kill everyone in sight and recover what was rightfully theirs. Implicitly arguing that America is a land that was built upon great crimes (Native American genocide, slavery, piracy), Carpenter extends the social message of Romero's work in novel ways.

The Fog gears up for a *Night of the Living Dead* style climax in which a band of survivors lock themselves inside a hilltop church for safety, only to discover that it hides the treasure that was stolen from the leprous mariners a century before. It's at this point that Carpenter's deft touch begins to falter and one can't help feeling that amidst all the dry ice and electronic synthesiser music, these zombies are rather vague phantoms whose impact suffers from them getting less screen time than they deserve.

As Carpenter falls back on yet another of his trademark siege set-ups – recalling the barricaded group dynamics of *Rio Bravo*, *The Birds* and *Night of the Living Dead* – *The Fog* squanders much of its originality. Indeed, all of Carpenter's zombie movies follow much the same siege pattern, from the scientists trapped in a church by ghouls led by rocker Alice Cooper in *Prince of Darkness* (1987) to space cops fending off zombie colonists on the surface of Mars in sci-fi outing *Ghosts of Mars* (2001). Still, *The Fog* remains a (second tier) horror classic. It received an inevitable, and inevitably pointless, remake in 2005 with Selma Blair stepping into Barbeau's shoes, lots of CG and a bunch of photogenic teens in the supporting roles.

In comparison Gary Sherman's *Dead & Buried* (1981) is a somewhat neglected genre piece. A small town horror thriller, it's set in the coastal community of Potter's Bluff where the local sheriff (James Farentino) is investigating a perplexing series of tourist murders. Showcasing some grisly special effects make-up by the legendary Stan Winston, Sherman's film also boasts an early role from Robert "Freddy Krueger" Englund and a script credit for Dan O'Bannon. The result was one of those little-known efforts that horror fans often become passionate about, much like the director's previous film *Death Line* (1972) which featured cannibals stalking commuters on the London Underground.

Although Sherman had originally planned to make a rather black comedy, the gore-hungry video market of the early 1980s meant that his financial backers were keen to play up the nastier elements of Winston's make-up effects – even ordering reshoots of the villain's acid-in-the-face demise to appeal to hardcore gore fans. Perhaps the most troubling sequence, though, involves the bandaged body of a badly burnt photographer who is attacked by the zombie townsfolk in the film's opening scene. Laid up in a hospital bed with his lips burnt off and his skin charred beyond all recognition, he receives a fatal hypodermic syringe to his one remaining eyeball during a visit from a sadistic zombie nurse. Ouch.

As the college-educated sheriff struggling to explain the sudden spike in the sleepy town's murder rate, Farentino holds the film together right up until its cheating ending where we realise just how much wool has been pulled over our eyes.

Predating David Lynch's obsession with small town values twisted into perversity, *Dead & Buried*'s ghoulish scares recall *Messiah of Evil* and *Deathdream*. It also creates a memorably freakish villain in the guise of the town's myopic mortician G. William Dobbs (Jack Albertson). His passionate interest in restoring dead bodies to lifelike beauty leads him to dabble in some questionable professional ethics.

A lap dissolve sequence in which he demolishes and then rebuilds a dead woman's skull in preparation for her open casket takes the film's obsession with dead flesh into disturbing territory, not least of all because its gory horrors are accompanied by the bubbly, upbeat strains of Glenn Miller's "Serenade in Blue". It's enough to ensure that, while the film's ending is something of a swizz, *Dead & Buried* is a memorable little chiller.

Most of the American movies that followed in its wake were best forgotten. The Italian zombie cycle frequently pushed the boundaries of what constituted acceptable violence, provoking repressive measures like the UK's Video Recordings Act along the way. In contrast the trashy American movies that dominated the 1980s rarely upset the censor at all in their desire to appeal to the teen market.

One sure sign that the zombie had gone from censors' nightmare to mainstream icon was its appearance in Michael Jackson's smash hit music video *Thriller* (1983). Poverty Row cheesiness segued into quick-cutting MTV visuals as Jackson's horror spoof video – directed by John Landis – riffed on vampires, werewolves and the living dead. Although the video's horror content was initially controversial, triggering complaints from parents concerned about its influence on the young, the singer's dance floor friendly song-and-dance routine effectively defused much of the criticism. The sight of Jackson sharing screen time with a motley collection of walking

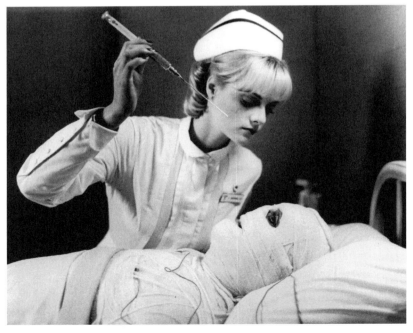

Dead & Buried (1981).

and *grooving* corpses helped make the zombie into a living room-friendly ghoul. After *Thriller* everyone and their grandmother knew what a zombie was.

Zombie movies remained largely marginal, though. Most outings were cheap and forgettable, occasionally enlivened by an odd bit of casting. Jack Bravman's tiresome *Zombie Nightmare* (1986) starred an aging Adam West from the original *Batman* TV show. Meanwhile, the execrable *Revenge of the Living Zombies* (1989) was produced, directed and bolstered by a central performance from Bill Hinzman, whose dubious claim to fame was that he'd starred as the first ghoul in Romero's *Night of the Living Dead* some twenty years earlier. That really didn't give him a license to dump this pile of steaming celluloid crud in our laps.

Armand Mastroianni's *The Supernaturals* (1986) featured a platoon of modern-day squaddies led by Nichelle Nichols (better known as *Star Trek*'s Lieutenant Uhura) who are attacked by zombie corpses from the Civil War. More Rebel zombies turned up to whistle Dixie in the cannily titled but dirt cheap *Curse of the Cannibal Confederates* (1982), in which hunters are set upon by zombies left over from the war. Then there was *Ghost Brigade* (aka *The Lost Brigade*, *The Killing Box*, 1992), a classier outing starring a host of famous and soon-to-be-famous faces: Martin Sheen, Ray Wise, Billy Bob Thornton and Matt LeBlanc (the film is not to be confused with Australia's 1988 *Zombie Brigade*, about dead Vietnam veterans who return to life after an unscrupulous property developer bulldozes their memorial).

A few filmmakers tried to separate themselves from this morass of cinematic detritus by creating novel genre combinations. Director Samuel M. Sherman showed a great deal of chutzpah but little talent in *Raiders of the Living Dead* (1985). The title promised an ingenious combination of zombies and Indiana Jones yet it actually delivered a bloodless and boring tale. The buddy-cop cycle got a taste of zombie action in 1988's *Dead Heat* penned by Terry Black – the brother of *Lethal Weapon* scribe Shane Black – and directed by Mark Goldblatt. Meanwhile, in Hal Barwood's *Warning Sign* (1985) the tense laboratory setting of *The Andromeda Strain* (1971) was invaded by the living dead as a biochemical research station is

quarantined and its staff are turned into pissed-off ghouls. Considering the quality of the movie they were in, who could blame them for being annoyed?

Other combinations were even less subtle. Krishna Shah's *Hard Rock Zombies* (1984) billed itself as a horror-musical featuring Nazi gags, "hard rock" music and dismembered hands. It took bargain basement cinema to new lows with a cameo from Adolf Hitler. More entertaining was the short-lived cycle of parodies of 1950s movies including Marius Penczner's *I Was a Zombie for the F.B.I.* (1984), John Elias Michalakis's rock 'n' roll *I Was a Teenage Zombie* (1986) and Fred Dekker's sci-fi *Night of the Creeps* (1986).

The latter was easily the best of the bunch, a cult sci-fi comedy in which slithery, slug-like aliens turn human hosts into zombies. Tom Atkins gets all the best lines as a grumpy cop who helps college teens defend their campus from attack: "Zombies, exploding heads, creepy-crawlies… and a date for the formal. This is classic, Spanky."

Night of the Creeps has established itself as one of the most fondly remembered B-movies of the 1980s. Its knockabout tone – similar to that of Dekker's later kid-friendly horror comedy *The Monster Squad* – gives it an unlikely *joie de vivre*. It manages to play with B-movie clichés while subverting them.

Not every 1980s horror movie was so clever. Indeed, some filmmakers seemed to be deliberately aspiring to match the Poverty Row horrors of the past. *Beverly Hills Bodysnatchers* (1989) had a half-baked plot reminiscent of dire Monogram efforts like *Bowery at Midnight*. Such a lazy lack of ambition was further confirmed with the release of two lazy compilation movies – Ken Dixon's *Zombiethon* (1986) and Kenneth J. Hall's *Linnea Quigley's Horror Workout* (1989) – which featured bits and pieces of footage trimmed from a variety of living dead films.

However awful they were, these various productions indicated that the zombie had finally begun to achieve a degree of widespread acceptance. Decades earlier such a range of mass-marketed zombie movies would have been impossible imagine, but by the mid-1980s producers clearly believed that the majority of cinemagoers (or videocassette renters) were familiar enough with the premise to make the living dead a safe gamble. The period even saw the release of two zombie-themed TV movies: *The Midnight Hour* (1985) and *From the Dead of Night* (1989). Sadly, neither made very much of the living dead concept – although the skateboarding zombie of *From the Dead of Night* probably deserves a special, dishonourable mention for its sheer stupidity.

If anyone was in any doubt that the zombie had started to claw its way into the mainstream, Dan O'Bannon's hugely successful *The Return of the Living Dead* (1985) offered proof enough. A horror comedy that emerged from the shadow of Romero's legacy, it effectively trashed *Day of the Dead*'s box office receipts when it went head to head with that more serious zombie outing. Faced with the prospect of Romero's dark and gloomy horror-drama, or the madcap energy of *The Return of the Living Dead*, American audiences chose the latter and lapped up its gross gags, gross nudity (actress Linnea Quigley became a cult star on the basis of her performance as a punk who strips off in a graveyard for a quick dance) and fast-moving, fast-talking zombies.

The idea was conceived by *Night of the Living Dead*'s co-screenwriter John Russo and was partly based on his novelised sequel to Romero's 1968 classic. Originally Tobe Hooper was in the frame to direct, but the project became mired in extensive legal wrangling with Romero's lawyers over who had the rights to the "Living Dead" title. By the time the dust settled and *The Return of the Living Dead* went into production in 1984, things had changed: Russo was no longer attached, Hooper had dropped out, and screenwriter Dan O'Bannon had reworked the script and was preparing to direct it himself.

The Return of the Living Dead arrived in cinemas in August 1985, a month after *Day of the Dead*'s release. The arrival of two zombie movies so close together inevitably confused audiences – and Romero was frequently linked to *The Return of the Living Dead* even though he wasn't involved in the series.[162]

It's difficult to imagine two more different movies: *Day* is intelligent, sophisticated splatter that aspires to be more than just a gore movie. *Return* is a breathless horror cartoon that aspires simply to make jaws drop to the floor through its sheer exuberant excess. "I just couldn't visualise a straight horror movie at this juncture in history," O'Bannon confessed to *Cinefantastique* magazine.[163]

At least *The Return of the Living Dead* was more than respectful when it came to doffing its cap to Romero's influence. The movie opens at a Kentucky warehouse belonging to the Uneeda Medical Supplies Company ("You need it, we've got it") where know-it-all, foreman Frank (James Karen) is showing off to young hire Freddy (Thom Mathews). Taking the new kid down into the basement, Frank talks to him about the movie *Night of the Living Dead* and reveals a corporate secret: the film was actually based on a real incident.

As Frank tells it, the dead really did return to life in Pittsburgh in the mid-1960s after an industrial chemical designed by the military for spraying on marijuana crops turned out to have an unusual effect on dead bodies. Hushed up by the government and the US Army, the incident became the inspiration for Romero's horror masterpiece.

Decades later, a couple of sealed drums containing desiccated zombie corpses and a copious amount of the reanimating chemical still exist. One particularly leaky barrel has ended up in this Louisville warehouse due to an admin error. Eager to impress his young protégé, Frank shows him where the deadly reanimating fluid is stored and accidentally releases a brains-hungry living dead ghoul.

Unfortunately, the 1968 movie wasn't an accurate version of the truth: once unleashed, these ghouls can't be killed with a shot to the head. In fact, they're almost completely unstoppable. Frank and Freddy manage to incinerate the ghoul in the nearby mortuary, but not before they've been exposed to the reanimating chemical and start to turn. Meanwhile, it turns out that burning the body simply contaminates the air and causing a toxic rain shower to reanimate the dead. In the graveyard, an illicit party hosted by a bunch of meathead punks is gatecrashed by the ravenous, reanimated dead.

With its madcap, take-no-prisoners energy, *The Return of the Living Dead* was a million miles removed from the dark pessimism of Romero's *Day of the Dead*. No philosophical musing here, just buckets and buckets of gore and a post-punk aesthetic in which anything goes (from nude punkettes to split-in-half zombie dogs). The gags fly thick and fast but can't keep up with the adrenalin-charged ghouls themselves – who tear around the screen at a breakneck pace while chattering away. "Send more paramedics" demands one smart zombie into a walkie-talkie after feasting on an unlucky ambulance crew.

At the heart of *The Return of the Living Dead* is a savage kind of comedy, a nihilistic punk mentality that considers nothing to be sacred. Featuring a band of grubby punks led by "Trash" (Quigley) and "Suicide" (Mark Venturini), the film is hardly coy about its attempt to appeal to the alienated teen audiences of mid-1980s shopping mall culture. It even has a soundtrack that features The Damned, The Cramps and The Flesheaters. In keeping with its attempt to be both hip, humorous and horrific, the end of the world is greeted with open arms by the filmmakers, who positively revel in the destruction of Louisville, KY.

Every attempt to deal with the crisis, from firing up the local morgue's incinerator to the military's decision to drop a nuke on the city simply makes the whole sorry mess much, much worse. The end result is the horror equivalent of *MAD Magazine* – a brash rejection of anything serious that invites us to giggle while the world goes up in smoke. It's an entertaining ride featuring some truly sunning special effects, not least of all the now infamous "Tarman" zombie, a dripping mass of putrid flesh. Yet, although it remains a firm fan favourite, *The Return of the Living Dead* ultimately has very little to say. Perhaps if someone had listened to the zombies' repeated demands for "Brains!" its legacy and influence might have matched its impressive box office returns.

The Return of the Living Dead's blend of punk nihilism and sick humour was successful enough to spawn several sequels. Ken Weiderhorn's unimaginatively titled *Return of the Living Dead Part II* (1987) did little except lamely retread the same material without a single glimmer of originality – actors James Karen and Thom Matthews were forced to reprise much the same roles and go through the lengthy process of being turned into zombies all over again.

A few years later Brian Yuzna's *Return of the Living Dead 3* (1993) tried to revive the franchise with a more leftfield approach, introducing a Romeo and Juliet love affair between hero Curt (J. Trevor Edmond) and his zombified girlfriend Julie (Mindy Clark). Julie's attempt to stave off her hunger for her boyfriends brains sees her piercing her dead flesh with nipple rings, chains and various body modification accoutrements – all of which

seems in keeping with the series's appeal to punk and Goth kids.

After a long hiatus, the series limped back again for *Return of the Living Dead: Necropolis* (2005) and *Return of the Living Dead: Rave to the Grave* (2005). Shot back-to-back in Romania and the Ukraine by director Ellory Elkayem – who had proved his genre mettle on arachnid horror *Eight Legged Freaks* – these two belated outings didn't save the franchise from spiralling into oblivion.

By playing up the comedy as well as the gore, the original *Return of the Living Dead* successfully broke out of the zombie ghetto and became a mainstream hit. The need to match horror with laughs as the 1980s became increasingly conservative was something that many filmmakers were becoming increasingly aware of.[164]

Sam Raimi's experience with *The Evil Dead* (1982) serves as an illuminating case in point. Though not strictly a zombie movie – its ghouls are dead bodies possessed by demons rather than walking corpses – Raimi's splatterfest follows Ash (Bruce Campbell), a hapless twenty-something who finds himself forced to confront demons from another dimension when a vacation in a log cabin goes horribly wrong. After his friends unleash the evil power of the Necronomicon, Ash has to fend off a seemingly never-ending array of demons, zombies and ghouls. Since none of these evil creatures can be "killed," he has to obliterate them, cutting up the dead bodies of his friends so that the evil spirits can't use them against him.

A groundbreaking example of what a budding filmmaker can do with a few bucks, a homemade Steadicam and some ingenuity in the special effects department, *The Evil Dead* was full of barf bag laughs – all of which were a result of Raimi's sheer unwillingness to compromise on the scares. Exaggerating the gore of the conventional horror film to epic proportions, *The Evil Dead* was so horrific it became hilarious.

When it arrived in the UK, the British Board of Film Classification was split. "Reaction within the BBFC was divided between those who felt the film was so ridiculously 'over the top' that it could not be taken seriously, and those who found it 'nauseating'".[165] It was passed for cinema showings with an X certificate and 49 seconds of cuts (mostly to scenes of axe violence, eye-gouging and a pencil being twisted in a leg).

On video cassette in the UK, though, the film become a notorious "Video Nasty" after it was included on the Director of Public Prosecution's list of video titles. Chased through the courts and seized from stores, *The Evil Dead* was vilified by politicians, moral guardians and media commentators as indicative of a specific kind of horror movie – a movie that could corrupt and deprave the young and innocent.

Raimi, who'd set out to make an outrageous scary movie rather than rip the social fabric of 1980s Great Britain apart, was understandably upset; particularly when the UK press and courts declared both the film and its American makers morally corrupt.

Raimi's response was to change his focus. Two years later he practically remade *The Evil Dead* in its sequel *Evil Dead II*. Mixing the splatter of *The Evil Dead* with *Three Stooges*-style slapstick, Raimi effectively pulled the rug out from under the censors' feet. If it was funny as well as violent, was it possible to brand it morally corrupt? Notably, the sequel received a much easier ride from Britain and America's moral guardians.

By the time of the third *Evil Dead* film, *Army of Darkness* (1992), the balance had tipped so far that the horror was virtually non-existent. Here Ash is cast back into the Middle Ages to battle yet more demons with his chainsaw and trusty "boom-stick". Despite the bigger budget and Campbell's enthusiastic performance, the splatter took a back seat. Still, that didn't stop the square-jawed actor becoming deified by fans for his effortless ability to dispatch hordes of zombie demons with a shotgun blast and a cry of "Groovy! Hail to the king, baby!"

Twenty years later, Raimi and Campbell produced a grim and rather po-faced reboot, *Evil Dead* (2013). Shot in New Zealand by Urugyan-born director Fede Alvarez, it was a totally unnecessary attempt to bring the franchise back from the dead. Refusing to be seduced by CG, Alvarez stayed with old school practical effects and stepped carefully around the humour. History had apparently affected horror fans' memories, since no one seemed to be able to agree whether the original *Evil Dead* was funny or violent.

For Alvarez, though, the reboot aimed to push boundaries. It was a gory movie designed to traumatise its audience, a throwback to the VHS-era. No matter how outrageous the gore becomes,

it's not supposed to be funny. Released almost thirty years after the Video Recordings Act became law in Britain, the new *Evil Dead* took the series full circle. Its appeal to horror fans was that it was a retro "Video Nasty".

"There is a line that Sam always talks about, the line between horror and comedy," Alvarez told interviewers. "You go too far and everyone starts laughing, but if you hit the right place everyone is scared to death. We were always standing on that line. And sometimes gore can be very funny, guts falling out blood splashing all over the place. It's not that kind of gory film. It is has a lot of blood. A lot of blood. I would come back home every day after shooting covered in blood… It is a very gory film. People had to cover themselves in plastic bags because there was blood and splatter everywhere."[166]

If there's a comparison to be drawn between the original *Evil Dead* series and the *Return of the Living Dead* films, it's that both indulge in a demented kind of gory comedy. Harking back to Romero's custard pie splatter in *Dawn of the Dead*, both series prove less interested in social commentary than physical comedy.

Bizarrely, their "splatstick" owes more than a nod to the work of slapstick comedians like Buster Keaton and Laurel and Hardy. "The Three Stooges were a great influence on [*The Evil Dead*]," Raimi admitted not long after *Evil Dead*'s release. "When the light bulb fills up with blood and the blood comes out of the sockets, there's a Stooges episode called "A Plumbing We Will Go" [where] they hook up all the pipes and it fills the light bulbs with water and they hook up the water supply to the electrical system. The gas ring pours water and out of the television pours water, so I just took that idea and entirely changed it to horror – they're so close anyway. The Stooges are *so* violent."[167]

Inviting audiences to either laugh or barf, splatstick was perfect for the zombie movie. In splatstick cinema, the human body becomes an object of ridicule rather than abjection – a faulty machine that doesn't seem to realise quite how ludicrously gross its mass of internal fluids and red matter actually is. Replacing slapstick soda siphons and custard pies with blood and pus, the audience gets the chance to laugh and scream (and possibly vomit) simultaneously. Naturally, almost every splatstick movie featured zombies: what other monster was better suited to express our revulsion towards the physical realm than a walking corpse?

Unlike the dark, unrelenting nihilism of the Italian zombie cycle, splatstick films confront the abject with a buoyant sense of playfulness. There is horror and disgust in their visions of bodily trauma and secretions. But it's neutered by the desire to play everything for yucky yuk-yuk-yuks. Judging by these movies, the uncaring universe that Fulci introduced audiences to apparently has its own internal sense of comic logic.

In *Evil Dead II*, Ash is forced to amputate his hand. This possessed zombie appendage then scampers off and continues to taunt him by very literally flipping him the finger. Just as Oliver Hardy was resigned to the fact that life was a never-ending series of pratfalls, so splatstick heroes have to accept that their bodies are awkward and often ludicrous hunks of flesh.

One of the finest splatstick zombie movies was Stuart Gordon's *Re-Animator* (1985). Released a couple of months after the first *Return of the Living Dead* outing, it was a gory comic book homage to writer H. P. Lovecraft, whose six-part short story series "Herbert West – Reanimator" was the film's loose source. Much like *Return of the Living Dead*, *Re-Animator* marked itself out thanks to its irreverent, anything-goes mentality.

Piling on the gags without losing sight of the gore or the scares, *Re-Animator* proved a brilliant blend of humour and horror. Gordon keeps his tongue firmly wedged in his very bloody cheek at all times. In this movie, zombiedom becomes the ultimate cosmic joke in an uncaring, cruel universe. When fanatical science student Herbert West (Jeffrey Combs) invents a serum that can bring the dead back to life, Gordon unleashes all manner of chaos including reanimated cats; writhing, snake-like intestines; and various morgue residents running amok.

West's chief antagonist is Dr Hill (David Gale), a faculty member at the Miskatonic University who discovers the wild-eyed student's experiments and plans to steal the serum for himself. In the ensuing chaos, Hill is killed and returns as a decapitated zombie. While Hill's cantankerous, disembodied head plots world domination, his body proves to be a real stumbling block to achieving his plans – quite literally, as the headless cadaver careens about the morgue knocking into doors and walls.

Shot in just eighteen days on a skimpy budget *Re-Animator* is, as intrepid *Fangoria* correspondent Chas Balun later argued, the horror movie equivalent of a Ramones song. "It calls to mind the primal power, the focussed ferocity and the gleeful sense of all-out fun found in all the best rock 'n' roll tracks. *Re-Animator* shares a common bond with the best kick-ass rock around too – a simple formula for success known by all True Believers: 'Three chords and the truth'."[168]

The punk rock analogy is an inspired way of understanding the appeal of *Return of the Living Dead*, *Re-Animator* and other similar splatstick comedies. These are stripped down, rollicking movies whose only aim is to push against the conventional, the stuffy and the boring. Convinced that enough comedy can let you get away with almost anything, these films push the boundaries of violence and gore with a nod, a wink and a ghoulish grin. Scaling the heights of bad taste, splatstick possesses a degree of outrageousness that few other horror movies can match (consider, for instance, the infamous scene of a decapitated zombie head giving head in *Re-Animator*).

The laugh or barf humour doesn't always defuse the horror behind such envelope-pushing assaults on the sanctity of the flesh, though. *Re-Animator* certainly courted its fair share of controversy and fell foul of the MPAA, who objected to the extent of its gore. "They told us we would have to cut everything after the second reel," claimed Gordon. "Too much blood; this has to go, that has to go… if we'd done everything they 'suggested' we'd have ended up without about a half hour of film left."[169]

In keeping with its punk mentality, the film was eventually released unrated to well-deserved acclaim. It was startlingly well received and spawned two sequels: *Bride of Re-Animator* (1991), which followed much the same pattern as the original while lampooning *The Bride of Frankenstein*; and *Beyond Re-Animator* (2003), which sent West to prison for his crimes against the dead.

Neither film matched its predecessor and the series currently hangs in limbo. In 2011 Gordon headed back to his roots in the theatre – he founded Chicago's famed Organic Theater Company in the 1970s – and revived the series for the stage as *Re-Animator: The Musical*. It was an unlikely, but critically acclaimed, return to form.

Undoubtedly the most influential splatstick filmmaker was New Zealand's Peter Jackson, whose love of the living dead gave the world two of the yuckiest zombie movies ever made. Shot over four years on a scraped together budget ("Mum & Dad" are pointedly credited as special assistants to the producer), *Bad Taste* (1987) is a perfect example of splatstick's lo-fi, lowbrow, DIY punk aesthetic. It comes with enough gleeful energy to sustain its shoddy production values and its cascade of gore is so relentless it papers over the film's various technical flaws.

Evolving from a short called "Roast of the Day", *Bad Taste* survived the departure of its original leading man (Craig Smith, who got married and couldn't commit his weekends to filming) after Jackson scored development cash from the New Zealand Film Commission. Jim Booth, his mentor at the Commission, advised him not to show the bureaucrats the rushes since "they wouldn't understand". He was right; when they finally saw it they were outraged.

The production's on-the-hoof ingenuity accounts for much of *Bad Taste*'s appeal. Its story of aliens turning the population of a small New Zealand town into denim wearing zombies becomes a jumping off point for a series of gross gags. Jackson delivers the bad taste promised by the title: characters sup from a bowl of vomit; there are AIDS gags, sledgehammer lobotomies and a climax involving a rebirth-by-chainsaw. It is, as Kim Newman described it in the pages of the UK's *Monthly Film Bulletin*, "some kind of triumph in its horror-comic verve, settling into the genre next to the excesses of *Dawn of the Dead*, *Street Trash* and *The Evil Dead*."[170]

Jackson's next zombie outing, *Braindead* (1992) was the apotheosis of the splatstick cycle, a catalogue of viscera that builds to a double climax: one featuring a giant zombie mother monster; the other featuring a thirty-five minute stretch of mayhem in which a house full of zombies and partygoers are reduced to mush by each other – and a lawnmower. Ambitiously set in 1950s New Zealand, *Braindead* proved to be the most technically accomplished film of Jackson's budding career, featuring a fully fledged storyline, a remarkable series of special effects, and a finely honed comic sensibility.

The film's hero is Lionel (Timothy Balme), a twenty five year old mummy's boy who's kept on a tight leash by domineering, widowed matriarch Vera (Elizabeth Moody). When local shopkeeper's daughter Pacquita (Diana Peñalver) asks Lionel out on an illicit date to the zoo, Vera follows to spy on them.

Snooping on the lovers between the animal cages, Vera gets bitten by a rare rat monkey. The creature carries a deadly disease that turns anyone infected by it into a zombie. Vera quickly falls ill and, not long after she scoffs a pet dog, she's declared dead by the district nurse. Of course, she quickly returns as ghoul then quickly disposes of the nurse – who also comes back as a ravenous zombie.

Crippled by a sense of social embarrassment, Lionel tries to cover up his mother's illness by locking the ghouls in the basement. He does his best to keep a lid on ever-growing family of ghouls, but they eventually break out and run riot in suburban Wellington.

Braindead takes the splatstick of *Bad Taste* to its inevitable – and hilariously yucky – conclusion. It's a truly outrageous film: zombies are cut up with lawnmowers, meat cleavers and kitchen appliances; a zombie baby in a romper suit goes on the rampage; and entrails slither around with a murderous will of their own (while the attached anus farts with the exertion).

It's not just the gore that's outrageous. Jackson gets great comic mileage by setting this bloody horror in the buttoned down world of 1950s New Zealand – where *The Archers* plays on the radio and the Queen's portrait hangs in the living room. This is an uptight world that can't cope with the embarrassingly gloopy and mucky realities of the body, a world that is too repressed for its own good.

As Lionel battles his enormous, pus-dripping zombie mother in the film's climax, *Braindead* even has the chutzpah to grapple with Freudian and Lacanian theories of the Oedipus Complex and the Monstrous Feminine. But it's real subtext is about another parent/child relationship: New Zealand bucking against the monstrous matriarchy of the Commonwealth. Being zombified in *Braindead* becomes a metaphor for New Zealand's experience of being ruled by the declining post-war British Empire. Unlike *Bad Taste*, *Braindead* is a film that resolutely refuses to live up to its title.

CHAPTER EIGHT

THE NEW DAWN OF THE DEAD

I. NIGHT OF THE LIVING DEAD REDUX

The 1990s began with an announcement that caused equal parts elation and despair among George Romero's loyal fans: *Night of the Living Dead* was to be updated for the new decade in a colour remake. Reactions were mixed. The news that Tom Savini was signed up to direct from a script by Romero was encouraging, but the fact that it was being backed by a big Hollywood studio, Columbia Pictures, was less so. Worse still Romero, who was acting as producer, seemed convinced that the main impetus behind the remake was economic rather than artistic. "From my standpoint," the director bluntly told *The Wall Street Journal*, "this [remake] is purely financial."[171] While such comments made the project seem alarmingly mercenary, those familiar with the disastrous distribution history of the original film could only sympathise with the director's motivation. Although the black & white drive-in classic had made millions of dollars following its release in 1968, none of the original filmmakers had seen anything like their fair share of the profits. Questionable distribution practices and bankruptcy filings had taken their toll. Most damaging, though, was the embarrassing realisation that the copyright line had accidentally been left off the original print's title – which allowed bootleggers to pirate the film without fear of legal repercussion.

In a belated attempt to claw back some extra dollars in revenue, a colourised version of the film was released on video in the 1980s. However, it did little to balance the books. The 1990 remake was designed to maximise the franchise's profitability with a big-budget publicity campaign.

The chief hurdle Savini faced in remaking the film was the over-familiarity of the living dead. "I had to try and make zombies scary again," he told *Cinefantastique* magazine citing Joe Piscopo's Miller Lite beer commercial (which parodied *Night of the Living Dead*) and Michael Jackson's *Thriller* video as two reasons why zombies had lost their shock factor. "I had to reiterate that these are dead people walking around [and I wanted] to reiterate in the audience's mind: death, dead, these are poor dead people."[172]

With Savini in the director's chair instead of handling special effects, it was left to make-up artists John Vulich and Everett Burrell to come up with a suitably scary collection of ghouls. "Because it's been done to death (pun intended) the image of the zombies as these horrendous, bloody, torn apart creatures just wasn't scary enough anymore," they told *Starburst*. "We wanted to make our zombies scary by injecting a strong sense of realism into their appearance. By going with a slightly emaciated look we wanted the audience to believe that they are their next door neighbours, accident victims, victims of disease and corpses which had long been laying in their graves and returned to life."[173]

The artists attended autopsies and studied concentration camp photos to help them discover the right degree of realism – an admission that stirred up some controversy at the time of the film's release.

Despite the good intentions of the filmmakers, things didn't turn out quite as planned. The shoot was fraught with tension and bickering as Savini fell out with certain members of the crew and became tied up in messy divorce proceedings at home. "There were people involved in the [original version of *Night*] who really resented the fact that George chose me to direct this movie. Some of them are directors themselves. They resented me." [174]

As a result, the finished film was only a shadow of what Savini had hoped to make: "It's forty percent – maybe forty percent – of what I'd intended to do," he explained years later. [175]

In spite of such troubling circumstances, the remake turned out to be a welcome addition to Romero's living dead universe. Returning to the original with a fresh eye, Romero and Savini crafted a thoroughly ironic pastiche that wasn't afraid to break with audiences' expectations. Typical of the script's iconoclasm is the opening graveyard scene, which deliberately wrong-foots anyone familiar with the 1968 film. Most fans thought they knew what to expect as Johnnie (Bill Moseley) and Barbara (Patricia Tallman) arrive at their father's grave. But Romero and Savini have plenty of tricks up their sleeve. The man who lumbers towards them turns out to be the cemetery's caretaker, not the zombie we expect. It's a cheeky reworking of one of the seminal moments in horror history and it elicits a knowing giggle from the audience that quickly turns to shock as a real zombie suddenly rushes into the frame and attacks Johnnie. We're left deliriously off-balance.

The most fundamental change in the new screenplay is its feminism. Focusing his attention on issues of gender rather than race, Romero plays down the role of black hero Ben (Tony Todd) in favour of transforming the character of Barbara. No longer the passive, near-catatonic victim of the 1968 film, she is now a proactive, gun-toting heroine. A clear descendant of Sigourney Weaver's ass-kicking Ripley in the *Alien* series, Barbara is the only member of the group who's capable of recognising the zombie threat for what it really is and responding to it in an effective manner. While the men argue over issues of territoriality (Who gets the gun? Who's in charge? Which is safer, the cellar or the ground floor?), Barbara faces up to

the return of the repressed that the zombies represent. Instead of barricading herself inside the house, she decides to confront the threat and goes outside among the slow-moving ghouls. In psychoanalytic terms, she's the only character who doesn't retreat into the compromised safety of the unconscious (the cellar, the attic) to try and escape the horror. Instead, she faces it head on.

For academic Barry Keith Grant, Barbara's transformation suggests that "Romero has returned to his original zombie narrative and fashioned a more politically progressive view than in the original, particularly in terms of the feminist issues raised by the first *Night of the Living Dead*'s influence on the subsequent development of the genre." [176] Although race recedes into the background, the remake "encapsulates the trilogy's depiction of patriarchy" by making "hysterical masculinity" more frightening than the zombies themselves. [177]

Romero's living dead trilogy has always been interested in subverting the conventions of gender roles. While the original character of Barbara may have been a terrified catatonic – prompting *Variety*'s reviewer to describe her as a "blathering idiot" – the heroines of *Dawn of the Dead* and *Day of the Dead* are strong, independent and resourceful women. Contrasting his heroines with the (macho, active) heroes and the (passive, feminised) zombies, Romero offers an understated critique of contemporary American culture. It's not just consumerism that turns us into soulless, shuffling zombies. Patriarchal culture does much the same ting – encouraging men to play violent war games that are braindead and driven by instinct.

As all-male SWAT teams and groups of survivalist rednecks run wild in the wake of the apocalypse, Romero suggests that a more rational response to the crisis may involve reconsidering traditional gender roles. Machismo will get you killed. Romero's heroines chart a different path as dynamic, rational and compassionate protagonists.

Of the three films in the original trilogy, *Dawn of the Dead* made the most of these gender issues. As Fran revokes her maternal, feminine status ("I'm not going to play den mother for you guys"), she initially seems determined to beat the boys at their own game, tooling up with all the symbols of patriarchal power from pistols to shotguns to helicopters. Playing both ends of the gender spectrum, she becomes a freakish symbol of extreme femininity and extreme masculinity combined: the scene in which she idly sits in one of the mall's beauty salons, caked in make-up, brandishing a revolver and admiring her reflection in the mirror makes her look like an Old West saloon girl and gunslinger rolled into one. It's a telling image of a woman being pulled in opposing directions.

By the time the bikers attack, Fran has realised just how dangerous this identity is. While Stephen is desperate to prove his shooting prowess and masculinity by battling the rampaging bikers, Fran embodies something different – a professionalism that allows her to be tough and sexy, masculine and feminine simultaneously. It's an identity that Peter seems to share, resorting to violence only when it's necessary and taking no pleasure in it. The insistent point of *Dawn of the Dead*, and the rest of the series, is that machismo is dangerous. Patriarchal culture, not the zombie, is the real monster.

The Savini-Romero remake of *Night of the Living Dead* makes this theme explicit. Like Fran, Barbara offers an alternative to machismo. She's a resolute professional whose response to the crisis is rational and yet still empathetic. In short, she's a survivalist who's willing to do whatever it takes to get through the living dead apocalypse without resorting to hysteria, vindictiveness or cruelty. While the men strut around the house "playing rooster," Barbara is the only person who manages to keep her head – something that, as we've already seen, always has great significance in Romero's universe.

The pivotal scene in this regard comes as Barbara tries to make the rest of the group understand that the hordes of ghouls outside aren't some strange breed of supernatural monster, but simply reanimated corpses. She realises that if they can be killed they can be defeated, which is why she objects to the hysterical reaction that everyone else has to the ghouls. To prove her point, she repeatedly shoots an approaching zombie in the chest while the rest of the group look on in shocked silence. "Is he dead? Is he dead?" she yells at them as the zombie continues its relentless advance. She then calmly puts a single bullet through the ghoul's forehead.

While it momentarily seems as though Barbara has slipped into hysteria, Romero's point is quite clear: Barbara is the only member of the group who hasn't lost her head. She's able to comprehend the facts of their situation and is capable of taking appropriate, effective action. The zombie threat isn't that dangerous at all – they can be stopped with a single bullet. All you need to do is remain calm, take a steady aim and have plenty of ammunition.

In contrast, Barbara's bickering male counterparts lose their heads at the first sign of trouble. They're too busy fighting with one another to make any effective plans. As Barbara tells them: "You can talk to me about losing it when you stop screaming at each other like a bunch of two-year-olds."

The extent to which Romero expects us to identify with Barbara's rationalism is apparent in the script's deft reversal of Cooper's death. In the original film, the cowardly businessman died after being shot by Ben in a moment of distinctly unheroic revenge. In the remake, Ben and Cooper have an extended – and utterly pointless – gunfight with each other while the zombies overrun the farmhouse. Their selfish and completely irrational actions destroy the group's chances of surviving the zombie attack. Only Barbara escapes, washing her hands of these pigheaded cowards characters and venturing out into the zombie-infested countryside alone.

When she returns to the farmhouse the next morning, Barbara discovers that Ben has become a zombie and that Cooper has survived the night by hiding in the attic. Emotionless, she shoots him in the head; then tells the posse of rednecks who she's travelling with that he was a zombie. It's a crowd-pleasing moment, in which Barbara takes revenge on the film's chief villain. But it's also a brilliant indication of Barbara's detached professionalism. Unlike the blind rage that leads Ben to kill Cooper in the original film, Barbara's violence is presented as an act of pragmatism rather than personal revenge. Barbara executes Cooper because his behaviour represents everything that is wrong with the dominant patriarchal order. People have died because of his arrogant, self-centred cowardice. Had Ben survived the night, we're left in no doubt that Barbara would have done the same to him. In this version of the story both men are as dangerous to those around them as one another.

The remake ends with Barbara surrounded by rednecks who cheerfully herd up the remaining living dead while taunting and torturing them. She looks on in disgust, muttering: "They're us and we're them." She may have the cold rationalism of a killer, but she can still empathise with the zombies. By failing to recognise the fact that the zombies were once human, the living risk becoming as dehumanised as the living dead. The film's conclusion suggests that while the zombie apocalypse may be contained, the patriarchal apocalypse in which rampant militarism, racism and sexism rule is only just beginning. The mask has finally slipped from the face of the civilised world and it seems that nothing can stop the new barbarism.

II. POVERTY ROW FOR THE MTV GENERATION (OR, CHILDREN SHOULDN'T PLAY WITH CAMCORDERS)

Savini's remake of *Night of the Living Dead* proved to be a modest critical and commercial success. It prompted Romero to give serious consideration to adding a fourth film to his original trilogy. Disappointed that the budgetary limitations of *Day of the Dead* had prevented him from bringing the story to a suitably grand conclusion, the filmmaker hoped that Savini's success might have a knock-on effect on his own plans. It was an idea that Romero repeatedly mentioned in interviews.

"I'd love to do a 1990s [instalment] that reflects the attitudes of this decade. It would be further on from the zombie rising, so there'd be fewer people but fewer zombies too, as they'd all have rotted away. And the zombies would just wander around us like the homeless or AIDS victims. They'd be kind of unwanted and annoying to have about, but you'd be used to them – you'd just step over them on the way to the shops. But there are so many fingers in the financial pie over the previous three films that I can't see it ever happening."[178]

In another interview in 2000, he continued: "For a long time I had this idea that I'd do one *Dead* film in each of the last four decades. And I jokingly said that maybe the last one should be called *Twilight of the Dead*, or, better yet, *Brunch of the Dead*, because I figured that the 1990s were all about ignoring problems anyway."[179]

Romero's legions of loyal fans were certainly excited, but their hope came to nothing. The filmmaker knew better than anyone that the logistics of such a post-apocalyptic conclusion to the series would require a budget bigger than any he'd be able to raise for an independent feature. Working within the Hollywood studio system was a possibility. But it would bring its own compromises, particularly the need to tone down his trademark splatter in order to secure the necessary rating. Plans for a fourth film, nominally titled *Dead Reckoning*, slowly withered and died.

As the decade continued, the chances of Romero finding anyone in Hollywood willing to back him in such a venture looked increasingly unlikely. American horror cinema was becoming increasingly mainstream. With franchises and personalities prized over innovative storylines, zombie movies were distinctly out of favour again. The biggest grossing horror stars of the decade were slashers like Freddy Krueger, Jason Voorhees, and Michael Myers; or the suave, intelligent cannibal Hannibal Lecter. Plans for a television series based on Romero's living dead trilogy were briefly mooted then quietly shelved. It seemed that the walking dead's time had been and gone.[180]

Although a few low-budget features went into production, they simply confirmed the bad news. Films as diverse as *The Laughing Dead* (1989), *The Dead Pit* (1989), *The Vineyard* (1989), *Nudist Colony of the Dead* (1991) and *My Boyfriend's Back* (1993) seemed destined to take the genre to new lows.

S. P. Somtow's *The Laughing Dead* had a busload of kids travelling to Mexico under the watchful eye of a Catholic priest. Once there, they become the victims of all kinds of Aztec shenanigans including a rather bizarre game of basketball between the living and the living dead.

The asylum-set story of Brett Leonard's *The Dead Pit* featured ghouls released from their eponymous pit by a ghostly doctor. They stalked the corridors of the hospital where he used to torture his patients. In *The Vineyard*, James Hong's

Chinese sorcerer tries to keep his youthful looks by killing pretty teens and burying them in his vineyard (the wine their decomposing bodies helps produce is apparently a very good vintage). Of course, they eventually crawl back from the grave to get their revenge.

Meanwhile, in Bob Balaban's tongue in cheek zombie love story *My Boyfriend's Back*, a high school student returns from the grave after being shot in a store robbery. He woos his prom queen girlfriend while trying not to eat her (literally, that is). The less said about *Nudist Colony of the Dead*, in which director Mark Pirro delivers a tiresome blend of musical numbers, naked performers and zombies at a nudist camp, the better. The title song's lyrics speak for themselves: "You'll be shaking in your boots, by corpses in their birthday suits. The horror mounts, the terror grows, these monsters have no use for clothes."

Zombies seemed destined to return to the graveyard. One group of fans were determined not to let the matter (or the dead) rest, though. In the absence of anyone making the kind of horror movies they wanted to watch, they decided to make their own instead. Inspired by the low-budget splatter tradition of the Italian cycle, these "Camcorder Coppolas" as they joking referred to themselves used the growing availability of cheap home video technology to produce their own independent features.

In much the same way as the Poverty Row studios of the 1940s had relied on the living dead to provide cheap horror scares, the Camcorder Coppolas took the living dead into the realm of energetic but decidedly amateur filmmaking. Dominated by a punk aesthetic in which technical ability was considered far less important than sheer enthusiasm, the shot-on-video (SOV) revolution was led by fans who were essentially teaching themselves the mechanics of filmmaking from the ground up – often while they were in the process of shooting. With little or no formal training, the results were often spectacularly bad. Eager directors roped in friends and family and forced them to fumble through semi-coherent scripts in productions plagued by horrendously incompetent sound, lighting, editing and camerawork. Amazingly, many of these truly amateurish productions were picked up for home video release by small, independent labels. They recognised that these films offered hardcore horror fans something that no one else at the time was.

The film that was largely responsible for initiating the SOV trend was J. R. Bookwalter's *The Dead Next Door* (1989). A true horror fan – and one time zombie extra on *Day of the Dead* – Bookwalter was fortunate enough to secure the patronage of director Sam Raimi while he was in production on *Evil Dead II*. Armed with a couple of thousand dollars of Raimi's money, Bookwalter put together enough additional cash to get his zombie opus off the ground and filmed and edited the production over the next four years.

Shot entirely in 8mm on a budget of around $125,000, the finished film is really little more than a home video feature marred by obvious budgetary constraints, some technical ineptitude and bad acting. Its moments of blackly comic hilarity were enough to make it into something of an underground horror hit, though, launching Bookwalter's career as an indie filmmaker.

Set in a post-apocalyptic world where the dead are inexplicably returning to life to feed off the living, *The Dead Next Door* is an uneven little film that cribs shamelessly from Romero. Rarely able to convince us that it's anything more than an enthusiastic fan film, it's let down by ketchup bottle gore effects, a cast who aren't always able to keep a straight face and threadbare production design that regularly verges on the unintentionally ludicrous (the cages that hold the captured zombies, for instance, are so flimsy they appear to have been made out of cardboard). It's only Bookwalter's occasional moments of ingenuity that propel the film forwards. These need to be patiently sought out, but are often worth the wait: a decapitated zombie head biting the fingers off a policeman's hand, only for the undigested digits to emerge from its bloody neck a few seconds later; or, a zombie armed with an electronic voice box whose cries of "Feed me, I'm hungry!" are eventually followed by a comical rendition of The Star Spangled Banner.

Despite its obvious shortcomings, the film was successful enough to trigger the SOV revolution. Soon backyard filmmakers all over America were turning to the zombie in the hope of aping Bookwalter's underground hit. The director was keen to distance himself from his many imitators simply because so many of the productions that clung to the coattails of *The Dead Next Door* were irredeemably bad.

"Right now I'm lumped in with every other loser with a camcorder, and it bothers me," Bookwalter complained. "A lot of people watch my movies and they see a big difference between what I'm doing and what the average Camcorder Coppola is doing, but the mentality is still there that I'm not making 'real' movies. So, I aspire to move up the next rung on the ladder."[181]

While it is easy to sympathise with Bookwalter's desire to put some distance between himself and the rest of the SOV crowd, the fact remained that *The Dead Next Door* was shoddy by mainstream standards. His follow-up, a sixty-minute feature entitled *Zombie Cop* (1991), added little to the zombie-with-a-badge theme that William Lustig's infinitely superior *Maniac Cop* (1988) had made its own.

As an amateur auteur, Bookwalter had plenty of company. Vaguely notable entries in the SOV cycle, which slowly evolved from camcorders to digital video as technology marched on, include *Working Stiffs* (1989), *The Zombie Army* (1991), *Living a Zombie Dream* (1996), *Meat Market* (2000), *Biohazardous* (2000), *Flesh Freaks* (2001), *Zombie Chronicles* (2001), *Zombie Campout* (2002), *Maplewoods* (2002), *Necropolis Awakened* (2003), *Hallow's End* (2003), *Blood of the Beast* (2003), *Dead Life* (2004), *The Legend of Diablo* (2004) and *The Stink of Flesh* (2004).

It wasn't a phenomenon limited to North America either: the poisonous *Zombie Toxin* (1998) was shot in England and a clutch of Irish fans produced the Emerald Isle's first zombie movie *Zombie Genocide* in 1993 (Irish film production being somewhat slower than Hollywood standards, another decade passed before zombies continued their assault in *Dead Meat* in 2004).

On the international film circuit, Germany became one of the most prolific producers of low-budget zombie horror with directors like Andreas Schnaas, Timo Rose and Olaf Ittenbach taking the living dead concept to the depths of the bargain basement. The list of dishonourable Teutonic cinema (some SOV, some a little classier) is a lengthy one that includes predominantly worthless trash like: *Zombie 90: Extreme Pestilence* (1990), the memorably titled *Urban Scumbags Vs. Countryside Zombies* (1992), *Premutos: Lord of the Living Dead* (orig. *Premutos: Der Gefallene Engel*, 1998), *Zombie: The Resurrection (1998), Mutation (1999), Legion of the Dead (2000), Midnight's Calling (2001), Mutation 2: Generation Dead (2001), Last Days of Humanity (2002) and Zombie Commando (2006).*

In other countries, SOV zombies proved equally popular. Argentina delivered madcap Peter Jackson homages in *Plaga Zombie* (1997) and its sequel *Plaga Zombie: Zona Mutante* (2001); Brazil stepped into the fray with the lo-fi but spirited *Zombio* (1999), and even France mustered a cheap *Re-Animator* rip off called *Trepanator* (1991) with a Jean Rollin cameo and a scene where a zombie rips its own head off and throws it after an escaping victim – in slow motion.

The undisputed king of the SOV era, however, was Kansas filmmaker Todd Sheets whose prolific output included *Zombie Rampage* (1991) *Zombie Bloodbath* (1993), *Zombie Bloodbath II: Rage of the Undead* (1994), *Zombie Bloodbath 3: Undead Armageddon* (2000) and many, many more. Sheets's one-man assault on the horror genre produced a stream of films some of which even he admitted were "unwatchable pieces of trashola". Looking through his oeuvre, it's difficult to find anything to counter that undeniably accurate assessment.[182] Lacking even the limited technical skill of Bookwalter, his movies are tedious exercises in zombie mayhem with little understanding of the bare essentials of cinematic storytelling.

Watching these Kansas backyard epics is rather like sitting through someone else's child's high school play; without any vested interest in the actors, you're left wincing at every mangled line of dialogue and stilted performance. With their extreme gore and micro-budgets these films were the bastard offspring of spaghetti horrors like *Zombie Creeping Flesh* and *Zombi Holocaust* crossed with the Poverty Row films of the 1940s.

During the SOV boom, Sheets proved unstoppable and impervious to bad reviews. Through his Extreme Entertainment production company, he built a career for himself an indie filmmaker. Clearly there was a niche market for his kind of no-frills, micro-budget zombie mayhem. The question was, why? A lot of the answer had to do with the gradual watering down of mainstream American horror in the 1990s as studio movies became increasingly homogenous, teen-focussed and unwilling to challenge the censors at the MPAA. The spectacle of violent bodily trauma offered by SOV films wasn't to be found in mainstream productions like *Scream*, which were only interested in appealing to the widest audience demographic possible.

It was a state of affairs that Sheets and his fellow filmmakers were keenly aware of. "Today it's all about what hot teen 'babe' is in the movie," Sheets complained in a mission statement he released online. "Or how many pop-hit bands are on the soundtrack, or how many endorsements and product tie-ins like Nike, Pepsi, etc. are in it, or how much it makes and costs to make. Who gives a shit?!? These twits, like the girl stars of *Scream* for instance, hate horror movies for the most part! The girls in *The Craft* were on TV interviews acting like they were embarrassed to be in a 'horror' movie… They all kept claiming that it wasn't fair to classify it as a horror-picture."[183]

Unlike the glossy, relatively high-budget productions that dominated 1990s studio horror – in particular the endless procession of serial killer movies targeted at the teenage demographic – the SOV market offered gore for gore's sake. Many of these films didn't bother to approach the MPAA for ratings, so circumvented the censors. Even if they did get apply for certification, it didn't matter if they received an NC-17 rating. It was considered a badge of honour and a sign that they hadn't sold out or skimped on the horror. While the results of their labours may not have been any good, these films did prove that there was an alternative to the dominant Hollywood hegemony.

Among the prevailing dross of the 1990s underground horror circuit, the odd gem did appear. The best example is Scooter McCrae's *Shatter Dead* (1993), an uneven but memorable SOV feature that offers a decidedly surreal take on the zombie apocalypse. Significantly, McCrae claimed that his inspiration for the film was his realisation that the Hollywood studios were no longer catering to the interests of horror fans like himself.

"I think that the major studios are incapable of producing what we used to know as the 'horror movie,' but they are certainly capable of producing what I would call a 'horror spectacle,' or what critics used to denigrate Dario Argento's films as being by calling them nothing more than 'scare machines'… Missing all the subtext of course. By

that they meant a film that was calculated to make the audience jump every few minutes with some kind of set piece scare or horrible death; and we all know how difficult that is, right…?"[184]

Eager to produce something radically different, McCrae wrote, directed and produced *Shatter Dead*. Combining the gauche pretentiousness of a film school project with occasional flashes of genre-bending brilliance, the film is set in a future world in which there is no more death. With the difference between life and death severely skewed, the living have taken to killing themselves young in order to keep their bodies youthful in living death. Once dead, these zombies can't be killed; the typical bullet to the brain does no more than mess up their faces.

The reason for this drastic change in life and death is apparently linked to the arrival of the Angel of Death, who comes to Earth in the guise of a woman and impregnates a mortal girl using a strap on dildo (none of this actually makes much sense within the film, but is heavily glossed in the video sleeve notes). "There's no more room in heaven, either" proclaims the tagline and with *Shatter Dead*'s decidedly leftfield sensibility established, the film proceeds to create a haphazard universe full of religious overtones and angst-ridden characters. Dismissing the empty gore shots of most SOV productions, this charts its own path and owes little more than a curt nod to Romero or any other zombie filmmaker.

In McCrae's film the dead coexist with the living, begging for food and spare change on the streets of this post-apocalyptic world and forming a new social underclass. "When death ends, life changes," argues the film and the implicit suggestion is that God has abandoned his creation, leaving the dead to wander without hope of redemption. Acting exactly like their living counterparts (they walk, talk and eat) these zombies aren't much of a threat, but their presence has had a disastrous effect on the global economy. Through this chaotic world wanders Susan (Stark Raven) a feisty, gun-toting heroine (albeit with a tendency to take her clothes off as often as possible) who vehemently hates the dead and is suspicious of the reconciliatory aims of the mysterious Preacher Man (Robert Wells).

Privileging grim surrealism over conventional horror, McCrae presents us with an upside down world which defies explanation. *Shatter Dead*'s catalogue of the sick, the perverse and the bizarre makes for memorable viewing: a gang of raiders attack the house where the woman carrying the Angel of Death's baby is hiding and shoot her with a shotgun, blasting the unborn foetus out of her belly; Susan's boyfriend slits his wrists, remarking "My sin is quite literally on my sleeve for eternity"; the zombies decide to hasten the deaths of the living by killing them themselves. A strange, frequently amateurish, but still quite ingenious, film *Shatter Dead* is a true genre oddity and a refreshing change from the rest of the decade's SOV zombie movies.

On the other side of the Atlantic, British director Andrew Parkinson's debut feature *I, Zombie: The Chronicles of Pain* (1998) may have been shot on 16mm but it shared the same DIY aesthetic as the American SOV market. A curious blend of extreme gore and existential angst, it tells the story of Mark (Giles Aspen), a young Ph.D. student who is bitten by a ghoul and slowly transforms into a zombie in a dank, West London bedsit. Isolated from his friends and family, and desperately in need of fresh flesh to survive, Mark preys on tramps and prostitutes to satisfy his bloodlust.

Described by its distributors as "an attempt to make the most relentlessly depressing film ever [...] a film with no jokes, no light relief, no MTV visuals, just an unrelenting downward spiral [into living death]", Parkinson's movie plays like a kitchen sink zombie drama as it casts an unflinching gaze over its hero's messy physical deterioration.[185] A stunning counterpoint to the teen horror that dominated the 1990s, this is a film with the courage not to pander to its audience, delivering instead a depressing and shocking onslaught of angst and gore.

Presenting the daily misery of Mark's condition with graphic and meticulous detail, Parkinson uses voiceover to great effect: "Had another black out this morning, woke up on the bathroom floor covered in puke. What a fucking mess." As Mark's physical state worsens, so too does his mental stability turning *I, Zombie* into the diary of a man in despair.

Reminiscent of the body horror of David Cronenberg's films, it certainly chronicles more than its fair share of pain, with some gruelling moments of self-inflicted violence. Patching his dead body together using a power drill and rusty metal sheeting, Mark is ultimately unable to save his decaying flesh. In the film's most wince-inducing moment, the hapless zombie accidentally pulls off his penis while masturbating. As much to do with the social and bodily alienation fostered by the AIDS crisis as zombies, Parkinson's grim nightmare is a disturbing example of a truly alternative horror cinema.

Parkinson's next feature film moved up to 35mm, demonstrating his ambition to strike out as an independent filmmaker. Replacing Mark's solitary suffering with that of a group of female zombies who live and feed together, *Dead Creatures* (2001) saw the director developing his technique and expanding his range. The film follows female zombies who pose as prostitutes to lure men back to their flat, and a zombie hunter who's determined to wipe out the scourge.

Parkinson's zombie apocalypse is a slow-burning event that unfolds at a steady pace. Groups of the infected hole up among the living, gradually spreading the disease as they feed. Where it will all end isn't certain, but it's a fascinating glimpse of an underground zombie community that gradually transforms the social order. It's also as far from the mainstream as one could image. As Parkinson told *Fangoria*, who released both films on their own in-house video label: "I don't think the audience for these films is massive but there are enough people out there who are tired of horror comedies and clever postmodern horror."[186]

Interestingly, *I, Zombie*, *Dead Creatures* and *Shatter Dead* fulfil Romero's aims for the 1990s zombie movie by tentatively approaching two of the issues that the Pittsburgh director had earmarked for his planned fourth film: homelessness and the impact of AIDS. In presenting their zombies as social outcasts rather than monsters, these films play up the 1990s concern with urban alienation and marginalisation and try – with varying degrees of success – to question our faith in social progress. From *I, Zombie*'s existential drama (in which Mark worries as much about paying his next gas bill as his deteriorating condition) to *Shatter Dead*'s panhandling zombies (one carries a sign reading, "Help. Dead. Sold arm for medical experiments. What next?"), the living dead become symbols of the forgotten underclass of the Reagan/Thatcher era.

III. OF DEATH, OF LOVE: AN INTERLUDE

I don't know how the epidemic started. All I know is that some people on the seventh night after their death come back to life… I call them "Returners" but frankly I can't understand why they're so anxious to return. The only way to get rid of them once and for all is to split their heads open – a spade'll do it or a dumdum bullet is best […] Is this the beginning of an invasion? Does it happen in all cemeteries or is [mine] the only one? Who knows? And in the end who cares? I'm just doing my job.

–Francesco Dellamorte (Rupert Everett) in *Dellamorte Dellamore*.

If the SOV phenomenon suggested that the zombie movie had moved beyond the world of Italian exploitation cinema into a cultural hinterland of fan productions, one 1990s movie redressed the balance. Michele Soavi's *Dellamorte Dellamore* (aka *The Cemetery Man*, 1993) starred Rupert Everett – possibly the most unlikely actor to appear in a modern zombie film – as a cemetery groundskeeper whose clients keep coming back to life. It became a perfect, if somewhat belated, swansong for the Italian cycle.

Loosely adapted from a popular mid-1980s Italian "*fumetti*" (an adult-focussed graphic novel) by Tiziano Sclavi entitled *Dylan Dog*, *Dellamorte Dellamore* follows Francesco on a blackly comic confrontation with death (and life). For reasons that are never explained, the dead bodies that are buried in the cemetery of the Italian town of Buffalora have a tendency to come back to life on the seventh night after their death. More concerned with keeping his job than in trying to explain the ins and outs of the matter to his bureaucratic superiors, Francesco simply deals with the zombies himself, quietly killing these "Returners" each night with the help of his retarded assistant Gnaghi (François Hadji-Lazaro) and an armoury full of hollow point bullets.

Francesco has been doing this for so long that it's become a matter of course. But after an erotic encounter with a woman known only as "She" (Anna Falchi), the widow of the town's most recently deceased, things start to go horribly wrong. Returning from his grave to find his wife and Francesco making the beast with two backs, Anna's husband is understandably annoyed and bites her in a fit of pique. Francesco is left with no choice but to live up to the Italian title's literal translation ("Of Death, Of Love") and shoot the woman he adores before she becomes a ghoul.

Except there's worse to come: Francesco later realises that She wasn't actually dead when he pulled the trigger. Driven insane by guilt and despair, he begins to lose his grip on the difference between the worlds of the living and the dead. Taking matters into his own hands, he starts killing the townsfolk *before* they're actually dead in order to save himself the trouble of dealing with them later. This prompts Death himself to pay him a rather peeved visit and demand that Francesco leave the dead and the living alone. Meanwhile, Francesco keeps running into women who look exactly like She and who seem to have the same amount of life expectancy.

According to Soavi, *Dellamorte Dellamore* "is not about the fear of dying; its concern is the fear of living."[187] Francesco's fear of life is all-too-apparent. Locking himself away behind the high walls of the cemetery grounds, he has effectively annexed himself from the land of the living. Francesco, an embodiment of 1990s apathy, turned sour, inhabits a world in which ignorance – and death – is bliss. At one particularly telling point in the story Gnaghi's television set broadcasts an important newsflash about the Gulf War, yet no one notices since they're too preoccupied killing the Returners.

Dellamorte Dellamore's nihilistic, fairy-tale tone stays faithful to Sclavi's original comic book. But, as the filmmakers themselves admitted, it has been considerably watered down. Screenwriter Gianni Romoli claimed that the original comic was "Too bitter, too negative and without any hope whatsoever […] Audiences would have slit their wrists watching a literal version of the book. I wrote five drafts of the script altogether, making the story less and less nihilistic, necrophiliac and pessimistic each time."[188]

As it stands, *Dellamorte Dellamore* is resoundingly bleak, although its moody tone is enlivened by some wonderfully sardonic humour. There are several deliciously perverse moments, from the reanimated severed head of the mayor's daughter that Gnaghi keeps inside a burnt-out TV set (they plan to get married) to the whole troupe of Boy Scouts who are killed in a traffic accident and then return en masse. Matching the script's dark wit, Soavi delivers an endless array of inventive camera angles and bold stylistic flourishes. One surreal shot is taken from *inside* the mouth of a decapitated head as it flies through the air while the film's concluding sequence makes an audacious reference to *Citizen Kane*.

Then there's the unlikely prospect of the film's star. More accustomed to costume dramas than blood and guts, Rupert Everett is an actor with a self-confessed hatred of the horror genre. No wonder he was so surprised to be eagerly courted by Soavi for the role of Francesco. The director handpicked him for the part because, somewhat bizarrely, the original comic book's zombie hunter was explicitly based on Everett's classical features (without the actor's knowledge). Soavi was determined to remain true to Sclavi's vision by casting Everett. According to one industry rumour, he even turned down a lucrative American offer to finance the film because the backers wanted him to cast Matt Dillon in the lead.

Everett was flattered by such attention into agreeing to make his horror debut despite his initial trepidation. In the end, the actor was impressed by the film's power: "Death here means emotional death, pop-arted into a mad, psychedelic fantasy" he said. "Sclavi's story is how he sees contemporary life in Italy: the people, the government, the mafia scandals, the bleak future. The living dead/Returners are us in effect, because we've all become so boring, so cauterised, so politically correct."[189]

It's telling that a Hollywoodised reboot – *Dylan Dog: Dead of Night* (2010) starring Brandon Ruth in the Everett role – ditched the Goth nihilism and Italian backdrop and took the concept to New Orleans instead. Paying lip service to the original Italian comic book, it recast its hero as a retired supernatural gumshoe and, inspired by *Buffy The Vampire Slayer*, followed him on a trawl through the city's underworld of vampire nightclubs and werewolf meat-packing warehouses. Along the way Dylan's recently deceased partner Marcus (Sam Huntington) returns as a slowly deteriorating zombie who has to choose between eating maggots or live human flesh. Updating the original robbed it of everything that made it work – not least of all its 1990s sensibility.

Back in 1994, Soavi claimed that he set out to make "a black fable about today's Blank Generation".[190] It's what gave *Dellamore, Dellamorte* its wickedly funny, sharply barbed vibe.

Trapped by his gloomy outlook and complete rejection of the world around him, Everett's cemetery slacker is significantly more zombified than any of the corpses that return from the dead. A fitting symbol of Blank Generation apathy and disengagement, Francesco is completely unable to find the energy to embrace life. As a result, he's only too eager to follow his charges to the grave: "Everything's shit. The only thing that's not shitty is sleep," he complains, adding, "I'd give my life to be dead." The joke is that in this cruel world there's not much chance of death being a very restful experience.

IV. THE RESIDENT EVIL EFFECT

As Romero battled to get his fourth zombie film off the ground, Bookwalter and Sheets played about in their backyards and Soavi brought the Italian cycle to a rousing climax, one intrepid member of the global entertainment industry was preparing to rescue the zombie from the margins. Determined to repackage the zombie as a mainstream monster and an icon of cool, this man was hell-bent on making a fortune out of the living dead. His credentials however, were rather unusual.

He wasn't a director or screenwriter but a producer. He didn't work in Hollywood but Tokyo. And he wasn't in the movie industry but the Japanese videogame market.

When Shinji Mikami was first given the brief for the project that would become one of the biggest selling videogames of the 1990s, he was spectacularly unimpressed. Summoned by the head of consumer research and development at Japanese videogame giant Capcom Inc., Mikami was told to develop a new horror adventure game for the emerging PlayStation console. His boss wanted him to emulate the model of *Sweet Home*, a best-selling haunted house game adapted from Kiyoshi Kurosawa's film of the same name. That title had been a huge success on the rival Nintendo console in Asia, and Capcom wanted to release something similar for the PlayStation.[191]

What surprised Mikami was how underdeveloped the brief was: all his boss wanted was a horror game that would garner a cult reputation among gamers in the lucrative PlayStation market. He wasn't concerned with what type of game it might be and he didn't have a long list of criteria that it had to adhere to.

"The director said, 'We don't have to sell a large number of games,'" Mikami later remembered. "Our goal is to create a game that is worth owning. It is enough if a total of 300,000 units for both Sony PlayStation and Sega Saturn can be sold.'"[192]

What they wanted was a prestige title that would help consolidate Capcom's reputation among owners of the new Sony console. What they got was *Biohazard* – released in Europe and America as *Resident Evil*. Premiering on the PlayStation in 1996, it became an overnight sensation. Over the next five years, it spawned five different versions and was so successful that it began to compete with the phenomenally successful *Tomb Raider* franchise in terms of multi-million dollar sales and brand name recognition.

"The main attraction of *Resident Evil* is FEAR," Mikami claimed. "I really wanted to make it as scary a game as possible."[193] With that in mind, he instructed his design team to focus on one particular horror monster: the walking dead.

Mikami had seen *Night of the Dead* while he was in junior high. But the main inspiration behind *Resident Evil* was Lucio Fulci's *Zombi 2*. "When I saw the movie I was dissatisfied with some of the plot twists and action sequences. I thought, "If I was making this movie, I'd do this or that differently." I thought it would be cool to make my own horror movie, but we went one better by making a videogame that captures the same sense of terror. I want *Resident Evil* to give the player the feeling that he's the main character in a horror movie.[194]

The game's set-up is deceptively simple as STARS (Special Tactics And Rescue Squad) officers are sent to the fictional Mid-West American town of Raccoon City to investigate a series of strange murders. Unbeknown to the team, an experimental virus has escaped from a secret laboratory belonging to the shadowy Umbrella Corporation and is turning the citizens of Raccoon City into flesh-eating zombies. When contact is lost with the first team, a second STARS group is sent to Raccoon and the player controls two of its members – Jill and Chris – as they search the eerie mansion where the outbreak is rumoured to have started.

Taking the films of Romero and Fulci as its starting point, *Resident Evil* single-handedly established the template for a new genre of videogame playing quickly dubbed "survival horror". Armed with a single gun and a limited amount of ammunition, *Resident Evil* plunges players into a game in which simple survival takes precedence over conventional ideas of winning. Since there are often too many zombies to be killed with the weapons available, survival depends on keeping your head.

Correctly guessing when to expend those ever-so precious bullets and when to simply run away from the advancing zombies is of vital importance, as is the ability to be able to rationally solve a set of basic puzzles. Perhaps that explains why the *Resident Evil* games were some of the first to star resourceful women as their player characters instead of the usual pixelated Rambo clones. As in Romero's films, macho heroics are of little use in the game's unforgiving world.

Moving through each level, players are confronted with a range of atmospheric locations that use carefully chosen sound effects like dripping water, breaking glass and the moans of off-screen zombies to heighten the tension. Much like a conventional horror movie, the game makes use of a creepy score interspersed with long sections of disturbing silence to help set up its scripted "shock" moments:

zombies smashing through the windows of a deserted hallway as the player's avatar walks along it or a pack of living dead dogs that suddenly leap into the playing area from off screen.

Forging similarities between the games themselves and the horror movies that inspired them seems to have been something of a deliberate ploy. The survival horror genre that *Resident Evil* helped to create – which evolved over the years through franchises like *Silent Hill*, *Left 4 Dead* and *Dead Space* – frequently draws on horror movies for inspiration and, more importantly, atmosphere.

As videogame commentator Steven Poole puts it, "Tense wandering in dark environments is interrupted with shocks, sudden appearances of blood-curdling monsters. Silence is interrupted by grating noise, making you jump and increasing your nervousness. The same sort of atmospheric virtue is present in the *Resident Evil* series of zombie videogames, which [...] lift wholesale the camera angles and action sequences from Romero's own classic zombie flicks such as *Dawn of the Dead*." What's interesting to Poole is why cinematic videogames so often take their cues from the horror genre. He suggests it's because "the horror genre can easily do away with character and plot; it is the detail of the monsters, the rhythm of the tension and shocks that matter."[195]

Intriguingly, the relationship between zombie movies and these videogames proved strangely reciprocal: *Resident Evil*'s success as a videogame franchise reinvigorated zombie cinema in the late 1990s and paved the way for the zombie renaissance that occurred in the 2000s. It was the first sign of the zombie's impending mutation into a crossmedia monster – a creature so adaptable it could jump from movies to games to comics and novels with ease.

Before the *Resident Evil* series, Asia's contribution to the zombie movie's evolution had been largely ignored in the West. That was rather ironic since Chinese folklore about the "jiangshi" – stiff-limbed, reanimated corpses that have some similarities with the Western concept of the zombie – actually dated back to the Qin Dynasty, if not earlier. Caught somewhere between a reanimated corpse and a vampire, the jiangshi were Chinese folklore staples.[196] From the 1970s onwards, Hong Kong cinema wasn't adverse to using zombie-like monsters. A handful of martial arts films employed

the reanimated dead among their chopsocky action sequences from the green-faced goons in the Shaw Brothers' *The Legend of the 7 Golden Vampires* (1973); the hopping zombie fighters of Hwa I. Hung's *Kung Fu Zombie* (1981); or the zombie sparring partners in Godfrey Ho's near-incoherent *Zombie Vs. Ninja* (1987). Other films gave the Western idea of zombies their own bizarre spins – not least of all *Revenge of the Zombies* (aka *Black Magic II*, 1976) which had a sorcerer in contemporary Hong Kong turning women into zombies by hammering nails into their craniums and using them as sex workers.

In contrast, Japan reached towards a sensibility that was closer to the apocalyptic, Western tradition. Cheap, end of the world movies like *The Living Dead in Tokyo Bay* (orig. *Batoru garu*, 1992) followed the now formulaic pattern of Romero's living dead outbreaks. Endearingly shoddy in the manner of the country's interminable *Godzilla* series, *The Living Dead in Tokyo Bay* has radioactivity from a crashed meteorite bringing the dead back to life to run riot through the capital while a perky Manga style heroine battles to save the day. It was distinctly undistinguished.

By the late 1990s, the Asian zombie movie found itself in the midst of an unexpected resurgence post-*Resident Evil*. A string of new releases featuring the living dead proved domestically successful and also had international appeal: Japanese entries included *Junk* (orig. *Shiryô-gari*, 1999), *Wild Zero* (1999), *Versus* (2000), *Stacy* (2001), *Battlefield Baseball* (orig. *Jigoku Kôshien*, 2003). In Hong Kong the slapstick antics of *Bio-Zombie* (orig. *Sang dut sau shut*, 1998; the title literally translates as "Petrified Fortune Corpse") proved surprisingly sweet.

"Where the hell are all these new Japanese zombie movies coming from?" wondered *Fangoria* magazine as these movies turned Japan into ground zero for the walking dead. Zombies were suddenly cool again and it was all thanks to the pixel ghouls of Shinji Mikami's survival horror console game.

None of these movies took themselves too seriously and, as *Junk*'s self-reflexive title hints, they weren't aiming for high art. They weren't even particularly frightening – especially not when compared to the J-horror menace of Japan's most successful horror movie of the period, *Ringu*. Instead they delivered throwaway bouts of zombie action.

Junk itself is as forgettable a film as one could ask for, a quick-paced no-brainer in which a couple of petty thieves are caught between the yakuza, the American military and flesh-eating ghouls after the usual army experiment goes balls up. Chock full of big guns, martial arts moves and entrail-ripping violence it's loud, it's brash and it amounts to very little. As far as director Atsushi Muroga was concerned, that was the whole point. "I kept the Japanese expression '*shitsu yori ryou*' in my mind at all times. This means 'less quality, more quantity.' I was geared to make the most extreme zombie film I could."[197]

Tetsuro Takeuchi's defiantly punkish *Wild Zero* is a similarly disposable trashfest that plays more like an ingenious promo video for its stars – riotous Japanese punk band Guitar Wolf – than a fully fledged horror film. Barefacedly acknowledging his lack of interest in cinema, the debut director made no secret of his belief that *Wild Zero* was meant as nothing more than a joke. "It's probably not a good idea for me to express this, but I'm not a person inspired by movies, someone who grew up with this school of ideas about movies being the best thing. I actually really hate that ideology."[198]

Wild Zero's kinetic style and deliberate flouting of the conventions of "good" moviemaking has a lot in common with a Troma Studios production. Chucking zombies, UFOs, aliens and manic teenagers into a fast-food blender of cross-cultural reference points, it's just as throwaway as the junk of *Junk* – although it's considerably wittier and much more fun.

Guitar Wolf's punk mayhem (sample lyrics "Blood Blood Baby Exploding Blood, Exploding Blood, Roaring Blood!") is perfectly suited to this kind of trash filmmaking. Their look – leather jackets and Elvis quiffs – suggests the band are more than happy to wear their influences on their sleeve. *Wild Zero*, which borrows liberally from movies like *Evil Dead II*, follows in the same vein.

Such tongue-in-cheek genre nods continued in Naoyuki Tomomatsu's bonkers *Stacy* in which girls aged between 15 and 17 suddenly start dying and coming back to life as wide-eyed, shuffling ghouls. Featuring zombie teens in sexualised school uniforms being blasted to bits by SWAT teams, it didn't take itself at all seriously – and it played the parody game with "Romero Repeat Kill" squads dispatched to kill the girls and chainsaws dubbed

"Bruce Campbell's Right Hand".

Of all these post-*Resident Evil* zombie outings, it's Ryuhei Kitamura's *Versus* that's the most visually impressive. It's also the most indebted to the aesthetics of videogames. No less trashy than *Junk*, *Wild Zero* or *Stacy*, this deliriously fast-paced film builds upon the kinetic visual style of über-cool Western movies like *The Matrix* and *El Mariachi* and videogames like *Street Fighter*.

Frantic, bloody and completely relentless, it pits its leather trench coat clad escaped convict Prisoner KSC2-303 (played by Tak Sakaguchi – an actor who looks rather disconcertingly like an Asian Johnny Depp) against an army of vengeful yakuza foot soldiers and zombies resurrected in a magical forest.

"Hong Kong and Korean movies are really powerful these days but Japanese films are not," explained the filmmaker when asked what inspired his distinctive visual style. "A director like John Woo has not appeared in Japan yet. I decided I would do it; I will direct great Japanese entertainment movies and show the samurai soul to the world."[199] The director's immodesty aside, there's an undeniable genius to *Versus*'s attempt to commit the frantic, multi-angle mayhem of a videogame onto celluloid.

Pilfering bits and piece of a dizzying array of American cultural products from *Highlander* to *Reservoir Dogs* and referencing every kinetic Asian movie of the last decade or so – including the director's earlier short *Down to Hell* (1996) – *Versus* offers breathtaking visual virtuosity and some decidedly bloody moments that are guaranteed to have horror fans cheering. In one sequence, the super-powered villain punches a hole through the head of a zombie creating a bloody tunnel between the front and the back of the ghoul's skull that the camera perilously zooms through. The following shot shows the gruesome aftermath of this exaggerated violence with hilarious irreverence: the zombie's eyeballs have been glued to the villain's hand by the sheer force of the blow.

Such audacity continued in *Battlefield Baseball*, a bizarre zombie/baseball movie hybrid about a game to the death (and beyond) between two league teams. Returning to the zombie genre after *Versus*, Tak Sakaguchi stars as an expert player called on to help a high school team defeat their ghoulish adversaries. Directed by Yudai Yamiguchi, screenwriter of *Versus*, *Battlefield Baseball*'s outrageous horror comedy cannily combined two of Japanese pop culture's great loves: the living dead and baseball.

When it came to genre-blending, though, *Battlefield Baseball* couldn't even start to compete with the wackiness of Takashi Miike's *The Happiness of the Katakuris* (*Katakuri-ke no kôfuku*, 2000). Hailed by critics as a cross between *Night of the Living Dead* and *The Sound of Music*, Miike's film was a high camp combination of thriller, family melodrama, horror movie and karaoke musical with a (sadly brief) scene in which zombies return from the grave for an impromptu song and dance number.

While Japanese cinema frequently used the success of the *Resident Evil* games as a jumping off point for unrelated zombie action, one Hong Kong movie was far more inventive. In *Bio-Zombie*, Hong Kong director Wilson Yip produced a witty homage to Romero and a forthright pastiche of the influence of videogames. Set in a suburban shopping mall, *Bio-Zombie* stars two loudmouthed VCD pirates, Woody Invincible (Jordan Chan) and Crazy Bee (Sam Lee), who get mixed up with an Iraqi biological weapon stored inside a Lucozade bottle.

After the virus is accidentally unleashed, residents of the shopping mall are transformed into zombies. Trapped inside this neon-lit prison of consumer goods, noodle bars and bootleg movie stores, Bee and Invincible join forces with the local beauty salon girls (Angela Tong and Tara Jayne) in a desperate escape attempt.

Making explicit references to the link between the living dead and videogames, *Bio-Zombie* includes a scene in which Bee, faced by zombies, has a sudden flashback to his hours of playing *House of the Dead*. Reliving his past glory in the video arcade, Bee has a flash of inspiration and realises that the best policy is to shoot the marauding ghouls in the head. Such knowing nods to the gaming world crop up again in a later tongue-in-cheek scene which stops the action in mid-flow as the principal characters' attributes, statistics and fighting abilities are flashed up on-screen. Such witty insouciance even extends to the film's loving Romero references, which encompass everything from the mall setting to Bee's blink-and-you'll-miss-it imitation of Scott H. Reiniger's escalator slide in *Dawn of the Dead*.

Lampooning the genre and its digital offspring, *Bio-Zombie* is one of the funniest horror comedies of the 1990s, a madcap adventure that blends the slacker ethos of Kevin Smith's indie cult favourite *Clerks* with Romero's apocalyptic vision. Invincible and Bee are an unlikely pair of heroes, who're more interested in watching *Titanic* for the umpteenth time and trying their luck with the salon girls than saving Hong Kong. Their foul-mouthed, cowardly antics in the face of the end of the world take Romero's obsession with bickering characters to a ludicrous extreme. An unofficial, and completely unrelated sequel, *Bio Cops* (orig. *Sheng hua te jing zhi sang shi ren wu*, 2000), followed much the same screwball tradition but couldn't recapture the magic.

V. BIG-BUDGET GHOULS

Resident Evil's success was something of a mixed blessing for George Romero. He was still struggling to get the planned fourth movie in his "Dead" series off the ground and had endured a frustrating period in Hollywood in the 1990s as a series of cherished projects stalled or got shelved. He'd earned more money out there that at any point in his career. But he was depressed by the endless meetings, studio politics and total lack of traction.

Yet, despite not having made a zombie movie since *Day of the Dead* in 1985, the Pittsburgh filmmaker was the "Don of the Dead" for a generation of zombie fans. His movies had become the touchstone for every zombie movie from Kansas backyard epics to Japanese comedies and games like *Resident Evil* and *House of the Dead*.

So when Capcom offered Romero the opportunity to direct a Japanese TV commercial for *Biohazard 2*, the second game in the series known as *Resident Evil* in the West, it made karmic sense. Romero hooked up with special effects legend Screaming Mad George (*Bride of Re-Animator*) and shot at the Lincoln Heights jail in downtown Los Angeles. After the 30 second commercial, featuring ghouls overrunning the Racoon City Police Department, aired on Japanese TV in 1998 it was quickly bootlegged.

For Romero, watching Capcom making millions out of the zombie apocalypse that his movies had popularised was slightly annoying. But when Capcom became interested in taking the *Resident Evil* franchise onto the big screen – encouraged by the box office success of *Lara Croft: Tomb Raider* (2001) – they invited Romero to write a screenplay. The filmmaker replaced original screenwriter Alan McElroy, creator of the Spawn comics and it was widely rumoured that he would direct as well. Although not a videogame fan, he had watched tapes of *Resident Evil* play-throughs and could see the crossover between his work and the games' taut survival horror.

Romero worked on the *Resident Evil* project through 1998 and 1999 turning in various drafts of a screenplay to Capcom and German production company Constantin Film, who'd purchased the movie rights. What happened next isn't clear. According to some sources, Romero's script was considered too much like *Dawn of the Dead* and not enough like *Resident Evil*.[200] He was dropped from the project and his dream of returning to the genre he loved died on its feet.

As Romero wrote on his personal website in July 2000, "The biggest damn shame was Resident Evil. We busted balls writing drafts of that screenplay. I'm talkin' marathons, seventy-two hours straight. I really wanted this project. I had directed a TV commercial for ResEv II, and being on the set again with zombies (by Screamin' Mad George), I was hooked. Deep in my heart, I felt that ResEv was a rip-off of *Night of the Living Dead*. I had no legal case, but I was resentful. And torn... because I liked the videogame. I wanted to do the film partly because I wanted to say, 'Look here! *This* is how you do this shit!'"[201]

News of the filmmaker's departure from the project was met with a howl of protest from hardcore horror fans. Romero, who had once railed against "The McDonaldization of America", seemed to have been sidelined by the corporate forces now running the movie business.[202] Big companies like Capcom and Sony didn't really have a place for a radical, indie filmmaker from Pittsburgh like Romero. He was too maverick, too difficult, too leftfield. He wasn't considered a safe pair of hands.

There was a suspicion that Romero's old school approach was too gory and that the *Resident Evil* movie was not going to be a rough and ready genre classic but a mainstream popcorn movie. It was indicative to some of the general trend in American horror as the golden age of the 1970s faded and a new, corporate sensibility took over. As one angry reader claimed on the letters page of *Fangoria* magazine, Romero's departure was symptomatic of a much wider issue, the general decline of American horror since the 1980s.

"It seems that no horror film can be released in this country without being watered down," the incensed fan wrote. "Another good example would be the *Resident Evil* movie, which began as a potentially kick-ass zombie flick and, after ditching George Romero's script due to its graphic nature, is now destined to be a horrid piece of shit. Studios seem to be making horror films for people who don't usually like horror films. Instead of movies like *Hellraiser* and *Evil Dead*, they are making horror films for teenage girls, like *Valentine*, and 'thrillers,' a term which is slowly becoming a euphemism for 'boring crap,' such as *What Lies Beneath*."[203]

As Camcorder Coppolas like Bookwalter and Sheets had complained years previously, the Hollywood horror movie had moved so far towards the mainstream that it was no longer effectively scary. The slew of jokey, self-reflexive sequel-driven horror movies initiated by Wes Craven's *Scream* (1996) was killing the genre in the eyes of many fans. It had encouraged studios to make overly formulaic, teen-focussed movies that were frequently more interested in comedy rather than horror.[204]

The tradition of low-budget films like *The Texas Chain Saw Massacre*, *The Last House on the Left* and even *Dawn of the Dead* had given way to the dominance of ratings-friendly, mainstream-orientated *product* that was almost completely devoid of guts (both literally and metaphorically). German-based Constantin Films may have not been a Hollywood production company, but they were eager to ape the American industry. The chances of *Resident Evil* being a meaty horror movie looked quite bleak.

British director Paul W.S. Anderson was announced as the new writer/director on the project by *Variety* in October 2000. The filmmaker's CV boasted the most commercially successful videogame adaptation in cinema history, *Mortal Kombat* (1995). An avid fan of videogames in general, and *Resident Evil* in particular, he looked like the perfect candidate for the project. Shooting was scheduled to start in Berlin in March 2001 with a $40 million budget.[205]

Not everyone was pleased about Anderson's involvement and gamers were particularly distressed when a plot synopsis suggested that the movie was straying far from Capcom's source material. Fan rage ignited on the Internet: petitions were set up, boycotts of Capcom games were suggested and the company's email address was posted on forums. Horror fans weren't very happy either as Romero's departure saddened many.

In interview, Anderson responded to concerns and distanced himself from Romero's influence. "You can't do today what filmmakers were doing twenty-five years ago," he argued. "Then, extreme splatter movies like *Dawn of the Dead* and Lucio Fulci's *Zombi* [sic] were everywhere, and gore was the *modus operandi* of the times. To be scary, rather than just gross, I knew we had to be radical with our conception of the undead. I watched every zombie film again before starting this and noticed how dated they all looked […] It's too easy to gross people out on a splatter level and far harder to scare them senseless. I made a deliberate choice in the script to be frightening rather than visceral – showing everything covered in blood or the usual Italian style exploitation and cannibalism is now such a dated and hokey approach. Ensuring things are shadowy and tension-filled is the best way to keep audiences shrieking and their nerves gangling. That's why I decided to direct the film after initially only wanting to write and produce it. I didn't trust anyone else to pull that chill-laden atmosphere off."[206]

Regardless of the director's accomplished PR spin, this was a decision that was clearly motivated by marketing rather than aesthetic considerations. The gore-lite approach would ensure that teenagers wouldn't be alienated and that the film could appeal to a mainstream audience beyond just core gamers.

The fact that the accountants at Capcom and Constantin were more concerned with profits than horror was no surprise. It simply made Anderson's convoluted explanations of his artistic intent rather redundant. In a final ironic twist to the affair, the film was released in the UK with a 15 certificate while the original videogame carried an 18 certificate for its scenes of pixelated gore.[207]

All in all, it was a bizarre situation. The *Resident Evil* movie was the first ever big-budget, mainstream zombie production in seventy years of living dead cinema. Yet it was apparently ashamed of its heritage and directed by a filmmaker keen to distance his work from the splatterfests of Romero, Fulci and others, the very films that the videogame's creator cited as his chief source of inspiration.

Working as a prequel to the games themselves, *Resident Evil* opens with heroine Alice (Milla Jovovich) waking up inside a deserted mansion with no idea of who she is or how she got there. Piecing together her identity, the amnesiac slowly realises that she is an employee of Umbrella, a shadowy multinational corporation that has been researching bio-chemical weapons in The Hive – an underground laboratory hidden beneath the mansion. After a lab accident, the virus is unleashed, contaminating the facility and turning the scientists into flesh-hungry ghouls.

Before Alice can remember her own part in the catastrophic events and her decision to blow the whistle on the corporation's dubious research programme, a military squad charged with re-securing the lab arrives and takes her into custody. As events unfold, the team is trapped in the complex by the facility's computer, The Red Queen – just one of a series of redundant *Alice in Wonderland* references. Surrounded on all sides by zombies as the facility enters its self-destruct sequence, the living face an against-the-clock battle to locate the anti-virus serum and escape The Hive before it explodes.

Designed with all the linear logic of the videogame that inspired it, the *Resident Evil* movie is a completely formulaic adventure in which characters progress from level to level by overcoming various obstacles. References to the film's digital inspiration are rife. At several points during the action a map of the facility flashes up on-screen showing our heroes' progress; in other sequences Anderson makes explicit nods to the *Resident Evil* game itself as zombified Doberman Pinschers pursue Milla Jovovich through the labs and the spectacular finale features The Licker, a mutant CGI zombie monster, in an echo of the traditional videogame "Boss Battle". Other nods prove more esoteric, such as the conversation about "The Nemesis Project" between the scientists who rescue the survivors from the lab (avid gamers will recall that Nemesis is an intelligent super zombie mutated from the original viral strain).

Juggling the need to appeal to gamers and non-gaming audiences, *Resident Evil* reskins the survival horror of its source into a sci-fi action movie where the zombies are little more than incidental cannon fodder. It certainly isn't much of a horror movie and proves far less scary than the *Resident Evil* games. Predominantly skimping on the gore, the film delivers only a handful of tense set pieces. The best of these is a scene where The Red Queen locks the military team in a corridor as she unleashes a series of laser beams that slice 'n' dice them to bloody bits. It's typical of the writer-director's magpie-like approach that this sequence is lifted straight from Vincenzo Natali's sci-fi horror *Cube* (1997). Ultimately however, it's the amount of attention given to The Licker that makes Anderson's intentions clear. More interested in this CG monster than any of the lo-fi ghouls dotted around the lab facility, *Resident Evil* rarely even feels like much of a zombie movie. Eager to appeal to the widest demographic possible, rather than deliver meaty horror, it's a movie that dumbs down the zombie genre for a quick buck.

The most incisive critical commentary on the film actually comes from star Milla Jovovich's throwaway comments to *Total Film* magazine. "We've got really infantile mentalities on this movie. We're like: 'It's gross – cool! It's disgusting – print it!' You have to think like a 15-year-old. Wet dress. Zombies. Guns. Cool!"[208]

Resident Evil was a commercial success, taking $102 million worldwide and doing gangbuster business on DVD. Sequels inevitably followed: *Resident Evil: Apocalypse* (2004), *Resident Evil: Extinction* (2007), *Resident Evil: Afterlife* (2010) and *Resident Evil: Retribution* (2012). Each new instalment was bigger than the last – with *Resident Evil: Afterlife* employing 3D for extra wow factor. Along the way, Alice was transformed too. Beginning as a fragile amnesiac, she was mutated by her exposure to the zombie T-Virus into a superhuman zombie basher. The claustrophobic survival horror of the videogame franchise gave way to outrageous ass-kicking action sequences.

In box office terms the films have become a billion dollar franchise, matching the videogame series and reviving its flagging fortunes. In critical terms, the *Resident Evil* franchise is considered something of a joke, but it's Anderson who's laughing all the way to the bank.

Resident Evil – as both a game and a film – was responsible for taking the zombie out of the margins and into the mainstream. Much was lost in the transition, and there was some irony in the fact that the zombie had finally met its match in a blockbuster movie franchise that was as soulless as it was.

VI. REBIRTH OF THE DEAD

The revival of the zombie and the start of its ascension to pop cultural dominance began in 2002 and evolved quickly. Within mere weeks of *Resident Evil*'s opening came a series of press releases and announcements suggesting that the monster had finally broken free of its marginal roots: a remake of *Dawn of the Dead* was greenlit; a big screen adaptation of the *House of the Dead* arcade game went into production; and, perhaps most exciting of all, George Romero announced at

Fangoria's Weekend of Horrors Convention in August 2002 that he was in serious talks with Twentieth Century Fox to complete the fourth and final instalment of his "trilogy" – provisionally dubbed *Land of the Dead* – with a $10 million budget and a planned R-rated release.

The most cheering sign of the zombie's return to cinematic health was actually something far more concrete than Romero's oft-announced plans for a new instalment in the series. It was the gradual –

indeed almost imperceptible – invasion of the living dead that was occurring. Zombies were everywhere, from UK television adverts for the new Mini Cooper car to multimillion-dollar American studio pictures. Gore Verbinski's *Pirates of the Caribbean: The Curse of the Black Pearl* (2003) starred a ragbag collection of ghostly zombie buccaneers led by Geoffrey Rush who were vaguely related to the aquatic ghouls of *The Zombies of Mora Tau* and *The Fog*. In the equally mainstream *The Haunted Mansion* (2003), Eddie Murphy proved that the spirit of Mantan Moreland lived on, facing a group of fugitives from the undertaker with only some cowardly comic mugging and a quick-witted wisecrack for defence: "Get back in your beds, man."

The greatest proof of the zombie's newfound acceptability was their appearance in the biggest blockbuster of the new millennium. In *The Return of the King* (2003), the final film in the *Lord of the Rings* series, the heroes raise a zombie army from The Paths of the Dead and lead them into battle against the forces of Mordor. Credit may have been due to J.R.R. Tolkien's original novels, but it was fitting that director Peter Jackson got the chance to return to his living dead roots even in the midst of making a $300 million blockbuster trilogy.

All in all, it seemed that there was no keeping a good corpse down. This suspicion was reinforced by the appearance of a crossover hit that managed to achieve mainstream success without compromising the genre's chief concerns, Danny Boyle's *28 Days Later* (2002). While the ghostly corpses of *Pirates of the Caribbean* and *The Return of the King* were far removed from the visceral flesh-eating ghouls of a thousand low-budget pictures, Boyle's film was the real deal.

As the first British zombie movie in years (albeit one that was eased into life with the help of American finance), the critical and commercial success of *28 Days Later* signalled that the genre had entered a new phase. Phenomenally popular with audiences on both sides of the Atlantic (though particularly in America, where the substitution of an alternative, darker ending helped its kudos among horror fans) it was hailed as the first visceral *and* intelligent zombie movie in recent memory.

Shot cheaply and quickly on digital video, *28 Days Later* had an indie movie's guerrilla feel and

style. Curiously, though, the involvement of a major studio prompted Boyle to be somewhat circumspect about the film's genre lineage. In interviews, he explicitly distanced himself from horror cinema in general and the Z-word in particular. "I suppose my trepidation about [calling it a horror movie] while we were making it was partly to do with how Fox was planning to market it. Are they going to turn this into a mainstream cult film for zombie fans?" the director mused to *Fangoria* magazine.[209] His fears seemed fair enough, but they did lead to some rather ridiculous comments as he tied himself up in semantic knots in his attempt to disown the film's heritage.

"I don't see *28 Days Later* as part of some zombie lineage. Zombie films are an entertaining part of the horror genre, but they are rooted in nuclear paranoia. Zombie addicts have another theory. They say it has to do with the shooting of Kennedy because you can only kill zombies by shooting them in the head. I don't really buy into that, but I can see the connection with nuclear power and what it will do to us – that whole 'living dead' thing. Those fears aren't so relevant anymore, but the idea of a psychological virus is fascinating."[210]

Eager not to associate his monsters with the mixed fortunes of the zombie genre, Boyle instead makes his ghouls descendants of the infected civilians of Romero's *The Crazies* or Rollin's *The Grapes of Death*. His raging sub-humans aren't zombies per se, but unfortunate victims of a plague that starts after an over-zealous group of animal rights activists accidentally release a man-made virus from a research laboratory in the pre-credits sequence. Tapping into millennial fears about biological warfare, chemical attacks and viral outbreaks, *28 Days Later* proved the perfect index of the Western world's post-9/11 apocalyptic anxieties. The fact that film's release coincided with the 2002/2003 SARS outbreak seemed less like serendipity than proof of how well it had plugged into the zeitgeist.

Twenty-eight days after the virus is unleashed motorcycle courier Jim (Cillian Murphy) wakes from a coma in an empty London hospital. Wandering outside, he discovers that the capital has become a ghost city. Walking through the streets, past overturned buses, looted shops and deserted tourist sites (Anthony Dodd Mantle's digital photography gives the looming spire of Big Ben an eerie presence), Jim eventually runs into a handful of survivors who are doing their best to avoid the "infected" – raging, fast-moving, highly contagious maniacs who have been transformed by the virus into a cross between rabid epileptics and psychotic Ebola carriers.

It turns out that the city has become a giant hot zone and, as a snatch of graffito sprayed onto a wall so eloquently puts it, "THE END IS EXTREMELY FUCKING NIGH". Banding together with fellow survivors Selena (Naomie Harris), cab driver Frank (Brendan Gleeson) and his daughter Hannah (Megan Burns), Jim makes his way north along the empty M1 motorway in search of military protection from the roaming bands of viral victims.

An apocalyptic fantasy in the characteristically British vein of H.G. Wells, John Wyndham or J.G. Ballard, *28 Days Later* is a masterful, sinewy little horror film. Unlike *Resident Evil* it's not ashamed of its zombies, whatever Boyle's personal hang-ups about the z-word itself might suggest. Frantic and furious, the film's infected are terrifying, highly contagious creatures with a habit of puking up their tainted blood over the living as the virus causes their internal organs to go into meltdown.

Boldly updating the zombie genre for the new millennium, Boyle and novelist-turned-screenwriter Alex Garland present us with an apocalypse that, they claim, is a reflection of our increasingly stressful social interactions.

"It started with road rage and cars, but now every inner-city hospital has to have security guards," explained Boyle. "Air rage, parking rage, trolley rage in the supermarkets. [We thought] what if we could employ *that* as the element that constitutes the zombies?"[211]

Employing the infected as a metaphor for the breakdown of the social structures governing our behaviour towards one another, the film suggests that anger – "rage" itself – has become the defining emotional response in late capitalist societies.

"Some people have a theory that it's democracy that does it – that people are waking up to the fact that democracy tells you all the time, 'You have a vote, you are important,' but the truth is you're not. Other people say it's actually a direct result of Thatcher. She said, 'There's no such thing as society, let's empower the individual,' but the truth is we are completely irrelevant. These moments of rage happen when people are not treated properly. I remember seeing this CCTV clip of a woman with parking rage. She was so furious that someone else was going for the same parking space that she repeatedly hammered her car into the other vehicle. The truth is this sort of thing is happening more and more. It's not some abstract monster, the monster is in all of us. We are all capable of flying into a violent rage."[212]

Murky and digital cinematography mimicks the grainy *vérité* of the ubiquitous inner-city CCTV camera, and *28 Days Later* questions where we are heading with brutal honesty. Turning the contemporary urban landscape into a vision of hell that owes as much to Hieronymus Bosch as Romero, the film presents us with a stark vision of social

28 Days Later (2002).

breakdown in which the infected are implacable automatons, consumed from within by the destructiveness of their own rage.

It makes for a startlingly efficient comment on all that's wrong with contemporary Western society. "It's a new kind of intolerance," is how Boyle describes the growing tide of rage. "It's not based on the usual factors that cause violence like race, religion or gender. It's a social rage that doesn't have boundaries defining it."[213]

Even when the survivors think they've found safety with a military squad led by Major West (Christopher Eccleston), they quickly find themselves in more danger than before. The pent up frustration of the all-male group soon explodes into violent rage as the squaddies decide to let off some steam by turning the women into unwilling concubines. Not even Jim, the film's nominal hero, is above such base human emotions. His own regression into savagery in the film's fraught climax suggests that the rage virus is in some ways already a part of all of us – just as in a traditional zombie movie we all carry the seeds of our own zombified deaths. When Jim appears in front of Selena, covered in mud and blood after butchering the soldiers, *28 Days Later* raises the very real possibility that he might be mistaken as "one of them" and struck down by the woman he's just fought so hard to save.

Such a bleak ending would certainly have been preferable – and more in keeping with the film's grim view of the state we're in – to the one that was shown to British audiences. After depicting The End Of The World As We Know It with grim fatalism, the UK edit of *28 Days Later* delivered a ludicrously optimistic conclusion in which the survivors discover that the infection never actually spread beyond the British Isles. Retreating to an isolated farmhouse and flagging down a passing airplane with the help of a homemade banner, they eventually get to live happily ever after. It was like a parody of a focus-grouped, studio-imposed finale.

28 Days Later was a surprise success. The flipside of *Resident Evil*'s glossy ghouls, it proved that the zombie genre still had the power to terrify, alarm and thrill. It was a lesson that other filmmakers around the world were trying hard to learn in the early 2000s. A new wave of films proved that the zombie's time was coming. Few shared the blockbuster chutzpah of *Resident Evil* or the visceral

punch of *28 Days Later* but their sheer diversity was, in retrospect, an indication of just how much mileage the revived zombie genre had in it.

In Australia, twins Michael and Peter Spierig's *Undead* (2003) was a knockabout Raimi-Jackson rip-off about aliens turning an Australian town into zombies. Fighting the hordes is an outback survivalist who's watched one too many John Woo movies (Mungo McKay) and an assorted band of hysterical nobodies who don't get killed off quickly enough.

Undead delivered a strange cross between *Night of the Living Dead* and *Close Encounters of the Third Kind*, although it wasn't enough to save this derivative effort from being just another apocalyptic zombie movie that overplays the stylistic flourishes without offering anything particularly new or interesting.

At least it was a few steps up from Uwe Böll's truly awful *House of the Dead* (2004) based on Sega's coin-op videogame. The script, co-written by Dave Parker who had previously made the not-bad postmodern zombie outing *The Dead Hate the Living!* (1999), featured ravers on a deserted island getting chomped by zombies. It was so thin it should have checked into a support group for anorexics. Böll did himself no favours by lazily (and nonsensically) editing footage from the coin-op into the live action of the movie – thereby proving that watching someone else play the game was more compelling than watching his movie.

Meanwhile, in Canada, Elza Kephart provided a welcome shot in the arm for zombie fans everywhere with the warm and witty *Graveyard Alive: A Zombie Nurse in Love* (2003), an irreverent black and white addition to the zombie canon in which ugly nurse Patsy (Anne Day-Jones) finds a new lease of life after being zombified. With newfound sex appeal this walking corpse becomes the ward's new hottie. It mischievously merged the camp melodrama of TV soap operas with zombie nurses and lots of off-the-wall humour.

Similarly camp humour cropped up *Dead & Breakfast* (2004), a likeable low-budget ghoul outing with an army of redneck zombies and some funny one-liners. Elsewhere, postmodern efforts like Spain's *Una de zombis* (2003) and the Czech Republic's *Choking Hazard* (2004), struck distinctively different paths with stories that don't so much wink at the audience as develop relentless facial tics.

The title of Miguel Ángel Lamata's Spanish effort translates as "A Film About Zombies", yet that barely scratches the surface of its appeal. If Tarantino ever made a zombie movie the result might be something like this. A *Pulp Fiction*-esque blend of narrative game playing and ghoulish off-the-wall humour in which a Goth shock jock (co-writer Miguel Ángel Aparicio) ditches his radio station to make the eponymous movie about zombies with the help of a fanboy mate. They end up in all kinds of trouble as the line between script and reality begins to blur and Satanic zombies roam the city at the behest of an underachieving villain whose aim is to conquer the world "a little bit at a time".

Achingly hip and brimming over with inventive energy, it bears some resemblance to cult Spanish director Alex De La Iglesia's films – *Acción Mutante* (1993) or *The Day of the Beast* (1995) – yet possesses a manic glee that's all its own. Memorable moments include a coke-snorting cat, a great gag about "Cannibal Remorse" – an existential sequel to *Cannibal Holocaust* – and various mindbending narrative slips as the story fractures and folds in on itself. It threatens to become tiresome – and to be honest it eventually does – yet there's no mistaking its welcome energy.

The same was true of Czech director Marek Dobes's *Choking Hazard*, an equally ironic and self-reflexive attempt to rejuvenate the tired old zombie formula. Here a bunch of philosophy students retire to an isolated hotel to discover the meaning of life with the help of a blind seminar guru (Jaroslav Dusek). A Jehovah's Witness pornstar gatecrashes the event, quickly followed by a horde of woodsmen zombies (dubbed "woombies") who appear out of nowhere dressed in black overcoats and hats to chomp on the living. There's no explanation for the chaos, just lots of gore, a string of silly jokes (including electrocuted zombies breakdancing in a pool of water) and a bizarre attempt to blend philosophy and the zombie apocalypse. The meaning of life we eventually learn is the balance of reason and instinct – the latter represented by the zombies themselves, of course. Running out of steam early on, its insouciance very nearly makes up for its faults.

The most successful reworking of the living dead formula was actually a British movie. While *28 Days Later* harked back to Ballard and Wyndham and post-apocalyptic BBC TV dramas like *Survivors* (1975–77), *Shaun of the Dead* took a much more upbeat approach. Its zombie apocalypse captured a different side of England: a land that was more green and pleasant.

Billed as "a romantic comedy, with zombies", *Shaun* proved as parochial as *28 Days Later* was ambitious, featuring a host of living dead in-jokes, plenty of riffs on 21st-century England and a smart awareness of the impact of the *Resident Evil* videogame on the zombie's changing fortunes.

Straight from the twisted imaginations of the slacker geniuses responsible for late-1990s Channel 4 sitcom *Spaced*, *Shaun of the Dead* is a quintessentially British tribute to Romero. Co-written by director Edgar Wright with star Simon Pegg, it's the story of a hapless twenty-something shop worker named Shaun (Pegg), whose life is thrown into turmoil when his girlfriend Liz (Kate Ashfield) dumps him. Simultaneously, an American deep space probe unexpectedly crashes to Earth unleashing a wave of radioactivity that turns the population of North London into zombies. It never rains…

Faced with an impending zombie apocalypse, Shaun and his stoner mate Ed (Nick Frost) battle the living dead ghouls, rescue Liz and save Shaun's mum Barbara (Penelope Wilton) – prompting Shaun to shout "We're coming to get you Barbara" in a nerdy fanboy nod to *Night of the Living Dead*.

Of course, this being merry ol' England, shotguns and shopping malls are in annoyingly short supply which means Shaun and Ed must fend off the zombies by throwing Dire Straits albums and pizza boxes at them, whacking them with spades and cricket bats and eventually taking refuge in the local pub.

The offbeat premise of this "zom-rom-com" was familiar to fans of *Spaced*. Back in 1999, an early episode of the sitcom featured its slacker hero (Pegg) dreaming that he was stuck in a live action version of the *Resident Evil* game after a heavy night of speed snorting and videogaming. In *Shaun*, the ghouls are real rather than just a figment of the hero's frazzled imagination. Blending zombie mythology with British suburban life, Pegg and Wright carefully sketch a twenty-something male slacker lifestyle dominated by PlayStations, spliffs and pints of lager. No sooner is that done, then set the living dead loose in it.

The chief joke is that everyone's so "spaced" by the dreary dullness of life in Britain that they don't notice the zombies' arrival. Shaun's job as a sales assistant in retailers Foree Electrics (a reference to *Dawn*'s leading man) is so crushingly soul-destroying that he fails to spot the tell-tale signs of the coming apocalypse and mistakes the zombies for listless commuters.

In one of the film's funniest sequences, he wanders down to the local newsagents on the morning of the dawn of the dead and is so crippled with a hangover from the previous night's boozing that he's completely oblivious to the chaos around him. "Sorry mate, haven't got any spare change," he mutters to a ghoul he mistakes for a homeless beggar.

"Much of the film is about the way city people conduct their lives and ignore each other and ignore other people," Pegg explained. "In London you can walk past someone who's dying in the street and just step over them – in some respects that's one of the things the zombies represent."[214]

For Wright, the movie satirises our attitude towards the rest of the world. "One of the inspirations for the script was that during the foot and mouth crisis I didn't read a paper for about two weeks and felt utterly stupid when I was watching the TV and saw footage of burning cows. I had to ask somebody what exactly foot and mouth was. A lot of people walk around in their own little bubble of their own problems and don't see wider things going on."[215]

Shuffling, lumbering brutes, the suburban living dead of *Shaun* are the complete opposite of *28 Days Later*'s raging commuters – something the film half-acknowledges with a gag in which a TV news report dismisses claims that the outbreak is attributed to "Rage infected monkeys".

Pegg and Wright were adamant in their decision to stay true to Romero's original trilogy and its painfully slow-moving monsters. "[The zombies in *Shaun of the Dead* are] very slow and almost inept and shambolic," Pegg told reporters. "They're without motive or moral rage. There's something kind of inexorable about it. They are death and they will get you in the end. We could all be in a room now with one and quite happily walk round and round the room and he'd never get you because he'd just be stumbling along. But eventually you'd have to go to sleep and when you did, he'd eat you.

There's just something really eerie about that."[216]

Even though they followed in the master's footsteps, Pegg and Wright were still worried that Romero might not approve of their cheeky spoof. After sending an advance copy of the film to the States for his blessing, they waited with baited breath for a response. "We were given his phone number. We basically called up the man who invented the contemporary movie zombie movie and he really, really enjoyed it! I was waffling on like a fanboy going 'I'm sorry that the zombies in our film reanimate straight away while, of course, in your films it takes about half an hour.' And he said: 'Simon, you know what? I don't mind.'"[217]

For Pegg, who'd spent his twenties watching *Dawn of the Dead* and battling walking corpses in the *Resident Evil* game, Romero's praise was the icing on this ghoulish cake: "It's amazing, because daddy approves! What more do you need? Everything else is just a footnote."[218]

Shaun of the Dead builds to a standoff between the survivors and the zombies in a local pub called The Winchester, which has a still-functioning Winchester rifle hanging over the bar. In a nice little touch, shooting the ghouls evokes memories of Shaun and Ed's videogaming sessions ("Reload!" Top Left! Nice Shot!") and although it doesn't have the big-budget gloss of *Resident Evil*, *Shaun* has far more to say about the way in which the PlayStation demographic of twenty-something males has helped revive the zombie as an iconic pop culture figure.

Pegg, an avid gamer, was adamant in his belief that the 1990s cycle of zombie videogames fuelled the movie boom. "I'd say *Resident Evil* [the game] is directly responsible for the renaissance in zombie films at the moment," he said in 2004. "It was a Japanese game but somehow they entirely captured the spirit of the Romero movies and they captured the creepiness of those very slow-moving lumbering zombies. People had forgotten the sheer creepy potential of those movie beasts."[219]

By 2004, though, people were beginning to remember again.

"When there's no more room in hell, the dead will walk the Earth" was the now-famous tagline of the original *Dawn of the Dead*. After Universal announced that it was turning its attention to Romero's 1978 classic, it looked like it might be necessary to add a postscript: "And when there's no more originality in Hollywood, lazy producers will remake anything that moves, shuffles or lumbers for a quick buck." As news came that Universal had hired director Zack Snyder – then best known for his homoerotic, Spartan battle movie *300* – to direct, horror fans groaned in unison.

An unnecessary rehash of a landmark genre film, the remake of *Dawn of the Dead* was forced into production without Romero's artistic blessing: "I'm not delighted that it's happening," claimed the Pittsburgh filmmaker in an interview with *Rue Morgue* magazine just before the film's release: "I don't have anything against it, I just thought it wasn't a very good idea."[220] Somewhat ironically, it seemed as though Romero's nihilistic vision of a consumer society forced to cannibalise itself in order to satisfy its never-ending greed had finally come full circle. Taking nothing but the basic pitch of the original – an unexplained plague causes the dead to return to life and eat the living, leaving a handful of survivors to hole up in an empty shopping mall – the remake completely dispatched with its characters and plot, cynically keeping only the zombies and the dollar-spinning title.

From the very first moment the production was announced, diehard fans raged against the remake and all it stood for. When the film's trailer was screened at a *Fangoria* convention in January 2004, magazine editor Antony Timpone found himself facing an angry crowd: "They booed. They hissed. They hated it."[221] According to screenwriter James Gunn, feelings among certain fans went to insane extremes: "I got death threats. I had people saying they wanted to shoot me, to kill me. I got long, rambling, schizophrenic letters sent to me through my managers. It was a trip [...] I know that I and a few of my friends loved *Dawn of the Dead*, but I did not know that there was this huge *Dead* underground out there."[222] To borrow a catchphrase from the screenwriter's *Scooby Doo* movies: zoinks!

With such negative audience expectation, Universal was forced to get the PR machine rolling as quickly as possible to justify the apparent "sacrilege" to the fans: "Making a zombie movie in the high $20-million range is a risky proposition," explained producer Eric Newman after he sweet-talked Romero's collaborator Richard P. Rubinstein into signing over the rights. "But as far as the genre goes this is the biggest title."[223]

As the release date neared, the filmmakers carefully reasserted their commitment to doing justice to Romero's vision. "This is a *re-envisioning* of a classic," director Zack Snyder explained in the UK press notes. "There was not, is not, a valid reason to 'remake' *Dawn of the Dead*. That's not what we set out to do, not what any of us wanted. There are some amazing updates of some great films – I love Kaufman's *Invasion of the Body Snatchers*, Carpenter's *The Thing*, Cronenberg's *The Fly*. They're great movies that add to rather than diminish the original films. We really saw this as a chance to continue the zombie genre for a new audience.[224]

There was a certain symmetry to Snyder, a former commercials director, stepping into the remake's hot seat. After all, Romero's own career had begun in the advertising industry. But, for some, it suggested that the remake would be nothing more than a souped-up, braindead exercise in style crafted to satisfy the restless "bigger-better-faster" tastes of a generation weaned on MTV.

In many ways, that's exactly what the finished film turned out to be. However, it was also reverential of its source material, glossily effective and more breathlessly exciting than any American horror movie of the previous decade. In an era when big-budget Hollywood horror was becoming increasingly equated with disposable popcorn fare – see the likes of *Ghost Ship* (2002), *Freddy Vs. Jason* (2003) or *Gothika* (2004) – the new *Dawn* delivered a degree of edginess and balls-to-the-wall action that was more than a little refreshing.

Engaging the adrenal gland rather than the brain, Gunn's script amped up the splattery action of Romero's original while simultaneously excising its vast chunks of social commentary. We're left with an upgraded, streamlined thrill-ride that races through the zombie apocalypse, aiming at getting its characters to the iconic mall as quickly as possible.

Our heroine is Ana (Sarah Polley), an ER nurse who clocks off work, goes to bed and literally wakes to the dawn of the dead as a zombified moppet invades her bedroom and bites her husband's neck open. Within seconds, he's bled to death and is up on his feet as one of the films' fast-moving ghouls, a bunch of manic Usain Bolts who are less walking than running dead.

As the city becomes infested by zombies, the social order quickly implodes and anarchy reigns.

Joining fellow survivors – including US Marine veteran turned cop Kenneth (Ving Rhames), electronic salesman Michael (Jake Weber), gangsta Andre (Mekhi Phifer) and his pregnant wife (Inna Korobkina) – Ana takes refuge in a suburban Wisconsin shopping mall while waiting for the military to come and rescue them. As the zombie hordes grow in size and the televisions fall silent, it's apparent that the end of the world really is nigh.

"America always sorts its shit out," whispers C.J. (Michael Kelly), one of the mall's redneck security guards after watching news footage of army grunts shooting civilians in a desperate bid to contain the infection. It's a tantalising, throwaway line that this equally throwaway adrenalin-fest never makes much of. Lacking the satiric bite that made the original so powerful, Snyder's film shows little interest in the mall location as a comment on American consumerism, reducing the introspective lull in the middle of Romero's film into a brief montage of its inhabitants screwing, playing basketball and sharing a communal dinner. That out of the way, the remake then races headlong towards its next action sequence.

Gunn, who cut his teeth at Troma Studios, has a keen eye for exploitation horror potential and Korobkina's pregnancy slowly builds towards an icky sequence that wouldn't have seemed out of place in *Zombi 3*. His screenplay delivers splatter but little that matters, though. It's a Romero-lite retread and by the time the survivors try to escape the mall in two customised buses that could have come out of *The A-Team*, it's obvious that this *Dawn of the Dead* doesn't want to engage the head.

Something more relevant may have been struggling to get out. What are we to make of the title sequence's stock footage of civil unrest being suppressed by riot police around the world? Or the ironic use of Johnny Cash singing "The Man Comes Around" on the soundtrack? The lengthy reality TV section in which the survivors watch news reports charting the escalating chaos on huge plasma screens in the mall's electrical goods store seems particularly poignant. Yet none of these things build towards anything in particular amid the apocalyptic chaos and social breakdown.

As with so many American horror films, it's the tongue-in-cheek irony that eventually defuses the film's build up. When original cast member Tom Savini appears on television as a tough-talking

redneck sheriff – "Somebody put another round in that woman over there, she's still twitching!" – the postmodern in-jokes threaten to turn the tension into giggles. It's something that's not helped by the appearance of Scott H. Reiniger as a gruff army general nor Ken Foree's solemn televangelist, who intones: "How do you think your God will judge you?" Rather than adding anything much to the production, such cameos simply seem *de rigueur* for any remake; the fact that Romero doesn't appear says more than the rest of them put together.

Gunn has claimed that his script was supposed to be "about human beings having their lives stripped away, and how they react to that," adding "What would people turn to? How would a person's religious beliefs be affected by the dead returning to life? Would you turn to your faith more? Or would you tend to think it's bullshit?"[225] However, the finished film actually has little interest in such philosophical issues.

Despite all the secondary religious waffling – Andre is momentarily concerned about all the bad things he's done in his life and rather self-centredly wonders if the apocalypse is his personal punishment – the film lacks the dark nihilism of Romero's trilogy. These walking dead are really just victims of a virulent plague and since anyone who dies without being bitten by the ghouls doesn't return to life, the hand-me-down "When there's no more room in hell" spiel seems rather redundant. Whatever the filmmakers may want us to believe, this isn't Judgment Day – just another common or garden viral outbreak.

Even without the dark satire, there's much to enjoy in the new *Dawn*. The film's chief pleasure stems from its resplendent goriness in which wooden sticks are stuck through zombie skulls, heads are blasted open with shotguns and special effects make-up designer David LeRoy Anderson unleashes 3,000 ghastly ghouls.

A million miles from the anodyne, censor-friendly world of *Resident Evil*, this *Dawn* delivers more gore than one can shake an amputated limb at. It also possesses a dark strain of comedy that owes a debt to the E.C. Comics tradition that was such an influence on Romero. The scene in which the survivors play a grim game of sniping – shooting at the massed ghouls with a high-powered rifle and picking out targets on the basis of their similarity to famous people – is chock full of gallows humour: "Jay Leno! […] Burt Reynolds! No, too easy. Aim for someone harder. Rosie O'Donnell! Tell him to shoot Rosie!"

With *Shaun* and *Dawn* becoming hits on both sides of the Atlantic, 2004 proved a vintage year for zombie fans. Rescued from the shadows, the living dead were finally getting the respect they deserved across a variety of different media. Like a viral plague, zombies were spreading across movies, videogames, books and comics.

In the world of games, *Resident Evil 4* gave the franchise a new lease of life with a buffed up, redesigned take on its survival horror which featured Spanish-speaking zombies, dark woods and a ghoul in a burlap sack hood revving a chainsaw. *Doom 3* rebooted its sci-fi ghouls for a new generation of gamers and Capcom's *Dead Rising* (released in 2006) delivered an open-world zombie apocalypse that was set in a shopping mall and clearly influenced by Romero.

Accompanying these new digital developments was a sudden explosion in zombie-themed comic books. Robert Kirkman's understated, monochrome outing *The Walking Dead* began in October 2003 with a dramatic, claustrophobic storyline that privileged character development over gore. It would soon become the preeminent zombie franchise of the burgeoning renaissance.

Elsewhere Steve Niles's comics *Remains* and *Wake the Dead* upped the blood and guts (*Remains* later became a passable TV movie). Simon Pegg contributed a zombie story to long-running British comic *2000 A.D.* and no less than George Romero himself kick-started D.C.'s *Toe Tags* series with a story from his own pen.

Meanwhile, Max Brooks's affectionate tongue-in-cheek tome *The Zombie Survival Guide: Complete Protection from the Living Dead* became a bookshop bestseller with some ingenious, deadpan advice about how to survive a zombie apocalypse.[226] It was the first step in a career that would take the author, son of comedian Mel Brooks, into blockbuster territory with his follow-up novel *World War Z*. He led the sudden charge of zombie writers who sprang up around 2004 – helped in part by the growth of e-books and self-publishing.

Romero had more than just comic books on his mind in 2004, though. A series of announcements throughout the late-1990s and early years of the new century alerted fans that Romero was keen to make another living dead film. The rumours were varied and contradictory: he was going to make a rock musical called *Diamond Dead* with Ridley Scott about a group of musicians brought back from the grave; he was going to make a fourth film in his Living Dead series; he was going to make a videogame called *City of the Dead*; he was struggling to find funding; he was going to work with Twentieth Century Fox; he'd refused to compromise on the gore by working with a studio.

In the spring of 2004, the gossip finally turned into hard facts. Romero was indeed interested in making both a zombie rock musical and a fourth film in his Living Dead series. Plus, after years of battling for funding, he was in the unlikely position of having both bankrolled at once. Understandably, it was the latter project that generated the most excitement and Romero's long-gestating *Land of the Dead* (previously entitled *Brunch of the Dead*, *Twilight of the Dead* and *Dead Reckoning*) was picked up by Universal, the studio that had distributed both the *Dawn* remake and *Shaun of the Dead*. Within twenty-four hours of the announcement, a cast was already locked in that included Dennis Hopper, John Leguizamo and Asia Argento.

Set after the events of *Day of the Dead*, *Land* takes place in a fortified city where the remaining human survivors of the zombie apocalypse are sheltering from the living dead. As the film's title suggests, the zombies have overrun everything. America has become the home of the grave and the land of the dead: a dank wasteland populated by "walkers" or, as some of the less sympathetic characters dub the ambling corpses, "stenches".[227]

What is left of the living living – as opposed to the living dead – can be found in a fortified urban compound (the location of this is never made clear, but in a nicely ironic touch it appears to be Romero's home town of Pittsburgh). It's a community split between the haves and the have-nots, governed by a ruthless, bespoke-tailored CEO called Kaufman (Dennis Hopper).

Kaufman claims to have been the architect of the city's fortifications – a walled compound protected on two sides by water – and he's using the current situation to profit from the misery of the impoverished survivors who're sheltering under his wing. Taking up residence in the plush corridors of Fiddler's Green, a luxury skyscraper apartment complex, Kaufman and his cronies preside over a post-apocalyptic community where the rich are getting richer and the poor are desperately trying not to become zombie chow.

An electric fence keeps most of the ghouls at bay, but also traps the living. Kaufman's idea of entertaining the masses is to profit from their baser instincts: "If you can drink it, shoot it up, fuck it or gamble on it, it belongs to him," one character remarks. His most recent idea is to use anyone who upsets him – including ex-hooker Slack (Asia Argento) – as live bait in gladiatorial zombie battles. What was threatened before in Romero's series has finally come to pass: the living are now more monstrous than the living dead.

One man who's realised this is Riley (Simon Baker). He's a burnt out forager who's been leading sorties into the nearby zombie-infested towns in a battle truck called Dead Reckoning. As a result of his hard work he's been able to secure the supplies needed to keep Kaufman eating fillet mignon and the impoverished simply eating. Disillusioned by the compound's escalating social collapse, Riley's eager to escape to Canada with his sharpshooter sidekick Charlie (Robert Joy). Even though he hates Kaufman's world of bourgeois comfort, Riley's uninterested in the revolution that's quietly fermenting on the streets beneath Fiddler's Green. He simply wants to get out while he still can.

Riley's best laid plans are complicated by two factors: the theft of Dead Reckoning by Cholo (John Leguizamo), who threatens to use it to destroy Fiddler's Green unless he's given a sizeable amount of money; and the evolution of the zombies, who are "learning to be us again" and have suddenly developed the ability to communicate, use tools and work as a group under the command of growling ghoul Big Daddy (Eugene Clark).

Enlisted by Kaufman to get Dead Reckoning back,

Riley heads out into zombie land with Slack and Charlie, while the zombies head towards Fiddler's Green, swimming across the expanse of water that had previously kept them at bay.

As the first film in Romero's "Dead" series to have the backing of a major studio, get released with an MPAA rating and spawn a slew of official studio merchandise including action figures, *George A. Romero's Land of the Dead* (to give the film it's full, if rather grand, title), marked a significant departure for the writer-director. Despite only being given a paltry $15 million budget, Romero managed to stay true to the ambitious vision of social collapse that he had once wanted to explore in *Day of the Dead* and had been talking about in interviews during the 1990s.

After two decades spent watching other directors derivatively tackle the zombie mythology he had forged himself, *Land of the Dead* was something of a high stakes gamble for Romero. In the years since 1985, the living dead had returned to cinematic health: wouldn't it be ironic if Romero, the man who had single-handedly invented the modern zombie, managed to kill them again once and for all with a glossy studio flop?

Fortunately, Romero proved to have lost none of his touch. In fact, given the variable output of his work after *Day of the Dead*, he actually seemed to have rediscovered some of the magic he'd mislaid. His Faustian pact with Hollywood didn't seem to

Land of the Dead (2005).

hamstring his artistic sensibilities either, and the impressive cast he gained as a result gave *Land*'s performances a professionalism that the earlier films in the series had sometimes lacked. Certainly, Romero relished working with a heavy weight like Dennis Hopper ("I want to play Steppenwolf whenever he comes on the set," the filmmaker joked to one reporter) and Asia Argento – daughter of Dario Argento, who'd been instrumental in getting *Dawn of the Dead* financed.[228]

Yet, compromises were inevitably made. Originally planning to shoot in his native Pittsburgh, Romero was reluctantly forced to relocate to Toronto to get the benefit of a couple of million dollars worth of tax breaks and the favourable currency exchange rates. During production, rumours circulated that Romero was battling the studio over both the budget and his trademark gore shots. More money was eventually found, which enabled him to shoot pick-ups: "Universal was more willing to pony up a little more dough," he later explained. "We got an extra few days to try and improve on some of the gore things and dance around the MPAA a little bit by doing the shadow thing and smoke thing to indicate what was going on without actually having it in your face."[229]

The result was a movie that could be released with an R rating in the US and, incredibly, a 15 certificate in the UK. Given that the film foregrounds some astonishingly brutal special effects sequences of zombie munching action – intestines being pulled from chest cavities, hands being shoved into mouths in search of tongues and, in the most squirm-inducing moment a navel piercing being ripped off – it's surprising that the film received such a lenient ride. Romero seems to have anticipated most of the censors' objections, filming in a dark murky grey that seems to have become *de rigueur* for most American horror movies in recent years, and hiding some of the more gory action behind foreground figures. Even still, the film's love of splatter is apparent: one of the most ingenious moments features a decapitated zombie who's inexplicably retained some motor function. A quick shake of its shoulders and its obvious why this is so – its head isn't missing, but hanging down its back by a thin piece of spinal cord. Catapulted over its shoulders, the head then proceeds to chomp on one of the unsuspecting living.

The zombies themselves are equally striking creations. Make-up artist Greg Nicotero, who originally assisted Tom Savini on *Day of the Dead*, took that film as his starting point and expanded on its vision of the ghouls as decaying lumps of flesh.

"A lot of what zombies look like in movies has to do with what we did for *Day of the Dead*," he told *Fangoria*. "The idea then was always to try and make their eyes look deeper set, so we built out the brows and they were a little caveman-ish, and their eyebrows disappeared. The joke was that you became a zombie and your eyebrows are gone. So here, we really wanted to present the facial structures of most of the people. Very rarely have we done brows – we've done enhanced cheekbones and the bridge of the nose and everybody either has custom dentures or we use a mouth rinse to make their teeth look grey. And before every take, we have them rinse their mouths with black mouthwash so their tongues are black, as if there's no living flesh in their mouths."[230]

The detail of the zombie make-up adds much to *Land of the Dead*'s aesthetic, ensuring that even though this is the most action-orientated film in Romero's series, the ghouls dominate the audience's imagination – and not even tongue in cheek cameos from Savini, Simon Pegg and Edgar Wright can detract from that.

The scene in which Big Daddy leads his zombie army towards Fiddler's Green – the ghouls silently emerging from the murky waters that surround the city – has a haunting quality that surpasses anything Romero has achieved before. The film may not be, as the overeager studio trailers claimed, "Romero's masterpiece". But it has undeniable moments of grandeur.

Fortunately, the studio-enforced shenanigans over gore, ratings and money did little to change Romero's vision of where the film was heading politically. "At this point in the story, the zombies are the majority, and we're taking up where we left off with Bub [from *Day of the Dead*], who was the first ghoul we saw with a hint of intelligence," explained Nicotero. "They've basically taken over, but there are still bands of [surviving] humans, and the story is all about their existence. It's intriguing how George has still been able to inject social relevance to today's culture [...] This one is going to be about greed and selfishness and money, and how that drives everyone. George's movies are always about one part of society consuming another, whether it's consumerism or wealth and power, and we're definitely going to stick with that."[231]

With the apartments of Fiddler's Green a more luxurious take on the shopping mall enclave from *Dawn of the Dead*, it's obvious that Romero has lost none of his anti-consumerist fervour even when taking a major Hollywood studio's dollar. Universal obviously realised that a financially successful Romero movie would need to be given some socio-political leeway in the subtext department to avoid angering both its director and fans – which leads one to speculate that Romero may have done more to popularise socio-political readings of film among horror fans than any other director living today.

Envisioning a world ruled by a rich cartel of Fiddler's Green residents – all suited and coiffured like a board of fat cat company directors – *Land of the Dead* wins few prizes for subtlety. But Romero does make some well-aimed jabs at the current American establishment. Kaufman and his cronies are, it seems, the zombie apocalypse's answer to Enron, a group of rapacious businessmen interested in fiddling as much green as they can.

The name "Fiddler's Green" evokes both corruption and a certain disregard for the situation happening beyond the limits of the skyscraper paradise: "fiddling while Rome burns".[232] In retrospect, though, the movie is also prescient about the financial crash that was lurking in the sidelines of the American economy in 2004. The credit and derivatives boom and bust would create the Occupy Wall Street movement and a sense of resentment against the wealthiest 1 per cent that *Land of the Dead* seems to sense coming.

Certainly Romero was keen to stress that the real villains of the movie weren't the ghouls. "It's not so much the zombies. Whatever commentary on consumerism is in *Dawn of the Dead* had nothing to do with the zombies. They're just sort of walkin' through all of this, man. It's really the humans and their attitudes – the same themes of people not communicating, things falling apart internally and people not dealing with it. If everybody just sat down in a room and tried to figure out an approach... But everyone is still working to their own agendas and not willing to give up life as it was. That's the theme that runs through all of this. And *Land*, I believe, has a little bit more of that.

The idea of building a society on glass, and not caring about what's going on around you – wearing blinders."[233]

Whatever one makes of Romero's rather disingenuous comment that his consumerist critique in *Dawn* had "nothing to do with the zombies" (what else were they but parodies of soulless consumerism?), this stands as an interesting statement of his intent in *Land*. The sense of a society in meltdown is keenly sketched throughout the film, although at times – as in the ragged revolution being fermented on the streets beneath Fiddler's Green – it's rather clumsy. Still, Romero's point is the same as it has been during the rest of the series, what is the difference between the zombies and us? Or as actor Robert Joy insightfully sums it up: "It makes you ask, 'When is the Other really the Other and when is the Other us?'"[234]

The zombies in *Land of the Dead* are definitely more central than in any other of Romero's living dead outings. While the previous three films in the series featured a black hero who was alive, *Land of the Dead* is the first to feature a black hero who is already dead. Big Daddy (Eugene Clark) is a distant cousin not only of Bub, the zombie with a brain from *Day of the Dead*, but also of Ben, Peter and John in the earlier films.

As a zombie who has regained the power of thought and speech – albeit limited – Big Daddy has jumped several steps up the living dead evolutionary ladder. He can remember his former job as a gas station attendant and is smart enough to lead his fellow zombies towards Fiddler's Green in an attempt to save them from extermination. No longer entranced by the "sky flower" fireworks displays that Kaufman uses to transfix the zombies, Big Daddy is a revolutionary: a zombie leading a living dead uprising. Under his command the ghouls relearn how to use the tools they have to hand, from meat cleavers to looted machine guns.

Romero styles this uprising in keeping with the rest of the series' racial undertones. Big Daddy is like a zombified Black Panther, a civil rights revolutionary who leads this living dead underclass on a riot against the Establishment. Clark, who plays the growling, raging zombie with quite remarkable conviction, overtly suggested as much in interview with *Fangoria*.

"I see Big Daddy as a man, a zombie, who is evolving and who realises, 'This is wrong!' All right? You don't come into our territory, we don't eat you – we'll leave you alone. You come in, you cause mayhem, and it's wrong. So… civil rights? I don't think there are any civil rights. It's zombie rights. Leave. Us. Alone! […] There are a lot of atrocities occurring. These events are happening within my world. And when Big Daddy sees people dying, and being slaughtered, it pains him. For me to play this role, there are some really dark places I'm going and it breaks my heart. Those moans and groans come from that place. Any oppressed people around the world, when they're in deep, deep pain, you don't hear words, you hear moaning and groaning."[235]

In Big Daddy, Romero rewires the zombie genre's rich racial history, styling his ghouls as an oppressed minority rising up against the fascist dictatorship of Kaufman's Fiddler's Green. It's the first film in the series to explicitly ask us to sympathise with the zombie horde and it extends Romero's living dead mythology in a way which none of his imitators have ever managed to do.

As Big Daddy leads his mixed band of zombies towards the compound, it's difficult not to read the conflict in racial terms. After all, Kaufman and his cronies have already revealed themselves as racists: Cholo is refused an apartment in the Green because he's the wrong sort of person (i.e., Hispanic); Kaufman employs the services of a black manservant (who, in a moment worthy of Willie Best himself, heads for the hills when the going gets rough). The zombie insurrection may recall the armed proletariat uprisings of both *Nightmare City* and *The Nights of Terror*, but Romero is the first filmmaker to link it with such an explicit racial theme. This could well be the zombie genre's answer to the Watts Riots.

What's striking is the fluidity of Romero's living dead metaphor. Previous entries in the series styled the ghouls as the dead of Vietnam, the silent majority of the Nixon era and vapid consumers. *Land*, meanwhile, turns them into an oppressed (ethnic) underclass. In Romero's hands, the zombie has a symbolic, metaphorical power unmatched by any other horror movie monster. His ability to reshape them for each decade has become his calling card and *Land of the Dead* proves to be no exception as it bravely tries to tackle the Bush administration, the War on Terror and the post-9/11 world.

Much of this was a result of timing. The original script for the film – written as *Dead Reckoning* – was penned before 9/11 and had to be radically altered after the attack on the World Trade Center, as certain scenes involving helicopters and skyscrapers suddenly seemed in rather bad taste. Romero reworked the film in the aftermath of 9/11 and so was able to incorporate the War on Terror into his vision of the zombie apocalypse. As he told a reporter from *The New York Times* during production: "The idea of living with terrorism – I've tried to make it more applicable to the concerns Americans are going through now."[236]

How successful this strategy is depends on how transparent one likes one's political subtext. Yet, regardless of the lack of subtlety, *Land of the Dead* stands as one of the first major blockbuster productions to openly criticise Bush's war record. Presenting Kaufman as a composite of George W. Bush and Defense Secretary Donald Rumsfeld, Romero makes his criticism of the regime more than transparent. After Cholo steals Dead Reckoning and threatens to destroy Fiddler's Green, Kaufman growls "We don't negotiate with terrorists" in an echo of that now famous presidential line. Cholo's response is equally fraught with real-world analogy: "I'm gonna do a jihad on his ass."

Making Kaufman into a symbol of the corporate interests underpinning the Bush government's desire to continue the War on Terror, *Land of the Dead* homes in on a society in which the leaders are willing to profit from a dangerous situation, exacerbating that situation in the process in order to make a profit. The link between this and critics of the White House – who contended that the post 9/11 terrorist threat was being used as an excuse for the occupation of oil-rich Iraq, the expansion of corporate America's coffers and the gradual erosion American civil liberties – is clear.

Pointing out the twenty-seven year difference between *Dawn* and *Land*' social commentary, Romero says: "The financial stakes are a little higher, too. In *Dawn*, it was just about getting a pair of Nikes. But, you know, this is the era of Halliburton."[237] It's unsurprising, then, that Kaufman should meet his end by being doused in petrol and set light by Big Daddy. Romero lost none of his darkly humorous touch during his sabbatical from the genre.

As the zombies invade the Fiddler's Green skyscraper, Romero restages a variation of the attack on the Twin Towers. Zombies pile through the lobby and wreak havoc on the inhabitants. Outside, suited residents of the apartment complex run terrified through the streets, a visual analogue of the footage of commuters in New York fleeing the collapsing World Trade Center. Around them, Kaufman's fascist bullyboys – a different kind of Homeland Security – try to stop the advancing ghouls with little success.

The question Romero poses is: who is the real terrorist? Cholo, who's threatening to destroy the city? The zombies; who, as Riley realises, are just looking for a place to call home? Or Kaufman and his cronies, who've brought this situation upon themselves as a result of their inhumane treatment of both the living and the ghouls? The correct answer isn't difficult to guess.

Romero's *Land of the Dead* is likely to become the yardstick by which the millennial revival of the zombie genre is measured. By focusing in on the War on Terror, the fourth film in his influential series gives some indication of what fuelled the sudden re-emergence of the genre in the early years of the 20th century. The obvious answer for this unexpected boom in zombie movies is to trace the trend back to the success of the *Resident Evil* games, which brought the living dead to the attention of a new generation who may have been unfamiliar with Romero's work.

That's certainly what the director's own take on the situation is. "I'm cynical enough that I don't think there's any particular reason or social zeitgeist that brings people to this material. One movie becomes a hit and everyone says let's go make a zombie film. I do think the *Resident Evil* videogames woke everyone up to the undead idea that had been lying dormant a while. Then *28 Days Later* and *Shaun of the Dead* added fuel to the flames. Those plus the *Dawn of the Dead* remake certainly helped the *Land* deal."[238]

Yet perhaps there's more to it than this. Romero's self-confessed cynical take on Hollywood's unerring ability to always play follow the leader doesn't explain why audiences have responded so favourably to zombies after 2002.

The spectre of several intertwined millennial anxieties, from SARS to global terrorism hangs over many of these films. The fact that the redux version of *Dawn of the Dead* concentrates on a group of heroes led by emergency service workers – a nurse, a policeman, and (at a push) a couple of security guards – seems rather significant in the post-9/11 world. So too does almost all of these recent zombie films' interest in viral outbreaks, diseases and death. As America and Europe braced themselves for another terrorist "spectacular" after 9/11, could the zombie be a response to contemporary anxieties?

The revival of the genre coincided with a historical moment that the zombie was more suited to than vampires, werewolves, serial killers or any of the other usual horror monsters. The genre's traditional use of biochemical warfare and toxic spills as the starting point for its living dead apocalypses had an added impetus after the anthrax scares, concerns about weapons of mass destruction, and fears about a "dirty bomb" being released in a major metropolitan centre that emerged after 9/11.

Shaun of the Dead's Simon Pegg noted that the zombie renaissance seemed to be feeding off these anxieties. "It's fear of each other. It's about fear of other human beings, and fear of ourselves. Weirdly enough, a parallel thing with [*Shaun of the Dead*] is that it's all about not noticing the threat around you. And now here we are in a situation where apparently we could be blown to smithereens at any point because of terrorism and it's a threat that we have not noticed gather up around us. It's very current, this whole thing: viral paranoia, fear of outsiders coming in, xenophobia, these bogeymen terrorists that are out there."[239]

As if to prove the point that zombie movies were reflecting contemporary concerns, a couple of months after the release of *Land of the Dead*, the world's news channel's were suddenly dominated by horrendous images from New Orleans in the wake of Hurricane Katrina. Tuning into CNN or the BBC, the scenes from the devastated city looked like the backdrop to a Romero movie: bewildered, scared civilians; looting and lawlessness; incompetent government agencies that failed to prevent the disaster or deal with its immediate aftermath effectively. The dead may not have been walking, but it all had an eerily familiar ring. There was a sense that the zombie was the perfect monster for the time.

PART TWO

ZOMBIES, ZOMBIES EVERYWHERE!

2004 – 2014

"APOCALYPSE IS TRENDING"
– *Night of the Living Dead: Resurrection* (2012)

CHAPTER NINE

TERROR OF THE ZOMBIE TERRORISTS

"THIS ELEPHANT IN THE ROOM, THIS IRAQ WAR STORY,
IS NOT BEING DRAMATISED."
– Joe Dante, director of *Homecoming*[240]

I. THE NIGHT IT CAME HOME

Zombie movies have always been an index of their times. They're such a supremely elastic metaphor for our darkest fears, easily adaptable to each era's gravest concerns. The zombie renaissance that began around 2001 was no different. Emerging in the shadow of the world-changing events of 9/11, the sudden revival of zombies in pop culture was inevitably coloured by the unfolding of the War on Terror.

The events of 9/11 didn't start the zombie boom; both *28 Days Later* and the *Resident Evil* movie were in production before the attacks. But it did put fuel in its tank, changing the course zombie cinema would take forever. Romero's satire in *Land of the Dead* gave the first hint of how world events might be reflected in zombie cinema. However, it was another veteran horror filmmaker who'd give us the most politically excoriating zombie movie of the 2000s – and, perhaps, the most politically excoriating zombie movie, period.

Joe Dante's *Homecoming* (2005) was made for the Showtime TV channel in the US as part of their *Masters of Horror* series. It was a reminder of just how powerful and transgressive the walking dead could be. No simple horror show, it tackled contemporary politics head-on with a dogged determination to get its message across.

Significantly – and, perhaps, surprisingly – *Homecoming* was only one of a handful of zombie movies to explicitly tackle the aftermath of 9/11, the War on Terror and the invasion of Iraq. *Land of the Dead* had staked out this ground first, although its anger was constrained within the limits of a studio movie distributed by Universal. *Zombies of Mass Destruction* (2008) would pick up the baton a few years later, a jokey satire of ordinary Americans' responses to 9/11 filtered through the lens of a zombie outbreak. *The Crazies* (2010) would boldly retool Romero's own Vietnam War horror for the era of Iraq. Other movies after 9/11 bore the stamp of the times in increasingly more apparent ways – even big budget blockbusters like *I Am Legend* (2007) and *World War Z* (2013) – although they largely refrained from overt political comment.

Homecoming takes its conceit from the short story "Death and Suffrage" by Dale Bailey, in which the dead return to life to vote for tougher gun-control laws. In Dante's movie the idea is repurposed for the Iraq War, allowing the filmmaker to take a swipe at George W. Bush's legacy. In *Homecoming*, the dead don't want to eat you, they just want to cast their vote – something which Republicans find more terrifying than cannibalism.

Homecoming begins with a Monkey's Paw-style wish. Slick Washington presidential speechwriter David Murch (Jon Tenney), aka "the smartest guy in D.C.", goes on a Larry King-style TV show to debate the Iraq War. He's confronted by an angry mother whose son died fighting overseas. "They told us there was a threat to America," she complains." But the weapons of mass destruction weren't there. The nuclear program wasn't there. The threat wasn't there."

It's a powerful piece of television and it's sure to hit the President's popularity ratings. Murch quickly defends government policy. He talks about his brother who died in Vietnam and breaks down in tears on live TV as he makes an emotive wish: "Believe me, if I had one wish I would wish for your son to come back," he tells the grieving mother. "Because I know he would tell us all how important this struggle is for the safety and security of all Americans."

Murch's shameless piece of media spin doctoring gets attention. In a world where media-savvy commentators are rarely authentic, his real tears shake up the political class in Washington D.C. "It was like so… *sincere*," marvels Jane Cleaver (Thea Gill), a rightwing constitutional scholar and bestselling author of lurid book *Subversion: How The Radical Left Took Over Cable News*. She's so impressed she hungrily beds him after the show.

On its own, Murch's wish doesn't do anything very much. But when the line is reused by POTUS himself – a figure who we never properly see, but whose voice recalls George W. Bush's Texan drawl – strange things happen. At the Dover Air Force Base in Delaware, where coffins of servicemen and women are draped in the Stars and Stripes, the dead suddenly start returning to life.

The President's insincere wish, his deliberate use of soundbite spin in the face of American dead in Iraq, forces the ghouls to march on Washington demanding the right to vote in the upcoming presidential elections. The ghouls arrive in the capital, calling out the politicians for being liars,

draft dodgers and morally bankrupt. Still dressed in their uniforms, these zombie soldiers prove a potent symbol of leftwing American disillusionment in the years before Obama's election.

Homecoming is a truly brilliant piece of agitprop filmmaking. It's literally dripping with caustic hatred for the politicians and spin doctors who led America into a war that the filmmakers obviously believe was built on a lie. Retooling the zombie movie as a vehicle of ideas rather than gore, Dante and screenwriter Sam Hamm deliver a strident, passionately political TV B-movie.

Unlike Romero's *Land of the Dead*, where the anti-Bush satire was veiled and subtextual, *Homecoming*'s overt polemic slaps audiences on both cheeks. No one could mistake this for just another silly zombie movie. It is an angry howl of rage.

Dante's imagery is part of the film's provocative appeal. At Dover Air Force Base, we see rows of military caskets draped with the Stars and Stripes – a side of the war that was banned from TV at the time. Later, as the voting dead become a problem for the Republicans, the ghouls are rounded up and interned in orange jump suits behind barbed wire fences in Guantanamo style concentration camps.

The zombies themselves aren't scary. In fact what's fascinating about the movie is the grace and respect with which the ghouls are treated – these, the filmmakers seem to be arguing, are the metaphorical representations of America's real dead. Instead, *Homecoming* presents Washington politicians and spin doctors as the monsters – ghoulishly feasting on the sacrifice made by America's soldiers.

Chief among the villains is Kurt Rand (Robert Picardo), a Karl Rove figure. Freely admitting that "We sold a war based on nothing but horseshit and elbow grease", he hopes that the zombie soldiers will eventually eat someone and give the authorities an excuse to round them up.

When the ghouls prove annoyingly restrained in their appetites, Rand helps rig the presidential elections so that the zombies' votes don't count – it's an act of fraud that explicitly recalls the controversy surrounding the Florida vote count in the Presidential elections in 2000. His actions are so shamelessly criminal and un-American that the war dead of WWII, Korea and Vietnam rise up in protest from their graves in Arlington National

Cemetery to depose the government.

Homecoming has a long cinematic lineage stretching from Abel Gance's *J'Accuse* to Bob Clark's Vietnam-era *Deathdream* and William Lustig's *Uncle Sam* (1996) – in which a soldier killed by friendly fire during Operation Desert Storm in Kuwait comes back from the dead on the Fourth of July to kill peeping toms, pacifists and corrupt politicians in a sly satire of patriotism run amok.

What gives *Homecoming* its power, though, is its furious anger. Turning the Republican "Support Our Troops" rhetoric back on itself, it's a movie that's fuelled by pure rage. "It's extremely biased and it's extremely unsubtle," Dante admitted after the film's premiere. "It's [like taking] a blunt hammer to the administration that's currently ruining the country."[241]

When *Homecoming* was broadcast in 2005, it was the first film to deal openly with the anger surrounding the Iraq War. The irony that it was a zombie movie that articulated the rage many felt about the invasion didn't escape the filmmakers. "It's fucking sick," Dante said. "This pitiful zombie movie is the only thing anybody's done about this issue that's killed 2,000 Americans and untold numbers of Iraqis."[242]

III. INSANITY IS INFECTIOUS

The opening match of a small town's high-school baseball season. A small crowd watches from the stands. It's a friendly, family atmosphere. Nothing unusual here. Nothing you couldn't find in a thousand American towns every week. This particular town is Ogden Marsh, Pierce County, Iowa. A locale billed by the local tourist board as "The friendliest place on earth".

Watching the ball game from the wings is Sheriff David Dutton (Timothy Olyphant) and his deputy Russell Clank (Joe Anderson). They're sipping coffee, commenting on the batter's swing. Suddenly, across the baseball diamond, a figure appears: a lone middle-aged man walking towards the players with a strange, dead eyed purpose. In his hand is a double-barrelled shotgun.

The sheriff drops his cup, coffee spilling over the concrete ground, and races forwards. He waves the players back into the dugout, tells his deputy to split left and cover him. Then he jogs up to the gunman, a local man called Rory Hamill (Mike Hickman), and blocks his way. You can tell that the sheriff would rather be anywhere else than there. But he has a job to do – "To protect and serve" – and he knows it.

His opening gambit – matter-of-fact surprise, not anger – is smart. "We've got a ball game going on. We're playing ball and you come out with a gun? What the hell are you doing? Rory, you're drunk. That's all…"

The man looks at the weapon, as if noticing it for the first time. Sheriff Dutton tries to talk him down, but it's quickly obvious that he's not getting anywhere. Hamill is altered, weird. The sheriff – what choice does he have? – puts a hand on his holster. In such a tinderbox situation that action is provocative enough to be a catalyst. In a flash: Hamill goes to fire his shotgun and Dutton draws his weapon and puts him down. BANG!

Instantly, the sheriff's face contorts in shock and despair. He rushes forwards, kneels beside the man. But it's already too late. The peaceful afternoon has been interrupted by a fatal police shooting. We're still reeling from the shock as two military jets suddenly scream overhead deafeningly and the film's title silently, imposingly flashes up on screen without fanfare: *THE CRAZIES*. This isn't just another crappy Romero remake like *Day of the Dead 2: Contagium* (2005) or *Night of the Living Dead: 3D* (2006).

Back in 1973, Romero made *The Crazies* for around $220,000. In 2010, the remake had a budget in the region of $20 million – an increase that went above and beyond inflation. For director Breck Eisner (*Sahara*) the justification for the remake was to be found in that budgetary jump.

"*The Crazies* was a *really* low-budget movie and it suffered from limitations in production. So, for me, *The Crazies* remake is about: What if Romero had had more money? What if he had had better actors? What would he have done in that scenario? Philosophically, I'm only interested in remaking a movie where I can do something different or improve upon a limitation that was presented to the filmmakers originally. With *The Crazies*, obviously the budget was a limitation."[243]

Eisner's *The Crazies* set the gold standard for zombie remakes in the 2000s. In box office terms its success ($54 million worldwide theatrically) was modest, especially when compared to Zack Snyder's 2004 *Dawn of the Dead* remake. But in artistic terms it completely justified itself, updating the 'Nam paranoia of Romero's original to the era of the Iraq War. Much like its predecessor, it isn't a zombie movie per se – its "crazies" are very much alive, not dead – but it has all the tropes of the classic zombie movie It's monsters are, like the zombies of *Night of the Living Dead*, what Romero always called "the neighbours".

The Crazies's plotting stays true to the original's simplicity: after the US military accidentally release a bio-weapon codenamed "Trixie" into the water supply of a small American town, the inhabitants begin to turn into rabid, violent ghouls. The army moves in and attempts to enforce quarantine and martial law with disastrous results as the civilian population – both infected and immune – fight back.

Delivering a sense of unease and disconnection reminiscent of the *Invasion of the Body Snatchers* movies, Eisner and screenwriters Scott Kosar (who worked on *The Texas Chainsaw Massacre* and *The Amityville Horror* remakes) and Ray Wright (who co-wrote the Pulse remake) quickly pull the rug out from under us. Everyone seems crazy here: from the clearly disturbed townsfolk developing 1,000-yard stares; to the mayor who point blank refuses to turn off the infected water supply ("You turn off the water, you're going to kill the crops. You kill the crops you're going to bankrupt every family in Pierce County"); and the military who shut down the town.

Sheriff Dutton quickly finds himself breaking the law, even shutting off the town's water against the mayor's explicit wishes, in order to do his job. It's a total reversal of the way things should be that suggests the world is beginning to lose its grip on sanity. Traumatised by the baseball pitch shooting, Dutton increasingly looks like a loose cannon. When his deputy worries that the act of "civil disobedience" in shutting off the water might cost his boss his job, Dutton responds, "That wouldn't be such a bad thing."

Meanwhile, the craziness infects the town – ordinary family men and women suddenly turning into homicidal maniacs. The transformation of the sane into the insane is what gives *The Crazies* its brilliant set pieces as the fabric of small town America is ripped apart. As the military arrives – soldiers clad in chemical-warfare suits, their invasion accompanied by an excess of military hardware – it's hard to believe this is happening on American soil. The gas-masked soldiers ignore the Dutton's pleas ("I'm the sheriff, she's a doctor – we know these people"). They act without the kind of compassion and understanding we've seen from Dutton. More damningly, they also act without reason.

Judy (Radha Mitchell), Dutton's wife and the

Still from Romero's original *The Crazies* (1973).

town's doctor, is pulled away from her husband because she has a temperature. No one listens to the explanation that she's pregnant, or that she's had a temperature for weeks. Instead, she's manhandled by military stooges in bulky spacesuits like she's some sort of E.T. The military doctors ignore her terrified pleas that she's pregnant, sedate her and strap her to a gurney. No one offers her a word of comfort. They treat her like cattle.

Like the original, the remake is a powerful indictment of the military and of martial law (it was financed by politically focussed film company Participant Media, who previously backed Al Gore's Oscar-winning documentary *An Inconvenient Truth* and oil thriller *Syriana*). In Eisner's version the heavy-handed tactics lead the townsfolk to rebel and, as a result, the military's chance to stop the spread of the virus is lost as their makeshift containment (concentration?) camp is attacked by insurgent local residents. In a country where carrying arms is a Second Amendment right, the military's tactics seem more than a little short-sighted.

Dutton himself eventually joins the growing guerrilla effort, teaming up with survivors as crazies and soldiers roam the county killing indiscriminately. As they escape, what follows is a series of set-pieces that are held together by the core characters: Dutton and his deputy, whose increasingly shaky grip on sanity is the film's ticking time bomb. Is Deputy Clank showing signs of infection? Or is his increasingly unhinged behaviour actually a rational response to the insanity of the authorities?

After a meeting with a scared soldier – who is initially so ill-informed he's terrified of taking his gas mask off, and later agrees to help them ("I didn't sign up to shoot unarmed civilians") – the film lays its theme bare. Dutton and co watch as a group of soldiers shoot a boy, then kill his grieving mother even though she offers them no threat at all. The bodies are quickly burned by a flamethrower, a shockingly throwaway moment of summary execution that brings home *The Crazies*'s real terror.

In the face of such institutional madness, the crazies themselves seem a lesser threat somehow. With their peeling skin, obsidian eyes and zigzagging veins full of black blood, they're suitably disturbing ghouls – make-up designer

Robert Hall worked on TV's *Buffy the Vampire Slayer* and also *Quarantine*, the US remake of Spanish zombie horror *[REC]* and its sequel.

Yet, the film's real horror is a political one. The realisation that a democratic nation like the United States of America could slide into martial law and toss citizens' rights aside so quickly is terrifying. As the forces of local law and order (the sheriff's office, the mayor's office and the local healthcare providers) are superseded by an unaccountable military machine working under shadowy orders, *The Crazies* returns to Romero's 1973 theme: can we trust our leaders? Can we trust our government? Is democratic stability a wafer-thin construct that can be rescinded without consultation?

The discovery that Trixie was a bio-weapon designed to destabilise the civilian populations of America's enemies offers a bleakly ironic additional layer to the film's events. Although it was on its way to be destroyed when the plane transporting it crashed in the local river, Trixie actually proves highly effective. This WMD opens up the film's political commentary as it updates Romero's 'Nam-era anger to the Iraq War.

"I really wanted to make *The Crazies* because of the times," Eisner said during the movie's preproduction. "I absolutely think what has happened in Iraq – and what is happening with our country and how our military has been used for abusive and oppressive way around the world – was a big point of what Romero was doing with *The Crazies* when he made it. Today it's a different war, a different time, but it's a very similar issue."[244] *The Crazies* repeatedly echoes the Iraq War. There is the spectre of Weapons of Mass Destruction (Hans Blix never found any in Iraq; but in *The Crazies* America itself has, perversely, more than its own fair share). There is also the idea of the American military destabilising civilian populations for tactical advantage. Charging into Ogden Marsh, the US military create a situation in which a besieged civilian population turns against them and takes up arms to defend itself. Previously peaceful citizens become makeshift guerrillas, and even the local forces of law and order turn against the invading soldiers. It seems like a mirror image of Baghdad during Operation Iraqi Freedom in 2003.

By destabilising the town, though, the military reveal themselves to be even crazier than the crazies themselves. One might be forgiven for remembering

Colin Powell's alleged accusation that certain colleagues in the Bush administration were "fucking crazies" in their approach to Iraq.

What's most interesting about *The Crazies*, though, is how it treats its homicidal ghouls. By 2010 the image of what we might call raging zombies – the furious, hating "infected" that first established themselves in *28 Days Later* – had become something of a genre staple.

Driven totally by rage, these creatures are "Terminators", single-minded in their relentless pursuit. But while the iconic cyborg of James Cameron's movie was calmly devoid of emotion, the raging, homicidal ghouls of *The Crazies* seemed to truly hate us.

Does that sense of hatred, that thirst for our annihilation seem familiar? Perhaps it's because it has a real-world parallel in the West's view of Islamic fundamentalism – a religious extremism that seems equally obsessed with hatred of us and a thirst for our annihilation. The raging zombies that increasingly appeared after *28 Days Later* – not just in *The Crazies* but in scores of zombie movies – are nothing less than jihadists. Driven by an unrelenting, all-consuming hatred for everything we hold dear, they are unwilling to listen to reason, impossible to placate.

Romero's dead were driven by appetite. They wanted to eat us, or, at second best, turn us into them (misery, after all, loves company). But the raging zombies that emerged after 9/11 aren't interested in consuming or subsuming us. They simply want to annihilate us, to make us literally nothing.

III. THE DEAD HATE THE LIVING

Why do they hate us?" was a meme that blossomed in 2001. Addressing a joint session of Congress ten days after 9/11, George W. Bush posed a historic question about the growing wave of terrorism. "Americans are asking: 'Why do they hate us?'" It wasn't a rhetorical question – his scriptwriters already had a pre-prepared answer. "They hate our freedoms," the President told his audience. "Our freedom of religion, our freedom of speech, our freedom to vote and assemble and disagree with each other."[245]

It was around this time that the idea of the raging zombie was born. In retrospect, it's clear that a large proportion of post-millennial zombie movies lost interest in death as one of the fundamental planks of the zombie myth. Instead, they began to treat the zombie as a physically and psychologically altered being – more often infected than dead, and intent on destroying the living. It was a change that swept away the graveyards, mortuaries and corpses of earlier zombie movies. After 2001, zombies became metaphors for viral outbreaks and diseases – a reflection, as we'll see, of our increasingly globalised world.

It is a transition that – much like Romero's introduction of cannibalism to the zombie myth in '68 – has had an irrevocable impact on the genre.

One of the chief characteristics of the millennial zombie is its fury, an unstoppable raging anger. No longer are zombies slow shufflers. They're now furies intent on destruction.

28 Days Later's rage virus – which riffed on news headlines about road rage and on the breakdown of fundamental human connections in modern, urban society – was the start of this. But it is tempting to argue that it has evolved into something more politically charged. The raging zombie is, from one perspective, a proxy for the jihadists who haunt Western society's paranoid nightmares. They're driven by hatred for us. They cannot be reasoned with, placated or calmed. Meanwhile, the heroes of contemporary zombie movies are reflections of the citizen-soldiers of 9/11 – ordinary men and women forced to undertake extreme acts of heroism in terrible circumstances.

Many of the movies in which these raging dead appear have tangential but unmistakable links to 9/11, the invasion of Iraq and the War on Terror. The leaping ghouls in *Evilution* (2007) escape a black ops military lab in Iraq where the US military is experimenting with an alien microbe that resurrects the dead; the airplane terror in both *Flight of the Living Dead: Outbreak on a Plane* (2007) and *Quarantine 2: Terminal* (2010) can't help but recall the 9/11 attacks; Britain's *Zombie Undead* (2010) begins with a terrorist bomb in Leicester creating ghouls; *Zombie Farm* (2007) sees a laughable "Taliban terrorist" in a dodgy headscarf poisoning the water supply in a Californian town; the prologue of *Vs The Dead* (2010) features zombie Taliban soldiers accidentally created by a US battlefield drug called "Round Two".

In *Planet Terror* (2007) a military bio-weapon designed for Iraq turns American citizens into zombified "sickos". Bruce Willis plays a special forces soldier who reputedly killed Bin Laden. "I put two in his heart, one in his computer," he growls. A few years later, the crossover between the world's (then) most wanted man and the zombie craze led to the not-as-fun-as-it-ought-to-be *Osombie* (2012), in which a living dead Osama leads jihadist ghouls against American forces from a cave in Afghanistan. *Ridge War Z* (2013) tells the story of a squad of US grunts overrun and massacred during a zombie outbreak – but its desert setting and unstoppable ghouls could just as well be insurgents in a Middle Eastern theatre of war.

9/11 itself informs *Zombies of Mass Destruction*, directed and co-written by Iranian-American Kevin Hamedani. It satirically dissects both xenophobia and homophobia after a terrorist zombie outbreak convinces a bigoted Pacific Midwestern town to turn against an innocent Iranian-American family and a visiting gay couple.

"Romero did an African-American in the late 1960s as a protagonist," Hamedani told *Fangoria*. "So we did a Middle Eastern and a gay guy, because it just seemed that for my generation – I'm in my mid-20s – that's our civil rights movement: the homophobia and then all the xenophobia that came to the surface after 9/11."[246]

In a similar vein *The Dead Live*, a barely watchable backyard epic about a TV news crew filming a zombie outbreak in Ohio, ends with a bathetic cry of "Let's roll!" – the same phrase used by one of the terrorist-fighting passengers on flight United 93 on 9/11. After the credits, an on-screen statement from the director shamelessly dedicates his barely incompetent movie to "the brave men, women and children who died as heroes on that fateful sunny morning of September 11th, 2001". To add insult to injury it then draws asinine comparisons between zombies and terrorists that have nothing to do with the movie itself. It's completely embarrassing.

In *28 Weeks Later* (2007), the sequel to Danny Boyle's influential retooling of the zombie myth, the US military has created a quarantined Green Zone on the Isle of Dogs in London. With its explicit militarisation – one sequence features a military helicopter being used as an aerial scythe against the ghouls – the film finds a bigger canvas for its raging, hating ghouls and its finale sees the infection spreading further afield into Europe with a shot of ghouls closing in on the Eiffel Tower.

Contagion. Inexplicable hatred. The spread of a virulent disease. Such imagery and language has as much to do with how the West conceives of Islamic terrorism as it does with how the filmmakers treat their "infected" zombies. Genre fans who argue themselves in knots over whether or not the ghouls of *28 Days Later* and its sequel deserve to be considered zombies blithely miss the point – the fundamental basis of the zombie myth has evolved in the years since 9/11.

In retrospect, *28 Days Later* achieved something quite remarkable. It achieved a tectonic shift in the plates of the zombie genre that proved as earthshaking as the moment Romero turned the Haitian zombie into a cannibal. Infected ghouls – and the rest of what critic Matt Zoller Seitz has called "zombies-by-proxy" – are the cornerstone of the zombie genre in the post-9/11 era.[247] Walking corpses have become raging haters.

Looking through the plots of low-budget, straight-to-DVD zombie movies it's obvious how fundamental the link between zombies and the War on Terror has become. The ghouls in *Awaken the Dead* (2006) are created by an unhinged CIA scientist who is fed up watching American troops die in futile incursions overseas. In *Bloodlust Zombies* (2011) a bereaved scientist (Janice Marie), whose husband was killed rebuilding schools in Afghanistan, creates a weaponised virus to turn civilians in hostile states against one another.

"That's insane," laments one of her colleagues. "When did being patriotic get so fucked up?" She snaps back: "Sending our best and brightest 5,000 miles away only to be stabbed in the back by the very people they're trying to help is fucked up." For the US military, zombie armies promise to be the ultimate chapter in American politicians' commitment to "war without casualties". It's an idea that gets its most fulsome expression in the final shot of zom-buddy-com *The Revenant* where the US military airdrops a squad of naked, citizen-soldier ghouls on Iran. Dick Cheney would approve.

Elsewhere, the ghouls as jihadists idea became a familiar trope. In *Dead Air* (2009) Bill Moseley stars as a shock jock whose rabid radio talk show homes in on the nation's mindset post 9/11: "Why are you so paranoid America?"His callers blame everything from tinned cat food to aliens to Muslims for their woes.

When Middle Eastern terrorists release "rabies bombs" in cities across the US, though, the streets are soon overrun by raging jihadist-style ghouls with bleeding eyes. "It happened, it finally happened," whispers one of the station's staffers – suggesting that a zombie outbreak is a logical extrapolation from the terror attacks of 9/11.

Using its "On Air" device to echo the tearful first-person statements recorded by callers to 911 operators during the WTC attacks, *Dead Air* also uses its ghouls as a stand in for Muslim fundamentalists. Determined to have it both ways, the screenplay reveals that the bio-weapon was actually created by the US military, adding a layer of left-leaning irony in the third act. "Where is the American media when Osama Bin Laden cashes his CIA paychecks?" demands lead terrorist Abir (Navid Negahban, later the bogeyman of US TV show *Homeland*). He proceeds to call out the American media and its citizens for being culpable in their own destruction.

Silly zombie musical *Song of the Dead* (2005) features a "Jihad Resurrection Virus" that creates "zombie terrorists". At a televised press conference the US president (Reggie Bannister, star of *Phantasm* and the hardest working man in horror) bursts into song while wearing a red, white and blue disco suit: "United we stand Muslims and Jesus/Christians and Jews/United we stand, the whole USA". Once again it turns out that it's actually the US government, not terrorists, who are responsible for the outbreak.

While most of these movies are ham-fisted in how they tackle their zombies-as-terrorists conceit, they illustrate how definitively the genre has been changed by the events of 9/11. But it's *The Crazies* that offers the most sustained and intellectually robust interrogation of the theme. Updating Romero's Nam-panic to the Iraq War, *The Crazies* features an abundance of military hardware and surveillance drones.

Its power, though, lies in its keen appraisal of how American citizens have lost faith in big government and in how it exploits fears about the collapse of democracy. By incompetently losing the Trixie WMD over the American Midwest, the US military create an army of crazies (jihadists) who want to destroy small town America (the parallels with US foreign policy in the Middle East fuelling terror attacks back home is pretty obvious).

At the same time, the military's murderous willingness to treat civilian casualties as necessary collateral damage is a disturbing echo of US policy in Iraq and Afghanistan. Unlike blockbuster *World War Z* (2013), which mirrors *The Crazies*'s ghouls-as-jihadists conceit, Breck Eisner's horror film doesn't assure us that everything will be all right by the time the credits rule. There is no Brad Pitt here to save the world. It is, instead, a rolling apocalypse.

As American foreign policy is recreated on home soil, Ogden Marsh's civilian population experience what it is to caught between military occupation and crazed zombie jihadists. Like all the best B-movies, *The Crazies* is infused with political and cultural anxieties that are well above its paygrade. As the Pentagon's eye-in-the-sky satellites keep everyone under surveillance, *The Crazies* ends with a truly terrifying twist: the next town could be yours. For Western audiences, it was a taste of how civilians in Iraq must have felt on a daily basis.

CHAPTER TEN

GHOULS ON FILM

"WHO'S GONNA BE LEFT TO WATCH?"
– Stranger (Martin Roach), *Dairy of the Dead* (2007)

I. ZOMBIE DIARIES OF THE DEAD

The camera shakes. A voice somewhere off-screen screams. An out of focus shadow appears in the corner of the frame. And across the nation there is the sound of box office cash registers going *ker-ching*! In the 2000s found footage movies became big business in Hollywood. *Paranormal Activity* (2007) set the trend, a $15,000 ghost story shot on consumer grade cameras becoming a $193 million worldwide hit after Paramount picked it up and released it in 2009. It was joined by *Cloverfield* (2008), a reskin of *Godzilla* relocated to New York. It was in many ways a cathartic replay of the 2001 World Trade Center attacks – a real-life terrorist atrocity that was similarly framed through the camcorder lenses of citizen journalists in downtown Manhattan.

It's no surprise that the rise of found footage movies corresponds with the evolution of our increasingly digital lives. In an era when we all now have a smartphone camcorder in our pockets, we've become used to seeing the news filmed by non-journalists on the ground.

It was inevitable that zombie cinema would be swept up in the tide. In 1978, Romero had made a cameo in *Dawn of the Dead* as a beleaguered TV news producer trying to hold things together as the world fell apart. Back then the networks were the channels you'd turn to in times of crisis. Today's digital landscape is different, though. If the dead walked tomorrow, the evidence would be on YouTube, Twitter and Facebook before it hit the BBC or CNN.

Events in the summer of 2012 proved the point.

In May, a new street drug known as "bath salts" exploded into public consciousness after the so-called "Miami cannibal attack". Car wash employee Rudy Eugene, allegedly high on bath salts at the time, stripped himself naked then attacked Ronald Poppo, a homeless man, under the MacArthur Causeway. He beat his victim unconscious, removed the man's trousers and then literally tried to eat his face off. When police officers arrived on the scene, Eugene ignored their orders to cease and desist this unprovoked act of cannibalism. They shot him dead.

The incident became international news and prompted semi-serious speculation that this might be how a zombie apocalypse would start. Reports of similarly bizarre cannibal incidents in the following months, all supposedly involving aggressors high on the illegal drug, only increased the press and public's hysteria. Twitter and Facebook lit up as people shared news reports of how bath salts were apparently turning rational people into slavering, superhuman zombie cannibals. The bath salts zombie meme went viral. By June 2012 the phrase "zombie apocalypse" was, for a brief time, the third most popular Google search.

The public hysteria over these attacks was so intense that the Centre for Disease Control in Atlanta took the unprecedented step of issuing a formal statement denying the existence of zombies. "CDC does not know of a virus or condition that would reanimate the dead (or one that would present zombie-like symptoms)," explained agency spokesman David Daigle.[248] His argument might have appeased conspiracy theorists if the CDC hadn't previously used zombies to publicise disaster preparedness.[249] Inevitably the hysteria inspired a zombie film, a maniacal punk DIY outing called – what else? – *Bath Salt Zombies* (2013).

The real intersection of our rapidly changing digital landscape and zombie movies had actually happened a few years earlier though. A cycle of found footage and mockumentary zombie movies had started retooling the traditional zombie apocalypse in novel and timely ways. It was a cycle that crossed continents, including Turkey's first zombie movie *Island: A Zombie Wedding* (orig. *Ada: Zombilerin Düğünü*, 2010), filmed on a wedding guest's camcorder; the Soviet Army found footage horrors of Dutch director Richard Raaphorst's deliriously bonkers *Frankenstein's Army* (2013); micro-budget US indie *Pretty Dead* (2013), a found footage tale of a medical student turning dead; the shot in twelve hours and mostly improvised (read: shouty and sweary) *Zombie Doomsday* (2010) in which a reality TV show crew is trapped in a restaurant during a zombie outbreak; and Ireland's *Portrait of a Zombie* (2012) which played like a subpar *Man Bites Dog* with ghouls.

Surprisingly enough, one of the first zombie movies in the found footage trend came from George Romero – a self-confessed relic of the analogue age. After *Land of the Dead*'s incendiary attack on Bush-era foreign policy, Romero turned his attention to something less politically charged

but equally timely. Like all his *Dead* films – movies that he calls "snapshots in time" – it reflected the period in which it was made back at us.[250]

Diary of the Dead (2007) tackled the rise of citizen journalism, YouTube and digital cameras. For a then 67-year-old filmmaker who has always been, by his own admission, uneasy with the online world, *Diary*'s contemporary feel was a pleasant surprise, even if its wide-eyed wonder at the power of the Internet had a slightly gauche feel. It also marked a deliberate departure from the earlier four films – a reboot of sorts.

Diary is inspired by everything from 9/11 to the YouTube generation to the looting of New Orleans after Hurricane Katrina.[251] The key to it, though, is Romero's sense of how the digital era has changed the media landscape. "All during the post-production on *Land*, I'd been watching Iraq on the 24/7 news and seen this incredible, ballooning growth of alternate media," the filmmaker later explained. "YouTube and so on – all of a sudden we're all somehow electronically connected to one another."[252]

Romero's reboot of his zombie apocalypse was an attempt to start a new *Dead* franchise that he would retain the rights to. *Diary of the Dead* broke with the chronology of the earlier *Dead* films (much like the Bond movies, Romero's zombie films are largely sequential, even though they're anachronistic in terms of being made across several different decades). It also broke with *Land of the Dead*, Romero's first studio zombie film.

Romero's experience with Universal had been a frustrating one. Although he had creative control over *Land of the Dead*, the film's distribution proved lacklustre. *Land* opened poorly theatrically sandwiched between *Batman Begins* and *War of the Worlds*, although it later did strong business abroad and on DVD. Uncomfortable working within the studio machine, Romero cashed in his chips and returned to his indie roots. Together with his producing partner Peter Grunwald, he teamed up with indie production company and distributor Artfire Films. *Diary of the Dead* ended up with an estimated $2 million budget – a far

Bath Salt Zombies (2013).

cry from the $15 million he had on *Land of the Dead*.

Diary of the Dead is set on the first night of the zombie outbreak, "the night everything changed". Caught up in the chaos are film students from the University of Pittsburgh, who are shooting a "silly mummy movie" in the woods when reports of the dead returning to life hits the news channels.

Convinced that the authorities are covering up the true scale of the problem, student director Jason (Josh Close) ditches the mummy movie. Instead, he decides to use his filmmaking skills to capture events as they unfold. Crowding into their Winnebago, the kids and their boozy, Eton-educated professor (Scott Wentworth) head out in search of safety.

Through their encounters, Jason remains committed to his documentary – much to the disgust of his girlfriend Debra (Michelle Morgan), who doubles as the film's narrator. She is appalled by his detachment. Jason is committed to getting the truth out there, uploading his film to the Internet so that a global audiences of truth-seekers can see how the authorities are covering up the disaster. Within eight minutes of its release, it gets 72,000 hits.

Although Romero plays fast and loose with found footage conventions – breaking the conceit that everything is filmed from a single camera perspective – *Diary of the Dead* illustrates how the media landscape has changed during the filmmaker's career. Today every kid with a smartphone can be a mini-Coppola, or their very own news channel. It's something that Romero is reticent about endorsing.

"By now we'd become part of it, part of 24/7," Debra laments as the movie unfolds. "It's strange how looking at it, seeing things through a lens, a glass – rose-coloured or shaded black – you become immune. You're supposed to be affected but you're not. I used to think it was just you out there, the viewers. But it's not. It's us too, the shooters. We become immune too. Inoculated. So that whatever happens around us, no matter how horrible it is, we just end up taking it in our stride. Just another day, just another death."

A self-confessed Luddite, Romero apparently doesn't see much potential in a society where everyone is a blogger, filmmaker or citizen journalist. "The mainstream had vanished," Debra

notes as *Diary*'s social collapse unfolds. "Now it was just us: bloggers, hackers, kids. The more voices there are, the more spin there is. Truth becomes that much harder to find. In the end it's just… noise."

For Romero, social media isn't a tool for revolution. He's inherently wary of celebrating a multiplicity of voices and mourns the loss of authority, consensus and Truth (with a capital T) that social media has brought about.

"In the old days there were three networks and all of a sudden Walter Cronkite is the most trusted man in America," he explained after the movie's release. "Everybody believes what he says, not even thinking. In those days we didn't even know it was being spun. We were very willing to just sort of listen to it and go along with it. I think the same thing is happening today. The problem is we're going along not with Cronkite, not with these three guys anymore, we're going along with 500 of them, a thousand, thousands of people, Arianna Huffington […] I'd almost rather be unknowingly manipulated, at least if the information is being managed, than just be subjected to this absolute confusion which just turns into noise."[253]

Another version of this story might have pitched Jason's documentary as a riposte to the edited and redacted network news – news that hastens the apocalypse by refusing to properly prepare citizens for what is coming. In the past, Romero was sceptical of the mainstream news – the TV network at the beginning of *Dawn of the Dead* runs an on-screen list of rescue stations, even though they're out of date, in a cynical attempt to win the ratings war.

Here, though, Romero seems equally cynical about the margins too. It feels like an old man's take on a contemporary revolution – a point of view that rails against the democraticisation of information because it's messy, inaccurate and overwhelming rather than accepting it as the price we pay for everyone having a voice and an online platform.

If that makes *Diary* sound preachy, well… it largely is. Romero's social satire, never particularly light on its feet at the best of times, hits the audience like an anvil dropped off the Eiffel Tower. As the kids continue their journey and Jason keeps filming his movie, *Diary*'s big point comes into focus: it's not just the zombies who are ghouls; the media are too. Voyeurism makes us all a little dead inside.

The Zombie Diaries (2007). Photo by Julian Newman Turner.

of Toronto-based Gaslight Studio – equal anything found in Romero's earlier outings.

At the same time, *Diary* is easily the most misanthropic film in the series. As Romero casts a weary eye over American's craven mainstream media and a narcissistic generation who can't see beyond their next selfie, the words of Fran in *Dawn of the Dead* still resonate: "We're blowing it ourselves". This is an American filmmaker, now exiled

It's something that Debra accuses Jason of, and that Romero himself expounded on in interviews: "During the shootings at Virginia Tech, people were filming out of the windows," the director noted. "CNN was asking flood victims [after Katrina] to send in pictures. We have all this information now, but it's not being managed."[254]

Fortunately, the film's road-movie structure compensates for its rather leaden satire. *Diary* runs from one encounter to another as Romero's students meet corrupt National Guardsmen, a deaf-mute Amish farmer (R.D. Reid) and a group of African-American looters led by Martin Roach, whose stately presence recalls the earlier films' black heroes.

Despite the heavy-handed messaging, there's a wry wit at work in *Diary*. It has a gleeful streak of gallows humour that isn't ashamed to chase a cheap splatstick gag. In the hospital, where the shell-shocked kids go to find help, they learn how to aim for the head, first with guns, then by using the paddles of a defibrillator to electrify a ghoul's noggin.

Later, dynamite, scythes and acid dispatch ghouls messily; and a swimming pool becomes a place to trap zombie "goldfish". These Looney Tunes gore sequences – staged by Oscar-winning zombie go-to-guy Greg Nicotero of KNB EFX, with the help

in Canada, who continues to be appalled by what has happened to his country since he made *Night of the Living Dead* in 1968. For him, the American nightmare continues – just in a more modern guise.

Misanthropy and video cameras make happy bedfellows. Over in the UK, around the same time as *Diary of the Dead*, filmmakers Michael Bartlett and Kevin Gates took a similar approach in *The Zombie Diaries* (2007). It documented a British living dead apocalypse through the lenses of several different characters carrying camcorders.

The Zombie Diaries divides its action into sections of found footage culled from different stages of the disaster: it opens with a TV news crew heading into the countryside to interview a poultry farmer, as rumours of an Asian bird flu pandemic circulate. Then it fast forwards into the coming apocalypse as the UK is overrun by ghouls, following a disparate bands of survivors, before switching back on itself to show us what happened to our original protagonists on that fateful first night.

Focussing on a moral collapse as much as societal one, *The Zombie Diaries*'s intimate, handheld shooting style gives an on-the-ground view of how things fall apart: London is in lockdown, and survivors are holed up on a farm scavenging for precious supplies. Like so many British zombie movies, it has a grubby, kitchen-sink realism –

which is quite at odds with the bait-and-switch DVD artwork that promises a zombie army on Tower Bridge. That was dreamt up by The Weinstein Company's marketing department after they bought the home entertainment rights.

The Zombie Diaries's big twist is that the living turn out to be more dangerous than the living dead – all too happy to indulge in a spot of rape and murder against their fellow survivors as the world crumbles. It's a theme over-familiar from a few hundred zombie movies, but it was deployed with enough gusto by Bartlett and Gates to produce a sequel titled *World of the Dead: The Zombie Diaries* (2011).

Here a group of British Territorial Army soldiers head out from their overrun compound in search of a coastal rescue, tramping across Sussex and being picked off one by one by ghouls and murderous bandits. The shakicam adds frisson to events and hides some of the production's obvious budgetary shortcomings.

Both *Zombie Diaries* films capture the intimate, existential horror of a world where authority has been replaced by individual points of view. Looking through a camera lens becomes a metaphor for the disconnect that's happening in the world as morality is eroded and the old certainties are demolished. Subjective reality is suddenly all there is – and in the absence of authority *World of the Dead*'s raiders happily kill and rape both the living and zombies with primal abandon.

The loss of moral compass that occurs when staring through a viewfinder is something that's replayed again and again in found footage zombie movies. Filmmaker Chad Ferrin tackled it in *The Ghouls* (2003), a bleak SOV production that crawls into the underbelly of Los Angeles where cannibal creatures survive by snacking on the drunk and destitute from the streets above. The ghouls aren't living dead, but the film's alternate title *Cannibal Dead: The Ghouls* shamelessly tried to cash in on the zombie renaissance.

Timothy Muskatell plays a world-weary "video vulture" roaming the city with his camera in search of gory crime footage for the TV news. When he discovers ghouls emerging from the sewers, he thinks he's found a ticket to riches and tries to catch the cannibals on film – a quest that will lead him to the brink of his sanity. Although it's badly shot on DV and riddled with terrible camera setups, bursts of jarring jazz saxophone and poor, often muffled, dialogue, *The Ghouls* takes no prisoners in its downbeat sense of one man's moral collapse. Desensitised to the gory horror he records on a daily basis, Muskatell's cameraman is arguably more ghoulish than the zombie creatures he's pursuing.

The cinéma vérité of Romero's grainy newsreel footage back in 1968 probably explains why so many zombie movies have tried to disguise the fantastical nature of their conceit – the dead walking – with a patina of realism. While scenes of newsreaders solemnly announcing the apocalypse straight to camera have become a z-movie cliché, a few films took the idea to its conclusion and featured news cameramen as their protagonists.

Crappy no-budget outing *The Dead Live* (2004) has a TV crew caught up in the rolling z-apocalypse. In *Feeding the Masses* (2004) a news reporter rails against media manipulation and propaganda as the dead walk, refusing to accept that TV should be the opiate of the masses as the world unravels: "The news ain't all it's cracked up to be these days…" *Dead Genesis* (2010), a return to the found footage style set after the zombie apocalypse has already happened, dispatches a pretty young filmmaker (Emily Alatalo) to the front line of the "War on Dead". Embedded with a dysfunctional group of guerrilla fighters, she's supposed to be making a pro-war propaganda film. Instead, she ends up revolted by her discovery of seedy zombie brothels, various acts of inhumanity and some vague War on Terror parallels. The living, she realises, may be even more dangerous than the zombies themselves.

If z-cinema's found footage movies teach anything, it's that filming the action doesn't absolve you from moral responsibility. "You can't film this!" someone yells in *Zombie Doomsday* as the cameraman watches a child being mobbed by ghouls. Turns out it's not just evil that triumphs when good men do nothing. Zombies win too.

II. PLAY, STOP, PAUSE, [REC]

[REC] (2007) is easily the most influential found footage zombie movie released in the 2000s. It unspools in a Barcelona apartment block where local TV presenter Ángela (Manuela Velasco, a real-life TV personality in Spain) and her cameraman Pablo (Pablo Rossi) are caught up in a terrifying viral outbreak. Accompanying a group of firefighters for the TV show *While You're Asleep* – "Who's awake to watch it?" is the standard quip – Ángela and Pablo get much more than they bargained for.

It begins with reports of an elderly woman trapped inside her apartment. However, this is just the tip of a very terrifying iceberg. It turns out that the apartment block has been contaminated with some kind of virus, possibly rabies. When the firefighters and police arrive to free the trapped woman, she responds by attacking them – ripping open the neck of a police officer who's trying to calm her.

Things quickly unravel into total chaos as *[REC]* proves it credentials as a visceral rollercoaster of a fright flick. Shooting everything through Pablo's camera, directors Jaume Balagueró and Paco Plaza succeed in immersing us directly in the action. Pretty soon the perky presenter, cops and firefighters are locked in the quarantined apartment building. Outside, the police drape the windows in thick plastic sheeting and helicopters circle overhead.

Right from the start, no one has much faith in the reassurances they're being given by the authorities. Ángela and Pablo keep the camera rolling because they suspect that the decision to enforce BNC (Biological, Nuclear, Chemical) procedures is a sign that they're dealing with more than just an outbreak of the flu or even rabies.

Pretty quickly, the tenement's residents become raging zombies – much in keeping with the infected-not-dead ghouls of *28 Days Later* – who thrash and roar with total hatred for the living. By the time a health inspector, dressed in a gas mask and contamination suit, makes a solo entry in the apartment block armed with a hypodermic, it's already too late. The infection has spread like wildfire.

[REC] (2007).

Moving from the fire station to the claustrophobic, tiled corridors of the apartment block, *[REC]*'s skill lies in its careful funnelling of the relentless action as Ángela and the ever-diminishing group of survivors are herded upwards towards the building's penthouse. What's waiting for them up there proves that this isn't a conventional zombie movie.

The rundown penthouse is an old-fashioned haunted house. It's papered with newspaper articles and a reel-to-reel tape recorder that reveals a surprising backstory about demonic possession and the Catholic Church. In the attic above the penthouse hides the film's chief ghoul, an emaciated monster with elongated limbs (played by Javier Botet, whose over-stretched arms and legs are a result of being born with Marfan Syndrome). By the time Ángela and the audience realise that the outbreak isn't a simple viral infection, or that *[REC]* isn't a simple zombie movie, it's too late. The only survivor is the video camera itself.

The visceral thrill of *[REC]* – a non-stop blur of shakicam angles, shouting characters and raging zombies – is its greatest strength. In Spain the film became 2007's biggest hit after *The Orphanage* and won two Goya Awards. At the 40th Sitges Film Festival the audience was filmed by a night-vision camera as they watched the movie. The footage of them cowering and jumping in fear was used in an innovative trailer that cheekily echoed the movie's own night-vision finale.

For all its rollercoaster thrills, though, *[REC]*'s biggest impact comes from its dark sense of betrayal. Every authority in the movie is either incompetent or complicit or both. It's a chain of shame that stretches from the police to the health inspectors, and right up to the Vatican itself. It turns out that the Catholic Church has failed everyone. It has been secretly investigating cases of demonic possession in an attempt to isolate the bio-chemical chain that turns a normal human being into a possessed monster.

In the penthouse, a priest has been performing hush-hush experiments on a possessed Portuguese girl named Tristana Medeiros, experiments that have inevitably got out of control. The eye-rolling stupidity of dabbling with such dangerous forces in an inhabited apartment block in the middle of Barcelona isn't lost on us. Nor is the fact that the Vatican tries to cover it up – another scandal to file alongside nepotism, corruption and child sexual abuse.

The name of Ángela's TV show, *While You Were Sleeping*, retrospectively reveals a cruel irony: this abuse of power has happened right under our noses, and has been committed by those we relied on for moral guidance (we discover elsewhere in the *[REC]* franchise that the Medeiros girl's suffering began when she was gang raped by a group of priests).

[REC] has so little time for organised religion, it doesn't even countenance the possibility of any of its characters grabbing a crucifix to fight off these demonic terrors. In the finale, shot in sickly green night vision, the camera itself becomes Ángela's talisman against evil. In a room crammed full of esoteric artifacts, newspaper cuttings and weird scientific paraphernalia, Ángela and Pablo hide behind the camera's safety like Van Helsing raising his crucifix to ward off Dracula. It's not just the zombies who are dead. Faith, in this movie, is too.

[REC] 2 (2009) picks up the story 70 minutes after the events of *[REC]* as a cocksure SWAT team rush to the quarantined apartment block, filming the action on their helmet cameras as they breach and clear. Taking a leaf out of the *Aliens* playbook, *[REC] 2* puts the original premise on steroids and swaps *[REC]*'s slow burn build-up for rollercoaster action.

On arriving at the apartment block, the SWAT team are ordered to escort Ministry of Health official Dr Owen (Jonathan Mellor) into the quarantined apartment block. As the superfast, super-angry ghouls attack, things go from bad to worse. Eventually Dr Owen reveals he's wearing a dog collar. He isn't a public health official; he's a priest on special assignment from the Vatican. His mission: to secure a sample of the possessed Medeiros girl's blood.

Fending off zombies with the help of mumbled prayers and rosaries, Dr Owen reveals that the possessed child from *[REC]* was being experimented on by an over-zealous priest. He was trying to determine the bio-chemical cause of demonic possession and create a vaccine. Quite why anyone would need to perform such experiments is never explained. Indeed, a few historical cases of demonic possession seem pretty innocuous compared to the city-wide contagion that seems to be brewing as a result of the Vatican's botched intervention in the Devil's work.

[REC] 2 rarely stops long enough to let us ask questions, though. As the SWAT team is decimated and a couple of teenagers with a camcorder sneak into the building, *[REC] 2* sets up a bold double found-footage conceit – the logic of which arguably doesn't bear too much thinking about.

The real pleasure, though, is the film's non-stop pacing and its ghoulish horror. The penthouse apartment itself becomes a place of utter dread, a twilight zone where things lurk in the dark that only a night-vision camera can see. Meanwhile, downstairs, a possessed teenager with tar-black eyes spouts obscenities with disturbing conviction. The film's trump card is its carefully crafted atmosphere; this isn't just some *Exorcist*-style case of possession confined to a single bedroom. We're left in no doubt that there's a very real chance that this is the beginning of a demonic pandemic that could spread across the globe from this ground zero in a Barcelona apartment block.

By the time Ángela makes a belated reappearance in *[REC] 2*'s third act, it's obvious that the *[REC]* franchise is a series with legs. The creepy finale promises to take us out of the apartment block and into the city proper as the demonic contagion spreads. The stakes couldn't be higher, not least of all because humanity's hand seems to be hamstrung by having the secretive, incompetent human representatives of the Lord on its side.

The first two *[REC]* films put modern Spanish zombie cinema back on the map. So it was somewhat inevitable that a cynical US remake would come along and ruin everything. *Quarantine* (2008), a shot-for-shot remake, managed to squander all of the original's power. Its modest box office success was largely due to the fact that US audiences hadn't had the chance to see the Spanish original in cinemas before *Quarantine*'s release.

Producer Roy Lee, best-known for bringing Asian horror hits like *Ringu* and *Ju-on* to the attention of American studios, snapped up the US distribution and remake rights to *[REC]* before the original movie was even finished. Sony Screen Gems then kept the finished Spanish movie on the shelf in the US while the English-language remake went into production. *[REC]* itself was belatedly released on US DVD in 2009.

In the remake, the zombie outbreak is just another virus, a super rabies strain unleashed by doomsday cultists whose existence is nothing more than a plot point MacGuffin. By losing the supernatural and religious element, *Quarantine* squeezes the life out of its predecessor.

For the Spanish filmmakers, the remake was a disappointment that they had no control over since Spanish production house Filmax Entertainment owned the rights to the franchise. They weren't involved creatively, nor were they even given the courtesy of being told that the rights had been sold. They found out by reading about it online.

"It was a bittersweet feeling," said director Paco Plaza after the event.[255] His co-director was even more candid. "It's impossible for me to like, because it's a copy," Jaume Balagueró explained. "It's exactly the same, except for the finale. It's impossible to enjoy *Quarantine* after *[REC]*. I don't understand why they avoided the religious themes; they lost a very important part of the end of the movie."[256] The remake did, however, convince him that Spanish cinema no longer had to feel limited. "Any non-English-speaking culture can now take on a Hollywood so bereft of ideas they're forced to look overseas for any originality."[257]

Despite referring to a DVD of *[REC]* on set, the American filmmakers and execs clearly didn't get what gave the original its unique power and its franchise potential. *[REC]* spawned sequels because its story hints at a much bigger world – of global conspiracies, a secret history of demonic possession and a brewing apocalyptic battle between heaven and hell. *Quarantine* sacrifices all of that for something mundane.

The sequel *Quarantine 2: Terminal* (2010) moved even further away from the supernatural and explicitly tapped into post-9/11 anxieties – in a similar fashion to the earlier *Flight of the Living Dead: Outbreak on a Plane* (2007) – with a half-baked story that traps a flight attendant and various other survivors of a bio-warfare terrorist attack in an airport terminal.

Still, even the Spanish *[REC]* franchise itself wasn't beyond getting lost. *[REC] 3: Genesis* (2012), directed by Plaza without Balagueró, completely dropped the ball. Rewinding from the events of the first two movies to the initial outbreak of the virus at a wedding ceremony, it ostensibly served as a prequel – albeit without giving us any insight into the demonic outbreak or the Medeiros girl's possession.

By the time the demonic zombies start pursuing a man dressed in a knockoff Spongebob Squarepants costume and the bride-to-be rips off her wedding dress and revs a chainsaw ("This is MY day!"), it's pretty obvious that *[REC] 3* isn't taking itself seriously. It feels like a footnote to a horror movie franchise that, if we're lucky, still has more to give.

III. DOCUMENTING THE DEAD

"We can't pretend they don't exist," explains a research scientist in *American Zombie* (2007). "It's not a disease, it's not a disability... it's a new population." While the idea of the dead returning to life to take up their place in society rather than eat the living wasn't new, Grace Lee's *American Zombie* was the first feature-length film to turn it into a socially conscious documentary (two short films had previously riffed on the same idea: the three-part, seven-minute *Zombie-American* in 2005; and the 28-minute *Rising Up: The Story of the Zombie Rights Movement* in 2009).

Positing a world in which the dead are returning to "life" as anything from mentally incapacitated ghouls to high-functioning, walking, talking almost-living humans, Grace Lee's mockumentary turns the zombie into a metaphor for social exclusion. Interviewing a diverse group of zombies – including a convenience store slacker cum zine-creator (Austin Basis), a florist who specialises in funeral-home arrangements (Jane Edith Wilson) and a cat-loving vegan (Suzy Nakamura) – Lee builds a portrait of a marginalised underclass trying to find their place in the world.

Returning to life with no memories of their past lives, or their violent deaths, these sympathetic zombies are lost souls cut adrift. Zombie-rights advocate Joel (Al Vicente) believes it's a problem the "revenants" have to face up to. His collective ZAG (Zombie Advocacy Group) offers legal advice and counselling services for his fellow ghouls with the slogan: "We're here! We're dead! Get used to it!"

For Lee, an Asian-American filmmaker who has previously tackled issues of race and selfhood in her work, the zombies are a metaphor for identity politics. What's interesting is the way she approaches zombiedom itself. It's not a single identity but a collective mass of individuals who are presented as being as rich and diverse in their opinions and temperaments as the living. Afflicted by skin problems, hair loss and the eternal suspicion of the living, the zombies are united by their existential need to find acceptance.

With Lee and fellow filmmaker John Solomon playing themselves within the movie, *American Zombie* also proves smart about the documentary form itself. Solomon has such hunger for a juicy tabloid story that he could be a cousin of the Timothy Muskatell's video vulture in *The Ghouls*. He's unconvinced by all the chatter about zombie art, labour relations and love affairs between the living and the living dead. His gut tells him there's a bigger story here – the revenants must be secretly eating human flesh. Nor is he afraid of confronting interviewees about what they might have hidden at the back of their refrigerators, either. Lee, in comparison, takes a more ethical and less confrontational approach with her subjects, delicately posing questions like: "Are you ashamed of being a zombie, Jenny?"

As events unfold, the filmmakers discover that everything is not quite as it seems. At the secretive annual zombie gathering "Live Dead", things get weird. "I like to call it Grace's personal horror film," Lee told *Fangoria*. "It's not a gorefest, but I've been in situations with documentary subjects where you think you can trust them, and they're normal, but it suddenly changes."[258]

By the time the final reel unspools, *American Zombie* turns threatening as these previously placid ghouls begin to show a more violent, less amenable side. Social inclusion, it turns out, can work both ways. If zombies can't be accepted back into polite society, then perhaps polite society will end up being assimilated into the zombie ranks.

If *American Zombie* highlighted social exclusion in America, *Harold's Going Stiff* (2011) did much the same for the UK. Yet where Lee's movie is sprawling and powered by a desire to delve into the margins of Los Angeles, Harold's focus is parochial and quintessentially British.

Presenting itself (at least initially) as a documentary, Keith Wright's movie begins not long after the UK is gripped by a degenerative neurological epidemic called Onset Rigours Disease (ORD). The symptoms are easy to spot. Men of a certain age afflicted with ORD start suffering from stiff limbs, then dementia and finally madness as they lose their mental faculties and become shuffling ghouls.

It is a public health catastrophe. Hospitals are full to bursting, community support groups struggle to pick up the slack and NHS health workers, like Harold's chubby and cheerful physiotherapist Penny (Sarah Spencer), make home visits to help the infirm.

The most famous sufferer is Harold Gimble (Stan Rowe), a pensioner from Barnsley who was the first recorded case. For some reason he is also experiencing the slowest rate of decline. Other sufferers are less fortunate, quickly becoming arthritic, demented and dangerous. As these ghouls rampage around the Barnsley countryside, they're chased down by a pack of roaming vigilantes.

Filmed over nine days in 2011 by a crew of six

Harold's Going Stiff (2011).

and funded by "two Tesco credit cards", *Harold's Going Stiff* is a bittersweet mockumentary that puts a human spin on the zombie movie (compare it with *Portrait of a Zombie*, a similarly cheap mockumentary shot in Dublin that lacks the innate warmth of Wright's film).[259] Taking a fly-on-the-wall approach, *Harold's Going Stiff* presents straight-to-camera interviews and observational scenes of Harold as he shuffles about his house, his body slowly locking up. It's less a zombie movie than a wry and melancholy take on the nature of aging, the isolation of the elderly and the fear of illness and death that's common to us all.

What makes it work is its low-key Northern humour. Harold's neurologist is named Dr Shuttleworth, presumably after the comic John Shuttleworth whose quirky, gentle style the film mirrors. The central innuendo of the title actually turns out to be the key to the movie's charm; the growing relationship between Harold and his young, unlucky-in-love physio Penny illustrates that all that stops us becoming zombies ultimately is our intrinsic humanity.

It's their shared personal connection – which moves through funny, nudge-wink physiotherapy sessions on Harold's bed, to impromptu relationship counselling and mugs of tea made with washing-up liquid instead of milk – that makes writer-director Keith Wright's mockumentary more than just a one-joke film. There is a real tenderness here as Penny begins to realise that Harold is part of a dying breed of gentleman, and that the rigidity of social mores means it's unseemly for her to end up dating an OAP.

There's also a typically British sense of the forgivable weirdness of others. An interview with a young man who insists on eating the banned Meat-a-Rino products responsible for the outbreak (even buying them from eBay to sate his hunger) is a great example of how the mockumentary format doesn't have to belittle its subjects to work. His eye-rolling awkwardness when admonished on camera by his mother is a comic treat worthy of Peter Kay. In keeping with its very British charm, *Harold's Going Stiff* is also the first (and, one suspects, the last) zombie movie to feature a ghoul being placated by a Scotch egg.

CHAPTER ELEVEN

DEAD GIRLS (AND BOYS)

"WE COULD KEEP HER…"
– J.T. (Noah Segan) *Deadgirl* (2008)

I. PORNO ZOMBIE APOCALYPSE

Zombies weren't the only things that shuffled out of the margins and into the mainstream during the 2000s. Porn did much the same – shuffling in a different sense perhaps – as the adult entertainment industry capitalised on the rise of digital distribution and the death of shame. No longer were zombie or skin flicks relegated to seedy cinemas or the top shelf of the DVD rack. They'd both become accepted, if not entirely *acceptable*.

The link between sexuality and movie zombies stretches back to the very beginning of the genre. In *White Zombie* Bela Lugosi's zombie master keeps the film's eponymous female ghoul locked up in his mansion. We see her playing the piano, beautiful and blank-eyed like a living doll – but one can't help wondering what else goes on between them off-screen. The film coyly teased 1930s audiences with her status as a sexual slave. What desires might an unscrupulous villain satisfy with a woman who is unable to say no?

Over the coming decades, the link between the zombie and sex became increasingly graphic and gratuitous. Both zombie horror and pornography are fixated by the flesh; both feature dead-eyed performers eating one another either literally or euphemistically; both thrived in the sleazy grindhouses of 42nd Street in the US.

By the 2000s, the blurring of the line between a certain kind of zombie movie and a certain kind of sex film occurred, making it impossible to tell one from the other. The trend stretched back to 1980 when Eurosleaze filmmakers like Joe D'Amato (aka Aristide Massaccesi) churned out sex/horror hybrids like *Erotic Nights of the Living Dead* and *Porno Holocaust*. By the 2000s, though, the dynamic between the two genres began to change. As the porn industry grew more lucrative and powerful – and adult entertainment productions tried harder to find a unique angle – the relationship shifted. Instead of horror movies with some hardcore porn, the new trend was porn movies with horror in them. Porn suddenly climbed on top.

The result was a cycle of hardcore porno zombie movies like *Dawn of the Head* (2006), *Night of the Giving Head* (2008), *Monster Tit Sex Zombies* (2008), *Dawna the Dead* (2010) and *I Can't Believe I Fucked a Zombie* (2011). Most of these use the zombie conceit to spice up what are pretty conventional porn films – even if making their performers join the ranks of the living dead seems a rather questionable way to arouse their audiences.

Occasionally, there's a modicum of wit. *Evil Head* (2012) is a crazed send up of the *Evil Dead* movies with porn star Tommy Pistol playing Ash. It gamely runs through the original movies' iconic moments: a passage is read from the Necronomicon (now a gory and hellish sex manual called the *Necrocumicon*), a demonic girlfriend is locked in the cellar and Ash performs his own chainsaw amputation. In between such plot points, the heavily tattooed starlets turn into demonic zombies. Then, inexplicably, they decide to head to the mall for some shopping. "Your credit card has been revoked!" yells Ash, revving his chainsaw.

Other porno zombie movies embraced the nihilism of zombie horror. *Porn of the Dead* (2006), a grainy, hardcore skin flick with no dialogue or plot, plays out its porno apocalypse with depressing seriousness. Punk filmmaker Rob Rotten sets up scenes of joyless, rough sex between men in decontamination suits and bloodsoaked zombie girls scored by a death metal soundtrack. If your idea of a fun night in is watching sleazy blokes nailing skanky women in dank workshops covered in plastic sheeting, Rotten has you covered.

Grub Girl (2006), a skin flick based on a comic called *Zombie Hooker* by Ed Lee, is little better. It opens with morgue attendants raping a corpse (Brittney Skye) killed by a radiation released from an experimental, fuelless jet plane. When their victim wakes up she kills her tormentors and gets a job as a hooker ("I'm dead anyway, what the fuck do I care?"). Hardcore sequences follow one after the other as the filmmakers assume that male audience like their women to be dead and loving it. "Don't act like you never thought of it [necrophilia] before," Skye says straight to camera as *Grub Girl* reaches its conclusion. "Why else would you be watching this crummy movie?"

Interestingly, the crossover flowed in the opposite direction as well. Non-porn zombie movies began to take a more salacious interest in bodily function beyond just eating. In *Mutant Zombie Vampires from the 'Hood!* (2008) C. Thomas Howell's cop and a bunch of gangbangers watch as radiation from a solar flare turns LA residents into hungry, horny ghouls who occasionally drop their trousers and pleasure themselves with severed heads. When Howell bangs a sexy scientist in full view of the up-for-it horde massed outside her safe house, the mutant zombie vampires storm the barricade, desperate to get in on the action.

In *Chillerama* (2011), a nostalgic anthology inspired by grindhouse cinema, a drive-in is overrun by "sex zombies" after a mysterious blue goo finds its way into the popcorn butter. The humping, ejaculating dead run rampage through the audience, fucking severed heads and stumps of legs with wild abandon. Proof that "When there's no more room in hell, the dead will fuck the earth". By the end, the heroine (Kaili Thorne) and her boyfriend (Corey Jones) shelter in their car while a horde of randy ghouls press their faces against the windows – a kind of living dead dogging.

The idea that zombies might want to bang your brains out rather than eat them gained traction in Japan. Director Naoyuki Tomomatsu (*Stacy*, *Zombie Self-Defence Force*) blended his experience of working in Japan's pink film industry and horror cinema to create *Rape Zombie: Lust of the Dead* (orig. *Reipu zonbi*, 2012) in which zombies run around Tokyo with their trousers around their ankles raping women indiscriminately.

As the city is overrun, lesbian nurse Nozomi (adult actress Arisu Ozawa) grabs a katana and takes refuge in a rural house with a few other capable women. They are determined not to let the *doku-otoko* ("poison men") inseminate them with their toxic sperm.

Taking its cue from *Dawn of the Dead*'s TV show interludes, *Rape Zombie* frequently cuts away to TV news reports where feminists and scientists debate whether this worldwide outbreak of male sexual violence against women is simply a new stage of human revolution, or proof that "all men are beasts". Meanwhile, jubilant women join the now all-female Japan Self-Defence Force for a two-hour crash course in automatic weapons and how to aim for the head – again, the one between the legs.

Lingering salaciously over scenes of sexual violence, director Tomomatsu apparently has no sense of just how offensive *Rape Zombie* is. Any hopes that it might be filed as an example of Swiftian satirical excess is undermined by the title song's lyrics which translate as "Rape zombie! Rape Zombie! Rape Zombie! Rape!" It sounds suspiciously like cheerleading. A low point comes when Nozomi explains how she became a lesbian after being gang raped by a sports team years before the outbreak begins. It's provocative potential in highlighting real misogyny and sexual violence is undermined by Tomomatsu's decision to flashback to the rape and replay it in graphic detail.

Tomomatsu seems convinced he's making a feminist statement by blaming men for being braindead, sex-obsessed ghouls – even before they're zombified. On the TV, a feminist commentator draws a pointed parallel between the outbreak's origins (supposedly, a man-made hole in the ozone layer) and the rape of Mother Earth. At the end of the movie, a zombie-raped victim gives birth to a glowing newborn who may, or may not, herald a new start; and North Korea nukes

Tokyo. The Communists blame the global outbreak on Japan's adult entertainment industry – and decide to hit the red button in response. Watching too much porn is clearly bad for your health. Watching *Rape Zombie*, though, isn't much better.

Zombie Babies (2011), a grubby and outrageous DIY effort from West Virginia, took the whole sex 'n' zombies crossover to its logical conclusion. Its concept – a backwoods abortionist's pain-free, late-term termination method leads to an outbreak of baby fetuses – was in such bad taste it's hard to forget. As a group of up-the-duff patrons and their partners find themselves besieged by tiny tot ghouls, filmmaker Eamon Hardiman crafts sequences that would make John Waters blush.

The grossest moment involves a crawling ghoul who sits on the face of a man who's been tied up and blindfolded on a bed, waiting for kinky sex. Mistaking the baby ghoul sitting on him for his girlfriend, the man proceeds to entertain it with his tongue… Compared to that, even *Grub Girl* and *Rape Zombie* seem reserved.

II. GENTLEMEN PREFER (DEAD) BLONDES

The question of what men might gain from the lawlessness of a zombie apocalypse was an issue that cropped up again and again throughout the 2000s. *The Zombie Diaries* and *World of the Dead* both feature living bandits sexually assaulting both the living and the dead. In *World War Z* (2013) even Brad Pitt's wife isn't safe from being groped and pawed by supermarket looters. Men, it seems, are always willing to take advantage of the walking dead.

Night of the Living Dead: Resurrection (2012), a forgettable low-budget British attempt to relocate Romero's classic to Wales, captured this rape panic succinctly. Its central characters are trapped in a farmhouse besieged by ghouls and hoodie-wearing videogame-obsessed chavs ("It's just like COD!") until the sole survivor, teenage Eve (Sarah Louise Madison), is finally rescued by the Welsh equivalent of Romero's rednecks. But her saviours aren't saviours at all. Eve is hooded and bound and bundled off as the leader issues a chilling order: "Stick her in the rape van".

What if zombies weren't monsters but also potential victims? In post-millennial zombie movies the idea that men might chase after anything with a pulse was given a new spin. Perhaps the porno filmmakers behind the likes of *Porn of the Dead* and *Grub Girl* were clear-eyed in their understanding of male libido. Maybe Lugosi's Murder Legendre was just ahead of the curve. After watching Marcel Samiento and Gadi Harel's provocative low-budget US indie *Deadgirl* (2008), you might be forgiven for coming to that conclusion.

Taking zombie sexual politics far beyond most viewers' comfort zones, *Deadgirl* begins as high school kids J.T. (Noah Segan) and Rickie (Shiloh Fernandez) find a naked girl (Jenny Spain) chained up in the basement of an abandoned mental asylum. Uncertain who she is or how she got there, J.T.'s first response isn't to call the cops but to wonder aloud if they could rape her. As inciting incidents go, it's a leap into the abyss that will make most viewers recoil… if not head for the nearest exit.

Rickie appeals to his friend's better nature. But when morality can't trump sexual desire, he sulkily departs. In his absence J.T. rapes the girl and, driven by bloodlust, ends up beating her to death while trying to subdue her. Only there's a catch. It turns out she's already dead. Even though J.T. knows he broke her neck she remains "alive". Even a gunshot to the torso won't kill her.

Faced with the ontological conundrum of a girl who is alive yet dead, J.T. decides this is every red-blooded man's dream come true: his very own living dead sex slave. Although Rickie voices serious doubts about the morality of raping a girl – even if she is one of the living dead – he's too busy moping after childhood sweetheart Joann (Candice Accola) to interfere. The object of his affection is dating one of the high school jocks and Rickie is powerless to do anything much about it. It's that sense of powerlessness that's at the heart of *Deadgirl*.

Slowly, J.T. starts to open up the secluded

basement to an ever-growing group of high school guys. They're all so horny that they're willing to overlook the practical reality of having a corpse as a sexual partner, from a general lack of personal hygiene to pus-dripping wounds. When the novelty begins to fade, they start to find new ways to abuse their victim even more – opening up her wounds to use as alternative orifices.

Mostly, though, they simply revel in the power they have over this slab of meat. Kept chained and gagged, this dead girl is a zombie cousin of the bound heroines of torture porn movies like *Hostel: Part II* (2007) and *Captivity* (2007). Jenny Spain imbues her ghoul with a surprising degree of humanity – certainly more than any of the boys display – making the viewing experience even more uncomfortable as a result.

Deadgirl offers a window onto teenage masculinity. It's an uncompromising critique of male libido that takes the feminist axiom that "all men are rapists" as its starting point. No one here emerges with a shred of decency apart from the dead, soulful-eyed victim herself. *Deadgirl* lays the male psyche laid bare and strips it down to its core motivations: sex, sex, sex; pause for a bit of violence; then more sex, sex, sex.

Eventually, as the film's tension escalates, J.T. and one of his buddies realise they have a way to make more zombies by getting their sex slave to bite anyone they bring to her. Pretty soon they're predatorily camping out at a petrol station, looking for fresh female victims to drag back to the basement. One dead girl clearly isn't enough. Dominance – and the sexual satisfaction it delivers – needs a steady supply of fresh meat.

Yet one of the most interesting things about the film is its suggestion that the boys' actions are born out of powerlessness and impotence. They don't have girlfriends; they're not jocks; they're bullied misfits in a town that seems – from the little we get to see of it – to be on the economic skids. Growing up in an era of global recession, these kids aren't masters of the universe. They're the next generation of Staples managers and they feel as powerless as the zombie they abuse.

The movie had a chilling, real-life echo a few years after its release – the 2012 Steubenville High School rape case, in which a drunk and incapacitated teenage girl was repeatedly sexually assaulted by football team players at a party. The strange synchronicity with *Deadgirl* became apparent when a video posted online showed an intoxicated student making fun of the victim by calling her "the dead girl".[260]

Deadgirl wasn't the only movie exploring the intersection of zombies, sex and death, although no other outing would match its stark rigour. Echoes of *White Zombie*'s sexual politics also reverberated in teen drama *Beneath the Surface* (2006) in which a cheerleader (Dominique Geisendorff) is killed by her jock boyfriend in a date rape gone wrong.

She's resurrected, via Haitian voodoo, by her lovesick emo admirer Ethan (Kyle Stanley), who keeps the dead girl locked in a wooden box under his bed. He's less interested in getting off with her than helping her remember what happened.

In between bouts of adolescent sentimentality, a *Bill & Ted* jokiness prevails: the dead girl is ordered to play guitar solos and gets a makeover by clueless Ethan in preparation for a date in the local mall ("She looks like Joan Rivers!").

A briefly outlined backstory tells us how French troops were attacked by zombies while invading Haiti in the nineteenth century – a rare example of a post-2001 zombie movie that bothers to use voodoo as its MacGuffin (lame indie comedy *My Dead Girlfriend* (2006) did something similar too). But expecting *Beneath the Surface* to join the dots between voodoo vengeance and the modern sex war is probably a little too optimistic.

A very different film, the elliptical and hypnotic indie *Make-Out With Violence* (2008) plays with similar themes to both *Deadgirl* and *Beneath the Surface*. Set over a languid school summer holiday it follows twin brothers Carol and Patrick Darling (Cody DeVos and Eric Lehning). The object of Patrick's affection is local gal Wendy (Shellie Marie Shartzer) who suddenly goes missing, then unexpectedly reappears as a stiff-limbed, blank-eyed zombie.

Deeply in love with her even though she's apparently (living) dead, Patrick hides her away and plays nursemaid – dressing her up and even tying her to a chair for a romantic dinner. His love, however, is sorely tested when the unresponsive girl scoffs a pet rat. Teenage romance was never supposed to be like this.

Directors The Deagol Brothers, actually the name for a collective of filmmaking friends, describe their film as "like Tarkovsky's *Solaris* crossed with *Weekend at Bernie's*". That description doesn't even begin to do justice to the film's languid Sofia Coppola meets George Romero vibe. Capturing a very adolescent sense of longing, while touching on sexual power games and male fantasy, *Make-Out with Violence* proves unique and strangely touching.

Zombies as a metaphor for the sex war itself became a recurring theme in the 2000s and played out in a series of cheesy B-movies. *Stripperland* (2011), a less-funny-than-it-thinks-it-is parody of *Zombieland* (2009), posits a virus turning the women of the world into living dead pole dancers. The male population is first aroused, then disturbed.

"Getting naked was great," complains the film's narrator Idaho (Ben Sheppard), "but we didn't know our moms and sisters would be turned into flesh-eating fantasy sex monsters that would treat us like food." Eventually Idaho and his friends meet a mad scientist convinced that the zombie virus will tilt the sex war back in men's favour. "We've been given a second chance to reshape the world so that the women dance to our tune instead of us dancing to theirs!" Cue scenes of hot ghouls in bikinis washing cars and ironing shirts.

Stripperland was part of an unlikely cycle of pornstar/stripper zombie movies that came to the unarguable conclusion that sex + zombies would attract the attention of men under the age of 30. The cycle began with *Zombie Strippers* (2007) and continued through *Zombies! Zombies! Zombies!* (aka *Strippers Vs Zombies*, 2007), which featured a cast of busty pole dancers fighting against crack whore zombies (who comes up with this stuff?) Neither should be confused with *Zombies Vs Strippers* (2012), in which a strip club becomes a convenient place to shelter during a zombie apocalypse.

Headlined by porn star Jenna Jameson, *Zombie Strippers* set the standard that the rest slavishly followed. It's an exploitation cash grab that has all the dead-eyed enthusiasm of a gyrating lap dancer asking you to stuff dollar bills in her garter. "We were joking around one day, trying to come up with the most commercial film we could think of," said producer Angela Lee of the project's genesis.[261]

It shows: everything here is designed to maximise revenues from casting former porn queen Jenna Jameson as one of the titular (heh, heh) pneumatic ghouls; to roping in poor old Robert Englund as the strip club proprietor who realises the living dead girls are pulling in more patrons than ever.

Zombie Strippers claims to be loosely based on Eugène Ionesco's 1959 stage play *Rhinoceros*, in which the inhabitants of a French town turn into rhinos – a metaphor for the seductive, beastly allure of Nazism and the French collaborators who worked with it. For writer-director Jay Lee, the producer's brother, who previously made the dire *The Slaughter* (2006) with her, the movie satirises "the brutal regime" of the Bush era: "The brutality is running amok, people are being mercilessly slaughtered, people seem to be ignoring it or accepting it and, at the same time, someone is making a buck off the whole thing."[262]

It's more tempting, though, to read *Zombie Strippers* – which features a viral epidemic that turns both strip club patrons and dancers into the living dead – as a parody of the entertainment industry itself. Much like the libidinous zombie strip club patrons, hungry exec producers lined up to invest in the movie thanks to its sells-itself title and the presence of Jenna Jameson in the lead.

"I never wrote a synopsis for the script," Lee

Zombie Strippers (2007).

boasted in one interview. "I'm actually convinced that a lot of people hadn't read the script. They actually went in and greenlit and went into executive positions of the film [without reading it]. I'm sure they thought *Zombie Strippers* with Jenna Jameson was all they needed."[263]

Jameson wasn't the only porn star to strip for the sake of zombie cinema. *Zombies Vs Strippers* co-stars hardcore performer Adriana Sephora, who sandwiched this in between her work on *Lesbian Love 2* and *This Ain't Avatar XXX 2: Escape from Pandwhora*. She gets the movie's funniest gag when she seduces the club bouncer Marvin (J. Scott), little realising he's just turned into a zombie. Taking a moment in the middle of their lovemaking session, she asks him what he likes best about her. "Braaiinnns" groans the ghoul. "Marvin!" she squeals in delight. "That's like the sweetest thing anyone's ever said to me!" A few seconds later, Zombie Marvin attacks her, ripping the skin off her face to reveal the muscles, tendons and eyeballs beneath. Sephora, who has shown so much on-screen during her porn career, has certainly never exposed that much before.

Even the uptight British got in on the act, although with less nudity. Silly but inoffensive *Stag Night of the Dead* (2011) featured a latex-clad stripper (nicely played by Sophie Lovell Anderson) and a stag party fighting zombies escaped from a

game of "Zomball", the post-apocalyptic answer to paintball. *Zombie Women of Satan* (2009) forced its female cast into burlesque corsets, where they bleed from all their orifices while a bare-breasted zombie lass in a wheelchair squirts toxic liquid from her nipples. It's like a *Carry On* movie directed by Rob Zombie.

Proving men are from Mars and women are from hell, *Doghouse* (2009) is the kind of Britzomcom that would likely have Germaine Greer shouting "Shoot it in the head!" (or, perhaps, the balls). It replayed the Lads Vs Zombettes idea with a bunch of 30-something blokes, led by perennial British geezer Danny Dyer, heading out to a sleepy village for a boozy weekend. There they discover a pack of jerky zombie women in slutty clothing – "zombirds" – who are the result of an accident involving a military bio-weapon.

Director Jake West (*Evil Aliens*) and screenwriter Dan Schaffer are smart enough to treat the film's outrageous misogyny with a nod and a wink. They ensure that Dyer's obnoxious, loud-mouth sexist gets his just desserts at the hands of the skimpily costumed, all-female zombie horde and even include gay character among the lad pack to try and balance things out. Still, it can't stop the movie from leaving a slightly bitter aftertaste: imagine *Zoo* magazine crossed with Hammer horror and you're pretty much there.

III. QUEERING THE ZOMBIE

In contrast with the hetero zombie movies that flashed some T&A and roped in strippers, a brief cycle of gay zombie movies combined sexual explicitness with a more rigorous take on the zombie's metaphorical potential.

One of the strangest uses of the zombie as a political metaphor was in Bruce LaBruce's high-minded, occasionally hardcore, queer zombie outing *Otto; Or, Up With Dead People* (2008), a German-Canadian co-production. Set in a not-too-distant future where the dead have apparently returned to life and formed an uneasy truce with the living, it follows a zombie hoodie named Otto (Jey Crisfar, a Brussels art student recruited by LaBruce from MySpace) as he stumbles around in search of

meaning. He is, in the words of the film's voiceover narrator, "a zombie with an identity crisis".

For La Bruce, a Canadian queercore artist, photographer and avant-garde filmmaker, Otto's personal plight is tied to much bigger social and political issues. This homeless gay ghoul is recruited by radical lesbian filmmaker Medea Yarn (Katharina Klewinghaus) who wants him to star in a political gay zombie porn flick. She praises the blank-faced Otto as "the gay Che Guevara of the undead". While her other zombies are simply gay men pretending to be ghouls, Otto is something else – something more *authentic*. Is he a victim of soul-destroying capitalism and homophobia? A revolutionary in waiting? Or just a bit of a misfit?

We're never quite sure.

As a movie, *Otto* is as politicised as Medea's porno *Up With Dead People* hopes to be. LaBruce has said he was inspired by the teenage alienation he noticed around his younger acquaintances and shocked to learn from a friend who worked on teen support hotlines that suicide rates for gay teens are much higher than their non-gay counterparts.

In response, *Otto* becomes a movie about queer identity, alienation and integration. Like the ghouls in *Shatter Dead*, *They Came Back* or *American Zombie*, Otto is trying to negotiate a relationship with the living – a mass of people who, he says, "all seem like the same person to me".

Speaking to *Filmmaker* magazine, LaBruce explained that his take on the zombie focused on it as a rich metaphor for the clash between consumerism and anti-capitalism.

"Zombies are the ultimate consumers. Like one of the characters says in *Dawn of the Dead*, the zombies are drawn to the shopping mall because it was the most important place in their lives. And of course the joke is that they act pretty much the same as zombies as they did when they were alive. In my movie I try to make a paradigm shift. I've made a movie in which the zombie becomes more human than the living. It's the living who represent violence, intolerance and consumerism, and it's the zombie who has become the victim – a sensitive figure with a conscience. Otto is the result of the deadening effects of a selfish, violent culture."[264]

Otto isn't your common or garden zombie. He isn't part of the mass – not even of zombies. He is set apart – a non-conformist in a world of homogeneity. "He doesn't fit in," says LaBruce, "he's more of an individual on the margins."[265] He's also a metaphor for the underbelly of gay culture that La Bruce suggests has been shut out and denied as queer identity politics have gone mainstream.

"If you've ever cruised a public toilet or a bathhouse, it's like *Night of the Living Dead*," LaBruce told one interviewer. "You've got people in this zombie-like trance, in dark shadows with disembodied body parts. And I don't mean that negatively; it's kind of exciting. But there is that aspect to gay culture and sometimes it can be kind of sad. In the drive of the gay movement to become mainstream, they have distanced themselves from the more extreme elements of the movement. Otto kind of represents that for me."[266]

Taking in queer identity politics, alienation, AIDS panic (the homosexual undead are described as a "plague") and anti-capitalism, *Otto* is a scattershot mess of a movie. But it is also a potent and bold attempt to retool zombie cinema – replacing apocalyptic gunfights with Godardian political commentary and a surprisingly tender love story.

Other recent gay zombie movies can't match *Otto*'s strangeness. They're more camp than political. *Creatures from the Pink Lagoon* (2006) was a gay B-movie spoof. Screaming queens fight "homosexual flesh-eating monsters" (aka zombies) created by mosquitoes buzzing around a local chemical plant. It's high camp, with some of the most outrageous gags this side of John Waters: "I just thought water sports would be a great ice breaker," says one guy as he breaks out the water pistols for a bit of frolicking fun. Meanwhile, the Philippines delivered something similarly frothy in the pro-tolerance themed, outrageously camp comedy *Remington and the Curse of the Zombadings* (orig. *Zombadings 1: Patayin Sa Shokot Si Remington*, 2011) in which a homophobic kid is cursed by a drag queen and turns effeminately gay on his 21st birthday. Cross-dressing zombies, "gaydar" ray guns and much light-hearted Filipino wackiness ensues. In comparison, *Otto* might as well have come from another universe.

LaBruce followed up *Otto* with *LA Zombie: Hardcore* (2010), and continued to carve his own path. Definitely not a flamboyant gay comedy, *LA Zombie: Hardcore* was banned from being shown at the 2010 Melbourne International Film Festival by Australia's Film Classification Board. It was the first time a film had been banned from Australia's film festival circuit since Larry Clark's skateboarder flick *Ken Park* in 2003. Ironically, the cut the Board was unimpressed by was actually the softer version, known simply as *LA Zombie*.

That wasn't the end of the controversy. After the film was screened illegally at the Melbourne Underground Film Festival, it prompted a police raid on the festival organiser's house (strangely, though, the police waited several months until November 2010 before conducting the raid – by which time the print of the film had apparently been destroyed).[267]

Unlike *Otto*, *LA Zombie: Hardcore* is violent

and explicit. Its chief zombie (played by French porn star François Sagat) is a ragged, unnamed blue-tinged ghoul with big, retractable teeth who wanders through the Los Angeles's homeless population after being washed up on the beach. He brings the dead back to (a semblance of) life by having sex with them. Penises slip into open wounds ("Zombie porn is practical: you can create your own orifice," the filmmaker argues in the movie's press pack) and black semen/blood is sprayed over faces. Is he a monster? An alien? A hero? Who knows… There's little dialogue and no real story – it's exactly what its title promises, a gay porno zombie movie set in LA.

Ultimately, the movie's rocky reception is more interesting than the film itself. Understandably, LaBruce turned the monumentally asinine approach of Australia's moral guardians into a victory for free publicity. In a press release, he

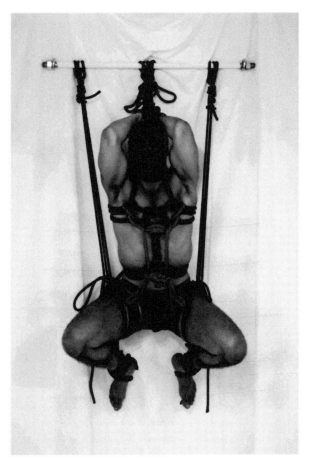

LA Zombie: Hardcore (2010).

lambasted the Australian Classification Board's willingness to pass "all manner of mainstream torture porn movies which feature, amongst other things, the rape and dismemberment of women." *LA Zombie: Hardcore* was he claimed – with jaw-dropping chutzpah – a comment on the epidemic of homelessness and a movie that "reaffirms life".[268]

After watching *LA Zombie: Hardcore*'s interminable scenes of necrophilia, not everyone might agree with that assessment – although it's pleasing to note that its zombie is smart enough to use proper protection when performing anal sex. Like all LaBruce's films, *LA Zombie: Hardcore* is more arty than genre, an avant garde attempt to blend gay sex/zombie films and social commentary. It's also proof that, when it comes to gay zombie porn, Andy Warhol's *Flesh for Frankenstein* was actually way ahead of its time. "To know death, Otto, you have to fuck life… in the gall bladder!"

Obsessed with new kinds of sexuality, La Bruce's films may be undisciplined and over-stuffed with incomplete ideas but they're a riposte to the assimilation of zombie culture that was happening at the time. While zombies were going mainstream, La Bruce's films remained shocking, banned and graphic outings that returned the zombie to its rightful, marginal status. The director's comments on Will Smith's *I Am Legend* (2007) – one of the first blockbuster zombie movies, as we'll see – are a glorious example of a filmmaker willing to speak out against multiplex blandness.

"I just saw *I Am Legend*, and I was thinking, 'If I made that film, the main character would definitely be watching porn and having sex with a blow-up doll, if not the dog!' But then again that movie was totally ideologically reactionary because the Will Smith character was supposed to be so pure and righteous that even when he's the last man on Earth he clings to monogamy and fidelity, not to mention Christianity. Don't get me started. For me, like Godard said, the sexual is political, and I've always used explicit sex to make certain political statements about gay representation, about defining and transgressing taboos, about issues of homosexual identity and difference, etc."[269]

Smith certainly wouldn't approve, but that image sums up everything that makes LaBruce's politicised, sexualised zombie cinema so wrong and yet so right.

CHAPTER TWELVE

IT'S EVERYWHERE!

"WHERE HAVE THESE ZOMBIES COME FROM?"
– Luv (Vir Das), *Go Goa Gone* (2013)

I. GLOBAL PANDEMIC

By the mid-2000s zombies were taking over the world. Z-culture had spread to even the most unlikely nations. Greece, Chile, Norway and Pakistan were among those who'd make their debut contributions to the genre as the zombie renaissance grew and grew. It seemed that the more popular zombies became, the more assured local producers could be that there was a viable, international market for their movies.

Greece broke new ground with its first zombie movie *Evil* (orig. *Το Κακό*, 2005) in which a demonic force escapes from a cave beneath Athens and turns citizens into rampaging ghouls. Shot for a few Euros, it was largely formulaic. But it featured a stunning climactic aerial shot in which its survivors huddle together in the centre circle of a football stadium as zombie hordes mass outside the building and swarm towards them in a pitch invasion from hell.

Norway made its Z-debut with audience pleaser *Dead Snow* (orig. *Død Snø* 2009), one of several goose-stepping ghoul movies from around the world that harked back to the likes of *Oasis of the Zombies* and *Zombie Lake*. Sweden made an unmemorable debut with the bargain basement *Die Zombiejäger* (2005), which turned Gothenberg into deadhead central. Iceland's embarrassing teens-with-a-videocamera epic *Knight of the Living Dead* (2005) was little more than a home movie.

South Africa's first foray into zombies was a medical experiment gone wrong in tense and lo-fi *Expiration* (aka *Rancid*, 2011). Serbia went straight to DVD with *Apocalypse of the Dead* (2009), a charmless production that let a flabby Ken Foree – star of the original *Dawn of the Dead* – top up his pension pot. Turkey got off the starting blocks with the found footage horror of *Island: A Zombie Wedding* (*Ada: Zombilerin Düğünü*, 2010).

Israel gave us *Cannon Fodder* (2013), which dabbled in local tensions as an army squad are sent into Lebanon to capture a Hezbollah leader and become surrounded by "biters". The film's anorexic political grandstanding – "What makes them different from us? The fact that they want to devour us? What have we been doing in this country for over 60 years!" – didn't add up to much. But it illustrated how adept zombie movies are at tackling local issues while playing to an international crowd.

In South East Asia, the Philippines gave us drag queen zombies in queer pro-tolerance comedy *Remington and the Curse of the Zombadings* (orig. *Zombadings 1: Patayin Sa Shokot Si Remington*, 2011). Malaysia dallied with talking, strategising ghouls in zom-com *Zombi Kampung Pisang!* (2007). Thailand joined the club with *Sars Wars: Bangkok Zombie Crisis* (2004) and the lone ghoul hitman of *Curse of the Sun* (orig. *Suriyakhaat*, 2004), summoned by gangsters to kill his own girlfriend. Dressed in black leather and armed with assault rifles, he cut an imposing, rather mournful figure. If John Woo made a zombie movie it would probably look a lot like this.

Meanwhile, Taiwan's debut *Z108* (2012) convincingly staged a SWAT vs zombies apocalypse, inspired in part by Indonesian action hit *The Raid*. Then it veered off into torture porn territory to focus on a maniacal rapist (writer-director Joe Chien) with a basement full of zombies chained to a manual electricity generator and a harem of living women he has kidnapped off the chaos-ridden streets. Getting off on scenes in which Chien beats, rapes and urinates on his victims (before torturing one with a live squid), *Z108* makes for uncomfortable viewing – even before the rapist keeps the toddler of one of the kidnapped women as a sex slave in waiting. One wonders how many of the 900 crowdfunding backers who supported the film's NT$10 million budget via social media knew about that before they signed up.[270]

While some countries made their debuts other, more prolific zombie-producing nations stuttered to a standstill. French horror may have been resurgent in this period, but it was largely zombie-free. *Mutants* (2008) found a unique setting for its breathless apocalypse in the French Alps; while the racist, in-your-face nastiness of *The Horde* (2009) set its action in a Parisian tenement block as cops and gangsters join forces against the dead.

In Italy, prolific hack Bruno Mattei ended a long and uninspired career with two ragged throwbacks – *Island of the Living Dead* (orig. *L'isola dei morti viventi*, 2006) and *Zombies: The Beginning* (orig. *Zombi: La Creazione*, 2007) – before his death in May 2007. The spaghetti ghoul cycle was later taken up by new arrivals Marco Ristori and Luca Boni. They continued the Fulci-Mattei-Lenzi tradition in the sub-par *Eaters: Rise of the Dead* (2010), which found distribution thanks to Uwe Böll and *Zombie Massacre* (aka *Apocalypse Z*, 2012).

In Böll's homeland, Andreas Schnaas continued to evade the clutches of the German cinema police with blind Templars and Nazis in *Don't Wake the Dead* (2008). A step up from Schnaas's efforts was Niki Drozdowski's desolate and ambitious *Extinction: The G.M.O. Chronicles* (2011), which was shot by filmmakers who'd obviously played too many videogames. Its ghoul pack ranged from shamblers to parkour runners, spitters and an eyeless screaming banshee similar to *Left 4 Dead*'s

terrifying Witch. *Extinction*, much like director Wolf Wolff's tale of bird flu zombies *The Beast Within* (2008), was cannily shot in English, not German, to maximise international sales.

There was more novelty elsewhere. *Toxic Lullaby* (2010) time-shifted between the 1970s and a post-apocalyptic future in which hippie heroine Eloise (Samantha Richter) wakes up in after taking a tab of LSD. Is she tripping or has the world really been overrun with zombie-like "Sleepers"? Marvin Kren gave the standard barricade-the-doors siege movie a fresh gloss of paint in *Rammbock: Berlin Undead* (aka *Siege of the Dead*, 2010). It cruelly posited the idea that staying calm might allow your body to fight off the zombie virus – and had nervous characters reaching for sedatives as fast-running ghouls lay siege to a Berlin apartment block.

Spain scored big with the *[REC]* franchise, although the fantastic *SexyKiller* (orig. *SexyKiller: morirás por ella*, 2008) deserved a better title, a lot more zombies (they turn up in the final reel as an afterthought), and a little more exposure for its stylish OTT Almovodar-tinged slasher/zombie mash up. In contrast, *Deadhunter: Sevillian Zombies* (2005), about a squad of ghoul exterminators in Seville, deserved even more obscurity than it achieved. Elsewhere in Europe, the Netherlands delivered a pleasingly energetic zom-com in *Zombibi* (aka *Kill Zombie!*, 2012), which pushed the *Shaun of the Dead* model to breaking point with silliness including the use of a tennis-ball launcher to deter zombies. *New Kids Nitro* (2011), a feature-length outing for a bunch of mullet-headed Dutch gross-out comedians, broke it completely.

Across the globe, New Zealand delivered ovine zombie comedy *Black Sheep* (2006) and insipid slacker zom-com *Last of the Living* (2008). Australia failed to match either of those in *Dead Country* (2008), where a crashed spaceship raises the dead from their graves in the town of... Romero. That tells you all you need to know about how original it is.

Canada, in contrast, proved a fertile ground for new films covering a spectrum that stretched from one of the finest zombie movies of the last fifteen years in *Pontypool* (2008), to a passable zom-com like *A Little Bit Zombie* (2011) or total clag like the misnamed *Vampires Vs Zombies* (2003), the dire futuristic French Canadian *Zombie Hunters* (2008), the botched *Autumn* (2008) based on David Moody's cult novel and *Zombie Doomsday* (2010), which came with a standalone documentary about making a no-budget zombie movie that was called, rather tellingly, *Another Zombie Flick* (2011).

A few stood out: *Severed: Forest of the Dead* (2004) found a superb setting in the Pacific Northwest where tree sap turns lumberjacks into ghouls (it's not to confused with *Forest of the Dead* (2005), a far inferior Canadian effort shot in 2001). *The Mad* (2006) was likeably demented and had Billy Zane fighting off flying beef patties infected with Mad Cow's Disease.

The endearing *Fido* (2006) gave us a post-apocalyptic reimagining of suburban 1950s America where zombies, including Billy Connolly's eponymous grunting ghoul, are kept as slaves to do the gardening and golf caddying. Like a Douglas Sirk melodrama with the walking dead, it strips away the veneer of this uptight, repressed suburb and takes Fido's kid owner (K'Sun Ray) on a journey to the city limits – where, it turns out, zombies mass outside this enclave of civilisation. Satirising conservative mores and America's racially segregated past, it also fed into the War on Terror theme of so many post-millennial zombie movies.

"I wanted to set it in the 1950s [because] I think there's this yearning by all of us in North America, Canada included, for that kind of simpler, sweeter time when everything was just right. I think it's a fallacy," explained director Andrew Currie. "I wanted to set it in the 1950s era [because] the politics that are going on today are all about building more fear, building the bigger fences, like Bush is talking about building the fence between Mexico and the States. Always keeping people afraid, as a way of justifying military spending, as a way of controlling the masses."[271]

In non-English-speaking territories, one of the biggest international surprises of the period was the arrival of Pakistan's first zombie movie *Zibahkhana* (*Hell's Ground*, 2007). Directed by English-born Omar Ali Khan, a diplomat's son and owner of a chain of Lahore ice cream shops, it's carefully aimed at the nation's cine-literate youngsters with a story about a group of Islamabad college kids getting lost in the wilds on their way to a rock concert.

Part slasher movie, part zombie flick, it tapped into a culture clash that echoes far beyond its nation's borders. "I don't get it about Pakistan. It's like the country's going psycho," complains one of the kids as they're abused and assaulted by a selection of rural freaks and geeks. "Fashion shows every day while half the country's back in the Stone Age."

As the brash youngsters get their comeuppance in the religiously uptight backwoods, *Zibahkhana* treads the same ground as classic American rural horror like *The Texas Chainsaw Massacre* or *The Hills Have Eyes*. Only here the horror isn't rednecks or inbred mutants. It's a conservative, fundamentalist evil. In a country where young men and women are still stoned to death under Sharia law for transgressions against sexual propriety, *Zibahkhana* knowingly sets

Zibahkana/Hell's Ground (2007).

its cool young kids against religious bigots.

The film's sari-wearing zombies highlight the clash between two very different Pakistans: the old Pakistan dominated by Islamic fundamentalists and the new Pakistan where free-wheeling, capitalist youth just want to have fun. When the film's chief villain arrives – a cross-dressing slasher, who wears a burka and wields a spiked ball on a chain – it's hard to shake the feeling that Khan is making a controversial point about the dangers of an Islamic fundamentalism that will make zombies of us all (although a passing plot point about the national scandal of polluted water in Pakistan may point to a more secular explanation of why the backwoods fields are teaming with the living dead).[272]

"Horror is at its most effective when it taps into real fears," explained the director. "Our real fears are connected to things that are sensitive politically and difficult to discuss. This is not a picture-postcard film. The kids in this film live in a bubble, and are confronted with another world and languages beyond that of the push-button city they inhabit. It captures the country's contradictions: it's a place where the magazines are full of cat-walk fashions, but which also suffers from Dark Age politics. There is such hypocrisy and double standards in Pakistan: we show Western films in which kids swear and smoke, but in our own films those images get censored. Yet the kids in this country are so bored that five out of ten are doped up with hashish."[273]

As South Asia went through rapid change, the zombie movie proved a useful sandbox in which to interrogate the cultural and social upheaval being experienced. "We only have ghosts and spirits in India. Where have these zombies come from?" asks Luv (Vir Das) in the likeable Indian zom-com *Go Goa Gone* (2013). It's a fair question. Zombies have never been typical monsters in the region, but their international popularity has meant that filmmakers from Islamabad to Goa have embraced them. Luv's buddy Hardik (Kunal Khemu) has a theory: "Globalisation! These foreigners have screwed us. First they brought HIV. Now zombies."

Go Goa Gone wears its hip credentials on its sleeve – lots of dope smoking, condom gags and Facebook references – but it takes pains to explain its ghouls to the audience as the characters debate whether the creatures are vampires, witches or ghosts ("Maybe they'll run away if we show them a cross…"). Ironically, though, globalisation has meant that the younger generation in developing nations are now well-versed in zombie lore gleaned from American and European horror movies and TV shows like *The Walking Dead*.

Rise of the Zombie (2013) takes a different tack. It treats its slowly zombified wildlife photographer (Luke Kenny) as patient zero for an Indian zombie franchise – following his solitary transformation into a ghoul with unflinching realism – all peeling skin, madness and gore – before setting up an apocalyptic sequel *Land of the Zombie* in its final five minutes.

Kenny, an influential Indian filmmaker, musician and celeb, is clearly trying to give India its very own, no-nonsense zombie franchise. "In 100 years of Indian cinema within the horror genre we haven't gone beyond the ghosts and spirits. Because we are a country that is so rooted in superstitions. But at the same time we also realise that we have the new generation that is glued to the international popular culture and zombies are a huge part of it."[274]

By the time British directors the Ford brothers set *The Dead 2: India* (2013) on the Indian subcontinent, it was obvious that many saw potential mileage in bringing the zombie myth to the land of *Slumdog Millionaire*. The zombie has become a useful lynchpin for filmmakers and distributors looking to international audiences.

South American filmmakers came to a similar conclusion. Brazil's long-standing love of ghouls pulled off something striking in *Mud Zombies* (orig. *Mangue Negro*, 2008), which featured mud-caked zombies crawling out of the mangrove swamps in a curious echo of the "Mud Men" from New Orleans-set videogame *Left 4 Dead 2*. Heavy on eerie atmosphere, *Mud Zombies* does well with very little – and puts low-budget American efforts like the atrocious *Swamp Zombies* (2005) to shame.

From Chile came *Descendents* (orig. *Solos*, 2008) – an artily downbeat apocalypse in which a girl (nine-year-old Camille Lynch) wanders across a post-apocalyptic landscape towards the coast. Her crayon drawings, the voiceover narration and a selection of confusingly frantic flashbacks vaguely piece the story together for us. It seems an airborne virus has turned the world's population into ghouls; the only uninfected survivors are soldiers in gas masks and a handful of children who've grown bloody gills on their necks.

Director Jorge Olguín goes all out for moodiness, shooting through filters to give the film a grey, ashen look that's slightly undermined by his choice of CG blood effects. He's less able when it comes to storytelling, though, and *Descendents* limps towards a WTF? ending that seems to have been spliced in from *Mega Shark Vs Octopus*.

In the Caribbean, Cuba made its zombie debut with *Juan of the Dead* (2011), a Spanish-Cuban co-production that is a textbook example of how low-budget, indigenous productions can leverage the zombie's international appeal. Written and directed by Alejandro Brugués, a graduate of Cuba's International School of Film and Television, the film arrived in a burst of publicity. Making the most of its Havana setting and shot in an energetic filmmaking style, *Juan* was adept at crossing over from the foreign film festival circuit to horror fans.

As Fidel Castro's ailing health and disappearance from public view prompted "Is he alive or dead?" speculation, *Juan of the Dead*'s poster proclaimed: "Fifty years after the Cuban revolution, a new one is about to start…" True, the movie itself wasn't revolutionary. But it was energetic and competently made, skilfully using CGI to transform Havana into a living dead wasteland.

Chock full of gags at the expense of Castro's regime, *Juan of the Dead* debates the benefits of communism and capitalism amid all the head trauma. When zombies attack, deadbeat forty-year-old slacker Juan (Alexís Diaz) seizes the opportunity the end of the world represents. He offers his crew's services as zombie exterminators and they do their best to make a dollar or two out of the chaos. This is the contradiction of a country where Communism rules but street-level capitalism dominates how people make ends meet. The authorities, meanwhile, insist the zombies must be political subversives.

A sense of just how badly the Communist regime has failed its people lingers over everything. The authorities are absent, distant voices heard on radio sets. No one comes to save the day. It's left to individuals themselves to fight the hordes. As Cubans try to flee to nearby Florida in a mass boat-people exodus, they're dragged into the sea by ghouls walking along the bottom of the ocean – a keen image of how trapped the island's populace feels. It also creates one of the best underwater zombie sequences since Fulci had a stuntman fight a shark in *Zombi 2*.

It's the filmmaking panache that gives *Juan of the Dead* its edge as much as its politicising. Brugués stages plenty of outrageous action – like a zombie trapped on a harpoon line, or a "handcuff tango" where Juan tries not to get bitten. He finishes it all off with a comic book credits sequence scored by Sid Vicious singing "My Way". If there's any justice, this movie will bring Cuba's moribund filmmaking industry back from the dead.

II. CHAVS, GANGSTERS AND LOST SOULS

The zombie revival that occurred in the mid-2000s stirred Britain's film industry into action too. There were found footage movies (*The Zombie Diaries* series and mockumentary *Harold's Going Stiff*, 2011), low-budget trendsetters (*Colin*, 2008) and bonkers passion projects (*The Veil*, 2005, shot over four years in black & white, running for 150 minutes and featuring a lead cast wearing face-hiding, dialogue-muffling gas masks).

Regional cinema gave us Leicester-set snoozer *Zombie Undead* (2010) and Nottingham apocalypse *Zombiehood* (2013). *Battle of the Bone* (2008) delivered an unlikely commentary on Northern Ireland's sectarian conflict, while its disappointing follow-up *The Knackery* (2010) swapped targets to take a swipe at reality TV – a redundant concept after *Dead Set* (2008) turned the Big Brother house into ground zero. Across the Irish Sea, Wales made an unlikely setting for a Romero rip-off in *Night of the Living Dead: Resurrection* (2012).

Further south, writer-director Matthew Hope's excitingly ambitious but deeply flawed *The Vanguard* (2008) set up camp in a Hertfordshire forest and delivered some of modern zombie cinema's most feral ghouls – leaping, howling, ape-like "bio-syns", styled after the primates in Kubrick's *2001: A Space Odyssey*.

Elsewhere, British z-cinema roped in some unlikely American stars – the time-ravaged Edward Furlong and Corey Feldman in *The Zombie King* (2012) – and reached to the corners of the Commonwealth in dire Cayman Islands comedy *Zombie Driftwood* (2010). The Queen would not have approved.

Scotland's *Outpost* series began in 2007 and spawned three dour, claustrophobic Nazi zombie movies that recreated Eastern Europe in the Scottish lowlands. Dumfries was also the location for a very different Scottish zombie movie, writer-director Kerry Anne Mullaney's *The Dead Outside* (2009). Set on a farm during an outbreak of a "neurological pandemic" it swapped dour, claustrophobic action for dour, claustrophobic character study. An invasion of Nazi ghouls might have distracted from its cheerless monotony as three protagonists go slowly mad in the dying Dumfries light.

Having said that, a random Nazi connection didn't do much for *Attack of the Herbals* (2011) a dull Scottish *Shaun of the Dead* wannabe about a crate of "crazy Nazi tea" that washes up on the Scottish coastline. Even though the mysterious crate's contents look like All Bran, the locals put the kettle on for a brew and turn into demon-voiced ghouls. They should have stuck to PG Tips.

A few low-budget British zombie movies marked an interesting departure from the past. *Colin* took the fairly unique approach of documenting a zombie apocalypse from the perspective of one of the shambling ghouls themselves.[275] Shot on a consumer camcorder with hardly any dialogue, it follows Colin (Alastair Kirton), a young man who is bitten during a zombie outbreak in London. As the city burns, the newly living dead Colin wanders the streets aimlessly, driven only by instinct.

It's one of several recent movies told from the zombies' perspective – a diverse list that encompasses likeable American POV comedies like *Wasting Away* (2007) and *Deadheads* (2011), and, elsewhere, Bruce LaBruce's daringly/incoherently radical *Otto; Or, Up With Dead People* (2008) and *LA Zombie: Hardcore* (2010). *Colin* separates itself from the pack thanks to the inspiring story of its no-budget production and its mournful take on living death.

Debut director Marc Price was working shifts answering the phones at a London courier firm when he set out to make a no-budget film using an old camcorder, some dumped tapes from a TV studio and a group of actors sourced on social networking sites. Made for £45, *Colin* is a landmark in no-budget indie horror filmmaking. "The plan was to make the film for absolutely nothing," Price later explained, "so we went over budget the day we spent money on tea and biscuits."[276]

When Price and his sales agent took the movie to Cannes, the novice director's life was transformed after the movie was picked up for distribution. It gave him a viable new career as a filmmaker and became the basis of a rags-to-relative-riches story to make many young zombie filmmakers green with envy.

Colin drifts around post-apocalyptic London like the hero of an eighteenth-century picaresque novel, stumbling in and out of trouble: being swept up in a zombie attack on a house, meeting (and biting) his still-living sister and finally being half-blown up by a hand grenade. He's a wide-eyed innocent, much like Candide, and we follow his journey through the apocalypse as if watching a fly-on-the-wall documentary.

With barely any dialogue, *Colin* is a minimalist, kitchen sink effort. Yet even though its hero is dead, the film isn't: there's an emotional core to it that centres on the relationship between Colin and his sister Linda (Daisy Aitkens). Refusing to believe that her brother is lost, Linda frantically tries to connect with him – showing him photos from his old life and finally bringing him to see their mother. She refuses to believe there's no trace of humanity left in this zombie.

By following Colin's perspective so relentlessly, director Marc Price asks us to do much the same. We empathise with Colin because even though he's dead, he's still human. We watch him trying to make sense of the world around him, picking up an MP3 player from a victim and gormlessly listening to music on it like the dim-witted British cousin of Bub the zombie in *Day of the Dead*.

The most ironic sequence involves Colin starring at a two-way traffic road sign, the arrows pointing in different directions and hinting at his own liminal state between life and death. As Colin stares at them – a moment that Price tellingly lingers on, letting us sense its import – we wonder if there is a glimmer of understanding in his eyes. Does he feel the misery of a damned soul? Does he realise that his personal purgatory will involve shuffling around the empty streets of suburban London moaning dejectedly for ever? He seems constantly on the cusp of understanding his predicament before it slips away from him again. Refusing to answer these questions, Price leaves us to simply connect with Colin on the most basic level – our shared humanity.

The film's power comes from actor Alastair Kirton, who manages to hint at much without overstepping the mark into cartoonish gurning. He imbues his monster with a fleeting sense of spark, a trace of life in something that should be lifeless. In doing so, he asks us to identify with that thin sliver of humanity that remains. What's interesting is how willing we are to be complicit in this. No matter how mindless or monstrous the classic Romero zombie is, it's always on one level still us.

By setting Colin up so sympathetically – in one scene he is harassed by other, meaner zombies, and in another he's mugged for his trainers by a pair of living thugs – Price and Kirton invite our empathy. It's something that the final moments of the film pay off – a tragic, melancholy finale that leaves Colin trapped somewhere between ignorance and understanding, a confusion that makes him all the more human.

"I think what really blindsided people was the emotional elements of the film," said Price. "That was the most obvious way to go for me, having a character you really cared about, a character the audience could really connect with. At the end of the movie they understand what his motivations are, even if he doesn't. The audience becomes linked to the character, following a zombie in different directions, that seemingly don't have any connection, but the more you watch the film, the more you see that everything does actually have a connection."[277]

Colin's muted sentiment wasn't typical of British z-cinema in the 2000s. In the 1990s, British movies became synonymous with "mockney" London gangsters, an East End renaissance that quickly stereotyped itself into a corner. Adding zombies to the mix was ill-advised but inevitable. *Devil's Playground* (2010) was the most lavish example, shot on a surprisingly big budget for a British B-movie.

After 30,000 human guinea pigs test out a new stamina supplement to help people cope with the stress of modern city living, 29,999 of them turn into black-veined, parkour ghouls. As London is overrun, the immune 30,000th test subject Angela (MyAnna Buring) is pursued across the city by her rogue cop boyfriend (Danny Dyer) and the drug corporation's fixer Cole (cockney hardman Craig Fairbrass). It turns out Angela's immunity is the key to solving the outbreak.

The leaping zombies (choreographed by parkour experts Urban Flow) are impressive, and the film's sense of apocalyptic scale is surprisingly ambitious, but too many characters and a leaden script soon bring it crashing back down to earth. Fairbrass, though, tackles his role with gusto, bish-bash-boshing zombie heads in with a hammer. Next time you need a nail in a wall, give him a bell.

The genre blending of *Devil's Playground* led to *Gangsters, Guns and Zombies* (2012), a much less ambitious, much jokier sub-*Lock, Stock and Two Smoking Barrels* romp that mixed bank robbers with zombie clowns, footballers and knights (an infected medieval re-enactment group) among all the effing and blinding. Jennie Lathan's turn as a potty-mouthed, shotgun-wielding nanna ("Really fuckface, do I look scared to you?") prefigured the strident OAPs of the much funnier *Cockneys Vs Zombies* (2012) – which proved that when there's no more room on EastEnders, cockney thesps will roam E14 looking for zombies to shotgun in the face.

To break the cliché of cockneys and gangsters, British zombie movies often looked further afield. *Decay* (2012), a no-budget, painfully amateur British indie shot by student physicists working at the CERN facility in Geneva, is strikingly set inside the claustrophobic tunnels underneath the Large Hadron Collider as the search for the God Particle accidentally turns staff into ghouls. The setting feels like a real-life analogue of the Umbrella Corporation's facilities in *Resident Evil*.

Other British zombie movies took the idea of confined space in a different direction. In *Stalled* (2012) maintenance man W.C. (screenwriter Dan Palmer) gets trapped in the lady's bathroom during the Christmas Eve office party. When a couple of hot girls start making out in front of the mirror, he can't believe his luck. But when the dead walk, he's trapped in a bathroom stall.[278]

Director Christian James pulls off the unlikely trick of keeping the action interesting even while

Decay (2012).

staying exclusively confined to the bathroom – apart from one hallucinogenic excursion into the offices beyond. Ingenious in its plotting – at one point the bloody contents of a sanitary towel bin are used to distract the ghouls; in another a dropped stepladder is put to good use – its zany comedy is carried off thanks to Palmer's likeable lead performance and his whispered romance with a trapped woman (voiced by Antonia Bernath) a couple of cubicles down.

Even more offbeat was criminally overlooked Wales-shot indie *Flick* (2007) which had an inventive visual style and a plot line that's so out there it sounds made up. It begins in sepia-tinged flashback to the 1950s, where stuttering Teddy Boy Johnny (Hugh O'Conor) commits murder on the dance floor after knifing a bunch of bullies who stop him from dancing with local beauty Sal (Hayley Angel Holt). His rampage ends with his car crashing into the local river and he becomes missing, presumed dead.

Years later, when his now-vintage car is hauled out of the water, the pissed-off Elvis fan stumbles back to life and drives around town wearing an algae-covered slim coat and brothel creepers. Hungry for revenge, he tracks down the now middle-aged rockers who wronged him, slicing them up with his flick knife.

On the trail is local detective Sgt Miller (Mark Benton, from TV's *Waterloo Road*) who's been teamed with Lt McKenzie, a one-armed cop on exchange from Memphis, Tennessee, played by Faye Dunaway. Yes, *Faye Dunaway*.

As the rockabilly ghoul slashes his way through the town, McKenzie pieces together the evidence and comes to the shocking conclusion that the dead killer is getting his ambulatory power from the sounds of the 1950s tunes playing from a local pirate radio station.

Working in the venerable tradition of camp British horror like *Psychomania* (1972), writer-director David Howard elevates the material into something visually exciting through the use of back projection, CG and an array of Dutch angles like a no-budget, Wales-shot *Sin City*. When the budget can't match the requirements Howard switches to garish comic book panels, and whenever the local pirate DJ plays 1950s rock, musical notes float across the screen.

Dunaway throws herself into her role as the disabled detective, crunching the testicles of hard-men club bouncers with her prosthetic limb and exploring an unexpectedly tender romance with Benton's down-at-heel copper. When she gets round to telling the story of how she lost her arm as a child and was ostracised until Elvis himself took her to her prom night, Howard's screenplay contrives to draw a surprisingly touching parallel between cop and stammering zombie. Both have been socially excluded because of their disability, and both have found solace in music. Meanwhile, as the algae-covered rockabilly ghoul, O'Conor teases out the pathos of a man who just wanted to dance.

III: HEART OF ZOMBIE DARKNESS

Not every UK movie was content to shoot on this Sceptred Isle. For British directors Howard J. Ford and his brother Jonathan, a trip to West Africa gave them the chance to create a Third World zombie movie that harked back to B-movies by the likes of Bruno Mattei and Lucio Fulci. Taking the genre back to its ancestral home, *The Dead* (2010) achieves something quite remarkable for a zombie movie: a sense of gravitas.

Filmed on location in Burkina Faso and Ghana, *The Dead* is a stunning achievement – a ravishingly beautiful gut muncher that uses its gorgeous African backdrops to brilliant effect. It's essentially an interracial road movie as stranded, white US Air Force engineer Lt Brian Murphy (Rob Freeman) hooks up with Sgt Daniel Dembele (Prince David Osei), an AWOL black soldier from a local regiment, as zombies ravage the African continent.

What begins as a wary acquaintance grows into a trusting friendship as they drive across the dusty roads of West Africa in a battered vehicle, harassed by slow-moving ghouls. They search abandoned mud huts, rescue a baby and fight zombies in the glare of the sun and in the dark of night. A movie of incident – but little plotting – it runs on pure survival horror adrenalin: count your bullets, keep on moving, try and stay safe. Its scares come from the knowledge that one slip, one mistake, one unchecked corner could lead to death and disaster.

Freeman, whose piercing, emotive eyes helps him bear a passing resemblance to Billy Bob Thornton, is the film's only white character. His relationship with Demeble (who Osei plays with quiet fortitude) naturally begs questions about the racial politics of setting a zombie movie in West Africa.

Sergeant Dembele's entrance, walking through a village calmly lopping off zombie heads and limbs with a machete, stirs memories of real-life African atrocities from the Congo to Rwanda. It's a rich symbolism that runs deep through *The Dead*, although the Ford brothers care careful to let it remain beneath the surface.

Certainly, the pairing of a white and black actor is loaded with potential meaning. "I don't understand the white man," complains Dembele after meeting Murphy. "Your soldiers come with guns to fight us. Your doctors come with medicines to save us." Angry that aid workers and UN forces have fled as the dead walk, Dembele's quiet fury can't help but prick the conscience of white audiences. There is a sense here that the zombies' arrival is just another example of how Africa is perpetually screwed over.

As far as much of the First World is concerned, the African heart of darkness has always been apocalyptic. Living on a continent where 852 million people are chronically or acutely malnourished makes zombies arguably less scary than not having enough food to feed your family. By taking us into a zombie-led African apocalypse, the Ford brothers both play into and challenge First World prejudices.

The ghouls themselves, who amble about with the slow creep of Romero and Fulci's zombies, possess an accusatory anger. They aren't raging, they aren't moaning – but their body language and piercingly fierce eyes (the West African extras are fitted with contact lenses) make them look as if they bear a very definite grudge. "Maybe we've been punished for our arrogance," suggests a village elder. "Perhaps nature has put in motion the ultimate solution to its problem. Man's greed has devoured this earth. Nature is restoring its delicate balance."

It's a throwaway line, familiar from a dozen zombie movies, but against the rich African backdrop it resonates with a newfound sense of poignancy. That is pretty much the whole modus operandi of *The Dead*, a movie that reinvigorates the genre's strongest tropes thanks to its setting.

It's also notable how visually arresting *The Dead*

is. The striking scenery is perfect for the task in hand and Jonathan Ford, who acts as cinematographer and co-director, uses it to brilliant effect. The abandoned air base the heroes eventually arrive at showcases the method: the constantly moving camera zips along the centre line of a sun-blasted runway as Murphy and Osei walk along it, giving us a sense of wide open spaces. In contrast, though, the buildings of the base are a nightmare – full of shadowy corners and dark corridors where Murphy dispatches a zombie with a fire extinguisher to the head.

The contrast between agoraphobic, sun-baked open spaces and claustrophobic darkness amps up the scare factor. As in Romero's movies, you have a sense that the zombies are all around the camera, forever ready to pop out and grab someone who doesn't have 20:20 vision. From the audience's point of view, this approach makes you feel constantly on edge. Nowhere is safe – danger is all around.

It's a feeling the directors playful toy with in a cheeky sequence in which the camera pans to follow the heroes' car and a zombie-esque scarecrow pops out of the edge of the frame. Few contemporary zombie movies have replicated that clammy sense of unease so brilliantly. *The Dead* stands as one of the most arresting z-flicks of the 2000s, overcoming its undernourished narrative and occasional missteps in performance.

IV. TURNING JAPANESE

Horror films aren't big in Japan, but Japanese horror films are big internationally. In the 1990s, Asian ghost stories like *Ringu* (1998) and *Ju-on: The Grudge* (2002) found a big audience in the English-speaking world and created a boom in J-horror that stretched all the way to Hollywood.

While the long-haired ghost girls of classic J-horror were stately spooks, a more disreputable kind of Japanese splatter movie grew out of the oddball strangeness of punkish gorefests like *Wild Zero* and *Stacy*. Delivering increasingly outrageous splatter films like *Tokyo Gore Police* (2008) and *The Machine Girl* (2008) pushed the boundaries of extreme gore while finding an appreciative audience on the international fantastic film festival circuit.

When Japan's oldest major movie studio Nikkatsu Studios founded its Sushi Typhoon label in 2010, it highlighted how these movies – which operate in the cut between the grindhouse, pink film pornography and insane splatter comedy – had become commercially successful cinematic exports. Zombies, with a growing dedicated fanbase, were an obvious hook for Japanese filmmakers to reach an international audience with.

"My investors actually requested that I make a zombie movie," explained Noboru Iguchi, director of the scatological *Zombie Ass: Toilet of the Dead* (orig. *Zonbi asu*, 2011). "I decided that if I was going to make a zombie movie it had to be really crazy and eccentric […] The president of the company is a huge fan of horror films and he particularly related to the idea that the characters can't stop farting. So I got the green light pretty much based on that."[279]

Zombie Ass is, in many ways, the epitome of the J-zombie cycle. Like all these films, it's driven by crappy VFX and a puerile desire to be as crass as possible. The sheer outrageousness of its premise does a better job of promoting it than a thousand press releases. After all, horror fans love to treat movies like a game of Top Trumps – in certain circles there's kudos in being able to say you've seen a movie where a tapeworm emerges from a man's arse and forces itself into a woman's mouth. J-splatter cinema works on the assumption that cult cinema fans will flock to anything if it's bizarre enough to come with bragging rights.

Zombie Ass features fecal zombies who crouch-walk backwards with their arses in the air, while phallic tapeworm monsters wriggle out from between their butt cheeks. A key sequence features a weight-obsessed model (Mayu Sugano) squatting over an outhouse latrine, while a shit-covered zombie (Demo Tanaka) emerges from the brown water below her. He reaches up to grab her behind. She screams "pervert!" and farts noxious yellow gas in his turd-spattered face. Clearly this is a movie that blurs the distinction between shit zombies and shit zombie movies.

Iguchi followed *Zombie Ass* with *Dead Sushi* (orig. *Deddo sushi*, 2012), an equally bizarre though rather more light-hearted outing in which California rolls and tamagoyaki fly through the air attacking people. Can killer sushi count as zombies? Who knows. It certainly wasn't a first, though. In knockabout zom-com *Big Tits Zombie* (orig. *Kyonyu doragon: Onsen zonbi vs sutorippa 5*, 2010) a bunch of chainsaw-wielding strippers fought zombie sushi *and* used wasabi sauce as a ghoul repellent.

Elsewhere the need to be more and more extreme in order to stand out began to take its toll. Sex – and sexual violence – was often a quicker way to achieve notoriety than sushi or scatology. *Attack Girls Swim Team Vs the Undead* (orig. *Joshikyôei hanrangun*, 2004) was part of a loose "Nihombie" trilogy bookended by *Zombie Self-Defence Force* (orig. *Zonbi jieitai*, 2005) and *Rika: The Zombie Killer* (orig. *Saikyô heiki joshikôsei: Rika – Zonbi Hantâ vs saikyô Zonbi Gurorian*, 2008). It lingered shamelessly over the pert nipples of its teen cast whether they were in their Lycra-snapping swimsuits or stripping off for lesbian shower scenes.

Not to be outdone, *Onechanbara* (aka *Onechanbara: Samurai Bikini Squad*, 2008) swapped the all-in-one swimsuits for bikinis and also gave its female zombie killer heroine a feather boa, cowboy hat and samurai sword for good measure. It left no doubt that these Japanese zombie films, with their pretty protagonists, were adolescent male fantasies that owed much to Japanese pop culture trends – sailor-suited schoolgirls, tentacle porn and manga action.

The small pool of male, Japanese filmmakers working on these films was telling. Naoyuki Tomomatsu graduated from the schoolgirls of *Stacy* way back in 2001 to the lively *Zombie Self-Defence Force* in 2006, then forced *Rape Zombie: Lust of the Dead* on an unsuspecting world in 2012. Special effects guru Yoshihiro Nishimura flitted between directing the likes of *Helldriver* (2010) and working on the make-up and creature design of *Zombie Ass* and *Dead Sushi*. The rather less frivolous *Yoroi: Samurai Zombie* (orig. *Yoroi: Samurai zonbi*, 2008) featured actor Tak Sakaguchi (*Versus*, *Battlefield Baseball*) stepping behind the camera to direct, while his former director Ryûhei Kitamura took scripting duties.

Not surprisingly, videogames were an influence too. *Onechanbara* grew out of a lacklustre game franchise in which its bikini heroine seemed only slightly less ridiculous than she did on-screen. *Zombrex: Dead Rising Sun* (2010) was an episodic series of films released on Xbox Live to promote Capcom's *Dead Rising* videogame franchise. Capcom also partnered with Sony to make two feature length CG animations based on its *Resident Evil* series – *Resident Evil: Degeneration* (2008) and *Resident Evil: Damnation* (2012). Both offered far more fan service than Paul W.S. Anderson's increasingly ridiculous girls 'n' guns live-action franchise bothered with.

There were occasional shifts of gear and hints at something slightly more interesting. *Yoroi: Samurai Zombie* at least tries to make its three towering ghouls in bushido armour scary – a rarity in a cycle that largely treats the walking dead as objects of ridicule (they were also presumably an influence on the WWII-era samurai ghouls in the Indonesia-shot *Dead Mine* (2011).

The quietly surreal and languorously paced *Tokyo Zombie* (orig. *Tôkyô zonbi*, 2005) exists in a category all its own. Its apocalypse is sliced into two distinct halves – first as a pair of ju-jitsu obsessed slackers try to escape the walking dead, then propelling us forward five years into a post-apocalyptic future where the rich entertain themselves by pitting living martial artists against zombies in gladiatorial conquests.

Ironically it took a Western director to make the most Japanese J-zombie movie. *Schoolgirl Apocalypse* (2011), written and directed by American expat John Cairns, sounds like it would be at home beside exploitation quickies like *Big Tits Zombie*. Yet, it's actually a more measured film with the creepily glacial pacing of a Kiyoshi Kurosawa movie.

"There is not enough domestic interest in horror to sustain a horror-film industry," explained Cairns of the film industry in his adopted country. "So most [producers] try to 'trend' something J-catchy with the words 'Sushi', 'Ninja' or whatever and toss a bunch of soft porn at it so it can sell abroad. There are some great films like *The Machine Girl* and *Zombie Ass* that are full of so much amazing creativity, but most of the time it seems like distributors and production companies keep blindly hurling money at the same trendy stuff until they go bankrupt. Japan has so much more to offer."[280]

Eschewing the usual goofiness, *Schoolgirl Apocalypse*'s coming of age story unfolds mysteriously as a migraine-inducing signal turns men into psychotic zombies and schoolgirl Sakura (Japanese gravure idol Higa Rino) leaves her home in search of safety. Armed with a bow and arrow – Sakura's a less-than-stellar archery student – she encounters different women each trying to cope in their own way with the crisis. The closest thing she has to a friend is a cartoon-animated blonde-haired foreign boy who springs to life out of her English textbooks.

Less interested in gore than evoking a strangely muted and elliptical atmosphere, Cairns manages to marry the apocalyptic tone of Kurosawa's *Kairo* (2001) with zombie-movie conventions. Empowering its female characters without lusting over them, *Schoolgirl Apocalypse* breaks with its predecessors and proves an uncharacteristically restrained and thoughtful entry in the Japanese zombie cycle.

Equally feminist in its intent was *Miss Zombie* (2013), written and directed by maverick Japanese filmmaker Sabu. Largely shot in black and white, it plays like a Japanese art house hybrid between *Deadgirl* and *Fido*. When a boxed ghoul, Shara (Ayaka Komatsu), is shipped to the house of Dr Teramoto (Toru Tezuka) the family's life is turned upside down. Accompanying the delivery is a set of instructions – feed her fruit and veg, never meat – and a pistol in case of emergency.

Initially treated like a servant, Shara mutely endures a repetitive life of cleaning and scrubbing, not to mention taunts and physical abuse from the local kids (she's the first and only running zombie I've ever seen sprinting *away* from the living – after they abuse her). Despite her ghoulishness, the sight of her buttocks bent over the flagstones as she scrubs tempts men to fantasise about turning her into a different type of slave – tellingly, actress Ayaka Komatsu is a Japanese gravure idol normally found posing in lingerie or swimsuits.

Building a creepy sense of foreboding before heading towards a revenge-tinged final act where a mother's love leads to madness, Sabu's provocative arthouse film joins *Schoolgirl Apocalypse* in being a welcome counterpoint to the drooling objectification of women in so much Japanese zombie cinema.

CHAPTER THIRTEEN

ZOMBIE DARWINISM

"NO LONGER DO THEY KILL ONE ANOTHER [...] NOW THEY BEGIN TO SEE..."
– Max (Ray Bullock Jr.), *The Vanguard* (2008)

I. NO MORE BOOM AND BUST

Over eight years between 2005 and 2013, more zombie movies were released around the world that in the monster's previous seven decades on screen combined. It's harsh but fair to say that only a handful of them were good, even fewer were competent and an embarrassing amount of them were – to use a technical film criticism term – utter shite.

Quality has never been zombie cinema's strength, nor has it seemed to matter. The enduring appeal of the zombie itself transcends the films it finds itself in. What is notable, though, is how flexible the zombie myth is. Every age has had the zombies it needs, or deserves, and the new millennium is no exception. The movement away from voodoo, and from Romero's cannibalism, gave us a new image of the zombie as an infected carrier, a viral terrorist and harbinger of social collapse. But the weakening of the central zombie myth also encouraged filmmakers to try their own versions of the classic formulas.

While Romero's standard outbreak – survivors trapped in an isolated location, unable to rely on incompetent or criminal authorities for help – remained the central inspiration for many unimaginative filmmakers, others pushed the genre in new directions.

The sheer diversity of zombie movies between 2005 and 2013 is staggering. There was a sudden boom in zombie Westerns, the most interesting of which was Romero's *Survival of the Dead* (2009) – a Western-by-stealth and, at the time of writing,

his last zombie film. There were also remakes, prequels and sequels for almost all of Romero's zombie films – all made without his blessing. There was an unlikely boom in that age-old subgenre of the Nazi zombie movie. There were novelty zombies. Comedy zombies. Native American zombies. Zombie musicals. Animal zombies.

Such desperate attempts to spruce up the zombie genre often felt like dressing up mutton as lamb – quite literally in the case of New Zealand's *Black Sheep* (2006), a black comedy about zombie sheep that ensured you'd never look at your Sunday roast in the same way ever again. *Poultrygeist: Night of the Chicken Dead* (2007) did much the same for chicken when a fast food joint built on a Native American burial ground unleashes feathered, finger-licking ghouls with giblets. *Zombeak* (2007) saw a horny Satan creating zombies after being trapped in the body of a sacrificial hen. In contrast with that, the CG crows infected with a zombifying strain of avian flu in *The Beast Within* (2008) seem pretty plausible.

Other attempts to stand out from the zombie crowd were less anthropomorphic. *Romeo & Juliet Vs The Living Dead* (2009), for instance, added a bunch of clown-faced zombies and faux-Elizabethan dialogue to Shakespeare's classic ("Didst thou observe the noble bitch slap he did apply?"). *Pathogen* (2006) stood out thanks to its twelve-year-old director Emily Hagins (but not much else). *A Little Bit Zombie* (2011) was funded by an innovative "My Million Dollar Movie" crowdfunding scheme (and was an enjoyable zom-com in its own right). *The Dead Can't Dance* (2011) earned its spurs as the first ever Native American zombie movie, and was good fun in a disarmingly modest way.

Other filmmakers simply thought that a novel setting might be enough. In other words, it's zombies… in the 'hood (*Hood of the Living Dead*, 2004; *Zombiez*, 2004; *Gangs of the Dead*, 2005; *Mutant Vampire Zombies from the 'Hood!*, 2008)… in a diner (*Die-Ner (Get It?)*, 2008, aka *KFZ – Kentucky Fried Zombie*)… in a college dorm (twice in *Dorm of the Dead*, 2006 and 2009)… at a school prom (*Dance of the Dead*, 2008)… in detention (*Detention of the Dead*, 2012)… on a college campus (*House of the Dead II*, 2005)… in a cheerleader camp (*Zombie Cheerleading Camp*, 2008)… in a fishing lodge (*Brain Dead*, 2007)… in the Large Hadron Collider (*Decay*, 2012)… in a bathroom (*Stalled*, 2012)… in a prison (*Shadow: Dead Riot*, 2005; *Living Dead Lock Up*, 2005; *Dead Men Walking*, 2005) or, even better, on Alcatraz (*Rise of the Zombies*, 2012)… in a grungy club (*Pop Punk Zombies*, 2011)… in a bar (*O.C. Zombies and the Slasher of Zombie Town*, 2008)… during a zombie walk (*The Dead Mile*, 2012)… in a mortuary (*Mortuary*, 2005)… in a bank (*Dead Heist*, 2007)… in a Vegas casino (*Remains*, 2011)… on a ranch for the mentally handicapped (*Special Dead*, 2006)… a school for special-needs kids (*Retardead*, 2008)… in the Caribbean (*Zombie Driftwood*, 2010; *Dead Season*, 2012)… or even on the red planet (*The Last Days on Mars*, 2013).

Unusual explanations for the zombie outbreak also proliferated. Mad cow disease got the blame in *The Mad* (2006), *Bubba's Chili Parlor* (2008) and *Zombieland* (2009) among others; it was a ouija board in *Platoon of the Dead* (2009); mobile phones in *Electric Zombies* (2005); TV and radio signals in *The Signal* (2007); back-street abortions in *Zombie Babies* (2011); bats in *The Roost* (2004); toxic dumping in *Grave Mistake* (2008); dishwashing soap (yes, really) in *Doghouse* (2009); a comet in *Days of Darkness* (2007) among many others; tree sap in *Severed: Forest of the Dead* (2004); a pirate's stolen gold in *The Curse of Pirate Death* (2006); cave water in *Special Dead* (2006); bottled water in *Zombie Exs* (2012); alien parasites in *Slither* (2006), *Zombie Town* (2006) and

Infection: The Invasion Begins (2009); alien micro-organisms in *GermZ* (2010); alien rectal probes in *Hide and Creep* (2004); a UFO in *Alien Zombie Invasion* (2011); an amnesia plague in *Fugue State* (2008); sugar in *Mutants* (2008); wine in *Attack of the Vegan Zombies* (2009); demons creating "Zemons" in *Dead Before Dawn 3D* (2012); a Cambodian scorpion in *Dead & Deader* (2006) and Lyme Disease in *Infected* (2012).

Drugs continued to be a good way of explaining why the living turn into drooling, braindead idiots. Dodgy Russian pills in *Goa, Goa, Gone* (2013); mashed up zombie brains make a super weed fertiliser in *Bong of the Dead* (2011); in *Brain Blockers* (2005) it's a cure all drug called Tryptophan (not to be confused with the amino acid of the same name); bad marijuana in *Detroit Blood City: Beaver Lake Zombies 2* (2005) and *Scream Farm* (2007); weight loss pills in *Zombie Planet* (2003); illegal fertility drugs in *Eaters: Rise of the Dead* (2010); a dodgy drugs trial in *Expiration* (2011); a street drug called Natas (Satan) in *Zombie Hunter* (2013) and the fabled Trioxin reanimating fluid is distilled into an ecstasy-like street drug in *Return of the Living Dead: Rave to the Grave* (2005) – sadly, the resulting ghouls aren't as loved up as one might hope.

Meanwhile, in a very different vein, a cycle of zombie Westerns desperately tried to enliven the Old West by populating it with new ghouls. Largely consigned to straight-to-DVD, these films were hamstrung by their makers' inability to take the frontier setting seriously. Schoolboyish *A Fistful of Brains* (2008) was like a zombie walk held at Knotts Berry Farm's Wild West stunt show. *Dead Noon* (2007) was little more than a calling card for its director's ability at knocking up CGI on a laptop. *The Quick and the Undead* (2006) showcased its director's love of Sergio Leone but, despite lots of close-ups of watchful eyes it was never good, just bad and ugly. *Undead or Alive: A Zombedy* (2007), directed by a former *South Park* staff writer, was typical of the tongue-in-cheek silliness as Geronimo curses the white race and raises the dead. It was tempting to wonder if every zombie Western took *Blazing Saddles* as its template rather than anything by John Ford or Howard Hawks.

Austere Canadian indie *Exit Humanity* (2011) suggested that director John Geddes had at least seen a few Terrence Malick movies. Languorously paced, infused with a grave voiceover by Brian

Cox, and divided into chapters by beautifully animated sections, it gave its story of a Confederate soldier (Mark Gibson) fighting ghouls on the frontier an unexpected gravitas.

Very different was *Gallowwalkers* (2012), a deliriously baroque fantasy Western that was shot in Namibia and starred Wesley Snipes as a gunman hunting down the men who raped and killed his girlfriend. With its S&M vibe, flayed ghouls and endless stretches of white desert sand, *Gallowwalkers* looked ravishingly weird – but its plot was totally incomprehensible.

Zombie Westerns were rare enough to be novel, but films without cowboy ghouls often needed to let their titles do all the heavy lifting. Who couldn't resist a movie called *Motocross Zombies from Hell* (2007) or *Fast Zombies with Guns* (2009)? Although resist you should. Others simply relied on unlikely sounding face offs to urge undemanding DVD buyers to pick them off the shelf: *Wiseguys Vs Zombies* (2003), *Ninjas Vs Zombies* (2008), *Santa Claus Vs The Zombies* (2010), *Vampires Vs Zombies* (2003), *Vs The Dead* (2010), *Humans Vs Zombies* (2011), *Cockneys Vs Zombies* (2012).

The Asylum's "mockbusters" – low-budget, me-too movies that ride on the marketing coattails of studio flicks – included a couple of zombie outings. *Dead Men Walking* (2005) made inventive use of a prison (including a location shoot at Lincoln Heights Jail in Los Angeles). *I Am Ωmega* (2007) cheekily tried to steal Will Smith's mojo in *I Am Legend* (2007). More successful was *2012: Zombie Apocalypse* (2011), starring Ving Rhames, which seemed to have been inspired by Valve's co-op zombie survival horror *Left 4 Dead*. It also featured crappy CG zombie tigers ("Here kitty, kitty!") for added WTF? value.

Meanwhile, *Abraham Lincoln Vs Zombies* (2012) tapped into Fox's $70 million flop *Abraham Lincoln: Vampire Hunter* (2012) and made a lot more money in terms of its budget to box office ratio.[281] Best of the bunch was *Nazis at the Center of the Earth* (2012), a busted OTT flush of Nazi zombies and Hitler's reanimated head on a robot's body. It's the closest The Asylum has come to pull off a living dead *Sharknado* (2013).

Elsewhere, a mini-run of zombie musicals proved that no one had learned the lesson of *Nudist Colony of the Dead* back in 1991. *Z: A Zombie Musical* (2006) gave us singing undead nuns in Texas. It really wasn't *The Sound of Music* with zombies. *Song of the Dead* (2005) enlivened its standard, Missouri-set zombie apocalypse by giving the ghouls a song-and-dance number: "Our brains are on fire for life/We want to taste as much as we like/I smell flesh and blood/Give me flesh blood…"

II. THE GOOSE-STEPPING DEAD

One of the strangest, most unexpected turns in zombie cinema was the resurrection of the dead and rotting Nazi zombie cycle. Laid to rest in the 1980s after filmmakers like Jess Franco and Jean Rollin had bled its lurid potential dry, it suddenly shambled back to life in 2001 with Rob Green's *The Bunker*. If it had been left to low-budget films – including shoddy DV backyard efforts *Operation Nazi Zombies* (aka *Maplewoods*, 2003), Ohio-shot zombie/werewolf mishmash *Zombies of War* (aka *Horrors of War*, 2006) and Andreas Schnaas's timewaster *Don't Wake The Dead* (2008) with its Nazis and Templar blind monks – it probably would have died all over again. But a handful of more polished efforts gave Nazi zombies an unexpected second wind.

In Scotland, the *Outpost* franchise became something of a surprise success. Director Steve Barker delivered the first *Outpost* (2007) with little fanfare. Shot in Dumfriesshire, it centred on a squad of mercenaries led by Ray Stevenson who head into an abandoned Eastern European WWII bunker looking for lost Nazi gold. What they discover instead are unkillable super soldiers who can apparently manipulate time and space, and a chess-playing catatonic ghoul dubbed "The Breather" (Johnny Meres) who becomes the series' underused chief villain.

Pitched as *Platoon* meets *The Sixth Sense* by producer Kieran Parker – who remortgaged his house along with partner Arabella Croft to raise £200,000 of the film's budget – *Outpost* became

Outpost (2007).

shoot, did little to progress the cycle much beyond its bare bones Nazi-ghouls-in-a-bunker conceit.

At the other end of the spectrum, *Nazis at the Center of the Earth*'s tale of Nazi zombies in the Antarctic clung to the coattails of Nazis-on-the-moon epic *Iron Sky* (2012) – a movie so offbeat that The Asylum should, by rights, have probably come up with it first. *Nazis at the Center of the Earth*'s bad-taste plotting featured Nazi torture porn (unusually grim by The Asylum's tongue-in-cheek standards); an equally nasty Nazi zombie gang rape; a non-consensual abortion; and Hitler's reanimated head (nicely played by James Maxwell) stuck on a cyborg chassis. By the time a flying saucer emerges from the polar ice cap to menace a passing fighter plane ("Target is covered with Nazi swastikas! I'm calling it hostile!"), *Nazis at the Center of the Earth* has earned itself a place in the footnotes of the dustbin of cinema history.

What drives the Nazi zombie cycle? In part, its appeal lies in the creeping dread that the Nazis, the ultimate 20th-century evil, might return from the grave as an unstoppable force. In each of these films, the implied desire to create a 1,000-year Reich is arguably more terrifying than the jack-booted ghouls themselves.

Outpost II taps into that, leaving the confines of the first film's bunker as the super-fast, super-strong Nazi zombies launch a Blitzkrieg across Europe. Hammering the living to death with their potato-masher grenades (surely not the smartest use of a live explosive?), the ghouls are terrifying in their mercilessly efficiency and unstoppable invulnerability. After NATO's attempt to halt the Nazi doomsday machine with an EMP blast fails, military commanders prepare a no-nonsense nuclear strike. The spread of Nazism – much like Islamic jihad – is simply too dangerous to take any chances with.

An unanswered question hovers over the goose-stepping ghoul cycle: is a Nazi zombie any scarier than just a plain Nazi Nazi? It's certainly obvious that the fascist ghouls don't owe much to the essential zombie myth – they're not cannibals, nor are they infectious. The ghouls in the *Outpost* series – styled individually as little more than chest-thumping, roaring football hooligans – don't seem likely masterminds of a Fourth Reich. The banality of evil suggests that Nazis are probably scarier when they're mundane and alive rather than when they're living dead.

an unlikely hit, in defiance of its muddy khaki palette, ill-defined characters and grim commitment to po-faced seriousness. Nazi zombies, it seemed, were back with a vengeance.

Clearly there was something in the ether. Around the same time hit videogame *Call of Duty: World at War* (2008) introduced a "Nazi Zombie" mode in which players had to survive against wave after wave of lumbering, living dead fascists. It helped turn the Nazi ghouls into iconic monsters who suddenly started popping up all over.

Blood Creek (2008) was a shelved project from director Joel Schumacher which improbably starred Michael Fassbender as a resurrected Nazi ghoul with a third eye in his forehead running amok in West Virginia (actually Romania). It was hard to tell whether it was dusted off and released in 2009 thanks to Fassbender's rising profile or the growing appeal of zombies in black leather SS trenchcoats. Over in Europe, *War of the Dead* (aka *War of the Dead: Stone's War*, 2011), an international co-production and Lithuania's biggest ever movie

Tellingly, *Outpost III: Rise of the Spetsnatz* (2012) dodged that question by heading back to WWII – a prequel in which a grizzled unit of Russian "Red Guard" soldiers discover a secret lab in the dog days of the war. Dour and dark, it played best as a beat 'em up with the Russian squad leader (Bryan Larkin) duking it out with Nazi zombies. It was like watching a gutter punch up outside a Govan pub.

Other films simply tried to amp up the horror of their villains. *Dead Mine* (2011), the debut film from HBO Asia and directed by British helmer Steven Sheil (*Mum & Dad*), had Japanese Imperial Guard fascist ghouls in full bushido armour chasing modern-day treasure hunters (seeking Yamashita's gold) around an abandoned mine. They're joined by Morlock-like, dehumanised ghouls – Australian POWs who were experimented on by Japan's real-life covert biological warfare experts Unit 731 in an attempt to create the ultimate obedient soldier.

Frankenstein's Army (2013) went even further, reengineering the Nazi zombie into a truly terrifying monster worthy of the name. Dutch commercials director cannily uses found footage, following a Soviet propaganda filmmaker Dimitri (Alexander Mercury) who's embedded with a rough and ready combat unit in East Germany when they stumble across a Nazi factory churning out a terrifying new kind of weapon. Filming in grainy 8mm, Dimitri captures the horror as the Soviets realise that Nazi mad science will stop at nothing to win the war.

Nodding towards videogames – in both its first-person perspective and echoes of Id Software's seminal 1992 shooter *Wolfenstein 3D* – *Frankenstein's Army* features "Zombots", grotesque man/machine assemblages dreamt up by Nazi scientist Viktor Frankenstein (Karel Roden), grandson of the infamous baron.

Emerging from the shadows, these surreal creations are blighted monsters. One walks on stilts like a human spider, another wears a huge diving helmet like the Big Daddies from *BioShock*. A third has an aircraft propeller in lieu of a head. They recall the crippled, cyborg WWI veterans of Otto Dix's painting *Die Skatspieler* (aka *Skat Players*, *Card-Playing War Cripples*, 1920), not to mention the gas-masked stormtroopers of his *Der Krieg* (*The War*) series.

Properly monstrous, these abominations are an affront not only to God but to science too. It's clear we're in the inhuman shadow of Auschwitz. But *Frankenstein's Army* doesn't want to be properly transgressive, just edgy enough to be noticed. Getting sillier with each passing minute – at one point Dr Frankenstein starts trying to meld Communist and fascist brains together, proclaiming "I can end the war by creating a new being!" – it ultimately plays its horror for midnight movie laughs and with one eye on the potential for a line of tie-in action figures.

In comparison, Tommy Wirkola's *Dead Snow* (orig: *Død snø*, 2009) embraces the essential silliness of Nazi zombies from the off as a group of likeable 20-something med students head out to an isolated log cabin in the Scandinavian wilderness for spring break. For the next 80 minutes they're terrified as Nazi zombies left over from WWII rise from the crisp, white snowdrifts in search of some stolen gold. It's like *Oasis of the Zombies* transplanted from the Sahara to the fjords of Norway.

The ghouls, dressed in grey Nazi uniforms and steel helmets, are led by Colonel Herzog (Ørjan Gamst), a fearsome-looking zombie with missing lips who likes to stand on hillsides watching the action through his binoculars. His ghouls use Blitzkrieg tactics and they're as fast and organised and as ruthlessly efficient as you'd expect zombie fascists to be.

Inspired by the "splatstick" of *Braindead* and *Evil Dead II*, Wirkola ratchets up the gore with a keen understanding of how a splatter movie can play to a crowded cinema on a Saturday night. Nazi heads are dropkicked, snowmobiles are used like *Braindead*'s lawnmower, and by the time the credits roll everyone – and the pure driven snow itself – is drenched in blood.

The best moments are, unsurprisingly, the funniest ones. A bitten survivor worries about becoming one of them but remembers he's half-Jewish (it doesn't stop him from taking a chainsaw to the offending appendage, just to be sure). A girl who tries to hide up a tree is forced to beat an angry crow to death in an effort to remain undiscovered. And the scene most likely to reduce an auditorium to shocked guffaws is when one escaping survivor is suddenly halted in mid-sprint because he's tethered to a tree by his intestines.

Dead Snow has little interest in the why or how and there's no appetite for exploring the history of

Norway's occupation during the Second World War. It exists purely for bloody thrills. It's fitting then that these Nazi zombies are treated more like party poopers than troubling, ambulatory remains of the Second World War's repressed memories.

They harass the good-looking, horny protagonists like the ultimate killjoys. That's fascism for you: ripping the intestines out of fun since 1933. Or as a mouthy soldier (Ali Craig) complains in *Outpost II*: "Nazis, mate. Proper cunts."

III. ANTI-ZOMBIE ZOMBIE MOVIES

When is a zombie not a zombie? In an era when zombies have metamorphosed from the shambling dead into the running infected, it's a question that crops up a lot. Today's zombies are often now zombies-by-proxy – infected stand-ins for jihad and viral pandemics.

At the same time, though, a few indie filmmakers have pushed the parameters of the zombie movie itself, breaking with the standard outbreak formula to reach for something unusual. So the question becomes: when is a zombie movie not a zombie movie?

Pontypool (2008), a Canadian indie locked inside a claustrophobic local radio station, starred Stephen McHattie (*Exit Humanity*, *A Little Bit Zombie*) as a talk-radio DJ reporting on a rolling apocalypse outside. Set in the small town of Pontypool, Ontario, and based on the boldly cerebral novel *Pontypool Changes Everything* by Tony Burgess, it stands as one of the most startling horror movies of the last decade.

Described by director Bruce McDonald (*The Tracey Fragments*) as "a zombie movie without any zombies", it begins with grizzled, cowboy hat wearing DJ Grant Mazzy (McHattie) encountering a strange woman in the snow on his way to work.[282] She babbles incoherently before vanishing back into the blizzard. Mazzy, a boozy, former big-time talk-show host who was fired from his last job for pushing things too far, is spooked by the incident. But it's only when reports of strange occurrences start coming over the wires while he's on air that he realises that something is very, very wrong in the town of Pontypool.

First adapted as a radio play, inspired in part by Orson Welles and the Mercury Theatre's famous 1938 broadcast of *War of the Worlds*, *Pontypool* is all about the power of language. It's a zombie movie inspired as much by William S. Burroughs

and Roland Barthes as George Romero. Its slightly bonkers premise is that the English language contains a virus: the infected start to lose their ability to find meaning in words, repeating phrases over and over again and eventually being driven to demented violence – at which point they try to bite the lips off their victims.

Daringly, McDonald and cinematographer Miroslaw Baszak (*Land of the Dead*) keep us locked inside the safety of the radio station for 90 minutes. "It's much more about what you don't see," he explained. "It's more about the theatre of the mind."[283] As a result, our only sense of the chaos happening outside comes from hysterical callers who offer terrified firsthand accounts of the infection's progress: a doctor's surgery "explodes" as a mob of chanting "conversationalists" literally cram themselves inside the building. Later, a chattering horde converges on a car while imitating – bizarrely – the sound of windscreen wipers.

Listening to the incoming reports, Mazzy and his radio team – frosty producer Sydney Briar (Lisa Houle, MacHattie's real-life wife) and sound engineer Laurel Ann Drummond (Georgina Riley) – can't quite believe what they're hearing. The reports simply don't make sense. The claustrophobic tension is ramped up brilliantly – although Burgess's offbeat suggestion they should keep the camera locked on McHattie's weather-worn face throughout the whole film might have been a step too far.

By the time French Canadian troops are sent in to quell what some are calling a separatist terror attack, and the authorities warn citizens to stop using the now dangerous English language and switch to French, *Pontypool* unravels into something more cerebral and leftfield than just another zombie flick. Indeed, it hardly has any on-screen zombies at all (although its chief ghoul, who bangs her head repeatedly against the DJ booth until the soundproofed plexiglass is a bloody mess, is one of the most disturbing zombies ever).

On the surface, *Pontypool* is a movie about talk radio and the power of words to inflame the passions. As Mazzy explains early on, his shockjock shtick is to piss the listeners off. Because a pissed-off listener keeps on listening – and probably calls up his pissed-off brother and makes him tune in too. Talk radio devalues language – turning it into a weapon of blunt-force trauma and infecting people with its virulence (it seems no accident that terms of hatred and endearment are posited as the chief carriers of the virus).

Pontypool hints at satire, but quickly backs away from it. This isn't a tub-thumping social commentary. Instead, it's more surreal and indefinable. In interviews Burgess gave a suitably cryptic explanation of the story's genesis.

"I had just finished a degree in semiotics so I had all this pent up theory shit in my head (Julia Kristeva's *Black Sun* in particular)," the novelist turned screenwriter told *Twitch*. "What I really wanted [to write was] a book about the sudden and convulsive end of the world that runs in two equal and opposite directions: it is most certainly happening AND it's not necessarily so. The language virus just fell in as an idea that allowed me to do these things. It wasn't, ultimately, French semioticians (or Laurie Anderson/William Burroughs) that helped me build it, but neo-platonic grammarians and occult memory theorists from the early modern period (what?!!?), Petrus Ramus' influence on Marlowe (the final scenes in the film are modelled on Marlowe's final scene in Faust – Oh my God, this sounds pretentious, but, whatever, you do what you do) and Giordano Bruno, Fucini and others who were convinced that rhetoric had the ability to change everything."[284]

To which one can only say, "whoa!".

Pontypool toys with post-9/11 anxieties, almost like a too-smart, college-educated cousin of the painfully on-the-nose *Dead Air*. There's talk of terrorism, there's a weird troupe of actors who turn up at the radio station in Middle Eastern garb to play out a scene from Lawrence of Arabia, and Mazzy's assistant is even an Afghanistan vet. What that amounts to, though, isn't clear.

Perhaps there's a sense that language, after all the "dodgy dossiers" and propaganda and political rhetoric that followed 9/11 and paved the way for the War on Terror, has been debased. Certainly Mazzy finds himself in an impossible situation: how can you safely report on a linguistic virus by talking about it on the radio? Are you warning people, or simply spreading the virus itself further?

At its heart, *Pontypool* is a film about selfhood, not terrorism. The voice of exposition is Dr Mendez (Hrant Alianak, a Canadian actor of Armenian descent whose presence suits the film's vague post-9/11 sensibility). He escapes the horde and arrives at the radio station as the ghouls start to break in. Explaining the linguistic basis of the virus, he convinces Mazzy and Sydney that they need to start communicating in pidgin French.

In the final third of the film, the acrimonious relationship between DJ and producer starts to blossom into something more tender. When Sydney becomes infected, Mazzy tries to help her fight off the virus – ascribing new meaning to old words. "Kill isn't kill. Kill isn't kill. Kill is kiss. What is kill? Kiss. Kill me."

A horror film unafraid to cite Roland Barthes, *Pontypool* builds towards a creeping dread – a sense of how precarious our sense of selfhood is. As words lose meaning and language turns on us, the infected spout gibberish like dementia sufferers. "This [movie] is all about the disconnection between people," said McHattie. "What we're afraid we might become: these babbling, meaningless parasites."[285] The death of words is the death of ourselves. It's a semiotic apocalyptic of nonsense/no-sense that will leave you truly scared... *scarred... scored... scorched.*

Mulberry Street (2006) – aka *Zombie Virus On Mulberry Street* – also begins with an unlikely, borderline ridiculous premise: mutated Manhattan rats are turning anyone they bite into humanoid rat-zombies. It then transforms into a grubby, grindhouse-era horror film worthy of the likes of Larry Cohen.

Delivering a hellish vision of the Big Apple's rottenness, Jim Mickle's film taps into a sense of post-9/11 anxiety but also themes of urban degeneration and blue collar suffering as the gentrification of Manhattan continues unchecked.

Its portrait of urban decay sits alongside its compelling sense of a Lower East Side tenement block community. Washed-up ex-boxer Clutch (played by Mickle's co-writer Nick Damici) is the ostensible hero. He's waiting for his daughter

Casey (Kim Blair), a battle-scarred veteran of Iraq, to return home.

Upstairs, pretty but exhausted Polish barmaid and single mom Kay (Bo Correy) takes a fancy to him, much to the annoyance of Clutch's black, gay friend Coco (Ron Brice) who's pining with unrequited love for him. On the top floor, a pair of crotchety old veterans (Larry Fleischman and Antone Paga) dodder about like Statler and Waldorf from *The Muppet Show*. Like its residents, the building is falling apart – left to rot by a property developer who wants the tenants out so Little Italy's gentrification can continue apace.

As the rat virus spreads and the infected turn into creepy rodent–human hybrids with crooked teeth and a hint of whiskers around their chops, the whole of Manhattan is locked down and the surviving characters struggle to survive – something they've been doing even before the rats arrived. Clutch, a former boxer, pummels ghouls with his fists; the bar where Kay works is overrun and you quickly realise it's risky betting on who will survive.

Mulberry Street is grim and gritty and offers a politically charged take on Manhattan's resilience after 9/11. The old codgers upstairs blame the outbreak on Bin Laden ("That rat bastard!") and there's also a real sense of a fractured, bickering community closing ranks to fight a common enemy.

In a passing (but pointed) scene, some of the building's middle-class residents decide to take their chances outside. The dad carries a toddler in his arms, and we know that this family isn't going to last more than a few minutes on the chaotic, blood-stained streets. It's incredibly distressing – but there's tellingly little sympathy for them. As they rush outside, one of the hard-nosed residents shouts after them, in typically blunt New York style: "Goddamn yuppies jumping the sinking ship! Go back to Connecticut!"

For all its War on Terror and class-war undertones, though, *Mulberry Street*'s most startling theme is its simmering love affair between Clutch and Coco. The bathrobe-wearing gay guy flirts relentlessly with hardman Clutch and is jealous of his growing love for Kay. But as the apocalypse unfolds, Kay is infected and Clutch unceremoniously dispatches her. Later, Coco is captured while escaping through a window and is dragged screaming down an apartment corridor, fingernails scraping along the floor as Clutch watches helplessly.

The couple's (b)romance comes to a head on the tenement building where the bitten, slowly transforming Coco meets Clutch and sniffs at his face – but doesn't bite him because Clutch is also infected (he's been bitten, he realises, in the fracas). They die in each other's arms – an image so striking you wonder if *Mulberry Street* has the potential to be read as a comment on gay New York and HIV/Aids.

Pontypool was a zombie movie without zombies. *Mulberry Street* was the Larry Cohen zombie movie Cohen never made. *The Battery* (2012), in contrast, was an anti-zombie movie set in the verdant backwoods of New England and barely bothered about its ghouls at all.

A two-handed character drama, *The Battery* followed a pair of survivors tramping across country after the zombie apocalypse had hit. Mickey (Adam Cronheim) and Ben (Jeremy Gardner) are former baseball players – a pitcher and a catcher "battery", an intuitive partnership that gives a team its power. Only in this changed, zombie-infested world they're no longer much of a team.

Mickey is a panty-sniffing, headphone wearing horny romantic. He can't adjust to the new world, insists on playing lottery scratch cards and has a phobia about killing zombies. Ben, in contrast, is on his way to becoming a grizzled mountain man. . He's thriving in the almost-empty landscape and is utterly annoyed by his buddy's inability to man up.

As they head across New England without any purpose other than staying alive, they raid houses wielding baseball bats. Mickey keeps his headphones on at all times, listening to CDs and dreaming about past girlfriends. Ben stays focussed on the present, draining the water from canned chicken to reuse in case their drinks bottles run dry.

They're an odd couple and an unlikely partnership. But the real cracks only begin to show after they discover a walkie-talkie and overhear chatter between a more organised group of survivors stationed at some mysterious place called "The Orchard". Mickey harbours hopes of discovering a new life, perhaps even the comfort of a girl's flesh against his own again. It helps that the voice on the radio belongs to Annie (Alana O'Brien), who Mickey instantly imagines to be some gorgeous babe. She warns him to stay away – telling him that the Orchard isn't what he thinks. But the lovesick dolt doesn't listen. It's the start of an obsession that will lead both him and Ben towards disaster.

Shot in 16 days for $6,000 on a Canon 5D DSLR and edited on Adobe Premiere, *The Battery* is a marvel of micro-budget filmmaking. It's also a refreshingly smart zombie movie. Largely uninterested in the ghoul pack, and frequently described as "an anti-zombie movie", it focuses on the relationship between its two leads.

"My intention was to explore human behaviour on an intimate scale," director Jeremy Gardner told critic Anne Billson. "Rather than watch the world burn, I thought it could be interesting to watch a psyche wither away. To watch one man become feral, and watch another one lose hope. It isn't exactly an original idea, but in all my years watching zombie movies, I hadn't seen it done that way."[286]

Released a few months after *World War Z*, *The Battery* is the total opposite of the epic, global Brad Pitt blockbuster: it's small and supple, intimate and daring. Gardner's skill lies in making us care deeply about these characters – a pair of regular guys just trying to find a way to live.

The Battery may well be the ultimate hipster zombie movie, its bearded protagonists mostly just hanging out against the backdrop of the z-apocalypse. It's knowing in its attempt to graft a character drama onto the zombie template, and bold in its artistic choices. One static, unbroken shot captures the guys taking pleasure in brushing their teeth after they unexpectedly find toothbrushes and paste. The music from Mickey's headphones – a hipster mix tape of Rock Plaza Central, Wise Blood and Sun Hotel – becomes the backbone of the film's floatily heartbroken atmosphere. This is a movie of loss and dissatisfaction, a post-apocalyptic tale about what it takes to keep on keeping on.

What's refreshing about *The Battery* is its reinvigoration of zombie formula. Despite eschewing the usual siege dynamics, it's a story of entrapment, both literally and metaphorically. The choices that these men make lead them to lose the freedom of the grassy woods as they end up locked inside their station wagon for the last 30 minutes of the movie.

It's an ironic echo of what has gone before.

Earlier, in an mad moment of hormonal horniness, Mickey is surprised in the car when a female zombie (played by production manager Elise Stella, and rather cruelly billed in the credits as "Fresh Slut Zombie") presses herself up against the window.[287] Watching her bra-less breasts against the glass, Mickey is aroused enough to start masturbating. He whacks off, his trousers around his ankles, while she moans dissatisfied outside, trying to get in. It's an outrageous moment and Mickey is totally mortified when Ben interrupts – first convinced Mickey's under attack and needs saving, then howling with laughter when he realises what's actually happening.

Later that scene is echoed and inverted when Mickey and Ben, after a violent encounter with Annie and her Orchard friends, are trapped in the station wagon and surrounded by a pack of moaning ghouls. This time there's no jerking off. Instead the two guys are forced to wait it out in the back of the car as the zombies press against the glass. Injured and alone and without the car keys, they're trapped.

It's a stunning sequence capped off by an 11-minute static shot of Ben as he convinces his partner to make a run for it. Waiting alone, pondering his fate, Ben is shocked when Mickey returns to the car – bitten and infected. As this battery team – so fractiously unsuited in their temperaments, desires and needs – finally falls apart, Gardner delivers one of the most mournful and downbeat zombie tales of the decade. It's a film about the cost of survival: the *Touching the Void* of zombie movies.

Taken together, these three indie movies – *Pontypool*, *Mulberry Street* and *The Battery* – were like a master class in zombie filmmaking. Brash and fresh, bold and daring, they were proof that no matter how over-saturated the zombie genre had become there was still space for talented filmmakers to mould and shape the zombie myth into something relevant and new. It was just a shame so few other zombie filmmakers could match them.

IV. ALL ROADS LEAD TO ROMERO

Being a horror fan in the 2000s meant enduring a pervading sense of déjà vu as Hollywood remake fever hit. As audience numbers fell to their lowest level for years, the studios retreated to safety – familiarity, tried-and-tested IP and established brand names calmed financiers' fears. Remakes, prequels and sequels were the talismans that warded off the spectre of box office failure. It was, in its own way, a cinematic reanimation of the dead.

While the *Transformers* franchise will no doubt stand in years to come as the pinnacle of Hollywood's creative bankruptcy, horror movies also became stuck in a rut as producers tried to lure the core demographic of 18–34-year-old males away from their Xboxes and into the multiplex. Properties as respected as *The Texas Chain Saw Massacre* (1974, remade 2003) and *A Nightmare on Elm Street* (1984, remade 2010) were fed into the machine. So too were outliers like *My Bloody Valentine* (1981, remade 2009) and even *Piranha* (1978, remade 2010). Any successful foreign movie – even something as strange and soulful as Swedish vampire movie *Let The Right One In* (2008, remade as *Let Me In* (2010)) – could expect an Americanised remake sooner or later, with varying results. Horror cinema was, it seemed, doomed in a cycle of eternal return.

Zombies weren't immune from the trend. Production on Spanish zombie movie *[REC]* hadn't even wrapped before it was snapped up for a US remake that left the original movie's American distribution on ice. The person who suffered the most was George Romero – he became a sitting target since his films were the genesis of the modern zombie myth and also, historically, tied up in a series of unfortunate rights deals.

In 2005 Taurus Entertainment released *Day of the Dead 2: Contagium* – a nonsensical title for a nonsensical sequel/prequel to Romero's 1985 movie. Its story about a military weapon turning inmates in a psychiatric institute into fast-running, still-talking ghouls had nothing to do with Romero's film apart from the cash-in title. It left Taurus Entertainment CEO J. Dudelson, who also served as the film's co-director, fighting something of a fan backlash.[288]

Not to be deterred, Taurus Entertainment followed *Day of the Dead 2: Contagium* with a straight remake of *Day of the Dead* (2007), produced with Emmett/Furla Films and shot in Bulgaria. Confusingly, it had no real connection to Romero's original, nor to Taurus Entertainment's own *Day of the Dead 2: Contagium*, or even Zack Snyder's remake of *Dawn of the Dead* – although the casting of Ving Rhames was clearly an attempt to force that misconception on unwary audiences (Universal, the studio behind the *Dawn* remake, retained their own sequel rights to that film – promising another layer of confusion for zombie fans should they ever decide to option them).

Directed by Steve Miner (*Friday the 13th Part 2*, 1981), the *Day of the Dead* remake starred Mena Suvari as a soldier whose Colorado hometown becomes ground zero for an outbreak of a flu-like virus that, it turns out, is actually a military bio-weapon. Stripping out everything from the original movie – the overrun Miami opening, the military bunker, the apocalyptic tone and Caribbean escape – the *Day of the Dead* remake instead features horny teenagers, Suvari's unconvincingly perky army corporal, and a town overrun by leaping, vaulting ghouls with the Spiderman-like ability to climb walls.

The only thing the remake retains is Bub, the mournful and iconic zombie with a soul. Pointlessly renamed "Bud" he becomes a mean-spirited gag – a "vegetarian" zombie who moons at Suvari like a lovesick puppy and is verbally and physically abused by Nick Cannon's motormouth soldier: "Why Thriller over here ain't trying to eat us?" To call it a travesty would only be scratching the surface of how insulting it is not only to Romero but to his fans too.

Night of the Living Dead was equally abused by those looking to cash in, spawning a stream of remakes and reimaginings thanks to its long-standing lack of copyright protection. Lame parody *Another Night of the Living Dead* (2011) mixed cheapo new footage with the black & white original. *Night of the Living Dead: Resurrection* (2012) cheekily transported the basic formula to Wales to little effect with a downbeat ending that it simply didn't earn.

While it was hard to take umbrage at such micro-budget imitators, Jeff Broadstreet's *Night of the Living Dead 3D* (2006) was a more insulting update that modernised the original with marijuana farms, zombie text messages ("Coming 4 U Barb") and silly 3D gimmicks like spades, zombie hands and even exhaled weed smoke jumping out of the screen.

Where Romero was coy about the cause of his outbreak in '68, Broadstreet decided to explain everything for fear of offending the hard of thinking. Mid-movie a local mortuary owner, Gerald Tovar Jr. (genre stalwart Sid Haig), unexpectedly pops up and spills the beans on his late father's unlicensed cremation practices. Toxic corpses and a pyrophobic mortician are, it turns out, to blame.

Depressingly, such nonsense had enough brand-name draw to spawn a prequel *Night of the Living Dead 3D: Re-Animation* (2011) that proved less interested in the living dead than Tovar Jr. (now played by Andrew Divoff from the *Wishmaster* series) and his money-grabbing brother (Jeffrey Combs, *Re-Animator*). Out-of-date Sarah Palin jibes and a Goth mortuary assistant (Robin Sydney) who has apparently wandered in from a Jörg Buttgereit movie did little to make up for the notable lack of screen time for the zombies.

Not every Romero remake was so pointless – Breck Eisner's *The Crazies* proved it was possible to reanimate an aging property without trashing it. After all, "reanimation" – as American cartoonist Winsor McCay had once explained – was an act of artistic appropriation that could offer old works of art a new lease of life. Far from simply creating a copy, reanimation could subvert and alter the original work of art in fascinating ways.

That theory got put to the test in *Night of the Living Dead: Reanimated* (2009). Around 130 artists and animators breathed new life into Romero's film by remaking it shot for shot in a variety of different animation methods, accompanied by the original audio track. Curated by conceptual artist Mike Schneider, *Night of the Living Dead: Reanimated* was a kaleidoscope of competing animation styles: stop-motion, Flash, rotoscoping, hand-drawn, Claymation, Lego,

machinima and 2-D cel animation.

It created some striking images, some silly and some powerful: sock puppet newsreaders on TV warning about the zombie outbreak, the cast suddenly turned into Barbie and Ken dolls, an 8-bit adventure game interface giving Barbara a list of options, or the use of machinima (based on "Garry's Mod" for *Half-Life 2*) for the film's downbeat ending. Turning the rednecks who shoot Ben into CG automatons had its own grim logic.

More art exhibit than a movie, *Night of the Living Dead: Reanimated* is arguably more suited to the walk in/walk out nature of a gallery. But it raised interesting questions about the nature of originality and remakes. "[The Internet has] put us up against the world and all of its history," Schneider told *Fangoria*. "When you see yourself as part of such a large system, it's easy to lose identity, and so we latch on to the choices we make to define us—such as what we consume: movies, music, games, food, etc. As a whole, society is struggling against this collective history and attempting to present it in its own image: remakes, reboots, revivals, revisions, adaptations, covers, mash-ups. What is all of this but one culture consuming another? In effect, the zombie serves as a perfect poster child for the era."[289]

Night of the Living Dead: Reanimated wasn't the only film to be self-aware in its attempt to remake a classic. Douglas Schulze's *Mimesis: Night of the Living Dead* (2012) tackled the same theme from a different perspective, highlighting its ambition in its esoteric title. When a group of fans attending a horror convention are invited to a party in an old farmhouse, they're given spiked beer and wake the next morning to find themselves in 1960s clothing and the house surrounded by shuffling ghouls.

They quickly realize they're being forced to play a live action role playing game – a more immersive spin on the traditional zombie walk. Yet unlike most LARPGs, this game is being played to the death in order to make this reimagining of *Night of the Living Dead* as realistic as possible.

The idea for *Mimesis* came from Schulze's trips to horror conventions. At one he witnessed a group of fans terrorising other convention goers by getting a little too boisterous in their role playing. "I got inspired at that point to say 'Wow, how far can a horror fan go, and what's the next level?' Hollywood

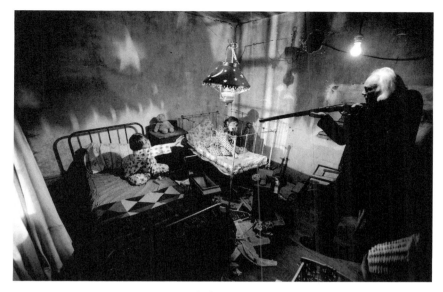

Survival of the Dead (2009).

is doing remake after remake, but where do you go after you keep remaking a movie?"[290]

Mimesis toys with that question, its ghoul pack led by a former funhouse employee (Dan Gerics) who's bored of scaring people for fun – he wants to do it for real. Stirring our nostalgia for the original, and openly copying Romero's Dutch camera angles, Schulze positions his film as a remake about remakes.

Although it does little to interrogate the ideas it sets up, it does leave us with a question. When it comes to remakes, who are the real zombies? Is it the filmmakers who are willingly cannibalising horror cinema in an effort to make a quick buck. Or is it us, horror fans, who mindlessly gobble up whatever reheated leftovers are put in front of us, hungry not for nourishment but doomed to consume for all eternity. The jury's still out on that one.

While others were remaking his earlier films, Romero himself was exploring pastures new. *Survival of the Dead* (2009), to date the sixth and most recent entry in his zombie series, was an unlikely zombie Western. Filmed on location in Ontario, Canada, and set on fictional Plum Island off the coast of Delaware, it follows immediately after the events of *Diary of the Dead* and focuses on the renegade National Guardsmen who briefly held up Jason and his fellow film students' Winnebago.

The grunts are lead by Sarge "Nicotine" Crockett (Alan Van Sprang), a hard-bitten soldier who's

become infamous after Jason uploads footage of the Winnebago stick-up to YouTube. "The fucking movie went out on the 'net, got millions of hits," he complains in his voiceover narration. "I became notorious, could have got an agent, made a fortune if there was anyone left to care. It had become an Us vs Them world. All we were looking for was a place where there was no 'Them'."

Crocket's squad of renegades are pretty professional: there's no-nonsense lesbian tomboy (Athena Karkanis) who's first seen masturbating in a jeep while opining that all the good men are dead, charmer Francisco (Stefano Di Matteo) who promises he could change her world in just five minutes and slightly slow but ever-so-loyal Kenny (Eric Woolfe).

Heading across the country to the coast, the group discover an armoured car stuffed with over $1 million in cash and a tag-along kid (Devon Bostick, who'd go on to star in zom-com *Dead Before Dawn 3D*). He shows them a YouTube video advertising help and shelter for survivors if they travel to a ferry terminal on the Delaware coast. It's clearly a scam but Crocket is taken in by the hard sell – an invitation to Plum Island where the zombie outbreak is contained. This plum sounds peachy, a Promised Land.

At the ferry terminal, the group discover Patrick O'Flynn (Kenneth Welsh), a grey-haired Irishman with a silver tongue and a wicked twinkle in his eye. It turns out he's been expelled from Plum Island by rival Irish patriarch Seamus Muldoon (Richard Fitzpatrick).

The two families – fishers and farmers – have been at each other's throats for decades. The zombie apocalypse has just given them something different to fight over. O'Flynn believes the returned dead should be exterminated for the sake of protecting the living. Muldoon disagrees, arguing that the dead are relatives and friends. "Maybe they're not dead," he suggests. "Maybe they've got a sickness." His solution isn't a bullet in the head but a form of pacification. He chains his zombie wife to the kitchen sink and the mailman to a post box, while theorising that it might be possible to teach the ghouls to eat something other than human flesh.

Survival of the Dead is Romero's sixth zombie film and arguably his most light-hearted since *Dawn*. It's replete with gore gags that continue his gradual transition from practical effects to CG. Early on, an M4 fired at point-blank range at a zombie's skull obliterates its head, and a scalp flops on the ghoul's remaining stump of a neck. Later, sticks of dynamite straight out of a Looney Tunes cartoon and a bunch of underwater ghouls add a layer of levity to the proceedings.

With its vision of two feuding families turning Plum Island into a standoff between two patriarchal ranch owners, *Survival* plays best as a Western-by-stealth. Romero, a long-time fan of John Ford and Howard Hawks, sneaks in farmhouses, assorted gunslingers, a corral and even a horse that's ridden across the open fields by a zombie, one of O'Flynn's twin daughters (both played by Kathleen Munroe, with and without zombie make-up).

One gets the sense that Romero, now in his 70s, is ticking a long-wished-for opportunity off his directorial bucket list. This could be his *El Dorado* (1966), and it's notable that, with the exception of the nameless teen kid, most of the characters here are over 30. It's an old man's movie.

Survival sketches out another typically bleak Romero portrait of human dysfunction – an early scene has Crocket's squad encountering a bunch of redneck hunters who've built a perimeter by sticking African-American zombie heads on spikes. We are doomed, it seems, to always be more dangerous than the living dead. As the range war escalates, O'Flynn and Muldoon's men end up cutting each other to ribbons, selfishly and inevitably ruining any chance of Plum Island becoming a sanctuary for the living. The film ends with the two now-zombified patriarchs approaching each other across an empty landscape and firing long-empty guns at one another in a classic Western gun duel – a pointless and futile cycle of violence that is self-sustained and never-ending.

The classic Western presents violence as the key to self-determination. But in Romero's zombie apocalypse we must – to quote an earlier movie in the series – stop the killing or lose the war. Perhaps that's why America, with its Second Amendment glorification of gun culture, is always destined to be overrun by ghouls. Gun-toting, redneck survivalism isn't a solution to a world in which the bodies of the dead get up and kill. It's a suicide note.

By the time *Survival* was released in 2010, though, few were interested in hearing Romero's warnings against violence and gun fetishism. Whatever the problems with Romero's film – and it vies with *Diary of the Dead* as the weakest of the filmmaker's zombie series – the audience just wasn't there for it.

As zombies became big business, from *Zombieland* (2009) to *The Walking Dead* TV show (2010–), Romero's intimate, low-key apocalypses no longer resonated. In the multiplex, redneck survivalists weren't the enemy – they were the heroes of zombie culture as it gatecrashed the mainstream.

CHAPTER FOURTEEN

ZOMBIES GO TO HOLLYWOOD (REDUX)

"THE ONLY WAY TO DO IT DIFFERENT WAS TO DO IT BIG…"
– screenwriter Damon Lindelof on *World War Z*.[291]

I. THE CROSSROADS OF THE WORLD

It's hard to pinpoint the exact moment when zombies burst out of their ghetto. The zombie renaissance hit around 2005, after the impact of *Resident Evil*, *28 Days Later*, *The Walking Dead* comic and the *Dawn of the Dead* remake had all been assimilated into the pop cultural ether. It quickly spread from the margins inwards.

As the renaissance became a boom, zombies became a transmedia monster, appearing in a swathe of movies, books, comics, videogames and merchandising. Zombie mania surpassed anything that vampires, werewolves or serial killers ever experienced. It was a confluence of the monster's flexibility and the rapidly changing media landscape of the mid-2000s. The Internet, cheap DV cameras and self-publishing all pushed zombies into becoming a pop culture phenomenon.

The growth of social media – and its ability to instantly share content – helped the zombie's dominance. You only needed one picture of something like a zombie-proof house – like the fortress-like "Safe House" designed by KWK Promes in Poland, which featured a drawbridge, moveable walls and impregnable shutters – to ensure saturation bombing of Facebook and Twitter. The *#zombies* hashtag – much like the monsters themselves – just keeps on coming.

What cultural factors spurred the rising, still ongoing, popularity of zombies? According to *TIME* magazine, who dubbed the zombie "the official monster of the recession", it's the economy, stupid.[292] As Lehman Brothers toppled in 2008, and the world entered a global recession unprecedented since the 1930s, the zombie's resurrection mirrored its arrival from Haiti during the Great Depression.

The contemporary zombie boom reached critical mass just as the financial system went into meltdown. The image of the zombie was suddenly everywhere: zombie banks were hungry for bailouts, zombie companies were being propped up by state aid and zombie countries were kept from failing by self-cannibalism as central banks consumed their own nation's debt through quantitative easing.

When Occupy Wall Street protestors dressed up as "corporate zombies" and shambled past the New York stock exchange carrying fistfuls of fake dollar bills in October 2011, it was obvious that a certain section of America felt like it was being zombified by the 1 per cent. Unlike in the 1930s, the zombie was no longer a metaphor for the public's anxiety – a bogeyman to keep one awake at night. It had been reclaimed and turned into an image of indictment, rebellion and resistance. To walk like a zombie was, on one level, to reject the very zombification that seemed to be happening everywhere.

Several commentators drew explicit comparisons between the social collapse of the zombie apocalypse and the economic downturn. In *Slate* magazine Torie Bosch penned the brilliantly titled essay "First, Eat All the Lawyers: Why The Zombie Boom is Really about the Economic Fears of White-Collar Workers".[293] Could the rise of zombies be tied to the collapse of the economy and white-collar fears of social anarchy? It was interesting that few zombie movies touched on the classic idea of the monster as an enslaved worker after 2005. The Haitian myth of the zombie worker vanished, perhaps because it was no longer necessary to be so explicit anymore.[294]

Zombies were once monsters of individual, very personal angst. But in the course of their evolution they transformed into harbingers of total social collapse – a systemic failure induced by a broken banking system where the cash points are about to run dry, or the anarchy of terror attacks like 9/11, or viral pandemics. The zombie apocalypse was no longer about the dead walking. It was about the precariousness of society and humanity itself.

Part of that precariousness led the First World to stop believing in its own impregnability. "The age of globalisation is the age of universal contagion," claim Hardt and Negri in their study of global capitalism, *Empire*. The zombie is, if nothing else, an anthropomorphised representation of that very contagion – the unchecked international flow of people, information, wealth and even viruses through increasingly porous national borders. Infected, disenfranchised and full of raging hatred, the zombie is possibly the first true monster of globalisation.[295]

From this perspective, the zombie's recent transformation from a monster of death into a creature of contagion makes sense. Zombie apocalypses are perfect metaphors for the fragility of our newly globalised world. Dead men walk, but the infected sprint. In a globalised world contagion – whether viral, financial or racial – is more threatening than death. Contagion corrupts the whole interconnected system, bringing the whole world to its knees. The smaller our world becomes, the more precarious it seems.

Inevitably, it would take a blockbuster to capture the epic scale of a truly globalised zombie outbreak. In 2013 it came in the shape of *World War Z*. Yet this wasn't the first Hollywood movie to tackle the resurgent zombie genre. *Planet Terror* (2007), *I Am Legend* (2007) and *Zombieland* (2009) offered different takes on the zombie apocalypse and a growing sense that zombies were becoming mainstream fare.

Ironically, Robert Rodriguez's *Planet Terror* harked back to Times Square exploitation, the zombie's spiritual, cinematic home. Released as part of the *Grindhouse* double bill, alongside Quentin Tarantino's B-movie *Death Proof*, *Planet Terror* was a postmodern homage to the sleazy exploitation outings that once kept 42nd Street's movie theatres in business.

Following in the footsteps of cheap grindhouse homages like *Bubba's Chili Parlor* (2008) and *Chillerama* (2011), it distinguished itself thanks to a $67 million budget (shared with Tarantino's movie). Gruff and sultry Rose McGowan stars as go-go dancer Cherry, who's trapped in a Texas town when an army bio-weapon ("Project Terror") unleashes zombies that munch her leg off. "No use crying over spilt milk," advises her boyfriend Wray (Freddy Rodriguez), as he fits her with an M4 assault rifle that doubles as an artificial limb.

Playing like an homage to Romero, Carpenter and Umberto Lenzi, *Planet Terror* feels schizophrenic – part blockbuster, part B-movie gorefest. Pus-dripping abscesses and jars of human testicles sit oddly alongside the presence of a major star like Bruce Willis, who plays a Bin Laden-killing soldier transformed into a flesh-melting zombie "sicko". As fun as it is, the fact that Rodriguez has spent millions of dollars recreating what Lucio Fulci used to knock out for peanuts feels like a joke without a punch line.

Blander but much more interesting as a mirror of its time was *I Am Legend* (2007) starring Will Smith. Based on Richard Matheson's vampire novel – previously filmed on the cheap as *The Last Man on Earth* with Vincent Price and *The Omega Man* with Charlton Heston – this studio tentpole featured CG zombie vampires that creep out of the shadows when the sun goes down.

Smith is military virologist Robert Neville, the sole survivor of a global pandemic that has turned the rest of mankind into bald, wide-mouthed ghouls. 1,001 days after the outbreak occurs, New York is deserted. The intersection of Broadway and 42nd Street – "The Crossroads of the World" – is no longer a throbbing metropolitan hub. Instead, a jungle has sprung up through the tarmac and a CG lion, presumably escaped from Central Park Zoo, hunts deer through the deserted streets.

It is enough to drive Neville slightly ga-ga. Accompanied only by his German Shepherd, he wanders the city chatting to store mannequins, listening to Bob Marley on his iPod and trying to invent a cure for the outbreak. When the sun goes down he barricades himself inside his fortified town house while the ghouls mass outside.

I Am Legend proved just how much zombie cinema was changing – it was now a bona fide blockbuster monster. Much was lost along the way, not least of all the original novel's ambiguous ending. Yet the sight of grey-haired Smith battling with loneliness and madness in a post-apocalyptic Manhattan was strikingly bold and far darker than one might expect from a movie released in the 2007 holiday season.

I Am Legend did disaster porn brilliantly, its vision of the Big Apple's collapse surprisingly chilling, even if its CG ghouls were wretchedly fake-looking. Offering audiences a glimpse of what the end of the world might look like on an epic scale – the need to close down several blocks of Manhattan on a Monday morning for filming won the filmmakers few friends – *I Am Legend* flirted with a darkness that was at odds with Smith's usually chirpy persona.

The fact that it takes place in Manhattan suggests it's another cathartic replay of 9/11, much like *Cloverfield* the following year. Yet what was fascinating about *I Am Legend* was how prescient it was. Hiding in his fortified Washington Square town house in Greenwich Village, Neville is the last New Yorker. He's tasked with repelling the raging mass that keeps coming night after night. Immune from the virus, he is Manhattan's last line of defence against the zombie infidels.

But he's also the keeper of the flame – the last shopper in New York, as well as its last man. In the daytime, while the ghouls sleep, Neville enjoys a

life of luxury – with the abandoned city as a his playground. Like the shopping mall in *Dawn of the Dead*, New York becomes a paradise of shopping and endless leisure: fast cars, iPods, a makeshift golf driving range on an aircraft carrier's deck. It is, according to academic Kirk Boyle's nuanced interrogation of the film in *Jump Cut*, a "consumerist fantasyland".[296]

In light of the fall of Lehman Brothers in 2008, *I Am Legend* seems strangely ahead of itself. Neville is, quite literally, one of the 1 per cent – his world of material plenty is threatened by the other 99 per cent who mass outside his door at night. The movie predates the Occupy Wall Street movement, yet it anticipates the battle between the haves and have-nots being fought on the streets of Manhattan a few years later.

In 2007, though, *I Am Legend* seemed more like a mirror of the War on Terror. In his review of the film on NPR.com, critic Bob Mondello contextualised *I Am Legend* against the backdrop of 2007's overt War On Terror movies like *Lions for Lambs*, *In the Valley of Elah* and *Rendition*. He suggested that *I Am Legend*'s plot played like an extended metaphor for US foreign policy and the rise of Islamic fundamentalism.

In *I Am Legend*, American scientists boldly create a virus to kill cancer, but it unexpectedly turns on them and makes people into zombies. For Mondello, it's hard not to see this as a reflection of US foreign policy. The decision to arm jihadists like Osama Bin Laden in the 1980s in order to fight Communism in Afghanistan was considered a noble cause. Yet it backfired when those same jihadists turned on their former paymasters in the years leading up to 9/11. Like the film's viral cancer, jihad proved hard to control and contain.

What's especially disturbing for Mondello is the implacable nature of the villains. "Even if [Neville] comes up with a cure, a way to make the nasty infected guys human again, they're just going to keep coming, banging their heads against plate glass, destroying the civilised world and – here's the kicker – either killing everyone they come into contact with or converting them into monsters just like themselves. And the only solution is to shoot them dead – or withdraw behind metal walls, into a fortress-like homeland. And that's not working. That's *I Am Legend* in a nutshell. A blockbuster for our time, no?"[297]

In *I Am Legend* the only response to such terror is, as Boyle points out, to retreat to the flag-waving small-town enclave of Bethel, Vermont – an image of "the neoconservative utopian vision".[298]

I Am Legend retools the subversive potential of the zombie movie and recasts it as a story of how one American hero's sacrifice can save the world from raging, jihadist ghouls. Once can only imagine the studio's notes on the film's original ending – which had Neville successfully negotiating with the ghouls' leader and recognising their essential humanity before abandoning the city to them. It was, unsurprisingly, scrapped. Instead, *I Am Legend* strips out the radicalism of films like *Dawn of the Dead*, *The Crazies* or *Homecoming* and recasts the zombie apocalypse as a neo-con fantasy.

II. BILL MURRAY'S A ZOMBIE (AND THAT'S OK)

If *Planet Terror* was a blockbuster homage and *I Am Legend* was a $150 million remake, the *Resident Evil* series was a law unto itself. From its beginnings in 2001, Paul W.S. Anderson's high-octane, low-budget sci-fi fantasies packaged the zombie into multiplex-friendly B-movies. The series, based on Capcom's videogame franchise and produced by German company Constantin Films, remains the most successful videogame-to-movie adaptation to date. As zombie movies they're rather less impressive – their ghouls relegated to mere cannon fodder for Milla Jovovich's alluring, ass-kicking heroine Alice.

With Sony Screen Gems behind it, the franchise was a huge draw internationally and, in particular, on DVD. It's been something of a constant during the zombie renaissance. The first two films led to *Resident Evil: Extinction* (2007), then leapt into 3D for the sequels *Resident Evil: Afterlife* (2010) and *Resident Evil: Retribution* (2012). Zombie movies for people who don't like zombie movies, the franchise is a canny way for Capcom to prop up interest in its *Resident Evil* videogame series. If you've ever wondered what "brand synergy" means, look no further.

Ruben Fleischer's *Zombieland* was something altogether less expected, a multiplex-friendly, action comedy that firmly cemented the zombie movie's mainstream appeal. Structured around a trip to a So Cal amusement park called Pacific Playland, *Zombieland* is less a road movie than a demolition derby through a zombie-infested America.

It opens with nerdy, OCD-challenged protagonist Columbus (Jesse Eisenberg, Hollywood's go-to-guy for geek chic and Woody Allen-style neurosis) listing the key rules needed to survive the dawn of the dead (The Double-Tap! Seatbelts! Cardio!). With Metallica's "For Whom the Bell Tolls" on the soundtrack and a slow-mo digital camera (the Phantom, shooting at 1,000 frames a second) recording the opening z-apocalypse montage, this is aimed at a generation weaned on Spike Jonze, not Romero – Fleischer, making his feature debut, cut his teeth on commercials and music videos.

After getting us up to speed on the apocalypse, Columbus meets redneck Tallahassee (Woody Harrelson), a man who treats zombie killing as sport and has an insatiable hunger for Twinkies. As these mismatched, unlikely buddies head across America they meet scam-artist sisters Wichita and Little Rock (Emma Stone and Abigail Breslin) – who initially con them, then end up pitching in with them. Heading west, the gang drive to zombie-infested Hollywood before making a pilgrimage to the Pacific Playground amusement park.

Zombieland itself exists purely to amuse, which may explain why it became the most commercially successful zombie comedy of the 2000s. It's a freewheeling, $23.6 million apocalypse full of madcap laughs (Zombie Kill of the Week: a piano dropped out of a window on a zombie's head) that's notably uninterested in Fulci-style splatter or Romero's satire.[299]

"The hardest part of the zombie apocalypse," goes the old Internet meme, "will be pretending I'm not excited," and *Zombieland* plays like a commercial for how enjoyable the undead could be. It exists purely to show us that bashing in zombies' heads is FUN!

Ever since Tom Savini sprayed a soda siphon in a zombie's blue face and trashed the Monroeville Mall in *Dawn of the Dead*, apocalyptic anarchy has been part of the zombie genre's appeal – a Dionysian revel that heralds the start of a new order; or, at the very least, the cleansing of the old corrupt one. Romero knew that such mindless behaviour made one worse than a zombie. But in *Zombieland* such revelry has no consequences. It's the movie equivalent of the sandbox found in the *Dead Rising* videogames – where it's often more fun to run around wearing a LEGO head and a mankini while beating zombies with a gigantic teddy bear than it is to actually complete the game's formal missions.

Destruction is *Zombieland*'s driving force. It culminates when the friends arrive at a roadside Indian trading post called Kemosabe's, a collection of Native American tourist kitsch. Deciding to trash the place, the group start out by knocking over a few knick-knacks then turn totally anarchic and destroy the entire shop – revelling in the freedom to act out that the end of the world offers. The destruction is presented as therapeutic – a release of pent up frustrations, grief over lost family members and personal insecurity – but really it's just an indicator of *Zombieland*'s comic nihilism.

"Part of the joy of the post-apocalyptic landscape, if there is joy to be had there, is that there are no rules," explained co-screenwriter Rhett Reese. "You can do things like walk into a store and break everything, which is something we always wanted to do as kids. We always wanted to go into a department store and trash the place because when does society ever allow you to do that? We were looking for the escapist fantasy in *Zombieland* with a little bit of violence and destruction, but it's safe because there are no consequences and you aren't hurting anybody."[300]

Presenting the apocalypse as a fun park, *Zombieland*'s landscape has no rapists or murderers, there are no real power struggles and none of the major characters suffer serious illnesses, bites or wounds. It operates instead as a wish-fulfilment fantasy. Want to drive a yellow Hummer? Here, take the keys. Want to bash someone's head? Go for it, they're dead. Want to shoot things? Check out this pick-up truck full of guns ("Thank God for rednecks!" yells Tallahassee as he fires his newly acquired Uzi into the air).

Killing is part of the film's taboo-breaking fun, and *Zombieland* revels in its heroes' murderous ability with shotguns, Uzis and, um, banjos.

Watching it, you realise that the allure of the zombie apocalypse on page and screen is that it allows its audience to indulge in a taboo fantasy: the desire to kill other human beings. In fact, *Zombieland* could be a guilt-free *Natural Born Killers* – which also starred Harrelson. Here victims of the heroes' murderous desires don't need to be mourned, because they're all already dead. The zombie apocalypse gives you a free pass.

The gun fetishism seems at odds with Romero's *Dawn of the Dead*, where redneck gun culture is a symptom of the collapse rather than a cure. The modern zombie movie, though, largely doesn't have time for such liberalism.

As one survivor in *Humans Vs Zombies* (2011) puts it, as he tools up in a hardware store and bashes zombies' heads in: "Damn, I will never get tired of this shit...!" Clearly, killing zombies is a redneck's dream come true. His worst nightmare, though, is *Fast Zombies with Guns* (2009). "Goddamn it," laments one good ol' boy, "I'm two days away from moving my furniture down to Carytown, Missouri, and now you tell me zombies have gone taken over the *gun store*? What is wrong with you Yankees?!"

Zombieland makes a virtue out its glibness, not least of all in a lengthy cameo from Bill Murray, who plays himself. Murray, it turns out, has survived the zombie apocalypse in Beverly Hills by disguising himself in corn starch make-up and venturing out of his mansion to wander among the living dead. "I like to get out and do stuff," he explains. "I just played nine holes at the Riviera." He entertains the kids, prancing around re-enacting *Ghostbusters* with a vacuum cleaner on his back.

It's hilariously silly, and played totally deadpan. Yet, it's also a fitting image of how devalued everything is in *Zombieland*. This is a world where nothing really matters and everything's a joke. When Murray is murdered – shot by nervy Columbus, who mistakes him for a real ghoul – he gets to utter the movie's funniest line. Asked if he has any regrets, he whispers, "*Garfield*, maybe..." before shuffling off this mortal coil.

After Murray's death, the film really has nowhere left to go. Its big finale in the Pacific Playland amusement park – where the characters use the rides as tools for evading and killing zombies – barely registers. It's infantile, but deliberately so. Murray's zombification is played for gags because in *Zombieland* there is no pathos. The zombies aren't our loved ones or even "the neighbours", they're merely target practise.

Far from promising that a new social order might emerge from the ruins of the old, *Zombieland* revels in its destruction. Its Gen Y heroes are too self-obsessed, short-sighted and flippant to do anything as altruistic as found a new world. All they want to do is have fun. Judging by the film's success – an impressive $102 million worldwide – it was a zombie fantasy that audiences shared too.[301]

II. SMALL SCREEN, BIG BITE

The biggest sign of the zombie's rehabilitation into the mainstream in the 2000s actually occurred on the small screen. Traditionally, television was the one medium that zombies never properly conquered – Romero's interest in producing a TV show spin-off of his living dead films came to very little back in the 1980s. The violence and gore of zombie movies was considered just too extreme for the small screen. But, two decades later, zombies were swarming all over terrestrial and cable TV in the US and Europe.

Masters of the Horror (2005–2007), Showtime's retro anthology series, was first out the gate. The first season gave us *Homecoming* and also the post-apocalyptic *Dance of the Dead* (2005) directed by Tobe Hooper. With its gyrating, OD'd corpses and careless clubbers, *Dance of the Dead* played like a satire of millennial nihilism. It was followed by *Haeckel's Tale*, a necrophiliac period horror set in the 1880s, based on a story by Clive Barker and directed by John McNaughton.

In the UK, Charlie Brooker's five-episode miniseries *Dead Set* (2008) offered a slyly satirical take on both the zombie apocalypse and reality TV as the Big Brother house becomes a refuge during a zombie outbreak. Gamely transforming host Davina McCall into a ghoul, it made a barbed point about how reality TV is making zombies of us all. In a very different vein, BBC TV show *In the Flesh* (2013–) was set after the zombie outbreak had been suppressed, and flesh-eating ghouls return to life thanks to a cocktail of neurological-enhancing drugs. Following teen former ghoul Kieren (Luke Newberry) as he returns to his bigoted Lancashire village, *In the Flesh*'s intriguingly nuanced drama boldly grappled with issues of integration and intolerance – not just towards zombies, but gay teens too.

Across the Channel on Canal+, French TV series *The Returned* (orig. *Les Revenants*, 2012–) became an international hit. Based on mournful French zombie movie *They Came Back* (2004), it offered a creepily off-kilter take on the zombie as the sentient dead start to return to life in a small alpine village. Far from wanting to eat the living, they try to reintegrate back into the community – but their intentions and the reasons for their return are shrouded in mystery and scored by an eerie Mogwai soundtrack.

The mother of all zombie TV shows is *The Walking Dead* (2010–), which premiered on AMC in the US on Halloween 2010. Based on the Image comic book by Robert Kirkman and artists Tony Moore and Charlie Adlard, *The Walking Dead* broke new ground in putting an undiluted version of zombie culture on the small screen. Inspired, like the comics themselves, by the classic Romero template, *The Walking Dead* impressed by refusing to tone or dumb down its zombie horror for TV. Interestingly, Romero was offered the opportunity to direct a couple of episodes, but turned them down because "My zombies are sort of my own. I didn't want to be a part of it."[302]

The Walking Dead was developed by showrunner Frank Darabont (director of *The Shawshank Redemption*) and his producing partner Gale Ann Hurd (*The Terminator*, *Aliens*) with comic creator Robert Kirkman acting as executive producer. It quickly became the most watched drama series on cable.

Darabont spent five years trying to get his pitch greenlit. "It was the first time I'd tried to set up a television series, and it sure seemed like a long time to be out there without a deal," he told *Deadline*. "It was considered pretty different and cutting-edge through most of that pitching process. My mantra had been that people were waiting for a really good zombie show. It takes a rare bit of courage to take a chance on something that hasn't been proven elsewhere."[303]

Set in Georgia, the first episode begins with wounded police officer Rick Grimes (Andrew Lincoln) waking up in hospital in the aftermath of a zombie outbreak. While he's been unconscious the world has changed irrevocably. Fighting his way back to his wife and son, Rick realises that the world he knew has gone, and he struggles to adapt to being a lawman in a lawless world.

Central to the drama was the question of how to survive and what the costs of survival would be. Not just in practical terms – although the creators' willingness to kill off key characters with unexpected abandon upped the stakes in that regard – but also the moral, emotional and spiritual cost.

A good man in difficult circumstances, Rick is both the last vestige of the old world's authority (he still has his uniform, badge and hat) and a symbol of a new, rapidly evolving pragmatism. Heading first into Atlanta in search of a CDC quarantine safe zone and then onto an isolated farm and, in the third season, a prison facility, Rick and his group of survivors find their old notions of how the world works interrogated at every turn. Less concerned with the zombies than the psychological impact of surviving at all costs, *The Walking Dead* isn't afraid to blur the lines between right and wrong, justice and necessity. Interestingly, when Glen Mazzara replaced Darabont as showrunner during the second season, he handed out copies of *Man's Search for Meaning* by Holocaust survivor and psychiatrist Viktor Frankl. It could double as the show's alternate title.[304]

The only character who thrives in this new world is Rick's twelve-year-old son Carl (Chandler Riggs). He carries less guilt and baggage from the world he barely remembers before the outbreak. In the comic, Kirkman presents Carl as both a scary psychopath in waiting and the most rational survivor – the one who has recognised that in a world where the dead walk, a moral compass is probably the least useful item one can have.

At its core, *The Walking Dead* taps into a very American narrative, the Western. Swapping zombies for injuns, it's a tale of heroic self-reliance in a frontier world without governance or authority. At once gunslinger and leader of a band of settlers, Rick is a throwback to the icons of the lawless West – he even wears a Stetson. What he slowly realises, as *The Walking Dead* unfolds, it that he is all alone. Authority in all its forms has failed: the CDC scientists at the end of the first season, the Bible-thumping religious belief of Herschel (Scott Wilson) in season two or the small-town American values preserved in aspic in Woodbury in season three.

Faced with creating a new order in a lawless land, Rick has to have the fortitude of the American cowboy – at once warrior, pacifier, family man and law-giver. The much-discussed scene, in season two, where Rick and his crew gun down a couple of fellow survivors they meet in an abandoned bar showcases the Western theme. Convinced that these men are a threat to his community – even though they have ostensibly done nothing wrong – Rick delivers frontier style justice. He shoots first, and shoots to kill. It highlights just how far he has come from the pilot episode, in which he humanely went out of his way to mercy kill a trapped, wounded ghoul that was unable to walk.

As academic Paul A. Cantor puts it, "By stripping away all the institutions that constitute modern civilisation, *The Walking Dead* gives us what the Western used to provide in American pop culture – an image of frontier existence, of living on the edge, of seeing what it is like to manage without a settled government, of facing the challenge of protecting oneself and one's family on one's own, of learning the meaning of independence and self-reliance."[305]

Given that idea of self-reliance, it's worth noting that *The Walking Dead* is a predominantly blue-collar show. In this new order, the middle classes have been destroyed – it's the mechanics, the police officers, the farmers, the hunters and poachers who thrive and survive. The people with calluses on their hands, not letters after their names.

"These highbrow zombie stories are not just about watching the newly humbled struggle to make sense of the topsy-turvy world," argues Torie Bosch in her essay "First, Eat All the Lawyers" in *Slate* magazine. "The suburbanite/urbanite viewer who can't hunt, can't slaughter animals, can't grow her own food, is meant to shudder at her ill-preparedness while watching. It's the existential fear of the economy writ large [...] Should the economy recover, I suspect that we will abandon zombies as entertainment. The zombie boom will be a reminder of the frightening uncertainties of this decade."[306]

It's tempting to describe *The Walking Dead*'s celebration of blue-collar skills and survivalism as the triumph of the redneck – a more sombre variation of the same kind of gun-toting prowess that *Zombieland* celebrates. Even though it's set in Georgia, it's a show with few black characters and few strong female roles. In the first season, as the apocalypse rolled out, the survivors were tellingly split into women and men, homemakers and protectors. The black characters were either the butt of racial hatred, or largely marginalised.

Meanwhile, the most popular character proved to be Daryl Dixon (Norman Reedus) – the motorcycle-riding, redneck hunter armed with a nifty crossbow.

As in the Old West, this new frontier is a land for white patriarchy – and specifically a rough-and-ready masculinity that knows one end of a crossbow bolt from another. It isn't just men who represent this masculinity – badass female characters like Andrea and Michonne do much the same. *The Walking Dead* doesn't fetishise guns 'n' ammo with the same carefree silliness of *Zombieland*. But it does suggest that surviving the zombie apocalypse is only likely to be possible in a land that has the Second Amendment. Messrs Smith & Wesson would approve.

III. WORLD WAR Z: IT'S THE ZOMBIES' WORLD NOW

When Max Brooks published *World War Z: An Oral History Of The Zombie War* in 2006, he couldn't have imagined that it was going to lead the zombie's charge into Hollywood. An episodic, meticulously researched tale of a global outbreak and its suppression, *World War Z* was the Sherman tank of zombie fiction. Nothing about it screamed blockbuster movie.

Brooks' first book, *The Zombie Survival Guide: Complete Protection from the Living Dead* (2003) read like a CDC handbook on disaster preparedness written by a comedian – appropriate since Brooks is the son of Mel Brooks. It was a tome of supremely practical, blackly comic advice about what to do in the event of a real zombie outbreak.

World War Z was something very different. In what was then a relatively under-populated niche of horror fiction, Brooks' novel became the zombie genre's *War and Peace* – a towering, epic achievement. It was also quietly subversive rather in the vein of Romero's films. In 300+ pages, Brooks takes a broad swipe at the lack of preparedness of world nations for a global catastrophe and the glacial slowness of bureaucratic institutions in responding to events on the ground. We get to see the duplicity of national governments when dealing with an international health crisis, and the inability of the US military to realise that shock-and-awe tactics don't work on an army of

undead ghouls indifferent to pain and ignorant of the notion of defeat.

World War Z was a novel born out of anxiety. "Since 2001, people have been scared," Brooks explained to *The New York Times*. "There's been some really scary stuff that's been happening – 9/11, Iraq, Afghanistan, Katrina, anthrax letters, D.C. sniper, global warming, global financial meltdown, bird flu, swine flu, SARS. I think people really feel like the system's breaking down."[307] His novel's success suggested that a large proportion of the world agreed with him – and enjoyed the cathartic release his vision of global collapse offered.

In 2007 news came out of Hollywood that a bidding war had been sparked for the novel's movie rights. *World War Z* didn't lend itself to the screen. It lacked a central hero since its epic story was recounted through various first-person viewpoints. It was also told in flashback *after* the war had finished. Yet its brand-name recognition alone made it highly attractive. Bidding for the rights were two production companies: Brad Pitt's Plan B and Leonardo DiCaprio's Appian Way. Plan B ultimately scooped the prize for an estimated $1 million.

Brad Pitt clearly saw the property as a potential star vehicle, and also, he said, as a chance to tackle more serious concerns. "Can we take this genre movie and use it as a Trojan horse for sociopolitical problems?" he pondered. "What would the effect on the world be if everything we knew was upside-down and pulled out from under us?" he asked.[308]

Good intentions don't always make good movies, nor do they make for smooth productions. *World War Z*'s torturous gestation has become the stuff of modern day Hollywood legend and for a while it promised to be the *Ishtar* of zombie cinema. A dirt-dishing piece in *Vanity Fair* magazine confirmed that the movie really was in big trouble. The first cut of the movie was greeted with silent dismay by Paramount execs who realised that its original ending wasn't working.

"It was just atrocious," Pitt later told *USA Today*. "You see some first cuts and you go, 'Oh, it's everything you want it to be and more.' It's working on certain levels that you didn't even understand when you were shooting it. Like, I had this feeling seeing *Moneyball*. And here was the exact opposite."[309] In a bold move, Paramount ordered extensive reshoots to replace the climactic 12-minute battle scene at a rumoured cost of $20 million.

Watching from the sidelines, Hollywood pundits were convinced they knew how this story would end. A studio gambling hundreds of millions of dollars on a zombie movie? A director and star at odds? Extensive reshoots? A delayed release date? All these things are normally signs that a movie is in deep, deep trouble – six feet under, in fact – before it's even released.

But *World War Z* wasn't that movie.

When it was eventually released in the summer of 2013, Brad Pitt's zombie apocalypse proved bigger than even the studio's own tracking estimated. It opened strong and took $202 million domestically, making $540 million in total worldwide.[310] It was the biggest box office hit of Pitt's career. Even before its theatrical run was over a sequel had been greenlit. The movie that many had written off as dead on arrival had come back from the grave.

World War Z owed little to Brooks' novel beyond its title. Instead, its vision of social collapse, raging ghouls and global pandemic was something that zombie cinema had been building to since 9/11. It was the first zombie movie to capture the zombie's new status as the poster child of globalisation. What's more, it was the first $200 million zombie movie. For the zombie – traditionally a low-rent and disreputable monster forever consigned to the

margins – this was a momentous turning point.

In terms of pure spectacle, *World War Z* amazes. Opening with UN troubleshooter Gerry Lane (Pitt) and his family trapped in downtown Philadelphia gridlock as the viral outbreak hits, it's paced even faster than its rabid ghouls. Within minutes Lane is ferrying wife and daughters through anarchy, pursued by raging virulents who pounce like hyenas and attack car windshields with their foreheads. Like the *Dawn of the Dead* remake, its overclocked, frenetic action is breathless and breathtaking – a merciless vision of how precarious everything we hold dear is.

Pitt, whose long-haired, bearded hippie demeanour and laidback charm is at odds with the global meltdown happening around him, is perfectly cast as the Everyman husband and dad trying to protect his family. For their sake, it's lucky that he just happens to be important enough for the UN to send a chopper into Philly to bring them to the safety of a UN fleet of aircraft carriers off the coast of Bermuda. In return for a guarantee of their safety, Lane is tasked with helping the UN track down the origin of the outbreak by finding the elusive "Patient Zero".

Globetrotting from the US to South Korea, Israel and a World Health Organisation research lab in Wales – the latter a result of the rewritten, somewhat hurried ending – Foster delivers stunningly destructive set-pieces that rival Roland Emmerich's back catalogue: zombies vs commuters on the streets of Philadelphia, a helicopter extraction from a tenement rooftop infested with Zeds, an outbreak on a plane flying at 30,000 feet, rampaging zombies ripping through crowds of civilians.

Biggest of all is a remarkable set-piece sequence set in Jerusalem. Arriving in Israel, Lane discovers that the authorities have been able to use their experience of fighting Islamic terrorists to keep the zombies at bay. In an eyebrow-raising moment, we're told that Israel's foreign policy has taken a liberal turn: the government has decided to rescue uninfected Palestinians because, in this zombie holocaust, we're all human.

Sheltering behind an enormous security wall, Jerusalem hopes to withstand the zombies. It's a questionably politicised moment, which led to suggestions that *World War Z* was pro-Israeli – and, more problematically, that it was delivering subtle propaganda for Israel's controversial, real-world security policy and treatment of Palestinians.

The Jerusalem sequence moves towards the film's most startling image: as jubilant refugees celebrate their newfound safety behind the towering wall, a headscarved Arab woman starts singing into a microphone. Yet the sound attracts the zombies beyond the wall, who storm Jerusalem like a Biblical plague, piling up against the enormous wall like ants to enable their brethren to throw themselves over the other side into the city. Chaos ensues as IDF troops open fire on the free-falling ghouls and helicopter gunships hover overhead. A few minutes later, Jerusalem's streets are awash with zombies and the city has been irreparably breached.

It seems pretty clear that *World War Z* envisions its raging zombies as suicidal jihadists willing to sacrifice their lives to penetrate an impregnable Israel. In doing so, it taps into the same War on Terror anxieties we've seen in everything from *28 Weeks Later* to *The Crazies* remake. The failure to contain Islamic fundamentalism doesn't just threaten Israel and the Middle East. It heralds the end of the world.

In fact, what's most striking about the sequence is the way in which it blames Palestinians for the disaster. Far from admiring Israel's post-apocalyptic inclusiveness, *World War Z* hints that it's a loose and liberal policy towards refugees that leads to Jerusalem's collapse. If Israel wants to save itself, the film implicitly suggests, it has to police its borders more rigorously.

Released against the backdrop of global financial recession, *World War Z* could also be read as a commentary on the economic downturn. As the US government retreats to aircraft carriers off the coast of Bermuda, the 1 per cent defend themselves against the 99 per cent all over again.

Elsewhere, the movie's globetrotting viewpoint captured the zombie's evolving role as the monster of globalisation. As Lane travels from nation to nation, *World War Z* reminds us how small and connected our world is – and yet, simultaneously, how vulnerable it is. Originating in rural Asia, *World War Z*'s zombie virus taps into anxieties about the blurring boundary between the First and Third Worlds and about the precariousness of international institutions. The virus spreads so quickly it takes nation states by surprise – especially the world's democracies. North Korea's iron fist serves it well – its infected are brutally rounded up in the first wave of the outbreak – but Europe and America are quickly overwhelmed.

Only a zombie would expect to find political subtlety in a $200 million movie. Sanitised to get a PG-13 rating in the US, and interested only in its own box office potential, *World War Z* was both the biggest zombie movie ever made and the end of zombie cinema as we know it. Safety comes first, which is why the book's political bite was extracted as ruthlessly as the teeth pulled from North Korean citizens' heads to stop the outbreak spreading.

The rewritten, reshot finale is a good example of the need to not upset. The original ending had lots of zombie-bashing spectacle, but its emotional tone was considered too dark. After Lane becomes stranded in Moscow, he joins the Russian zombie-killing militia and realises that the cold will stop the ghouls: it's simply a matter of letting them freeze to "death".

By the time he eventually gets back in telephone contact with his wife in the US, though, he realises that things have changed. She assumed he was dead and – in order to save their children from starvation – has shacked up with another man (Matthew Fox, fleetingly seen in the movie in its released cut). She has traded her body for food and shelter. When Lane realises this, he dies a little inside and turns into a brutal, zombie-stomping warrior who leads a final charge into Moscow's Red Square. In the final moments of the original ending he makes an epic journey in search of his family. He arrives back in the US bloodied, weary and on the ragged edge – the war still ongoing.[311]

The rewrite, by Damon Lindelof and Drew Goddard (former *Lost* scribes), swaps all this misery for a quieter, *Splinter Cell*-style stealth sequence set inside a zombie-infested WHO laboratory in Wales. It is abrupt, disjointed and tonally awkward, but is totally risk free and delivers a misty-eyed, if rather muted, victory that the original ending lacked.

In the finished version, Lane realises that the zombies ignore the sick and dying. After injecting himself with a virus in the WHO lab, he is able to walk among them with a kind of viral camouflage inside his body. It sets the ground for a sequel well, although the ending itself is presented as such a small-scale victory that it seems odds with the globetrotting spectacle of the rest of the movie.

Will there be another one? Of course there will. *World War Z* did unexpectedly well as audiences forgave its missteps and plot holes for the chance to see the zombie apocalypse play out in IMAX 3D. It may not have been a perfect movie, but it was a timely one – perfectly positioned to capitalise on the growing sense that this was the zombie's moment.

Brad Pitt wasn't the only person chasing ghouls in 2013. A completely different zombie movie was *Warm Bodies* (2013), which gave the walking dead an unlikely crack at ousting vampires as romanticised *Twilight*-style sex symbols. Written and directed by Jonathan Levine, and based on Isaac Marion's Young Adult novel, *Warm Bodies* became a sleeper hit that earned $116 million worldwide.

"I just want to connect," complains shuffling corpse R (Nicholas Hoult, once the boy in *About a Boy* but now all grown up). It's the zombie apocalypse and the ghouls have taken over the world. Unlike most zombie movies, though, *Warm Bodies*'s hero is ranked among the dead. For reasons that are never properly explained, he's remained cognisant and wanders around an abandoned airport terminal. "Why can't I connect with people? Oh, because I'm dead," he jokes. "I have a hard time piecing together how this whole apocalypse thing happened. It doesn't really matter, this is who we are now."

While R is still able to think and yearn, most of the other zombies are the standard Romero-style ghouls. Even worse are their cousins the "Bonies" – skeletal monsters who'll "eat anything with a heartbeat". R doesn't like the Bonies, nor does he like eating people's brains – although if he does, he gets a pleasing flash of who they were and a little infusion of their memories (the movie's best, if most nonsensical, conceit).

Mostly, R likes hanging out in an abandoned 747, where he surrounds himself with trinkets from the old world – the zombie answer to Ariel from *The Little Mermaid*. He listens to Bruce Springsteen a lot and radiates adolescent longing from under his hoodie. He's a keeper.

A chance encounter with pretty teen Julie (Teresa Palmer), a blonde Kristen Stewart lookalike, inspires R not only to feel but also speak. They share an unlikely connection – one that's even more unlikely since it's born after R eats her boyfriend. She forgives him, falls in love with him,

and their teen passion enlivens the whole zombie horde – teaching the ghouls how to evolve back towards their previous selves. It seems John, Paul, George (Harrison that is, not Romero) and Ringo were right: all you need is love.

Replaying *Romeo and Juliet* with zombies, *Warm Bodies* keeps R and Julie separated not only by life and death, but also by their feuding families. R belongs to the ghoulish hordes, where the Bonies have no use for the lyrical awakening of the living dead rank and file. They just want to see the living destroyed. Julie, in comparison, lives in a fortified city where her zombie-hating dad (John Malkovich, phoning in a performance long distance) is the weasley, dictatorial leader.

Before anyone can put a pox on anyone else's house though, the two lovers are wooing one another – a nice riff on the classic balcony sequence undercut by a curious moment when R sleeps on Julie's floor (which begs all kinds of questions about what kind of necrophilia this teen romance is toying with). Their love isn't tragic but invigorating – all conflict neatly resolved in a damp-squid third act that throws away everything in order to find a happy ending in this tale of a girl and her dead boy.

Like the *Twilight* series, *Warm Bodies* takes a classic horror monster and turns it into a romantic shadow of its former self. Yet while vampires have always been romanticised creatures, zombies have never had a dandy's air, nor a lover's passion. They're dead, after all. *Warm Bodies* ignores all that and turns R into a too-cute cipher for adolescent awkwardness. "This date is not going well," he complains to himself as he silently, awkwardly tries to woo his living girlfriend. "I want to die all over again."

Warm Bodies showcases just how far the Hollywood-friendly zombie had come from its origins as a dead man walking. A monster that previously represented death, decay and putrescence had become a sex symbol teen pinup. Audiences watching this 12-rated (PG-13 in the US) zombie movie could have been forgiven for thinking that the zombie phenomenon had jumped the shark.

In many ways, though, the syrupy confection of *Warm Bodies* was the final stage of a cycle that had started a few years earlier. The concept of the touchy feely, sympathetic zombie had evolved out of low-budget comedies like the Samantha Mumba-starring *Boy Eats Girl* (2005), the John

Hughes-esque buddy movie charm of *Deadheads* (2011) and the Billy Connolly starring *Fido*. Zombies with problems – like Steve (Kristopher Turner) in *A Little Bit Zombie*, hungry and crafty George (Carlos Larkin) in *George: A Zombie Intervention* (2009), Colin (Alastair Kirton) in *Colin* or the "Zombies Anonymous" support group attendees in *Last Rites of the Dead* (2006) – tried to convince us that all a zombie really needs is a good hug. *Warm Bodies* was just the next step up: all a zombie really needs is a good shag.

If *Warm Bodies* was cloyingly sweet, *R.I.P.D.* (2013) was a strictly nonsensical take on zombie lore. Playing like *Men in Black* meets *Hellboy* with a side order of *Dead Heat*, this $130 million movie had about as much life in it as an on-ice heart en route to an organ recipient. In fact, it bears all the hallmarks of being dreamt up in a Monday morning marketing meeting by studio execs who'd downed one too many double espressos.

Ryan Reynolds does his usual likeable shtick as a recently deceased cop who was killed by his dirty partner. Trapped in purgatory, he's offered a chance to return to earth by joining the Rest In Peace Division, a celestial law-enforcement agency.

Partnered with an equally dead frontier lawman (Jeff Bridges, still in *True Grit* mode), Reynolds is tasked with taking down "Deados" – CG zombies who have disguised themselves as human and who roam the Earth. In their true form the ghouls have blubber bellies, overslack jaws and a curious aversion to curry ("Maybe it's the cumin").

Disastrously short on ideas and largely incoherent, *R.I.P.D.* is a shockingly shoddy blockbuster, a cookie-cutter piece of studio product that has been test-screened to within an inch of its life. For anyone weaned on Romero and Fulci, or even Zack Snyder, it's also a travesty of a zombie movie that barely deserves the name. It's indicative of the bastardisation of zombie cinema that going mainstream threatens to inflict on the genre.

In their own ways, *World War Z*, *R.I.P.D.* and *Warm Bodies* all prove that zombies have as much to lose as gain by turning respectable. But with

zombies so popular, and profitable, it seems unlikely that Hollywood is going to stop until the boom is well and truly over. Zombies were worth an estimated $5.74 billion to the global economy in 2011 – and that figure has surely risen fast since then.[312] Even in an age where bank bailouts have made a billion dollars seem small, that's still a lot of living dead moolah.

How ironic that the zombie, once a metaphorical critique of consumerist excess, is now devouring pop culture and emptying the wallets of legions of fans in the process. Whether you like or loathe the new crop of zombie products, such commodification is undeniably a betrayal of everything the zombie has historically represented. Zombies were traditionally horror cinema's disreputable little secret, monsters that were hidden away in the cultural basement like the ghoul in Fulci's *The House by the Cemetery*.

Today, though, they're out in the open and being commoditised to hell and back. Zombie LEGO, zombie dolls, zombie cupcakes, zombie boardgames, zombie survival kits and even zombie-killing weapons are all parting consumers with their cash. *World War Z* is, as critic Ann Billson noted, "the great zombie sell-out".[313] Zombies haven't just invaded the Monroeville mall; they've set up shop there. It's rather like the moment in *Blade: Trinity* where Dominic Purcell's Dracula-a-like villain wanders into a goth shop and becomes incensed when he sees vampire dildos and Count Chocula cereal diminishing his legacy of evil.

Zombies have taken over the world. They've marched on Hollywood. They've infected movies, novels, comics, music, videogames and the Internet. But their ascendance has come at a price. In becoming so ubiquitous, these monsters have lost something fundamental. They've shed their radicalism, their subversive edge and their transgressive appeal. What was once marginal has been subsumed back into the mainstream. The zombie will never be the same again.

Hollywood may be crazy for zombies. But Zed? Zed's dead, baby.

CHAPTER FIFTEEN

TALKING 'BOUT ZOMBIES

AN INTERVIEW WITH GEORGE ROMERO

I've wanted to interview George Romero for most of my career as a journalist. Over the years, two proposed interview slots for different magazines I was freelancing for at the time got bumped at the last minute. It seemed like it was destined not to be. So, I was immensely grateful when the chance finally came to speak to the man credited as the "Don of the Dead" even if it was only on the telephone and not in person.

The truth is: George Romero hates doing press. Being wheeled out by distributors for junkets, round tables and meet 'n' greets always makes him miserable. "I don't like being trotted out and put on a stage," he admits, "but unfortunately most of my films don't have movie stars in them so I'm the guy who gets sent around to do these things."

This time, though, he's in his apartment in Toronto, the city where he took up residence after leaving Pittsburgh, Pennsylvania, and he's ready for a good chinwag. "Hey, this is easy," he tells me, "I'm sitting here in my living room and it's comfortable, you know?" His instructions via a pre-interview email were hospitable. "Get a jug of Scotch, or the elixir of your preference, and we'll spend a drunken hour or two on the phone."

And so it happens that at 10pm on a Monday evening, I sat down with a couple of beers and dialled Romero's number.[314] For a man who's spent his career hanging out in cemeteries and playing with dead things, Romero is full of life – a warm, congenial raconteur whose stories are peppered by his rumbling, infectious laugh and the odd dash of dated-yet-still-cool hipster speak, man.

So what do you ask the Don of the Dead? Well, it would seem churlish not to ask him about zombies, although his filmography has been about more than just those fugitives from the undertaker. His career as modern American cinema's most respected horror auteur has taken in vampires, mental monkeys and even Arthurian knights on motorbikes. Yet what's interesting about Romero is that he remains a true independent – one of the godfathers of indie cinema in fact.

Forget Sundance; Pittsburgh became the honorary home of American indie cinema when Romero shot *Night of the Living Dead* there in 1968. It was only supposed to be a cheap exploitation flick, yet it spoke to something deep within the American psyche and tapped into the spirit of the times: Vietnam, the civil rights struggle and the deeply ingrained fear of what Romero likes to call "the neighbours". Forty-six years later, the zombies Romero saved from the pop cultural graveyard are still among us. They've become, thanks to him, creatures that just won't die. Romero proves modest as hell when you try to praise him for that, preferring to laugh uproariously until his guffaws compete with his hacking cough ("I'm a smoker, man"). He takes a sip of his Scotch and the interview begins…

George Romero, the zombie master.

Looking around at all the zombie movies today, you must feel like James Whale with *Frankenstein*. You've created a monster, haven't you?

I don't know, man. I never realised there was a trend happening. Everyone always says "Well, you fathered the modern zombie". But I didn't call them zombies in the first film because I didn't think that's what they were. To me, back then, zombies were still those guys down in the Caribbean who were doing the wet-work for [Bela] Lugosi. Now people talk about the zombie age and how there are zombies all over the place. I think it's videogames that have really kept the creature alive, much more than films [...] I kind of think of it as my private Idaho, in a way. I have my own attitudes about what these creatures are. They could be any worldwide disaster – an earthquake, a hurricane or whatever. It's just something that completely upsets the status quo. My stories are really about the humans who just carry on with their own foibles and their own interests and their own concerns, despite being faced with this extraordinary phenomenon. They're still just worried about themselves and their own petty worries. If there's any sort of a message that runs through all of my films, it's that. People aren't able to stand up and face the reality, they'd rather keep on keeping on.

With so much money being made off the back of zombies, though, don't you feel slightly annoyed it's not going into your pocket? Right from the beginning, with the copyright problems over *Night* and then rip-off unofficial sequels like Lucio Fulci's *Zombi 2* [*Zombie Flesh Eaters*] with *Dawn of the Dead*, you always seem to be losing out…

I guess that's true but – and maybe this is going to sound strange – but I want to say, "Frankly Scarlett, I don't give a damn". My thing is my thing. I've always done my own thing with it. I'm not trying to do gore for gore's sake. I'm trying to tell stories, maybe cautionary tales, that have a little bit of social satire. Maybe everyone else is out there doing what they want to do. It has no effect on me. Of course it's irritating. When they called me up to do a script for *Resident Evil* I said yes precisely because of what you're talking about. I thought I should get a piece of this action. They wound up not liking the script. It was Constantin, a German company. Capcom [who published the game] liked my script and I thought maybe we're all set here. I'll make a movie that I won't have to take the blame for because it's not mine and I can just have fun with dead things for a change without having to worry about the message or anything else. It wound up not happening because they just didn't like the script.

Your last movie, *Survival of the Dead* was described by some as a "zombie Western". Is that how you saw it?

It's not really a Western. There are some Western outtrappings to it and I had some fun with that because I'm an old John Ford fan and so I could steal a few shots from him. But it's not period at all. It's set on a little island off the coast of Delaware and there's a fishing family and a farming family who've been feuding forever. On the island they use horseback instead of autos, and so there are some elements that make it look a bit like a Western.

Still, horses in a Romero movie! That's a first for you, no?

Yep, it was fun. I just wish I'd had better trained horses. But it worked out fine.

Never work with children, animals or zombies…

Yeah, I just can't seem to escape. I've done everything from cockroaches to monkeys and now horses. I keep digging my own grave by writing these things into my scripts. It's my own damn fault.

You directed the Japanese commercial for Biohazard 2 [the Japanese title for the first Resident Evil game sequel], didn't you?

Yes, that's how I first got into the game. I'm not a gamer myself. I was introduced to the game when they came to me and asked me to shoot the commercial. They basically acknowledged that they were sort of ripping me off [laughs]. So I agreed to do it. I think it only ran in Japan. But it was a fun exercise. So I asked them "What's going on with the movie? Is there an opportunity to get in on that?" and they said "Sure, we'd love to have you." So I took the bait on that, but they wound up not liking my script and that was the end of that. That was the only period when I was irritated. I was faced with the reality that somebody is making *lots* of money on this. But again that's never been my goal.

Did you ever see Lucio Fulci's Zombi 2?

I guess I never saw it. No, I don't run after these things [laughs].

So what is your goal these days?

Well, I'm at the age now where I'm just happy to be able to keep working. We've found some business partners, a company called Artfire [who funded *Diary of the Dead* and *Survival of the Dead*]. They've been wonderful and they're willing to let me keep creative control. I'm just having fun, man. It's almost like it's an annuity. I don't want to use the word "retirement", but it's easy. I get to do exactly what I want to do and nobody messes with it. It's like the old days. But I'm way beyond trying to play for a hit movie. I don't give a damn, man. I have a very comfortable new life up here in Canada and I think maybe I'll live a lot longer if I don't sweat it.

Night of the Living Dead is the Citizen Kane of horror movies…

[laughs]

No seriously! Can you understand what terrified audiences about it back in '68?

I've tried to figure that out. It was new, it was unrelenting in a way. It was something people hadn't seen. Nor did they expect. Horror films back then were a pretty simple formula. You upset the status quo, then you restored it again. But we didn't restore it. It was a pretty unrelenting movie and shattered some taboos and all of that. But I don't think that's what scared people. I think maybe the scary parts of it, what was scaring people, was the traditional things that go bump in the night – dead things walking around out there. I think there are elements of the films – that claustrophobic feeling that you have that you can't escape these films… actually they're easy enough to escape but there's more of them and they just keep coming and they're unrelenting… And it's the neighbours, *dead* neighbours. The neighbours are scary enough when they're alive! I don't know… I've had people come to me and say, "*Dawn of the Dead* scared the crap out of me!" But to me it's not a scary film at all. It's almost a balls-out comedy. It's a comic book. I don't see it that way, but I've never gone for scares beyond the obvious – here's a jump and I'll make you jump. But I've never tried to frighten you on any primal level. They're much more comic book.

The most famous review of Night of the living Dead came from Roger Ebert, who told the story of how he saw the movie surrounded by terrified six-year-olds who'd been dropped off at the cinema by their parents…

I feel terrible for those kids! [Laughs] We didn't make the movie for those kids. Of course, in those days they used to have these double bills. I don't know, it was probably on with *The Beast from 20,000 Fathoms* or something. It's much more hard-hitting. But I don't know if this film would have scared me as a kid. I think I might have been bored, you know: "This is going nowhere. No giant tarantula, nothing is happening!"

The horror of Night of the Living Dead has a lingering quality. There's a religious element to it: if people are dying and coming back to life, where is God? Is there no heaven? Are we all just walking hunks of meat. It's very stark, isn't it?

I think that's very true. But I don't know, I've seen both perspectives written: "Well, it gives hope for an afterlife" or, "No, it says there's no God and we're just walking garbage." I've seen both perspectives written. But I have to say, I never thought that deeply about it. Obviously we'll sit around and bullshit about it – even when making the new film I'll do that with my producer or my editors. But that's not a motivation in making these films, or telling the stories.

To me the story is just the dead are coming back to life. It's *quite* unbelievable… Do they shit? I don't know! There are all these unanswered questions! I mean, they do a lot of eating, what happens to the… [laughs]. So, I've just taken complete license with this idea of it's a complete sea change; something has completely changed the rules whether you want to think it's God or the Devil or a scientific phenomenon, something has changed the rules. My stories are just about how people respond to it, or fail to respond to it.

At least with the first three films they were ten years apart apiece and I was able to put a completely different surface on them and talk about a completely different time in North America. The last three have been in rapid succession, so I haven't really had that much else to talk about except for the new media in *Diary*. I suppose a lot of people related *Land* to the Bush administration… There were certain conscious tongue-in-cheek references to that in there.

You've always been a very independent filmmaker. Where does your scepticism about Hollywood and the studios come from? Was it coming of age in the 1960s?
I think that's certainly where it all started. I didn't join the [filmmakers'] guilds for years. I kept saying, "Who needs it?" I was sort of the Robert Rodriguez of the 1960s and 1970s. I was approached often right after *Night of the Living Dead* – "Come make movies with us, come play in our playpen" – and the deals were always [bad]. You could never have your own way and I got really frustrated. I've made two studio films – *Creepshow* we made independently and it was picked up by Warner Bros., and I made two films for Orion. *Land of the Dead* was Universal, although we were going through Mark Canton, an independent. He was running interference for us there. Universal pretty much left us alone. But it was because it was a very specific thing that they wanted and they'd made money with the remake of *Dawn of the Dead*. Normally, I just don't like the way [studio films] work. It's never your own project. You have to even use gaffers and keys who are studio-approved. It's wonderful to work with friends – people you've worked with before – because start-up costs are very high and having to explain yourself takes up valuable time. When you're working with buddies it's cake. Everybody walks in and goes, "Yeah, I get it".

On *The Dark Half* I was forced to use a studio-approved DP [Tony Pierce-Roberts] and he and I were like oil and water, you know? In the end we wound up, I think, doing pretty good work. But it took a long time for him to leave Merchant Ivory in the closet [Pierce-Roberts had shot Merchant Ivory's costume drama *Howard's End*] and understand that we were making a different kind of film!

I can imagine the "discussions" you must have had on that movie…

Oh, it was unbelievable. He was expected to win an Oscar for *Mr and Mrs Bridge* and so as far as the studio was concerned, if Tony wrote a memo saying "George is being unreasonable," the studio would instantly agree that I was being unreasonable. It's so political and it took weeks for us to work through this stuff and that's just wasted time. We finally did and we became friends and in the end I think we did good work together. But who needs all that stuff?

I guess the film that encapsulates this independent spirit is *Knightriders*, which I'm guessing you'd say is one of your most personal films. It's a real hippie movie, isn't it?
Oh completely! We were so lucky to find Ed [Harris], who was willing to go along with it. It's a very personal film. It's the only film that I've ever made that is in part about *me* and about my journey – although I haven't killed myself yet [laughs]. But yeah, it was really about me… and not only me, there were a bunch of us who were working together in Pittsburgh against the system at that time. You're quite right to notice that, because that's exactly where it came from.

It's all about selling out and the price of idealism. In the 1960s, were you into the love beads and the LSD and everything else? Or was it more about a state of mind than all the stereotypical trappings?
It was much more about a state of mind. Of course, we all did a little dope and did some of this and some of that. But I was never an activist; I was never out there looking to set up a commune or anything like that. I wanted to make movies and we were doing it at the time and I guess just those attitudes were reflected in some of our films. There's a little film that no one has ever seen called *There's Always Vanilla*, which is probably also pretty reflective of who were at that time. There was a bunch of us. I suppose in a way we were our own little commune. We went through some real hard times, sleeping on the couch in the office and not being able to rent an apartment. And then after a couple of years we started to make some money doing commercials and industrial films. We were able to buy some equipment and you know actually pay the light bills, and that's when we decided to make *Night of the Living Dead*.

You started filmmaking when you were a kid, throwing burning dummies off rooftops in the Bronx for an 8mm film called *The Man From The Meteor*, right?
Oh my God, how do you know all this stuff? Jesus! Yeah, I did this little… I mean, I always wanted to make

movies. I never thought I could do it as a career. My dad was a commercial artist who actually did posters and banners for films. That was the closest that I ever came to the industry. I thought you had to be born royalty to make films. My uncle was one of the first guys to buy a home movie camera and so, of course, I got hold of it, and I don't think he hardly ever used it, I always had it. And I was always screwing around trying to make a little movie. I made this thing called *The Man From The Meteor* and I got arrested for throwing this burning dummy off a roof. It wasn't a full-sized dummy. But I guess you're not supposed to do that in New York!

And is the movie lost or does it exist somewhere in a shoebox?
Oh yeah, yeah, yeah it's lost... There's no vestiges of it, no footage anywhere.

What did you enjoy about filmmaking at such a young age? Was it the storytelling aspect or was it having your own little "crew" of childhood friends?
Yes, exactly. It was just buddies who were sort of interested in it, all the while laughing up their sleeves, you know: "What the fuck are we doing?!" But I was able to convince them to go along somehow and that's sort of been the story of my life, you know, convincing people to play along for a while and see what happens. When you have a couple of successes that gets a lot easier! But yeah, I loved movies. It's what I did. I was just this chubby little Catholic kid. Never had a date, never had anything like that. My parents rented me a tuxedo for the senior prom in high school and I just went down to Manhattan and saw movies... I never went to the prom! I guess I looked a bit overdressed [in the cinema]! I was pretty much a loner as a kid and a bit shy, maybe that's part of it. It's hard to even express it. But I just loved movies. It was pretty similar to the Scorsese experience, I think – having had some conversations with him years later.

Did you and Martin Scorsese know each other as children? Were you from the same neighbourhood?
Not exactly. He was in Brooklyn, I was in the Bronx – these are enemy territories. For some reason we both loved *The Tales of Hoffman*. My aunt and uncle took me kicking and screaming to see that movie when I was, I don't know, maybe twelve. It was probably around 1952. I was determined not to like it. I wanted to go and see Lex Barker, the new Tarzan! But *Tales of Hoffman* just knocked me out. It turned me on to classical music. It's a

fantasy, of course, and I just thought it was beautiful. And the tricks that [Michael Powell] was using – in-camera techniques, shooting in reverse, double exposures, things like that – blew my mind. I was like a kid watching *Jurassic Park*. It seemed accessible to me and it made me want to do it.

Scorsese loved it too, right?
Yeah he did. Back in those days if you wanted to watch a film at home you had to go rent a projector and rent a 16mm print. So whenever I'd saved up enough money I'd go down to this placed called Janice Films and rent *The Tales of Hoffman*. And one day it was out! Now this was a film that no-one ever took out. So I was like, "OK, who the hell took it out?" And they said, "Oh, some kid in Brooklyn." Years later, I learned that it was Scorsese. Whenever one of us wanted to take it out and it wasn't there, it was the other guy who had it! But anyway, Powell's the cat who made me really want to try to make movies. Oddly, it wasn't *Tarantula* or the *50ft Woman*, it was *Hoffman*.

Talking of Powell, I was reading about your desire to do a remake of *Peeping Tom*...
Oh, I would love to... But who knows all this stuff?! Who have I said this too? How does it even get out?

It's the Internet age, George, there are no secrets any more!
What did I eat tonight, do you know?

Not yet. But I'll Google it in the morning. But tell me about Powell...
My editor Michael Doherty and I were in London promoting *Land of the Dead* and the National Film Theatre were doing a retrospective on Powell. Michael, the editor, and I were on our way to Edinburgh where Thelma [Shoonmaker, Powell's widow] was visiting. So we went to a screening of *Peeping Tom* and we both afterwards over coffee said, "Wow, you know you could make this movie today and you might even be able to make it stronger." I went through all my things about I can't step on the toes of my God, my idol, but I thought, well I'll talk to Thelma about it. I have *not* gotten up courage yet. I sat with her and had dinner with her and I couldn't bring myself to mention it to her. It's a bit bold of me to think of doing that. I've sort of decided to maybe write a spec script and send it to her and see if I can get her nod on it.

Anyway, that's in the wind. There's nothing real at all to do with that. It's something that I'd really like to take a try at it, principally because I feel that I owe something to Michael. I'm not standing here thinking I know how to do it better. Nor would I want to do it shot-for-shot, you know like [Gus Van Sant's] *Psycho*. I'd want to sort of make it my own, but as much as possible acknowledge Michael's influence on my work and what I've done. It's odd, I've never had a film where I could actually steal from Michael. People have said that some of my stuff is Hitchcock-like. I don't quite see that. I think maybe Welles. I think I've probably stolen more shots from Welles than anybody else. The only time I ever felt I was sort of approaching Powell or *Hoffman* was, oddly, in *Creepshow*, because of all the colour splash and the episodic nature of it and all of that. All through the making of *Creepshow*, I was fondly remembering *Hoffman*.

Just to backtrack a little bit, when we were talking about your childhood, what did your parents think of your filmmaking ambitions? Did they see *Night of the Living Dead*?
They did. I brought a 16mm print home to show my folks. They sort of dutifully watched it and basically said at the end of it, "Well maybe you should think about getting a job". But they were loving. I had a wonderful home life, I mean I truly did. I had two parents who couldn't have been more loving and nurturing and they just sort of put up with whatever I wanted to do and I think that was part of my eventually feeling emboldened enough to go and do something which wasn't normal! Particularly in Pittsburgh at that time.

They were good Catholics too, weren't they? And Catholicism always breeds a certain type of horror movie – the blood, the flesh, hell…
I'm sure that influence is there because it's very hard to erase all of that. No matter how hard you think you've risen completely out of it, it's never completely gone. There's always some little nagging thing there.

And yet ironically, one of your greatest horror movies is *Martin*. It's almost a secular vampire movie – about doing away with the mythology…
It's my favourite film of mine, it remains my favourite. I just thought wow… again it has that ingrained thing, he's been told all his life by the family that, "You carry the gene, you're Nosferatu!" It's ingrained in there. The black & white sequences are probably representative of films that he's seen or whatever, but he's too shy to open the door to any real relationship even though he's very honest about it. He calls into a radio show and basically

confesses. He never lies.

You once said no one would ever let you do a rom-com if you went in and pitched for one… Would you like to do one? With Sandra Bullock maybe?
I don't think so, no. I was just saying that I never get those phone calls and I don't. It's not the way my mind works. I'd love to do a real great melodrama without any of the horror. I have a couple of ideas but again I don't know that I'm ever going to be able to… As I said earlier, I'm sort of beyond the age of wanting to go out and pitch and go through all the ordeals and run the gauntlet. I just don't care enough about it. I'm beyond wanting to go through all the resistance of [puts on a prissy movie exec voice] "Well, what qualifies you to do this?" I'm really finished with all that.

But you haven't always been outside the system. Tell me about working in Hollywood in the 1990s. You had lots of projects that didn't get made, right?
I loved a couple of those projects. But it was the most disappointing period of my life. I made more money over those seven or eight years than I've ever made in my life, you know. It was, "Write a script. Write it again, write it again, write it again…" and they kept sending cheques. Then eventually, they don't make the movie.

We had a housekeeping deal at New Line. We pitched them an idea called *Cartoon* – it was basically a completely live-action cartoon. They said no to it, then along came *The Mask*. Then we pitched this thing called *Before I Wake* which was an old-fashioned ghost story that I loved and still love and they said "No". Then they did *In the Mouth of Madness* instead. So we wound up sitting there for two years with very expensive offices and never making a movie.

The moment we got out of there, MGM had seen the script for *Before I Wake* and they called us in and we started to develop that. At the same time, Universal called us in to try and develop *The Mummy*. Of course, my *Mummy* was not anything like the one they eventually made. It was much more deferential to the original, it was much more romantic with a love story and all of that. It was Boris Karloff. They green-lit it! It was unqualified: we're going to make this movie. It was greenlit. But MGM would not let us out of the contract on *Before I Wake*. We're talking twelve days before the contract ran out. MGM said, "No, we're going to make *Before I Wake*, we're not letting you go, we're going to make this movie." So, the two studios wound up in a pissing contest. MGM didn't make *Before I Wake* and by then

The Mummy was gone. It was a huge disappointment.

What happened then was Chris Columbus picked up *Before I Wake*, after MGM said no. He said, "We're going to make this and if I say we're making a movie, the movie gets made." Right in the middle of that, Chris went out and made *Jingle All The Way*. You know, $30 million went to The Schwarz [Arnold Schwarzenegger] and it hit the skids. All of a sudden Chris's movies were not automatic anymore and so we needed *stars*... and it just got so frustrating. I still love *Before I Wake* and we're still trying to untangle it but the problem is all the expenses of three studios are on it. There was another one called *Moon Shadows* that was in that group that I'd really love to try to do. But you never know what's around the corner.

Well I guess the proof of that is how *Land* and then *Diary* brought you back in a way that you weren't expecting. This whole new zombie wave that came out of nowhere...
I wasn't expecting it, and as I said, I've never understood it. "Zombies are hot? Really?!" I guess I've benefited from that in that we got to make these films. But let me tell you, I would have said no to both of these last two films [*Dairy* and *Survival*] if they had come with baggage. I just don't want to do it.

We met these people [Artfire] who are willing to finance the movies and give us creative control and they're wonderful partners. I'm very grateful for that. I have a new little career going here making these smaller films that are films that I really care about and really want to make. I'm doing sort of what I want to do and people are letting me do it and man, I couldn't ask for anything more. I don't have to go to pitch meetings, I don't have to go out there and compete, I don't have to fly out to LA and appear in front of the board. It's terrific.

Horror seems very different today than it was during your career. Do you get the whole torture porn thing?

Were you glad you weren't part of that?
I am glad, I do say that. We just did a day of reshoots in a studio here where they're prepping *Saw VII*, or whatever the hell it is, in 3D! I just said to myself, "Yikes, I'm glad I'm not stuck in that." I don't get it. I frankly don't get that stuff. I think it's just sort of cruelty. I guess what bothers me is that no one is using it as parable; or if they are, I don't get it. Maybe I'm just an old-fashioned guy. I don't know. I don't want to sit there for two hours and watch people being tormented.

What kind of horror do you watch these days? Guillermo Del Toro?
Guillermo [Del Toro] I love, I love *Pan's Labyrinth*. I don't put those in the same category. I mean I think he's a true poet. I've been a fan of his since *Cronos*. He's an amazing guy, he doesn't give in, he doesn't relent. I think he's a wonderful filmmaker. I don't put his stuff in the same boat as my stuff. I think it's a couple of notches up.

Finally, before you go. One last question: should zombies run or not?
No! Their ankles would snap! Except in the remake of *Dawn* the ones that run aren't really dead. In *28 Days* they're not really dead. Shit, I don't know. I actually had this conversation with Guillermo where I said, "I blame you for this!" Because he did these fast vampires in *Blade II* they were just *wibb-wibb-wibb* scurrying across the walls. There's just something about that speed that some people find frightening. I guess it's like a spider speed or something. I don't find it frightening. Again, I guess I'm a child of the old movies where the Mummy was terrifying to me because it moved slow, you could run away... but it just kept coming, you couldn't stop it. It was this inexorable force that would get you one way or another. I prefer that, it was more agonising. If these things suddenly come running around the corner and you're dead in two seconds, to me there's nothing to that.

SOMETHING TO DO WITH DEATH

I can vividly remember when I first fell in love with the zombie. It was one late evening in 1988. I turned on the television set and was greeted with the sight of a ghoul's head being chopped open by a whirling helicopter rotor blade. Fake-looking blood spilled out of its brainpan and gushed over its face as it staggered a few steps forward and collapsed. A man dressed in a SWAT uniform looked on with an expression of grim bemusement that matched my own.

The film was the original *Dawn of the Dead* and the programme was Channel 4's *The Incredibly Strange Film Show*, hosted by Jonathan Ross. I had no idea what the movie was, but I quickly became engrossed by the story of a bearded Pittsburgh filmmaker called George Romero and his love of zombies. There were clips from *Martin and Knightriders*, some black & white footage of zombies milling around outside the farmhouse of *Night of the Living Dead*, lots of scenes from the mall in *Dawn of the Dead* and a clumsy sequence involving a mad make-up man (Tom Savini, I later learnt) who used latex appliances to turn Jonathan Ross into a ghoul.

Watching the footage from *Dawn of the Dead* came with a strange sense of déjà vu. That was mainly because – as I later realised – I'd once played a computer game called *Zombi* (Ubisoft, 1986) that took its entire storyline from Romero's film. It was an adventure role-playing game in which you had to guide a band of survivors trapped in zombie-infested mall. Compared to today's videogames this Commodore Amiga title was simple stuff, but it was terrifying in the way the eerie calm would be punctured by the arrival of a zombie – each attack prompted some frantic keyboard hammering, then a long trudge down to the freezer compartment in the basement where the body could be dumped to stop it from reanimating.

I never could work out what I was supposed to do to stop the rising tide of the living dead (the copy of the game I had was in French, for starters). After I saw Romero's heroes blockading the mall doors I realised where I'd been going wrong. So that was what the trucks were for!

What had me hooked as I watched *The Incredibly Strange Film Show*, though, were Romero's zombies. Growing up in the era of video nasties, my school playground had been full of kids boasting about how they'd seen everything from *The Exorcist* to *The Evil Dead*. Stories of crucifixes inserted in unlikely orifices and rape by tree had been retold over and over again (it was an all-boys school); so too had tales of demons under the floorboards in woodland cabins or Michael Myers using a Jacuzzi to burn a woman's face off. But no one had ever talked about zombies – or if they had, they hadn't captured the sheer terror of these ghouls.

So Romero's monsters were a revelation to me. Shuffling, lumbering corpses: they were at once ridiculous and yet strangely terrifying. And what scared me more than the ghouls themselves was the foreboding sense of apocalyptic finality that accompanied them. Seeing Fran, Peter, Roger and Stephen hiding out in the shopping mall as the world collapsed sent shivers down my spine. What would I do if the world ended? Where would I go? How long would I survive?

That night I had terrifying dreams of being chased by hundreds of ghouls breaking through barricades, grasping through open doorways and windows. Nowhere was safe. I woke up the next morning still terrified, but convinced that I had to watch every single zombie movie there was.

The love of the apocalypse is something shared by every fan of zombie movies. That's because – regardless of whether or not they replay Romero's classic scenario of the living dead taking over the world – zombie movies are always about The End. Full of literal images of death, the genre taunts us with a vision of the permanent full stop that awaits us all as bodies decay and the mind switches off. It's the genre's most enduring quality.

Hopefully this book has succeeded in tracing some of the reasons why the zombie entered Western culture in the way it did in the early part of the twentieth century. Imperialism, racial anxiety and fears about brainwashing have all had their part to play in the zombie's evolution and popularity. But it was 9/11 that has fuelled the zombie movie's unstoppable renaissance and new-found blockbuster status. Zombie movies thrive in times of economic and social uncertainty, offering a vision of the world we thought we knew turned upside down. As the world faces the future with a sense of trepidation, and zombies have gone from the margins to the mainstream, it seems that the end of zombie pictures is not yet.

ZOMBIE FILMOGRAPHY

The aim of this extended filmography is two-fold. Firstly, to offer a dip-in/dip-out collection of credits and background information on every title mentioned in the course of this book. Secondly, to give some detail on films and TV shows that there wasn't an opportunity to discuss in the main text.

The entries here catalogue everything I've been able to source and see up to the start of 2014. Much has changed since the original filmography was compiled in the early 2000s, not least of all the availability of titles as the zombie boom has helped forgotten movies return from the dead, so to speak.

Obscure films that I previously watched on grainy VHS tapes shipped from mail order stores like Video Search of Miami in the US are now widely available on Blu-ray. Many other titles, including some that I was forced to write about from (sometimes embarrassingly imperfect) memory, are now on DVD, Netflix or even YouTube. What a brave new world it is for deadheads! The original filmography was written in haste under duress, and it was a late addition to the book. This new version is revised and updated and corrects many errors and omissions. All dates are actual copyright dates, not release dates.

For reasons of space, I've focussed on feature-length films – anything over 70 minutes – although a few outings with a shorter running time have slipped in. I've had to ignore short films, documentaries and animated films. While this list may not contain every movie ever made that has a zombie in it, it hopefully includes every movie that's been important to the genre's development. For that reason it also includes films – like *Invasion of the Body Snatchers* – that are influenced by, or have been an influence on, the genre's evolution.

Happy browsing!

13 EERIE
2012, CANADA

Dir: Lowell Dean. Prod: Don Carmody, Kevin DeWalt, Mark Montague. Sc: Christian Piers Betley
Cast: Katharine Isabelle, Michael Shanks, Brendan Fehr, Brendan Fletcher, Nicholas Moran

Forensics students arriving an isolated, island "body farm" get to try out their CSI skills on a bunch of corpses under the watchful eye of their grumpy professor. The island used to house a state penitentiary where the authorities were experimenting on death row inmates and now the bodies won't stay still. *American Mary* and *Ginger Snaps* star Katharine Isabelle leads the students being chased by smart, fast-moving, orange jump suited ghouls in this average Canadian zombie/slasher. Somebody call William Petersen, quick!

28 DAYS LATER
2002, UK/USA

Dir: Danny Boyle. Prod: Andrew Macdonald. Sc: Alex Garland
Cast: Cillian Murphy, Naomie Harris, Megan Burns, Brendan Gleeson, Christopher Eccleston

28 days after the apocalypse, London is deserted and the whole of the UK has been evacuated. Motorcycle courier Jim (Cillian Murphy) wakes up to find himself one of the few survivors of a viral outbreak that turns those infected into raging homicidal maniacs. Danny Boyle's digitally shot sci-fi horror harks back to the Terence Fisher invasion movies of the 1960s and the novels of J.G. Ballard, with its stark vision of social collapse. Followed by *28 Weeks Later* (2007).

28 WEEKS LATER
2007, UK/US/SPAIN

Dir: Juan Carlos Fresnadillo. Prod: Enrique López-Lavigne, Andrew MacDonald, Allon Reich. Sc: Juan Carlos Fresnadillo, Rowan Joffe, Enrique López-Lavigne, Jesús Olmo
Cast: Robert Carlyle, Rose Byrne, Jeremy Renner, Harold Perrineau, Catherine McCormack

28 Days Later: a sinewy horror movie arrives that reboots the zombie flick for the 21st century, making deadheads very happy indeed. Five years later: director Danny Boyle and writer Alex Garland F-off into the *Sunshine*, taking star Cillian Murphy with them, and pass the sequel reigns to Spanish helmer

Juan Carlos Fresnadillo (*Intacto*). 98 minutes later: you wonder what went wrong after this slapdash rehash regurgitates its predecessor with all the finesse of a zombie puking blood-vomit. It's a frantic, dumbed down follow-up that delivers jolts but little that lingers. Come back Danny Boyle, your infected zombies miss you...

2012: ZOMBIE APOCALYPSE
2011, USA
Alternative title: Zombie Apocalypse
Dir: Nick Lyon. Prod: David Michael Latt. Sc: Brooks Peck, Craig Engler
Cast: Ving Rhames, Taryn Manning, Johnny Pacar, Gary Weeks, Lesley-Ann Brandt

The Asylum – producers of mockbusters like *Titanic II*, *Transmorphers* and *Snakes on a Train* – delivers another Z-grade zombie knockoff as a bunch of survivors battle through the infested streets of America in an attempt to reach the coast. Ving Rhames leads the pack, wielding a sledgehammer. Together the group resemble the survivors from the *Left 4 Dead* games – melee combat is their favoured approach – and the location-to-location progression with little plot only heightens the sense that this is a videogame made film. It also features the first zombie tigers, ropey CG creations that let Rhames deliver the best line: "Bad kitty!" For an Asylum movie, it's not bad.

ABRAHAM LINCOLN VS ZOMBIES
2012, USA
Dir: Richard Schenkman. Prod: David Michael Latt. Sc: Richard Schenkman
Cast: Bill Oberst Jr., Baby Norman, Bernie Ask, Jason Hughley, Jason Vail

The Asylum has no shortage of chutzpah. *Abraham Lincoln Vs Zombies* cheekily sucks publicity from 20th Century Fox's blockbuster *Abraham Lincoln: Vampire Hunter* and retools the 16th president of the United States as a zombie killer armed with a decapitating scythe. Sadly, the fun is all in the title as this plodding cash-grab does little with its premise – although Bill Oberst Jr. delivers a spirited performance as the bearded prez as he slaughters antebellum ghouls, reunites with his long-lost love (a Savannah prostitute, no less!) and meets various historical personages including Teddy Roosevelt and cowboy Pat Garrett.

ACHURAS
2003, URUGUAY
Dir: Manuel Facal. Prod: Pablo Praino, Manuel Facal. Sc: Manuel Facal
Cast: Claudia Sturla, Marcos Duran, Pablo Praino, Cynthia Contrera, Guillermo Cardoza

Shot on a video camera that's probably older than most of its teen protagonists, this punk, lo-fi effort scores points for being Uruguay's first zombie outing... but little else. When their head teacher goes missing, a bunch of teens hold a party to celebrate – only to discover that his voodoo cursed corpse has been dumped in the bathroom and has come back to life. In the middle of the chaos big-toothed, bespectacled nerd Ariel (producer Pablo Praino) goes loco and tries his hand at raising his dead mates as zombies, before going after pregnant Andrea (Claudia Sturla) with a hedge strimmer. The filmmakers cite Troma as a reference point, but it's actually more like Uruguay's answer to *Zombie Bloodbath*. The version I saw had no subtitles, atrocious ADR and frequently looked like it was completely out of focus. With a bit of ingenuity they could have presented it as a found footage movie.

AFTER EFFECT
2010, USA
Alternative title: The Removed
Dir: David McElroy. Prod: Timothy "TC" Christian, Marc Menet, David McElroy. Sc: David McElroy, Marc Menet
Cast: Tuckie White, Matthew Lucki, Jake Hames, Alja Jackson, Kristina Geddes

Volunteers on an earn-quick-cash medical experiment become unwitting victims of the military's search for a new bio-weapon. Among the human guinea pigs is Lacie (Tuckie White) who quickly realises that the trial is turning her fellow volunteers into homicidal zombies. South Africa's *Expiration* (2011) was a much better spin on similar material – although it didn't have a cameo from Daniel Baldwin as an ethically-challenged senator.

THE AFTERMATH

1980, USA
Alternative title: Zombie Aftermath
Dir: Steve Barkett. Prod: Steve Barkett. Sc: Steve Barkett
Cast: Steve Barkett, Lynne Margulies, Sid Haig, Christopher Barkett, Alfie Martin

The green-faced ghoul on the original video sleeve promises lots of zombie mayhem as two US astronauts return to earth to find the world's population wiped out by a nuclear war. Cities are reduced to rumble and gangs of "mindless battered monsters" roam the streets. It's the perfect apocalyptic set-up. Except *The Aftermath* only has three mutant ghouls, who appear for a couple of minutes halfway through then vanish again. The rest of the film follows spaceman Steve Barkett as he befriends a cute moppet kid and battles an evil (non-zombie) outlaw played by Sid Haig. Horror legend Forrest J. Ackerman makes a brief appearance as a museum curator who lives just long enough to pass on some vital plot information. "They returned from space expecting a hero's welcome. They were met by something very, very different," says the video sleeve. If you were expecting zombies, you'll be equally disappointed…

AFTER THE DAY
2006, USA
Dir: Brett Mauser. Prod: Amanda Nutting, Bradley Bates. Sc: Brett Mauser
Cast: Trey Bayer, Sergio Cantu, Amanda Nutting, Violet Saenz-Arocha, Bradley Bates

2012: a nuke goes off in the US. Three survivors bicker about what to do while making vague plans to find their friend who went out to get cigarettes just as the warhead detonated. By 2017: the Communists have invaded, California has become a monarchy, *Dumb & Dumber* zombies roam the streets and a couple of people have turned into zombie-killing vampires. Apparently improvised and shot for peanuts, *After the Day* is the viewing equivalent of being water boarded. Scarily it was somehow followed by a sequel, *After the Day 2: Before the Knight* (2009).

THE ALIEN DEAD
1980, USA
Alternative title: It Fell From the Sky
Dir: Fred Olen Ray. Prod: Chuck Sumner, Fred Olen

Ray. Sc: Fred Olen Ray, Martin Alan Nicholas
Cast: Buster Crabbe, Raymond Roberts, Linda Lewis, Mike Bonavia, George Kelsey

Meteorites turn the living into zombies in this cruddy effort starring an aging Buster *Flash Gordon* Crabbe as a small-town sheriff responsible for investigating the strange goings on. The zombies spend most of their time hanging out in the Florida swamps, preying on bare-breasted swimmers and occasionally emerging to drag unlucky souls down to their doom. Pretty dismal for all concerned.

ALIEN UNDEAD
2008, AUSTRALIA
Alternative titles: The Dark Lurking, Alien Vs Zombies: The Dark Lurking
Dir: Greg Connors. Prod: Stuart Wall. Sc: Greg Connors
Cast: Tonia Renee, Bret Kennedy, Ozzie Devrish, Roslyn Van Doorn, Dirk Foulger

Alien Vs Zombies. What a title! It's not, sadly, an accurate one. This horrendously confused Ozploitation sci-fi horror filches liberally from *Alien* and *Resident Evil* but makes very little sense. A group of mercenaries and some scientists are trapped in an underground lab when the facility goes into lockdown. Apparently the scientists have been experimenting with Satan's DNA, discovered by the Nazis in WWII (!), and now various zombie-esque "minions" are running amok. A messy and incoherent throwback to VHS era clag.

ALIEN ZOMBIE INVASION
2011, USA
Dir: Joey Evans. Prod: Chris Daly. Sc: Joey Evans
Cast: Renee Wiggins, Larry Jack Dotson, Christopher Cassarino, Shane Land, Dana Wokas

Aliens create and control zombies in this sub-par effort from the filmmaker behind the much funnier *Bubba's Chili Parlor* (2008) that's very (very, very) loosely based on the Stephenville, Texas UFO sightings of January 2008. It's dull and tedious and relies on both zombie and redneck cliché. "Isn't that Mrs Johnson? I thought you said she was beautiful back in the day?" a kid asks his dad as a fat, lascivious ghoul approaches. The dad nods, unfazed.

"Well she's gotten real damn ugly now…" Yawn.

AMERICAN ZOMBIE
2007, USA
Dir: Grace Lee. Prod: In-Ah Lee. Sc: Rebecca Sonnenshine, Grace Lee
Cast: Austin Basis, Suzy Nakamura, Al Vicente, Jane Edith Wilson, John Solomon

As the walking, talking dead try to find a way to live among the living, a documentary director makes a film about their attempts to integrate back into society. But her reportage leads to some awful truths. A brilliantly fresh spin on familiar zombie fare.

ANOTHER NIGHT OF THE LIVING DEAD
2011, USA
Dir: Alan Smithee. Prod: Alan Smithee. Sc: Alan Smithee
Cast: Sam Ronick, Samantha Falk, Stephanie Hovers, Daniel Martin, Butch Everhart

The curse of the copyright returns as a bunch of losers retool Romero's classic mixing new and old footage and a lot of puerile nonsense: a total travesty. Sam Ronick plays a nerdy kid who's spliced into the farmhouse as Romero's survivors fight the ghouls. What does it add? Not a lot apart from some *Mystery Science Theater 3000* style japes and zombies farting.

APOCALYPSE OF THE DEAD
2009, SERBIA/ITALY/SPAIN
Alternative titles: Zone of the Dead, 2012: Apocalypse of the Dead
Dir: Milan Konjevic, Milan Todorovic. Prod: Vukota Brajovic, Loris Curci, Zeljko Mitrovic, Milan Todorovic
Sc: Vukota Brajovic, Milan Konjevic
Cast: Ken Foree, Kristina Klebe, Emilio Roso, Miodrag Krstovic, Vukota Brajovic

Opening with a quote from Schiller, shot in Serbia, produced by an Italian and starring everyone's favourite zombie slayer Ken Foree (from the 1978 *Dawn of the Dead*), this straight to DVD oddity is a mishmash of half-baked ideas, although it makes history as Serbia's first zombie movie. After NATO troops accidentally release a green chemical gas from a goods train, everyone who dies turns into… yep, you guessed it. The groan-inducing screenplay, full of total inanities, treats viewers like idiots and even gets its star to repeat a version of his now famous "No more room in hell" speech. If you can survive the perpetual shakicam without a fit of nausea, there's one decent moment worth searching out – when Foree has to walk through a "minefield" of sleeping zombies, terrified that they may spring into action at any moment.

ARMAGEDDON OF THE DEAD
2008, USA
Alternate title: Risen
Dir: Damon Crump. Prod: David Talbot, John Franklin, Damon Crump. Sc: David Talbot
Cast: Gigi Erneta, Joe Thackery, Jason Harper, Stephen Lee, Karim Irteimeh

"A mother must do everything she can to find her child…" When a train transporting toxic chemicals derails just north of Waco, Texas the resulting spill causes an outbreak of raging ghouls. Trapped in the chaos are a couple of parents (Gigi Erneta and Joe Thackery) who've left their toddler daughter with her grandparents. They're now racing across town to get back to her as zombies with bleeding eyes and a taste for flesh stumble around the streets. They hide out in a rescue centre where they meet a muslim AK (Karim Irteimeh) who responds to taunts from rednecks that he's a terrorist by proving his mettle as a zombie fighter. Bland and facile in its political correctness this lame low-budget outing barely musters enough power for a disturbance let alone Armageddon. For a more interesting take on parenthood during a zombie outbreak try the Australian short film "Cargo" (2013).

ARMY OF DARKNESS
1992, USA
Alternative titles: Army of Darkness: The Medieval Dead, Evil Dead 3
Dir: Sam Raimi. Prod: Robert Tapert, Bruce Campbell
Sc: Sam Raimi, Ivan Raimi
Cast: Bruce Campbell, Embeth Davidtz, Marcus Gilbert, Ian Abercrombie, Richard Grove

Poor old Ash finds himself flung back in time to the 15th-century to battle yet more demons in the final part of Raimi's *Evil Dead* trilogy. Armed with his trusty chainsaw and shotgun he's out to destroy the pesky Necronomicon once and for all. Not many zombies, although there are plenty of demonic Deadites and an army of skeletons who have a bone to pick with our weary hero. Memorable one-liners ("Well, I've got news for you pal, you ain't leadin' but two things: Jack and shit... and Jack just left town") and plenty of chainsaw action keep things fresh. But by this point the franchise was beginning to run out of steam.

THE ASTRO-ZOMBIES
1967, USA
Alternative titles: Space Zombies, Space Vampires
Dir: Ted V. Mikels. Prod: Ted V. Mikels. Sc: Ted Mikels, Wayne Rogers
Cast: Wendell Corey, John Carradine, Tom Pace, Joan Patrick, Tura Satana

Carradine's mad scientist has created a sci-fi Frankenstein's monster out of bits and pieces of body parts. Does it obey orders? Yes, but only when those orders are to go on a killing-spree. A script full of pseudo-scientific twaddle and a monster that's clearly a bloke in a cheap joke store mask make this a lamentable addition to the zombie genre. Four decades later Mikels revived this long dormant, non-franchise with *Mark of the Astro-Zombies* (2002), *Astro Zombies: M3 – Cloned* (2010) and *Astro Zombies: M4 – Invaders from Cyberspace* (2012). Talk about coming back from the dead.

ATTACK GIRLS SWIM TEAM VS THE UNDEAD
2007, JAPAN
Original title: Joshikyôei hanrangun
Alternative title: Undead Pool
Dir: Kôji Kawano. Prod: Yoji Hirako, Masami Teranishi. Sc: Satoshi Ohwada
Cast: Sasa Handa, Yuria Hidaka, Ayumu Tokito, Hiromitsu Kiba, Kiyo Yoshizawa

This stand out title is a typical throwaway movie from Asian production house Switchblade Pictures. At a Japanese high school, the swim team discover that a classroom vaccination program is turning staff and pupils into crazed zombies. Can the girls swim team save the day? Nope. Well what about new pupil – and former trained assassin – Aki (Sasa Handa)? Maybe. Shamelessly lingering over its female cast in swimsuits, all pert nipples and buttock snapping elastic, this daffy horror is less interested in its zombies than leering, random lesbianism, severed toes and a "crotch laser beam" that gives us gore cinema's answer to a bukakke party. It's irredeemably puerile and not a little creepy.

ATTACK OF THE HERBALS
2011, UK
Dir: David Ryan Keith. Prod: David Ryan Keith.
Sc: Alisdair Cook, Liam Matheson, David Ryan Keith
Cast: Calum Booth, Steve Worsley, Liam Matheson, Claire McCulloch, Richard Currie

Made for a rumoured £15,000, this redundantly anodyne Scottish zombie comedy plays like a cross between *Local Hero* and *The Crazies*. When city boy Jackson (Calum Booth) returns to the Scottish coastal town he grew up in, he's given the cold shoulder by the locals. Years ago, Jackson inadvertently screwed up the town's lobster fishing industry triggering a mini economic depression – and now an evil, golf-playing entrepreneur (Liam Matheson) is about to buy the town for a song. When a crate of mysterious, but highly addictive, tea is washed ashore, Jackson plans to sell it and save the town. Little does he realise he's dosing up his friends, neighbours and dear old granny on a experimental Nazi drug that will turn them all into zombie-like villains...

ATTACK OF THE VEGAN ZOMBIES
2009, USA
Dir: Jim Townsend. Prod: Jim Townsend. Sc: Jim Townsend
Cast: Christine Egan, H. Lynn Smith, Jim Townsend, Kerry Kearns, Natalia Jablokov

Failing crops and spiralling debts convince a vineyard owner (Christine Egan) to dabble in witchcraft in an attempt to save the family farm. A year later the winery is back on track with a bumper harvest. But it comes at a price: people are turning into green-skinned zombies hungry for grapes and attracted to anyone who's been quaffing wine. The herbivore ghouls don't make an appearance until the last twenty minutes, but they can shoot vines out of their mouths so they're almost worth waiting for. It's no *Grapes of Death*, though.

AT TWILIGHT COME THE FLESHEATERS
1998, USA
Dir: Vidkid Timo. Prod: Vidkid Timo and Jim Buck.
Sc: Vidkid Timo
Cast: Jim Buck, Vidkid Timo, Kiki Ann Karrion, Lew R., Chris Sheridan

Zombie cinema's first gay porno zombie outing works as both a skin flick and a cheesy horror spoof thanks to an ingenious movie-within-a-movie set-up. A couple of guys plan to spend an evening at home watching a video called *Night of the Living Dead*. The rejigged Romero classic opens with Barbara (filmmaker Vidkid Timo in drag) sucking off her brother Johnny on their mother's grave while doing her best to ignore his attempts to scare her ("They're coming to rape you Barbara. They're going to gangbang you Babs!"). Pretty soon sex-crazed zombies are on the loose and Barbara's forced to take refuge in an isolated farmhouse with an assortment of other survivors. Lots of hardcore gay sex punctuates the action and there are funny parodies of *Night of the Living Dead*'s key scenes including a zombie girl who kills her mother with a hairdryer. At one point the black hero decides to relieve his pent-up tension by masturbating over the kitchen floor of the besieged farmhouse – which pretty much sums up the iconoclastic nature of this outrageous spoof. Quite what Romero would make of it all is debatable.

AUTOMATION TRANSFUSION
2006, USA
Alternative title: Zombie Transfusion
Dir: Steven C. Miller. Prod: Geoffrey James Clark, Jeremy McCormick, William Clevinger Sc: Steven C. Miller
Cast: Garrett Jones, Juliet Reeves, William Howard Bowman, Rowan Bousaid, Ashley Elizabeth Pierce

A zombie outbreak at a high school quickly turns Orlando, FL into running dead central as a bunch of cardboard cut-out teens fight raging zeds. About fifteen minutes from the end a fat bloke in combat fatigues turns up to blame it all on Vietnam era experiments on the dead. The rest of the running time of this shoestring DIY effort is little more than an SFX showreel scored by death metal. Heads are ripped off, jaws are torn off and a foetus is pulled from a pregnant woman's belly. Gore, gore, gore – but nothing more.

AUTUMN
2008, CANADA
Dir: Steven Rumbelow. Prod: Anton Brejak, John Dunlop, Steven Rumbelow, Matthew Stone, Michael Summerfield. Sc: David Moody, Steven Rumbelow
Cast: Dexter Fletcher, Dickon Tolson, Lana Kamenov, Anton Brejak, David Carradine

Everyone is dead in the blink of an eye in *Autumn*, a zombie apocalypse that doesn't believe in hanging around when it comes to ending the world. As a small band of unaffected survivors (led by Dexter Fletcher) group together to figure out what just happened, the corpses get up and start to walk – first stumbling around, passively aimless, then slowly showing signs of evolving into something more threatening. David Moody self-published his novel *Autumn* in 2001 and discovered a hungry audience, leading to a long-running series of zombie e-books and later print titles. It's a smart, engrossing spin on the usual z-apocalypse. Director Steve Rumbelow's adaptation has the right sense of growing, sweaty-palmed menace but its disjointed, technically shambolic and often artily self-indulgent approach is a real disappointment. Meandering like one of the first day ghouls, *Autumn* proves a shocking waste of a great idea.

AWAKEN THE DEAD
2006, USA
Dir: Jeff Brookshire. Prod: Michelle Brookshire, Jennifer Kilpatrick. Sc: Jeff Brookshire
Cast: Gary Kohn, Lindsey Morris, Nate Witty, Paul Dion Monte, Will Harris

A priest with a shady past battles the newly awakened dead in a no-budget effort that's so grainy it looks like it was shot on an iPad during a Sahara sandstorm. Focussing on a diverse bunch of survivors (including a Jehovah's Witness, a survivalist and the daughter of the CIA spook responsible for the outbreak), writer-director Jeff Brookshire is more interested in character development than gore. It's just a pity his characters are so terminally dull. Paul Dion Monte, who plays the film's ill-fated survivalist, has a string of bit parts in Sylvester Stallone movies on his résumé...

it turns out he's Sly's cousin.

AWAKENING: ZOMBIE NIGHT 2
2006, CANADA
Dir: David J. Francis. Prod: Mike Masters. Sc: David J. Francis, Mike Masters
Cast: Steve Curtis, Sharon DeWitt, Dan Rooney, Kari Grace, John Paris

"No actual zombies were harmed in the making of this production" has become a sure way of spotting a low-budget, low-on-ideas zombie movie – it's just a pity you have to wait until the end credits before you see it flash up on screen! It's no surprise David J. Francis's second entry in his *Zombie Night* series uses it – this is a cookie cutter, shot on the cheap Canadian zombie flick in which a group of survivors try to get through the z-apocalypse. It's saying something that the most memorable moment is when two women decide to have a "You bitch!" catfight in the middle of the climactic ghoul attack.

BAD TASTE
1987, NEW ZEALAND
Dir: Peter Jackson. Prod: Peter Jackson. Sc: Peter Jackson, Tony Hiles, Ken Hammon
Cast: Terry Potter, Peter O'Herne, Craig Smith, Mike Minett, Peter Jackson

Intergalactic aliens invade New Zealand in this lo-fi but delightfully inventive gross out zombie comedy. A squad from the Astro Investigation Defence Service (AIDS, ahem) are dispatched to battle the intergalactic bullies and end up fighting off zombies, giggling their way through the ridiculous dialogue and getting mucky as the special effects team try their best to live up to the film's title. The lowest point involves one of our heroes having to sup from a bowl of vomit, plus there's a rousing chainsaw/rebirth climax designed to make you larf till you barf. Shot on 16mm over several years as the cast and crew scrimped and saved enough money to complete it, *Bad Taste* puts the threadbare filmmakers of the SOV cycle to shame. It may be bargain basement cinema yet it comes with more wit and ingenuity than any of the American backyard epics that followed it. Jackson eventually went on to make *The Lord of the Rings* trilogy – which surely must be one of the most incredible career arcs in the history of modern cinema.

BATH SALT ZOMBIES
2013, USA
Dir: Dustin Mills. Prod: Clint Weiler. Sc: Dustin Mills
Cast: Brandon Salkil, Jeremy Ryan, Ethan Holey, Bella Demente, Rip Slabcheek

Credit where it's due: this punk DIY effort cleverly surfs the wave of media hysteria that erupted over "bath salts" (synthetic cathinones) in 2012. It's a scrappy affair thrown together with likeable brio by prolific, no-budget filmmaker Dustin Wayde Mills.

THE BATTERY
2012, USA
Dir: Jeremy Gardner. Prod: Jeremy Gardner, Douglas A, Plomitallo, Adam Cronheim, Christian Stella. Sc: Jeremy Gardner
Cast: Jeremy Gardner, Adam Cronheim, Alana O'Brien, Larry Fessenden, Niels Bolle.

Two baseball players hang out in the aftermath of the dead walking in this lo-fi, low-budget but bracingly well-written indie. One of the best movies to come out of the zombie boom.

BATTLEFIELD BASEBALL
2003, JAPAN
Original title: Jigoku kôshien
Dir: Yudai Yamaguchi. Prod: Ryuhei Kitamura.
Sc: Yudai Yamaguchi
Cast: Tak Sakaguchi, Atsushi Ito, Hideo Sakaki

The team responsible for hyperkinetic Asian zombie outing *Versus* continue their assault on the genre with this manic zombie sports movie in which two high school teams battle it out on the baseball diamond. Reworking the no-holds barred craziness of *Versus*, this simply swaps samurai swords for baseball bats as the human players of Seido High face the notoriously deadly (and completely living dead) team from Gedo High. Fortunately, Seido have a secret weapon: a legendary player not afraid of facing down a bunch of grey skinned ghouls. Best not to ask why or how, just sit back and enjoy this outrageous, home-run-hitting comedy-horror.

BATTLE OF THE BONE
2008, UK
Dir: George Clarke. Prod: George Clarke. Sc: George Clarke
Cast: Shane Todd, Alan Crawford, Laura Jenkins, Michael Sloan, Graeme Livingstone

"For over 300 years now, Northern Ireland has suffered under the constant argument between Protestant and Catholic religions, ever since William of Orange landed on these shores in 1690: an argument that has gotten out of control ever since terrorist organizations formed on both sides." So begins *Battle of the Bone* a rambunctious Belfast-set zombie movie that's as interested in kung fu and parkour as it is in talking about the Troubles. When drug-fuelled zombies invade the streets of the city on 12 July – the day of Orangemen marches and inevitable sectarian conflict – a small band of friends have to fight their way to safety. Camcorder Coppola George Clarke has a terrible sense of pacing and storytelling, but a great eye for kinetic action. By the time the finale wraps up the zombie threat with a call to both sides of the Irish Problem to join forces against the living dead, it's clear that this amateur movie's politics may be facile, but its heart's in the right place. Clarke followed it up with *The Knackery* (2010).

THE BEAST WITHIN
2008, GERMANY
Alternative title: Virus Undead
Dir: Wolf Wolff, Ohmuthi. Prod: Jie Lin. Sc: Wolf Jahnke
Cast: Philipp Danne, Birthe Wolter, Anna Breuer, Nikolas Jürgens, Marvin Gronen

Shades of *The Birds* in this not-bad German outing in which attempts to create a vaccine for avian flu results in a zombie outbreak (oops!) Competently shot, with some unexpectedly ambitious stunts, it's a couple of cuts above the work of Schnaas and Offenbach and the film's growling, pustulated ghouls are suitably gross and nasty. Pity the Euro teen characters – all speaking English for maximum international appeal – are so terminally dull. The CG crows aren't exactly convincing, either.

BENEATH THE SURFACE
2006, USA
Dir: Blake Reigle. Prod: Blake Reigle. Sc: Blake Reigle
Cast: Kyle Stanley, Dominique Geisendorff, Christian Munden, Brett Lawrence, Jerry Schumacher

An emo teen resurrects the high school girl he loves after she's date raped by a football jock in this clumsy indie. Notable for its unfashionable mentions of Haiti and voodoo in its backstory, but little else.

BEVERLY HILLS BODYSNATCHERS
1989, USA
Dir: Jonathan Mostow. Prod: P.K. Simonds Jr., Jonathan Mostow. Sc: P.K. Simonds, Jr.
Cast: Vic Tayback, Frank Gorshin, Art Metrano, Rodney Eastman, Warren Selko

This straight-to-video outing feels more like a modern spin on the Poverty Row movies of the 1940s than a Troma outing and it has the distinction of being the feature debut of director Jonathan Mostow (*U-571*, *Terminator 3: Rise of the Machines*). Two slackers (Rodney Eastman and Warren Selko) are sent to work in a funeral home where the mob-connected owners are experimenting with reanimating the dead (what a great line of business to be in when your best customers are mobsters). The kids help out by stealing bodies, but when the recently deceased Don is revived things get out of hand. A flat and unfunny hybrid of *Prizzi's Honor* and *Re-Animator*.

THE BEYOND
1981, ITALY
Original title: E tu vivrai nel terrore! L'aldilà
Alternative titles: L'au-delà, Die Giesterstadt der Zombies, Seven Doors of Death
Dir: Lucio Fulci. Prod: Fabrizio De Angelis
Sc: Dardano Sacchetti, Georgio Mariuzzo, Lucio Fulci
Cast: Katherine [Catriona] MacColl, David Warbeck, Sarah Keller [Cinzia Monreale], Antoine Saint John, Veronica Lazar

The second film in Fulci's loose zombie trilogy finds New York girl Liza moving down to New Orleans to renovate an old hotel. She doesn't realise that the hotel houses the body of a dead painter murdered decades earlier, nor that it's about to become a gateway to hell. A genre classic.

BEYOND RE-ANIMATOR
2003, SPAIN
Dir: Brian Yuzna. Prod: Julio Fernández, Brian Yuzna.
Sc: José Manuel Gómez, Miguel Tejada-Flores
Cast: Jeffrey Combs, Jason Barry, Elsa Pataky, Simón
Andreu, Bárbara Elorrieta

Dr Herbert West gets banged up in the third film in
the *Re-Animator* series. Fortunately, prison proves
to be the perfect place to continue his re-animating
experiments and it's not long before the dead start
walking all over again. A lifeless corpse of a movie,
this disappointing sequel only springs into action
for a bonkers scene involving a silhouette fight
between a rat and a severed (but reanimated) penis.
Cthulhu only knows what H.P. Lovecraft would
make of that one.

BEYOND TERROR
1980, SPAIN
Original Title: Más allá del terror
Alternative title: Au delà de la terreur
Dir: Tomás Aznar. Prod: Francisco Ariza. Sc: Tomás
Aznar
Cast: Francisco Sánchez Grajera, Emilio Siegrist,
Alexia Loreto, Andrée van de Woestyne, David Forrest

This obscure Spanish film plays like *The Last
House on the Left* of zombie cinema. Bikers rob a
roadside diner, kidnap a wealthy couple then head
for the countryside. Along the way, they leave a
trail of brutal murders – even bludgeoning an old
woman's pet dog to death – then hide out in a
ruined church. Eventually they get their just
desserts: the crypt beneath the church inexplicably
spews forth cobwebbed zombies, among whom
are the bodies of all their victims – including the
dog! Solemnly paced and not especially interesting,
Beyond Terror spends most of its time following its
protagonists as they hang out and bicker among
themselves. The desiccated zombies owe a nod to
the Blind Dead yet the climactic gory death scenes
are more *Scanners* than de Ossorio.

BIG TITS ZOMBIE
2010, JAPAN
Original title: Kyonu doragon: Onsen zonbi vs
Sutorippa
Alternative title: The Big Tits Zombie
Dir: Takao Nakano. Prod: Seiji Minami, Hideaki

Nishiyama. Sc: Takao Nakano
Cast: Sora Aoi, Risa Kasumi, Mari Sakurai, Tamayo, Io
Aikawa

One minute and forty seconds into this Japanese
splatter epic, a cute girl in cowboy boots revs up a
chainsaw and slices a zombie in half from the brain
down to his crotch. At the two minute mark, her
equally under-dressed friend stabs a zombie
through its mouth with a samurai sword. If you
haven't already guessed what kind of movie you
were about to see from the title, you can no longer
claim ignorance. Playing like Japan's answer to
Tarantino and Rodriguez's *Grindhouse*, *Big Tits
Zombie* follows a bunch of strippers (led by adult
actress Sora Aoi) who discover a zombie-spewing
portal to hell under their club. It's daft and likeable,
if totally disposable.

BIKER ZOMBIES FROM DETROIT
2001, USA
Dir: Todd Brunswick. Prod: Tommy Brunswick. Sc: John
Kerfoot
Cast: Tyrus Woodson, Jillian Buckshaw, Joshua Allan,
Jeffrey Michael, Rob Roth

They're bikers, they're zombies and they're from
Detroit. Can we leave it at that? No? OK then.
This utter waste of videotape follows a demon
recruiting hardened criminals for his zombie army.
He sends his minions to kill our hero, who then
returns as a zombie who refuses to join the Harley-
riding ghouls. "Evil never looked so bad" according
to the tagline. And neither did backyard cinema…

BIO COPS
2000, HONG KONG
Original title: Sheng hua te jing: sang shi ren wu
Alternative title: Bio-Crisis Cops
Dir: Wai-Man Cheng. Prod: Wong Jing. Sc: Chuek-Hon
Szeto
Cast: Stephen Fung, Sam Lee, Alice Chan, Wai Ming
Chan, Chun Lai

An unofficial sequel to *Bio-Zombie*, this Hong
Kong comedy gives us a new cast (Lee is the only
familiar face) and a slightly different premise. The
result is entertainingly daffy. A CIA-funded
experiment to create "Painless Warriors" for use in
Iraq gets out of control when the project's boss,

Harry, is bitten by the first test subject. After turning into a flesh-eating, green-goo-dribbling zombie, Harry takes over a country police station and infects everyone he comes across. Out to stop him are Sam Lee's cowardly triad, copper Stephen Fung and feisty heroine Alice Chan. Lee steals the show by replaying much the same slapstick role as he did in *Bio-Zombie*, and there's a half-assed subtext about viruses, AIDS and safe sex. The best moments include Lee pretending to be one of the zombies (stumbling around with his arms outstretched) and an utterly silly gag in which the heroes use gas-filled condoms as weapons against the randy "Zombie New Humans".

BIO-DEAD
2009, USA
Dir: Stephen J. Hadden. Prod: Manfred Drews
Sc: Stephen J. Hadden
Cast: Matthew Norton, Derek Long, Jacob W. Gentry, Tony Williams, Rick Hall

After a biological terrorist attack decimates SoCal killing 12 million people, a recon team in hazmat suits heads into the contaminated zone to investigate an abandoned office block. Foolishly removing their gas masks just minutes after arriving ("My neck's fucking killing me, I've got a headache, I've been wearing this goddman suit for 12 hours!") the elite team of idiots wander around the building encountering weird zombie-like creatures that may or may not be hallucinations caused by the bio-weapon (if only they'd followed protocol!) and generally freaking out. Shot on the cheap and badly paced, this VOD thriller delivers some gore – including a nasty torture sequence involving a blowtorch – and owes more to *The Crazies* than the walking dead its title implies. Pro tip: if you're issued with a gas mask, wear it soldier!

BIO-ZOMBIE
1998, HONG KONG
Original title: Sang faa sau si
Dir: Wilson Yip. Prod: Joe Ma. Sc: Matt Chow, Wilson Yip, Siu Man Sing
Cast: Jordan Chan, Sam Lee, Angela Tong, Yiu-Cheung Lai, Emotion Cheung

Hong Kong's New Trend Plaza Mall becomes the site of a zombie outbreak after an Iraqi biological weapon hidden in a Lucozade bottle sets the living dead loose. So that's what happened to those missing weapons of mass destruction…! An unofficial sequel – *Bio Cops* – followed.

BIOHAZARDOUS
2000, USA
Dir: Michael J. Hein. Prod: Howard Hein. Sc: Michael J. Hein
Cast: Sprague Grayden, David Lee Garver, Al Thompson, Tom Cahill, Will Durham

In Hillsdale, New Jersey a new facility belonging to dastardly corporation GenTech Industries starts spawning out zombies after an experimental bio-weapon gets loose. Caught up in the chaos are a bunch of partying teens who've got their B&Bs ("beer & bones", apparently) ready for a night of fun; a pair of cops; and a bunch of right wing religious nutters who break into the GenTech complex to prove to the media that the nefarious company is trying to play God. The zombies are dressed in white lab coats and shamble about in doddery Romero fashion – arms out, necks crooked. Dull, lacking in horror and totally unconvincing *Biohazardous* also features one of the flimsiest barricades ever erected to stop the dead. It doesn't even block the doorway properly!

BLACK SHEEP
2006, NEW ZEALAND
Dir: Jonathan King. Prod: Philippa Campbell.
Sc: Jonathan King
Cast: Nathan Meister, Danielle Mason, Peter Feeney, Tammy Davis, Glenis Levestam

Years after Peter Jackson put Kiwi zombie cinema on the map, *Black Sheep* takes the gory glory of splat-flick *Braindead* in a totally different direction as genetically-altered zombie sheep swap grass for human flesh. It's a problem for ruthless farm owner Angus (Peter Feeney) but it's even worse for his ovinophobic, city slicker brother Henry (Nathan Meister) who's left to fight the woolly horde when big bro gets turned into a human ram (Weta, Jackson's special effects company, handled the gore and ovine creatures). Director Jonathan King delivers several outrageous gags as the z-sheep go baaaa-d.

BLED WHITE

2011, USA
Dir: Jose Carlos Gomez. Prod: Kelli Tidmore. Sc: Jose Carlos Gomez
Cast: North Roberts, Matthew E. Prochazka, Colleen Boag, Christian Rogala, Bruce Spielbauer

Everyone knows the dead eat the living. But what happens when the living eat the living too? This wintry indie zombie apocalypse from Illinois follows a band of the living who're turning their fellow survivors into fillet steak in order to survive. It thinks it's poignant and melancholy. It's actually overwrought and silly. And any bloke who keeps a zombie girl chained up in his bathroom really deserves everything he gets.

BLOOD CREEK
2008, USA
Alternative title: Town Creek
Dir: Joel Schumacher. Prod: Paul Brooks, Tom Lassally, Robyn Meisinger. Sc: David Kajganich
Cast: Henry Cavill, Dominic Purcell, Emma Booth, Michael Fassbender, Rainer Winkelvoss

Goodbye, good taste: say what you like about Joel Schumacher's bonkers Nazi zombie horror flick, it isn't easily forgotten. How many movies feature a zombie horse biting people… with its guts hanging out… on fire? Shot in 2007, then name-changed, shelved and finally dusted off to capitalise on Michael "Magneto" Fassbender and Henry "Superman" Cavill's sudden fanboy fame, *Blood Creek* is dumb, gory post-pub fun. Fassbender stars as a *Hellraiser*-style zombie Nazi terrorizing modern-day West Virginia, clad in a black leather Waffen-SS trenchcoat and sprouting a third eye in his forehead. Hey Joel, 1984 called: they want their video nasty back.

BLOODLUST ZOMBIES
2011, USA
Dir: Dan Lantz. prod: Dan Lantz, Adam Danoff. Sc: Dan Lantz
Cast: Alexis Texas, Janice Marie, Adam Danoff, Robert Heath, Catherine White
Porn star Alexis Texas headlines this low-rent zombie effort. When a weaponised virus escapes from a corporate lab, the facility goes into lockdown and traps staff – including a secretary (Texas), the creator of the virus, and a playboy sales rep – in the building. Largely ignorable, its only claim to fame is its starlet. She delivers a couple of softcore sex scenes, then gets drenched in blood after hacking up ghouls with a fire axe (it prompts a strip scene with a ludicrous nod to Lady Macbeth as she cleans herself up at a bathroom sink: "It won't come off of me! Get it off of me!"). By the final reel she's wearing a gas mask and chemical warfare suit like a reject from *The Crazies*. Texas should think about finding new representation… Sasha Grey's agent got her a gig with Steven Soderbergh.

BLOOD MOON RISING
2009, USA
Dir: Brian Skiba. Prod: David C. Hayes, Laurie Love, Neal Trout. Sc: Brian Skiba, Laurie Love
Cast: Laurie Love, Neal Trout, Kent Welborn, Davina Joy, Jose Rosete

Blame Rodriguez and Tarantino for this one: a cowboy back in the Wild West inadvertently dooms the world when he finds an amulet that opens up the gates to hell. His Satanist wife Lucy (Laurie Love) makes a deal with the Devil and before you know it a bunch of zombies and werewolves are wandering around a Wild West movie set in the 1970s (I think). Love plays a dual role – as a gun-toting heroine and slinky, latex-clad Satanist – while director Brian Skiba tries to give this a retro grindhouse vibe with cheesy dialogue, a scratched print and a missing reel. But the all-too-knowing irony is very 2009 and the jerky zombies don't get to do much apart from mop up bullets. Ron Jeremy makes a cameo and sticks around long enough to join their ranks.

BLOOD OF GHASTLY HORROR
1971, USA
Alternative titles: Fiend with the Electronic Brain, Man with the Synthetic Brain, Psycho a Go-Go
Dir: Al Adamson. Prod: Al Adamson. Sc: Dick Poston, Chris Martino
Cast: John Carradine, Kent Taylor, Tommy Kirk, Regina Carrol, Roy Morton
John Carradine's paying the bills again as a mad scientist (is there any other kind?) experimenting on a Vietnam vet and turning him into an electronically controlled killer. Eventually, the vet's father (who's also a mad scientist) decides to take

revenge on him for this travesty, using his knowledge of voodoo learned in the jungles of Jamaica to create two zombies. It reworks footage from Adamson's earlier outings *Psycho a Go-Go* (1965) and *Fiend with the Electronic Brain* (1965), although it's very unlikely you'll actually care. Despite having two mad scientists, there's an alarming shortage of zombie action.

BLOOD OF THE BEAST
2003, USA

Dir: Georg Koszulinski. Prod: Georg Koszulinski.
Sc: Georg Koszulinski
Cast: Derrick Aguis, Joshua Breit, Sharon Chudnow, Matt Devine, Georg Koszulinski

Essentially nothing more than a standard SOV zombie flick – featuring campers caught in the Deep South as the living dead run amok – this overcomes the limits of its basic plotting with some innovative visuals and an imaginative backstory. Set in the year 2031, *Blood of the Beast* takes place in a future where the human race has been rendered infertile after a global biochemical war. Genetic engineering has taken over what was once God's work, but now something's amiss and the "first strain" of clones are flipping out and turning into flesh munching ghouls. Director Koszulinski delivers a memorably avant-garde zombie apocalypse using stock WWI footage, an ambient soundtrack and some impressive tricks (the last thirty minutes switches to black & white and uses title cards for the dialogue, like an old silent movie). If only all no-budget zombie flicks showed this much imagination.

BLOODSUCKERS FROM OUTER SPACE
1984, USA

Dir: Glen Coburn. Prod: Rick Garlington. Sc: Glen Coburn
Cast: Thom Meyers, Laura Ellis, Dennis Letts, Robert Bradeen, Big John Brigham

The title says it all really. Texan farmers are turned into bloodsucking zombies that growl at the camera after an extra-terrestrial wind (!) blows through town. A dull horror comedy that fails on both counts, it's barely worth reading about let alone watching. *Invasion of the Bodysnatchers* meets absolute stupidity.

BLOODY BILL
2004, USA

Alternative title: Death Valley: The Revenge of Bloody Bill
Dir: Byron Werner. Prod: David Michael Latt, David Rimawi, Sherri Strain. Sc: Matthew Yuan, John Yuan
Cast: Chelsea Jean, Jeremy Bouvet, Gregory Bastien, Matt Marraccini, Scott Carson

No frills horror production house The Asylum deliver Wild West ghouls in this threadbare schedule filler set in the desert ghost town of Sunset Valley (pop. 99 and soon to be rising) where zombies run amok. On the menu are coke snorting drug dealers and a bunch of good looking debating students. The town is apparently cursed by Bloody Bill (Jeremy Bouvet), a racist confederate soldier who the original townsfolk killed back in the day (as retold via scratchy b&w footage). The real curse, though, is on whoever's unwary enough to rent this – unless of course your idea of fun is overbearing heavy metal, ragged-ass ghost zombies and migraine-inducing editing effects.

BLUE SUNSHINE
1977, USA

Dir: Jeff Lieberman. Prod: George Manasse. Sc: Jeff Lieberman
Cast: Zalman King, Deborah Winters, Ray Young, Robert Walden, Mark Goddard

The drugs don't work in Jeff Lieberman's tale of acid anxiety as a bad batch of LSD called "Blue Sunshine" turns ex-hippies into bald zombie maniacs several years after they first turned on, tuned in and dropped out. After one of the freaks runs riot, hero Jerry is left carrying the can and hits the road to prove the link between the acid tabs and the killings. Getting great mileage out of the fact that the killers are former hippies who're now respectable, white-collar professionals, this high concept little shocker comes with plenty of social satire.

BONE SICKNESS
2004, USA

Dir: Brian Paulin. Prod: Brian Paulin, Rich George.
Sc: Brian Paulin
Cast: Darya Zabinski, Ruby Larocca, Rich George, Brian Paulin, Kevin Barbare

The appropriately named Morbid Vision Films presents this gory, gloopy, unrelentingly ugly special effects showcase that's a Niagara Falls of DIY grue. Alex (Rich George) is suffering from a bone disease, prompting his morgue attendant buddy (writer-director Brian Paulin) to cook up an alternative medicine from discarded corpse parts (say what?). Meanwhile, out in the graveyard skeletal zombies are rising to rip the intestines out of buck naked actresses (say what what?) and a group of raspy-voiced goblins are annoyed about humans stealing corpses before they can feast on them (OK, I give up). This is how they make backyard zombie flicks in Massachusetts, apparently.

THE BONEYARD
1989, USA
Dir: James Cummins. Prod: Richard F. Brophy.
Sc: James Cummins
Cast: Ed Nelson, Deborah Rose, James Eustermann, Denise Young, Norman Fell

Bring on the zombie poodle! Director James Cummins's naff but undeniably lively tale about zombie kiddies and an ancient Chinese curse ought to be nothing more than a throwaway horror flick – high on the gore and the cheese. Instead, it turns into a cult oddity thanks to some hilariously bad special effects involving animatronic zombie monsters. A pair of cops and an overweight psychic find themselves trapped in the county morgue with the living dead nippers (officially known as "kiyoshi" demons) as all hell breaks loose. In the midst of the ensuing chaos, a poodle laps up some gunk and finds itself turned into a seven-foot zombie pooch. Silly, sick and undoubtedly a classic… of sorts.

BONG OF THE DEAD
2011, CANADA
Dir: Thomas Newman. Prod: Jodi Thomas. Sc: Thomas Newman
Cast: Simone Bailly, Mark Wynn, Jy Harris, Barry Nerling, Vince Laxton

It's Cheech and Chong meet the walking dead: after a meteor falls from space turning half the world into zombies, a couple of enterprising stoners (is that an oxymoron?) use ghoul brains as a "fucked up zombie fertiliser for growing killer weed." When their stash runs dry they head into the Danger Zone for more zombie goo – a road trip that finds them encountering a Nazi zombie called Alex (Barry Nerling) and a badass Milla Jovovich asskicker (Simone Bailly). Shot in 15 days but in post-production for a couple of years, this mashed up zom-com is cursed by terrible ADR. But it was clearly a labour of love for Thomas Newman who wrote, directed, edited it and also composited 355 VFX shots by himself on his Mac.

THE BOOK OF THE ZOMBIE
2010, USA
Dir: Scott Kragelund, Paul Cranefield, Erik Van Sant.
Prod: Scott Kragelund, Paul Cranefield, Erik Van Sant.
Sc: Erik Van Sant
Cast: Brian Ibsen, Larisa Peters, Andrew Loviska, Paul Cantu, Adrienne Maclain

Mormon zombies terrorise a small town in Utah. It's certainly an attention-grabbing pitch but nothing in this over-long (even at 63 minutes), micro-budget flick lives up to its promise. As the door-knocking, God-bothering ghouls attack, a few survivors head to a medieval-themed bar where a suit of armour and crossbows come in useful – although the best thing to kill zombies of the Mormon faith is caffeinated drinks. Nice dig at Scientology at the end.

BOWERY AT MIDNIGHT
1942, USA
Dir: Wallace Fox. Prod: Sam Katzman, Jack Dietz.
Sc: Gerald Schnitzer
Cast: Bela Lugosi, Wanda McKay, John Archer, Lew Kelly, Tom Neal

Bela Lugosi plays a dual role as both a philanthropic psychologist and a murderous gangster in this Monogram chiller. The Bowery Mission is a front for his criminal activities, but it also makes the perfect hiding place for the bodies of his victims. Little does he realise that his sidekick is secretly reanimating the dead on the sly. A truly dire Poverty Row schedule filler.

BOY EATS GIRL
2005, IRELAND/UK
Dir: Stephen Bradley. Prod: Ed Guiney, Andrew Lowe.

Sc: Derek Landy
Cast: David Leon, Samantha Mumba, Tadhg Murphy, Laurence Kinlan, Sara James

A book of voodoo rituals lets a grieving mother bring her lovesick, suicidal son Nathan (David Leon) back from the dead in this Irish zombie outing. Wandering through school with strange hunger pangs, zombie Nathan triggers a z-apocalypse that spills out of the playground onto the High Street. Will he romance girlfriend Jessica (Samantha Mumba) or eat her? Think TV's *Waterloo Road* crossed with *My Boyfriend's Back* (1993) with a fun bypass. The screenwriter is Derek Landy, author of the far superior *Skullduggery Pleasant* novels.

BRAIN BLOCKERS
2005, USA
Dir: Lincoln Kupchak. Prod: Tim Everitt, Lincoln Kupchak. Sc: Lincoln Kupchak, Keith Myers
Cast: Timmi Cragg, Matt Shevin, Ned Liebl, Crystal Day, Diora Baird

"*The Sound of Music* is a movie. *Steel Magnolias* is a movie. This is just a waste of my time." So complains a lab assistant (Timmi Cragg) whose boyfriend makes her watch shitty zombie movies in this… utterly shitty zombie movie. Meanwhile her boss, a nefarious doctor (Edwin Craig), is battling the FDA as he develops a cure-all medicine "Tryptophan" that actually… well, you can guess the rest. The zombies can't really compete against the amorous, youthful cast who all need to get a room or ten.

BRAINDEAD
1992, NEW ZEALAND
Alternative title: Dead Alive
Dir: Peter Jackson. Prod: Jim Booth. Sc: Stephen Sinclair, Fran Walsh, Peter Jackson
Cast: Timothy Balme, Diana Peñalver, Elizabeth Moody, Ian Watkin, Stuart Devenie

Fondly loved among zombie fans, this amps up the lo-fi gore of Jackson's debut *Bad Taste* with brilliantly yucky results. After a stop-motion rat monkey bites his beloved mother during a trip to the zoo, shy little Lionel (Timothy Balme) watches as she turns into a slavering zombie. Struggling to keep her and her victims under lock and key in the basement while romancing local shopkeeper's daughter Paquita, Lionel's sitting on a powder keg of pent up zombie rage. Needless to say, the zombies finally escape during a house party and Jackson and his special effects team take the splatter to the limit. It's a truly astonishing film with scenes involving a garden lawnmower, an oversexed pair of zombies (who produce a living dead baby) and a truly audacious Oedipal climax in which Lionel must face down his hideously mutated, gigantic mother. The zenith of zombie splatstick, it's impossible to see how it could ever be topped.

BRAINDEAD
2007, USA
Dir: Kevin Tenney. Prod: Daniel Duncan, Dennis Michael Tenney, Kevin Tenney
Cast: Joshua Benton, Sarah Grant Brendecke, David Crane, Andy Forrest, Alexandra Goodman

Attack of the alien-infected, amoeba-controlled zombies! When a comet hits the Earth near a deserted fishing lodge, an angler is turned into a mutant, black tar spewing ghoul. Barricading themselves in the lodge are a couple of convicts, some hot skinny dipping lesbian hikers, a preacher and his amply bosomed hot secretary (see a pattern yet?). Not much here beyond an 1980s vibe and decent make up effects; but the amoeba-controlled zombie angle mirrors the real-life *Ophiocordyceps unilateralis* fungus that attacks and controls the brains of rain forest ants. If a fungus-controlled ant had been in charge of *Braindead*, it might have been more fun.

BRIDE OF RE-ANIMATOR
1989, USA
Alternative title: Re-Animator 2
Dir: Brian Yuzna. Prod: Brian Yuzna. Sc: Woody Keith, Rick Fry, Brian Yuzna
Cast: Jeffrey Combs, Bruce Abbott, Claude Earl Jones, Fabiana Udenio, David Gale

More goretastic splatter from Lovecraft fanatic Brian Yuzna as Miskatonic University's finest student, Herbert West, resumes his re-animating experiments in this frantic, blood-drenched sequel. Frankenstein references abound as West creates a patchwork corpse – the bride of the title – and dubs her "what no man's mind and no woman's womb ever dreamed of". Dr Hill returns as a still-severed head (although now with added bat wings) and takes command of an army of zombies eager to destroy West once and for all. H.P. Lovecraft was no doubt throwing up in his grave, but chances are he was laughing too.

BUBBA'S CHILI PARLOR
2008, USA
Dir: Joey Evans. Prod: S. Mike Davis. Sc: Joey Evans
Cast: S. Mike Davis, Camille Rocha, Audrey Elizabeth Evans, Ramie Mercado, Bradley Maroney

Growing out of a 2005 short of the same name, this patchy but inoffensive outing from Texas features contraband beef from a government research lab that turns rednecks into ghouls. Leading the fight back is likeable chef Bubba (S. Mike Davis) who's also, unwittingly, responsible for the outbreak. Fortunately, there's no shortage of weapons ("This is Texas, even my grandmother has a gun!") which allows for the usual run and gun DIY action. The grindhouse vibe is heightened thanks to some vintage style commercial spots – including some from Bubba's restaurant itself. Director Joey Evans went on to make *Alien Zombie Invasion* (2011).

THE BUNKER
2000, UK
Dir: Rob Green. Prod: Daniel Figuero. Sc: Clive Dawson
Cast: Charley Boorman, John Carlisle, Jack Davenport, Christopher Fairbank, Nicholas Hamnett

Not much of a zombie movie since its corpses are little more than a final-reel plot device. However this is worth inclusion here on the basis of its heritage, which owes as much to the Nazi zombie cycle as its more obvious influence, Michael Mann's *The Keep*. Trapped in an isolated anti-tank bunker during the final days of 1944, a German platoon begins to crack up as shell-shocked dismay gives way to edgy paranoia. Meanwhile, in the labyrinth of tunnels under the bunker, strange things start happening. Have the Americans infiltrated the complex, or is something evil lurking in the darkness? Building towards a rather ridiculous denouement that may or may not feature the dead returning to life, *The Bunker*'s contribution to the Nazi zombie cycle is stylish yet ultimately unmemorable.

BUTTCRACK
1998, USA
Dir: Jim Larsen. Prod: Cindy Geary. Sc: Jim Larsen
Cast: Doug Ciskowski, Caleb Kreischer, Rob Hayward, Kris Arnold, Mojo Nixon

From the anus it came and to the anus it can return: this is definitely the arse-end of the zombie genre. Troma goes for broke in this tale of a man who kills his overweight roommate only to be shocked when the dead bloater's sister resurrects him with a voodoo spell. He enlists the help of a mad Bible-bashing preacher played by cult rockabilly musician Mojo Nixon and things trundle along until a gore soaked climax. With a title like that, what were you expecting? High art?

A CADAVER CHRISTMAS
2011, USA
Dir: Joe Zerull. Prod: Daniel Rairdin-Hale. Sc: Daniel Rairdin-Hale, Hanlon Smith-Dorsey, Joe Zerull
Cast: Dan Hale, Hanlon Smith-Dorsey, Yosh Hayashi, Ben Hopkins, Jessica Denney

A nerdy university janitor (Dan Hale) fends off zombies with a mop. Nope it's not the *Toxic Avenger* but a lightweight zom-com about cadavers taking over a university building. Starting out as a short and then expanding into a feature, *A Cadaver Christmas* does its best to look like an old-fashioned grindhouse pic with faux scratched film stock and stylised lighting. Story-wise there's not much to it as the janitor enlists the help of some blue collar stereotypes (cop, barman, drunk) to help him stem the zombie tide. The jokes are inoffensive, the festive setting is pretty inane (honourary mention to the zombie skewered on a Christmas tree). Props to whoever wrote the final, post-credits line, though: "New Year's is gonna be hell!"

LA CAGE AUX ZOMBIES
1995, USA
Dir: Kelly Hughes. Prod: Kelly Hughes. Sc: Kelly Hughes
Cast: Cathy Roubal, Eric Gladsjo, J.R. Clarke, William

Love, Betty Marshall

Imagine *The Rocky Horror Picture Show* shot on home video and full of zombies. That's what this enthusiastic but terrible SOV effort wants to be. A wife running away from her drug dealer husband gets mixed up with a bunch of cross-dressing ghouls after a plane carrying football players crashes and the buff boys come back from the dead. Before long, zombies in jockstraps and trainers are roaming the streets and attacking anyone they can get their well-manicured hands on. With gore made out of baked beans and a whole troupe of exquisitely dressed drag queen zombies, this is so camp it might as well have come with its own set of tent poles. The title is a riff on French classic *La cage aux folles* (1978) and there's even a cameo from Russ Meyer favourite Kitten Natividad – who gets her ample (if ageing) breasts out for a pair of zombie boys to suck milk from. Bizarre and definitely best left to the terminally curious.

CANNON FODDER
2012, ISRAEL
Dir: Eitan Gafny. Prod: Tom Goldwasser. Yafit Shalev, Eitan Gafny. Sc: Eitan Gafny
Cast: Liron Levo, Yafit Shalev, Roi Miller, Emos Ayeno, Gome Sarig

Israel's first zombie movie follows a squad of special forces soldiers, led by Liron Levo (*Munich*), who head into Lebanon to arrest a senior Hezbollah commander. So far, so incendiary. Once over the Northern Border they're attacked by raging Arab ghouls ("We've never seen insurgents like these!") and discover an elaborate conspiracy to wipe out the Hezbollah leadership and prevent war. Wearing its paper-thin political allegory on its sleeve (Israel's security policy creates an army of ghouls who want to destroy it), this delivers pretty standard zombie action led by a distinctly unlikable group of macho, racist grunts. By the final reel it goes completely OTT as the heroes face off against an army of the infected with knives and a couple of empty guns. Disappointing.

THE CAPE CANAVERAL MONSTERS
1960, USA
Dir: Phil Tucker. Prod: Richard Greer. Sc: Phil Tucker

Cast: Katherine Victor, Scott Peters Linda Connell, Jason Johnson, Billy Greene

Katherine Victor, the evil scientist from *Teenage Zombies* (1957), returns for more ghoulish boredom as aliens attempt to sabotage the US space program by taking over the bodies of a couple killed in a car crash. Backyard 1960s nonsense from the man behind the execrable *Robot Monster*, it's notable only for its willingness to play up the grotesque dead-ness of its aliens' human bodies.

THE CASTLE OF THE MUMMIES OF GUANAJUATO
1973, MEXICO
Original title: El castillo de las momias de Guanajuato
Dir: Tito Novaro. Prod: Rogelio Agrasánchez.
Sc: Rogelio Agrasánchez
Cast: Superzán, Blue Angel, Tinieblas, Zulma Faiad, Maria Salomé

A crazed doctor (Tito Novaro, who doubles as director) needs the blood of terrified victims. What better way to secure it than to send out his midget henchmen to raise an army of momias. The latex-masked ghouls lurch stiffly about as the midgets blow whistles to command them. They invade a village and kidnap the inhabitants. Back at the doctor's lair they string up the skimpily-dressed unfortunates and torture them with medieval looking implements. While the victims scream, a trio of masked wrestlers (Superzán, Blue Angel, Tinieblas) investigate and eventually whup the ghouls back to their graves. A surprisingly nasty addition to the momias series.

THE CHILD
1977, USA
Alternative titles: Kill And Go Hide, Zombie Child
Dir: Robert Voskanian. Prod: Robert Dadashian.
Sc: Ralph Lucas
Cast: Laurel Barnett, Rosalie Cole, Frank Janson, Richard Hanners, Ruth Ballan

Children shouldn't play with dead things... tell that to antisocial, troubled brat Rosalie (Rosalie Cole) who uses her mysterious telekinetic powers to raise zombie playmates from a local graveyard. Her new nanny Alicianne (Laurel Barnett) is intrigued by the motherless girl's strangeness and her trips to the cemetery. Pretty soon, Rosalie is using her "friends" to kill the adults who annoy her – the decaying, grey-blue ghouls creep out of the graveyard, their flesh peeling as they go on a murder spree. Under the watchful eye of exploitation producer Harry Novak, director Robert Voskanian ratchets up the tension with a disturbing and overbearing piano-pounding score and handheld camera sequences as he builds towards a tense finale where Alicianne and Rosalie's older brother are trapped in a lumber mill. A blend of *Night of the Living Dead* and *Carrie*, it's laced with a druggy, hypnotic quality that makes up for some of its rougher edges.

CHILDREN OF THE LIVING DEAD
2001, USA

Dir: Tor Ramsey. Prod: Karen Wolf. Sc: Karen Wolf
Cast: Tom Savini, Martin Schiff, Damien Luvara, Jamie McCoy, A. Barrett Worland

"Bred from the creators of classic horror *Night of the Living Dead* comes the long-awaited sequel" hypes the DVD tagline, but you'll struggle to find George Romero's name here. Instead, the people in the dock for this travesty are his collaborators John A. Russo, Bill Hinzman and Tom Savini. It opens with a zombie outbreak in Pennsylvania (where else?) then fast-forwards fourteen years to follow a property developer who disturbs the gravesite of a rubber-faced zombie villain named Abbott Hayes. Hayes raises a zombie army to attack the town in a climax that looks more like a post-pub car park brawl than the end of the world.

CHILDREN SHOULDN'T PLAY WITH DEAD THINGS
1972, USA

Alternative title: Revenge of the Living Dead
Dir: Benjamin Clark. Prod: Benjamin Clark, Gary Coch. Sc: Benjamin Clark, Alan Ormsby
Cast: Alan Ormsby, Valerie Mamches, Jeff Gillen, Anya Ormsby, Paul Cronin

A theatre troupe of hippies gets more than they bargained for when their nihilistic leader, Alan, takes them out to a burial island for some spooky hi-jinks. Chanting a spell to raise the dead from their graves, Alan gets a shock when they actually do come back. Ghoulish fun.

THE CHILDREN
1980, USA

Alternative titles: The Children of Ravensback
Dir: Max Kalmanowicz. Prod: Max Kalmanowicz.
Sc: Carlton J. Albright, Edward Terry
Cast: Martin Shakar, Gil Rogers, Gale Garnett, Jessie Abrams, Shannon Bolin

Strange things start happening in the sleepy town of Ravensback after a busload of school kids goes missing. It turns out that a leak from the local nuclear power plant has turned the nippers into zombies with pale complexions and black fingernails. Reunited with their parents, the radioactive zombie kids cause havoc. Since they're impervious to bullets, someone comes up with the smart idea of simply chopping the kids' hands off – resulting in lots of mutant moppets holding their spurting limbs in the air. It's a daft as it sounds and the scene in which a radioactive little girl microwaves her mother by hugging her is unintentionally hilarious.

CHILLERAMA
2011, USA

Dir: Adam Green, Joe Lynch, Bear McCreary, Adam Rifkin, Tim Sullivan. Prod: Cory Neal, Andrew Mysko, Jason R. Miller. Sc: Adam Rifkin, Tim Sullivan, Adam Green, Joe Lynch
Cast: Adam Rifkin, Sarah Mutch, Ray Wise, Lin Shaye, Tania Raymonde

Closing night in the last drive-in in America brings lots of horror spoofery in this fun little grindhouse tribute. Joe Lynch's segment "Zom-B-Movie" features a bunch of sex-crazed dead who run riot in the drive-in after blue sex goo gets laced into the popcorn butter. It's icky and silly and outrageously features zombies humping anything with a pulse.

THE CHILLING
1989, USA

Dir: Jack A. Sunseri, Deland Nuse. Prod: Jack A. Sunseri.
Sc: Jack A. Sunseri
Cast: Linda Blair, Dan Haggerty, Troy Donahue, Jack de Rieux, Ron Vincent

Deep-frozen zombies thaw out after a lightning bolt hits a cryogenic chamber in Jack A. Sunseri's low-budget "chiller". Linda Blair and Dan

Haggerty (aka Grizzly Adams) swallow their pride to star as a research assistant and a hirsute security guard at the state of the art laboratory. As hilariously cheesy, green-faced zombie ghouls wrapped up in aluminium shrouds run amok, it's left to Blair and Haggerty to work out why the corpses are returning as killers and how not to wince at lines like "Those frozen TV dinners out there are starting to get to you."

CHOKING HAZARD
2004, CZECH REPUBLIC
Dir: Marek Dobes. Prod: Marek Dobes, Narek Oganesjan. Sc: Stepan Kopriva
Cast: Jaroslav Dusek, Jan Dolansky, Eva Nadazdyova, Anna Fialkova, Kamil Svejda

Philosophy students battle living dead zombie woodsmen ("woombies") in this frantic Czech horror comedy. The mashed-up ghouls in black trilbies look like distant cousins of Freddy Krueger but can't compete with the madcap comedy and clever-clever asides on Nietzsche, Jung and John Lilly. "We came here looking for sense and we found nonsense," opines one of the students as zombies trap them in an isolated country hotel. Indeed.

CHOPPER CHICKS IN ZOMBIETOWN
1989, USA
Original title: Chrome Hearts
Dir: Dan Hoskins. Prod: Maria Snyder, Nancy Paloian. Sc: Dan Hoskins
Cast: Jamie Rose, Catherine Carlen, Lycia Naff, Vicki Frederick, Kristina Loggia

Those trash merchants at Troma Studios strike again. This time they've got a fun premise, though: a posse of leather-clad, female bikers ride into the town of Zariah (population: 127) and discover zombies terrorising the living. The ghouls are the creations of the town's mortician, who's implanted the corpses with electronic devices so he can use them as slave labour in a radioactive tin mine (let's see, so far the plot's ripped off *The Plague of the Zombies*, *Dawn of the Dead* and *Dead & Buried*). As usual with Troma this is crude stuff but there's little nudity or gore. Two useless pieces of trivia: eagle-eyed viewers will spot a pre-fame Billy Bob Thornton among the cast; and, according to

legend, the MPAA refused to rate the film under its original title of *Cycle Sluts Vs. the Zombie Ghouls*.

CITY OF ROTT
2005, USA
Dir: Frank Sudol. Prod: Frank Sudol. Sc: Frank Sudol.
Cast: Frank Sudol

One man studio Frank Sudol, an assistant animator on the *South Park* movie, creates a stunning 2D animated zombie apocalypse in this novel outing in which the human race is almost wiped out by parasitic worms in the water supply. An old man on a walker wanders through a ravaged city looking for a new pair of slippers while talking to his walking aid and occasionally using it to bash zombies' brains in. It's distinctive and occasionally funny but might have worked better as a short. The slow old guy on a walker gag was used to better effect in *Cockneys Vs Zombies* (2012).

CITY OF THE LIVING DEAD
1980, ITALY
Original title: Paura nella città dei morti viventi
Alternative titles: La ciudad de los muertos vivientes, The Gates of Hell, Ein Zombie hing am Glockenseil
Dir: Lucio Fulci. Prod: Giovanni Masini. Sc: Lucio Fulci, Dardano Sacchetti
Cast: Christopher George, Katriona [Catriona] MacColl, Carlo De Mejo, Antonella Interlenghi, John Morghen [Giovanni Lombardo Radice]

The first film in Fulci's zombie trilogy begins with a priest in New England hanging himself. His suicide opens a gateway to hell and our heroes have until All Saint's Day to close it, otherwise the dead will rise from their graves and take over the world. It would be simple if it weren't for all the zombies, crazed rednecks and plagues of maggots hindering them. A true classic.

COCKNEYS VS ZOMBIES
2012, UK
Dir: Matthias Hoene. Prod: James Harris, Matthias Hoene, Mark Lane. Sc: James Moran, Lucas Roche
Cast: Rasmus Hardiker, Harry Treadaway, Michelle Ryan, Jack Doolan, Georgia King

This silly but fun low-budget British zom-com gets a lot of mileage out of its wonderful title.

Construction work for the 2012 Olympics unleashes long-buried ghouls on England's capital. The city's only hope is a bunch of bank robbers (among them former Albert Square resident and Bionic Woman Michelle Ryan) and a bunch of care home escapees led by Alan "Rent-a-Gangster" Ford. The old lags tool up with semi-automatic weapons and a double-decker bus, and the gags range from "Knees Up Mother Brown" stereotypes to a very slow (and very funny) scene in which a shambling ghoul tries to catch a wrinkly on a zimmer frame: RIP Richard Briers.

COLIN
2008, UK
Dir: Marc Price. Prod: Marc Price. Sc: Marc Price
Cast: Alastair Kirton, Daisy Aitkens, Kate Alderman, Tat Whalley, Leanne Pammen

Using a borrowed camcorder and editing on his laptop, director Marc Price proves that it's possible to make a zombie movie for next to nothing. What sets *Colin* apart from the usual SOV zombie movie is the originality of its premise: it follows Colin (Alastair Kirton) as he's bitten and joins the shambling hordes of living dead roaming through suburban London. Much like another micro-budget British movie, *I, Zombie: The Chronicles of Pain* (1998), Colin takes a documentary approach to its subject. Impressive in its scope and in its single-minded devotion to telling a zombie apocalypse from a ghoul's perspective, it's a modest but memorable debut.

CORPSE EATERS
1974, CANADA
Dir: Donald R. Passmore, Klaus Vetter. Prod: Lawrence Zazelenchuk Sc: Lawrence Zazelenchuk
Cast: Michael Hopkins, Ed LeBreton, Helina Carson, Michael Krizanc, Terry London

A deservedly obscure Canadian effort, Passmore's film follows four aging swingers who ought to know better than to venture into a graveyard and summon Lucifer. Old Nick doesn't show up but several flour-covered, cobwebbed zombies rise from their graves to wreak havoc. The heroes end up in hospital, where reality blends with a series of blood-soaked nightmares; meanwhile, there are various strange goings on down at the Happy Halo funeral home where the dead are also returning to life. Mercifully, the dull proceedings are over in under an hour.

CORPSES
2004, USA
Dir: Rolfe Kanefsky. Prod: Tanya York, Mark Headley. Sc: Rolfe Kanefsky
Cast: Jeff Fahey, Tiffany Shepis, Stephen W. Williams, Robert Donavan, Melinda Bonini

In a suburban undertaker's chapel, the dead are returning to life thanks to an experimental green embalming fluid that lets a mortician (Robert Donovan) resurrect corpses for an hour at a time. Before you can say "*Re-Animator!*" the ambling, goofy dead are getting into trouble – robbing pawn shops and even streetwalking with retarded abandon. You feel slightly sorry for them – not least of all because they're trapped in a horror comedy with neither scares nor laughs.

COWBOYS & ZOMBIES
2010, USA
Alternate title: The Dead and the Damned
Dir: Rene Perez. Prod: Mattia Borrani. Sc: Rene Perez
Cast: David Lockhart, Camille Montgomery, Rick Mora, Robert Amstler

Gold Rush miners crack open a green glowing rock that turns the Wild West into zombie central in this shot on DV pantomime horror Western. The ghouls – whose leprous mugs look like they've just stuck their faces in a big, gooey bowl of Eton Mess – are wrangled by bounty hunter Mortimer (David Lockhart, who sounds like he's still waiting for his voice to break) and his Native American prisoner (Rick Mora). There's one horse, lashings of comedy CG blood, and all of the female cast are required to remove their blouses at regular intervals... and occasionally run from zombies for maximum bounce effect.

THE CRAZIES
1973, USA
Alternative title: Code Name: Trixie
Dir: George A. Romero. Prod: A.C. Croft. Sc: George A. Romero, based on an original script by Paul McCollough
Cast: Lane Carroll, W.G. McMillan, Harold Wayne

Jones, Lloyd Hollar, Lynn Lowry

A chemical spill turns the inhabitants of a rural American town into homicidal "crazies" in Romero's faux-zombie outing. The military quickly step in to seal off the community, herding the townsfolk around while clad in biochemical warfare suits. Resenting the military's heavy-handed approach some non-infected citizens head out into the countryside to fight a guerrilla war that's curiously reminiscent of America's misadventures in Vietnam.

THE CRAZIES
2010, USA
Dir: Breck Eisner. Prod: Michael Aguilar, Rob Cowan, Dean Georgaris. Sc: Scott Kosar, Ray Wright
Cast: Timothy Olyphant, Radha Mitchell, Joe Anderson, Danielle Panabaker, Christie Lynn Smith

Unnecessary Hollywood remake #4,321? Refreshingly, no. This slick, sick retread of George Romero's B-movie strips the '73 original down and pumps it full of popcorn. Same premise – US bio-weapon turns a redneck town into psycho-zombie central – but the execution swaps Romero's politicising for big, skin-crawling scares (pregnant woman in pitchfork panic!) and a great star turn from Timothy Olyphant. If today's filmmakers must insist on remaking vintage fan favourites for the multiplex, then this'll do as a benchmark.

CREATURES FROM THE PINK LAGOON
2006, USA
Dir: Chris Diani. Prod: Chris Diani, Peter Torr, Lisa Anne Glomb. Sc: Chris Diani, Basil Harris
Cast: Nick Garrison, Lowell Deo, Evan Mosher, Vincent Kovar, John Kaufmann

Straight to DVD, shot in black & white and a high camp parody of 1950s monster movies, this harmless comedy is notable as one of the few (non-hardcore) gay zombie movies around – but for little else. In 1967 a lake house party goes wrong after problems at the local chemical plant cause mosquitoes to turn gay men into zombies. What can save the living? Only Judy Garland show tunes! "Mary, zombies or not, I know a show tune loving friend of Dorothy when I see one!"

CREATURE WITH THE ATOM BRAIN
1955, USA
Dir: Edward L. Cahn. Prod: Sam Katzman. Sc: Curt Siodmak
Cast: Richard Denning, Angela Stevens, Michael Granger, S. John Launer, Gregory Gaye

An ex-con and his scientist partner reactivate the bodies of the dead to take revenge on the gangster who double crossed them in this no-frills zombie flick from director Edward L. Cahn. Making heavy weather of its radioactive trappings, this pulp tale follows the police's efforts to track down the zombie assassins and their living masters – culminating in a pitched battle between cops and ghouls.

CREEPSHOW
1982, USA
Dir: George A. Romero. Prod: Richard P. Rubinstein. Sc: Stephen King
Cast: Stephen King, Hal Holbrook, Adrienne Barbeau, Fritz Weaver, Leslie Nielsen

Scripted by Stephen King, this portmanteau horror collection looks back to the days of E.C. horror comics of the 1950s with a nostalgic eye. The five episodes contain two zombie storylines. In "Father's Day", a rich brat watches in horror as her cranky dad returns to life and demands his Father's Day cake. In "Something To Tide You Over," a cuckolded husband buries his cheating wife and her lover up to their necks in sand on a deserted beach and leaves them at the mercy of the incoming tide. Later, they come back as salty, seaweed-covered zombies in search of revenge.

LA CRUZ DEL DIABLO
1974, SPAIN
Alternative title: The Cross of the Devil
Dir: John Gilling. Sc: Juan José Porto, Jacinto Molina
Cast: Ramiro Oliveros, Carmen Sevilla, Adolfo Marsillach, Eduardo Fajardo, Emma Cohen

Chiefly notable for briefly starring skeletal zombies filched from the *Blind Dead* films, this Spanish production by Hammer exile John Gilling is otherwise zombie-free. Ramiro Oliveros plays a drug addled writer who leaves England for Spain to visit his sister, only to discover she's been murdered. The Templars and their Satanic rites have a role in the film's backstory, but don't make much of an appearance in the actual film itself. Occasionally cited as an unofficial addition to De Ossorio's series it adds little to the *Blind Dead* franchise beyond a footnote. Taken on its own merits, though, it manages to build a suspenseful Gothic atmosphere by making the most of its hero's fractured mental state.

CURSE OF PIRATE DEATH
2006, USA

Dir: Dennis Devine. Prod: David S. Sterling. Sc. Jeremiah Campbell, Steve Jarvis
Cast: Randal Malone, Syn DeVil, Ron Jeremy, Mitch Toles, Monte Hunter

ARRR, landlubbers! Here be no sign of Johnny Depp, just a bunch of underpaid hopefuls padding out their CV. 100 years ago – that's a maths fail right there – the fearsome buccaneer Abraham LeVoy aka Pirate Death (Mitch Toles) lost all his loot after the inhabitants of a coastal town rebelled against him. Now he's back from the dead as a zombie pirate to stalk a bunch of college kids who've discovered his gold. This no-budget backyard epic features a fat bloke in a joke-store pirate costume running around shouting "ARRR!" and killing people while death metal pounds on the soundtrack. It feels like a porno with no sex – something not helped by the sight of actress Syn DeVil baring her over-inflated life preservers and ex porn stud Ron Jeremy making a cameo. The only break in the tedium comes when Pirate Death is confused by a swimming pool ("What do ye call this body of water? No fish, no sharks. Hmmm, clever…"). But a second later he's shouting "ARRR! YOU STOLE MY TREASURE" again and skewering more unfortunates on his sword. Mesmerisingly awful.

CURSE OF THE CANNIBAL CONFEDERATES
1982, USA

Alternative titles: The Curse of the Screaming Dead
Dir: Tony Malanowski. Prod: Tony Malanowski. Sc: Lon Huber
Cast: Steve Sandkuhler, Christopher Gummer, Judy Dixon, Rebecca Bach, Jim Ball

"The South shall rise again… and again," screams the tagline for Troma's Confederate ghoul pic in which a bunch of city 20-somethings on a deer hunting trip awaken the dead. Heading into a cemetery the scruffy dropouts steal an old book, only to realise it's a Confederate general's diary that chronicles the torture and abuse he and his men suffered at the hands of the Union. After an interminable wait and much pointless dialogue, cannibal ghouls in military uniforms eventually claw their way out of the ground looking for some kind of vengeance – although quite what the longhaired hippie kids have done to deserve the gut munching isn't really clear. With technical specs on a par with a Guatemalan snuff movie from 1964, this scare-free, ineptly shot snoozer deserves its rep as one of the worst zombie films ever made.

THE CURSE OF THE DOLL PEOPLE
1960, MEXICO

Original title: Muñecos infernales
Alterntive title: Devil Doll Men
Dir: Benito Alazraki. Prod: Guillermo Calderón. Sc: Alfredo Salazar
Cast: Elvira Quintana, Ramón Gay, Roberto G. Rivera, Quintin Bulnes, Alfonso Arnold

The film that kick-started the enchilada zombie cycle is pretty unremarkable. Four amateur archaeologists stir up trouble for themselves when they pinch a stone deity from an ancient Haitian temple. Ignoring warnings about a curse, they set off home with their booty but are soon being punished by the temple's priest. He sends out doll people – midget actors – who kill them one by one. The dolls are supervised by a towering, straggly-haired zombie slave named Sabud who's intent on fulfilling his master's desire to wipe out everyone connected with the desecration. A few creepy scenes – midget doll people on the bed! – don't add up to much.

CURSE OF THE MAYA
2004, USA

Alternative titles: Dawn of the Living Dead, Evil Grave: Curse of the Maya
Dir: David Heavener. Prod: David Heavener. Sc: David Heavener
Cast: David Heavener, Joe Estevez, Amanda Bauman, Andrew Crandall, Lauren Aguas

You know how it goes: you buy a house in the California desert so your wife (Amanda Bauman) can recover from her drug addiction and before you can even unpack the kettle zombies are crawling out of their graves to attack you… What's that? The house was built on a Mayan graveyard? Well that'll teach you not to skimp on a full survey won't it? Alternating its DVD rental sleeves between titles *Dawn of the Living Dead* and *Curse of the Maya*, this badly-shot nonsense makes the most of its barren desert location where wind turbines spin on the hillside and burnt-looking Joshua trees are silhouetted against the sky. It turns out that the family who used to live in the house were killed by a lunatic gunman and now they're back for blood. The vengeful Mayan zombies – especially the one that pops out of a car boot – are good, raggedy value. But you'd have to be dead and buried not to see the plot twist coming.

CURSE OF THE SUN
2004, THAILAND
Original title: Suriyakhaat
Dir: Kittipong Panyataweesap. Prod: Pornphan Bannajtrakul, Kittipong Panyathaweesub. Sc: Kittipong Panyathaweesub
Cast: Paul Carey, Sitiporn Niyom, Ornjira Lamwilai, Pairoj Jaisingha

A woman's dead boyfriend becomes an unstoppable zombie hit man sent to kill her in this overblown, action-packed Thai thriller. Summoned from the dead by gangsters to finish a botched assassination, the black leather-clad, scarred-faced ghoul (Paul Carey) stalks hospital corridors in search of the woman he once loved. Tooling up with assault rifles – even after losing an arm – he's a formidable foe for the cynical cop (Sittiporn Niyom) on the case. "It's not possible for the dead to get up and start killing people," he complains as the ghoul runs amok. As zombies go, this one arguably owes more to Arnie's T-800 than Romero.

DANCE OF THE DEAD
2008, USA
Dir: Gregg Bishop. Prod: Ehud Bleiberg, Gregg Bishop. Sc: Joe Ballarini
Cast: Jared Kusnitz, Greyson Chadwick, Chandler Darby, Carissa Capobianco, Randy McDowell

It's prom night, the most important night of the year if you're 17, popular and horny. Only this year the prom is being gatecrashed by an army of living dead ghouls who've emerged from the local cemetery. Well, I say "emerged" but they've actually leapt out of their graves, bouncing out of the earth like gymnasts on a trampoline before racing off faster than Olympic relay runners. Fending off the ghouls are a bunch of high school no-hopers including Jimmy (Jared Kusnitz) and the geeks from the Sci Fi Club. Memorable moments include a punk band pacifying a dance floor of ghouls with their chords; the high school coach going all Rambo on the living dead's asses; and a pair of horny teens getting it on as they turn into ghouls. A likeable prom-zom-com to file alongside *Night of the Creeps* and *My Boyfriend's Back*.

DANCE OF THE DEAD (MASTERS OF HORROR)
2005, USA
Dir: Tobe Hooper. Prod: Lisa Richardson, Tom Rowe. Sc: Richard Christian Matheson
Cast: Jonathan Tucker, Jessica Lowndes, Ryan McDonald, Marilyn Norry, Lucie Guest

Tobe Hooper directs the third episode in Showtime's *Masters of Horror* TV series. Set in a post-apocalyptic, post-WWIII America, it centres on a nu-metal club called the Doom Room where Robert Englund's creepy MC uses OD'ed, twitching zombies for sex and as on-stage dancing entertainment. It's based on a story by Richard Matheson, adapted by the novelist's son for TV. But, despite its pedigree, it never rises much beyond dull schedule filler.

DARK ECHOES
1986, AUSTRIA/YUGOSLAVIA
Alternative titles: The Curse of Gohr, Deep Echo
Dir: George Robotham. Prod: George Robotham. Sc: George Robotham
Cast: Karin Dor, Joel Fabiani, Wolfgang Brook, James Dobson, Fred Tully

Veteran Hollywood stuntman George Robotham takes his first (and last) stint behind the camera for this aquatic tale of zombie horror which kicks off with a skeleton faced zombie in a captain's outfit swimming out of a sunken wreck and heading towards the surface. The voiceover tells us that an excursion boat sank on this Austrian lake a hundred years ago, killing Captain Ghor and his eighty passengers. Ever since then, the villagers have been convinced that the ghost of Gohr will return to take his revenge on them – which he eventually does. Set in a *Heidi*-style Austrian locale, with plenty of underwater scenes (one of Robotham's stunt specialities apparently), this obscure zombie flick proves better than one might expect with some occasional chills. Gohr himself is rather ridiculous, though – and is ultimately defeated once the American clairvoyant called in to solve the mysterious murders realises that the monster's afraid of mirrors!

DAWNA OF THE DEAD
2010, USA
Dir: Laume Conroy. Sc: Laume Conroy. Sc: Laume Conroy
Cast: Zoe Mathews, Aiden Starr, Gwen Foxxx, Roxy, Ginger Cash

Porn stars in high heels totter through the ankle-level mist of a deserted graveyard. Dawna (Zoe Mathews) masturbates on her boyfriend's grave, triggering a zombie apocalypse as skull-faced ghouls claw their way out of the ground in search of sex. That's about it for plot as the raggedy-clothed zombies get on with the XXX action. Naked girls suck bloody cocks in sepulchres and occasionally munch on intestines marinated in karo syrup. Director Laume Conroy scratches up the print and puts crackles on the synth soundtrack *Grindhouse*-style but the search for an authentic horror vibe doesn't really deliver. It ends with Dawna wandering through a sunlit cemetery the next morning in what could be an outtake from a Jean Rollin movie.

DAWN OF THE DEAD
1978, USA
Alternative titles: Zombie, Zombies: Dawn of the Dead
Dir: George A. Romero. Prod: Richard P. Rubinstein. Sc: George A. Romero
Cast: David Emge, Ken Foree, Scott H. Reiniger, Gaylen Ross, David Crawford

The sequel to *Night of the Living Dead* has a new set of characters trying to survive the zombie apocalypse by hiding out in a shopping mall. When a rampaging band of bikers attack the mall, though, the zombies stumble back into the neon-lit consumer paradise. More action, more comedy, more social commentary, more gore. Thank you, Mr. Romero.

DAWN OF THE DEAD
2004, USA
Dir: Zack Snyder. Prod: Marc Abraham, Eric Newman, Richard P. Rubinstein. Sc: James Gunn, based on George Romero's 1978 screenplay
Cast: Sarah Polley, Ving Rhames, Jake Weber, Mekhi Phifer, Ty Burrel

A full-throttle adrenalin ride into the clammy claustrophobia that made the original so terrifying, this delivers a pared down version of the story and squeezes great mileage out of the set-up as a small band of civilians led by Sarah Polley's resourceful nurse and Ving Rhames's police officer wait (hopelessly) in a shopping mall for help to arrive as the living dead mass outside, hungry for their flesh.

DAWN OF THE HEAD
2006, USA
Dir: Ivan. Prod: Tom Byron. Sc: Ivan
Cast: Gia Paloma, Angelina Bonet, Ashley Gracie, Genesis Skye, Memphis Monroe

This parody porn movie's title and advertising copy ("When Hell is full, the horny shall spank on Earth!") set the tone. Lots of hardcore sex as Z.i.P.S., aka the Zombie Patrol Squad, track down victims of a new zombie drug. Their motto? "We Serve. We Protect. We Bukkake if we have to!" A bizarre crossover between zombie horror and XXX filmmaking.

DAWN OF THE MUMMY
1981, USA
Alternative title: El despertar de la momia
Dir: Frank Agrama. Prod: Frank Agrama. Sc: Daria Price, Ronald Dobrin, Frank Agrama
Cast: Brenda King, Barry Sattels, George Peck, John Salvo, Ibrahim Khan

A bunch of insipid fashion models find themselves pursued by a rampaging mummy and his zombie minions in this gory but pointless attempt to blend the zombie and mummy cycles of the period. The mummy is an ancient pharaoh awakened from his tomb; his servants are bald, decomposing ghouls who rise up out of the desert sand. The gore's the main emphasis (the promise of sex is a red herring), although nothing here is particularly innovative or even well executed.

DAY OF THE DEAD
1985, USA
Alternative title: Zombie 2
Dir: George A. Romero. Prod: Richard P. Rubinstein. Sc: George A. Romero
Cast: Lori Cardille, Terry Alexander, Joseph Pilato, Jarlath Conroy, John Amplas.

It's the end of the world as we know it. A handful of survivors are desperately trying to find a cure for the fact that the dead won't stay dead. Hiding out in a missile silo, they bicker and fight with one another in a grim vision of apocalyptic dysfunction. The third movie in Romero's series is darker than the rest and considerably gorier, yet it has a remarkably upbeat ending.

DAY OF THE DEAD
2007, USA
Dir: Steve Miner. Prod: Boaz Davidson, James Glenn Dudelson, Randall Emmett, George Furla. Sc: Jeffrey Reddick
Cast: Mena Suvari, Nick Cannon, Michael Welch, AnnaLynne McCord, Stark Sands

Not a sequel to Universal's super-charged *Dawn of the Dead* remake, this lame outing from Taurus Entertainment reboots Romero's original for a shameless cash grab. It's a shadow of the earlier film and its hyper-kinetic, Spiderman-style zombies are totally daft. Mena Suvari stars as an army officer trapped in a small US town when a military bio-weapon turns the populace into zombies. Ving Rhames takes the Joe Pilato role – and gets to eat his own eyeball.

DAY OF THE DEAD 2: CONTAGIUM
2005, USA
Dir: Dir: Ana Clavell, James Glenn Dudelson. Prod: James Glenn Dudelson. Sc: Ryan Carrassi, Ana Clavell
Cast: Laurie Maria Baranyay, Steve Colosi, John F. Henry, Justin Ipock, Julian Thomas

Not a sequel, not a remake, not a prequel: what is *Day of the Dead 2: Contagium?* No one knows, least of all the filmmakers themselves. Bearing no link to Romero's movie, nor production company Taurus Entertainment's other *Day of the Dead* movie, this transparent attempt to rip off fans is set in a mental hospital where a virus turns patients into ghouls. Dire.

DAY X
2005, USA
Dir: Jason Hack. Prod: Julie Bounds. Sc: Jason Hack
Cast: Ken Edwards, Jason Brenizer, Caitlin Cagle, Blair Cox, Avi Hartman

More low-budget apocalyptic nonsense. Here an airborne virus called "Series 14" turns the world's population into burnt-looking ghouls. Shady government security driver Frank Chambers (Ken Edwards) hides out in a warehouse with a bunch of survivors who aren't too sure about his backpack full of guns or the injured blonde girl (Caitlin Cagle) he's carrying with him. The usual bicker-run-fight plotting is vaguely enlivened by Edwards's decision to throw himself into the material, a series of video diaries from a scientist working on the virus and Cagle's slightly bizarre Patient X who's immune to the virus and can stop the infected by biting them back. Never seen that in a zombie movie before.

THE DEAD
2010, UK
Dir: Howard J. Ford, Jon Ford. Prod: Howard J. Ford. Sc: Howard J. Ford, Jon Ford
Cast: Rob Freeman, Prince David Osei, David Dontoh, Ben Crowe, Glenn Salvage

Relocating the zombie apocalypse to West Africa this ambitious road movie follows two men – one American, one African – on a cross country road trip to safety. Making fantastic use of its locations, it is a visually stunning achievement with a retro Romero/Fulci vibe. One of the best zombie movies of the 2000s.

DEAD AIR
2009, USA
Dir: Corbin Bernsen. Prod: Chris Aronoff, Jesse Lawler, Corbin Bernsen. Sc: Kenny Yakkel

Cast: Bill Moseley, Patricia Tallman, Navid Negahban, David Moscow, Joshua Feinman

When Middle Eastern terrorists release a biological weapon at a basketball game in Los Angeles, shock jock Logan (Bill Moseley) and his team (including Patricia Tallman, who joined Moseley in the 1990 reboot of *Night of the Living Dead*) lock themselves in their radio station and continue broadcasting. Although it's pretty rudimentary, this TV-movie style horror is clumsily committed to its probing of America's post-9/11 psyche. The radio show set-up involves lots of citizen-journalist descriptions of off-screen atrocities, capturing the intimate feel of voicemails and 911 emergency recordings made by the victims of the WTC attacks. But it's no *Pontypool* and its ghouls – with bleeding eyes and demonic roars – aren't nearly scary enough.

DEAD & BREAKFAST
2004, USA
Dir: Matthew Leutwyler. Prod: E.J. Heiser, Jun Tan. Sc: Matthew Leutwyler
Cast: Ever Carradine, Brent David Fraser, Bianca Lawson, Jeffrey Dean Morgan, Erik Palladino

From the moment the distinctive comic book titles begin, you know that this teen horror is going to tick more than the usual boxes. And it does, with an outrageously funny "splatstick" vibe that's completely over the top. A group of more-likeable-than-usual teens stop off in a small town bed & breakfast (hence the terrible titular pun) and end up in all kinds of zombie trouble as a voodoo box and flesh-hungry Texans make their stay a misery. It's off-the-wall stuff with a rockabilly gas station attendant turned narrator who pops up to sing us through the plot developments, and more decapitations, amputations and chainsaw action than a Friday night shift in the Miskatonic University morgue. The zombies are redneck Texan ghouls who owe more to *Deliverance* than Romero and have the added benefit of still being able to talk: "Hey David," mischievously shouts one of the kids turned living dead, "did you ever tell Sara that you fucked my cousin?"

DEAD & BURIED
1981, USA
Dir: Gary A. Sherman. Prod: Ronald Shusett, Robert

Fentress. Sc: Ronald Shusett, Dan O'Bannon
Cast: James Farentino, Melody Anderson, Jack Albertson, Dennis Redfield, Lisa Blount

More North American small town zombie chaos as local sheriff Dan Gillis (Farentino) investigates a spate of murders in the sleepy community of Potters Bluff. As tourists are killed in strange and brutal ways, Gillis eventually tracks the murders back to the townsfolk themselves and discovers some rather nasty truths about his wife. The chief villain is William G. Dobbs, the town's undertaker; to say any more would spoil all the fun.

DEAD & DEADER
2006, USA
Dir: Patrick Dinhut. Prod: Mark A. Altman, Mark Gottwald, Chuck Speed. Sc: Steven Kriozere, Mark A. Altman
Cast: Dean Cain, Susan Ward, Guy Torry, Peter Greene, Natassia Malthe

A squad of US special forces soldiers in Cambodia are infected by zombifying scorpions that burrow under the skin in this SyFy TV movie. Returning home, Green Beret Lt Bobby Quinn (Dean Cain) finds himself transformed into a zombie Wolverine – he's got no pulse but he's super strong and self-heals. The rest of his squad aren't so lucky, they're just green-goo-dribbling zombies. As the authorities close in, Quinn goes AWOL from Fort Preston army base with motormouth chef (Guy Torry) and a hot barmaid (Susan Ward). Much knockabout bro horror humour ensues and for added annoyance it's laced with sub-Tarantino pop culture chatter about *Star Wars* and superheroes (Cain played Supes on TV in *Lois & Clark*). Eventually Peter Greene pops up and reveals the body burrowing scorpions are a yucky version of the fountain of eternal youth. Not nearly as much fun as it thinks it is.

DEAD & ROTTING
2002, USA
Dir: David P. Barton. Prod: Trent Haaga. Sc: Douglas Snauffer, David P. Barton
Cast: Stephen O'Mahoney, Tom Hoover, Debbie Rochon, Trent Haaga, Jeff Dylan Graham

Tempe Entertainment and Full Moon Pictures

team up for this low-budget zombie horror produced by Trent Haaga (*Deadgirl*). When a trio of blue collar workers (Stephen O'Mahony, Trent Haaga, Tom Hoover) assault a local inbred kid, his witch mother (Barbara Katz-Norrod) curses them with some black magic. Transforming herself into a sexy seductress (Debbie Rochon) the wizened crone seduces the men and curses them to turn into rotting zombies. A modern day Poverty Row production.

DEAD BEFORE DAWN 3D
2012, CANADA
Dir: April Mullen. Prod: Tom Doiron, April Mullen. Sc: Tom Doiron
Cast: Devon Bostick, Martha MacIsaac, Christopher Lloyd, Brandon Jay McLaren, Brittany Allen

When nerdy Casper (Devon Bostick, the nameless kid from *Survival of the Dead*) looks after an occult store for the afternoon, there's one simple rule: don't touch the urn containing a demon spirit or bad things will happen. He does. They do. The rest of this lightweight Canadian high school zom-com unfolds painlessly enough as Casper and his mates fight off zombie demons. Christopher Lloyd gives the comedy a bit of juice as Casper's granddad, and director April Mullen (the first female helmer to shoot in stereoscopic 3D, apparently) and screenwriter Tom Doiron take roles in front of the camera too.

THE DEAD CAN'T DANCE
2011, USA
Dir: Rodrick Pocowatchit. Prod: Rodrick Pocowatchit, Deanie Eaton. Sc: Rodrick Pocowatchit
Cast: Rodrick Pocowatchit, Guy Ray Pocowatchit, T.J. Williams, Randall Aviks, Wade Hampton

Native Americans Dax (writer-director Rodrick Pocowatchit) and his brother Ray (Guy Ray Pocowatchit, his real life sibling) are on a road trip with Ray's son (T.J. Williams) when a mysterious event turns all the white people in Kansas into dumb ghouls. It turns out that Native American blood is immune to the plague – a delicious irony that feckless, but racially proud, Comanche Ray wastes no time in pouncing upon: "We were the first ones here. We'll be the last ones to leave. That's poetic justice." Heading for a rescue station, the family learns a hard lesson about the ties that bind and what it means to survive. Described by its director as a Native American *Shaun of the Dead*, this goes for laughs with scenes set in a zombified strip club and a horde attack in a kid's playground. But it's a shame that the zombies – including a gormless, radio-loving ghoul dubbed Stupid (Wade Hampton) – are barely able to take themselves seriously.

DEAD COUNTRY
2008, AUSTRALIA
Dir: Andrew Merkelbach. Prod: Andrew Merkelbach. Sc: Anthony Davis, Clifford Hoeft, Kaye Redhead
Cast: Ted V. Mikels, Gia Paloma, Rob Kellum, Andrew Merkelbach

Backyard filmmaking Australian style: when an intergalactic criminal who looks (if you squint a lot) like fat Elvis lands on Earth, his spaceship inadvertently causes the dead to walk in the Outback town of Romero. Zombie extras, including a Santa ghoul drooling at a girl with her top off, stumble around and occasionally get bashed by nunchucks. It's scrappy and dull and spawned an unnecessary sequel *Deader Country* (2008). The alien visitor is played by filmmaker Andrew Merkelbach who also ropes in Ted V. Mikels, of *The Astro-Zombies* infamy, for a cameo.

DEAD CREATURES
2001, UK
Dir: Andrew Parkinson. Prod: Andrew Parkinson, Jason Shepherd. Sc: Andrew Parkinson
Cast: Beverley Wilson, Antonia Beamish, Brendan Gregory, Anna Swift, Bart Ruspoli

A group of women infected with the same unexplained virus from Parkinson's earlier film *I, Zombie* struggle with the knowledge that they're facing inevitable zombiedom. Posing as prostitutes they occasionally bludgeon johns and carve up their corpses – operating more out of necessity than pleasure. Adding to their woes is the fact that they're being tracked by a self-styled zombie hunter who wants to eradicate the plague before it spreads even further. British zombie miserabilism – a Ken Loach movie with ghouls.

THE DEAD DON'T DIE

1975, USA
Dir: Curtis Harrington. Prod: Henry Colman. Sc: Robert Bloch
Cast: George Hamilton, Ray Milland, Linda Cristal, Ralph Meeker, Joan Blondell

Robert "*Psycho*" Bloch scripted this zombie TV movie. George Hamilton stars as a man in 1930s Chicago trying to uncover the truth behind his brother's conviction for murder most foul. Lots of shenanigans involving reanimated dead bodies ensue and, although the movie never quite lives up to its screenwriter's pedigree, there's a scary moment in a funeral home where the dead just won't die.

DEAD DUDES IN THE HOUSE
1991, USA
Alternative titles: The Dead Come Home, The House on Tombstone Hill
Dir: Jim Riffel. Prod: Jim Riffel, Melissa Lawes, Marc Bladis. Sc: Jim Riffel
Cast: Mark Zobian, Victor Verhaeghe, Douglas F. Gibson, Naomi Kooker, John Cerna, Sarah Newhouse

A group of kids fixing up a dilapidated, cursed house discover that neither the building nor its previous owner – a creepy looking old lady (Douglas F. Gibson, in *Mrs Doubtfire* drag) – are ready for it to be repossessed. They're killed off one by one in a variety of gruesome ways, then their mangled bodies are resurrected as sarcastic zombies to menace the others. "I often wondered what goes on inside that head and now I'm going to find out," one dead dude tells his terrified girlfriend. "I'm going to take that piece of wood and bash your skull in and take a look-see." There's much body trauma with carpentry tools but not a lot else, and the kids' clothes date it terribly.

DEADER COUNTRY
2010, AUSTRALIA
Dir: Andrew Merkelbach. Prod: Andrew Merkelbach
Sc: Andrew Merkelbach, Ben Trebilcook
Cast: Ted V. Mikels, Gia Paloma, Rob Kellum, Andrew Merkelbach, Ben Trebilcook

More walking dead alien nonsense in the Australian Outback: this sequel is less coherent, features more writhing, tattooed ladies and sees the return of filmmaker Andrew Merkelbach and his trenchcoat. This time there's a plan to transport the zombies to the moon but what's more unbelievable is that Merkelbach manages to convince so many actresses to strip for his camera. Either there's a lack of things to do in Victoria, Australia or he pays them a lot of money.

DEAD GENESIS
2010, USA
Dir: Reese Eveneshen. Prod: Reese Evenshen, Justin Dmitruk, Peter Szabo. Sc: Reese Eveneshen
Cast: Emily Alatalo, Lionel Boodlal, Colin Paradine, Erin Stuart, Tom Parkinson

Documentary filmmaker Jillian (Emily Alatalo) gets more than she bargained for when she heads out to the front line of the war against the zombies (which it turns out is, rather curiously, a pretty deserted forest). Teaming up with a group of guerrillas Jillian tries to make a film about the War On Dead to buoy the civilian population holed up in the few remaining cities, but finds more questions than answers. Writer-director Reese Eveneshen sets up an interesting world then lets it all fall apart as budget constraints and a lack of purpose leave this running-around-the-woods outing less than the sum of its parts.

DEADGIRL
2008, USA
Dir: Marcel Sarmiento, Gadi Harel. Co-Prod: Cynthia Graner. Sc: Trent Haaga
Cast: Shiloh Fernandez, Noah Segan, Candice Accola, Eric Podnar, Jenny Spain

The evil that horny men do… A bunch of emasculated high school kids find a zombie woman chained up in an abandoned hospital. Do they rescue her? Kill her? Try to help her? Nope, they rape her. Repeatedly. This provocative indie zombie movie puts masculinity under the microscope. It's not your usual zombie movie. Before this, screenwriter and prolific deadhead Trent Haaga scripted Feeding the Masses (2004), co-starred in The Ghouls (2003) and produced and co-starred in Dead & Rotting (2002).

THE DEAD HATE THE LIVING!
1999, USA

Dir: Dave Parker. Prod: Kirk Edward Hanson, Dana Scanlan. Sc: Dave Parker
Cast: Eric Clawson, Jamie Donahue, Brett Beardslee, Wendy Speake

"Kids would race to see a living dead movie with a real corpse in it. It would be the ultimate!" Pitched somewhere between *Children Shouldn't Play with Dead Things* (1972), *The House of Seven Corpses* (1973) and *Rise of the Damned* (2011), this self-reflexive horror movie is set in an abandoned hospital where aspiring filmmakers discover a real dead body and decide to use it in their horror flick, only to unleash Dr Eibon (Matt Stephens, channelling Rob Zombie) and his ghoul horde. Wearing his horror cred on his sleeve, writer-director Dave Parker follows the write-what-you-know rule and tries to give us z-cinema's answer to *Scream* as characters riff on genre lore ("He's going to be the next David Warbeck…"). Parker went on to script the *House of the Dead* (2003) – perhaps the very definition of one step forwards, two steps back.

DEADHEADS
2011, USA
Dir: Brett Pierce, Drew T. Pierce. Prod: Andy Drummond, Brett Pierce, Drew T. Pierce, Kevin Van Hagen. Sc: Brett Pierce, Drew T. Pierce
Cast: Michael McKiddy, Ross Kidder, Markus Taylor, Thomas Galasso, Natalie Victoria

"In a world of putrid zombie movies, *Deadheads* is a breath of fresh air!" reckoned Bruce Campbell and who's going to argue with The Chin? Following a pair of cognisant zombies (Michael McKiddy and Ross Kidder) who wake up, find themselves dead and become bickering buddies, this knockabout comedy road movie plays like a living dead answer to John Hughes. Early scenes get good mileage out of these two zombies being the only thinkers among the mass of braindead brain-munchers and replay a *Night of the Living Dead* siege with its two chief ghouls trying to pass unnoticed inside the barricades. Supporting characters – like bumbling zombie giant Cheese (Markus Taylor) and a cracked 'Nam vet (Harry Burkey) – give it life, while the rom-com plotting adds (against the odds) some heart. Good fun.

DEAD HEAT
1988, USA
Dir: Mark Goldblatt. Prod: Michael Meltzer, David Helpern. Sc: Terry Black
Cast: Treat Williams, Joe Piscopo, Lindsay Frost, Darren McGavin, Vincent Price

It sounds like 1980s video trash, it looks like 1980s video trash, and by God it *is* 1980s video trash. Starring none other than Treat Williams, an actor who could teach Rutger Hauer a few things or two about bad movies, this living dead buddy picture plays like a zombie *Lethal Weapon* (it's written by Terry Black, brother of Shane). Williams and Piscopo are cop partners with a difference – Detective Roger Mortis (Williams) is recently deceased and has been resurrected. He has only a few hours to work out why the city is being overrun by bizarre zombies. Totally ridiculous – check out the zombie Peking duck attacking our heroes in a Chinese restaurant – this trashy cheesefest is silly enough to have attained cult status. It was undoubtedly a huge influence on *R.I.P.D.* (which makes me like it even less).

DEAD HEIST
2007, USA
Dir: Bo Webb. Prod: David Eubanks, James Register. Sc: Anghus Houvouras, Eric Tomosunas
Cast: Big Daddy Kane, Brandon Hardin, DJ Naylor, Dominic L. Santana, E-40

Dawg! Nigga! Wassup? If *Boyz 'n' the Hood* had zombies in it, this Florida-shot, modern day blaxploitation horror might play like a me-too imitator. When a bunch of street corner gangbangers storm a small town bank, hotheaded crew leader Ski (Brandon Hardin) and one-last-job veteran Jackson (DJ Naylor, a dead ringer for a gone-to-seed Vin Diesel) are trapped inside while zombie/vampires roam outside. The first 45 minutes of this urban thriller is enjoyably badass. As soon as the ghouls arrive, though, it unravels into nonsense. "These things have been slowly travelling South," explains an anonymous ex-government scientist/homie known only as Hunter (Big Daddy Kane) as he witters on about ghouls, new moons, blood experiments and his dead wife. Riiiigghhht… Director Bo Webb clearly thinks he's making the zombie version of *Blade*. Who's going to break the bad news to him?

DEADHUNTER: SEVILLIAN ZOMBIES
2005, SPAIN
Dir: Julián Lara. Prod: Julián Lara. Sc: Julián Lara
Cast: Beatriz Mateo, María Miñagorri, Julián Lara,
José Manuel Gómez, Jesús Gallardo

Zombies roam the streets of Seville, tracked by a squad of "deadhunters" in this amateur Spanish video outing. Shot guerrilla style with limited special effects (the heroes' guns shake a lot when shot, but don't actually fire) this doesn't take itself too seriously. Spanish celeb Leonardo Dantés makes a cameo to distracts some zombies with his famous "El baile del pañuelo" (The Handkerchief Dance).

THE DEAD INSIDE
2013, UK
Dir: Andrew Gilbert. Prod: Andrew Gilbert, Julian Hundy. Sc: Andrew Gilbert, Julian Hundy
Cast: Luke Hobson, Nicky Paul Barton, Roger Fowler, Samuel Hogarth, Elizabeth Quinn

Shot for £15,000 by misappropriating the filmmakers' student loans, *The Dead Inside* is undoubtedly a remarkable achievement for its young crew. But it's a fairly interminable 116 minutes for viewers thanks to stilted dialogue and its non-professional cast. A night out turns sour for Tom (Nicky Paul Barton) and his mates when a bunch of ghouls storm out of the men's toilets and overrun the city. As a by-the-numbers on-the-cheap apocalypse quickly unfolds, the kids take shelter in a school with a few cut-off-from-their-unit squaddies. It's *28 Days Later* reimagined by a bunch of GCSE Media Studies students.

DEAD IN THE WATER
2006, USA
Dir: Marc Buhmann. Prod: Emily Faith Cook, Jennifer Hellwig, Cannon Kinnard. Sc: David Moore
Cast: Alissa Bailey, Megan Renee Burgess, Mike Parrish, Bill Zasadil, Jacob Paque

"We're under attack from zombies! It's fucking *Thriller* out there!" An isolated lake cabin... A group of barely-likeable 20 somethings... A bunch of zombies emerging from the murky depths...

This plodding, straight-to-DVD indie zombie thriller feels over-familiar, although it does throw a couple of curve balls into its mix. The zombies are a boat load of Christian campers who drowned on the lake and are now coming back from the murky depths to recover a lost ring. The living fall in and out of love, argue a lot, reveal past rape trauma, and basically fail as human beings as the zombies attack. For novelty value, the zombies are slowed down by people reciting the Lord's Prayer (or are they?). Shame the ironic movie geekiness in the script – "Please do not get all Frodo on me, OK?" – is so grating.

DEADLANDS: THE RISING
2006, USA
Dir: Gary Ugarek. Prod: Lisa Brandt, Brian Wright, Gary Ugarek. Sc: Gary Ugarek
Cast: Dave Cooperman, Gary Ugarek, Michelle Wright, Brian Wright, Connor Brandt

Backyard filmmaking nonsense from Baltimore: after a bio-weapon hits the US and zombie stumble about, a few survivors must... well, survive. As a viewer, I know how they feel. Clocking in at just 61 minutes this fragmented and tired-looking micro-budget effort has little to recommend it unless you're one of the filmmaker's family. Amateur actors voice bad dialogue about whether to go ask the dentally-challenged gas station attendant the way to the rescue station or not and, in an unintentionally funny scene, a cop warns a homeowner to close her windows because there's rioting going on nearby. It spawned a better sequel *Deadlands 2: Trapped* (2008).

DEADLANDS 2: TRAPPED
2008, USA
Dir: Gary Ugarek. Prod: Gary Ugarek, Chris Kiros, Elias Dancey. Sc: Gary Ugarek
Cast: Jim Krut, Joseph D. Durbin, Christopher L. Clark, Josh Davidson, Ashley Young

"It has the potential of taking over its host... even beyond the point of death!" Scientists prepping a nefarious new bio-weapon refuse to wait 60 days for further tests before running a live test on unsuspecting civilians under the Pentagon's watchful eye. And – wouldn't you know it? – it turns everyone into zombies. Baltimore filmmaker

Gary Ugarek ups his game in this bigger, more polished sequel to/reboot of *Deadlands: The Rising* (2006) with our heroes are trapped in a cinema as ghouls attack. But a better screenplay might have saved us from the clichéd survivor drama.

DEAD LIFE
2004, USA

Dir: William Victor Schotten. Prod: Joseph J. Zetts. Sc: William Victor Schotten
Cast: Michael Hanton, Joseph J. Zetts, Ashleigh Holeman, Jayson Garity, Bruce Taylor

"Tell you what man... Dave hit that sonuvabitch over the head with a frying pan and he still kept coming!" An outbreak of a zombifying strain of Necrotising Fasciitis M ravages a Midwest neighbourhood in this DIY effort that resembles its corpses – shambolic and lifeless, but refusing to give up. As the ghouls attack, a bunch of guys sitting on lawn chairs put down their six packs and fight back. The zombies shake their heads violently – possibly trying to keep up with the throbbing speed metal that scores the whole sorry movie. Some kinetic editing tricks try to jazz things up, but look out of place given that this impenetrably murky movie seems to have been shot on an 8mm camera dating back to the Soviet era. Meanwhile, the inevitable penis munching scene is handled with distressing enthusiasm by all concerned.

THE DEAD LIVE
2004, USA

Dir: Darrin Brent Patterson. Prod: Darrin Brent Patterson. Sc: Darrin Brent Patterson
Cast: Tom Hughes, Mike "Joe Joe Little" Jones, Emily Hughes Jr., Brandy Patterson, Mike Berube

When a TV news crew at a hostage siege witness the dead starting to walk, an ambitious young journo (Emily Hughes) realises she's got one hell of a scoop and heads out to the mortuary to follow up her lead. Bad idea. So is enduring this amateurishly acted, shot and plotted zombie apocalypse from Ohio that redefines the scope of the word incompetent (and would probably spell it wrong for good measure). It's notable only for drawing silly comparisons between its backyard action and 9/11 in its end credits. It ends with a SWAT officer gunning down an All-American zombie cheerleader with a shout of "Let's roll!" before threatening "To Be Continued ???" Please, sweet Jesus, no.

DEADLY FRIEND
1986, USA

Dir: Wes Craven. Prod: Robert M. Sherman. Sc: Bruce Joel Rubin
Cast: Matthew Labyorteaux, Kristy Swanson, Michael Sharrett, Anne Twomey, Anne Ramsey

Bedroom scientist Paul (Matthew Labyorteaux) brings his girlfriend back to life as a robot zombie after her nasty dad kills her in a fit of rage. He sticks a microchip in her brain and hey-presto the appliance of science keeps the grave at bay and gives her the opportunity to kill off a few of the enemies she made while alive. Craven was definitely having an off day when he agreed to helm this little chiller filler, although it racks up some bad movie value. Paul's *Short Circuit* style yellow robot is hilariously cheesy; the nonsensical twist ending is all kinds of wrong; and the now-restored basketball to the head death scene is a gory treat.

THE DEADLY ORGAN
1965, ARGENTINA

Original title: Placer sangriento
Alternative title: Feast of Flesh

"A real man, so groovy... A whole man... But that haunting music...!" A maniac in a zombie mask is preying on young girls, turning them into his sex slaves using hypnotic organ music in this lurid, if rather plodding, 1960s exploitation outing. Made in Argentina, and later dubbed into English and released in the US, it's a time capsule of the psychedelic era. After the Love Drug killer's used and abused victims are found dead with hypodermics sticking out of their chests, the police investigate and interrogate one near-victim after dosing her up with lysergic acid! Full of salacious sexual interludes it's a hysterical warning about the dangers of sex, drugs and rock 'n' roll. No, wait... sex, drugs and wah-wah organ music. A downer like that is enough to give anyone a bad trip.

DEAD MEAT
2004, IRELAND

Dir: Conor McMahon. Prod: Edward King. Sc: Conor McMahon

Cast: Marian Araujo, David Muyllaert, Eoin Whelan, David Ryan

Billed as the first ever Irish zombie movie – although it came ten years after the largely forgotten *Zombie Genocide* (1993) – Conor McMahon tapped into early 2000s anxieties about mad's cow disease, foot and mouth and contaminated food products. As an infection spreads through the Irish countryside turning people into homicidal ghouls, Helena (Marian Araujo) is trapped in the wilds and teams up with a gravedigger (David Muyllaert) and a potty-mouthed coach (Eoin Whelan, who also starred in McMahon's short *The Braineater*). Playing to the fan audience – producer Ed King founded Dublin's annual Horrorthon – this expertly delivers the gory goods as vacuum cleaners are shoved in zombies' faces and shovels are embedded in their heads. Modest but fun.

DEAD MEN DON'T DIE
1990, USA
Dir: Malcolm Marmorstein. Prod: Wayne Marmorstein. Sc: Malcolm Marmorstein
Cast: Elliott Gould, Mark Moses, Philip Bruns, Mabel King, Melissa Anderson

Dead men might not die, but Elliott Gould's career sure goes into cardiac arrest in this abysmal comedy about a TV anchorman who's killed by gangsters. Conveniently, he's brought back to life as a zombie by a black cleaning lady with voodoo powers and goes live on the air and flushes out his killers. Ghastly.

DEAD MEN WALKING
2005, USA
Dir: Peter Mervis. Prod: David Latt, David Rimawi, Sherri Strain. Sc: Mike Watt
Cast: Bay Bruner, Brick Firestone, Chriss Anglin, James Ferris, Robert James

"I do not enjoy shooting staff members, godammit!" This Asylum movie offers great twist on the standard zombie virus patient zero storyline as a newly-infected victim (Brandon Stacy) is arrested and locked up in Harwood Maximum Security Prison. On his trail is Sam(antha) Beckett (Bay Bruner) from the CDC, who's worried he's been exposed to an experimental biotoxin. Before you know it, the prison guards are overrun by blood spitting ghouls and the Federal Emergency Management Agency is freaking out. Ugly production design, bad lighting and a shortage of cash don't help this cheapo effort convince. But it throws itself into its cell block riot of the raging dead with gusto. I'm guessing the filmmakers were familiar with *Zombie Death House* (1988).

THE DEAD MILE
2012, CANADA
Dir: K.J. Kleefeld. Prod: K.J. Kleefeld. Sc: K.J. Kleefeld
Cast: Shawn Roe, Krystle Mintonye, Sean Dykink, Wade Sun, Julia Kruis

It was inevitable that an enterprising indie filmmaker was eventually going to realise that a zombie walk is the perfect cost-cutting opportunity to shoot a lot of zombies. Filmed at Calgary's annual zombie walk this harmless zom-com follows comic store clerk Tyler (Shawn Roe) and his friends who're trapped on the streets when a real-life zombie infects the ketchup-spattered walkers. How meta is that? Sadly it's a one gag movie, yet it lumbers along innocently enough and sets up a novel finale at a hockey ring as zombies slip and slide across the ice.

DEAD MINE
2011, INDONESIA
Dir: Steven Sheil. Prod: Catherine Davila, Daniel Davila, Nick North, Mike Wiluan Sc: Steven Sheil, Ziad Semaan
Cast: Miki Mizuno, Sam Hazeldine, Ario Bayu, Les Loveday, Carmen Soo

The Descent meets Nazi zombies in this Indonesian-shot B-movie about a group of treasure seekers who discover a WWII Japanese bunker hidden in an abandoned mine. Deep inside, the Japanese army has been breeding Imperial Guard super soldiers. A competent B-movie from the man who directed British kitchen sink horror *Mum & Dad*.

DEAD MOON RISING
2007, USA
Dir: Mark E. Poole. Prod: Mark E. Poole. Sc: Mark E.

Poole
Cast: Jason Crowe, Mike Seely, Erica Goldsmith, Gary Williams, Tucky Williams

Proudly boasting "the largest zombie scene ever filmed" this Louisville indie zom-com is small in every other way. At the Cheapskate Car Rental office manager and narrator Jim (Jason Crowe) gets a break from disciplining his customer-baiting team when a zombie apocalypse breaks out. While Jim talks straight to camera, a few survivors band together in the usual fashion, tooling up with weapons including an Arnie style mini-gun. The zombie horde scene comes as a pack of bikers take on the zombies on the city's streets. It apparently features 1,200 extras – which is an incredible logistical achievement. Otherwise, though, this is standard backyard filmmaking.

THE DEAD NEXT DOOR
1989, USA
Dir: J.R. Bookwalter. Prod: J.R. Bookwalter. Sc: J.R. Bookwalter
Cast: Peter Ferry, Bogdan "Don" Pecic, Michael Grossi, Jolie Jackunas

Ripping off Romero, backyard filmmaker J.R. Bookwalter presents us with a post-apocalyptic America in which zombies have been unleashed by a viral outbreak. Zombie Squads have been despatched to try and stem the tide of the living dead, but they're fighting a losing battle. Meanwhile, scientists are trying to find a cure for the virus and a weird redneck religious cult is planning to put the dead to alternative uses. Gory, cheap and silly.

DEAD NOON
2007, USA
Dir: Andrew Wiest. Prod: Marianne Myers, Matthew Taggart. Sc: Keith Suta, Matthew Taggart, Andrew Wiest
Cast: Kane Hodder, Robert Bear, Scott Phillips, Elizabeth Mouton, Robert Andrus

After an infamous rootin', tootin' bad guy called, um… Frank (Robert Bear) beats the devil at poker, he demands a little more fun before his soul burns in hell for eternity. So, zombie gunfighters and sub-Harryhausen CG skeletons head back to our time to take revenge on the descendant of the original sheriff who sent Frank to Boot Hill. Really it's little more than an excuse for flashy filmmaker Andrew Weist to show off what he can do with some self-taught green screen effects and fast-paced editing. No movie with flaming skull zombie gunslingers has any right to be this dull.

THE DEAD ONE
1961, USA
Alternative title: Blood of the Zombie
Dir: Barry Mahon. Prod: Barry Mahon. Sc: Barry Mahon
Cast: John McKay, Linda Ormond, Monica Davis, Clyde Kelly, Darlene Myrick

Belly dancers, voodoo superstition and a honeymoon on a New Orleans plantation pad out this threadbare and thoroughly stilted early 1960s effort. Newlyweds played by MacKay and Ormond find their passion thwarted when a jealous cousin raises a ghoul from the dead to kill them. The pallid zombie mistakes a belly dancer for the bride and murders her, alerting the real targets to the danger.

THE DEAD OUTSIDE
2009, UK
Dir: Kerry Anne Mullaney. Prod: Kris R. Bird. Sc: Kerry Anne Mullaney, Kris R. Bird
Cast: Alton Milne, Sandra Louise Douglas, Sharon Osdin, Vivienne Harvey

There are few female filmmakers in this book, so *The Dead Outside* is notable for being directed and co-written by Kerry Anne Mullaney, making her feature debut. Set in the wilds of Scotland, this lo-fi British outing pares down the usual post-apocalyptic set up as a man and two women find themselves thrown together on an isolated farm while infected ghouls wander outside. Concentrating on the psychological effects of the apocalypse, this micro-budget character piece delivers a moody rural ambiance and some solid jump shocks. It's undermined by confusing editing and a sense of over-familiarity as its characters descend into loneliness and madness.

THE DEAD PIT
1989, USA

Dir: Brett Leonard. Prod: Gimel Everett. Sc: Brett
Leonard, Gimel Everett
Cast: Cheryl Lawson, Danny Gochnauer, Stephen
Gregory Foster, Jeremy Slate, Joan Bechtel

A surreal nightmare of a movie, the only thing
that's really scary about this is just how bad it is.
The spirit of ghastly Dr Ramzi haunts a creepy
insane asylum. He used to perform bizarre
experiments on the inmates but now he's after
patient Jane Doe (she can't remember her real
name) – despite the fact that he's been dead for two
decades. He eventually gives up the ghost (so to
speak) and brings his long dead victims back to life
as zombies to wander through the hallways instead.

DEAD SEASON
2012, USA
Alternate title: Running Dead
Dir: Adam Deyoe. Prod: Adam Deyoe, Loren Semmens.
Sc: Adam Deyoe, Josh Klausner, Loren Semmens
Cast: Scott Peat, Marissa Merrill, James C. Burns,
Corsica Wilson, Marc L. Fusco

When sledgehammer wielding survivor Elvis (Scott
Peat) and Tweeter (Marissa Merrill) escape Florida
on a boat headed for a Caribbean island, they get
more than they bargained for. The island isn't safe
– it used to be a military testing ground, it's
irradiated to hell, there are "walkers" and it's run
by a collective of former soldiers running low on
food and willing to eat anything. Yes, anything.
Competently made, if relentlessly bleak, this low-
budget indie makes the most of its Puerto Rico
locations which compensates for the ropey script
and tired the-living-are-more-dangerous-than-the-
dead theme.

DEAD SET
2008, UK
Dir: Yann Demange. Sc: Charlie Brooker
Cast: Jaime Winstone, Andy Nyman, Kevin Eldon,
Adam Deacon, Davina McCall

"Big Brother House, this is Davina. You are live on
Channel 4. Please do not swear." Written by
Guardian columnist, professional TV cynic and
committed deadhead Charlie Brooker, this Channel
4 TV series riffs on the *Big Brother* reality show as
the BB house becomes the only sanctuary during

an outbreak of the living dead. Spread over five
episodes it's full of gory zombie action but also
plenty of satirical swipes at a TV culture that turns
viewers, contestants and media suits into braindead
ghouls. Iconic *Big Brother* presenter Davina
McCall's game agreement to play along, and be
zombified, gives it extra bite.

DEAD SNOW
2009, NORWAY
Original title: Død Snø
Dir: Tommy Wirkola. Prod: Terje Strømstad, Tomas
Evjen. Sc: Tommy Wirkola, Stig Frode Henriksen
Cast: Vegar Hoel, Stig Frode Henriksen, Charlotte
Frogner, Lasse Valdal, Evy Kasseth Røsten

Norway delivers comic book Nazi zombies in this
crowd pleasing horror. Director Tommy Wirkola
later parlayed its success into a Hollywood career
on *Hansel & Gretel: Witch Hunters* (2013) but
cared enough to return for *Dead Snow: Red Vs
Dead* (2014).

DEAD SUSHI
2012, JAPAN
Original title: Deddo Sushi
Dir: Noboru Iguchi. Prod: Motohisa Nagata, Yoichi
Sakai, Mana Fukui. Sc: Noboru Iguchi
Cast: Rina Takeda, Kentaro Shimazu, Kanji Tsuda, Toru
Tezuka, Takamasa Suga

Killer sushi goes on the rampage as director
Noboru Iguchi – *Zombie Ass: The Toilet of the
Dead* (2011) – delivers the first zombie sushi
movie. The plot is nothing more than a peg to hang
the outrageous concept on: shy Keiko (Rina
Takeda) offends her sushi chef dad with her poor
culinary skills and is sent to work as a waitress in
an inn where the food unexpectedly comes to life.
Typically bonkers J-splatter moments – like a
woman who thinks she's taking a hot shower but is
actually being geysered by arterial spray from a
decapitated body – pale into insignificance when
compared to the sight of zombie sushi flying
through the air with a desire to kill. Oh and did I
mention there's a giant fish-head zombie and a
flying California roll battleship? Tuck in.

THE DEAD UNDEAD
2010, USA

Dir: Matthew R. Anderson, Edward Conna. Prod: Edward Conna, Matthew R. Anderson, Edward Plumb. Sc: Edward Conna
Cast: Luke Goss, Cameron Goodman, Joshua Alba, Johnny Pacar, Laura Kenley

Not vampires. Not zombies. What are they? According to Luke Goss's vampire soldier his prey are "ZeeVees". Well that's a new one. Don't expect much sense from this confused action horror B-movie in which a team of tooled-up vampire soldiers (veterans of conflicts from the Viking Wars to Vietnam, apparently) hunt down the ZeeVee ghouls. A bunch of kids in a motel are caught in the crossfire as the two supernatural sides duke it out in tiresome fashion – the pumped up, special forces vamps bringing big automatic guns to the party. Not vampires, not zombies, not ZeeVees, just Zzzzzzzs.

DEATH WARMED UP
1984, NEW ZEALAND
Dir: David Blyth. Prod: Murray Newey. Sc: David Blyth, Michael Heath
Cast: Michael Hurst, Gary Day, Margaret Umbers, Norelle Scott, William Upjohn

It may be confusing, but there's a memorable nastiness to David Blyth's island-set tale in which a mad neurosurgeon operates on people's brains, turning them into zombie killers. Maybe it's just the Kiwi accents, or maybe it's the wall-to-wall splatter that gives this otherwise silly outing a bit of an edge. Scarily, director Blyth graduated to the *Mighty Morphin' Power Rangers* TV series.

DEATHDREAM
1972, USA/CANADA
Alternative titles: Dead of Night, The Night Andy Came Home
Dir: Bob Clark. Prod: Bob Clark. Sc: Alan Ormsby
Cast: John Marley, Lynn Carlin, Henderson Forsythe, Richard Backus, Anya Ormsby

The follow-up to *Children Shouldn't Play With Dead Things* is a very different beast. Focussing on the Vietnam experience, Clark and Ormsby follow dead war veteran Andy, who's willed back to life by his desperate mother. He returns home as a blood-drinking ghoul and proceeds to leave a trail of death and destruction in his hometown. Throwaway horror comedy or poignant Vietnam-era satire?

DECAY
2012, UK
Dir: Luke Thompson, Michael Mazur. Prod: Michael Mazur, Luke Thompson, Burton De Wilde. Sc: Luke Thompson
Cast: Zoë Hatherell, Tom Procter, Stewart Martin-Haugh, Sara Mahmoud, William P. Martin

Shot at the CERN facility in Switzerland by Ph.D. students who were part of the search to discover the Higgs boson, this zombie movie is definitely a one-off. Sadly, it's also pretty amateurish with its non-professional cast and crew struggling to bring the story of zombies created by radiation from the Large Hadron Collider to life. The setting is atmospheric and memorable; the rest of the movie isn't much. Newsflash: particle physicists can't act. Who'd have thunk it?

DELLAMORTE DELLAMORE
1993, ITALY/FRANCE
Alternative title: Cemetery Man
Dir: Michele Soavi. Prod: Tilde Corsi, Giovanni Romoli, Heinz Bibo, Michele Soavi. Sc: Gianni Romoli
Cast: Rupert Everett, François Hadji-Lazaro, Anna Falchi, Mickey Knox, Fabiana Formica

Rupert Everett is an incongruous lead in this belated – but masterful – addition to the Italian zombie cycle. A caretaker at the Buffalora Cemetery, he faces a regular onslaught of "Returners" who need to be dispatched with dumdum bullets. Easily one of the best zombie films of the 1990s and the pinnacle of spaghetti zombie movies.

THE DEMENTED
2012, USA
Dir: Christopher Roosevelt. Prod: Shirley Craig, Steven R. Monroe, Danny Roth, Damiano Tucci, Christine Holder, Mark Holder. Sc: Christopher Roosevelt
Cast: Sarah Butler, Kayla Ewell, Richard Kohnke, Brittney Alger, Ashlee Brian

Horny rich teens down in the bayou find their weekend rudely interrupted when unknown terrorists launch ballistic missiles at the Gulf Coast. What a bummer. It gets worse: a bio-weapon in the warheads turns the citizens of Louisiana into bloodthirsty ghouls who're attracted by sound (a rare moment of originality) and want to chomp on these trust fund babies. As the military quarantines the area, the kids must race to the nearby university for a (implausible) helicopter extraction – a run and dodge sequence that delivers one good scare as they inch through a corridor of dormant zombies who're waiting for a sound to wake them. Otherwise, it's by-the-numbers, straight-to-DVD guff.

DEMONS
1985, ITALY
Original title: Demoni
Dir: Lamberto Bava. Prod: Dario Argento. Sc: Dario Argento, Lamberto Bava, Dardano Sacchetti, Franco Ferrini
Cast: Urbano Barberini, Natasha Hovey, Karl Zinny, Fiore Argento, Paola Cozzo

With so much spaghetti talent behind the camera you could be forgiven for expecting more from this disposable gorefest. Aimed squarely at the American teen horror fan it's a wonderfully nasty, but ultimately empty, tale about some ordinary Joes given free tickets to a movie premiere. For some unexplained reason, they find themselves trapped in the auditorium as Evil Dead-style zombie-demons attack. Sounds silly? Well it is, but the team play it straight, piling on buckets of blood 'n' gore and an eardrum thrashing soundtrack designed to stop you from questioning the ridiculousness of the action. It was followed by Bava's Demons 2 (1986), which basically relocated the action to a high-tech tower block and Demons 3: The Ogre (1988), which had absolutely nothing to do with the first two films except for its cash-in title.

DEMONS 3
1991, ITALY
Original titles: Demoni neri
Black Demons, Demoni III
Dir: Umberto Lenzi. Prod: Giuseppe Gargiulo.
Sc: Olga Pehar
Cast: Keith Van Hoven, Joe Balogh, Sonia Curtis, Philip Murray, Juliana Teixeira

Completely unrelated to Lamberto Bava's Demons trilogy (see above), this late Italian entry from Umberto Lenzi takes place in Brazil where six black zombies hound some white teenagers as punishment for years of European imperialism. Or maybe just for the hell of it.

DESCENDENTS
2008, CHILE
Original title: Solos
Dir: Jorge Olguín. Prod: Ana María Aguilar.
Sc: Carolina García, Jorge Olguín
Cast: Camille Lynch, Karina Pizarro, Cristobal Barra, Carolina Andrade, Rosa Luiz Ramos

I wonder how many careless DVD renters have confused this with the George Clooney comedy The Descendents? Hard to imagine a more striking contrast. Shot in Chile in English, this arty and downbeat apocalypse follows a nine-year-old girl (Camille Lynch) as she wanders across a war-torn landscape towards the coast. Her crayon drawings, voiceover narration and a selection of confusingly frantic flashbacks half-piece the story together: an airborne virus has turned the world's population into ghouls and the only uninfected survivors are soldiers in gas masks and a handful of children who've grown bloody gills on their necks. Director Jorge Olguín goes all out for moodiness, shooting through filters to give the film a grey, ashen look that's slightly undermined by his choice of CG blood effects. He's less able when it comes to storytelling, though, and Descendents limps towards a WTF? ending that seems to have been spliced in from Mega Shark Vs Giant Octopus.

DETENTION OF THE DEAD
2012, USA
Dir: Alex Craig Mann. Prod: Michael Mann, Brooke Anderson. Sc: Alex Craig Mann
Cast: Jacob Zachar, Alexa Nikolas, Christa B. Allen, Jayson Blair, Justin Chon

Heads down toilets, jocks vs nerds: this high school zombie comedy has its cookie cutter characters – jock, Goth chick, druggy, cheerleader – take refuge in the school's "Savini Library" when the dead walk. Gore gags, put downs and asides on the zombifying nature of high school cliques follow. Funniest moment is the Goth chick Alexa Nikolas delivering a pledge of undying love for zombie cinema's maestro: "If I ever meet George Romero, I'm gonna seduce him and bear him little zombie babies… but then they'll probably eat us, which would be kinda sad cos that would mean no more living dead movies." Otherwise, this is tumbleweed central.

DETROIT BLOOD CITY: BEAVER LAKE ZOMBIES 2
2005, USA

Dir: Mike Hartman. Prod: Mike Hartman. Sc: Mike Hartman
Cast: Joe Morse, Lawrence J. Straughen, Angela Roberts, Josh Hooper, Lisa Lechniak

"Beaver Lake Zombies" (2003) was a crappy 59 minute short. Here filmmaker Mike Hartman expands his follow-up into a feature. Bad marijuana (who'd smoke orange weed?) turns Michigan residents into talking zombies. It's a badly shot, no budget DIY effort laced with bro stoner humour: on meeting a zombified friend, a dodgy Russian mafia type decides "You look like you've eaten bad pussy or something". Yawn.

DEVIL HUNTER
1980, SPAIN/GERMANY/FRANCE

Original titles: El caníbal, Jungfrau unter Kannibalen, Il cacciatore di uomini
Alternative titles: The Man Hunter, Mandingo Manhunter
Dir: Clifford Brown [Jesús Franco]. Prod: Julian Esteban Gomez. Sc: Julius Valery, Clifford Brown [Jesús Franco]
Cast: Al Cliver [Pier Luigi Conti], Ursula Fellner, Robert Foster [Antonio Mayans], Gisela Hahn, Werner Pochath

After a famous young actress is kidnapped in an undisclosed Caribbean location, Vietnam vet Al Cliver is dispatched to pay the ransom and get her back. Aside from the kidnappers and the jungle cannibal tribe, Cliver finds himself at the mercy of a towering black zombie who wanders through the undergrowth eating (in every sense) any women he comes across. Franco's on familiar territory with this cannibal-zombie-sex-horror hybrid that's as irredeemably racist as it sounds.

DEVIL'S PLAYGROUND
2010, UK

Dir: Mark McQueen. Prod: Freddie Hutton-Mills, Bart Ruspoli, Jonathan Sothcott. Sc: Bart Ruspoli
Cast: Danny Dyer, Craig Fairbrass, Myanna Buring, Jaime Murray, Shane Taylor

London's burning, London's burning… forget the engine, fetch Danny facking Dyer. British cinema's eternal cockney geezer finds himself in a shiny suit battling 28 Days Later-style raging zeds in this surprisingly ambitious London-set apocalypse.

DEVIL STORY
1986, FRANCE

Original title: Il était une fois… le diable
Dir: Bernard Launois. Sc: Bernard Launois
Cast: Véronique Renaud, Marcel Portier, Catherine Day, Nicole Desailly, Christian Paumelle

A possessed horse, an Egyptian mummy, a spooky shipwrecked galleon and a deformed monster bearing an uncanny (or is it simply unashamed?) resemblance to the Toxic Avenger are among the pleasures to be searched out in this rare Euterciné flick. The chief monster is a deformed zombie-esque creature in a Nazi uniform terrorising the French countryside. It keeps coming even after it's head is stoved in by the devil horse. A sequence in which the spit-dribbling mummy raises a dead woman from her grave adds to the ramshackle chaos of the plot.

DEVIL'S KISS
1973, SPAIN

Original title: La perversa caricia de Satán
Alternative title: The Wicked Caresses of Satan
Dir: Georges Gigó. Sc: Georges Gigó
Cast: Silvia Solar, Olivier Matthau, Evelyne Scott, Daniel Martin, Jose Nieto

"I have finished. It wasn't easy, but in the end I succeeded in reconstructing his head." Once an obscure genre entry but now released on Arrow DVD, this dull Spanish chiller combines black magic and mad science as a medium (Silvia Solar), assisted by a professor (Olivier Matthau), raises the dead to get revenge for her husband's death. The striking ghoul they create and control telepathically looks like zombie cinema's answer to Caliban, a turquoise-tinted, bald and bare-chested monster who could be inspired by the genie in The

Thief of Baghdad. He wanders around the chateau strangling busty maids and assorted other victims before rotting away after spotting a crucifix. "Boredom is contagious…"complains the chateau's libertine owner. He's not wrong.

DIARY OF THE DEAD
2007, CANADA

Dir: George A. Romero. Prod: Peter Grunwald.
Sc: George A. Romero
Cast: Michelle Morgan, Josh Close, Shawn Roberts, Amy Lalonde, Joe Dinicol

The zombies may be dead but George Romero's taste for social commentary isn't in *Diary of the Dead*, his fifth zombie movie. Some 40 years after the Pittsburgh filmmaker unleashed the modern zombie movie in *Night of the Living Dead* (1968), he returns to dissect our media-saturated culture as it heads down the YouTube. Josh Close stars as Jason, a student filmmaker who copes with the zombie apocalypse by shooting it on his camcorder and uploading the footage to the Internet.

DIE AND LET LIVE
2006, USA

Dir: Justin Channell. Prod: Justin Channell, Zane Crosby.
Sc: Justin Channell, Zane Crosby, Josh Lively
Cast: Josh Lively, Zane Crosby, Sarah Bauer, Ashley Goddard, Jonas Dixon

Zombies break out of a pharma company's lab and invade a house party where a bunch of kids are trying to get off with one another in this scrappy teenage effort. It feels like it was thrown together by a few mates for a laugh. Pizza, beer, sex and zombies all get a look in and there's an inevitable cameo from Lloyd Kaufman, irrepressible cheerleader of indie horror filmmakers everywhere. The production company is IWC (Idiots With Cameras) Films – which is a little harsh, but in keeping with the general not-taking-ourselves-seriously tone.

DIE-NER (GET IT?)
2008, USA

Alternative title: KFZ – Kentucky Fried Zombie
Dir: Patrick Horvath. Prod: David Cummings, Mark Johnson, Seth Allen Martin. Sc: Patrick Horvath
Cast: Joshua Grote, Liesel Kopp, Jorge Montalvo,
Maria Olsen, Larry Purtell

Ken (Joshua Grote), a charming serial killer, holes up in a diner and finds his victims returning to life in this low-budget, offbeat zombie comedy. Less interested in the usual living dead apocalypse than in charting the power plays between the killer and his latest quarry (a bickering married couple), this simply lets the ghouls run occasional interference. The zombified cook and waitress have a habit of wandering out of the walk-in refrigerator at inconvenient moments – such as when a Sheriff stops for coffee – causing Ken no end of trouble and testing the limits of his nihilistic take on the world. A pleasingly unusual, if not entirely successful, attempt to do something different with the standard zombie movie.

DIE YOU ZOMBIE BASTARDS!
2005, USA

Dir: Caleb Emerson. Prod: Haig Demarjian, Caleb Emerson. Sc: Caleb Emerson, Haig Demarjian
Cast: Tom Gerstmar, Pippi Zornoza, Geoff Mosher, Jamie Gillis, Jennifer K. Beal

Die You Zombie Bastards! is apparently "The world's first EVER serial killer, superhero, Rock 'n' Roll zombie road movie romance." And far be it for this writer to disagree! A sub-Troma trash epic, this backyard offering throws everything into the mix: green-skinned, purple-haired zombies, a rubber-faced villain, former porn stud Jamie Gillis (*Night of the Zombies*), cannibal killers, stop motion animation and black & white segments. It's zany, off-the-wall humour is funny for about five minutes and it looks like it was made for the price of a Big Mac. Seriously, don't bother.

DISCIPLE OF DEATH
1972, UK

Dir: Tom Parkinson. Prod: Tom Parkinson, Charles Fairman [Mike Raven]. Sc: Churton Fairman [Mike Raven]
Cast: Mike Raven, Ronald Lacey, Stephen Bradley, Marguerite Hardiman, Virginia Wetherell

Eighteenth-century Cornwall is the setting for this pointless British outing. After blood is spilt at an abandoned manor house, demonic lead actor Mike Raven returns from hell and sows the seeds of destruction through the local community by sacrificing the local women to his lord Satan. Lots of sub-Dracula moments see Raven trying to pitch himself somewhere between Bela Lugosi and Christopher Lee. However, the film is ultimately little more than a curiosity piece as oo-ar accents, a vampiric dwarf and assorted English Gothic trappings pad out the interminable dullness. The only reason for its inclusion here is that Raven surrounds himself with zombie-like female slaves – although, for all it matters to the movie's plot they could just as well be vampires, demons or shape-shifting aliens from the planet Zartoff. Tellingly, producer/writer Churton Fairman was actually Raven himself working under a pseudonym.

DOCTOR BLOOD'S COFFIN
1960, UK

Dir: Sidney J. Furie. Prod: George Fowler. Sc: Jerry Juran, James Kelly, Peter Miller
Cast: Kieron Moore, Hazel Court, Ian Hunter, Kenneth J. Warren, Paul Stockman

Young Dr Peter Blood returns home to Devon after a spell in Vienna convinced that he can resurrect the dead through the use of heart transplants. Preying on the locals, he paralyzes them with curare then kills them in a series of botched attempts to prove his hypothesis. Blood finally succeeds and brings the dead husband of his new girlfriend back to life. Neither the zombie nor his widow is particularly impressed. Funny that.

DR ORLOFF'S MONSTER
1964, SPAIN

Original titles: El secreto del doctor Orloff, Les maîtresses du docteur Jekyll
Alternative titles: Brides of Dr Jekyll, Dr Jekyll's Mistresses
Dir: Jesús Franco. Prod: Manus Lesaeur. Sc: Jesús Franco
Cast: Hugo Blanco, Agnès Spaak, Marcelo Arroita-Jauregui, José Rubio, Pastor Serrador

After inheriting some groundbreaking research into "ultrasonics" from a dead colleague, Dr Jekyll is able to resurrect his dead brother-in-law Andros as a zombie. The arrival of Andros's daughter Melissa complicates matters, though. Especially once she catches sight of her reanimated father.

DR SATAN VS. BLACK MAGIC
1967, MEXICO

Original title: El Dr Satán y la magia negra
Dir: Rogelio A. González. Prod: Sidney T. Bruckner.
Sc: José María Fernández Unsáin
Cast: Joaquín Cordero, Noe Murayama, Sonia Furio, Luz María Aguilar

A Mexican horror movie sans wrestling, this follows two warring sorcerers (Dr Satan and "Black Magic") who're out to destroy each other. It's bonkers, surreal and OTT and among its catalogue of weirdness are two rather pert zombie girls.

DOGHOUSE
2009, UK

Dir Jake West. Prod: Mike Loveday. Sc: Dan Schaffer
Cast: Danny Dyer, Stephen Graham, Noel Clarke, Emil Marwa, Lee Ingleby

A boozy weekend away for a group of 30-something lads to celebrate a mate's divorce is ruined by a pack of zombie women in this outrageously sexist British horror-comedy. Director Jake West (*Evil Aliens*) redeems himself with enough self-awareness of the sexual politics at play and by giving his hard men actors (Danny Dyer, Noel Clarke, Stephen Graham) an unexpected, sentimental seam to mine.

DON'T WAKE THE DEAD
2008, GERMANY

Dir: Andreas Schnaas. Prod: Thomas Buresch, Oliver Wiebelitz. Sc: Klaus Dzuck, Ted Geoghegan
Cast: Ralph Fellows, Sonja Kerskes, Fiana de Guzman, Carolin Schmidt, Cristiane Malia

Andreas Schnaas hires out a Gothic castle and rips off the blind monks of *Tombs of the Blind Dead* (1971) in this throwback to the Eurotrash movies of the 1970s. A bunch of girls arrive at the castle only to discover that it's home to Templar zombies who rise every 66 years to feast on the living. The last time they rose from their tombs was during WWII in the midst of a Nazi orgy. So this time around the living face not only lumbering Nazis but also the Blind Dead. By Schnaas's standards, it's not bad. But that isn't saying much.

DOOMED
2006, USA
Dir: Michael Su. Prod: Hoby Ruhaas. Sc: Patrick McManus, Sean O'Bannon
Cast: Drew Russel, Kara Schaaf, M.C. Brown, Edwin Villa, Aaron Gaffey

Murderers, thieves, hackers and prostitutes get a chance at a pardon and $50 million in cash in a futuristic TV show called *Survival Island 2020*. The aim of the game? To survive on an island where zombies – the leftovers from some vague military experiment gone wrong – run free. A mismatched bunch of contestants bicker and fight while Michael Su (*The Revolting Dead*, 2004) inserts CG sequences showing their progress on the island ("Isola de Romero", natch) and punctuates each fight with on-screen scores ("KILL SHOT * 550 POINTS"). The fast-moving, grey-skinned ghouls are dressed in army camo and growl a lot. If you're only going to watch one zombie survival game show then this is certainly better than *The Knackery* (2010).

DORM OF THE DEAD
2006, USA
Dir: Donald Farmer. Prod: Jackie Napoli. Sc: Donald Farmer
Cast: Ciara Richards, Adrianna Eder, Jackey Hall, Tiffany Shepis, Andrea Ownbey

"Where *Mean Girls* meet *Dead Girls*!" promises the tagline for this tawdry trawl through softcore sex scenes and gore that has none of the snappy pizzazz of the Tina Fey scripted teen comedy it name checks. After Haitian zombie blood causes an outbreak of you know what at Arkham University (actually Tennessee Technical University), filmmaker Donald Farmer (once a zombie extra in *Day of the Dead*) throws together lesbian sex scenes and unconvincing zombies. It's sleazy and dull. Unlike *Dorm of the Dead* (2009) which was merely tired and dull.

DORM OF THE DEAD
2009, USA
Dir: Tobias Canto Jr., Tyrel Good. Prod: Chelsea Benson, Max Johns. Sc: Tobias Canto Jr., Mike Joyner, Jimmy Anthony Donahue, John Strong
Cast: Aaron Sosa, Ryan DeLuca, Dana DiRado, Michael Curbs Miller, Brian Oviedo

"I hate the week after Spring Break, everyone brings some sort of sick shit with them!" So moans one of the characters in this shot on video indie about a bunch of college kids swept up in the zombie apocalypse. As usual, various survivors – a sarcastic Goth girl; a preppy black guy; a geek armed with Romero style big glasses and a Thor hammer; and the baby-faced kid brother who was just visiting – battle the zombies as the infection spreads across the University of Arizona campus. True, this unassuming little movie doesn't have a shred of originality but the amateur filmmakers doubtlessly consider simply completing it a major achievement. Not to be confused with *Dorm of the Dead* (2006).

DYLAN DOG: DEAD OF NIGHT
2011, USA
Dir: Kevin Munroe. Prod: Ashok Amritraj, Scott Mitchell Rosenberg, Gilbert Adler. Sc: Joshua Oppenheimer, Thomas Dean Donnelly
Cast: Brandon Routh, Sam Huntington, Anita Briem, Taye Diggs, Peter Stormare

Dylan Dog (Brandon Routh) is a paranormal investigator dragged out of retirement when his assistant (Sam Huntington) is murdered by one of the werewolves that live in New Orleans alongside unsuspecting humans (and some rather more suspecting zombies and vampires). Riffing on *Buffy the Vampire Slayer* with a smidgeon of *Kolchak: The Night Stalker* this is a Hollywood-ised, and frankly rather bland, companion to *Dellamorte, Dellamore* (1993).

THE EARTH DIES SCREAMING
1964, UK
Dir: Terence Fisher. Prod: Robert Lippert, Jack Parsons
Sc: Harry Spalding
Cast: Willard Parker, Virginia Field, Dennis Price, Thorley Walters, Vanda Godsell

After aliens invade the Earth with gas attacks and clunky robots, a handful of British survivors find themselves trapped in a provincial town. They watch in horror as the invaders reanimate the dead and use them as cheap soldiers in the skirmish. In a daring act of bravery our plucky heroes attack the broadcasting antenna that's transmitting the aliens' radio waves and turn the tide of the war.

EAT ME!
2010, USA
Dir: Katie Carman. Prod: Katie Carman, Elizabeth Lee
Sc: Elizabeth Lee
Cast: Elizabeth Lee, Jun Naito, Ivy Hong, Chesley Calloway, Chad Michael Wyckoff

"I hate the Boroughs, please take me home!" A New York garage band escapes the zombie apocalypse in their Brooklyn basement, smoking blunts and guzzling beer without realising that the world has ended outside. Much bitchy slacker bickering – which the filmmakers clearly think is hilarious – keeps the stoned characters busy as they try to evade the ghouls outside. In between arguments they take out zombies with drumsticks and brooms, and complain about "demotivated" ghouls. Ho, ho.

EATERS: RISE OF THE DEAD
2010, ITALY
Dir: Marco Ristori, Luca Boni. Prod: Marco Palese, Filippo Corradin. Sc: Marco Ristori, Germano Tarricone
Cast: Alex Lucchesi, Guglielmo Favilla, Claudio Marmugi, Rosella Elmi, Elisa Ferretti

"Uwe Böll presents…" is about as frightening as this Italian gut-muncher gets. It opens with increasingly far-fetched news reports documenting infection, quarantine and the fall of mankind: "The Pope committed suicide at 9 o'clock this morning by shooting himself in the head". Then it spirals into a derivative, but competently made, post-apocalyptic chaos. After dodgy fertility drugs wipe out humanity, a couple of hardmen wander the ruins. They bring in feral ghouls for scientists to run dodgy experiments on, uncover some unpalatable truths about the outbreak and fight Seig Heiling neo-Nazis. I spent most of the running time trying to work out if lead actor Lucchesi, a dead ringer for an Italian Johnny Harris, was really bald or wearing a latex skull cap.

ELECTRIC ZOMBIES
2005, USA
Dir: John Specht. Prod: John Specht. Sc: Richard Novosak, John Specht
Cast: Paul Wendell, Jonas Moses, Richard Novosak, John Specht, Ali Jenkins

"Zeus 1374–1374 Order test: self-kill. Mutilation. Mask location. Unit 148 pick up at test end. Authorisation Zeus 1374. End." This nonsensical little movie from Missouri babbles incoherently for 90 minutes before finally self-destructing under the weight of its own narrative and technical incompetence. On the surface it's an appealingly high concept idea: military-made cellphones are turning people into brainwashed zombies using experimental microwave transmissions from an orbiting satellite. The technology was originally used to destabilise foreign states. Now a corrupt US senator is using a batch of phones to kill prostitutes and drug dealers in St Louis. Just for kicks. Hoping for Stephen King's *Cell*? Expect disappointment. This movie has no zombies, just a couple of brainwashed Manchurian Candidates. It chiefly revolves around spies, cops, politicians and gangbangers shouting at one another incessantly, while director Jon Specht positions his camera at a variety of angles… none of them straight. Beyond dreadful.

ENTER… ZOMBIE KING
2003, CANADA
Alternative title: Zombie King and the Legion of Doom
Dir: Stacey Case. Prod: Bill Marks, Steve Solomos.
Sc: Bill Marks, Sean K. Robb.
Cast: Jules Delamore, Rob "El Fuego" Etchevarria, Jennifer Thom, Raymond Carle, Sean K. Robb

The spirit of El Santo lives on in this lurid and kinetic Canadian B-movie that's set in a world where masked wrestlers and zombies wander around without anyone batting an eyelid. Aristotle-quoting masked muscleman Ulysses (Jules Delamore) is on a mission to track down a bunch of wild zombies after an attack in a parking lot, a crime initially blamed on his old ringmate Tiki (Rob Etcheverria). What they discover is masked villain Zombie King (Nicholas Sinn) and his henchmen who're planning to take over the world with genetically-altered ghouls. Going all out for cult status *Enter… Zombie King* is something of an acquired taste. But its procession of tattooed ladies, wrestling bouts and comic book riffs impresses thanks to its sure-footed certainty of purpose and tone. The end credits thank Romero, Stan Lee and Jack Kirby but not – strangely enough – El Santo.

EROTIC NIGHTS OF THE LIVING DEAD
1980, ITALY
Original title: Le notti erotiche
Alternative titles: In der Gewalt der Zombies, Le notti erotiche dei morti viventi, Sexy Nights of the Living Dead
Dir: Joe D'Amato [Aristide Massaccesi]. Sc: Tom Salina [Aristide Massaccesi]
Cast: Laura Gemser, George Eastman [Luigi Montefiori], Dirce [Patrizia] Funari, Mark Shannon [Manlio Cersosimo]

A yachtsman takes a couple of tourists to a distant Caribbean island and runs into a horde of native zombies in this rough and ready effort from Joe D'Amato. As our heroes are torn between making the beast with two backs and fighting off the living dead, things quickly get messy.

EROTIC ORGASM
1982, ITALY
Original title: Orgasmo esotico
Alternative titles: Exotic Orgasm
Dir: Lee Castle [Mario Siciliano]
Cast: Marina [Frajese] Lotar, Sonia Bennett, Michel Curie, Peter Brown, Joe Mignano [Eugenio Gramignano]

A virtually incomprehensible hardcore sex flick from Mario Siciliano (although it's sometimes also attributed to Joe D'Amato, aka Aristide Massaccesi), *Erotic Orgasm* features lots of explicit orgies and a couple of zombies. There's hardly any dialogue but the plot appears to involve a black witch, who uses her supernatural powers to turn the inhabitants of a remote Mediterranean villa into zombie sex slaves. Possessing all the skewered logic of a bad hash dream, it combines endless hardcore porn sequences with a fair few sex toys and a dreadful Eurotrash elevator Muzak score. Given that the zombies are little more than actors caked in pallid make-up and – in the case of a zombie woman who comes back to give her boyfriend head – an overabundance of blue eye shadow, it's never as interesting as it might sound.

EVIL
2005, GREECE
Original title: To kakó
Dir: Yorgos Noussias. Prod: Yorgos Noussias.
Sc: Yorgos Noussias
Cast: Meletis Georgiadis, Argyris Thanasoulas, Pepi Moschovakou, Stavroula Thomopoulou, Mary Tsoni

When an ancient evil buried in a cave beneath Athens is disturbed by construction workers, a zombie outbreak engulfs the Greek capital. The nation's first zombie movie unspools at a cracking pace, bitten victims turned into ghouls in a heartbeat in football stadiums and nightclubs. Surviving the carnage is a small band of ordinary citizens, including a grumpy cabbie (Argyris Thanasoulas). For reasons known only to the filmmakers, they all seem to have *Matrix*-style martial arts powers. Much rollicking zombie fighting fills the sparse running time as forks are stabbed into eyeballs and everyone turns into Bruce Lee on speed. Aside from a throwaway gag comparing the outbreak to the 1967 coup d'état, though, this has little to say.

THE EVIL DEAD
1982, USA
Dir: Sam Raimi. Prod: Robert Tapert. Sc: Sam Raimi
Cast: Bruce Campbell, Ellen Sandweiss, Hal Delrich, Betsy Baker, Sarah York

Sam Raimi's thundering gorefest is a classic but whether or not it really deserves to be billed as a zombie movie depends on how strict you want to be about your living dead ghouls. It seemed prudent to include it anyway, just because it was such an influence on Peter Jackson's zombie flicks *Bad Taste* and *Braindead*. Ash and his mates head out to a log cabin in the woods for some R&R only to reawaken an ancient evil that turns their trip into a living hell. As the put upon everyman facing up to demons with a habit of possessing the bodies of his friends, Bruce Campbell became an overnight horror star. Bonkers sequel *Evil Dead II* (1987) basically remade its predecessor with demented Three Stooges-style slapstick, chainsaws and dancing zombie girlfriends.

EVIL DEAD
2013, USA

Dir: Fede Alvarez. Prod: Robert G. Tapert, Sam Raimi, Bruce Campbell. Sc: Fede Alvarez, Rodo Sayagues Cast: Jane Levy, Shiloh Fernandez, Lou Taylor Pucci, Jessica Lucas, Elizabeth Blackmore

Uruguayan writer/director Fede Alvarez's reboot of Sam Raimi's demonic zombies classic was shot on digital in New Zealand and uses janky, old skool practical effects (25,000 litres of blood, 300 litres of vomit), more out of nostalgia than necessity. Sick and slick, it's a proper and respectful remake. It's telling they dropped the definite article off the title, though: even Alvarez knows there's only one *The* Evil Dead.

EVIL HEAD
2012, USA
Dir: Doug Sakmann. Prod: Joanna Angel, Mitch Fontaine. Sc: Doug Sakmann, Joanna Angel Cast: Joanna Angel, Tommy Pistol, Kleio, Veruca James, Danny Wylde

The *Evil Dead* movies get an indulgent, porno parody makeover in this outing from Burning Angel Entertainment. Surprisingly faithful to its source material this keeps Ash, the Book of the Dead, the cabin in the woods and the chainsaw. Meanwhile the performers – including three of the most heavily inked actresses I've ever seen – breathlessly make the beast with two backs. No bloke seems to mind screwing demonically possessed zombie girls… until they bite his testicles off.

EVILUTION
2007, USA
Dir: Chris Conlee. Prod: Eric Peter-Kaiser, Brian Patrick O'Toole. Sc: Brian Patrick O'Toole Cast: Eric Peter-Kaiser, Tim Colceri, Sandra Ramirez, Noel Gugliemi, Guillermo Diaz

Military scientists in Iraq create zombie supersoldiers using a microscopic extraterrestrial parasite. Inevitably, the ghouls get out of control and the lab facility is bombed to oblivion. That's the breathless opening five minutes of *Evilution*, full of raging parkour zombies in combat fatigues. You might as well switch off at that point, since the rest of the movie slows to a turgid crawl as the base's only survivor (Eric Peter-Kaiser) returns

Stateside to continue experimenting with the parasite *Re-Animator* style. Comedy gangbangers, a love interest (Sandra Ramirez) and a military hitman keep things trundling along until the late return of the living dead. Duller than it promised.

EXHUMED
2003, CANADA
Dir: Brian Clement. Prod: Brian Clement. Sc: Brian Clement
Cast: Hiroaki Itaya, Masahiro Oyake, Rei Kido, Claire Westby, Moira Thomas

It's always rewarding to watch an indie filmmaker consolidating their talent and upping their game. Canadian writer-director Brian Clement (the *Meat Market* movies) does exactly that in an ambitious anthology of three living dead stories. "Shi No Mori" is the first and boldest instalment – it's in Japanese and features a samurai and a monk fighting the living dead, and each other, in a haunted forest. The second, "Shadow of Tomorrow", throws zombies into a detective noir parody shot in b&w. Finally, "Last Rumble" sees werewolf rockers and vampire mods fighting each other while post-apocalyptic Nazis build an army of zombies. Great to see a micro-budget movie with ambition.

EXIT HUMANITY
2011, CANADA
Dir: John Geddes. Prod: Jesse Thomas Cook, Matt Wiele, John Geddes. Sc: John Geddes
Cast: Brian Cox, Mark Gibson, Dee Wallace, Bill Moseley, Stephen McHattie

Handsomely shot in Ontario's Beaver Valley this Civil War Western features the dead returning to life and a weighty voiceover from Brian Cox. It's a cut above most zombie Westerns.

EXPIRATION
2011, SOUTH AFRICA
Alternative title: Rancid
Dir: Alastair Orr. Prod: Ryan Macquet, Alastair Orr, Phil Gorn. Sc: Alastair Orr, Jonathan Jordaan
Cast: Michael Thomspon, Brandon Auret, Ingeborg Riedmaier, Ryan Macquet, Craig Hawks

"It's not a medical test, it's a test to build

monsters…" Four medical guinea pigs sign up for a well paid but mysterious drugs trial, then wake up months later in a dank, abandoned hospital. What they don't know is that zombie-like participants of the previous trial are in the building with them – and the scientists responsible are watching on surveillance cameras, trying to keep the whole thing from unravelling. Shot in South Africa on little money, this tense lo-fi movie makes clever use of grainy security cam footage, bloodsoaked ghouls called "anomalies" and a maze-like setting. It's a little too histrionic for its own good before its final, inevitable, switchback.

EXTINCTION: THE G.M.O. CHRONICLES
2011, GERMANY
Dir: Niki Drozdowski. Prod: Niki Drozdowski, Daniel Buder. Sc: Niki Drozdowski, Ralf Betz
Cast: Daniel Buder, Luise Bähr, Klaus Ebert, Tobias Kay, Lee Rychter

"Nothing on the radio. Even the test signal has gone out. That can't be good." Hiding out in an abandoned Cold War military base as the zombie apocalypse rolls out, ex-soldier Tom (Daniel Buder) keeps track of the unravelling global situation while giving shelter to any survivors he finds. Shot in Germany but with English dialogue, *Extinction*'s desolate, gunmetal visuals are more arresting than its over-egged drama. Strong action scenes make the most of the evolving zombies – which range from classic shamblers to runners to spitters and an eyeless screaming banshee reminiscent of *Left 4 Dead*'s Witch. It's also the first time someone's lured a zombie into a car, jumped out the far side, shut the doors on them and then torched the vehicle. Innovative!

THE FACE OF MARBLE
1946, USA
Dir: William Beaudine. Prod: Jeffrey Bernerd.
Sc: Michel Jacoby
Cast: John Carradine, Claudia Drake, Robert Shayne

John Carradine is up to his old tricks again in this voodoo-themed Monogram outing, resurrecting the dead and a Great Dane dog just for the hell of it. The corpses act more like ghosts than zombies. Whatever they are, this is just another Poverty Row schedule filler.

FAST ZOMBIES WITH GUNS
2009, USA
Dir: Bennie Woodell. Prod: Ken Svitak, Megan Darrow, Nick Green, Chris Malec, Keisha Malec. Sc: Bennie Woodell
Cast: Leena Kurishingal, Tony Swansey, Will Cummings III, Dennis Doornbos, Ken Svitak

Gangsters poison a federal witness with biohazardous material and inadvertently spark a zombie apocalypse in this mind-numbingly terrible backyard epic from Illinois. Incompetently shot, written, acted and (most of all) lit, it's a murky, pointless exercise in tedium. The film's big idea is promised by its title: these zombies fire guns. Together with the lack of FX make-up budget and the atrocious lighting, all that actually means is it's hard to distinguish the living from the living dead. It's so indescribably inept on every level, it makes Umberto Lenzi's *Nightmare City* (1980) – which popularised the idea of gun-toting ghouls – look like high art.

FEEDING THE MASSES
2004, USA
Dir: Richard Griffin. Prod: Ted Marr. Sc: Trent Haaga.
Cast: Billy Garberina, Rachel Morris, Patrick Cohen, Michael Propster, William DeCoff

When it comes to social critique, zombie movies are often about as subtle as an elephant. This on-the-nose, micro-budget outing is more like a herd of the beasts. As the world is consumed by the "Lazarus Virus", stoner news cameraman Torch (Billy Garberina) questions the network's decision to pump out propaganda reassuring citizens that the situation is under control. Refreshingly ambitious but painfully underpowered, *Feeding the Masses* takes 85 minutes to achieve what Romero managed in the first ten minutes of *Dawn of the Dead*. Screenwriter Trent Haaga progressed to *Deadgirl*, a much more polished exploration of the zombie genre's potential for social critique.

FIDO
2006, CANADA
Dir: Andrew Currie. Prod: Blake Corbet, Mary Anne Waterhouse. Sc: Robert Chomiak, Andrew Currie, Dennis Heaton
Cast: K'Sun Ray, Billy Connolly, Carrie-Anne Moss,

Dylan Baker, Henry Czerny

Once upon a time real stars didn't play zombies. But by the mid-2000s zombies were becoming so popular that that old truism was overturned. Billy Connolly stars as Fido, a grunting, domesticated zombie slave in Andrew Currie's sweet satire of 1950s suburbia. Think *Pleasantville* with ghouls. Connolly's delicate, dialogue-free turn gives zombie cinema one of its most sympathetic monsters since Howard Sherman picked up a Gillette in *Day of the Dead* (1985). Meanwhile, the film's veiled commentary on American race relations in the 1950s is nicely understated.

FISTFUL OF BRAINS
2008, USA
Dir: Christine Parker. Prod: Bret Harris, Christine Parker, Edward Warner, Bill Mulligan. Sc: Christine Parker
Cast: Jaqueline Martini, Conrad Osborne, Darrell Parker, Edward Warner, Wayne Bates

The Old West fills up with amateur actors and raggedy ghouls in a no frills production full of silliness and unconvincing attempts at period detail. When a snake oil salesman flogs a tonic that turns the living into cannibal ghouls who like to snap their teeth noisily, the sheriff (Darrell Parker) of a small frontier town grabs his six shooters to fight back. Terrible acting, awful cinematography and atrocious sound recording make this very tiresome.

FLESH FREAKS
2001, USA
Dir: Conall Pendergast. Prod: Conall Pendergast. Sc: Conall Pendergast
Cast: Eshe Mercer-James, Etan Muskat, Ronny Varno, Erica Goldblatt, Clayton Hayes

"He just kept killing and killing and killing until everyone of them was dead…" This amateur outing is made by students in Toronto and it unexpectedly beefs up its DV production with some footage from a trip to Central America. Heading into the jungle to investigate some Mayan ruins, archaeology student Barry (writer-director Conall Pendergast) unleashes a zombie controlled by alien parasites that kills his entire digging team. Pretty soon outrageously decomposed, ghouls with pulsating craniums are slaughtering students back in Toronto, slashing them with scalpels and sickles. They're controlled by bug-like aliens inside their heads (which eventually make a hilarious appearance, erupting from the zombies' skulls). Enthusiasm isn't enough to overcome the dire production values and technical incompetence.

FLICK
2007, UK
Dir. David Howard. Prod. Rik Hall. Sc. David Howard
Cast: Hugh O'Conor, Faye Dunaway, Mark Benton, Liz Smith, Michelle Ryan

Visually inventive and with a bonkers plot, *Flick* ought to be better known. Instead it's an undiscovered B-movie treat, a British zombie film featuring a teddy boy ghoul (Hugh O'Conor) who comes back from the dead in the Welsh town of Port Talbot to avenge himself on the rockers who did him wrong. Faye Dunaway is the one-armed, Elvis-loving cop on exchange from Memphis, Tennessee who's on his trail. Yes, you read that right.

FLIGHT OF THE LIVING DEAD: OUTBREAK ON A PLANE
2007, USA
Dir: Scott Thomas. Prod: David Shoshan, Scott Thomas. Sc: Scott Thomas, Mark Onspaugh, Sidney Iwanter
Cast: David Chisum, Kristen Kerr, Kevin J. O'Connor, Erick Avari, Richard Tyson

Blame Samuel L. Jackson… Onboard an American flight to Paris, crew and passengers face more than just deep vein thrombosis when a CGI storm causes an "outbreak on a plane". Down in the hold, a medical company is transporting its top secret research project into reviving the dead; in the turbulence, ghouls are unleashed. Is this energetic B-movie indicative of American post-9/11 anxieties? Or, is it just a dumb attempt to swap slithering serpents for hyperfast zombies? No one says: "I have had it with these motherfucking zombies on this motherfucking plane!" Which is a shame, really. For another take on the whole zombies at 30,000 feet idea try *Quarantine 2: Terminal* (2010).

THE FOG

1979, USA
Dir: John Carpenter. Prod: Debra Hill. Sc: John Carpenter, Debra Hill
Cast: Adrienne Barbeau, Jamie Lee Curtis, Janet Leigh, Tom Atkins, Hal Holbrook, John Houseman

Antonio Bay's celebrating its hundredth birthday when a dark, dank fog rolls in off the ocean. Soon the townsfolk are turning up dead as sea-faring zombies emerge from the mist to kill off the ancestors of the town's founding fathers who did them wrong. Radio DJ Stevie tries to warn the townsfolk as she broadcasts from the lighthouse but it's too late – the ghouls are everywhere. The survivors eventually decide to barricade themselves in the local church, then realise that that's where the ghouls' stolen gold is hidden. Uh-oh. A very poor remake followed in 2005.

FOREST OF THE DEAD
2005, CANADA
Dir: Brian Singleton. Prod: Brian Singleton. Sc: Brian Singleton, Mark S.
Cast: Chris Anderson, Erin Brophy, Brandi Boulet, Elaine Cummings, Heather Duthie

Not to be confused with the superior *Severed: Forest of the Dead* (2004) this DIY backwoods apocalypse has campers turning into zombie cannibal fiends. One-man studio Brian Singleton apparently poured his own money into the venture, working weekdays and shooting at weekends for several weeks – then coming back to the project a few years later to finish it for a DVD release as the zombie boom kicked off. Despite his commitment, it's a total bomb – amateur acting, production values and far from impressive zombies who emerge from the woods to eat the vacationing living. Even the jokes are dead on arrival.

THE FOREVER DEAD
2007, USA
Dir: Christine Parker. Prod: Christine Parker, Bill Mulligan, Mike Jones. Sc: Christine Parker
Cast: Bill Mulligan, Libby Lynn, Jessie Walley, Ryan Williams, Brian Chippewa

"We have a problem… the rabbit's *gone*!" When a bunny infected with a zombie virus escapes from a lab, the clock's ticking on the zombie apocalypse.

Out in the woods little "Lupus" twitches his nose, then growls and viciously attacks rednecks (complete with bunny POV shots) before the virus starts to spread human to human. Shot on a camcorder with acne-covered actors, this backyard zombie movie skips from one gory scene to another, unhindered by ideas of plot or character development. Eventually it sticks its bickering survivors in a house and give us interminable flashbacks to the virus's creation. It might be serious, it might be a joke – damningly, it's impossible to tell. The zombie bunny hops about a bit and ends up half-dead and still flapping around after being killed by a cat – at which point the filmmakers switch to a furry puppet on a string. Catching myxomatosis would be more enjoyable than this.

FRANKENSTEIN'S ARMY
2013, NETHERLANDS/USA/CZECH REPUBLIC
Dir: Richard Raaphorst. Prod: Nick Jongerius, Daniel Koefoed, Todd Brown. Greg Newman. Sc: Chris W. Mitchell, Miguel Tejada-Flores
Cast: Robert Gwilym, Hon Ping Tang, Alexander Mercury, Luke Newberry, Joshua Sasse.

A Soviet infantry squad and a propaganda filmmaker discover that the grandson of Baron Frankenstein is alive and well and working for the Nazis in this found footage horror. Superb "zombot" creature designs give director Richard Raaphorst's grindhouse throwback its *raison d'être*.

FROM THE DEAD OF NIGHT
1989, USA
Dir: Paul Wendkos. Prod: Barbara Black. Sc: William Bleich
Cast: Lindsay Wagner, Bruce Boxleitner, Diahann Carroll, Robin Thomas, Robert Prosky

Writer Bill Bleich takes zombies onto the small screen again after *The Midnight Hour* (1985) in this equally lame TV movie. Lindsay Wagner stars as Joanna, a woman who's had a near death experience involving a cat and a swimming pool (don't ask… Or laugh). Now it seems a whole host of strangers are out to kill her, so where better to go for some calm relaxation than Mexico's Day of the Dead festival? It all adds up to a risible plot in which zombie spirits from the afterlife – dubbed "walkers" – try and make Joanna join them. If it saves us having to watch this dross, they're welcome to her.

THE FROZEN DEAD
1966, UK
Dir: Herbert J. Leder. Prod: Herbert J. Leder.
Sc: Herbert J. Leder
Cast: Dana Andrews, Anna Palk, Philip Gilbert, Kathleen Breck, Karel Stepanek

A Nazi scientist reanimates the dead in the English countryside in this cheap and forgotten British outing from '66. An impressive cast – including Dana Andrews as the villain and a bit part for Edward Fox as a zombie – can't mask the general whiff of cheesiness. There's much fun to be had with a reanimated head in a box, though.

FROZEN SCREAM
1975, USA
Dir: Frank Roach. Prod: Renee Harmon. Sc: Doug Ferrin, Michael Sonye, Celeste Hammond
Cast: Renee Harmon, Lynne Kocol, Wolf Muser, Thomas McGowen, Wayne Liebman

"I'm aware that we've had some minor malfunctions, the cranial circuitry will have to be perfected…" Hooded, frozen zombies run amok in this cheesy 1970s outing about mad doctors (Lee James and Renee Harmon, who sports a ridiculous accent of obscure origin) searching for the secret of life and death. Their experiments aren't going very well, creating not eternal life but an army of zombie killers. They're kept in the freezer and occasionally let out to go on the rampage with axes and knives, hoods pulled down over their gurning faces. Meanwhile, a cop (Thomas Gowen) investigates the deaths of a string of med students, his voiceover unhelpfully drowning out other characters' dialogue as they talk! Badly made, incompetently plotted; it's pretty dire.

FUGUE STATE
2008, USA
Dir: Tim McClelland. Prod: Tim McClelland, Rob Ellis.
Sc: Tim McClelland
Cast: Brian Lucero, Jocelyn Tucker, Justin Tade, Michele Spiro, Gary Dannenbaum

A mysterious amnesia plague sweeps across the globe. As society crumbles a cop (Brian Lucero) finds himself in the New Mexico desert, holed up with a strange and dysfunctional family. The plague is a mental disorder that turns the infected into zombie-like victims. Writer-director Tim McClelland puts a fresh conceptual spin on the zombie genre, but doesn't have the budget to deal with the interesting version – instead he locks us in the desert with loco protagonists and a Dolby battering sound mix. Disappointing.

GALLOWWALKERS
2012, USA/UK
Dir: Andrew Goth. Prod: Jack Bowyer. Sc: Joanne Reay, Andrew Goth
Cast: Wesley Snipes, Kevin Howarth, Riley Smith, Tanit Phoenix, Simona Brhlikova

Mired in development hell for several years after star Wesley Snipes was convicted of tax evasion, this ravishingly shot film is a narrative mess. It's set in an alternate universe where the Old West setting is full of skinless, demonic ghouls and where laconic living dead gunfighter Aman (Snipes) searches for vengeance. A hallucinogenic, hyper-kinetic comic book horror, it features a Klaus Kinski style zombie villain (Kevin Howarth) whose flayed, skinless body is straight out of *Hellraiser*; his mummified, crucified son who he hopes to bring back to life; and a henchman with a vicious pineapple spiked helmet. Supermodel Tanit Phoenix plays a sneak thief tart. Her heaving bosom gets so much screen time one assumes it must have its own agent.

GALLERY OF HORROR
1966, USA
Alternative titles: Alien Massacre, The Blood Suckers, Dr Terror's Gallery of Horrors, Return from the Past
Dir: David L. Hewitt. Prod: David L. Hewitt, Ray Dorn.
Sc: Gary R. Heacock, David Prentiss
Cast: Lon Chaney Jr., John Carradine, Rochelle Hudson, Roger Gentry, Mitch Evans

This cheapo American horror anthology offers up five different tales of terror that cover everything from vampires in Victorian England to bewitched clocks. In "Monster Raid" a scientist (Ron Doyle) experiments with an immortality formula and returns from the grave as a burnt-looking ghoul to take revenge on his lab assistant and his adulterous wife. In "The Spark of Life" one of Dr Frankenstein's protégés (a gone-to-seed Lon Chaney Jr.) manages to bring an executed killer back from the dead. Bad move, obviously.

GANGS OF THE DEAD
2005, USA
Alternative titles: Last Rites, City of the Dead, 48 Weeks Later
Dir: Duane Stinnett. Prod: Duane Stinnett, Todd Ocvirk
Sc: Duane Stinnett, Krissann Shipley
Cast: Noel G, Howard, Ethan Ednee, Ryan King, Dayanah Jamine

Corn rows and the walking dead: two gangs – one Latino, one African-American – are trapped in a deserted corner of LA after microbes from a meteor turn the world into flesh-eating ghouls. The plot is non-existent and the zombies are slow and dim-witted – although arguably brighter than the unimaginative characters who treat the apocalypse as a chance to try out for the Darwin Awards as they bicker, swagger, fight, and die. "Y'all don't like dark meat," one black gangsta tells the ghoul pack as they prepare to chomp on him. "Check this out, we can all go down to my Aunt May's house and she can make us some hams and macaroni cheese and greens… OK, kill the greens."

GANGSTERS, GUNS AND ZOMBIES
2012, UK
Dir: Matthew Mitchell. Prod: Clare Pearce.
Sc: Matthew Mitchell, Taliesyn Mitchell
Cast: Vincent Jerome, Huggy Leaver, Fabrizio Santino, Cassandra Orhan, Frank Rizzo

Lock, Stock and Two Smoking Zombies. This low-budget British indie delivers plenty of mockney gangster shtick as a group of bank robbers find themselves on the run just as the world is overtaken by a zombie apocalypse. It should be wearisome but director and co-writer Matt Mitchell doesn't set his sights too high and livens up his generic zombie apocalypse with some potty-mouthed characters and novelty ghouls (Clowns! Footballers! Knights!) A modest addition to modern Brit z-cinema to set alongside the *Devil's Playground* (2010) and *Cockneys Vs Zombies* (2012).

GARDEN OF THE DEAD
1972, USA
Alternative title: Tomb of the Undead
Dir: John Hayes. Prod: Daniel Cady. Sc: Jack Matcha
Cast: Phil Kenneally, Duncan McLeod, John Dullaghan, John Dennis, Marland Proctor, Lee Frost

A group of chain-ganged prisoners in an isolated work camp get high on formaldehyde fumes in this dreadful zombie shocker. After a prison break goes wrong the bodies of dead inmates are slung in shallow graves soaked in formaldehyde and – through some inexplicable chemical process – the dead return to life as fast-moving ghouls armed with pick-axes. Lots of boring action sequences pad out the (mercifully) brief running time, until the prison guards realise that the best way to keep a bunch of sexually-pent up zombies quiet is to give them some female company and then catch them with their pants down. Awful.

GEORGE: A ZOMBIE INTERVENTION
2009, USA
Dir: J.T. Seaton. Prod: Brad Hodson, J.T.Seaton. Sc: J.T. Seaton, Brad Hodson
Cast: Peter Stickles, Michelle Tomlinson, Carlos Larkin, Shannon Hodson, Eric Dean

Micro-budget filmmaking doesn't have to be terrible: this cheap 'n' cheerful effort zips along nicely, beginning with a cartoonish school slideshow that preps us on the rules of the zombie outbreak. Not much later we meet George (Carlos Larkin), a sentient zombie who's trying to live among the living without eating them (and not succeeding terribly well). One of several "touchy feely" zombie films that tackled the idea of making zombies sympathetic protagonists – the most obvious being *Warm Bodies* (2013) – this has George's friends hiring an interventionist to help him fight off his more anti-social desires. Ironic and daffy, it delivers a few good chuckles with an offbeat take on addiction.

GERMZ
2010, USA
Dir: J.T. Boone, John Craddock. Prod: John Craddock
Sc: J.T Boone
Cast: Maguerite Soundberg, Michael Flores, Bernard Setaro Clark, Mark Chiappone, Jody Pucello

A crashed satellite unleashes an alien germ that turns the inhabitants of a rural American town into flesh-hungry cannibals. "Alien? As in foreign?" wonders likeable sheriff's deputy (Michael Flores). No such luck. Distributed by *Fangoria*'s DVD label – whose marketing bods shamelessly added the "Z" to the original title *Germ* – this backwoods horror never really gets going.

THE GHOST BREAKERS
1940, USA
Dir: George Marshall. Prod: Arthur Hornblow Jr.
Sc: Walter DeLeon
Cast: Bob Hope, Paulette Goddard, Richard Carlson, Paul Lukas, Willie Best

Bob Hope teams up with Willie Best as a radio show host and his valet who end up in a haunted Cuban castle. The castle has been inherited by Paulette Goddard, who's being spooked out of the place by the zombie son of the former housekeeper and a collection of bad guys desperate to get their hands on the silver mine buried beneath the foundations.

GHOST BRIGADE
1992, USA
Alternative titles: Grey Knight, The Killing Box, The Lost Brigade
Dir: George Hickenlooper. Prod: Brad Krevoy, Steve Stabler. Sc: Matt Greenberg
Cast: Corbin Bernsen, Adrian Pasdar, Ray Wise, Cynda Williams

Civil War zombie ghouls attract an unlikely cast in this threadbare production. Martin Sheen, Ray Wise, Billy Bob Thornton and Matt LeBlanc are among the famous faces as a band of unkillable Confederate soldiers go on the rampage. Caught somewhere between ghosts and living dead ghouls, these creatures aren't really zombies but a mishmash of horror conventions (they're wounded by silver and can't cross running water). It doesn't add up to anything very much (and there are rumours of post-production tampering). Oh, and if the portentous voiceover about the horror of war occasionally sounds as if it's been lifted straight out of *Apocalypse Now* that may be because Hickenlooper also directed the Francis Ford Coppola documentary *Hearts of Darkness: A*

Filmmaker's Apocalypse (1991).

GHOST TOWN
1988, USA
Dir: Richard Governor. Prod: Larry, Carroll, Tim Tennant. Sc: Duke Sandefur
Cast: Franc Luz, Catherine Hickland, Jimmie F. Skaggs, Penelope Windust, Bruce Glover

For a while this ropey outing was the closest anyone had come to making a zombie Western (today there are now several more, although we're still waiting for a great – or even halfway decent – one). Here modern day sheriff's deputy Langley (Franc Luz) is on the trail of a kidnapped girl when he finds himself stuck in a supernatural ghost town lorded over by a decaying zombie-ghost called Devlin. Can he save the girl and free the town's spirits from their purgatorial existence?

GHOSTS OF MARS
2001, USA
Dir: John Carpenter. Prod: Sandy King. Sc: Larry Sulkis, John Carpenter
Cast: Ice Cube, Natasha Henstridge, Jason Statham, Pam Grier, Clea DuVall

John Carpenter takes the zombie movie into space for some laughable shenanigans on Mars in this thrash-metal living dead flick. Vengeful red planet demons possess the bodies of dead colonists and head out to attack cops transporting one of the galaxy's most dangerous criminals, Desolation Williams (Ice Cube). Yes, it's *Assault on Precinct 13* (1976) all over again, just set in 2176 and with zombie ghouls who look like they've escaped from a Slipknot concert.

THE GHOUL
1933, UK
Dir: T. Hayes Hunter. Prod: Michael Balcon. Sc: Roland Pertwee, John Hastings Turner
Cast: Boris Karloff, Ernest Thesiger, Cedric Hardwicke, Dorothy Hyson, Anthony Bushell

Karloff's feted return to Britain after making his name in America isn't a patch on his Universal efforts. Playing a dying Egyptologist who uses an occult amulet to bring himself back from his coffin (or rather sarcophagus), the star himself is on fine form. It's just the rest of the movie that's terrible as subplots involving the assembled mourners and thieves who want to steal the gem take their toll. It doesn't help that the only surviving print is in an awful state. Still, Karloff's hulking, ape-like ghoul is an interesting take on the zombie – a thuggish villain who kicks in windows and bends open bars with his bare hands while sporting a dreadfully decomposed face and thick, bushy eyebrows.

THE GHOULS
2003, USA
Alternative title: Cannibal Dead: The Ghouls
Dir: Chad Ferrin. Prod: Cad Ferrin, Nicholas Loizides, John Santos. Sc: Chad Ferrin
Cast: Timothy Muskatell, Trent Haaga, Tina Birchfield, Gil Espanoza, Casey Powell

Under Los Angeles, cannibal ghouls live in the sewers preying on the drunk, drugged and homeless. This bleak SOV effort has terrible production values, but a handful of interesting thoughts about how our media culture makes desensitised zombies of us all. Imagine *C.H.U.D.* (1984) remade by Abel Ferrara.

GHOUL SCHOOL
1990, USA
Dir: Timothy O'Rawe. Prod: Timothy O'Rawe. Sc: Timothy O'Rawe
Cast: William Friedman, Scott Gordon, Paul Venier, Nancy Sirianni, Ed Burrows

"I think they're putting a little bit too much chlorine in the pool!" When a couple of thugs accidentally release toxic chemicals in a high school gymnasium, the swim team turn into sharp-toothed, blue-tinged ghouls. Pretty soon zombies in Speedos and Lycra swimsuits are running down the corridors eating students and it's left to a couple of *Fangoria*-reading nerds (William Friedman, Scott Gordon) to save the day. A scrappy, crappy effort *Ghoul School* fails on just about every level, not least of all its cheesy, DIY gore. Jackie "The Joke Man" Martling's comedy try out is a sole high point.

GO GOA GONE
2013, INDIA
Dir: Raj Nidimoru & Krishna DK. Prod: Saif Ali Khan, Dinesh Vijan, Sunil Lulla. Sc: Raj Nidimoru & Krishna DK
Cast: Saif Ali Khan, Kunal Khemu, Vir Das, Anand Tiwari, Pooja Gupta

Three slacker friends head out to Goa from mainland India for a weekend of raving, only to discover that a new Russian pill is turning partygoers into ghouls. Playing to an upwardly mobile, urban audience, the first Bollywood zom-com is bright and fluffy with an anti-drugs message, a crazed Russian mafia gunman (Saif Ali Khan) and an inventive use of cocaine to pacify its army of stumbling, dead ravers. The Harold and Kumar style antics and cowardly banter of the three heroes is played strictly for laughs. "I'll take the hot one, you take the pissed off one, you take the fat one," plans Hardik (Kunal Khemu) as they're surrounded by three zombie girls. "Why do I always get the fat one?" complains Bunny (Anand Tiwari). "I want the hot one!"

GOESHI
1981, SOUTH KOREA
Alternative title: Strange Dead Bodies
Dir: Kang Beom-gu. Prod: Jeong Woong-gi. Sc: Ju Dong-woon
Cast: Yu Kwang-ok, Kang Myeong, Park Am, Hwang Ok-hwan, Hong Yun-jeong

Incredibly obscure, this 1980s South Korean zombie movie exists as a bootleg taken from its original domestic VHS release. That means it has no subtitles but even if you don't speak Korean it's obvious that it owes debt to Grau's *The Living Dead at Manchester Morgue* (1974). The basic plot revolves around a hitchhiker and a female motorist, en route to visit her sister, who discover a transmitter in the countryside that's turning people into zombies. Key elements from Grau's film are repeated – like the heroine being attacked by the first ghoul while she tries to escape in her car; and the bullying police inspector investigating the sudden spike in the murder rate – and the atmosphere is suitably downbeat and eerie. I'm still not sure what the transmitter is for (presumably an electronic pesticide?) but it's apparently being supervised by an American scientist. The zombies lurch slowly out of the undergrowth in a sinister fashion, noses bleeding and eyes red-ringed as if they're terminally hungover.

GORE WHORE
1994, USA
Dir: Hugh Gallagher. Prod: Hugh Gallagher. Sc: Hugh Gallagher
Cast: Audrey Street, Brady Debussey, D'Lana Tunnell, John McLaughlin

No budget, no brains, no taste. Gallagher's z-grade effort stars Audrey Street as a zombie/vampire prostitute who's escaped from a scientist's lab with his newly-invented reanimating serum. On her trail is a deadbeat private investigator who slowly realises there's more to this hooker than meets the eye. "In my death the tables are turned and paybacks are a motherfucker" she hisses as she hangs out in a graveyard, dosing herself up on the green glowing serum using a hypodermic/dildo combo. She's also brought a few corpses back from the dead as playmates. The dedication to penis-slicing woman-spurned Lorena Bobbitt suggests this wants to be a feminist spin on *Re-Animator*, although I'm not sure Camille Paglia would approve. Over a decade later the porno *Grub Girl* (2006) made this look surprisingly tame.

GORE-MET, ZOMBIE CHEF FROM HELL
1986, USA
Dir: Don Swan. Prod: Don Swan. Sc: Don Swan, Jeff Baughn, William Highsmith
Cast: Theo Depuay, Kelley Kunicki, C.W. Casey, Michael O'Neill, Jeff Baughn

"This will be your eternal curse! You will lust for flesh when you do not have it and despise it when you do!" Goza (Theo Depuay) is a cursed priest from the Middle Ages who's forced to spend a living dead eternity munching human flesh. We meet him in 1986 at his Deli and Beach Club where he parades around in a Hawaiian shirt and uses his customers to make burgers and stews (surely not the most sustainable business model). Chiefly remembered thanks to its title, this micro-budget cannibal epic is a zombie movie in name only.

THE GRAPES OF DEATH
1978, FRANCE
Original title: Les raisins de la mort
Alternative title: Pesticide

Dir: Jean Rollin. Prod: Claude Guedj. Sc: Jean Rollin, Christian Meunier
Cast: Marie George Pascal, Felix Marten, Serge Marquand, Mirella Rancelot

Wine contaminated by a bad pesticide causes a strange form of zombification in Jean Rollin's Gallic horror. Heroine Elizabeth finds herself at the mercy of a gang of putrefying locals as the wine's effect devastates rural France. Teaming up with a pair of non-wine drinkers she makes her way to the supposed safety of a mountaintop vineyard, but it's actually ground zero for the disaster. Rollin's attempt at gore *à l'américaine* may not be one of his most typical films, but it's moody and distinctive stuff.

GRAVE MISTAKE
2008, USA
Dir: Shawn Darling. Prod: Shawn Darling. Sc: Shawn Darling
Cast: Seth Darling, James Blackburn, Wendy Andrews, Stephen Eckles, Benjamin Palmer

When the zombie apocalypse comes the weirdest things can happen. Toxic dumping makes the dead walk in this by-numbers, no-budget offering from New Mexico. Leading a band of survivors to the local hardware store, mechanic Mike (James Blackburn) meets a bloke in a medieval suit of armour who throws himself into slaying the ghouls while yabbering courtly dialogue: "Our enemies are numerous as if hell itself had sent its legions upon the face of the earth. For these are some… evil dead." It's a momentary diversion in an otherwise pointless backyard outing. Producer-writer-director Shawn Darling does his own VFX and compositing – and you can see the joins.

GRAVESTONED
2006, USA
Dir: Michael McWillie. Prod: Michael McWillie, Steve Terrell, Max Steward. Sc: Michael McWillie
Cast: Eryn Brooke, Ron Britton, Summer Borden, Ivan Jones, Everett Burns

"I don't know who this Shakespeare guy is but he needs to come in for a rewrite!" So begins *Gravestoned*, a movie that combines stoners, a film-within-a-film horror director with delusions of grandeur, a one-armed zombie and a Scotty dog (random trivia: director McWillie is a dog artist who was once invited to paint a picture of President Bush's Scotty dog, Barney). During a night shoot in a misty cemetery the pot-smoking cast and crew are attacked by a ghoul with one arm, a machete and a plastic bag over his head. He's the former owner of the movie's most realistic "prosthetic" limb which was sourced by a couple of gangsta dope peddlers eager to break into the movie biz. Barely coherent, you'll need more than a few blunts to see you through it.

GRAVEYARD ALIVE: A ZOMBIE NURSE IN LOVE
2003, CANADA
Dir: Elza Kephart. Prod: Patricia Gomez, Elza Kephart, Andrea Stark. Sc: Elza Kephart, Patricia Gomez
Cast: Anne Day-Jones, Karl Gerhardt, Samantha Slan, Martha Brooke, Barbara Bacci

Billed as *General Hospital* meets *Night of the Living Dead*, this feminist zombie picture is a welcome riposte to the almost exclusively male-dominated movies in the rest of this filmography. Taking the eroticism of the vampire mythology and grafting it onto a living dead soap opera set in a hospital, debut writer-director Elza Kephart delivers a fantastic homage to the low-budget horror movies with some beautiful cinematography (it's shot in black & white in the old Techniscope format) and a very funny line in camp humour. The zombie nurse is Patsy Powers (Anne Day-Jones), an ugly duckling whose prettier, blonder, sexier peers mercilessly ridicule her for being a plain Jane. Then an encounter with a zombie patient transforms her into a sexy ghoul (complete with all the necessary curves) and she's able to woo the handsome Dr Dox. Loving, warm and witty it's a real indie treat that reinvigorates zombie conventions.

GRAVEYARD DISTURBANCE
1987, ITALY
Original title: Una notte nel cimitero
Dir: Lamberto Bava. Prod: Massimo Manasse, Marco Grillo Spina. Sc: Dardano Sacchetti, Lamberto Bava
Cast: Gregory Lech Thaddeus, Lea Martino, Beatrice Ring, Gianmarco Tognazzi, Karl Zinny

What's more disturbing? This lame TV movie's distinct lack of gore or the realization that it's directed by Lamberto Bava, scion of Italian horror's greatest dynasty? Thieving teenagers find themselves in trouble when they accept a bet to hide in some deserted catacombs. Needless to say, they're not as deserted as they thought, which leads to all kinds of encounters with various monsters and a few rotting corpses.

GRAVEYARD OF THE LIVING DEAD
2008, GERMANY
Dir: Marc Rohnstock. Prod: Ramon Kaltenbach, Christian Reckert, Martin Rüdel, Marc Rohnstock, Lars Rohnstock. Sc: Marc Rohnstock
Cast: Stefan Rüdel, Alexander Reckert, Lars Rohnstock, Marc Rohnstock, Ramon Kaltenbach

Gonzo German splatter filmmaker Timo Rose makes a "special appearance" in this micro-budget outing. That probably tells you all you need to know about its quality. In a German laboratory, scientists in Marigold gloves are doing experiments on a corpse in Speedos, with inevitable results. Meanwhile, a gang of black-wearing Goth kids on a picnic to a graveyard encounter the blood-splattered escapees from the lab. Their blood then causes the dead to rise from their graves. Rohnstock throws together no-budget, no-nonsense gore – a messy "Last Supper" feeding scene, amputations with axes and chainsaws, and head trauma with a rake. But if you're hoping for anything more than a DIY punk outing, you'd better look elsewhere. The credits – where several cast/crew members get 10+ mentions each – could well be the basis for a drinking game.

GROUND ZERO
2010, USA
Dir: Channing Lowe. Prod: Channing Lowe, David Garcia, Aaron Peterson. Sc: Steve Darling, Channing Lowe, Aaron Peterson
Cast: Mike Langer, Sahna Foley, D.L. Walker, Chris Harvey, David Candland

When a group of "cleaners" are sent to a warehouse to wipe away all traces of a corporate assassination, they don't expect the bodies to start returning to life. It turns out that their client is developing germ bio-weapons and that the dead bodies are activists who were trying to expose the dodgy experiments.

This indie horror spends a long time setting up its sub-*Pulp Fiction* cleaner characters – led by henpecked Jairus (Mike Langer) and badass blonde Greer (Sahna Foley) – by which point the zombies become something of an afterthought. I wouldn't trust these guys to clean up a kitchen counter, let alone a zombie outbreak.

GRUB GIRL
2006, USA

Alternative title: Ed Lee's Grub Girl
Dir: Craven Moorehead.
Cast: Brittney Sky, Charmane Star, Teanara Kai, Eva Angelina, Gigi

Based on the comic *Zombie Hooker* by Ed Lee, this porno is less interesting than it sounds. After a nuclear powered jet leaks radiation everywhere, a young woman (Brittney Sky) ends up "on a slab in some lab" where she's raped by a couple of scientists before reanimating, killing them and going off to work as a zombie hooker (a "grub girl"). Being dead has its advantages – she can't catch diseases, can't feel pain – but it also means she's abused by every sicko she meets (her pimp's only rules: Johns can't break any bones or cut off any parts). Eventually turning on the men who are doing her wrong, she goes into business on her own opening a grub brothel full of dead hookers. Zombie sisters are doing it for themselves.

HAECKEL'S TALE – MASTERS OF HORROR
2006, USA

Dir: John McNaughton. Prod: Tom Rowe, Lisa Richardson. Sc: Mick Garris
Cast: Derek Cecil, Leela Savasta, Tom McBeath, Steve Bacic, Gerrard Plunkett

George Romero was originally slated to direct this episode of the *Masters of Horror* series, but dropped out due to scheduling conflicts. He's replaced by John McNaughton (*Henry: Portrait of a Serial Killer*) who does good work with a Hammer-style period drama set in the 1800s. Haeckel (Derek Cecil), is a scientist researching the reanimation of the dead who becomes obsessed with black magic. He encounters a money-grabbing necromancer (Jon Polito) who is resurrecting the dead for sexed-up shenanigans with a farmer's young wife (Leela Savasta). "It's the most horrible story ever told… that a woman would have carnal knowledge of the dead!" Indeed.

HALLOW'S END
2003, USA

Dir: Jon Keeyes. Prod: Brandon Baker, Richard T. Carey, Faras Rabadi. Sc: Christopher J. Burdick
Cast: Stephen Cloud, Brandy Little, Amy Jo Hearron, Amy Morris, Jim Dunn

"The Devil is real. He is! I met him. I knelt down and kissed his backside. Mmmmm…" Set in a haunted Halloween house in the town of Hallow's End run by college students for charity, this underpowered B-movie eventually turns into risible nonsense after much interminably pointless exposition and too-much character conflict (secret lesbian trysts – because, why not?) It's chief idea is pretty simple: an ancient occult volume turns the kids into their Halloween costumes – pirates, ghosts, zombies and vampires – after scheming Heidi (Amy Morris) makes a pact with Satan and promises to sacrifice all her friends. It looks like a TV movie and it amounts to very little of note. There are *Scooby Doo* episodes with more scares.

THE HAPPINESS OF THE KATAKURIS
2000, JAPAN

Original title: Katakuri-ke no kôfuku
Dir: Takashi Miike. Prod: Hirotsugu Yoshida. Sc: Kikumi Yamagishi
Cast: Kenji Sawada, Keiko Matsuzaka, Shinji Takeda, Naomi Nishida, Tetsuro Tanba

A demented remake of Korean film *The Quiet Family*, this dispenses with everything apart from the basic premise: a laid-off family leave the big city to open a guesthouse in the mountains. After their first guest commits suicide, the family decide that the best way to keep the tragedy quiet is by burying the body out in the woods. Pretty soon, all of their lodgers end up dead by dawn, creating a pile of corpses that have to be discreetly disposed of. An all-singing, all-dancing karaoke epic, this features a brief scene in which the dead guests return from the grave for a quick dance number.

HARD ROCK ZOMBIES
1984, USA

Dir: Krishna Shah. Prod: Krishna Shah. Sc: Krishna

Shah, David Ball
Cast: E.J. Curcio, Geno Andrews, Sam Mann, Mick Manz, Jennifer Coe

A rock band is brought back from the grave in this supposedly outrageous, but really rather dull horror comedy featuring Adolf Hitler, a midget Nazi attacking a cow and lots of rock music. It's brash, it's loud, and it's very 1980s. Beavis and Butthead would approve. Everyone else is advised to bring earplugs.

HAROLD'S GOING STIFF
2011, UK
Dir: Keith Wright. Prod: Richard Guy. Sc: Keith Wright
Cast: Stan Rowe, Sarah Spencer, Andy Pandini, Phil Gascoyne, Lee Thompson

A bittersweet British mockumentary, *Harold's Going Stiff* focuses on a strange neurological virus that causes its victims to become stiff-limbed. Gentle and observational, it's not your ordinary zombie movie but a poignant and very funny take on old age and isolation.

HELLDRIVER
2010, JAPAN
Original title: Nihon bundan: Heru doraibâ
Dir: Yoshihiro Nishimura. Prod Yoshinori Chiba, Hiroyuki Yamada. Sc: Yoshihiro Nishimura, Daichi Nagisa
Cast: Yumiko Hara, Eihi Shiina, Yurei Yanagi, Kazuki Namioka, Kentaro Kishi

Helldriver begins with its emo schoolgirl heroine Kika (Yumiko Hara) pole-dancing around a zombie's over-elongated spinal column, and gets increasingly ridiculous. Ash from a falling meteor causes citizens in the northern half of Japan to turn into antler-headed monsters. While politicians argue over whether the dead have rights or not, Kika heads into the wilderness in search of her evil mother – a zombie queen sitting on top of a giant man-mountain of ghouls. It's extremely violent, bizarre and demented. It's also surprisingly incoherent and dull.

HELLGATE
1989, SOUTH AFRICA
Dir: William A. Levey, Prod: Anant Singh. Sc: Michael

O'Rourke
Cast: Ron Palillo, Abigail Wolcott, Carel Trichardt, Petrea Curran, Evan Klisser

A town with a secret, a beautiful female zombie, a magical crystal and a campfire ghost story do little to enliven the horrors of *Hellgate* as a girl raped and murdered in the 1950s is brought back to life by her embittered father. Complete drivel that went straight to video for very obvious reasons. However, the exploding goldfish deserves an honorary (posthumous) mention for services to horror cinema…

HIDE AND CREEP
2004, USA
Dir: Chuck Hartsell, Chance Shirley. Prod: Chuck Hartsell, Stacey Sessions, Chance Shirley. Sc: Chance Shirley
Cast: Barry Austin, Melissa Bush, Chris Garrison, Chris Hartsell, Chuck Hartsell

"There are only about three good American zombie movies and Romero made all those…" Sadly, nothing in this micro-budget zom-com proves that statement wrong, but it's a step or two up from the usual backyard nonsense that comes out of the US. Shot on 16mm and later spruced up for a DVD release by The Asylum, its zombies-in-a-redneck-town premise is enlivened by some funny gags (like why a strip mall isn't a good place to wait out the z-apocalypse) and a Kevin Smith vibe (the hero is a video store clerk weary of explaining widescreen letterboxing to his clientele).

HOMECOMING – MASTERS OF HORROR
2005, USA
Dir: Joe Dante. Prod: Lisa Richardson, Tom Rowe. Sc: Sam Hamm
Cast: Thea Gill, Jon Tenney, Terry David Mulligan, Beverley Breuer, Robert Picardo

Released as part of ShowTime's *Masters of Horror* series, this politicised zombie movie reworks *Deathdream* and the classic Monkey's Paw conceit as dead soldiers return from the Iraq War and demand the right to vote. Unlikely to be on George W. Bush's Netflix queue.

HOOD OF THE LIVING DEAD

2004, USA
Dir: Jose Quiroz, Eduardo Quiroz. Prod: Jose Quiroz, Eduardo Quiroz. Sc: Jose Quiroz, Eduardo Quiroz
Cast: Carl Washington, Chris Angelo, Brandon Daniels, Jose Rosete, Victor Zaragoza

"How the fuck do you explain a dead muthafucka wandering around eatin' people alive?" The mean streets of Oakland make an unlikely setting in this gangbanging zombie flick. When his brother Jermaine (Brandon Daniels) is killed in a drive-by-shooting science lab worker Ricky (Carl Washington) uses his access to rainbow-coloured test tubes to raise him from the dead. Jermaine then stumbles around the neighbourhood taking chunks out of people while Ricky tries to track him and a few other zombies down. Dour, cheap and very, very dull.

THE HORDE
2009, FRANCE
Original title: La Horde
Dir: Yannick Dahan, Benjamin Rocher. Prod: Raphaël Rocher. Sc: Juliette Baumard Cast: Claude Perron, Jean-Pierre Martins, Eriq Ebouaney, Aurélien Recoing, Doudou Masta

Watch enough zombie movies and you'll know that certain places are better to hide in during a living dead attack than others (the shopping mall in *Dawn of the Dead* is infinitely more hospitable than the morgue in *The Beyond*, for instance). In *The Horde*, a kinetic French zombie/gangster mash-up, the protagonists are trapped inside a condemned high-rise while ghouls mass outside. Clearly, there's no way to go but up. The same could be said for *The Horde* itself, a grubby exercise in brutality with a crack den aesthetic and a selection of disreputable heroes: a Nigerian drug dealer, bent cops and a racist veteran of the Second Indochina War who dubs zombies "Chinks". Playing to the gore crowd, *The Horde* conjures up some outrageous violence (heavy machine guns; hand grenades shoved into zombie mouths), yet it's misogynous and racist and rarely half as much fun as it seems to think it is.

HORRID
2011, USA
Dir: James Pronath. Prod: Mike Jorgenson, Jim Van

Vonderen, James Pronath. Sc: James Pronath
Cast: Kevin Kiser, Liz Ribarchek, Kyle Berg, Amber Rae Halama, Roland James Williams

"It's not a disease. It's a cure for disease..." A trio of guys on the worst bachelor party in cinema history end up in the Wisconsin woods just as infected patients escape from a nearby lab (what are the chances, eh?). Short on cash and originality, *Horrid* pits pepperoni pizza faced zeds against the 20-something guys as the scientists responsible for the cure-all virus try to stop the outbreak. Apparently one of the earliest patients was so hungry for flesh he devoured his own arm. You'll probably want to eat your own eyeballs Ving Rhames-style by the 20-minute mark.

HOUSE OF THE DEAD II
2005, USA
Dir: Mike Hurst. Prod: Mark A. Altman, Mark Gottwald. Sc: Mark A. Altman
Cast: Emmanuelle Vaugier, Ed Quinn, Victoria Pratt, Nadine Velazquez, Billy Brown

A sequel to one of the worst videogame-to-movie adaptations ever made, *House of the Dead II* sees Brit Michael Hurst replace Uwe Böll in the director's chair as a college campus is overrun by ghouls. Two scientists (Ed Quinn and Emmanuelle Vaugier) are dispatched to contain the outbreak, along with an elite (read: inept) special forces team. Inevitably, they get more than they bargained for as the "Category 1" threat spirals out of control. The bulk of the movie is a dull mishmash of ill-conceived gore, illogical scripting and supporting actress T&A (including a scene where a soldier abuses a buxom dead zombie for a photo opportunity. Stay classy, guys). Is it better or worse than the atrocious original? Is a snail quicker than slug...?

HUMANS VS ZOMBIES
2011, USA
Dir: Brian T. Jaynes. Prod: Niko Foster, Brian T. Jaynes, Bruce Kahn. Sc: Devan Sagliani, Brian T. Jaynes
Cast: Madison Burge, Frederic Doss, Melissa Carnell, Chip Joslin, Jonah Priour

Humans Vs Zombies is a college tag game between two teams. *Humans Vs Zombies* the movie is a half-baked attempt to do something with that concept, as a group of college kids play the game for real when a viral outbreak reaches their Texas campus. Other than the references to the game in the opening sequence, this is just your bog-standard survivors vs zombies micro-budget movie.

HORROR EXPRESS
1972, SPAIN/UK
Original title: Pánico en el transiberiano
Dir: Gene [Eugenío] Martin. Prod: Eugenio Martín, Bernard Gordon. Sc: Arnaud d'Usseau, Julian Halevy, Eugenío Martin
Cast: Christopher Lee, Peter Cushing, Alberto de Mendoza, Silvia Tortosa, Julio Peña, Telly Savalas

The Trans-Siberian railway is the setting for this alien invasion movie featuring a couple of zombies. The real star of the show is a two-million-year-old alien monster that thaws out in transit and goes wild. The creature has the ability to erase men's minds, turning them into blank-eyed zombies. It's great fun, with Lee and Cushing playing the material for all its worth. "What if one of you is the monster?" demands one of the passengers when they discover that the creature has the ability to jump into people's bodies. "Monster?!" replies an incredulous Cushing, "We're British, you know."

HORROR HOSPITAL
1973, UK
Alternative title: Computer Killers
Dir: Antony Balch. Prod: Richard Gordon. Sc: Antony Balch, Alan Watson
Cast: Michael Gough, Robin Askwith, Vanessa Shaw, Ellen Pollock, Dennis Price

Directed by legendary British distributor and avant-garde filmmaker Antony Balch several years after he'd collaborated with William S. Burroughs on *The Cut Ups* and *Towers Open Fire*, this is a quite unique attempt to turn trash horror into something more. It fails dismally, but it's never less than cheesily entertaining. A hippie (Robin Askwith from the *Confessions...* sex comedies) gets more than he bargains for when a weekend break in a country retreat turns nasty. Brittlehouse Manor is a "health resort" that's definitely bad for your health as experiments on the guests turn them into braindead zombies. Throw in a weird mud creature,

leather-clad biker boys, and an evil dwarf butler and you have one of the most surreal trash horror movies of the 1970s.

THE HORROR OF PARTY BEACH
1963, USA
Alternative titles: Invasion of the Zombies
Dir: Del Tenney. Prod: Del Tenney. Sc: Richard Hilliard
Cast: John Scott, Alice Lyon, Allan Laurel, Eulabelle Moore, Marilyn Clarke

I Eat Your Skin (1964) director Del Tenney's currency in zombie circles is pretty low even by this variable genre's standards. This ludicrous beach movie cum rock 'n' roll horror flick does little to endear him either. Partying teenagers are attacked on the sandy beaches by mutant sea monsters after toxic sludge is dumped into the water. The monsters don't have much to do with zombies (other than the fact that the dim-witted cast call them that) but look more like The Creature from the Black Lagoon with a hotdog in his mouth. Oh and there's a dance number called "The Zombie Stomp" thrown in for good measure. They should have just had a clam bake instead.

HORROR OF THE ZOMBIES
1973, SPAIN
Original title: El buque maldito
Alternative titles: The Ghost Galleon, Ghost Ship of Blind Dead, La noche del buque maldito, Ship of Zombies, Das Geisterschiff der schwimmenden Leichen
Dir: Amando de Ossorio. Prod: J.L. Bermúdez de Castro. Sc: Amando de Ossorio
Cast: María Perschy, Jack Taylor, Bárbara Rey, Carlos Lemos, Manuel de Blas

A publicity stunt featuring bikini-clad babes tempts the Templars out of hiding in this nautical entry in the *Blind Dead* series. Set out on the ocean wave, it follows a pair of models lost at sea and the attempts of a rescue party to save them. A ghostly galleon containing the Templars unexpectedly interrupts the proceedings – by sailing in and out of some vaguely explained inter-dimensional portal – leaving the protagonists trapped aboard until the spooky shoreline conclusion. Best not to dwell on the footage of the galleon itself, which looks decidedly like a miniature model floating in a pond.

HORROR RISES FROM THE TOMB
1972, SPAIN

Original title: El espanto surge de la tumba
Dir: Carlos Aured. Prod: Ricardo Muñoz Suay.
Sc: Jacinto Molina
Cast: Paul Naschy [Jacinto Molina], Emma Cohen, Vic Winner [Victor Alcazar], Helga Liné, Betsabé Ruiz

Years before Arnie, Paul Naschy's 15th-century warlock promised "I'll be back". He wasn't joking. Resurrected as a disembodied head in a box, Naschy stalks this trashy Spanish horror resurrecting the dead for nefarious purposes and growling lines like "You will return my body to me that for centuries has been separated from me, allowing my soul to wander through the shadows!" Its Gothic horror is typically overblown and there's an all-too brief scene in which noisy, gargling zombies attack a house and are fought off with shotguns and fire.

HOT WAX ZOMBIES ON WHEELS
1999, USA

Dir: Michael Roush. Prod: Mike J. Roush, Bob Yesk.
Sc: Elizabeth Bergholz
Cast: Jill Miller, Gwen Somers, Tre Lovell, Jon Briddell, Kimberly Johnson

"Zombie or not zombie, wax or no wax, nobody two times me!" Shot in twelve days in sunny California, *Hot Wax on Wheels* weighs in with copious amounts of naked flesh as a dominatrix zombie biker (Gwen Somers) opens up a "hot wax" beauty salon in a small fishing town and invites the inhabitants to get rid of their "pesky body hair". Pretty soon sex-crazed, fur-free "zombies" are on the loose as the hot wax therapy has unexpected side-effects. It's down to lingerie store owner Sharon (Jill Miller) to save the day with a blower full of hair shavings. Put it on a double bill with Troma's *Chopper Chicks in Zombietown* (1989).

HOUSE
1985, USA

Dir: Steve Miner. Prod: Sean S. Cunningham. Sc: Ethan Wiley
Cast: William Katt, George Wendt, Richard Moll, Kay Lenz, Michael Ensign

Friday the 13th's Sean S. Cunningham teamed up with executive producer Roger Corman for this 1980s horror-comedy about a haunted house. William Katt's Vietnam vet turned novelist moves into his dead aunt's spooky home only to find himself haunted by ghosts, flying gardening implements and the zombified remains of "Big Ben", a comrade in arms who he left behind in Southeast Asia. Cheesy horror comedy at its stinkiest.

THE HOUSE BY THE CEMETERY
1981, ITALY

Original title: Quella villa accanto al cimitero
Dir: Lucio Fulci. Prod: Fabrizio De Angelis.
Sc: Dardano Sacchetti, Giorgio Mariuzzo, Lucio Fulci
Cast: Katherine [Catriona] MacColl, Paolo Malco, Ania Pieroni, Giovanni Frezza, Silvia Collatina

Bob (Giovanni Frezza) and his parents move into a Victorian house in New England that formerly belonged to a family named Freudstein. Little do they realise that the zombified remains of the evil Dr Freudstein are still in the basement and that he's attacking anyone who ventures downstairs. A typically surreal addition to Fulci's zombie trilogy, this doesn't stand up to scrutiny but give yourself over to its strangeness and it delivers all the primal terror of a Grimm fairy tale.

THE HOUSE OF SEVEN CORPSES
1973, USA

Dir: Paul Harrison. Prod: Paul Lewis, Paul Harrison.
Sc: Paul Harrison, Thomas J. Kelly
Cast: John Ireland, Faith Domergue, John Carradine, Carole Wells, Jerry Strickler

"Eight graves! Seven bodies! One killer... and he's already dead!" enthused the posters. Shame the movie didn't live up to the hype. A bunch of witless horror filmmakers manage to accidentally raise the dead while shooting a zombie movie in a spooky old mansion where John Carradine works as a caretaker (that should've put off most location scouts for starters). As they're picked off one by one, the production is put on hold, which is a shame since the director of the film-within-the-film gets some great lines as he shouts at his truly rubbish cast: "You're supposed to be going into a trance, not having an orgasm!" It turns out a ragged ghoul is killing off the principal cast, re-enacting the violent deaths of the family who used to own the mansion.

HOUSE OF THE DEAD
2003, CANADA/USA/GERMANY
Dir: Uwe Böll. Prod: Uwe Böll, Wolfgang Herold, Shawn Williamson. Sc: Mark Altman, Dave Parker
Cast: Jonathan Cherry, Tyron Leitso, Clint Howard, Ona Grauer, Ellie Cornell

The 1998 arcade game gets a pointless big screen adaptation. Quite how a game that was as simplistic as blasting zombies with a light gun seemed like the perfect movie idea is quite an enigma. Certainly the finished product doesn't bear much relation to the game, with some dumb kids heading out to a deserted island for a rave (sponsored by videogame creators Sega, no less) and ending up among the living dead instead. Personally, I'd rather spend 90 minutes watching someone else playing the arcade machine than sit through this lame collection of inept scares, footage culled from the videogame and braindead movie in-jokes. To stave off boredom, keep a look out for a zombie cameo from former *Fangoria* editor Tony Timpone.

THE HOUSE ON SKULL MOUNTAIN
1974, USA
Dir: Ron Honthaner. Prod: Ray Storey. Sc: Mildred Pares
Cast: Victor French, Janee Michelle, Jean Durand, Mike Evans, Xernona Clayton

This blaxploitation Old Dark House movie has a dying Haitian immigrant, Pauline Christophe (Mary J. Todd McKenzie), summoning her disparate great-grandchildren to her bedside. By the time they arrive on her Georgia estate on Skull Mountain, though, she's already kicked the bucket – and an inevitably bloody struggle ensues for control of her fortune. The estate's butler and voodoo priest Thomas (Jean Durand) knows more than he's letting on, menacing the guests with snakes, voodoo dolls and ouangas. Badly dated, this voodoo horror only manages to summon up a zombie in its final scene as Pauline is brought back from the dead. She bursts into the house in a puff of smoke, white haired and dusted in flour as if she's just blown up the oven while doing some

baking. For a proper blaxploitation zombie movie try *Sugar Hill* (1974).

I AM LEGEND
2007, USA
Dir: Francis Lawrence. Prod: Akiva Goldsman.
Sc: Mark Protosevich, Akiva Goldsman
Cast: Will Smith, Alice Braga, Charlie Tahan, Salli Richardson, Willow Smith

Will Smith is the last man on earth in this adaptation of Richard Matheson's seminal vampire/zombie horror novel. New York has never looked emptier.

I AM ΩMEGA
2007, USA
Dir: Griff Furst. Prod: David Michael Latt, David Rimawi, Paul Bales. Sc: Geoff Meed
Cast: Mark Dacascos, Geoff Meed, Jennifer Lee Wiggins, Ryan Lloyd

The Asylum try to steal some of *I Am Legend*'s audience share with this pointless, low-budget update of the classic Richard Matheson story. Martial artist Mark Dacascos stars as the last man on earth who spends his days shooting zombies in the mouth and trying not to go loopy with loneliness. A Skype call from the last woman on earth – hey, the Internet was designed to survive a nuclear war, so why not a zombie outbreak? – gives him a newfound purpose and pits him against a couple of hillbilly bandits. It's competent enough not be dreadful, but it's unlikely Will Smith and Warner Bros. lost much sleep over it.

I CAN'T BELIEVE I FUCKED A ZOMBIE
2011, USA
Dir: Rodney Moore. Prod: Rodney Moore. Sc: Rodney Moore
Cast: Caroline Pierce, Rachel O, Harper Leigh, Nikki Daniels, Rodney Moore

Filmmaker and adult actor Rodney Moore sets up a plotless tale of zombified women with insatiable appetites. The girls are dead-eyed and soulless, and shuffle about blankly, moaning "Fuck me" straight to camera. Pretty much like 99 per cent of all adult actresses, then. Unlike in Moore's earlier *Night of the Giving Head*, they don't look dead or infected and there's no real explanation for their state. Put this on a double bill with *Deadgirl* for maximum irony.

I EAT YOUR SKIN
1964, USA
Alternative titles: Voodoo Blood Bath, Zombies
Dir: Del Tenney. Prod: Del Tenney. Sc: Del Tenney
Cast: William Joyce, Heather Hewitt, Walter Coy, Dan Stapleton, Betty Hyatt Linton

More monochrome monsters from the indefatigable Del Tenney, director of *The Horror of Party Beach* (1963). This time he heads out to the Caribbean with a story about a playboy novelist and his publisher who get caught up in a voodoo conspiracy. The film's zombies are woeful creations that look as if they've been dunked head first in a mud bath. Their eyes are so full of gunk it's a wonder they can see to walk, let alone swing their machetes. Padded out with native voodoo rituals in which bikini-clad ladies gyrate round campfires and a ridiculous scene in which our heroes don a pair of voodoo masks to infiltrate a ceremony, it's pitiful even by Tenney's standards. There's no skin eating, and the less said about the crummy lap-dissolve sequence, in which we see a man being turned into a zombie, the better for everyone concerned.

I SELL THE DEAD
2008, USA
Dir: Glenn McQuaid. Prod: Larry Fessenden, Peter Phok. Sc: Glenn McQuaid
Cast: Dominic Monaghan, Ron Perlman, Larry Fessenden, Angus Scrimm, John Speredakos
Larry Fessenden's indie production company Glass Eye Pix pulls off a rambunctious period horror in this fog-shrouded, Dickensian tale of 18th-century grave robbers (played by Fessenden and Dominic Monaghan). Their employers are medical doctors searching for the secrets of immortality and their stock in trade is a supernatural collection of vampires, aliens and a few grey-skinned bandaged zombies who they dig up from crossroads. It's a fantastic, refreshingly original horror movie with comic book verve and an entertainingly manic edge – a shame, for the purposes of this book at least, that its zombies are little more than incidental.

I WALKED WITH A ZOMBIE
1943, USA
Dir: Jacques Tourneur. Prod: Val Lewton. Sc: Curt Siodmak, Ardel Wray
Cast: James Ellison, Frances Dee, Tom Conway, Edith Barrett, James Bell

Frances Dee stars as a naïve young nurse sent out to look after the catatonic wife of a plantation owner in the West Indies in this beautiful gothic tale. Uncertain whether to believe the local island superstition about voodoo and magic, she becomes embroiled in the family's affairs, encounters a striking native zombie, and begins to question her faith in the rational world.

I WAS A TEENAGE ZOMBIE
1986, USA
Dir: John Elias Michalakis. Prod: Richard Hirsh, John Elias Michalakis. Sc: James Martin
Cast: Michael Rubin, Steve McCoy, George Seminara, Robert Sabin, Cassie Madden

This throwback to the 1950s starts a bunch of thirty-year-old high school kids falling foul of a crazed gangster who sells them bad weed. After knocking him off they dump him in the river for good measure, little realising that the water is contaminated with radioactive sludge. He comes back as a green-faced ghoul and kills one of their buddies, Dan (Rubin). Thinking on their feet, the guys chuck Dan in the water and wait for him to come back too. A rather lame horror comedy spoof, this stars a pair of green-faced zombies who don't seem particularly dead. Dan's more interested in chatting up cute-but-clumsy Cindy than actually eating anyone. Fortunately, the kindly soda storeowner is on hand with some advice about dating the living: "You couldn't expect Cindy to be wanting to raise zombie babies now could you?"

I WAS A ZOMBIE FOR THE F.B.I.
1984, USA
Dir: Marius Penczner. Prod: Marius Penczner, Nancy Donelson. Sc: Marius Penczner, John Gillick
Cast: James Rasberry, Larry Raspberry, Christina Wellford, John Gillick

Welcome to Pleasantville, USA (population 711). When aliens takeover the local Health Cola factory they use carbonated drinks and a flying "zomball" to make upstanding American citizens into mindless zombie slaves. Can FBI Agents Rex Armstrong (James Rasberry, without a "p") and Aloyious "Ace" Evans (Larry Raspberry, with a "p") save the day before the whole nation is turned into *Invasion of the Body Snatchers* rejects? A lovingly retro throwback to 1950s sci-fi made by students at Memphis University, this features blank-eyed "zomboid" automatons, a stop-motion alien creature and real ingenuity in recreating the 1950s on a budget. A pity it never really capitalises on its zombies, nor delivers on its fantastic title.

I, ZOMBIE: THE CHRONICLES OF PAIN
1998, UK
Dir: Andrew Parkinson. Prod: Andrew Parkinson.
Sc: Andrew Parkinson
Cast: Giles Aspen, Ellen Softley, Dean Sipling, Claire Griffin, Andrew Parkinson

Andrew Parkinson, Britain's first zombie auteur, delivers a thoughtful take on the horrors of joining the ranks of the living dead in this depressingly grim tale in which a Ph.D. student is bitten by a ghoul and endures a lonely and agonising slide into living death in a London bedsit. Kitchen sink zombie body horror.

THE INCREDIBLY STRANGE CREATURES WHO STOPPED LIVING AND BECAME MIXED-UP ZOMBIES!!?
1963, USA
Alternative title: The Teenage Psycho Meets Bloody Mary
Dir: Ray Dennis Steckler. Prod: Ray Dennis Steckler.
Sc: Gene Pollock, Robert Silliphant
Cast: Cash Flagg [aka Ray Dennis Steckler], Brett O'Hara, Atlas King, Sharon Walsh, Madison Clark

After a visit to a funfair fortune teller called Madame Estrella, mixed-up beatnik kid Jerry (Cash Flagg, aka director/producer Ray Dennis Steckler) is turned into a homicidal zombie maniac. Hypnotised by a psychedelic spinning wheel and sent out to do the madame's dirty work, he proves an effective killer until she fears that he's remembering too much about his adventures. So she does what any self-respecting evil gypsy hypnotist would do – douses him in acid and throws him in the cage at the back of her tent that's

full of her other zombified victims. It's campy, trashy and not half as much fun as the infamous title promises.

INFECTED
2012, USA
Alternative title: Infection Z
Dir: Glenn Ciano. Prod: Chad A. Verdi, Gino Pereira, Noah Kraft. Sc: Glenn Ciano, Robert Rotondo Jr.
Cast: Michael Madsen, William Forsythe, Christy Romano, Tom DeNucci, Johnny Cicco

"Do not give in to the maddening compulsion to eat human flesh" This low-rent horror plays fast and loose with "infected" conventions as Michael Madsen, William Forsythe and a bunch of less famous (but perhaps less down on their luck) actors deal with a blood virus that "takes your soul and destroys you from the inside". The ghouls talk and connive, infected by a virus that is a mutated form of Lyme Disease. Meanwhile, Madsen has a terrible voiceover and the dead-eyed sadness of a man who remembers working with Tarantino.

INFECTION: THE INVASION BEGINS
2009, USA
Dir: Howard Wexler. Prod: Bryan Brewer, Mark Brewer, Howard Wexler. Sc: Bryan Brewer
Cast: Lochlyn Munro, Kelly Pendygraft, Brian Guest, Bryan Brewer, David Jean Thomas

In a future comprised of shoddy green screen CG and weird monorail trains, an intrepid reporter uncovers an alien invasion cover up. Back in 2009, where the movie proper takes place in flashback, an asteroid crashed onto Earth and unleashed alien tapeworms that turn the inhabitants of a small American town into parasitical zombies – more brainwashed *Invasion of the Body Snatchers* pods than *Night of the Living Dead* ghouls. Shot like a bad TV movie and written like a high school drama assignment, this is memorable only for using caffeine as an antidote to the zombie-slug menace – see also *The Book of Zombie* (2010). Someone should have done a sponsorship tie-in with Coca-Cola.

ISLAND OF THE LIVING DEAD
2006, ITALY
Original title: L'isola dei morti viventi

Dir: Bruno Mattei. Prod: Gianni Paolucci. Sc: Antonio Tentori, Bruno Mattei, Gianni Paolucci
Cast: Yvette Yzon, Alvin Anson, Ronald Russo, Ydalia Suarez, Jim Gaines

Bruno Mattei's penultimate film is a throwback to his 1980s zombie heyday when he was making junk epics like *Zombie Creeping Flesh* (1980). Shot on horrendous-looking DV, it opens with Conquistadors facing a horde of rotting zombies before jumping to the present where a band of treasure hunters search for lost Spanish loot. Ending up on an uncharted island near the Philippines the group – including resourceful Sharon (Yvette Yzon) who survives to star in sequel *Zombies: The Beginning* (2007) – are attacked by decaying native and Conquistador ghouls. In an era when the living dead have become proxies for infection and terrorism, this takes zombies back to their roots in First World imperialism and native superstition. It's cheap, cheesy and ridiculous – and Mattei's slapdash approach to filmmaking is as hilariously awful as it has ever been. But there's something eternally creepy about dead bodies wrapped in white sheets and tied with ropes slowly coming back to life

ISLAND: A ZOMBIE WEDDING
2010, TURKEY
Original title: Ada: Zombilerin Düğünü
Dir: Murat Emir Eren, Talip Ertürk. Prod: Murat Emir Eren, Talip Ertürk, Cicek Kahraman. Sc: Murat Emir Eren, Talip Ertürk
Cast: Ozan Ayhan, Cansel Elcin, Sirri Süreyya Önder.

Turkey's first zombie movie, directed by two former film critics, covers up its threadbare production values by adopting the tried-and-tested found footage method. When a group of wedding guests head to an island to celebrate the nuptials of a friend, the party is overrun by bloodied ghouls with a jerky, see-sawing gait. No one's quite sure where they came from (is it some kind of toxic coal smoke, or bad seafood?) and no one really cares. One guest shoots the entire movie from the hip on his camcorder while the rest try to survive the by-the-numbers plot. The Turkish setting gives it some vague novelty value, but it's really just another generic found-footage movie complete with green-toned night-vision scenes, much survivor bickering

and the inevitable finale in which the mainland turns out to be already overrun. The zombie actors sport unconvincing make-up and some vaguely comical, *Dawn of the Dead*-style facial expressions.

IN THE FLESH
2013, UK
Dir. Jonny Campbell. Prod: Ann Harrison-Baxter, John Rushton. Sc: Dominic Mitchell
Cast: Luke Newberry, Steve Evets, Ricky Tomlinson, Marie Critchley, Steve Cooper

In the very near future, a global zombie outbreak has been stopped thanks to the development of a drug that can turn the walking dead into "Partially Deceased Syndrome" sufferers. As neurological ability returns, the walking dead are left with guilty flashbacks to their flesh eating days and the government's desire to reintegrate them into society proves fraught. The living are paranoid and scared, uneasy around these former "Rotters" – something Kieren (Luke Newberry) discovers when he returns to his Lancashire home town where the local vicar (Kenneth Cranham) spouts anti-zombie rhetoric. Offering a smart reassessment of the usual zombie narrative, this BBC drama imaginatively uses the monster to tackle ideas of alienation and assimilation – a metaphor for everything from xenophobia to homophobia.

INVASION OF THE BODY SNATCHERS
1956, USA
Dir: Don Siegel. Prod: Walter Wanger. Sc: Daniel Mainwaring
Cast: Kevin McCarthy, Dana Wynter, Larry Gates, King Donovan, Carolyn Jones

The body snatchers might not be zombies, yet they had a huge impact on Romero's *Night of the Living Dead* (1968) and so deserve a mention. Alien seedpods land on earth and replicate the living while they sleep, creating perfect copies that take the place of the original humans. As the number of these alien doppelgängers increase, a small-town doctor is inundated with people complaining that their loved ones are, well, different. Expertly tapping into America's Cold War fears, the film's central conceit – that the country is being overtaken by people who look like us but aren't us – prefigured Romero's mass zombie apocalypse. Siegel's film was influential enough to be remade several times. In 1978, Philip Kaufman's outing updated the story to San Francisco and tackled the soullessness of the Me Generation. In 1993, Abel Ferrara set the action on an authoritarian military base in *Body Snatchers*. In 2007 the highly-troubled remake *The Invasion* saw Nicole Kidman and Daniel Craig fighting the invaders – it was a critical and commercial flop.

THE INVASION OF THE DEAD
1972, MEXICO

Original title: Blue Demon y Zovek en La invasión de los muertos
Alternative title: Invasion of Death
Dir: Rene Cardona Sr. Prod: Rene Cardona Jr., Enrique Rosas. Sc: Rene Cardona Jr.
Cast: Francisco Javier Chapa del Bosque " Zovek", Blue Demon, Christa Linder, Raúl Ramírez, Carlos Cardán

No sign of El Santo in this Mexican movie, which skimps on the wrestling in favour of pitting heroes Zovek and Blue Demon against living dead ghouls reanimated by the impact of an extra-terrestrial object on the Earth. Escapologist Zovek died during production, which explains the weird changes in tone between his scenes and those starring Blue Demon – it's all a bit Ed Wood. The zombies, who rise from their graves in a memorable scene, are distinctive in that they have retained enough of their motor function and memory to be able to use cars and helicopters in their attempt to take over the world. But, unlike some of their Mexican brethren, they don't look particularly dead.

INVASION OF THE ZOMBIES
1961, MEXICO

Original title: El Santo contra los zombies
Alternative titles: Santo Vs the Zombies
Dir: Benito Alazraki. Prod: Alberto López. Sc: Benito Alazraki, Antonio Orellana
Cast: Santo el Enmascarado de Plata, Lorena Velázquez, Armando Silvestre, Jaime Fernández, Dagoberto Rodríguez, Irma Serrano

Mexican wrestler El Santo began his zombie battles in this Mexican quickie about a hooded madman who launches a wave of ghouls on an unsuspecting world. The zombies are all former criminals brought back from the dead and kitted out with high-tech remote control systems that make them virtually unstoppable. Fortunately, Santo is on hand to dispense some rough justice: saving orphaned kids from the rampaging zombies, then tracking the ghouls back to their master and whupping the hell out of him.

INVISIBLE INVADERS
1959, USA

Dir: Edward L. Cahn. Prod: Robert E. Kent. Sc: Samuel Newman
Cast: Philip Tonge, John Agar, Jean Byron, Robert Hutton, John Carradine

Invading aliens reanimate the bodies of the dead and use them as shock troops in an attempt to take over the Earth. Scientist Adam Penner (Philip Tonge) and his military assistant Major Bruce Jay (John Agar) retreat to a high-tech government facility to cook up a weapon that will save the day, eventually realising that sound waves will halt the attack. One of director Cahn's better efforts – although that isn't saying much.

ISLE OF THE SNAKE PEOPLE
1968, MEXICO/USA

Original title: La muerte viviente
Alternative titles: Cult of the Dead
Dir: Juan Ibáñez. Prod: Luis Enrique Vergara. Sc: Luis Enrique Vergara, Jack Hill
Cast: Boris Karloff, Tongolele [Yolanda Montes], Julissa, Carlos East, Rafael Bertrand

The legendary Boris Karloff was seriously ill by the time he starred in this dire Mexican horror for Jack Hill (*Spider Baby*, *Foxy Brown*), and it probably hastened the old ghoul's demise. A French military governor arrives on a South Pacific island along with a young temperance worker who quickly attracts unwanted attention of the voodoo variety. A snake cult intend to use her as a human sacrifice while her evil uncle Carl van Molder (Karloff, staying mostly seated) summons legions of living dead ghouls in preparation for the return of voodoo god Baron Samedi.

J'ACCUSE
1937, FRANCE

Alternative titles: That They May Live
Dir: Abel Gance. Prod: Abel Gance. Sc: Abel Gance, Stève Passeur
Cast: Victor Francen, Line Noro, André Nox, Jean Max, Marcel Delaître

In the fields of Flanders, soldier Jean Diaz (Victor Francen) agrees to take the place of a father of four on a suicide mission into enemy territory. It turns out to be the final day of the war and, although several of the platoon are killed, Diaz survives and returns home a changed man. Back in France, he discovers a new kind of unbreakable "steel" glass that he hopes will put an end to war for good. Then the military pinch his invention and decide to use it for less amenable purposes. This prompts Diaz to call the fallen dead of all nations from their graves in order to warn the world about the horror of war.

JOHNNY SUNSHINE MAXIMUM VIOLENCE
2007, USA

Dir: Matt Yeager. Prod: Sean-Michael Argo, Eric Halsell. Sc: Sean-Michael Argo
Cast: Shey Bland, John Patrick McCauley, Eric Halsell, Sean-Michael Argo, Casey Halsell

What kind of films will people want to watch after the z-apocalypse? Snuff movies, of course. After "The Rising" transforms the globe, a masculine-named, zombie-slaying, porn starlet called Johnny Sunshine (Shey Bland) makes a killing by killing on-screen. Dressed in black leather bondage gear she plays for the camera ("This isn't an execution, it's entertainment") and has built up a loyal audience. But when her fame eventually plateaus, her producer hatches a plot to have her killed on-screen – a ratings winner, clearly. A messy, barely coherent post-apocalyptic film laced with fetish fantasy and a lot of sexual violence.

JUAN OF THE DEAD
2011, SPAIN/CUBA

Original title: Juan de los Muertos
Dir: Alejandro Brugués. Prod: Gervasio Iglesias, Inti Herrera. Sc: Emilio Vasquez, Alejandro Brugués
Cast: Alexis Díaz de Villegas, Jorge Molina, Andrea Duro, Andros Perugorría, Jazz Vilá

Cuba's first zombie movie has slacker Juan leading a bunch of cynical no-hopers against the ghouls as Havana is stormed by the living dead. Although the authorities claim they are US-funded dissidents, Juan knows better and seizes the opportunity to make a quick buck. Fun, fast-paced and shot with verve, this Third World z-flick has more panache than most low-budget US outings could even dream of.

JUNK
1999, JAPAN

Original title: Junk: Shiryô-gari
Dir: Atsushi Muroga. Prod: Tadao Masumizu, Isao Kurosu. Sc: Atsushi Muroga
Cast: Kaori Shimamura, Yuji Kishimoto, Osamu Ebara, Tate Gouta, Miwa

It looks like junk, it plays like junk, heck it's even called *Junk*. No prizes for guessing that this bottom of the barrel gore effort is as trashy as its title playfully suggests. After a secret US military installation in Japan invents a serum that can bring the dead back to life, a gang of jewel thieves are caught between their yakuza bosses and some hungry ghouls. There's lots of frantic gunplay in the vein of *Versus* – just without the style.

KILLING BIRDS
1988, ITALY

Original title: Uccelli assassini
Alternative titles: Raptors, Zombie 5: Killing Birds
Dir: Claude Milliken [Claudio Lattanzi]. Prod: Aristide Massaccesi. Sc: Daniel Ross [Daniele Stroppa]
Cast: Lara Wendel, Robert Vaughn, Timothy W. Watts, Leslie Cummins, James Villemaire

Ornithologists and zombies? You've gotta be kidding. If only director Claudio Lattanzi was. Kids in the Louisiana swamps get more than they bargained for while looking for woodpeckers (!) when they encounter Vaughn's blind Vietnam vet. Returning from his tour of duty years previously, the vet murdered his cheating wife then had his eyes pecked out by swamp birds as punishment. Now he's being harassed by zombies – who take time out from tormenting him to pick off the dumb kids. So, is it a movie about killer birds, killing birds, killer zombie birds, zombie bird killers or something altogether different? Who knows and, frankly, given the lack of suspense who really cares? The college student heroes spend most of the movie running around as a couple of mummified zombies give chase, then Vaughn finally pops up in the last two minutes to half-heartedly offer an iffy explanation of the horror and face his fate. Maybe director Lattanzi (apparently replaced during shooting by Aristide Massaccesi) was trying to highlight the rarely acknowledged link between *The Birds* and *Night of the Living Dead*... or maybe it's all just a crock.

KING OF THE ZOMBIES
1941, USA
Dir: Jean Yarbrough. Prod: Lindsley Parsons.
Sc: Edmond Kelso
Cast: Dick Purcell, Mantan Moreland, John Archer, Joan Woodbury, Henry Victor

Mantan Moreland gets all the best gags in this horror comedy about three Americans who crash land their plane on a Caribbean island. There they discover a villainous scientist and his house full of zombies. To make matters worse, the scientist turns out to be a Nazi spy who's using voodoo to interrogate a captive American officer. This is Poverty Row's best zombie film... which admittedly isn't saying much.

KISS DADDY GOODBYE
1981, USA
Alternative titles: Caution, Children At Play, Revenge of the Zombie; Vengeful Dead
Dir: Patrick Regan. Prod: Alain Silver. Sc: Ronald Abrams, Patrick Regan, Alain Silver, Mary Stewart
Cast: Fabian Forte, Marilyn Burns, Jon Cedar, Marvin Miller, Chester Grimes

After their daddy's killed by nasty bikers, two psychic children manage to bring his corpse back from the grave to wreak revenge. Lame horror notable only for featuring a rare appearance by *Texas Chain Saw Massacre* scream queen Marilyn Burns and for its unusual casting – the unconvincing kids are the director's real-life children.

THE KNACKERY
2010, UK
Dir: George Clarke. Prod: George Clarke. Sc: George Clarke
Cast: George Clarke, Graeme Livingstone, Alan Crawford, Gary Whelan, Iain Boden

In a near future Belfast, a group of contestants enter "The Knackery", a disused industrial site fitted with cameras, to win cash prizes by fighting each other and an army of boiler-suited, feral ghouls. It's all part of a reality TV show – like *The Running Man* with no Arnie but lots of zombies. Impressively made in just five weeks on a £100 budget, George Clarke's follow-up to *Battle of the Bone* (2008) sadly lacks its political bite or any semblance of sense. Instead, it combines half-arsed satire with a lot of chopsocky martial arts to little purpose. One word review: knackered.

KNIGHT OF THE DEAD
2013, USA
Dir: Mark Atkins. Prod: Erica Steele, Mark Atkins, Michael Lurie. Sc: Jeffrey Giles, Mark Atkins
Cast: Feth Greenwood, Vivien Vilela, Lee Bennett, Dylan Jones, Alan Calton

Pus, pus everywhere... The Black Death spawns zombies in this medieval zombie movie that wants to be *Game of Thrones* but looks more like a weekend convention of live action role playing fanatics. As a group of knights lead the Holy Grail through plague-hit England, they find themselves trapped in a valley of living dead peasants. With its cheap production design and mud splattered costumes, it's like a po-faced *Monty Python and the Holy Grail*. Director, cinematographer, co-writer and producer Mark Atkins is a veteran of mockbusters studio The Asylum but this isn't on par with his *Jack the Giant Killer* (2013) or *Battle of Los Angeles* (2011) – which is saying something. It's also not to be confused with Iceland's *Knight of the Living Dead* (2005).

KNIGHT OF THE LIVING DEAD
2005, ICELAND
Dir: Bjarni Gautur. Prod: Bjarni Gautur, Steinar Geirdal, Andri Kjartan, Siggi Jökull. Sc: Bjarni Gautur, Höddi Björnsen
Cast: Höddi Björnsen, Infernus Kjartan, Steinar Geirdal, Bjarni Gautur, P.N. Guin

Iceland's first zombie movie is a backyard epic shot by a bunch of teens on video using beer money as a production budget and a bottle of ketchup (literally) for gore. In medieval times, a knight and Viking go toe-to-toe in a distant land – actually someone's back garden – before being struck down by a bolt of red CG lightning. Centuries later they're resurrected by a group of bumbling drunk teens to continue their fight. Lloyd Kaufman of Troma fame and prolific zombie screenwriter Trent Haaga lend undue credibility by taking brief cameos (shot while they were attending the Icelandic Independent Film Festival). It's really little more than a 15-year-old's home video with wink-wink asides commenting on the awfulness of the script and a knight wearing what looks to be a metal bucket on his head. The end credits try to excuse wasting your time, while being offensive: "This movie took pretty long to make and it's pretty lame but hey at least we're not gay."

KUNG FU ZOMBIE
1982, HONG KONG
Original title: Wu long tian shi zhao ji gui
Dir: Hwa I Hung. Prod: Pal Ming. Sc: Hwi I Hung
Cast: Billy Chong, Lau Chan, Kei Ying Cheung, Yung-Moon Kuan

What is this obsession with martial arts zombies? At least this fast-paced farce from Hong Kong features some fun, decomposing ghouls. Some hopping corpses are brought back from the dead for a flurry of chopsocky action after a thief gets a priest to dabble in black magic. A tale of revenge, kung fu fighting and several different vampire/zombie/corpses, it delivers enough manic laughs to be a memorable favourite among both zombie and martial arts fans. Hero Billy Chong went on to star in horror comedy *Kung Fu from Beyond the Grave* (1982) opposite vampires, sorcerers and a couple more fugitives from the undertaker.

LA ZOMBIE: HARDCORE
2010, USA
Dir: Bruce LaBruce. Prod: Arno Rok, Bruce LaBruce, Robert Felt, Matthias von Fistenberg, Damian Todaro, Jürgen Brüning, Jörn Hartmann. Sc: Bruce LaBruce
Cast: François Sagat, Rocco Giovanni, Wolf Hudson, Eddie Diaz, Andrew James

Bruce LaBruce's follow up to *Otto; Or, Up With Dead People* (2008) caused controversy after being banned in Australia. Unlike *Otto* it's a hardcore zombie porn flick that mixes graphic sex, necrophilia and a shambling zombie/alien who brings the dead back to life by having sex with them (instead of eating them). It was released in vanilla and hardcore versions, neither of which have much in the way of dialogue.

LAND OF THE DEAD
2005, USA
Alternative title: George A. Romero's Land of the Dead
Dir: George A. Romero. Prod: Mark Canton, Bernie Goldmann, Peter Grunwald. Sc: George A. Romero
Cast: Simon Baker, John Leguizamo, Dennis Hopper, Asia Argento, Robert Joy

After a two-decade wait, Romero delivered the fourth entry in his zombie series. The dead have taken over the world, trapping a few survivors in a post-apocalyptic gated community where the line between haves and have nots is starkly drawn. Intelligent ghouls, Dennis Hopper, and a veiled allegory on Bush Jr.'s America. God bless you, Mr R.

THE LAST DAYS OF HUMANITY
2002, GERMANY
Dir: Peter Dubiel. Prod: Peter Dubiel, Martin Faltermeier. Sc: Peter Dubiel
Cast: Stefan Eger, Sandra Feld, Peter Dubiel, Martin Hager

A handgun blasts a zombie in the head, squirting a geyser of blood into the air. A machete staves a zombie's head in, squirting more gore skywards. A car boot decapitates a ghoul, leaving its twitching body to pump out claret onto the tarmac. See a pattern here yet? This 60-minute, micro-budget German zombie effort charts the last couple of days of humanity after the dead start to walk without the budget or technical skill to even make its gore convincing (check out the guy dreaming about flashing his ribcage while in the bathtub). No subtitles.

THE LAST DAYS ON MARS
2013, IRELAND/UK
Dir: Ruairi Robinson. Prod: Michael Kuhn, Andrea Cornwell. Sc: Clive Dawson
Cast: Liev Schreiber, Elias Koteas, Romola Garai, Goran Kostic, Johnny Harris

In space, no one can hear you scream "Braaiinnnsss!" 19 hours before a 6 month mission on Mars ends, scientists led by Elias Koteas discover a bacterial strain that – rather inconveniently – starts turning them into zombies. Shot in Jordan on a shoestring blockbuster budget, this international co-production has a United Nations cast and a starring role for Liev Schreiber and his befuddled squint as he battles his raging crew mates. It's *Ghosts of Mars* meets *Alien* – perfectly serviceable, totally unoriginal.

THE LAST MAN ON EARTH
1964, USA/ITALY
Alternative titles: L'ultimo uomo della terra
Dir: Sidney Salkow (US), Ubalda Ragona (IT). Prod: Robert L. Lippert. Sc: Logan Swanson [Richard Matheson], William F. Leicester
Cast: Vincent Price, Franca Bettoia, Emma Danieli, Giacomo Rossi-Stuart, Umberto Rau [Raho]

Vincent Price stars as the eponymous Last Man, the only survivor of a virulent plague that's turned the planet's population into blood hungry ghouls. Barricading himself in his suburban house, Morgan fights off the creatures while piecing together his own involvement in the apocalypse. A masterful classic – and a huge influence on a certain Pittsburgh filmmaker too.

LAST OF THE LIVING
2008, NEW ZEALAND
Dir: Logan McMillan. Prod: Logan McMillan. Sc: Logan McMillan
Cast: Morgan Williams, Ashleigh Southam, Robert Faith, Emily Paddon-Brown, Mark Hadlow

Three slacker blokes survive the zombie apocalypse by hanging out on their sofa and playing videogames in this Kiwi comedy: "It's fun, I used to be an accountant..." Their fuck-it-all ethos crumbles when they meet sassy scientist Stef (Emily Paddon-Brown) who's working on a cure for the viral plague. Can they save the planet and win the girl? Possibly. Will you care? Unlikely. New Zealand's rep as the home of *Braindead* (1992) and *Black Sheep* (2006) gains little from this insipid zom-com.

LAST RITES OF THE DEAD

2006, USA
Alternative title: Zombies Anonymous
Dir: Marc Fratto. Prod: Brandi Metaxas, Frank Garfi, Andrew Dantonio. Sc: Marc Fratto
Cast: Gina Ramsden, Joshua Nelson, Christa McNamee, Gaetano Iacono, Constantine Josiah Taylor

The alternate title – *Zombies Anonymous* – gives a better sense of this grubby little pic's pretensions to social satire, something that makes it reminiscent of 1990s favourite *Shatter Dead* (1993). After being killed by her gangbanger boyfriend, Angela (Gina Ramsden) comes back as a zombie and journeys through support groups ("Hi, my name is Lewis and I am mortally-challenged") before hooking up with living dead militants. Meanwhile, her zombie-hating boyfriend has joined a vigilante group dedicated to wiping out ghouls. You can guess where this ends, can't you? A few half-explored asides – the scene where Angela applies for a job after caking herself in a skin care product called Lookalive is a high point – don't really justify sitting through the other 95% of this.

THE LAUGHING DEAD
1989, USA
Dir: S.P. Somtow [Somtow Sucharitkul]. Prod: Lex Nakashima. Sc: S.P. Somtow
Cast: Tim Sullivan, Wendy Webb, S.P. Somtow, Premika Eaton, Patrick Roskowick

A Catholic priest takes a bunch of terrible thespians to Mexico on an archaeological dig, only to be confronted with lots of supernatural Aztec shenanigans when they stumble across "The Festival of the Laughing Dead". Unmemorable low-budget horror that's managed to worm its way into the genre history books because of the scene in which the living play a bunch of blue-tinged zombies at basketball. It's far less zany than it sounds and does little to make up for the wooden acting, poverty-stricken production design or bizarre "Aztec" costumes. In the end, there's little for anyone to laugh about, living or dead.

THE LEGEND OF DIABLO
2004, USA
Dir: Robert Napton. Prod: Robert Napton, Victor Garcia, Neal Fredericks. Sc: Karl Altstaetter, Robert Napton

Cast: Fred Estrada, Lindsey Lofaso, Mario Soto, Calvi Pabon, Gabriel R. Martinez

Given that the zombie myth entered America from Haiti, it's strange how many films have linked the walking dead with Aztec and Mayan history (see for instance *The Laughing Dead*, *Museum of the Dead*, *Flesh Freaks*, *Curse of the Maya*). This terminally boring DV horror revolves around a 16th century demon called Azar who terrorised Mexico before being imprisoned by the Aztecs in some kind of shoebox. He's released by a modern day, small town sheriff in California (doh!) and begins to possess anyone he encounters, turning them into zombies. As the raspy-voiced demon runs around with infrared vision, an FBI agent, a priest and the sheriff's daughters try to save the planet by putting Azar back in his box. Azar orders his zombies to go forth and spread the word – but since all they do is groan (and run like cowards when shot at) a global demonic apocalypse might be a while coming.

THE LEGEND OF THE 7 GOLDEN VAMPIRES
1973 UK/HONG KONG
Alternative titles: Dracula and the Seven Golden Vampires, The 7 Brothers Meet Dracula
Dir: Roy Ward Baker. Prod: Don Houghton, Vee King Shaw. Sc: Don Houghton
Cast: Peter Cushing, David Chiang, Julie Ege, Robin Stewart, Szu Shih

Dracula heads East in this uneasy blend of Hammer and the Shaw Brothers. Peter Cushing stars as Van Helsing, tracking the Count through China after discovering that he's teamed up with the seven vampires of the title. With the help of several kung fu fighters Van Helsing launches an attack on the neck-nippers who're terrorising local villagers. In the ensuing chaos, the Hong Kong acting contingent get to show off their revered martial arts skills using the vampires and their zombie helpers as chopsocky fodder. Looking decidedly dated even on its release in 1973, this film still has a few moments of power – although the green-faced zombies are seriously underused.

LEGION OF THE DEAD
2000, GERMANY
Dir: Olaf Ittenbach. Prod: Michael J. Poettinger,

Claudia Quirchmayr. Sc: Olaf Ittenbach
Cast: Michael Carr, Russell Friedenberg, Kimberly Liebe, Matthias Hues, Hank Stone

Olaf Ittenbach writes and directs movies that are so bad they're hypnotic. After delivering geysers of gore in German splatter epic *Premutos – Lord of the Dead* he went to America to film this barely coherent horror movie that traps a bunch of disparate characters in a Texan bar as zombie-esque demons mass outside. The screenplay veers around like a drunk driver – serial killers, drifters, undead hitmen – and Ittenbach was apparently unhappy with the butchered cut that was released. In truth it's not much of a zombie movie. Scratch that, it's not much of a movie period.

LET'S SCARE JESSICA TO DEATH
1971, USA
Dir: John Hancock. Prod: Charles B. Moss Jr. Sc: Ralph Rose, Norman Jonas
Cast: Zohra Lampert, Barton Heyman, Kevin O'Connor, Gretchen Corbett, Alan Manson

The hippie dream turns sour in this lyrical, haunting horror movie. Released from a sanatorium, Jessica (Zhora Lampert) heads out to an isolated farmhouse in the Connecticut countryside with her husband Duncan and friend Woody. There they discover a young hippie girl named Emily hiding out in the house and offer to let her stay. As Emily seduces Duncan, Jessica starts to lose her marbles. She's convinced that she's in contact with the spirit of a dead Victorian girl who used to live in the house. She also starts to believe that the townsfolk are a bunch of zombie ghouls intent on making her into one of them. Lacking in sensationalism, director John Hancock's creepy little movie has slipped into obscurity: a shame since it's a fascinating take on the way the LSD-era blurred the line between sanity and madness.

LINNEA QUIGLEY'S HORROR WORKOUT
1989, USA
Dir: Hal Kennedy [Kenneth J. Hall]. Prod: Fred Kennamer. Sc: Hal Kennedy
Cast: Linnea Quigley, B. Jane Holzer, Amy Hunt, Victoria Nesbitt, Kristine Seeley

Quigley is best known for her naked appearance as

a punkette in *The Return of the Living Dead* (1984). By 1989, she was famous enough to front this lame collection of clips from her forays into the horror genre. Judging by its salacious treatment of the star, this is aimed squarely at teenage boys. Some zombie relief arrives when a few ghouls attack Quigley while she jogs through a graveyard. Since they're so unfit, she takes them through a workout routine. Imagine *Thriller* meets an exercise video, then try and come up with one single reason why you'd want to watch this junk. If the words "Linnea Quigley's boobs" spring to mind, this one is probably for you.

A LITTLE BIT ZOMBIE
2011, CANADA
Dir: Casey Walker. Prod: John Griffith, Casey Walker. Sc: Trevor Martin, Christopher Bond
Cast: Kristopher Turner, Crystal Lowe, Shawn Roberts, Kristen Hager, Emilie Ullerup

When Steve (Kristopher Turner) takes his prissy bride-to-be Tina (Crystal Lowe) to the family's cabin in the woods to bond with his sister and her husband, he gets bitten by a zombie mosquito. Before he can even look over the wedding's seating plan he's eating pet rabbits, got no pulse and has brains on the brain. With a couple of ghoul hunters (Stephen McHattie and Emile Ullerup) on his trail, Steve throws himself on his fiancé's mercy. He's still the same sweet Steve, right? Just a "little bit" zombie, no? A brain-munching supermarket sweep, some gloopy body deterioration and a pink stun gun inject laughs into this easygoing, crowdfunded indie.

LIVELIHOOD
2005, USA
Dir: Ryan Graham. Prod: Ryan Stachurski, Ryan Graham, Tracey Graham, Stephen B. Thomas, Nikc Miller. Sc: Ryan Graham, Tracey Graham, Curtis Crispin
Cast: Steven B. Thomas, Michelle Trout, Scott P. Graham, Amy Smith, Mike Bennett

American Zombie (2007) focussed on existential and social problems caused by the dead returning to life. Sod that, says this micro-budget American comedy as it plays their return for yuck-yucks. Among the corpses that won't lie down are a big-haired rock musician (Steve Thomas) who's still boasting to groupies about his prowess ("Rigor mortis, baby!"); a cuckolded office worker (Scott P. Graham) and a spiteful, tapioca-obsessed mother-in-law (Michelle Trout). A few choice commercial interludes – including a music video for the anti-zombie song "Leave the US to the Livin'" and an advert for "Intestine-Tact", the undead's answer to rotting insides – satirise America's impulse to either reject or exploit these poor returners. It's as silly and lightweight as it sounds.

LIVING A ZOMBIE DREAM
1996, USA
Dir: Todd Reynolds. Prod: Todd Reynolds. Sc: Todd Reynolds
Cast: Amon Elsey, Michelle White, Mike Smith, Frank Alexander, Mike Strain Jr

A near silent, angst-ridden tale of jealousy and revenge this tortured SOV movie from Springfield, Missouri plays like some kind of avant garde art experiment gone wrong. When a nameless man (Amon Elsey) discovers his brother is banging his girlfriend behind his back he decides to get his revenge. He conspires with a loin-cloth wearing local psychopath – every town has one of those, doesn't it? – to have the brother killed. Then, for inexplicable reasons, he decides to kill the psycho. For even more inexplicable reasons the psycho then returns as a zombie to drool blood on his killer's chest while he sleeps. Meanwhile, televisions flicker static, the soundtrack thrums ominously, the camera flips drunkenly and hardly anyone says anything. It's like aliens abducted David Lynch and forced him to mate with Uwe Böll.

THE LIVING DEAD AT MANCHESTER MORGUE
1974, SPAIN/ITALY
Original title: No profanar el sueño de los muertos, Non si deve profanare il sonno dei morti
Alternative titles: Da dova vieni?, Don't Open the Window, Invasion der Zombies, Let Sleeping Corpses Lie, Le massacre des morts-vivants, Zombi 3
Dir: Jorge Grau. Prod: Manuel Pérez García, Edmondo Amati. Sc: Sandro Continenza, Marcello Coscia
Cast: Ray Lovelock, Christine Galbo [Cristina Galbó], Arthur Kennedy, Jeannine Mestre, Fernando Hilbeck

An experimental pest-control machine using high

frequency sound waves reactivates dead bodies in this Spanish-Italian answer to Romero. Shot in the Peak District, it follows antiques dealer George (Ray Lovelock) and his unlucky travelling companion Edna (Christine Galbo) as they fight off zombies and a disbelieving fascist policeman (Arthur Kennedy). Though none of the film takes place in the eponymous Manchester morgue, it'd be churlish to moan too loudly since this proves to be a landmark zombie movie.

THE LIVING DEAD GIRL
1982, FRANCE
Alternative titles: La morte vivante
Dir: Jean Rollin. Prod: Sam Selsky. Sc: Jean Rollin, Jacques Ralf
Cast: Marina Pierro, Françoise Blanchard, Mike Marshall, Carina Barone, Fanny Magier

Nobody makes films about death quite like Jean Rollin. This lyrical and tragic necrophiliac tale is like a personal daydream about death. After barrels of toxic waste are accidentally spilled in the crypt of the Valmont chateau, the corpse of young Catherine Valmont (Marina Pierro) is revived from the dead. She begins feeding on anyone who ventures into the catacombs, ripping their throats open with her fingernails then sipping their blood. Catherine's childhood friend Helene eventually realises that she's come back to life and helps her dispose of the bodies while teaching her how to talk again. Blood drenched eroticism that's completely obsessed with a romantic image of (living) death, this recalls Rollin's vampire movies.

THE LIVING DEAD IN TOKYO BAY
1992, JAPAN
Alternative titles: Batoru garu: Tokyo crisis wars
Dir: Kazuo "Gaira" Komizu. Prod: Kazuo "Gaira" Komizu. Sc: Daisuke Serizawa
Cast: Cutei Suzuki, Kera, Keiko Hayase, Kenzi Ohtsuki

Self-explanatory title, throwaway movie. A meteor strikes the coast of Japan, unleashing a cloud of DNA-mutating fumes that turn the living into ghouls. Chaos reigns as the army try to prevent the usual band of scientists from finding a cure – they'd rather inject the living with the zombification virus in order to control them. Making her way through the anarchy is Keiko, the battle girl of the original

Japanese title (Batoru garu). Clad in a black leather combat suit and armed to the teeth, she's on a mission to find her father but isn't averse to doing some zombie killing along the way. The destruction of Tokyo is reminiscent of the Godzilla cycle and full of the same anti-military posturing – which is ironic seeing how Battle Girl turns guns and combat gear into fetish objects.

LIVING DEAD LOCK UP
2005, USA
Dir: Mike Hicks, Mario Xavier. Prod: Mario Xavier.
Sc: Mike Hicks, Mario Xavier
Cast: Mario Xavier, Natalie Morales, Miguel Angel Novo, Mike Hicks, Hess Wesley

Long before The Walking Dead made the zombies-in-a-prison concept mainstream, no-budget Z-cinema had explored the idea too. Here a jail called Stone Gate Penitentiary hides a gruesome secret – decades earlier 47 inmates died at the hands of a ruthless warden who dabbled in the occult. When a present day car thief (co-director Mario Xavier) is sent there for a two-year sentence, he discovers zombies rising up from their mass grave after some blood is spilled in a brawl. Xavier films himself in the shower a lot, the zombies lumber down corridors and it's all shot in tight angles to disguise the fact that it's not really taking place in a prison. Lock it up and throw away the key. It was followed by two short film sequels.

THE LIVING IMPAIRED
2005, CANADA
Dir: Michael Fox. Prod: Michael Fox. Sc: Michael Fox
Cast: Skratch Bastid, Charles T. Conrad, JuJu, Allison Leadley, Jonathan Saunders

The Cinema Impaired would be a better title for this backyard effort from Nova Scotia. Set on 31 October – "Eve of All Hollows" (sic) according to a helpful on-screen legend – this zombie apocalypse is shot in b&w and has occasional bursts of silent movie style piano slapstick music on the soundtrack for good measure. As zombies and vampires roam the streets, the kids drink beer and generally goof off. The town of Halifax needs to clamp down hard on films being shot without permits.

THE MAD

2006, CANADA
Dir: John Kalangis. Prod: Robert Wilson, Patrick Cameron, Harvey Glazer. Sc: Kevin Hennelly, John Kalangis, Christopher Warre Smets
Cast: Billy Zane, Maggie Castle, Shauna MacDonald, Evan Charles Flock, Jordan Madley

"Has your beef been acting strangely?" Mad Cow disease gives this splatstick Canadian comedy some meat, as a doctor (Billy Zane) and his daughter (Maggie Castle) discover "organic" meat turning rednecks into cannibal killers with low IQs. Burger patties jump around on plates, Zane proves surprisingly likeable and the screenplay throws out some choice gags – from a zombie losing a fight with an ice machine to Zane struggling to cope with the death of his girlfriend ("She's not your girlfriend any more. She's a puddle of blood and guts that smells like Chanel No 5"). A late left turn into slasher movie territory doesn't do it much favours, but until then it's a foodie zombie horror to file alongside *Dead Meat* (2004), *Poultrygeist: Night of the Chicken Dead* (2007) and *Dead Sushi* (2010).

MAKE-OUT WITH VIOLENCE
2008, USA
Original title: Zombie Lover
Dir: The Deagol Brothers. Prod: The Deagol Brothers
Sc: The Deagol Brothers, Eric Lehning, Cody DeVos
Cast: Eric Lehning, Cody DeVos, Leah High, Brett Miller, Tia Shearer

If Sofia Coppola, George Romero and Wes Anderson collaborated on a zombie movie they might come up with something like this whimsical study in summer longing and teen angst. Telling the story of a bunch of kids who find and decide to keep a zombified girl – who was once their classmate – it's a truly original, indie zombie flick.

THE MAN THEY COULD NOT HANG
1939, USA
Dir: Nick Grindé. Prod: Wallace MacDonald. Sc: Karl Brown, George Wallace Sayre, Leslie T. White
Cast: Boris Karloff, Adrian Booth, Robert Wilcox, Roger Pryor, Don Beddoe

Karloff's back from the grave again in this 1939 tale of a mad scientist experimenting on reviving the dead, who ends up swinging from a noose himself. Not exactly a zombie movie, but part of a brief series of films Karloff made during the period about men returning from beyond the grave. See also *The Ghoul* (1933) and *The Walking Dead* (1936).

MANIAC COP
1988, USA
Dir: William Lustig. Prod: Larry Cohen. Sc: Larry Cohen
Cast: Tom Atkins, Bruce Campbell, Laurene Landon, Richard Roundtree, William Smith

"You have the right to remain silent... forever," groans the tagline of this creaky 1980s horror flick penned by B-movie maestro Larry Cohen. When a series of murders involving a killer in a cop's uniform are reported in New York City, the boys in blue start taking flak for police brutality. Detective McCrae (Tom Atkins) traces the murders back to former NYPD officer Matthew Cordell (Robert Z'Dar), jailed for mistreating perps. Funny thing is, though, Cordell's been dead for years. Hands up, the zombie cop back from the grave idea is more than a little ropey. Still, this disposable exploitation effort scores a few points thanks to its unflinchingly downbeat take on the rottenness at the core of the Big Apple. Acting as judge, jury and executioner rolled into one, the cadaverous copper has the whole concept of Zero Tolerance bang to rights. Followed by *Maniac Cop 2* (1990), *Maniac Cop 3: Badge of Silence* (1993).

LA MANSIÓN DE LOS MUERTOS VIVIENTES
1982, SPAIN
Literal Title: The Mansion of the Living Dead
Dir: Jesús Franco. Prod: Emilio Larraga. Sc: Jesús Franco
Cast: Candy Coster [Lina Romay], Robert Foster [Antonio Mayans], Mabel Escaño, Eva León, Albino Graziáni
Four oversexed German lesbians find their dream holiday in the Canary Islands turning into nightmare in this dodgy "sexploitation" effort from prolific purveyor of trash Jess Franco. Taking Amando de Ossorio's *Blind Dead* films as his starting point, Franco cooks up a far-fetched tale about a monastery hiding some 18th-century zombie monks. They're damned former members of the Spanish Inquisition who dress in white cowls and have what looks to be copious amounts of antiseptic cream smeared on their faces. The monks

kidnap, try and rape the girls to punish them for their rapacious sexual appetites; later they decide that one of the women is a fabled saviour who can free them from their purgatory. Franco's keen awareness of the religious fervour and sexual sadism running through the *Blind Dead* films can't be argued with. But his decision to present both the Sapphic sex scenes and grim torture-rape sequences as equally titillating is unpleasant.

MAPLEWOODS
2002, USA
Alternative titles: Operation: Nazi Zombies
Dir: David B. Stewart III. Prod: Robert Schiller, Thomas Reilly, Joseph DeChristopher Sr. Sc: David B. Stewart III
Cast: Thomas Reilly, Elissa Mullen, Christopher Connolly, John Weidemoyer, John Martineau

Originally released as *Maplewoods* (boring!) then retitled *Operation: Nazi Zombies* (that's more like it!), this atrocious backyard epic doesn't work under any title. Badly shot on digital video in Pennsylvania, it sets up a conceit that it would be hard to go wrong with – modern day US special forces soldiers fighting zombies created by Nazi research in WWII – then proceeds to get it totally wrong. Despite the DVD art featuring pics of Hitler, there aren't actually any Nazi zombies here per se. What there is: hamfisted direction and risible acting, night scenes so dark it's impossible to see what is happening, sound recording that veers from blaring to inaudible in the course of single scenes and special forces soldiers whose idea of camouflage is wearing bright white security guard shirts in a forest. Want to see soldiers blasting S.S. ghouls? Then this isn't the movie you're looking for…

MEAT MARKET
2000, CANADA
Dir: Brian Clement. Sc: Brian Clement
Cast: Paul Pedrosa, Claire Westby, Alison Therriault, Teresa Simon, Chelsey Artensen

Canadian "Camcorder Coppola" Brian Clement takes us on a sub-Romero apocalyptic adventure in his above average SOV gorefest. Wince at the scenes cribbed so shamelessly from *Dawn of the Dead* (including a SWAT team tenement building raid and a suicidal copper blowing his brains out)

and focus instead on Clements's occasional bursts of vigour as heavily made-up zombies wander through deserted stretches of British Columbia. Our heroes are enigmatic survivalists who team up with a couple of "vampyros lesbos" armed with laser guns and a masked El Santo-style wrestler named El Diablo. The girls do some heavy petting, there are lots of tattoos and some over-enthusiastic zombie gore. Scariest thing of all, though, is the sex scene involving a bloke in leopard-skin underpants. Now that's grim. Followed by *Meat Market 2* (2001), *Meat Market 3* (2006).

MESSIAH OF EVIL
1972, USA
Alternative titles: Dead People, Return of the Living Dead, Revenge of the Screaming Dead, Deep Swamp
Dir: Willard Huyck. Prod: Gloria Katz. Sc: Willard Huyck, Gloria Katz
Cast: Michael Greer, Mariana Hill, Royal Dano, Elisha Cook Jr., Joy Bang

This gets an A for effort. Young Arletty (Mariana Hill) goes in search of her father in the spooky Californian town of Point Dune only to discover a horde of zombies masquerading as townsfolk who are apparently the result of some centuries old curse. Lots of atmospheric scenes set in the deserted town give way to some memorable shock sequences and an overly complicated plot that will leave most viewers completely confused. When it works, it's like *Deliverance* meets *Night of the Living Dead* meets *Days of Our Lives*.

THE MIDNIGHT HOUR
1985, USA
Dir: Jack Bender. Prod: Ervin Zavada. Sc: Bill Bleich
Cast: Lee Montgomery, Jonna Lee, Shari Belafonte-Harper, LeVar Burton
Dim-witted high school kids in have no one to blame but themselves as zombies walk the streets in this camp but insipid horror-comedy made for TV. After chanting an ancient spell in a graveyard on Halloween, the kids watch in horror as vampires, werewolves and ghouls pop up all over town (the joke being that because everyone's in costume they fit right in). Hero Phil (Lee Montgomery) eventually saves the day by reciting another spell that sends them all back from whence they came – if only he'd thought of that sooner

we'd have been spared the tedium. It's like *American Graffiti* meets *Thriller*... but that actually makes it sound fun.

MIDNIGHT'S CALLING
2000, GERMANY
Dir: Timo Rose. Prod: Timo Rose, Yazid Benfeghoul.
Sc: Timo Rose
Cast: Yazid Benfeghoul, Andreas Schnaas, Erich Amerkamp, Ricky Goldberg, Jens Massman

Things you might think while watching *Midnight's Calling*: 1) I have no idea what's going on. 2) Ha, ha, ha, look at the size of that exit wound. 3) This probably wouldn't make any more sense with English subtitles. In fact, it might make less sense. 4) Who is this lunatic keeping women chained up in their underwear? 5) Aren't those actresses cold? 6) Is this shot more in focus than the others, or is it just me? 7) A spade really isn't a sword and attempts to cut someone's head off with it are doomed to failure. Between co-directing *Mutation* (1999) and going solo on *Mutation 2: Generation Dead* (2001), German splatter helmer Timo Rose threw himself into this micro-budget zombie outbreak. There are no English subtitles, but it's bare bones narrative wise: people bicker, zombies stumble, blood spurts, it eventually ends. Proof that knowing how to turn a camera on doesn't make you a filmmaker.

MIMESIS: NIGHT OF THE LIVING DEAD
2012, USA
Alternative title: Mimesis
Dir: Douglas Schulze. Prod: Kurt Eli Mayry, Gavin Grazer, Douglas Schulze. Sc: Joshua Wagner, Douglas Schulze
Cast: Courtney Gains, Allen Maldonado, David G.B. Brown, Lauren Mae Shafer, Taylor Piedmonte

Every time you blink there's another take on *Night of the Living Dead*, which is forever cursed by being accidentally out in the public domain. This 2012 outing is more of a direct homage than a remake as a group of horror convention attendees are drugged at a party and wake up in a recreation of the movie as faux ghouls amble about outside.

MONSTER BRAWL
2011, CANADA

Dir Jesse T. Cook. Prod: Jesse T. Cook, John Geddes, Matt Wiele. Sc: Jesse T. Cook
Cast: Dave Foley, Robert Maillet, Art Hindle, Herb Dean, Jimmy Hart

In the red corner, weighing in at 454 lbs and 193 years old is the legendary Frankenstein's monster. In the blue corner, still going after death is 312 lbs of rotten corpse, Zombie Man. Who will win this deathmatch? Taking its cues from a WWF tournament, this story-lite horror comedy pits various classic monsters against each other in a wrestling ring in a Deep South graveyard. Bouts are interspersed with trash talking and vital statistics, but this one-joke movie is a bellyflop not a piledriver smackdown.

MONSTER TIT SEX ZOMBIES
2008, USA
Dir: Mark Stone. Prod: Mark Nicholson. Sc: Mark Stone
Cast: Abbey Brooks, Ricki White, Crystal Ashley, Daphne Rosen, Soleil

In the Carpathian mountains Dr Von Chunkenstein creates "sex zombies with big... no... huge... no... MONSTER TITS!" Featuring a bunch of porn stars with enormous breasts this hardcore outing throws in some sub-*Young Frankenstein* spoofery as the Dr and Igor create sex slaves, turn themselves into girls for a lesbian romp and generally muck about on a creaky old laboratory set full of glowing, smoking test tubes. A very silly XXX horror parody.

MONSTROSITY
1963, USA
Alternative titles: The Atomic Brain
Dir: Joseph Mascelli. Prod: Jack Pollexfen, Dean Dillman Jr. Sc: Vy Russell, Sue Dwiggins, Dean Dillman Jr.
Cast: Marjorie Eaton, Frank Gerstle, Frank Fowler, Erika Peters, Judy Bamber

Mad scientist Dr Frank (Frank Gerstle) is trying to transfer the aging brain of Heddy March (Marjorie Eaton), his pinched and mean employer into a new body. It's not as easy as it looks though. All the doc's been able to produce so far are various "monstrosities" including a woman with a cat's brain, a man with a dog's brain and a zombified chick whose cerebral matter is no longer firing on all cylinders. Trash cinema, although not without perverse enjoyment.

MORBUS
1982, SPAIN
Dir: Ignasi P. Ferré. Prod: Carles G. Gatius. Sc: Isabel Coixet
Cast: Mon Ferré, Carla Day, Juan Borras, Victor Israel, Juan-Antoni Crespi

The weirdest thing about this surreal Spanish sex/zombie farce is that it's written by Isabel Coixet, who would graduate to critically acclaimed dramas like *My Life Without Me*. Not much chance of acclaim for this cheap and sexed up exploitation effort, though. Available only in poor-quality bootlegged prints without English subtitles, it's a pretty confusing movie: a chemist creates a serum that can, it seems, raise the dead. There's a lot of stripping off, much letching and some *Carry On*-style humour. In one scene the chemist is forced to seduce a gay security guard who is immune to this female assistant's wiles. A couple of zombies later pop up and terrorise a prostitute and a novelist who's writing a zombie movie while staying in a remote woodland house. My Spanish isn't great, but I suspect even a native speaker might struggle to follow this confused and painfully unfunny fugue of a movie.

MORTUARY
2005, USA
Dir: Tobe Hooper. Prod: Tony Didio. Sc: Jace Anderson, Adam Gierasch
Cast: Dan Byrd, Alexandra Adi, Denise Crosby, Rocky Marquette, Stephanie Patton

Tobe Hooper, director of *The Texas Chain Saw Massacre* and *Poltergeist*, almost tackles zombies in this bland straight-to-DVD outing. *Star Trek: The Next Generation*'s Denise Crosby heads to a small town to run a funeral home, little realising that it's cursed by a strange evil – or is it just black mould in need of some bleach? – that reanimates the dead. I'd love to see Hooper return to form by directing an honest to goodness z-flick. Neither this supernatural nonsense, nor *Masters of Horror – Dance of the Dead*, are it.

MOTOCROSS ZOMBIES FROM HELL
2007, USA
Dir: Gary Robert. Prod: Heidi Meier. Sc: Gary Robert
Cast: Jason McClain, Dave Competello, Rachel Diana, Chris Saphire, James Fuentez

When motocross racer Cody (Jason McClain) meets the rival Skullz team he doesn't realise that the guys under the helmets are actually biker zombies. Summoned in a Satanic rite by their manager (Chris Saphire) the ghouls tempt Cody and his friends to their doom, eventually trapping them in a desert house full of stumbling living dead corpses. This no brains, no budget DV effort is running on fumes. It's a long 76 minutes.

MUD ZOMBIES
2008, BRAZIL
Original title: Mangue Negro
Dir: Rodrigo Aragão. Sc: Rodrigo Aragão
Cast: Kika de Oliveira, Walderrama Dos Santos, Ricardo Araújo, André Lobo, Markus Konká

In Brazil's mangrove swamps, the local villagers eke out a precarious living digging up crabs from the thick oozy mud. Times are hard and crab fishermen are heading deeper and deeper into the mangroves to make ends meet. One polluted patch is rumoured to be a "terrible place" – a bottomless swamp that can suck men down to their deaths – and it's now spawning mud-caked zombies. An atmospheric choice of locale make this lo-fi Brazilian effort memorable as it shares some of the surreal edginess of Fulci's Caribbean set *Zombie Flesh-Eaters* (1979). A shame it squanders the audience's goodwill with a couple of silly production decisions – like having its aging female characters campily played by men in drag. It's not, as is sometimes claimed, the first Brazilian zombie movie: *Zombio* has that honour, although hardly anyone saw it. *Mud Zombies* spawned a loose "eco trilogy" from director Aragão that included *The Night of the Chupacabras* (2011) and the fish-zombies of *Black Sea* (2013, sadly unavailable at press time).

MULBERRY STREET
2006, USA
Alternative title: Zombie Virus on Mulberry Street
Dir: Jim Mickle. Prod: Adam Folk, Linda Moran.

Sc: Nick Damici, Jim Mickle
Cast: Nick Damici, Kim Blair, Ron Brice, Bo Corre, Tim House

"He turned into a big fuckin' rat! We had to lock him in the closet!" This creepily effective low-budget horror features a virus passed from rats to humans that turns the infected into humanoid rodents – all snarling teeth, feral screeching and a taste for flesh. Are they zombies? Well, the film's alternate title (*Zombie Virus on Mulberry Street*) seems to think so and its bleak, unflinching view of a Manhattan apocalypse owes a clear and deep debt to the z-genre and, in a sense, 9/11.

THE MUMMIES OF GUANAJUATO
1970, MEXICO
Original title: Las momias de Guanajuato
Dir: Federico Curiel. Prod: Rogelio Agrasanchez.
Sc: Rafael Garcia Travesi
Cast: Blue Demon, Mil Máscaras, Santo, Manuel Leal, Elsa Cárdenas

In Guanajuato's famed museum, the dead are restless. When towering, former wrestler Satan (Manuel Leal) and his fellow zombies march out into the city, it's down to Blue Demon, Mil Máscaras and El Santo to stop the decomposing ghouls. Satan has a beef to settle with the man in the silver mask but the bulky wrestlers are a step ahead of the dead. Simultaneously both wacky and dull.

MUSEUM OF THE DEAD
2003, USA
Dir: James Dudelson. Prod: James Dudelson, Ana Clavell. Sc: Jason Rainwater
Cast: Nathaniel Arcand, Tanya Vidal, Vivian Lucas, Pepe Pena, Ryan Barreras

Before he produced the atrocious *Day of the Dead* (2007) remake and its prequel, James Dudelson made this unconvincing horror where a couple of girls are locked in a Sunset Boulevard museum filled with cheap Aztec "exhibits". As grey-blue skinned zombies shamble around attacking them, the girls realise they're trapped in a spooky maze – which lets the no-budget production designers get away with reusing the same corridor, shot from different angles. Very poor.

MUTANT VAMPIRE ZOMBIES FROM THE 'HOOD!
2008, USA
Alternative title: The Undead
Dir: Thunder Levin. Prod: George P. Saunders.
Sc: George P. Saunders, B. Thunder Levin
Cast: C. Thomas Howell, Tyshawn Bryant, Rachel Montez Collins, Johanna Watts, Robert Wu

"It's the end of the world, yo!" Hard to dislike a movie title like *Mutant Zombie Vampires from the 'Hood!* – especially when it stars C. Thomas Howell alongside a bunch of talking zeds ("What the fuck are you?!", "Hungry!") Director and co-writer Thunder Levin, who later graduated to The Asylum's *Sharknado* (2013), keeps the action and the gags flowing as Howell's cop and an alliance of Afro-Asian gangbangers team up to survive. It turns out radiation from a solar flare has affected the limbic section of the brain that controls hunger, thirst and sex, exacerbating these needs to psychotic proportions. Which is why we get to watch a ghoul getting oral relief from a severed head. Some images you just can't un-see...

MUTANTS
2008, FRANCE
Dir: David Morley [Morlet]. Prod: Alain Benguigui, Thomas Verhaeghe. Sc: Louis-Paul Desanges, David Morlet
Cast: Hélène de Fougerolles, Francis Renaud, Dida Diafat, Marie-Sohna Condé, Nicolas Briançon

Set in the inhospitable landscape of the French Alps this ferocious, exhausting apocalyptic thriller takes no prisoners. Pregnant heroine paramedic Sonia (Hélène de Fougerolles) endures a catalogue of misery: first watching her boyfriend "turning" as they hole up in an abandoned medical facility; then fighting him off once he's become one of the feral, obsidian-eyed ghouls out to get her. Wintry in both setting and tone this draws on the best of recent "New French Extremity" horror to deliver a muted, endurance-testing riposte to *28 Days Later*.

MUTANTS
2008, USA
Dir: Amir Valinia. Prod: Matt Keith, George M. Kostuch. Sc: Jodie Jones, Samuel W. Sullivan, Evan Scott
Cast: Michael Ironside, Louis Herthum, Tony Senzamici,

Steven Bauer, Sharon Landry

Imagine if sugar was engineered to be more addictive than cocaine and caffeine combined, and turned users into zombies. Far-fetched? Yep, but that's par for the course in this talky, schlocky Z-grade effort about a nasty corporation engineering hopped up, diabetic ghouls desperate to munch on brains… no, wait… er… sugar cane crops. Looks like someone took William Seabrook's idea of "dead men working in the cane fields" a little too literally. Endless flashbacks, huge chunks of exposition, and not a lot of zombie action do little to engage. Every now and then Michael Ironside turns up on-screen to gargle gravel: "Listen up men, we cannot let this infection get to the population. You kill everything that moves!" Not to be confused with the superior French film of the same name.

MUTATION
1999, GERMANY
Dir: Timo Rose, Marc Fehse. Prod: Timo Rose. Sc: Timo Rose
Cast: Julianne Block, Mark Door, Marc Fehse, Timo Rose, Carsten Fehse

Mutation, directed by Timo Rose and Marc Fehse, is one of several German zombie splatter micro-budget epics to emerge since the 1990s. It's proved remarkably impervious to critical commentary, spawning a director's cut and a couple of sequels despite the fact that it's a shuddering mess of a movie. It opens with a 30-minute pre-credits prologue about Nazi attempts to create "supermen" using a chemical compound known as K7B. Then it heads to the modern day where K7B is discovered and fought over by shady underworld types who manage to kickstart a zombie apocalypse. Despite a surprisingly ambitious canvas of locations, *Mutation* delivers little more than dull gunfights and zombie attacks, some spirited no-budget gore, and a near-incomprehensible story told through impenetrable editing. It's undeniably enthusiastic, but it's also totally and utterly artless. Rose progressed to *Mutation 2: Generation Dead* (2001) and *Mutation III: Century of the Dead* (2002), then edited the two sequels together into *Mutation: Annihilation* (2006). How can one atrocious SOV movie spawn so many atrocious iterations?

MY BOYFRIEND'S BACK
1993, USA
Dir: Bob Balaban. Prod: Sean S. Cunningham. Sc: Dean Lorey
Cast: Andrew Lowery, Traci Lind, Danny Zorn, Edward Herrmann, Matthew Fox

"Why is everyone making a big deal about this? I've only been dead one day!" Love is stronger than mortality in this high school rom-com. After being shot in a robbery, high school kid Johnny (Andrew Lowery) is determined not to stay six feet under. Crawling out of his newly dug grave, he heads off to woo Missy (Traci Lind, *Fright Night II*), the love of his life. She's conflicted about dating a dead guy – especially when his ear falls off while they're making out – but he won't take no for an answer. Spoofing the zombie genre, this offbeat comedy is like a goofy precursor to *Warm Bodies* (2013). Producer Cunningham made his name on the *Friday the 13th* series and also gave us the zombie flick *House*.

MY DEAD GIRLFRIEND
2006, CANADA
Dir: Brett Kelly. Prod: Anne-Marie Frigon. Sc: John Muggleton
Cast: Brett Kelly, Caitlin Delaney, John Muggleton, Anastasia Kimmett, Jason Daley

While most zombie movies were shifting to infections and viruses, this yawn-inducing zom-com has magic resurrecting the dead. When teacher Steve (director Brett Kelly) reverses his car over girlfriend Amy (Caitlin Delaney) he decides to use her black magic paraphernalia to try and bring her back. Naturally she returns as a ghoul and the next 70-odd minutes see bumbling Steve trying to keep his zombie girlfriend a secret – and prevent her from eating anyone. Pretty lame.

NAKED LOVERS
1977, FRANCE
Original title: La fille à la fourrure
Alternative titles: The Porno Zombies, Starship Eros, The Girl in the Fur Coat
Dir: Claude Pierson. Prod: Claude Pierson. Sc: Élisabeth Leclair
Cast: Ursula White, Alain Saury, Didier Aubriot, Alban Ceray, Barbara Moose

This French porno flick finds a newly remarried widower (Alain Saury) being haunted by his dead spouse's corpse. She pops up at his bedroom window while he's bedding his new wife and causes all kinds of trouble by turning various horny couples into zombies. Although there's some chatter about the ghouls being aliens, all their make-up actually consists of is some rather bizarre eye shadow. The rest of the movie concentrates on a series of sexual couplings intercut with hardcore close-ups of throbbing genitalia. It builds towards a scene in which zombie couples get naked in a forest and go at it with all the synchronised timing of a Busby Berkeley musical. The tone is pure Rollin – erotic surrealism on a shoestring budget – but the hardcore goes far beyond the master's customary tits 'n' ass trappings and heads towards the kind of explicitness normally found in Massaccesi's porno zombie films.

NAZIS AT THE CENTER OF THE EARTH
2012, USA
Alternative title: Bloodstorm
Dir: Joseph J. Lawson. Prod: David Michael Latt.
Sc: Paul Bales
Cast: Dominique Swain, Josh Allen, Christopher K. Johnson, Jake Busey, James Maxwell

Nazis hiding in the Antarctic plot the Fourth Reich in this bad taste offering from The Aslyum in which super soldiers play second fiddle to Hitler's reanimated head grafted onto a mechbot chassis. Entertainingly terrible.

THE NECRO FILES
1997, USA
Dir: Matt Jaissle. Prod: Matt Jaissle. Sc: Todd Tjersland, Sammy Shapiro
Cast: Isaac Cooper, Steven Sheppard, Gary Browning, Christian Curmudgeon, Jason McGee

A crazed and crazy low-budget "erotic" horror movie, *The Necro Files* is in a class of its own. Opening with a protracted rape scene, it follows a serial sex offender Logan (Isaac Cooper) who is being chased two care-worn cops. After Logan is shot and killed, he's resurrected from the dead by some clumsy Satanists and returns to continue his rape spree as a zombie with a decaying face and an over-sized penis. Featuring some of the worst acting ever committed to celluloid, lots of sex and bondage, a blow-up doll (which the zombie takes a shine to), several zombie rape scenes and a flying zombie baby (actually a kids' plastic doll) that zips through the air attacking people, *The Necro Files* defies film criticism. *The Necro Files 2* followed in 2003.

NECROPOLIS AWAKENED
2003, USA
Dir: Garrett White. Prod: Duke White. Sc: Garrett White
Cast: Duke White, Brandon Dubisar, Garrett White, Coren Slogowski

This micro-budget, amateur indie is a family affair. Writer-director Garrett White ropes in his brother Brandon and their dad Duke on both sides of the camera. In the deserted Oregon town of Sky Hook, Nefarious Thorne (Brandon White) is using genetics research to create an army of zombies. Fly in the ointment is Bob (Duke White), who's holding out in the hills and is being hunted down by Thorne's hitmen (Duke and Brandon White and Brandon Dubisar). It's crazily ambitious and opens with an insane car chase that would give *Mad Max* a run for its money. Zombie king Thorne wears bizarre eye goggles as he experiments on his subjects and threatens to invade the next door town with his army of slightly dunderheaded zombies. The actors ham it up and shout themselves hoarse and the team's technical skills are impressive. Curiously, though, despite being insanely OTT, it's all a bit dull.

NECROVILLE
2007, USA
Dir: Billy Garberina, Richard Griffin. Prod: Billy Garberina. Sc: Billy Garberina, Adam Jarmon Brown
Cast: Brandy Bluejacket, Adam Jarmon Brown, Mark Chavez, Billy Garberina, Gene Grant

The star of *Feeding the Masses* and *The Stink of Flesh* steps behind the camera as co-director for this slacker zom-com about a pair of video store clerks, Jack and Alex (Garberina and Adam Jarmon Brown), who get a job with Zom-B-Gone exterminators. There's plenty of work for them – the town is overrun with zombies, werewolves and vampires – but none of these are as frightening as

Alex's ballbusting girlfriend (Brandy Bluejacket). Passable micro-budget fare.

NEITHER THE SEA NOR THE SAND
1972, UK
Alternative title: The Exorcism of Hugh
Dir: Fred Burnley. Prod: Peter Fetterman, Jack Smith.
Sc: Gordon Honeycombe
Cast: Susan Hampshire, Michael Petrovitch, Frank Finlay, Michael Craze, Jack Lambert

A supernatural romance featuring a corpse who comes back from the grave, Gordon Honeycombe's adaptation of his own novel is laced with British miserablism. Susan Hampshire plays an unhappily married woman who heads out to Jersey in the bleak midwinter for some peace and quiet. There she falls into bed with lighthouse keeper Petrovitch. Tragedy strikes when he dies while the couple are enjoying a dirty weekend in Scotland. But he's not dead for long and returns from the grave as a taciturn zombie to continue their doomed affair. Despite the breathless scenes of Hampshire and Petrovitch romping, it's a glum little outing – and possibly the nearest zombie cinema has ever come to a Bergman movie.

NEON MANIACS
1986, USA
Dir: Joseph Mangine. Prod: Steve Mackler, Christopher Arnold. Sc: Mark Patrick Carducci
Cast: Allan Hayes, Leilani Sarelle Ferrer, Bo Sabato, Donna Locke, Victor Elliot Brandt

A forgotten relic of the 1980s VHS era, this low-budget curio falls several notches short of the cult appeal of, say, Night of the Creeps (1986). In San Francisco a bunch of damned lost souls emerge from one of the towers of the Golden Gate Bridge and venture out into the night to kill randy teens. The ghouls – misshapen, distinctive baddies including a towering samurai warrior, a caveman and a soldier – pursue the kids through woods and on a subway train, and eventually invade a high school "battle of the bands" Halloween concert. Fortunately, the kids have realised that the monsters melt into bubbling goo when hit with water and so break out the squirt guns and fire hoses to save the day. Imagine The Monster Squad crossed with Hellraiser – although that promises far more than these neon maniacs can deliver.

NEW KIDS NITRO
2011, NETHERLANDS
Dir: Steffen Haars, Flip Van Der Kuil. Prod: Hans De Weers, Reinout Oerlemans. Sc: Steffen Haars, Flip Van Der Kuil.
Cast: Huub Smit, Tim Haars, Wesley Van Gaalen, Steffen Haars, Flip Van Der Kuil

The second gross-out movie from Dutch comedy troupe the New Kids throws some zombies into the mix to spice things up. The big-haired, loud-mouthed, lager-swilling anti-heroes from Masskantje are fighting a war with a rival gang from the nearby village of Schinjdel, when a zombie outbreak – caused by a glowing green meteor landing in a cow pasture – gives them a new foe to fight. Much shouting of "kut!", a lot of fried meat products on sticks and a scene where Richard (Huub Smit) strips naked to fight a zombie horde. Because, why wouldn't you?

NIGHT LIFE
1989, USA
Alternative title: Grave Misdemeanours
Dir: David Acomba. Prod: Charles Lippincott. Sc: Keith Critchlow
Cast: Scott Grimes, Cheryl Pollak, Anthony Geary, Alan Blumenfeld, John Astin

A teenage undertaker's assistant thinks he has problems with bullies, unrequited love and all the other woes of adolescence. Then his tormentors die in a car crash and come back from the grave to really make his life hell. Fairly standard 1980s teen horror in the same vein as The Lost Boys (1987), just without the budget.

NIGHT OF THE COMET
1984, USA
Dir: Thom Eberhardt. Prod: Andrew Lane, Wayne Crawford. Sc: Thom Eberhardt
Cast: Robert Beltran, Catherine Mary Stewart, Kelli Maroney, Sharon Farrell, Mary Woronov

Dodgy synthesiser music, yellow legwarmers and big perms: welcome to the 1980s. After Earth celebrates the flyby of a comet unparalleled in size since the death of the dinosaurs, two sisters wake up to find the world's population turned to red dust. It seems the comet was more powerful than anyone imagined, leaving the girls stuck in a deserted LA with only a few pissed off zombies for company. There's a breezy energy flowing through the script of this low-budget sci-fi outing, though zombie fans will be disappointed that the ghouls seem to be little more than an afterthought. After our teen heroines go shopping (to the sound of Madonna's "Girls Just Wanna Have Fun") and tool up with guns ("The Mac-10 submachine gun was practically invented for housewives") writer-director Thom Eberhardt loses his way with a plot about some infected scientists trying to use the girls to produce a serum. Fun but far from great.

NIGHT OF THE CREEPS
1986, USA
Dir: Fred Dekker. Prod: Charles Gordon. Sc: Fred Dekker
Cast: Jason Lively, Steve Marshall, Jill Whitlow, Tom Atkins, Allan Kayser

Beginning with a bunch of aliens who look like naked Teletubbies, this throwback to the days of 1950s sci-fi is supremely ridiculous, with a plot involving alien parasites turning whitebread American high school kids into slavering zombies. The outbreak is all the fault of Chris (Jason Lively) and his best mate J.C. (Steve Marshall) who try to steal a corpse from their campus's science labs but end up releasing the alien parasites from cryogenic suspension. With the help of a grumpy cop (Tom Atkins) and Chris's girlfriend (Jill Whitlow), they set out to put things right. Cue lots of zombies on campus, a zombified dog and a coach-load of frat boy zombies going on a rampage in tuxedos. With its retro monster movie feel this has become a cult B-movie, and it's hard not to lap up lines like, "OK girls, there's good news and there's bad news. The good news is your dates are here. The bad news is they're dead."

NIGHT OF THE DAY OF THE DAWN OF THE SON OF THE BRIDE OF THE RETURN OF THE REVENGE OF THE TERROR OF THE ATTACK OF THE EVIL MUTANT HELLBOUND FLESH-EATING SUBHUMANOID LIVING DEAD, PART II
1992, USA
Dir: Lowell Mason. Prod: Lowell Mason. Sc: Lowell Mason

Cast: Lowell Mason

One-man comedy factory Lowell Mason takes Romero's original movie, drops the soundtrack and dubs his own version by voicing all the characters. It's hard to know what's more offensive, the stream of racist, homophobic, sexist wisecracking or the complete lack of respect for the movie itself (it's probably the former). For more in a similar vein see *Another Night of the Living Dead* (2011).

NIGHT OF THE GIVING HEAD
2008, USA
Dir: Rodney Moore. Prod: Rodney Moore. Sc: Rodney Moore
Cast: Scott Lyons, Nikki Rhodes, Jack Vegas, Caroline Pierce, Samantha Sin

"Is any man's penis safe? Sperm zombies attack!" That's about as much plot as there is as porn stars turn into ravenous cock-obsessed zombies. Apparently it's all thanks to rays from a passing comet, or something. But seriously, looking for plot here is like trying to find a genuine virgin on YouPorn.com. The ghoul girls stumble around hungry for men, sucking them dry before moving on to the next. The lumbering gait and a dash of make-up gives them a vague zombie look, as does the final sequence, where an army of naked adult actresses do the old drag 'n' stumble towards the camera, is the weirdest zombie walk ever. Director Rodney Moore went on to make *I Can't Believe I Fucked a Zombie* (2011). Personally, I can't believe I watched this junk.

NIGHT OF THE LIVING DEAD
1968, USA
Alternative titles: La noche de los muertos vivientes, La nuit des morts vivants
Dir: George A. Romero. Prod: Russell Streiner, Karl Hardman. Sc: George A. Romero, John Russo
Cast: Duane Jones, Judith O'Dea, Karl Hardman, Marilyn Eastman, Keith Wayne

The granddaddy of the modern zombie movie, *Night of the Living Dead* sticks its characters in an isolated farmhouse then sets a horde of ghouls on them. It's a brilliant, seminal horror film and the most influential zombie outing ever made.

NIGHT OF THE LIVING DEAD
1990, USA
Dir: Tom Savini. Prod: John A. Russo, Russ Streiner.
Sc: George A. Romero
Cast: Tony Todd, Patricia Tallman, Tom Towles, McKee Anderson, William Butler

Make-up master Tom Savini steps into the director's chair for this remake of the original 1968 *Night of the Living Dead* with a script – and a blessing – from Romero. Although it closely follows the original's plot, there's one very significant change: instead of being hysterical, Barbara now takes charge while Ben and Cooper bicker and everyone else sits around uselessly. Playing with the radical shifts in gender politics that have occurred since 1968, this is a cleverly ironic rehash of Romero's masterpiece.

NIGHT OF THE LIVING DEAD 3D
2006, USA
Dir: Jeff Broadstreet. Prod: Jeff Broadstreet. Sc: Robert Valding
Cast: Brianna Brown, Joshua DesRoches, Johanna Black, Greg Travis, Sid Haig

Another year, another unauthorised remake of the 1968 masterpiece thanks to its botched copyright history. A tacky attempt to update the original for the modern multiplex (Weed! Sex! 3D!), this cheap knockoff drags *Night of the Living Dead* into the 21st century. After Barb (Brianna Brown) is attacked in a graveyard by reanimated ghouls, she's saved by Ben (Joshua DesRoches) – now a white kid on a motorbike. They take refuge in a farmhouse where a bunch of rednecks run a weed farm. Shot in 20 days, it shows little respect for Romero or the intelligence of audiences.

NIGHT OF THE LIVING DEAD 3D: RE-ANIMATION
2011, USA
Dir: Jeff Broadstreet. Prod: Jeff Broadstreet. Sc: Jeff Broadstreet
Cast: Andrew Divoff, Jeffrey Combs, Sarah Lieving, Robin Sydney, Adam Chambers

A prequel to *Night of the Living Dead 3D*, this rewinds to the beginning of the zombie outbreak at the Tovar family funeral home. Crappy CG gore and cheap 3D combine with a ramshackle plot.

NIGHT OF THE LIVING DEAD: REANIMATED
2009, USA
Curator: Mike Schneider
Voices: Duane Jones, Judith O'Dea, Karl Hardman, Marilyn Eastman, Keith Wayne

Conceptual artist Mike Schneider curates a shot for shot animated remake of *Night of the Living Dead* with the help of over 100 artists. A fascinating experiment.

NIGHT OF THE LIVING DEAD: RESURRECTION
2012, UK
Dir: James Plumb. Prod: Andrew Jones. Sc: James Plumb, Andrew Jones
Cast: Sule Rimi, Kathy Saxondale, Lee Bane, Terry Victor, Rose Granger

Shot on a limited budget in Wales this British movie takes Romero's 1968 original to the Valleys as zombies attack an isolated farmhouse. The kitchen sink realism isn't best served by the obvious lack of production cash or professional actors.

NIGHT OF THE LIVING DORKS
2004, GERMANY
Original title: Die Nacht der lebenden Loser
Alternative title: Revenge of the Teenage Zombies
Dir: Matthias Dinter. Prod: Philip Voges, Mischa Hofmann. Sc: Matthias Dinter
Cast: Tino Mewes, Thomas Schmieder, Manuel Cortéz, Collien Fernandes, Nadine Germann

It's jocks vs nerds at Friedrich Nietzsche High School. Nothing unusual there. Until an urn of zombie ashes from Haiti is used in a Satanic ritual involving a frozen supermarket chicken (the aim: to raise Kurt Cobain from the dead). Not long afterwards, the school's three biggest losers (Tino Mewes, Manuel Cortez, Thomas Schmieder) are killed in a car crash and transformed into superpowered zombies. Which comes in handy when jocks are trying to flush your head down the toilet… A German spin on the high school zom-com – think *My Boyfriend's Back* meets *Revenge of the Nerds* – this is less terrible than its title suggests.

THE NIGHT OF THE SEAGULLS
1975, SPAIN

Original title: La noche de los gaviotas
Alternative title: Don't Go Out At Night, Night of the Blood Cult, Night of the Death Cult, La playa de los sacrificios, Terror Beach
Dir: Amando de Ossorio. Prod: José Angel Santos.
Sc: Amando de Ossorio
Cast: Víctor Petit, María Kosti, Sandra Mozarowsky, José Antonio Calvo

The final film to feature the Blind Dead (not counting their brief appearance in John Gilling's *La Cruz del Diablo* in 1974), this has a deeper resonance than any of the earlier movies in the series. In a small coastal village the inhabitants keep the Templars at bay by handing over women for them to sacrifice to an aquatic god. Shades of H.P. Lovecraft abound, yet what really stands out is the mythology in which the spirits of the girls become seagulls circling the village. Neatly tying into the beach ending of *Horror of the Zombies*, this builds into a fittingly austere climax to the series.

NIGHT OF THE SORCERERS
1973, SPAIN
Original title: La noche de los brujos
Dir: Amando de Ossorio. Prod: José Antonio Pérez Giner, Luis Laso Moreno. Sc: Amando de Ossorio
Cast: Simón Andreu, Kali Hansa, María Kosti, Lorena Tower [Loretta Tovar], Joseph [José] Telman

Shot between *Return of the Blind Dead* and *Horror of the Zombies*, this mishmash of voodoo, vampires and zombies proves a dreadful stain on de Ossorio's reputation. The opening scenes of voodoo practitioners being slaughtered by white colonials in turn of the century Africa set the stage for a clumsy tale about Europeans getting their just desserts from indigenous peoples. In the present, white scientists conducting a photographic survey of animals on the verge of extinction run into trouble when they encounter a female vampire and her black native zombies. She turns the women in the expedition into scantily clad vampires in leopard skin furs who leap through the jungle in slow-mo. Racist, risible and completely redundant, it's an undistinguished effort.

NIGHT OF THE ZOMBIES
1981, USA

Alternative titles: The Chilling, Gamma 693, Night of the Wehrmacht Zombies, Night of the Zombies II
Dir: Joel M. Reed. Prod: Lorin E. Price. Sc: Joel M. Reed
Cast: Jamie Gillis, Ryan Hilliard, Ron Armstrong, Samantha Grey, Juni Kulis

In the snowy hills of Bavaria, German and American soldiers left behind after the end of WWII keep themselves going by using military chemicals originally designed to put wounded soldiers into a state of suspended animation. In order to stop themselves falling apart, the zombies need to get a regular quota of Gamma 693 and human flesh, but their survival is threatened by a badass CIA agent (Jamie Gillis). It's difficult to know what's more laughable, the poverty-stricken production design (check out the Pentagon's sparsely furnished offices), the cruddy sound and visuals or the lamentably fake skeletons that are left behind when the zombies die.

NIGHT MARE CITY
1980, ITALY/SPAIN
Original title: Incubo sulla città contaminata, La invasión de los zombies atómicos. Alternative title: City of the Walking Dead
Dir: Umberto Lenzi. Prod: Diego Alchimede. Sc: Piero Regnoli, Antonio Corti, Luis Maria Delgado
Cast: Hugo Stiglitz, Laura Trotter, Maria Rosaria Omaggio, Francisco Rabal, Mel Ferrer

Director Lenzi always claimed that his radioactive killers weren't zombies, but there's no disguising the debt *Nightmare City* owes to the rest of the Italian zombie cycle. The nightmare begins as an airplane lands and radioactive killers charge down the gangway to feast on the living. As the unnamed city is overrun, reporter Miller (Hugo Stiglitz) and his wife (Laura Trotter) head out into the countryside to take shelter in a deserted theme park (!) A true guilty pleasure, this lamentably bad but hilariously silly Italian exploitation classic features fast, smart ghouls who attack the city's key installations with all the strategic planning of a band of heavily-armed insurgents. The set-piece TV station invasion sequence pretty much sums up the whole movie: chaotic, ludicrous and full of body-ripping trauma (one poor lass has a breast ripped off in gruesome close-up; fortunately for her, it's clearly made out of latex). As for the cyclical ending, well that has to rank as one of zombie cinema's most ridiculous moments.

THE NIGHT SHIFT
2010, USA
Dir: Thomas Smith. Prod: Erin Lilley. Sc: Thomas Smith
Cast: Khristian Fulmer, Erin Lilley, Jonathan Pruitt, Jordan Woodall, Soren Odom

Set in a graveyard *The Night Shift* inevitably draws a comparison with *Dellamorte Dellamore* (1994) – and comes off worst. Cemetery caretaker Rue Morgan (Khristian Fulmer) is unlucky in love, has a talking skeleton (voiced by Soren Odom) for a sidekick and is having his heels nipped by Confederate era soldier who wants his job. Oh and Rue's also dead, a sentient zombie charged with looking after the cemetery's unruly residents. Taking place in a mythical alternate universe infested with zombies, werewolves and even the Grim Reaper, this wacky but underpowered zom-com is hard to dislike... Shame it flaps around pretty lifelessly for 120 minutes before finally giving up the ghost.

THE NIGHTS OF TERROR
1980, ITALY
Original title: Le notti del terrore
Alternative titles: Burial Ground, Le manoir de la terreur, La noche del terror, Die Rückkehr der Zombies, Het Schrikkasteel der Zombies, Zombie 3, The Zombie Dead
Dir: Andrew White [Andrea Bianchi]. Prod: Gabriele Crisanti. Sc: Piero Regnoli
Cast: Karin Well, Gian Luigi Chirizzi, Simone Mattioli, Antonietta Antinori, Roberto Caporali

This classic Italian *morti viventi* movie finds a handful of bourgeois holidaymakers trapped in a country mansion by marauding zombies. Resurrected from a crypt in the grounds by a hapless professor, the Etruscan undead lay siege to the mansion, arming themselves with pitchforks, scythes and other farming implements. Despite the best efforts of the living, these slow-moving ghouls quickly overrun the estate, upsetting the sex-obsessed characters' plans for nookie.

NINJAS VS ZOMBIES
2008, USA
Alternative title: Zombie Contagion

Dir: Justin Timpane. Prod: William Stendeback, Brian Anderson. Sc: Justin Timpane
Cast: Cory Okouchi, Dan Guy, Daniel Ross, Carla Okouchi, P.J. Megaw

Nerdgasm alert! This backyard horror from Virginia improbably thanks Joss Whedon in its final credits, though is thankfully self-aware enough to add the caveat "Who doesn't know we exist". When a Satanic ritual brings 20-something Eric (P.J. Megaw) back from the dead as a soul-sucking warlock he raises an army of zombie ghouls to attack his former friends. Fortunately the friends are blessed with magic powers (including a nifty "Elsewhere!" teleport spell) and sick martial arts skills that are showcased in several interminable bouts of "fighty time". It's cheap, very dull and very nerdy – like a DIY role-playing game scenario put on film. Never say never, but I suspect that call from Mr Whedon may be a long time coming.

NINJA ZOMBIES
2011, USA
Dir: Noah Cooper. Prod: Michael Castro. Sc: Noah Cooper, Michael Castro
Cast: Michael Lee, Michael Castro, Arun Storrs, Chris Kulmann, Edward Lee Miller

Shot on the cheap, *Ninja Zombies* is little more than a geeky fan movie made by a bunch of hopeful filmmakers. On his 25th birthday slacker landlord Dameon (Michael Lee) discovers an ancient trunk containing a magic "Hell Sword" handed down from his Japanese ancestors. Pretty soon his student house share is overrun by ninja zombies in black pyjamas. Much laughably silly nerd dialogue ensues and even more laughable, super slow fighting sequences complete with dodgy CG blood. Lloyd Kaufman makes a cameo – wittering on about chicken zombies – and the whole thing feels like a companion piece to the equally nerdy, amateur outing *Ninjas Vs Zombies* (2008). Zombie ninjas, much like zombie Westerns, really shouldn't be this difficult to get right. Sigh.

NUDIST COLONY OF THE DEAD
1991, USA
Dir: Mark Pirro. Prod: Mark Headley. Sc: Mark Pirro
Cast: Deborah Stern, Tony Cicchetti, Rachel Latt, Braddon Mendelson, Jim Bruce

Possibly the worst film in this entire filmography, and that's quite a feat given some of the competition here. Mark Pirro's zombie musical begins with the mass suicide of a group of nudists, who decide to kill themselves after their camp is closed down by puritan officials to make way for a religious retreat. Later the naked folk (who aren't actually naked at all, but dressed in modesty-maintaining body stockings) come back from the grave to terrorise the living and punish them for their narrow-minded ways. Ignore the intriguing title; this is utterly dreadful. Heck, there aren't even any nudie cutie corpses. What kind of a cheap trick is that to pull on us?

LA NUIT DE LA MORT!
1980, FRANCE
Dir: Raphaël Delpard. Prod: Raphaël Delpard.
Sc: Raphaël Delpard, Richard Joffo
Cast: Isabelle Goguey, Charlotte de Turckheim, Michel Flavius, Betty Beckers, Michel Debrane

A spooky nursing home is the setting of this obscure French zombie effort, which revolves around the entertaining conceit of the old literally sucking the life out of the living. A young nurse (Isabelle Goguey) arrives to start work at the chateau but quickly realises that something's up after one of her friends disappears. Her investigations eventually reveal the chateau's dark secret: the witch-like, piano-playing proprietress and the residents are feasting off the nurses. Plenty of brooding atmosphere and a final reel full of splatter – including severed hands and gouged eyeballs – make up for the slow pacing. *Naked Lovers* helmer Claude Pierson is credited as a producer.

OASIS OF THE ZOMBIES
1982, SPAIN/FRANCE
Original titles: La tumba de los muertos vivientes, L'abîme des morts vivants
Alternative titles: Der Abgrund der lebenden Toten, Bloodsucking Nazi Zombies, The Oasis of the Living Dead, Le tresór des morts vivants
Dir: A.M. Frank [Jesús Franco]. Sc: A. L. Mariaux [Marius Lesoeur], Jesús Franco
Cast: Manuel Gélin, Eduardo Fajardo, Lina Romay, Antonio Mayans, Javier Maiza

The premise of this Franco atrocity is all-too-simple. Snotty nosed rich kids head out to Africa in search of some lost Nazi gold. They find it. Nazi zombies claw their way out of the sand. There's chaos and lots of bodies. The End. Franco was hardly on top form when he sat behind the camera for this Eurotrash exploitation outing, but it did relatively good business among curiosity seekers – especially when it was released under the title *Bloodsucking Nazi Zombies*. What self-respecting horror fan could resist a come on like that? As a side note, *Oasis* exists in two alternate edits: a gorier, Spanish-only version and a substantially re-worked Euurociné version with alternate footage and music. The latter is the English-dubbed international release and is the most widely available.

O.C. BABES AND THE SLASHER OF ZOMBIETOWN
2008, USA
Dir: Creep Creepersin. Prod: Nikki Wall, Matt Wall, Allyson Clark. Sc: Creep Creepersin
Cast: Elissa Dowling, Monique La Barr, Julie Rose, Ashley Tompakov, Noelle Balfour

"If you ever masturbated in a public bathroom, you'll love O.C. *Babes and the Slasher of Zombie Town...*" So promises the outrageous trailer for this terrible, no-budget zombie movie set in Orange County where a zombie attack traps a bunch of O.C. kids in the crappiest bar ever seen on film... with a serial killer thrown in for good measure. Barely clocking in at 70 minutes, it's inexplicably padded out by footage from the original *Night of the Living Dead*. Romero's monochrome ghouls make up about 99.99% of the film's zombie action. Clearly there wasn't even a budget for a bottle of ketchup. It's one of the worst movies in this book – alongside the likes of *Zombiez*, *Nudist Colony of the Dead*, *Santa Claus Vs The Zombies* and *The Curse of Pirate Death*... But the OTT trailer is hilarious.

OFFICE OF THE DEAD
2009, USA
Dir: Matthew Chung. Prod: Karen Shih, Teddy Chen Culver. Sc: Matthew Chung
Cast: Teddy Chen Culver, Shawn Parikh, Christina July Kim, Robbie Daymond, Don Jeanes

"I have been kissing his ass for hours and now he's dead!" When tech giant LifeCorp tries to invent a computer program to rewire negative thoughts into positive ones, it inevitably goes badly wrong: rewired, zombified corporate suits end up wandering the company's HQ while software engineer Ben (Teddy Chen Culver) and his colleagues fight back with keyboards and golf clubs. Satirising the inanities of corporate culture – the most aggressive zombies turn out to be the ones from sales; they also have the hardest heads to crack! – this zom-com wants to be z-cinema's answer to *Office Space*. It never quite finds enough spark to work – and it's telling that the 70 minute running time includes at least 10 minutes of "making of" interviews with the cast. Still, the moment where the heroes try to blend in among the angry office drone ghouls by bitching each other out is a nice take on the zombifying atmosphere of the modern workplace. For a variation on the same theme see *Working Stiffs* (1989).

OH! MY ZOMBIE MERMAID
2004, JAPAN
Original title: Â! Ikkenya puroresu
Dir: Naoki Kubo. Prod: Ganari Takahashi. Sc: Izô Hashimoto, Naoki Kubo
Cast: Shinya Hashimoto, Sonim, Shirô Sano, Nicholas Pettas, Urara Awata

STOP! There are no zombie mermaids in this movie, which is a real disappointment. There are, however, bonkers El Santo-style Japanese wrestlers having an in-house smackdown while a TV producer tries to bump up his ratings and a woman develops a scaly skin problem. It's not totally zombie-free – a random ghoul pops up near the end – but it's not a zombie movie and definitely not a zombie mermaid movie. Surely some enterprising filmmaker out there could bang out *Mermaids Vs Zombie*s for us?

ONECHANBARA
2008, JAPAN
Alternative title: Onechanbara: Samurai Bikini Squad
Dir: Yôhei Fukuda. Prod: Hideyuki Sakurai, Keisuke Ueno, Masanori Kawashima, Ryo Murata.
Sc: Yasutoshi Murakawa, Yôhei Fukuda
Cast: Eri Otoguro, Manami Hashimoto, Tomohiro Waki, Chise Nakamura, Tarô Suwa

When the zombie apocalypse comes you need the essentials: samurai sword, cowboy hat and, um, a feather boa and a bikini. Based on an equally disappointing Japanese videogame series, this piles on the sleazy objectification of hot women and gushing geysers of gore. Aya (Eri Otoguro) is a dead-inside zombie slayer who fights the dead while wearing very little. She's searching for the mad scientist responsible for the apocalypse and his assistant, her school-uniform wearing younger sister (Chise Nakamura). It's pretty subpar even by videogame movie tie-in standards – ropey VFX work spoiling the occasional moment of verve, like Aya fighting through a corridor full of poncho wearing ghouls, her katana glittering with mystical energy like it's been buffed by power-ups. The whole movie is, beyond the eponymous outfit, surprisingly unmemorable. A direct-to-DVD sequel *Onechanbara: The Movie – Vortex* followed in 2009.

ONE DARK NIGHT
1982, USA
Alternative titles: Entity Force, A Night in the Crypt, Night of Darkness
Dir: Tom McLoughlin. Prod: Michael Schroeder.
Sc: Tom McLoughlin, Michael Hawes
Cast: Meg Tilly, Melissa Newman, Robin Evans, Leslie Speights, Donald Hotton

A sorority house initiation rite goes badly wrong in this cheap shocker. Spending the night in a mausoleum, Julie's spooked not only by the location but also by the attempts of her so-called friends to freak her out. The high school pranks turn deadly serious, though, when the spirit of a Russian psychic raises zombies to attack the girls. Since the psychic uses telekinesis to move the corpses around, we're greeted to the rather ungainly sight of cadavers floating through the air in pursuit of their victims. Suffice to say it's a silly tweak of zombie mythology that nobody else bothered to imitate.

ORGY OF THE DEAD
1965, USA
Alternative title: Orgy of the Vampires
Dir: A.C. Stephen [Stephen C. Apostolof]. Prod: A.C.

Stephen [Stephen C. Apostolof]. Sc: Edward D. Wood Jr. Cast: Criswell, Fawn Silver, Pat Barringer, William Bates, Mickey Jines

Softcore horror merges with dancing zombie go-go-ghouls in this atrocious and completely un-erotic outing from the pen of Ed Wood. It's little more than a succession of topless "damned" zombie women dancing on gravestones as the emperor of the dead – played by Wood favourite Criswell – judges them on their ability. Or, perhaps, lack thereof. A couple who died in a car crash in the opening five minutes are forced to watch the shenanigans – mainly because they're tied up and terrorised into paying attention by the Wolfman and a Mummy. You, dear viewer, don't have that excuse.

OSOMBIE
2012, USA
Dir: John Lyde. Prod: John Lyde, Paul D. Green. Sc: Kurt Hale
Cast: Corey Sevier, Eve Mauro, Jasen Wade, Danielle Chuchran, Paul D. Hunt

Released alongside *Zero Dark Thirty* – Kathryn Bigelow's Oscar winner about the hunt for Osama Bin Laden – this low-budget outing asks the burning question of the post 9/11 world: what if OBL came back as a ghoul and triggered the zombie apocalypse? In Afghanistan (actually Utah) a group of US Navy SEALS and a yoga teacher (!) are on a mission to kill the zombified OBL. The gun-heavy action suggests someone's been playing too much *Call of Duty*. (Want to see a Barrett .50-cal fired at close range into a tunnel full of zombie Taliban? Of course you do!) The jokey dialogue is less clever than it thinks it is ("What did the zombie eat after it got its teeth pulled? The dentist!") and, despite a legion of bearded, turban-wearing Taliban zombies, *Osombie*'s quick 'n' cheerful production doesn't come close to delivering on the novelty title's WTF? promise.

OTTO; OR, UP WITH DEAD PEOPLE
2008, GERMANY/CANADA
Dir: Bruce LaBruce. Prod: Jürgen Brüning, Bruce LaBruce, Jörn Hartmann, Jennifer Jonas, Michael Huber. Sc: Bruce LaBruce
Cast: Jey Crisfar, Katharina Klewinghaus, Susanne Sachsse, Marcel Schlutt, Guido Sommer

Traditionally gay zombie movies are XXX pornos like *At Twilight Come the Flesheaters* (1998) or fluffy comedies like *Creatures from the Pink Lagoon* (2006). This queer cinema/zombie crossover is something very different – the production company is called Existential Crisis Productions which tells you all you need to know about its pretensions. Canadian director Bruce LaBruce, a self-described "reluctant pornographer", presents a politicised, Marx-quoting zombie movie which takes a swipe at capitalism along with a hardcore orgy scene in which a zombie screws a stomach wound. It's ambitious, sometimes startling, often boring and largely a mess but its hoodie-wearing, emo-kid protagonist Otto (Jey Crisfar, who LaBruce found via MySpace) has a poignant sadness about him that's hard to forget. La Bruce returned to zombie cinema with the more extreme *LA Zombie: Hardcore* in 2010.

OUANGA
1934, USA
Alternative titles: Crime of Voodoo, Drums of the Jungle, The Love Wanga
Dir: George Terwilliger. Prod: George Terwilliger. Sc: George Terwilliger
Cast: Fredi Washington, Philip Brandon, Marie Paxton, Sheldon Leonard

Caribbean plantation owner Adam finds himself trapped by the amorous attentions of neighbour Klili. Troubled by her confused racial identity (she's black but light-skinned enough to pass as white), Klili rejects her native foreman's offers of romance in favour of dispatching two zombies to abduct Adam's fiancée. In a striking shot, she raises the zombies out of their dug up coffins and they lumber into line like sleepwalkers. As these burly black musclemen abduct the screaming Eve, it's pretty obvious what kind of white fears the film is playing on. Still, the zombies are ineffective villains, obeying Adam's commanding voice even though Klili has ordered them only to listen to her. Perhaps they were simply swayed by his God-given white authority?

OUTPOST
2007, UK

Dir: Steve Barker. Prod: Arabella Page Croft, Kieran Parker. Sc: Rae Brunton
Cast: Ray Stevenson, Julian Wadham, Richard Brake, Paul Blair, Brett Fancy

Shot and financed in Scotland, this dour Nazi-zombies-in-a-bunker outing proved unexpectedly successful in reviving the fascist ghoul cycle and spawned an unlikely franchise.

OUTPOST II: BLACK SUN
2011, UK
Dir: Steve Barker. Prod: Arabella Page Croft, Kieran Parker. Sc: Steve Barker, Rae Brunton
Cast: Richard Coyle, Catherine Steadman, Clive Russell, Michael Byrne, David Caltagirone

In *Outpost II* Nazi hunter Lena (Catherine Steadman) finds herself co-opted into a mission to shut down the nefarious machine from the first movie. She teams up with a renegade physicist (Richard Coyle, doing a passable American accent to help international sales), and a squad of wry British rapid-reaction special forces as things inevitably go wrong. Shot in Scotland and part funded by Dumfries and Galloway council, this is as bleak as its predecessor, but its willingness to tackle an inherently silly conceit with serious gusto pays dividends.

OUTPOST III: RISE OF THE SPETSNAZ
2013, UK
Dir: Kieran Parker. Prod: Arabella Page-Croft, Kieran Parker. Sc: Rae Brunton
Cast: Bryan Larkin, Iván Kamarás, Velibor Topic, Lawrence Possa, Alec Utgoff

War, what is it good for? Zombie movies, according to Scottish production house Black Camel Pictures, whose third entry in the *Outpost* franchise continues in the same muddy, po-faced vein as its predecessors. Beginning in WWII, where a grizzled Russian squad ambushes a Nazi convoy, it leads right back to the now infamous bunker where the Nazis are dabbling with "Promethean fire" to create super soldiers. Director Kieran Parker cites *Cross of Iron, Come and See* and *Where Eagles Dare* as influences. The ghouls themselves are mostly interchangeable, with the exception of the giant zombie played by mixed martial artist James

Thompson.

PARANORMAN
2012, USA
Dir: Sam Fell, Chris Butler. Prod: Arianne Sutner, Travis Knight. Sc: Chris Butler
Cast (voices): Kodi Smit-McPhee, Tucker Albrizzi, Anna Kendrick, Casey Affleck, Christopher Mintz-Plasse

A cousin of kiddie-Goth outing *Coraline* (it's made by the same animation studio), *ParaNorman* is a stop motion animated kids adventure about high haired geek Norman (voiced by Kodi Smit-McPhee) who sees dead people. Saving his town from founding father zombies resurrected by a 300 year-old witch, bullied Norman learns how to stop being afraid and fight back. Wearing eclectic influences from Steven Spielberg, Tim Burton and Ruggero Deodato on its sleeve, this isn't afraid to scare with rotten-toothed, green-faced Puritan zombies in buckled pilgrim hats who are forever losing bits of their decaying bodies. It's frequently too good for kids – especially its pleasingly knowing asides on the conventions of the z-genre: "Zombies take over the world and we lock ourselves in a LIBRARY? There's an adult video store right across the street!"

PATHOGEN
2006, USA
Dir: Emily M. Hagins. Prod: Megan Hagins, Emily M. Hagins. Sc: Emily M. Hagins
Cast: Rose Kent-McGlew, Alec Herskowitz, Tiger Darrow, Tony Vespe, Alex Schroeder

A lot of backyard American zombie movies feel pretty juvenile; only *Pathogen* has the excuse of having been made by a middle schooler. Emily Hagins was 10 when she wrote the script for this Austin apocalypse and 12 when she directed the story of tainted water turning her local community into zombies. Filming between classes and homework, with the help of supportive parents, Hagins delivers a zombie movie that's no worse than many backyard epics made by filmmakers twice her age. More interesting than the movie itself is how her passion made her into something of an inspirational indie icon – as documented in the feature length making-of documentary *Zombie Girl: The Movie* (2009).

THE PEOPLE WHO OWN THE DARK
1976, SPAIN
Original title: Último deseo
Dir: Léon Klimovsky. Prod: Miguel F. Mila. Sc: Vicente Aranda, Gabriel Burgos, Joaquim Jorda
Cast: Nadiuska, Alberto de Mendoza, Teresa Gimpera, Paul Naschy [Jacinto Molina], Maria Perschy

Some Marquis De Sade-loving libertines manage to survive a nuclear war while making merry in a castle dungeon in this entertaining slice of post-apocalyptic sci-fi starring Paul Naschy. Meanwhile, the rest of the local populace are turned blind by the flash of the blast (shades of John Wyndham's *The Day of the Triffids*). With society on the verge of collapse, the libertines and their whores hole up in the chateau, but soon find themselves besieged after foolishly angering their blind neighbours. Quite how all of the sightless maniacs managed to find sunglasses to put over their burnt-out eyes remains unexplained, yet this little thriller zips along so quickly you probably won't have time to care. For a Naschy movie, it's not bad.

PET SEMATARY
1989, USA
Dir: Mary Lambert. Prod: Richard P. Rubinstein. Sc: Stephen King
Cast: Dale Midkiff, Fred Gwynne, Denise Crosby, Brad Greenquist, Michael Lombard

This King-scripted shocker (adapted from his own novel) was originally touted by producer Rubinstein as a directorial project for their mutual friend George Romero. Along the way things changed, and Lambert took over the reins to deliver a slick but rather ineffective film. The title refers to a children's cemetery for dead pets built, it transpires, over an old Indian burial ground that retains magical properties. When Midkiff's three-year-old son is killed by one of the huge trucks that thunders past their far-from-idyllic home, he buries the boy in the cemetery only to see him return as a nasty little zombie armed with an equally nasty scalpel blade. At its best when dealing with the psychological horror of confronting the dead returned to "life", this never quite manages to fulfil its promise, and soon degenerates into a shock-o-rama of hackneyed nastiness. Followed by franchise killer *Pet Sematary Two* (1992).

PIRATES OF THE CARIBBEAN: THE CURSE OF THE BLACK PEARL
2003, USA
Dir: Gore Verbinski. Prod: Jerry Bruckheimer. Sc: Ted Elliot, Terry Rossio
Cast: Johnny Depp, Geoffrey Rush, Orlando Bloom, Keira Knightley, Jack Davenport

A rollicking, swashbuckling adventure, Gore Verbinski's mammoth box office hit about pirates and lost Aztec treasure gets by on its sparky script and an audacious (over) performance from Depp, who bases his character on The Rolling Stones's Keith Richards. It also dips it toes into the zombie genre with a bunch of pirates led by Rush who're actually living dead ghouls (their true form can be seen when they're caught in the moonlight). The pirates are cursed to spend eternity as zombies unless they return every last coin of their plundered loot.

PLAGA ZOMBIE
1997, ARGENTINA
Dir: Pablo Parés, Hernán Sáez. Prod: Pablo Parés, Berta Muñiz, Hernán Sáez. Sc: Pablo Parés, Berta Muñiz, Hernán Sáez
Cast: Pablo Parés, Berta Muñiz, Hernán Sáez, Walter Cornás, Diego Parés

A hugely influential film in its native Argentina – where it helped birth that country's indie horror scene – *Plaga Zombie* is a backyard epic that's rarely much better than amateur. Made for about $120, this SOV effort excels thanks to its gross out chutzpah that pushes the DIY make-up and grue to the mucky limit as a trio of slackers are exposed to a zombifying alien virus. It's very *Braindead* and throws everything it can think of at the screen – wrestlers, gore, kung fu zombies, more gore, men in black, even more gore, and giggling zombies armed with a lawn mower. *Fangoria* magazine championed it in the States giving it a lot of exposure and helping to spawn a franchise.

PLAGA ZOMBIE: ZONA MUTANTE
2001, ARGENTINA
Alternative title: Plaga Zombie: Mutant Zone
Dir: Hernán Sáez, Pablo Parés. Prod: Walter Cornás, Pablo Parés, Berta Muñiz, Hernán Sáez, Paulo Soria. Sc: Pablo Parés, Hernán Sáez

Cast: Berta Muñiz, Pablo Parés, Hernán Sáez, Paulo Soria, Esteban Podetti

Picking up right where the previous movie left off, this energetic and confident sequel sees the trio of Argentinean zombie fighters (Berta Muñiz, Pablo Parés, Hernán Sáez) bathed head to toe in blood in the aftermath of the alien zombie invasion of their town. With a government conspiracy underway, they're trying to get out of Dodge fast, but need a map because the town is cut off. It sets the stage for epic fight scenes that would make Mexico's El Santo blush. There's not much sense or subtlety but there's no denying its made-by-fans-for-fans energy. Highpoints include a musical number for leopard leotard wearing wrestler John West (Muñiz) and a homage to the farting zombie intestines from Peter Jackson's *Braindead*. Followed by *Plaga Zombie: Zona Mutante: Revolución Tóxica* (2011).

THE PLAGUE OF THE ZOMBIES
1966, UK
Dir: John Gilling. Prod: Anthony Nelson Keys. Sc: Peter Bryan
Cast: André Morell, Diane Clare, John Carson, Alexander Davion, Jacqueline Pearce

An English country squire kills off the villagers under his charge and resurrects them as cheap labour for his tin mine in this Hammer picture. London doctor Sir James (André Morell) teams up with the village G.P. (John Carson) to trace the cause of the illness and discovers that the squire has been dabbling in voodoo. The scoundrel!

PLANET TERROR
2007, USA
Dir: Robert Rodriguez. Prod: Robert Rodriguez, Quentin Tarantino, Elizabeth Avellán. Sc: Robert Rodriguez
Cast: Rose McGowan, Freddy Rodríguez, Josh Brolin, Marley Shelton, Michael Biehn

This retro zombie movie played as part of the *Grindhouse* double bill with *Death Proof*. Rose McGowan stars as go-go dancer Cherry, who's trapped in a Texas town after an army bio-weapon unleashes zombies. Gloopy and outrageous, it's pure trash… in the best possible sense.

PLAN 9 FROM OUTER SPACE
1958, USA
Dir: Edward D. Wood Jr. Prod: Edward D. Wood Jr. Sc: Edward D. Wood Jr.
Cast: Gregory Walcott, Mona McKinnon, Duke Moore, Tom Keene, Vampira [Maila Nurmi]

Aliens are resurrecting the bodies of the dead to conquer the Earth in this Golden Turkey winner from Ed Wood Jr., infamous for being crowned American cinema's most incompetent filmmaker. Eager to save us from destroying our planet and the rest of the universe, the meddling aliens are eventually stopped by a police detective and a navy pilot who don't take kindly to being told that all earthlings are idiots. The film was, rather tragically, Bela Lugosi's final role. He died during filming and, in true Wood style, was replaced by a "double" twice his size who kept a cape over his face for the rest of the production.

PLATOON OF THE DEAD
2009, USA
Dir: John Bowker. Prod: Joe Sherlock, John Bowker. Sc: John Bowker
Cast: Tyler David, Tom Stedham, Chris Keown, Ariauna Albright, Michelle "Ame" Mahoney

J.R. Bookwalter's Tempe Entertainment sends viewers into a coma again with another no-brains, no-budget, no-entertainment zombie outing. Here a global war between zombies and humans has been started by a bunch of teens playing around with a "store-bought Ouija board" (damn those pesky kids). A few years into the future three soldiers wander through the woods armed with laser guns while blasting zombies in gas masks. It has all the technical skill of a home video and is about as fun as root canal.

PONTYPOOL
2008, CANADA
Dir: Bruce McDonald. Prod: Jeffrey Coghlan, Ambrose Roche. Sc: Tony Burgess
Cast: Stephen McHattie, Lisa Houle, Georgina Reilly, Hrant Alianak, Rick Roberts

One of the smartest and most daring zombie movies of the last decade, *Pontypool* hardly has any ghouls, or any gore. Set in a local radio station, it's a film about linguistics and the living dead ("The *Finnegan's Wake* of zombie movies" as *New York Magazine* memorably put it). A unique and thrilling triumph.

POP PUNK ZOMBIES
2011, USA
Dir: Steve Dayton. Prod: Steve Dayton, Brian Leis.
Sc: Steve Dayton, Brian Leis
Cast: Adam Hatfield, Ian Kane, Nick Marinucci, Erin Wheelock, Laura Savage

Is punk dead? When pop impresario Dameon David (Adam Hatfield) resurrects a recently-deceased guitar band The Vicious Vegans (take that, Simon Cowell), the public's split between couldn't-care-a-less gig goers and politicised protestors. But after the zombie band is unleashed from their restraints by the pro human jobs lobby, the zombie infested venue is locked down by the city authorities and lovelorn Eddy (Ian Kane) fights to save his ex-girlfriend. Shot on video, this dull and totally amateur outing adds little to the zombies-with-guitars cycle started by *Hard Rock Zombies* back in 1984. If only the ghoul band's lyrics – "No, I won't feel no pain/Someday I'll sleep again" – extended to the audience.

PORN OF THE DEAD
2006, USA
Dir: Rob Rotten. Prod: Not listed. Sc: Rob Rotten

Hardcore porn from filmmaker Rob Rotten and Punx Productions, the people behind porno horrors like *Texas Vibrator Massacre*. No plot or dialogue, just a lot of sex between blokes in decontamination suits and various zombie women covered in boot polish and blood. It includes the now de rigueur blowjob-gone-wrong scene and a soundtrack of thrash metal from the likes of Decapitated, Blood Red Throne and Gorerotted. Ugly, ugly, ugly.

PORNO HOLOCAUST
1981, ITALY
Alternative titles: Holocausto Porno
Dir: Joe D'Amato [Aristide Massaccesi]. Prod: Franco Gaudenzi. Sc: Tom Salina [Aristide Massaccesi]
Cast: George Eastman [Luigi Montefiori], Dirce Funari, Annj Goren, Mark Shannon, [Manilo

Cerosimo], Lucia Ramirez

More inimitable sex-zombie action from Joe D'Amato as scientists visit an island inhabited by a radioactive mutant zombie with a huge penis. Scenes of hardcore sex eventually give way to some splatter as the zombie goes on the rampage, killing the men and raping the women. Nasty, indefensible and memorable for all the wrong reasons.

PORTRAIT OF A ZOMBIE
2012, IRELAND
Dir: Bing Bailey. Prod: Bing Bailey, Laura Morand Bailey. Sc: Bing Bailey, Laura Morand Bailey
Cast: Patrick Murphy, Geraldine McAlinden, Rory Mullen, Paul O'Bryan, Sonya O'Donoghue

Shot on a RED 4k camera on the streets of Dublin, this ambitious, no-budget mockumentary follows the Murphys, a rough and tumble Irish family coping with newly zombified son Billy (Patrick Murphy). He's patient zero in an outbreak that's traced back to a meat packing plant and his plight – raging on a bed in the family's terraced house, straight-jacketed and muzzled – attracts the attention of a preening American filmmaker (Todd Fletcher). Mixing talking head interviews with a few gory moments, *Portrait of a Zombie* is formally daring and it hints at a satire of media manipulation worthy of *Man Bites Dog*. Veering uncertainly between laughs and seriousness, though, it never delivers on its promise. However there is a delicious moment where a pro-zombie, pro-vegetarian, eco-friendly campaigner realises that letting zombies eat the living – even though meat is murder – might reduce the world's carbon footprint.

POULTRYGEIST: NIGHT OF THE CHICKEN DEAD
2007, USA
Dir: Lloyd Kaufman. Prod: Andy Deemer, Kiel Walker. Sc: Gabriel Friedman, Dan Bova, Lloyd Kaufman
Cast: Jason Yachanin, Kate Graham, Allyson Sereboff, Robin L. Watkins, Joshua Olatunde

Directed by Troma president and co-founder Lloyd Kaufman, this outrageous zombie comedy starts with a zombie hand bursting out of a graveyard, where an amorous couple are getting it on. The ghoul inserts his dead finger into the unsuspecting man's anus, who thinks his girlfriend has just discovered her kinky side. Do I need to go on? OK, then… the graveyard is actually an ancient Native American burial ground. When a fast food chicken outlet builds a new store on the hallowed ground, zombie chicken ghouls are unleashed. Covered in feathers and with beaks for noses, the KFC ghouls run amok. Scenes of a fat man blasting out diarrhoea like Old Faithful, lots of gratuitous breast meat bouncing around and a gory climax in which the zombie chickens start serving up buckets of man meat kind of detract from the subtext about America's white guilt over Native American genocide. Finger lickin' good? Cluck off, no. But it's a true Troma original.

PREMUTOS: LORD OF THE LIVING DEAD
1997, GERMANY
Original title: Premutos: Der Gefallene Engel
Dir: Olaf Ittenbach. Prod: Andre Stryi, Michael Muller, Olaf Ittenbach. Sc: Olaf Ittenbach
Cast: Andre Stryi, Ella Wellmann, Christopher Stacey, Anke Fabre, Fidelis Atuma

Someone once told me they invented a drinking game based on the body trauma in *Premutos*. Take a shot for each severed head, and a double for a skinned corpse. Personally, I'd be drunk before the opening credits had finished… German director Olaf Ittenbach's backyard zombie epic is possibly the goriest movie since Peter Jackson departed New Zealand for Hollywood. Insanely ambitious, Ittenbach takes us from the Crusades to WWII to Christ's crucifixion to the present where goofy Matthias (Ittenbach) ends up awakening Premutos, the original fallen angel, and unleashing a horde of ghouls. Ittenbach has a modicum of talent and even less money, but there's no questioning his love of gore: eviscerations, flayed corpses, zombies attacked with chainsaws and cinema's first zombie vs tank battle (even demonic zombies can't argue with heavy artillery) before ending it all with a bodycount (139 apparently). Bad. Yet totally unforgettable.

PRETTY DEAD
2013, USA
Dir: Benjamin Wilkins. Prod: Joe Cook, Benjamin Wilkins, Jon Michael Kondrath. Sc: Benjamin Wilkins
Cast: Carly Oates, Ryan Shogren, Quantae Love, Emily Button, Dave Matos

An intimate zombie apocalypse begins with med student Regina (Carly Oates) suffering a near-fatal reaction to a snort of cocaine. Over the coming weeks, she slowly transforms – a slowing pulse and taste for raw bacon giving way to sucking the blood out of tampons then eating the pizza delivery guy. Telling its story through found footage, this slowburning micro-budget effort harks back to the birth-of-a-zombie cycle started by *I, Zombie: The Chronicles of Pain* (1998) with a winning central performance from Oates. It also cleverly leverages pop science discussions of the parasitical fungus that creates "zombie ants" that made headlines in 2012. Iffy reactions of the supporting cast – would any boyfriend really tolerate her snacking on human tissue pilfered from the hospital? – drag it down. It works best when it captures the pathos of this woman's attempt to fight the alien urges that are slowly consuming her.

PRISON OF THE DEAD
2000, USA
Dir: Victoria Sloan. Prod: Vlad Paunescu. Sc: Matthew Jason Walsh
Cast: Patrick Flood, Jeff Peterson, Samuel Page, Kim Ryan, Michael Guerin

The music video visuals, floppy haircuts and talk about voodoo dates this low-budget DVD filler from Full Moon Productions to its turn of the millennium genesis. When a spoilt rich kid dies in mysterious circumstances, his paranormal-obsessed, coke-snorting Manhattanite friends arrive to pay their (dis)respects at a spooky castle that was once a prison for witches. Playing about with a Ouija board raises the castle's executioners from their (apparently very shallow) graves. Dressed in medieval gear, the ghouls stalk through endless clouds of dry ice – their eyes glowing red as they chase down the brattish characters. Life sentences are shorter than this.

PRINCE OF DARKNESS
1987, USA
Dir: John Carpenter. Prod: Larry J. Franco. Sc: John Carpenter
Cast: Donald Pleasence, Jameson Parker, Victor Wong, Lisa Blount, Dennis Dun

Carpenter's apocalyptic answer to *The Exorcist*

and *The Omen* has nerdy physicists checking out a strange container hidden in the basement of a rundown inner-city church. Inside is the Antichrist, who's about to unleash a reign of terror. Strangely, he begins this grandiose plan by turning a few of the local bums (including rocker Alice Cooper) into zombies.

PSYCHOMANIA
1972, UK
Alternative titles: The Death Wheelers, Death Wheelers Are... Psycho Maniacs
Dir: Don Sharp. Prod: Andrew Donally. Sc: Arnaud d'Usseau, Julian Halevy
Cast: George Sanders, Beryl Reid, Nicky Henson, Mary Larkin, Roy Holder

When the leader (Nicky Henson) of a British biker gang known as The Living Dead dies in a road accident, he's buried upright, sitting on his beloved bike. Pretty soon, though, there's a revving in the graveyard as he bursts out of the ground with his motor running. The biker has realised that the way to cheat death is to commit suicide while having complete faith in the fact that he will return from the dead. He proceeds to convince the rest of his gang to crash and burn so they can return and join him on a living dead rampage across the Home Counties. Pure 1970s camp.

QUATERMASS 2
1957, UK
Alternative title: Enemy From Space
Dir: Val Guest. Prod: Anthony Hinds. Sc: Nigel Kneale, Val Guest
Cast: Brian Donlevy, John Longdon, Sydney James, Bryan Forbes, Vera Day

Redoubtable American scientist Professor Quatermass (Brian Donlevy) returns in this sci-fi offering from Hammer. As a wave of meteorites crashes into the Earth, they release a gaseous alien parasite capable of turning the human race into mindless zombie slaves. The aliens' plan is to colonise the planet by recalibrating the atmosphere; Quatermass discovers their secret plant and leads a band of resistance fighters against them.

QUARANTINE
2008, USA

Dir: John Erick Dowdle. Prod: Doug Davison, Roy Lee, Sergio Agüero. Sc: John Erick Dowdle, Drew Dowdle
Cast: Jennifer Carpenter, Jay Hernandez, Steve Harris, Johnathon Schaech, Columbus Short

Rushed into production by Sony Screen Gems, this American remake of *[REC]* lazily reproduces the original almost shot-for-shot. It's less a remake than an example of how little faith US studios have in American audiences' willingness to sit through subtitled movies. Adding to the irony, it hamfistedly ditches one of the two elements that made *[REC]* such a hit. While director John Erick Dowdle (*Devil*) keeps the "found footage" approach, he excises the supernatural element in favour of a scientific explanation for the zombie outbreak. Gone is the deeply Catholic horror of *[REC]*, replaced by something much more mundane. Jennifer Carpenter exercises her lungs as the TV reporter dragged into events, but she is no Manuela Velasco. The tragedy is that the politics of distribution meant that the Spanish original was shunted to a DVD release in the US after the remake had its theatrical run.

QUARANTINE 2: TERMINAL
2010, USA
Dir: John G. Pogue. Prod: Doug Davison, Roy Lee, Sergio Aguero, Marc Bienstock. Sc: John G. Pogue
Cast: Mercedes Masöhn, Josh Cooke, Mattie Liptak, Ignacio Serricchio, Noree Victoria

Bearing no relation to the Spanish sequel *[REC] 2*, this follow-up to the US remake of *[REC]* is largely set in an airport. Here passengers and flight crew are trapped in a quarantine lockdown after their flight is targeted by doomsday cult terrorists with a rabies-like bio-weapon. Scrappily shot and with a lower budget than its predecessor this clips along entertainingly enough – although it seems to have killed the US remake cycle stone dead.

THE QUICK AND THE UNDEAD
2006, USA
Dir: Gerald Nott. Prod: Gerald Nott, Clint Glenn. Sc: Gerald Nott
Cast: Clint Glenn, Nicola Giacobbe, Parrish Randall, Erin McCarthy, Dion Day

In the near future, a viral outbreak has left the

American West overrun by infected ghouls. Retaking the new frontier are bounty hunters on motorbikes who head into the wilderness to slaughter ghouls – snipping off their pinkie fingers as proof. As the pool of ghouls dries up, though, the latter-day cowboys are fighting one another for the last remaining zombie scalps. Not to be confused with *Undead or Alive* (2007), nor the non-zombie, Sam Raimi Western *The Quick and The Dead* (1995).

RAIDERS OF THE DAMNED
2005, USA
Dir: Milko Davis. Prod: Milko Davis. Sc: Mike Ezell
Cast: Gary Sirchia, Laura Zoe Quist, J.C. Austin, Thomas Martwick, Russell Reed

Robed, desiccated Blind Dead style zombies attack a DIY CG helicopter with catapults and bows and arrows. A towering wall blocks off a mysterious land. A team of scientists crash in zombie territory. For about three minutes, *Raiders of the Damned* looks like it might set itself apart from the usual low-budget zombie fare. It does, but not in a good way. Taking a leftfield approach to the genre, director and producer Milko Davis shows ingenuity in his production design, but has absolutely no idea how to tell a coherent story. Despite its DIY epic feel, this is barely watchable.

RAIDERS OF THE LIVING DEAD
1985, USA
Dir: Samuel M. Sherman. Prod: Dan Q. Kennis. Sc: Samuel M. Sherman, Brett Piper
Cast: Scott Schwartz, Robert Deveau, Donna Asali, Bob Allen, Bob Cacchett

Not the Indiana Jones meets zombies knockoff you might expect, but a curiously lifeless tale about a teenager (Scott Schwartz) and a reporter (Robert Deveau). They uncover living dead antics at a former prison and destroy half a dozen zombies using a homemade laser-beam gun built out of a laserdisc player. It's a movie of non sequitirs and endless, but unilluminating, plot exposition that'll leave you scratching your head wondering what on earth the point of it all is. A few ghouls stumble about to little purpose.

RAMMBOCK: BERLIN UNDEAD
2010, GERMANY
Alternative title: Siege of the Dead
Dir: Marvin Kren. Prod: Sigrid Hoerner. Sc: Benjamin Hessler
Cast: Michael Fuith, Anka Graczyk, Theo Trebs, Emily Cox, Steffen Münster

A Berlin apartment block is under siege in this short but intense German outing that's a cut above most of the nation's zombie flicks – although, given that we're talking about the land of Schnaas, Ittenbach and Rose, that is damning with faint praise. Trapped inside the block are a handful of scared residents, plumber's mate Harper (Theo Trebs) and lovelorn middle aged dweeb Michael (Michael Fuith) who's looking for his girlfriend. What distinguishes *Rammbock* isn't its anti-love story, nor its innovative use of a shopping trolley. It's the film's fresh take on viral contagion. Here the infection is triggered by excess adrenalin. If the infected can stay calm – and crack out the sedatives – there's a chance their bodies can fight off the virus. But it's hard to relax when half of Berlin is after you…

RAPE ZOMBIE: LUST OF THE DEAD
2012, JAPAN
Original title: Reipu zonbi
Dir: Naoyuki Tomomatsu. Prod: Masahiro Mikami. Sc: Naoyuki Tomomatsu, Jirô Ishikawa
Cast: Arisu Ozawa, Asami, Yui Aikawa, Saya Kobayasi, Takeshi Nakazawa

Bad taste pushes beyond all boundaries in this J-splatter flick from the director of *Stacy* and *Zombie Self-Defence Force*, as men turn into sex-crazed, raping ghouls. Scenes of gleeful women arming themselves with semi-automatic rifles and shooting men in the penis can't counter the amount of salacious titillation that dominates every rape. All in all, it's the kind of movie you'd expect to see on *Japanorama*, sandwiched between a segment on eel soup and vending machines selling schoolgirls' panties. Quickly followed by *Rape Zombie 2* and *Rape Zombie 3* (both 2013).

RE-ANIMATOR
1985, USA
Dir: Stuart Gordon. Prod: Brian Yuzna. Sc: Dennis Paoli, William J. Norris, Stuart Gordon

Cast: Jeffrey Combs, Bruce Abbott, Barbara Crampton, David Gale, Robert Sampson

Mad scientist Herbert West (Jeffrey Combs) may come straight out of the fiction of H.P. Lovecraft, yet the rest of this sick little movie is pure Gordon-Yuzna. Reanimating the dead with the help of a glow-in-the-dark serum, West is a precocious student at the Miskatonic Medical School run by Dr Hill (David Gale), who wants to claim the compound as his own. As the experiments get out of control and West struggles to reanimate the dead without them turning into mindless zombies, this blackly comic horror races towards a truly outrageous blood-splattered finale. Spare a thought for West's poor moggy too...

[REC]
2007, SPAIN

Dir: Jaume Balagueró, Paco Plaza. Prod: Julio Fernández. Sc: Jaume Balagueró, Luis Berdejo, Paco Plaza
Cast: Manuela Velasco, Ferran Terraza, Jorge-Yamam Serrano, Pablo Rosso, David Vert

Zombies are caught on video in this rollercoaster Spanish horror movie about a quarantine apartment block. When firemen are called to a Barcelona flat, perky TV reporter Ángela (Manuela Velasco) and unseen lenser Pablo (Pablo Rosso) tag along hoping for a scoop; what they discover instead is a zombie-infested apartment block that's suddenly quarantined... trapping the film crew inside and kickstarting a franchise that was quickly remade for US audiences.

[REC] 2
2009, SPAIN

Dir: Jaume Balagueró, Paco Plaza. Prod: Julio Fernández. Sc: Juame Balagueró, Manu Díez, Paco Plaza
Cast: Jonathan Mellor, Manuela Velasco, Óscar Zafra, Ariel Casas, Alejandro Casaseca

James Cameron laid down the golden rule for sequels in *Aliens*: take the original and max the mofo out. Spanish directors Jaume Balagueró and Paco Plaza obviously studied Big Jim's playbook. *[REC] 2* amps up the action, as a cocksure SWAT team get swatted, then adds meat to the original's

skeletal backstory and hints at a viable franchise. It takes one big idea – basically *The Exorcist* with shotguns – and sticks it on [FF]. It doesn't hit [II] until everyone's either dead, possessed or a gibbering wreck. A great example of a sequel that surpasses the original movie. What a pity *[REC] 3* dropped the franchise ball.

[REC] 3 GENESIS
2012, SPAIN
Dir: Paco Plaza. Prod: Julio Fernández. Sc: Luiso Berdejo, David Gallart, Paco Plaza
Cast: Leticia Dolera, Diego Martin, Ismael Martínez, Àlex Monner, Borja Glez Santaolalla

A prequel not a sequel, *[REC] 3* rewinds to the start of the rabies-like demonic outbreak that powered the first two movies in the franchise, but swaps the stripped down thrills of its predecessors for a shonky story and splatstick humour. On its own terms it's a passable movie; as part of the *[REC]* series it's a travesty. It barely advances the series' mythology at all, with the exception of one throwaway idea (when glimpsed in mirrors, the zombies are revealed as misshapen demons). Hopefully a future *[REC] 4* will return the series to its gory glory and continue the main Ángela plot line.

RED LIPS: EAT THE LIVING
2005, USA
Dir: Donald Farmer, Chuck Angell, Wes Human. Prod: Donald Farmer. Sc: Donald Farmer, Maria Ortiz
Cast: Debbie Rochon, Maria Ortiz, Linda Royer, Bryan Dorris, Jim O'Rear

Prolific scream queen Debbie Rochon stars in this DIY horror anthology by a bunch of filmmakers from Tennessee. In a Manhattan bar she meets Mircarla (Maria Ortiz) who talks to her about vampirism and tells her four creepy stories about zombies (it would probably help if the bar wasn't pumping out death metal during these conversations, but what can you do?) In the first tale, a husband tends his zombie bride. In the second, a group of survivors fight off a zombie attack. The third features a videotape with prophetic powers, and the final segment stars a mountain-man zombie looking for revenge. Nice anthology set-up. Pity the stories are scrappy and the production values lamentable.

REDNECK ZOMBIES
1987, USA
Dir: Pericles Lewnes. Prod: Edward Bishop, George Scott, Pericles Lewnes. Sc: Fester Smellman
Cast: Lisa DeHaven, William Benson, James Housely, Anthony Burlington-Smith, Martin Wolfman

The best description of this low-budget trash comes from the over-egged trailer: "Swilling toxic moonshine they become flesh-eatin', bloodthirsty kinfolk from hell... They become REDNECK ZOMBIES!" A cheap 'n' cheerful effort from the Troma team, this distant, inbred cousin of *The Grapes of Death* combines all the usual sick jokes, sexual innuendo and politically incorrect humour you'd expect from the studio with some really gory special effects. It's billed as making "*Day of the Dead* look like *Mary Poppins*" – which is proof that Troma's marketing campaigns are always more interesting than the finished products.

REMAINS
2011, USA
Steve Niles' Remains
Dir: Colin Theys. Prod: Andrew Gernhard, Zach O'Brien. Sc: John Doolan, Steve Niles
Cast: Evalena Marie, Grant Bowler, Anthony Marks, Lance Reddick, Miko Hughes

Things to do in Reno when you're dead... After a nuclear blast turns citizens of "The Biggest Little City in the World" into ghouls, casino worker Tom (Grant Bowler) and coke fiend cocktail waitress Tori (Evalena Marie) team up to bicker, fight and occasionally screw their way through the apocalypse. Based on Steve Niles's comic miniseries, this Chiller channel TV movie stays true to the source's imperfections: horribly flawed but weakly written characters and a killer lack of narrative drive. The spiky relationship between the charismatic Bowler (familiar from TV's *Ugly Betty*) and hotpants and cowboy boots wearing Marie just about sustains the interest, while the somnambulist zombies slowly evolve into something potentially much scarier. A valet-parking-gone-wrong scene is a hoot, the magician's rolling ball escape rather less so. All in all, its casino setting turns into a busted flush. It's not a

patch on Niles's vampire outing *30 Days of Night*.

REMINGTON AND THE CURSE OF THE ZOMBADINGS
2011, PHILIPPINES
Original title: Zombadings 1: Patayin Sa Shokot Si Remington
Dir: Jade Castro. Prod: Raymond Lee. Sc: Raymond Lee, Jade Castro, Michiko Yamamoto
Cast: Mart Escudero, Lauren Young, Kerbie Zamora, Janice de Belen, John Regala

As a child, bigoted homophobe Remington (Mart Escudero) liked nothing better than making fun of the gay men in his town. But, after being cursed by a transvestite, he finds himself turning into a screaming queen on his 21st birthday. The horror! Meanwhile, a serial killer armed with a gaydar gun is tracking and killing gay men, resulting in a sudden rash of cross-dressing zombies. This Filipino queer zom-com is a charming, day-glo fantasy (love the rainbow street disco) with a winning turn from Escudero. Sadly, the zombies are a bit of a footnote.

REQUIEM DER TEUFEL
1993, GERMANY
Dir: Jan Reiff. Prod: Andrea Leukel. Sc: Jan Reiff
Cast: Andrea Leukel, Jan Reiff, Joachim Schultz, Michael Faulk, Thomas Palmer

This slow-paced, soap opera-style German SOV outing – never released with English subtitles, but thankfully dialogue-lite – is more domestic than most of its fellow backyard epics. After a husband finds his wife has been cheating on him, he decides to settle scores, first by frying her in the bathtub with a hairdryer, then shooting her lover and even offing a passerby who witnesses the crime. That's the first half hour. The second half follows the lone murderer as he's hounded by his victims, inexplicably returned from the dead as zombies (or perhaps just figments of his imagination). They creep about his house at night, poison his schnapps, put razor blades in his spaghetti bolognese and hack his leg off with power tools. Divorce might have been a better option.

RESIDENT EVIL
2002, UK/GERMANY/FRANCE/USA
Alternative title: Resident Evil: Ground Zero

Dir: Paul W.S. Anderson. Prod: Bernd Eichinger,
Samuel Hadida, Jeremy Bolt, Paul W.S. Anderson.
Sc: Paul W.S. Anderson
Cast: Milla Jovovich, Michelle Rodriguez, Eric Mabius,
James Purefoy, Martin Crewes

Based on the best-selling videogame, Paul W.S.
Anderson's take on the zombie goes for high-
concept gloss and videogame references over
horror heritage. Milla Jovovich stars as an
amnesiac woman caught up in a zombie outbreak
at a secret underground laboratory in Raccoon
City owned by the Umbrella Corporation.

RESIDENT EVIL: AFTERLIFE
2010, CANADA/GERMANY
Dir: Paul W.S. Anderson. Prod: Bernd Eichinger,
Samuel Hadida, Don Carmody, Robert Kulzer, Jeremy
Bolt, Paul W.S. Anderson. Sc: Paul W.S. Anderson
Cast: Milla Jovovich, Ali Larter, Kim Coates, Shawn
Roberts, Sergio Peris-Menchet

Opening with an army of Alice clones attacking an
Umbrella lab, the fourth *Resident Evil* film mixes
non-stop 3D action, shoddy CG and outrageously
OTT pandering to the series's fanboys (and girls)
as Alice (Jovovich) escorts survivors to an Alaskan
safe haven known as Arcadia. The zombies are
little more than a diversion from all the densely-
plotted franchise mythology and big explosions.

RESIDENT EVIL: APOCALYPSE
2004, FRANCE/CANADA/UK/USA
Dir: Alexander Witt. Prod: Jeremy Bolt, Paul W.S.
Anderson, Don Carmody. Sc: Paul W.S. Anderson
Cast: Milla Jovovich, Sienna Guillory, Oded Fehr,
Thomas Kretschmann, Jared Harris

The sequel to Anderson's 2002 smash hit, this
picks up where the first movie left off with
Jovovich's heroine Alice waking up to find Raccoon
City overrun with zombies. Teaming up with a
band of plucky survivors, she searches for the
missing daughter of one of the Umbrella scientists
responsible for the outbreak and battles Nemesis
– a Herman Munster look-alike armed with an
RPG. There's the occasional welcome gag – after
blasting away one of the Damien Hirst-esque
zombie dogs, a character mutters: "Stay!" – but for
the most part this is a zombie movie in name only.

RESIDENT EVIL: DAMNATION
2012, JAPAN
Original title: Biohazard: Damnation
Dir: Makoto Kamiya. Prod: Hiroyuki Kobayashi.
Sc: Shotaro Suga
Cast: Matthew Mercer, Dave Wittenberg, Wendee Lee,
Val Tasso, Robin Sachs

Four years after *Resident Evil: Degeneration*
(2008), Capcom and Sony returned with this
sequel. A big jump in the quality of the animation
isn't matched by the still crippled storytelling. This
time Kennedy is in Eastern Europe, where a former
Soviet state mired in civil war becomes ground
zero for a new T-virus outbreak. Densely plotted
and overlong, it's hamstrung by its over-reliance on
keeping franchise fans happy. Anyone not well-
versed in *Resident Evil* lore – the Lickers, Las
Plagas, the dastardly Umbrella Corp., etc – is likely
to be left scratching their head. Although you've
got to love the scene where a tank takes out an
oversized mutant ghoul.

RESIDENT EVIL: DEGENERATION
2008, JAPAN
Original title: Biohazard: Degeneration
Dir: Makoto Kamiya. Prod: Hiroyuki Kobayashi.
Sc: Shotaro Suga
Cast: Paul Mercier, Alyson Court, Laura Bailey, Roger
Craig Smith, Crispin Freeman

Set after Raccoon City has been nuked back to the
Stone Age, *Resident Evil: Degeneration* picks up
the story with more faithfulness to the Capcom
series than Paul W.S. Anderson's multiplex fodder
has ever managed. When a US airport is overrun
with ghouls, franchise favourites Claire Redfield
and Leon S. Kennedy team up to save a slimy
Senator; and then, in the aftermath, work out who
was responsible for the bio-weapon attack. CG
animation stuck in the uncanny valley combines
with shonky, videogame-quality dialogue to create
a fan-friendly mélange of *Resident Evil* clichés.
Personally, I'd rather play *Left 4 Dead 2* in versus
mode.

RESIDENT EVIL: EXTINCTION
2007, GERMANY/UK/USA
Dir: Russell Mulcahy. Prod: Jeremy Bolt, Paul W.S.
Anderson. Sc: Paul W.S. Anderson

Cast: Milla Jovovich, Oded Fehr, Ali Larter, Iain Glen, Ashanti

Director Russell Mulcahy cut his teeth on Duran Duran videos in the 1980s before graduating to the slick high-octane excitement of *Highlander*, so it's no surprise the third instalment in the *Resident Evil* movie series looks seductive. As ever, it's a 12-year-old fanboy's wet dream: guns, zombies and Milla Jovovich slinking around while handing zombies their asses. This time she's off to the Nevada desert, goes a bit Mad Max, and gets attacked by zombie crows. Meanwhile, the filmmakers come to the smart conclusion that the only thing better than one Milla is a million of them – and so cook up a cloning plot device that delivers exactly that. It's probably the best movie in the series, for whatever that's worth.

RESIDENT EVIL: RETRIBUTION
2012, CANADA-GERMANY
Dir: Paul W.S. Anderson. Prod: Paul W.S. Anderson, Jeremy Bolt, Robert Kulzer, Don Carmody, Samuel Hadida. Sc: Paul W.S. Anderson
Cast: Milla Jovovich, Michelle Rodriguez, Kevin Durand, Sienna Guillory, Shawn Roberts

Captured by Umbrella (again), Alice (Jovovich) fights her old friend Jill Valentine and another Red Queen supercomputer in a last ditch attempt to save what remains of humanity. In other words: sexy catsuits, 3D slow-mo action combined with ADHD storytelling and not much else. Modern cinema's equivalent of a post-pub kebab.

THE RESURRECTION GAME
2001, USA
Dir: Mike Watt. Prod: Amy Lynn Best, Bill Homan and Mike Watt. Sc: Mike Watt
Cast: Ray Yeo, Kristen Pfeifer, Francis Veltri, Amy Lynn Best, Bill Homan

Shot in Pittsburgh, the zombie capital of the world, this self-styled 16mm "zombie noir" found fame when it was circulated among horror fans as a bootleg workprint. Set in the future where zombies have become an accepted factor of everyday life, it follows an ex-cop and his buddies as they uncover the damning conspiracy that surrounds the return of the dead. Filmmaker Mike Watt went on to

write *Dead Men Walking* (2005).

RETARDEAD
2008, USA
Dir: Dan West, Rick Popko. Prod: Dan West, Rick Popko. Sc: Dan West, Rick Popko
Cast: Paul Weiner, Beth West, Dan Burr, Rick Popko, Dan West

A vague sequel to no-budget fecal creature feature *Monsturd*, this has the nefarious Dr Stern (Dan Burr) returning to take over a school for special needs adults so he can inject them with a serum designed to make them super smart. Unfortunately, it turns them – and pretty much everyone else – into super dumb zombies. Cops and a serial peeping tom who leaves "pecker snot" on windowsills are on the case. No prizes for political correctness or good filmmaking as the zombie apocalypse unfolds in this Troma-style outing. Stick it on a double bill with the funnier, if no less offensive, *Special Dead* (2006).

THE RETURNED
2012, FRANCE
Original title: Les Revenants
Dir: Fabrice Gobert, Frédéric Mermoud. Prod: Simon Arnal, Caroline Benjo, Jimmy Desmarais, Barbara Letellier, Carole Scotta. Sc: Fabrice Gobert, Emmanuel Carrère, Fabien Adda, Nicolas Peufaillit
Cast: Anne Consigny, Frédéric Pierrot, Clotilde Hesme, Céline Sallette, Samir Guesmi

"Are we sure I'm not a zombie?" A world, and a continent, apart from *The Walking Dead*, this French TV drama unfolds with mysterious obliqueness. In an Alpine village the dead return to life but instead of moaning they simply try to fit back in among the living – an impossible task. Based on the French film *They Came Back* (*Les Revenants*, 2004) this is a bold and unconventional take on the zombie – less a horror show than a rumination on grief, community and resurrection.

RETURN OF THE BLIND DEAD
1973, SPAIN
Original title: El ataque de los muertos sin ojos
Alternative titles: Return of the Evil Dead, Die Rückkehr der reitenden Leichen
Dir: Amando de Ossorio. Prod: Ramón Plana.

Sc: Amando de Ossorio
Cast: Tony Kendall [Luciano Stella], Fernando Sancho, Esther Ray [Esperanza Roy], Frank Blake [Braña], Lone Fleming

The first sequel to *Tombs of the Blind Dead* (1971) bears no relation to its predecessor other than the return of its cowled ghouls. Here a rural village's festive celebrations are interrupted when a group of Templars rise from their tombs and cut a bloody swathe through the processions. It turns out that the village idiot has resurrected them in a fit of revenge for his mistreatment, using a kidnapped woman as a blood sacrifice. Several flashbacks flesh out the mythology surrounding these eyeless zombies, yet the main focus is on the village's preparations for their festival (which celebrates the five hundred year anniversary of the Templars' demise). As the dead attack, charging through the town on horseback, the living hide inside the cathedral for safety but don't last long against the sightless corpses.

THE RETURN OF THE LIVING DEAD
1984, USA
Dir: Dan O'Bannon. Prod: Tom Fox. Sc: Dan O'Bannon
Cast: Clu Gulager, James Karen, Don Calfa, Thom Mathews, Beverly Randolph

According to Dan O'Bannon's tongue in cheek pastiche of *Night of the Living Dead*, Romero's original movie was based on historical fact. The dead really did return to life in Pittsburgh in 1968 after the accidental release of a pesticide designed to be sprayed on marijuana crops. Although the incident was hushed up, the corpses of the original zombies were sealed in canisters that, as a result of a bureaucratic cock up, are sitting in a medical supply company's warehouse in Louisville, Kentucky. Two foolish workers manage to release the gas precipitating a mass zombie apocalypse in which the country is overrun by brain-munching ghouls. Sadly, Romero's shoot 'em in the head strategy no longer works since these bodies just keep on going even without any brain tissue: "You mean the movie lied?!"

RETURN OF THE LIVING DEAD: PART II
1987, USA
Dir: Ken Wiederhorn. Prod: Tom Fox. Sc: Ken Wiederhorn
Cast: James Karen, Thom Mathews, Dana Ashbrook, Marsha Dietlein, Michael Kenworthy

Just when you thought it was safe to be dead, Dan O'Bannon passes the reins to Ken Wiederhorn for this lame retread of the first film. Another canister is opened, releasing yet more toxic gas and another horde of zombies. Matthews and Karen even reprise much the same roles as before, this time as a gravedigger and his boneheaded assistant. Rehashing the plot of the first film isn't the height of postmodern irony just evidence of poverty in the ideas department.

RETURN OF THE LIVING DEAD 3
1993, USA
Dir: Brian Yuzna. Prod: Gary Schmoeller, Brian Yuzna. Sc: John Penney
Cast: J. Trevor Edmond, Mindy Clarke, Kent McCord, Basil Wallace, James T. Callahan

This time it's love as Brian Yuzna steps into the director's chair and delivers *Romeo and Juliet* for zombies. After his girlfriend Julie (Mindy Clarke) is killed in a traffic accident, army brat Curt (Edmond) uses his dad's experiments with the military chemicals of the first two films to bring her back to life as a ghoul. Escaping the army base, they hide out in the sewers with Curt's dad and an angry gang of thugs in pursuit. Julie spends most of her time trying not to chow down on Curt, eventually realising that she can dampen her taste for flesh through self-harming. It all leads to a body modification makeover in which she covers herself in homemade piercings. Ouch.

RETURN OF THE LIVING DEAD 4: NECROPOLIS
2005, USA
Dir: Ellory Elkayem. Prod: Anatoly Fradis, Steve Scarduzio. Sc: William Butler, Aaron Strongoni
Cast: Aimee-Lynn Chadwick, Cory Hardrict, John Keefe, Jana Kramer, Peter Coyote

Shameless in its dollar-driven resurrection of a franchise that probably ought to have stayed dead, this belated sequel heads to Romania where production and Peter Coyote's accommodation is cheap. Coyote, the only notable actor here, is responsible for experimenting with the barrels containing Trioxin-245 and turning kids into ghouls. Trying to stop him are a bunch of cookie cutter teens who discover that zombies still have a military value even after the Cold War. It's witless and dull and totally depressing – even more so when you realise that director Ellory Elkayem once made the not-bad spider movie *Eight-Legged Freaks*... Shot back to back with *Return of the Living Dead 5: Rave to the Grave*.

RETURN OF THE LIVING DEAD 5: RAVE TO THE GRAVE
2005, USA

Dir: Ellory Elkayem. Prod: Anatoly Fradis, Steve Scarduzio. Sc: William Butler, Aaron Strongoni
Cast: Jenny Mollen, Cory Hardrict, John Keefe, Aimee-Lynn Chadwick, Peter Coyote

Another failed attempt to resurrect the *Return of the Living Dead* franchise. This time the barrels of military zombie liquid become the basis for a new street drug – named, what else?, Z – that turns ravers into ghouls at a Halloween party. This is a sequel that totally manages to trash the goodwill fans felt towards the long-running series, not least of all by undercutting the franchise's most iconic ghoul the "Tar Man". Future sequels, at this point, look very unlikely.

RETURN OF THE ZOMBIES
1972, SPAIN/ITALY

Original titles: La orgía de los muertos, L'orgia dei morti
Alternative titles: Die Bestie aus dem Totenreich, Beyond the Living Dead, Dracula – The Terror of the Living Dead, The Hanging Woman
Dir: José Luis Merino. Prod: Ramona Plana. Sc: José Luis Merino, Enrico Colombo
Cast: Stan Cooper [Stelvio Rosi], Maria Pía Conte, Dianik Zurakowska, Pasquale Basile, Gérard Tichy

Paul Naschy plays a supporting role as a necrophiliac gravedigger in this grim Spanish-Italian offering. While he does his own brand of icky experimentation on the dead, a mad scientist (Gérard Tichy) is actually bringing other corpses back to life for some murderous antics. Shades of Jess Franco's classic Spanish exploitation flick *Dr Orloff's Monster* abound, although here there's more than one ghoul wandering through the countryside indiscriminately killing people. Gothic

atmosphere is ladled on to little purpose – although the brief scene where hero Serge (Stan Cooper) confronts a ghoul who's brought a knife to a gun fight is memorable.

THE REVENANT
2009, USA

Dir: Kerry Prior. Prod: Liam Finn, Kerry Prior, Jacques Thelemaque. Sc: Kerry Prior
Cast: David Anders, Chris Wylde, Louise Griffiths, Jacy King, Eric Payne

After he's killed in Iraq and his body is shipped home, US soldier Bart (David Anders) inexplicably returns to life – if puking up black goo, staring through milky white corneas and thirsting for blood counts as living. Confused about why he's returned as a vampire-zombie hybrid, Bart teams up with his stoner buddy (Chris Wylde). Together they roam LA as nocturnal vigilantes, killing scumbags and sucking them dry. Kerry Prior, an accomplished VFX artist on films including the *Nightmare on Elm Street* franchise, delivers much buddy movie hilarity – and a killer final twist that Dick Cheney would love.

THE REVENGE OF THE LIVING DEAD GIRLS
1986, FRANCE

Original title: La revanche des mortes vivantes
Dir: Pierre B. Reinhard. Prod: Jean-Claude Roy.
Sc: John King
Cast: Veronik Catanzaro, Kathryn Charly, Sylvie Novak, Anthea Wyler, Laurence Mercier

"I'm careful. It's safe here. They're all dead!" Jean Rollin's *The Grapes of Death* had wine turning Frenchmen into ghouls. Here porn director Pierre B. Reinhard takes the same idea but swaps wine for milk and Frenchmen for pretty girls and amps up the exploitation vibe with lashings of softcore titillation. When a batch of milk is sabotaged with chemicals by environmental activists, a group of girls fall down dead after drinking it. But, when the rest of the chemicals are dumped in their graveyard, they're resurrected as decayed ghouls badly in need of some moisturising body lotion. They go on a murderous, horny rampage – their first victim gets a stiletto heel in her eye; a later girl is gang-raped and menaced with a sword; a third has her unborn baby turn zombie. Outrageously sleazy, it veers between outright nastiness and total silliness (at one point the ghoul girls drive off in a Rolls Royce…!). An alternate ending – where the ghouls are revealed as nothing more than eco-activists wearing rubber masks – pushes the limits of credibility but explains the dodgy zombie make-up and their ability to put the pedal to the metal.

REVENGE OF THE LIVING ZOMBIES
1989, USA
Alternative titles: Flesheater: Revenge of the Living Dead, Zombie Nosh
Dir: Bill Hinzman. Prod: Bill Hinzman. Sc: Bill Hinzman, Bill Randolph
Cast: Bill Hinzman, John Mowood, Leslie Ann Wick, Kevin Kindlin

Talk about delusions of grandeur. After starring as the opening cemetery ghoul in Romero's 1968 classic, Hinzman took it upon himself to teach zombie cinema a few tricks. The result was this trashola tale in which he stars as a corpse buried for centuries and accidentally dug up by a rural farmer. Cue yet another zombie apocalypse as Hinzman and fellow ghouls gatecrash a Halloween barn party (they get to eat a bloke dressed as Dracula), rip open busty women's blouses and generally make a nuisance of themselves before the rednecks break out the shotgunzzzzzzzzz.

REVENGE OF THE ZOMBIES
1976, HONG KONG
Alternative titles: Black Magic II, Bewitch Tame Head
Dir: Ho Meng-Hua. Prod: Run Run Shaw. Sc: I Kuang
Cast: Ti Lung Tanny, Lo Lieh, Liu Hui-Ju, Lily Li, Lin Wei-Tu

From the moment black magician Kai Chang (Lo Lieh) forces a pretty girl to her knees and parts her hair to reveal a huge nail in the top of her head, this Hong Kong outing takes an invigoratingly fast and loose approach to zombie mythology. As the nail is removed with a pair of pliers, the pretty girl decays into a rotten corpse. Meanwhile, in a city hospital a young doctor (Lin Wei-Tu) suspects a sudden rash of flesh-eating cases he's seeing are linked to some kind of black magic. It turns out that Lo Lieh is creating an army of corpses to work as zombie prostitutes, using wax dolls to kill his enemies and enticing lactating ladies into letting him slurp their breast milk. Bonkers and surreal,

this romps through love spells, mutant foetuses, and a Where Eagles Dare-style cable-car fight. It's a bizarre ride.

REVENGE OF THE ZOMBIES
1943, USA
Alternative titles: The Corpse Vanished
Dir: Steve Sekely. Prod: Lindsley Parsons. Sc: Edmond Kelso, Van Norcross
Cast: John Carradine, Gale Storm, Robert Lowery, Bob Steele, Mantan Moreland

A lame retread of Monogram's earlier King of the Zombies (1941), this reprises much the same material with Mantan Moreland and friends falling foul of a Nazi scientist who's trying to create a race of zombie super-soldiers.

REVOLT OF THE ZOMBIES
1936, USA
Alternative title: Revolt of the Demons
Dir: Victor Halperin. Prod: Edward Halperin. Sc: Howard Higgin, Rollo Lloyd, Victor Halperin
Cast: Dorothy Stone, Dean Jagger, Roy D'Arcy, Robert Noland, George Cleveland

During the First World War, the Allies discover that Cambodian priests are in possession of a mind control technique that can brainwash people into becoming fearless zombie soldiers. A team of scientists is dispatched to the East and one of the group decides to use the power to bind the whole of Cambodia to his will. His aim? To blackmail his girlfriend into marrying him. It must be love.

THE REVOLTING DEAD
2004, USA
Dir: Michael Su. Prod: Jason Herbst, Tye Beeby. Sc: Daniel Benton, Michael Su
Cast: Shelley Delayne, Aaron Gaffey, Bokahra Robinson, Michael Falls, Lindsey Lofaso

Incompetent grave robbers and a vengeful priestess who can shoot CG magic bolts from her fingers cause the dead to rise in an amateurish, shot-on-DV outing. Called up by a pagan witch, the zombies claw their way out of their shallow graves and lurch around like orangutans on crack while making bizarre guttural noises. Even with that in mind, it's unclear whether the filmmakers think they're making a parody or not. It's revoltingly acted, revoltingly written and has a truly revolting scene where a half naked man is thrown into a coffin containing a decomposing corpse. Yucky.

RIDGE WAR Z
2013, USA
Dir: Alek Gearhart. Prod: Alek Gearhart. Sc: Alek Gearhart
Cast: Dominique Marsell, Travis O'Leary, Will Le Fevre, Kyle Gordon, Dane O'Leary

One disappointment of *World War Z* was the failure to put the novel's Battle of Yonkers sequence – an epic military disaster in which the US army is defeated by a horde of Zeds – on-screen. Sadly, any hope that *Ridge War Z*, a cheapo tale of grunts under attack, might pick up the slack are quickly dashed as the exciting *Zulu*-with-zombies premise is neutered by the lack of budget. During the zombie wars a 100-strong unit of US soldiers are overrun on a desert hilltop by about 20 hoodie-wearing zeds. Telling the story in flashback, with a *World War Z*-style narrator who's writing a book about the "Glory Ridge" stand, this micro-budget feature from one-man studio Alek Gearhart begins with a Siegfried Sassoon quote and quickly unravels into portentous, rah-rah-rah nonsense about honour and sacrifice. The setting is literally a sandbagged hilltop, the zombies barely have any make-up and the whole thing is faintly ludicrous.

RIKA: THE ZOMBIE KILLER
2008, JAPAN
Original title: Saikyô heiki joshikôsei: Rika— Zonbi Hantâ vs saikyô Zonbi Gurorian
Dir: Ken'ichi Fujiwara. Prod: Kenjiro Nishi, Masami Teranishi. Sc: Takeyuki Morikaku, Ken'ichi Fujiwara
Cast: Risa Kudô, Takeshi Yamamoto, Kêsuke, Mai Minami, Tsugumi Nagasawa

Another gonzo "J-ombie" movie. This time an euthanasia drug designed to combat the nation's aging population goes wrong, producing shambling, slapstick ghouls. When schoolgirl Rika (Risa Kudô) has her arm chopped off in a zombie attack, her senile surgeon/samurai grandpa sews her on a new one – turning her into the cute-as-a-button monster-slaying zombie hunter of the title. Much tongue-in-cheek, surreal nonsense ensues,

from a ghoul boss who looks like a Middle Earth reject to a friendly talking zombie fitted with a face mask to prevent any involuntary snack attacks.

R.I.P.D.
2013, USA
Dir: Robert Schwentke. Prod: Michael Fottrell, Neal H. Moritz, Mike Richardson. Sc: Phil Hay, Matt Manfredi
Cast: Jeff Bridges, Ryan Reynolds, Kevin Bacon, Mary-Louise Parker, Stephanie Szostak

Based on the Dark Horse comics by Peter M. Lenkov, this sees a dead cop (Ryan Reynolds) taking a purgatorial posting with the Rest In Peace Department. He's teamed up with Jeff Bridges's tobacco chewing, near-incoherent Wild West lawman. Together they track down "Deados" – CGI zombies that could have escaped straight out of *Resident Evil*. Expensive to make, tiresome to watch. It's like someone spent $130 million remaking *Dead Heat* (1988).

RISE OF THE DAMNED
2011, CANADA
Dir: Michael Bafaro. Prod: Jody York, Timothy Marlow, Gabriel Paul Napora. Sc: Neil Every
Cast: Liane Balaban, Colin Cunningham, Erin Karpluk, Erica Cerra, Jessica Kate Meyer

Stop me if you've heard this one before. Hapless indie filmmakers head into an abandoned mental asylum (St Raimi's hospital, no less) to make a horror movie. But down in the basement there's a mad scientist experimenting with nanotechnology who's creating disfigured zombies. Troubled heroine Jessie (Liane Balaban), whose family died in an unexplained car crash, feels like she's been here before. She's not the only one. There's inventive use of a hospital gurney as a zombie battering ram and Luiz Guzman finds himself in a room full of twitching corpses. But mostly it's just another insipid, low-budget horror destined to clog up Netflix's algorithms.

RISE OF THE UNDEAD
2013, USA
Dir: Nick Woltersdorf. Prod: Nick Woltersdorf.
Sc: Nick Woltersdorf, Dietrich Hanson
Cast: Nick Woltersdorf, Dietrich Hanson, Annie Jacobs, Nathaniel Walker, Emma Walker

This underachieving DIY indie from a teenage director opens with a couple of Russian soldiers in charity shop uniforms arguing over a secret bioweapons programme – which appears to be run out of a suburban starter home. After a zombie virus escapes from the former USSR, the world – or rather, a few streets in Washington State – is overrun with ghouls. We're forced to suffer through 70 minutes of appalling acting and learning on-the-job filmmaking. In the past home movies like this used to gather dust on top of aspiring director's wardrobes. Isn't the digital era wonderful?

RISE OF THE ZOMBIE
2013, INDIA
Dir: Devaki Singh, Luke Kenny. Prod: Devaki Singh, Luke Kenny, Reshma Mehta, Om Sawant. Sc: Devaki Singh
Cast: Luke Kenny, Kirti Kulhari, Ashwin Mushran, Benjamin Gilani, Prem Thapa

This Hindi zombie movie ditches the usual Bollywood gloss for a dark and disturbing tale of one man's decent into zombiedom. When wildlife photographer Neil (Indian VJ, musician and producer Luke Kenny) is jilted by his girlfriend, he abandons the city for a solitary trek in the wilderness to get his head together. But after he's bitten by an insect he starts to transform – peeling skin and a taste for bugs giving way to a hunger for human flesh. The opposite of *Go Goa Gone* (2013), *Rise of the Zombie* follows in the austere, nauseating footsteps of *I, Zombie: The Chronicles of Pain* (1998) and contrasts this patient zero's deterioration with glossy flashbacks to his earlier, urban life. Impressively shot and acted, it's let down by its over-familiarity. The last five minutes propel us into a more exciting Indian zombie apocalypse, but sadly it's nothing more than a tease for sequel *Land of the Zombie*, scheduled for 2014.

RISE OF THE ZOMBIES
2012, USA
Alternative title: Dead Walking
Dir: Nick Lyon. Prod: David Michael Latt. Sc: Keith Allan, Delondra Williams
Cast: Mariel Hemingway, Ethan Suplee, Levar Burton, Danny Trejo, Heather Hemmens

After a waterbourne microbe turns San Francisco and the rest of the world into ghouls, scientist Mariel Hemingway searches desperately for a cure. It feels like The Asylum's take on *The Walking Dead* – something summed up in its me-too alternate title *Dead Walking*. There's a small role for rent-a-Mexican Danny Trejo, but the best moment is a dodgy CG shot of zombies climbing out of the water and up the struts of the Golden Gate Bridge.

ROBBERY OF THE MUMMIES OF GUANAJUATO
1972, MEXICO
Original title: El robo de las momias de Guanajuato
Dir: Tito Novaro. Prod: Rogelio Agrasanchez.
Sc: Francisco and Miguel Morayta.
Cast: Mil Máscaras, Blue Ángel, El Rayo de Jalisco, Julio César Agrasánchez, Mabel Luna

In *Invasion of the Zombies* in 1961 Santo chased down ghouls who were being used to rob jewellery stores. Here, it's the momias themselves that have been snatched – rasied from their catacombs by a mad scientist and mad magician tag team. The zombies are dispatched to work in a radioactive mine – in what looks to be a direct lift from Hammer's *The Plague of the Zombies*. On the case of the stolen mummies is masked wrestler Mil Máscaras and his friends. Given it features cute girls in miniskirts, midget henchmen, masked wrestlers, masked zombies, brain implants and black magic, it's pretty lame. The scenes of the ghouls in ragged suits working in the mine are pleasingly creepy (although the saxophone jazz score adds little). Hi-ho, hi-ho! It's off to work we go…

ROMEO & JULIET VS THE LIVING DEAD
2009, USA
Dir: Ryan Denmark. Prod: Jason Witter, Ryan Denmark.
Sc: Jason Witter, Ryan Denmark
Cast: Hannah Kauffmann, Jason Witter, Mark Chavez, Kate Schroeder, Kevin R. Elder

Baz Luhrmann and Leonardo DiCaprio were sadly engaged elsewhere when this Elizabethan mash-up rolled into production, but the influence of *Romeo + Juliet*'s stylised, pop update of the Bard is all over this camp comedy. Witter, who produces, writes and stars as the living dead Romeo, had previously made *Hamlet the Vampire Slayer* and this take on English literature's greatest romance is equally silly in its attempt to mix faux-Shakespearean dialogue with college jock humour and a few clown-faced zombies. Taking the play as a jumping off point this has the star-crossed lovers separated not only by family ties but also their living/living dead states. Juliet (Hannah Kauffmann) is a living Capulet, Romeo (Witter) is a living dead Montague. The best gags revolve around the script's playful use of Shakesperean language ("How can you love a zombie? The blood of your kinsmen lie in their unholy bowels!"). The worst are, quite literally, in the toilet (in one scene a constipated Capulet is attacked while on the loo and literally shits himself in fear). It goes on far too long – a short would have been funnier – and it's hard to escape the feeling that someone on the team is very proud of their English Lit degree. *Pride and Prejudice and Zombies* it ain't.

THE ROOST
2004, USA
Dir: Ti West. Prod: Susan Leber, Ti West. Sc: Ti West
Cast: Tom Noonan, Karl Jacob, Vanessa Horneff, Sean Reid, Wil Horneff

Four bickering teens end up lost in the batty backwoods in Ti West's DIY, lo-fi horror throwback that makes a virtue of its writer-director's obvious love of VHS era nasties. Trapped on a farm when their car breaks down, the kids discover a barn full of vampire bats that turn their victims into zombies. Nodding to *The Birds* and *Night of the Living Dead*, West crafts effective scares accompanied by a jangling, nerve-shredding soundtrack that is arguably more assaultive than anything on-screen. The tacked on creature feature bookends, featuring a camp TV horror host (Tom Noonan), detract from what is otherwise a raw and remarkable calling card for a young director.

ROUTE 666
2001, USA
Dir: William Wesley. Prod: William Wesley.
Sc: William Wesley, Thomas N. Weber, Scott Fivelson
Cast: Lou Diamond Phillips, Lori Petty, Steven Williams, L.Q. Jones, Dale Midkiff

They're on a highway, a highway to HELL! A bunch of Feds (led by Lou Diamond Phillips and Lori Petty) arrest a mafia accountant (Steven Williams, doing a subpar Danny Glover impression) in the New Mexico desert. After taking a detour down an abandoned desert road – "Route 666" – they're hunted by grey and leathery ghost-zombies. The ghouls were once part of a 1960s prison chain gang, murdered by their guards after a botched escape attempt. Armed with pickaxes and pneumatic drills, the ethereal zombies shuffle down the highway causing mayhem until Phillips realises one of them is his dad (!) and saves the day.

SANTA CLAUS VS THE ZOMBIES
2010, USA
Dir: George Bonilla. Prod: George Bonilla. Sc: George Bonilla
Cast: Billy W. Blackwell, Alex del Monacco, Claude D. Miles, Cassidy Rae Owens, Tony Armstrong

Kids! If you're naughty, Father Christmas won't bring you a lump of coal. He'll bring you a DVD of *Santa Claus Vs The Zombies* and make you watch it on a loop until New Year's Eve. An amateur production shot in Kentucky on crappy DV, this has a bloke in a Santa suit, a couple of elves and a terminally annoying suburban family taking shelter as zombies attack. Shonky scenes featuring the US President coordinating the zombie battle from his bunker would make even Ed Wood Jr. roll his eyes.

SANTO AND BLUE DEMON AGAINST THE MONSTERS
1968, MEXICO
Original title: Santo y Blue Demon contra los monstruos
Dir: Gilberto Martínez Solares. Prod: Jesús Sotomayor Martínez. Sc: Rafael García Travesí, Jesús Sotomayor Martínez
Cast: Santo el Enmascarado de Plata, Blue Demon, Jorge Radó, Carlos Ancira, Raúl Martínez Solares Jr.

Zombies compete for ring space with a host of Universal creature-feature characters in this overstocked Mexican wrestling horror. Santo's hot on the trail of a mad scientist who's rounding up all the bad guys in Mexico – including a vampire, a werewolf, a Cyclops and Frankenstein's monster – to terrorise the local populace. Blue Demon goes bad and Santo gets to whup some monster ass. The zombies are little more than green-skinned hangers-on and are upstaged by their evil compadres.

SANTO AND BLUE DEMON IN THE LAND OF THE DEAD
1969, MEXICO
Original title: El mundo de los muertos
Alternative title: The Land of the Dead
Dir: Gilberto Martínez Solares. Prod: Jesús Sotomayor Martínez. Sc: Rafael García Travesí, Jesús Sotomayor Martínez
Cast: Santo el Enmascarado de Plata, Blue Demon, Pilar Pellicer, Carlos León, Antonio Raxel

More Mexican wrestling mania sees masked muscleman El Santo taking on a witch and her zombie bullyboys. Not even the flashbacks to the 17th century, a trip to red-tinted hell, or a small role for an evil Blue Demon (his soul has been captured) can do much to detract from the poverty-stricken production. The zombies are merely perfunctory, grey-skinned extras. Nice to see El Santo's 17th-century ancestor had the same dress sense, though (give or take some additional frilly cuffs).

SANTO VS. BLACK MAGIC
1972, MEXICO
Dir: Alfredo B. Crevenna. Prod: Lic. Jorge, Garcia Besne. Sc: Rafael García Travesi, Fernando Osés
Cast: Santo, Elsa Cardenas, Sasha Montenegro, Gerty Jones, Fernando Oses

Shot in Haiti, this takes Santo the silver-masked wrestler to the birthplace of the modern zombie – though to little purpose other than to give the crew some time in the Caribbean. Santo arrives in the region under government orders to prevent a new explosive, more powerful than the H-bomb, from ending up in the wrong hands. As soons as he arrives in Port-au-Prince he's assailed by Haitian ghouls controlled by a voodoo priestess (Sasha Montenegro). The first zombies are pretty mindless and are scared off by a cross-shaped tyre iron. Later ones abseil into Santo's hotel room to deposit snakes on his bed or grapple him with sleeper holds. The location shoot makes it more exotic than most Santo outings and the black Haitian zombies are creepily effective – the scene where they spin and and shield their eyes from an improvised crucifix is a throwaway twist on zombie lore.

SARS WARS: BANGKOK ZOMBIE CRISIS
2004, THAILAND
Original title: Khun krabii hiiroh
Dir: Taweewat Wantha. Prod: Uncle, Kim.
Sc: Kuanchun Phemyad, Taweewat Wantha, Sommai Lertulan, Uncle
Cast: Supakorn Kitsuwon, Suthep Po-Ngam, Phintusuda Tunphairao, Lena Christensen, Somlek Sakdikul

An African mosquito causes a new outbreak of a particularly virulent strain of SARS in Thailand in this knockabout, slapstick comedy. When a Bangkok high rise is quarantined, a sword-wielding martial artist (Supakorn Kitsuwon) goes inside to retrieve a kidnapped girl (Phintusuda Tunphairao) from a bunch of incompetent and sexually amorphous thugs. As the sharp-toothed ghouls multiply, chaos ensues: Thai drag queens scream, a giant CG zombie snake slithers, and *The Matrix* gets ripped off a lot. Pitched somewhere between Hong Kong's *Bio-Zombie* (1998) and Japan's *Wild Zero* (1999) this demented ludicrous cult movie never even hints at taking itself seriously. Gotta love that the government's solution to the outbreak is a batch of "Stop Virus Bullets", and the zombie that eats a cat, a fluffy tail hanging out of its mouth.

SCARED STIFF
1952, USA
Dir: George Marshall. Prod: Hal B. Wallis. Sc: Herbert Baker, Walter DeLeon
Cast: Dean Martin, Jerry Lewis, Lizabeth Scott, Carmen Miranda, George Dolenz

Director George Marshall shamelessly retreads his earlier outing *The Ghost Breakers* for a quick buck, but the forgettable zombie here isn't a patch on Noble Johnson's striking ghoul from the original film. In the leads, Jerry Lewis and Dean Martin replace Willie Best and Bob Hope respectively. Lewis is a bumbling, stumbling waiter, and Martin is a suave nightclub singer. Together they're roped into helping a damsel in distress as the mob, ghosts and a haunted castle on "Lost Island" prove too much for her to handle. If you're gonna call anyone in a spot like this, Jerry Lewis should not be your first choice. Or second. Or third. Or fourth.

SCHOOLGIRL APOCALYPSE

2011, JAPAN

Original title: Sêrâ-fuku mokushiroku

Dir: John Cairns. Prod: Yukie Kito. Sc: John Carins

Cast: Rino Higa, Max Mackenzie, Asami Mizukawa, Kaoru Nishida, Mai Tsujimoto

After men start turning into zombies and attacking women, schoolgirl Sakura (Rino Higa) travels in search of shelter armed with a bow and arrow. Meeting various women – a soccer mom with a zombified son, a blind scientist and a psychotic punk just out to have fun – Sakura begins to have strange visions of a caucasian boy who may, or may not, hold the key to the apocalypse. Mysterious and bewitching, this has the enigmatic appeal of less splattery, more arthouse J-cinema – and it's potentially also a feminist riposte to *Rape Zombie: Lust of the Dead* (2012).

SCREAM FARM
2007, USA

Dir: Jim O'Rear. Prod: Jim O'Rear. Sc: Jim O'Rear

Cast: Jim O'Rear, Ted Alderman, Kimberly Lynn Cole, Maria Kil, Brit Hunter.

Backyard filmmaking at its dullest. A batch of tainted weed ends up in the hands of some kids trying to set up a haunted house on a farm, and it's not long before the gangster it belongs to (played by filmmaker Jim O'Rear) turns up looking for his stash. Cue kids fighting stoner zombies and gangster thugs. O'Rear gets to choose his own demise – devoured by a zombie girl in hotpants – but the rest of us are left counting down the minutes to the credits.

THE SERPENT AND THE RAINBOW
1987, USA

Dir: Wes Craven. Prod: David Ladd, Doug Claybourne. Sc: Richard Maxwell, A.R. Simoun [Adam Rodman]

Cast: Bill Pullman, Cathy Tyson, Zakes Mokae, Paul Winfield, Brent Jennings

Wade Davis's book gets the blockbuster treatment with Wes Craven directing. Dr Alan (Bill Pullman) is a white American sent to Haiti to uncover the zombification drug for a giant pharmaceutical corporation. Once on the island, though, his presence gains the unwanted attention of one of the corrupt regime's more notorious torturers, who

also happens to be a voodoo priest. Playing up the psychological dimension of voodoo – "The soul begins and ends with the brain" – this centres on Davis's suggestion that zombification is a drug-induced psychological state used by secret societies to control the island's populace. Significantly, the film's chief zombie Christophe (Conrad Roberts) is a former grade school teacher turned into living dead slave as punishment for his radical political views.

SEVERED: FOREST OF THE DEAD
2004, CANADA

Alternative title: Severed

Dir: Carl Bessai. Prod: Cynthia Chapman, Andrew Boutilier. Sc: Carl Bessai, Travis McDonald

Cast: Paul Campbell, Sarah Lind, Julian Christopher, J.R. Bourne, Michael Teigen

The Pacific Northwest gives this gritty, checked-shirted horror an austere backdrop as tree sap turns loggers into jerky zombies with greenish-yellowish skin. Trapped in the woods with the logging crew are tree-hugging environmental protestors and the son of the company's CEO (Paul Campbell). Shot on Vancouver Island, *Severed: Forest of the Dead* – not to be confused with the much inferior *Forest of the Dead* (2005) – makes fantastic use of its dense forests and autumnal vibe. It is bleak and no-nonsense, and annoyingly runs out of steam about halfway, though it's not without flashes of cruel wit. See, for instance, the moment when zombies attack a bunch of environmental protestors who have chained themselves to tree trunks and thrown away the keys...

SEXYKILLER
2008, SPAIN

Original title: Sexykiller: Morirás por ella

Dir: Miguel Martí. Prod: Jaume Roures, Tedy Villalba. Sc: Paco Cabezas

Cast: Macarena Gómez, Alejo Sauras, César Camino, Ángel de Andrés López, Juan Carlos Vellido

If Pedro Almovódar got stoned and watched a double bill of *Scream* and *Re-Animator* he might have come up with *Sexykiller*, a delightfully perverse Spanish horror parody. Psychotic med student and *Cosmo*-reading fashionista Bárbara (Macarena Gómez) teeters around in high heels, serial killing any man who takes her fancy. Things get complicated when a couple of fellow students invent a device to read the brains of the recently dead – and the cadavers unexpectedly reanimate and go in search of their drop-dead gorgeous killer. Stylish and garish, it's great fun.

SHADOW: DEAD RIOT
2005, USA
Dir: Derek Wan. Prod: Csaba Bereczky, Carl Morano.
Sc: Michael Gingold, Richard Siegel
Cast: Tony Todd, Carla Greene, Nina Hodoruk, Michael Quinlan, Cat Miller

Co-penned by *Fangoria* regular Michael Gingold and directed by Derek Wan, this crosses zombies with the classic "women in prison" movie. It's a full on exploitation movie with a Satanic dead killer Shadow (Tony Todd) stalking the cells of a penitentiary, while new inmate Solitaire (Carla Greene) dodges his supernatural attacks and the Sapphic attentions of her fellow prisoners in the shower. What you get is more girl on girl action than an issue of *Hustler*, dialogue so cheesy it should come with crackers, a zombie baby biting its mother's nipple off, and a bunch of banged up zombie convicts. It's the best zombie women-in-prison movie ever made. It's also the *only* zombie women-in-prison movie ever made.

SHANKS
1974, USA
Dir: William Castle. Prod: Steven North. Sc: Ranald Graham
Cast: Marcel Marceau, Tsilla Chelton, Philippe Clay, Cindy Eilbacher, Helena Kallianiotes

French mime artist Marcel Marceau stars as Malcolm Shanks, a puppeteer who helps a scientist experimenting with reanimating dead animals using electrical currents. After the scientist dies, Malcolm continues the experiments and creates corpse "puppets" that he uses as jerky slaves. But when a biker gang arrives, things get out of control. Director William Castle is better known for his cheapo horror flicks – *House on Haunted Hill* (1959) and *Homicidal* (1961). This, his last film, is something quite different. A surreal, near-silent fairy tale oddity it's just crying out for a Tim Burton remake.

SHATTER DEAD
1993, USA
Dir: Scooter McCrae. Prod: Scooter McCrae.
Sc: Scooter McCrae
Cast: Stark Raven, Flora Fauna, Daniel Johnson, Robert Wells, Marina Del Rey

Touted by many as the finest example of ambitious SOV filmmaking, *Shatter Dead* is crammed full of good ideas – some of which fall by the wayside as the slipshod production takes its toll. Stark Raven plays a young woman who hates zombies. That's a bit of a problem, since the end of death has meant that zombies are now everywhere. As the living die and keep on living, the fabric of society is on the verge of collapse. Director Scooter McCrae's refreshingly leftfield approach to the genre isn't afraid to delve into exploitation territory with lots of gore and plenty of provocative sex.

SHAUN OF THE DEAD
2004, UK/USA/FRANCE
Dir: Edgar Wright. Prod: Nira Park. Sc: Edgar Wright, Simon Pegg
Cast: Simon Pegg, Kate Ashfield, Lucy Davis, Nick Frost, Dylan Moran

The film that single-handedly saved contemporary British horror, *Shaun of the Dead* is billed as "romantic comedy with zombies" (or "zom-rom-com"). Pegg plays a 29-year-old shopworker who finds his life thrown into chaos when his girlfriend Liz (Kate Ashfield) dumps him and a deep space probe unexpectedly returns to earth and turns the population of North London into zombies.

SHIVERS
1975, CANADA
Alternative titles: The Parasite Murders, They Came From Within
Dir: David Cronenberg. Prod: Ivan Reitman. Sc: David Cronenberg
Cast: Paul Hampton, Joe Silver, Lynn Lowry, Allan Migicovsky, Susan Petrie

In a purpose-built apartment block named Starliner Towers, an unhinged medical researcher has been experimenting with strange turd-like parasites. They're designed to replace failing organs, but actually turn their victims into sex-crazed maniacs.

As the epidemic spreads through the humdrum middle-class world of the complex, the inhabitants' sexual desires are unleashed with murderous results. Can the complex's doctor (Paul Hampton) and his pretty nurse (Lynn Lowry) prevent the spread of the infection? Or will they fall victim to the horny grannies and pre-pubescent kids stalking the hallways? The maniacs of Cronenberg's sexually charged horror movie may not be zombies in the strictest sense, but the revolt of the flesh over the brain that they represent owes a considerable debt to Romero.

SHOCK WAVES
1976, USA
Alternative titles: Almost Human, Le commando des morts vivants, Death Corps
Dir: Ken Wiederhorn. Prod: Reuben Trane. Sc: John Harrison, Ken Wiederhorn
Cast: Peter Cushing, Brooke Adams, Fred Buch, Jack Davidson, Luke Halpin

"There is danger here, danger in the water" warns Peter Cushing in this eerily atmospheric chiller featuring Nazi zombies. Genetically engineered during World War II, these super soldiers were designed to man submarines that would never have to come up to the surface. Foolishly, the test subjects were "cheap hoodlums and thugs and a good number of pathological murderers and sadists." Will mad scientists never learn? Now they're back from the deep, wreaking havoc on some tourists who've been stranded on the island. Emerging from the water in German uniforms and goggles to strangle or drown their victims, they're a striking collection of aquatic ghouls.

SICK BOY
2012, USA
Dir: Timothy T. Cunningham. Prod: Blayne Gorum, Timothy T. Cunningham. Sc: Timothy T. Cunningham
Cast: Skye McCole Bartusiak, Marc Donato, Debbie Rochon, Greg Dorchak, Pierre Kennel

A babysitting job from hell: hired to look after a mysteriously ill kid, slacker childminder Lucy (Skye McCole Bartusiak) spends most of her day surfing the net and busting moves in the mirror to gangsta rap. It's an easy gig: she's not even supposed to interact with the sick child locked in a bedroom downstairs, just house sit while his mom's out. But the strange noises on the baby monitor and the big padlock on the kid's bedroom door inevitably pique Lucy's curiosity, with disastrous results. Keeping its zombie kid under wraps until the final ten minutes, this micro-budget snooze-a-thon squanders its promising premise. It's poorly written, badly acted and shot on ugly DV. Don't worry about nightmares… it'll make you sleep like a baby.

THE SIGNAL
2007, USA
Dir: David Bruckner, Jacob Gentry, Dan Bush. Prod: Jacob Gentry, Alexander Motlagh. Sc: David Bruckner, Jacob Gentry, Dan Bush
Cast: Justin Welborn, Anessa Ramsey, AJ Bowen, Cheri Christian, Scott Poythress

"Have you got the crazy?" A mysterious broadcast signal turns the inner-city inhabitants of Terminus, USA into crazed psychopaths in this above-average Atlanta-shot indie. Made by three filmmakers, it moves through three very different "Transmissions" – the opening chaotic horror giving way to satirical black humour then a tense finale. Cleverly exploring modern paranoia, it also raises an interesting question: when people are beating each other to death on the street, how can you tell the difference between those exposed to the signal, and those who are simply trying to defend themselves?

SILENT HILL
2006, US/FRANCE/JAPAN
Dir: Christophe Gans. Prod: Don Carmody, Samuel Hadida. Sc: Roger Avary
Cast: Radha Mitchell, Sean Bean, Laurie Holden, Jodelle Ferland, Alice Krige

Based on the survival horror videogame franchise, *Silent Hill* does a good job of translating the games' shocks to the screen. The best scene is easily the "zombie nurses" sequence: these nightmare caregivers jerk and stutter around in their blood-spattered porno nurse uniforms with their heads hidden under thick bandages before attacking one another with scalpels. It's reminiscent of the video for Michael Jackson's *Thriller*, but the real horror is in how these ghouls manage to combine nubile sexiness with all the un-nameable dread of a Francis Bacon canvas. The film was the first in an ongoing, increasingly lacklustre franchise.

SILENT NIGHT, ZOMBIE NIGHT
2009, USA
Dir: Sean Cain. Prod: Wes Laurie, Sean Cain. Sc: Sean Cain
Cast: Jack Forcinito, Andy Hopper, Nadine Stenovitch, Felissa Rose, Tim Muskatell

"I hate to break it to you but I don't think Santa's coming this year…" This Christmas-set zombie apocalypse races out of the starting gate at a clip, then slows down to a snooze as it turns into a talky relationships drama. Caught in the chaos as the dead walk are borderline psychotic policeman Frank (Jack Forcinito), his about-to-leave-him wife (Nadine Stenovitch) and Frank's kid partner (Andy Hopper) who has the hots for his missus. Holed up in an apartment, the threesome largely ignore the ghouls outside. Instead they witter on about their feelings and play drunken games of truth or dare. It has the intimacy of a stage play, but its soap opera isn't involving enough to keep it interesting. The Christmas setting gives us a fat zombie in a Santa suit, but not much else.

THE SLAUGHTER
2006, USA
Dir: Jay Lee. Prod: Calvin Green, Judy T. Marcelline, Michael J. Zampino. Sc: Jay Lee
Cast: Jessica Ellis, Zak Kilberg, Jen Alex Gonzalez, Brad Milne, Terry Erioski

A naked zombie demon woman terrorises horny, dope-smoking teens sent to clean up a cursed, isolated house in a film that's reminiscent of *Dead Dudes in the House* (1991). Writer-director Jay Lee and his sister producer Angela Lee clearly see the horror genre as a get-rich-quick formula – piling on the T&A and gory, budget kills in an appeal to teenage hormones. The demon's victims eventually return as zombies – prompting a character to wonder if they're slow, old skool Romero-style lumbering ghouls or the fast, new infected kind: "New zombies – we may be fucked." Forgettable filler – although it is hilarious that Lee's script is laced with anti-capitalist asides given that his follow up, *Zombie Strippers* (2007), is totally cynical in its commercialism. It's as though Lee said "fuck it" and stopped fighting against the zombifying forces of late capitalism.

SLITHER
2006, USA
Dir: James Gunn. Prod: Paul Brooks, Eric Newman. Sc: James Gunn
Cast: Michael Rooker, Nathan Fillion, Elizabeth Banks, Tania Saulnier, Brenda James

Dawn of the Dead remake writer James Gunn directs this gloopy, retro B-movie in which an alien parasite turns Michael Rooker into a monstrous squid creature and the inhabitants of a South Carolina hick town into jerky zombies. The alien-controlled ghouls themselves don't turn up until the 60-minute mark, but their stop-motion-esque body movements and hive-mind witterings are well worth waiting for. Raiding his VHS collection to affectionately steal ideas from *Shivers*, *Society* and *Night of the Creeps*, Gunn delivers a treat for anyone who grew up in the 1980s.

SOLE SURVIVOR
1982, USA
Dir: Thom Eberhardt. Prod: Don Barkemeyer. Sc: Thom Eberhardt
Cast: Anita Skinner, Kurt Johnson, Caren Larkey, Robin Davidson, William Snare

A woman who cheats death by surviving a plane crash is chased by zombies who have come to take her down to hell. Riffing on classic spook movie *Carnival of Souls* (1962), this intermittently creepy movie makes the ghosts into ghouls to little real purpose.

SONG OF THE DEAD
2005, USA
Dir: Chip Gubera. Prod: Anlon O'Brien, Gene Ertel, Chip Gubera, James Robert Swope. Sc: Chip Gubera
Cast: Kate Gorman, Travis Hierholzer, Steve Williams, Conrad Gubera, Reggie Bannister

A zombie musical from Missouri, this grew out of writer/director Chip Gubera's 2004 short of the same name, but arguably isn't suited to feature length. When terrorists allegedly release a bio-weapon over the US, the Jihad Resurrection Virus does its work turning citizens into flesh-hungry ghouls. Zombies and survivors break out into show-stopping numbers at every opportunity – the funniest being by the survivor, who confesses to being a serial killer in song. If you're looking for zombies' answer to *The Rocky Horror Picture Show*, however, you'll be very disappointed.

SPACE ZOMBIE BINGO
1993, USA
Dir: George Ormond. Prod: George Ormond.
Sc: George Ormond, John Sabotta
Cast: William Darkow, Ramona Provost, Hugh Crawford, Dan Levine, John Sabotta

"Flesh eating robot zombies from outer space" attack in this Z-grade Troma nonsense that parodies 1950s alien invasion movies. The robot ghouls – in black wetsuits and wearing welder's helmets – clomp about and are later accidentally turned giant-sized by nuclear radiation. Songs, newsflashes and much silliness pad out the paper-thin plotting. There's also a reminder never to call invading zombie robots names. "He called us bozos! Remove his organs of sexual reproduction and throw them away!"

SPECIAL DEAD
2006, USA
Dir: Thomas L. Phillips, Sean Simmons. Prod: Sean Simmons, Owen Simmons, Gia Natale, Jared Tweedie, Carl Storm, Thomas L. Phillips. Sc: Jared Tweedie
Cast: Jay Brubaker, Amy Wade, Gia Natale, Anthony Rutowicz, Haneka Haynes

Set on Camp Special Dude, a ranch for the developmentally challenged, this bad taste comedy feels like a zombie movie made by the Farrelly brothers. Despite its offensive set up and willingness to use its physically and mentally challenged characters for jokes, it's actually pretty inclusive in its equal opportunity insults. When contaminated water from an underground spring turns people into ghouls with peeling faces, the camp's kids and counsellors must work together to survive. In the best tradition of Troma, the jokes fly thick and fast: a zombie with tourettes who shouts obscenities at his victims before he attacks; a girl in a wheelchair wielding a chainsaw on an impossibly long extension cord; and a chomping zombie's

mouth stopped by filling it with glue. There's also a song in which a counsellor confesses his lust for the female stars of 1980s sitcoms that ends: "It doesn't matter what I say, you're all retarded anyway…" Deliberately offensive, guiltily amusing.

STACY
2001, JAPAN
Dir: Naoyuki Tomomatsu. Prod: Hiromitsu Suzuki, Naokatsu Ito. Sc: Chisato Ogawara
Cast: Natsuki Kato, Toshinori Omi, Chika Hayashi, Shungiku Uchida, Yasutaka Tsutsui

Sometime in the 21st century, teenage girls aged between 15 and 17 start spontaneously dying and returning to life as zombies known as "Stacys". Impossible to stop, short of chopping them up into itty bitty pieces, these zombies prove a threat to civilization itself, which is why the UN has ordered special "Romero Repeat Kill" squads set up to re-kill the ghoulish girls all over again. Hacking up the bodies with chainsaws, the squads dump the still "live" remains into garbage bags to be burnt. Four interconnected storylines follow a scientist experimenting *Day of the Dead*-style, a doll-maker who falls in love with a teenage girl knowing that she's likely to die soon, a bunch of martial-arts girls dedicated to killing Stacys and some soldiers who are having trouble coping with the horror of the schoolgirl apocalypse. One of the chief templates for Japan's distinctive "J-ombie" trend.

STAG NIGHT OF THE DEAD
2011, UK
Dir: Napoleon Jones. Prod: Napoleon Jones.
Sc: Napoleon Jones
Cast: Sebastian Street, Sophie Lovell Anderson, Bruce Lawrence, James G. Fain, Joe Rainbow

The classic British stag night – a naked groom, booze and strippers – gets a unique twist in this indie comedy. Dean (Sebastian Street) is the groom, dragged off by his mates for a game of "Zomball" – paintball with tasers and ghouls. Set in a future where a zombie outbreak has been averted, this beery, blokey comedy features a midget; an annoying, virginal wise-arse called DJ Ronnie (Joe Rainbow) aka "the hymen-breaker"; and a few stumbling ghouls wandering former RAF Bentwaters in Suffolk. It doesn't live up to its tagline: "Six stags. One stripper. A million zombies. You do the maths…"

STALLED
2012, UK
Dir: Christian James. Prod: Richard Kerrigan. Sc: Dan Palmer
Cast: Tamaryn Payne, Mark Holden, Antonia Bernath, Sarah Biggins, Marcus Kelly

Ingeniously set almost entirely in an office bathroom, this unlikely British comedy uses the limitations of its confined space to its advantage as nerdy maintenance man W.C. (screenwriter Dan Palmer) tries to work out how to escape from the ghouls crowding outside his cubicle. It's not exactly *Shaun of the Dead*, but it's a surprisingly entertaining ride with some great gags – the demise of Jeff from IT (Mark Holden) thanks to a severed finger fired from a bra deserves a special place in any list of movie deaths.

STATE OF EMERGENCY
2011, USA
Dir: Turner Clay. Prod: Turner Clay, John Will Clay. Sc: Turner Clay
Cast: Jay Hayden, Tori White, Scott Lilly, Kathryn Todd Norman, McKenna Jones

The DVD box art promises a man with a hunting rifle facing down a horde of living dead. The movie can barely muster more than a couple of ghouls. When a chemical plant explodes in Montgomery Country, Nowheresville, USA, and the authorities impose quarantine, a handful of citizens led by Jim (Jay Hayden) fend off bloody-eyed ragers on an abandoned farm. The bulk of what follows is a meandering bickering-survivors drama with barely any undead – a shame, since when writer-director Turner Clay finds the budget for the odd zombie attack he reveals a decent eye for action.

STIFF ODDS
2004, USA
Dir: Caleb Allen. Prod: Alison Allen. Sc: Caleb Allen, Lauryn Wood
Cast: Gabe Strachota, Kate Delaney, Cory Pearson, Lauryn Wood, Matt Desreuisseau

This truly, truly awful, no-budget video production

is so bad it's virtually unwatchable. When a couple of Goth punks steal some caskets from a graveyard, the corpses inside them come back to life and escape in their car. Meanwhile the Grim Reaper – a bloke in a shiny red body suit and spider-leg dreadlocks – skips around the cemetery for comic effect. He also runs the "Bet Your Dead" (sic) betting shop for reasons that are never made clear. This celluloid travesty unfolds with endless, goofy non sequiturs in place of comedy and there is much Goth-stoner trippiness. Schools should show this to kids; it's the most convincing anti-drugs movie I've ever seen. Just say no.

THE STINK OF FLESH
2004, USA
Dir: Scott Phillips. Prod: Shannon Hale. Sc: Scott Phillips
Cast: Diva, Kristin Hansen, Kurly Tlapoyawa, Ross Kelly, William Garberina

Here's a horny little zombie outing: after the dead overrun the world, a wandering zombie slayer gets abducted by a pair of swingers looking for some post-apocalyptic between-the-sheets action. Terrible acting and an over-eager profusion of bare flesh and gore can't disguise the dearth of ideas here as characters ponder the state of sexual morality in a world where the dead have returned to life: "The way the world is today, what counts as a crime any more?" There are asides on the relative merits of living dead sex slaves ("She'd be pretty fucking hot if she weren't decomposing") and a yucky answer to that age old question: do zombies poo?

STONED DEAD
2006, USA
Dir: Ray Etheridge. Prod: Migdalia Etheridge, Ray Etheridge. Sc: Ray Etheridge.
Cast: Ben Daniels, Oscar A. Diaz, Sergio Vigano, David Cabrera, Paul Nicholson

"This is wrong! You're actually playing with a human being here!" Two American missionaries straight out of Bible school are missing in Panama. The only clue is a cryptic note delivered to their church. On the case are a couple of private investigators linked to the CIA who head into the jungle (actually the gardens of Saint Thomas

University in Florida) on the promise of a huge payout. What they find are blank-looking zombies in brown monks' robes who have been brought back from the dead by a combination of voodoo and coca leaves to work as free labour in the drugs trade. This z-grade, shot-on-video outing intercuts archive footage from Central America and never looks anything more than totally amateur.

STORM OF THE DEAD
2006, USA
Dir: Bob Cook. Prod: Ginger Brigham, Bob Cook. Sc: Bob Cook
Cast: Jason Todd Smith, Karin Justman, Debra Cassano, Brian Renner, Bill Zientek

When Hurricane Katrina hit the Gulf Coast in 2005, the images on CNN of devastation, civil collapse and widespread looting looked like something out of a zombie movie. Not long later this low-budget effort combined the two ideas: after a Category 5 hurricane triggers martial law in Florida, a squad of militia track and kill a looter in the swamp. Unfortunately for them, his grandmother is a voodoo priestess who calls him back from the dead. Not a bad idea for a movie, but it's a pity the zombie only features in about three scenes. The rest of this dull outing involves a lot of wandering through swamps with the soldiers and voodoo priestess and some half-baked moralising about the dangers of martial law.

STRIPPERLAND
2011, USA
Dir: Sean Skelding. Prod: Shawn Justice, Sean Skelding. Sc: Brad McCray, Shawn Justice
Cast: Ben Sheppard, Maren McGuire, Ileana Herrin, Jamison Challeen, Daniel Baldwin

Shamelessly ripping off *Zombieland*, this retools the basic plot and characters but makes the zombies into living dead strippers. Heh. On the road are Jesse Eissenberg and Woody Harrelson lookalikes, now called Idaho and Frisco (Ben Sheppard and Jamison Challeen) who are hoping to get somewhere where women aren't "exhibitionist man eaters". A carbon copy of its A-list inspiration – right down to a voiceover stuffed with rules and Frisco's obsession with Danish (read: Twinkies) – this weird little parody

fails to deliver laughs, or even much zombie stripping. In place of a Bill Murray cameo we get Daniel Baldwin as a tracksuit-wearing rapper called Double D.

SUGAR HILL
1974, USA
Alternative titles: Voodoo Girl, The Zombies of Sugar Hill
Dir: Paul Maslansky. Prod: Elliot Schick. Sc: Tim Kelly
Cast: Marki Bey, Robert Quarry, Don Pedro Colley, Betty Anne Rees, Richard Lawson

After heavy-handed thugs beat her fiancé to death, Sugar Hill calls on voodoo god Baron Samedi to help her get revenge. He appears with some cobwebbed black zombies – former slaves who died being shipped to the New World – and lets Sugar have some fun killing off the men who prevented her from walking down the aisle. The first blaxploitation zombie movie.

THE SUPERNATURALS
1986, USA
Dir: Armand Mastroianni. Prod: Michael S. Murphy, Joel Soisson. Sc: Joel Soisson, Michael S. Murphy
Cast: Maxwell Caulfield, Nichelle Nichols, Talia Balsam, Margaret Shendal, LeVar Burton

This 1980s outing for Civil War zombies – see also *Curse of the Cannibal Confederates* (1982) and *Ghost Brigade* (1992) – features a platoon modern-day soldiers on a training exercise in Alabama. Out in the woods they're attacked by crusty and wizened Confederate ghouls, who shuffle through the mist to pick them off one by one. The living soldiers are led by a gruff, no-nonsense sergeant (Nichelle Nichols, *Star Trek*) and the dead rebels are resurrected by a cute moppet kid who survived being made to walk through a minefield back in 1865. A pity the silly supernatural plot and shonky pacing keeps the impressive ghouls off-screen for so long. In its best moments this is zombie cinema's answer to *Southern Comfort*.

SURVIVAL OF THE DEAD
2009, USA/CANADA
Dir: George A. Romero. Prod: Paula Devonshire. Sc: George A. Romero
Cast: Alan Van Sprang, Kenneth Welsh, Kathleen

Munroe, Devon Bostick, Richard Fitzpatrick

Currently the last entry in Romero's *Dead* series, this takes him into John Ford territory as two feuding Irish families fight each other during the zombie apocalypse. It's a lesser entry in the series, but it's great to see Romero still playing with dead things.

THE SWAMP OF THE RAVENS
1973, SPAIN/USA
Original title: El pantano de los cuervos
Dir: Michael Cannon [Manuel Caño]. Prod: Fernando M. Hernandez, Javier Molina. Sc: Santiago Moncada
Cast: Raymond Oliver [Ramiro Oliveras], Marcia [Marcelle] Bichette, Fernando Sancho, William Harrison, Mark Mollin [Marcos Molina]

Shot on location somewhere in South America (possibly Ecuador), this atmospheric mad scientist chiller follows Dr Frosta (Raymond Oliver) as he tries to revive the dead. He's not very successful, which is why the swamp behind his isolated shack-cum-laboratory is littered with the corpses of his previous victims. In between scenes they occasionally bob up to the surface for added frisson. Kidnapping his ex-girlfriend, Frosta kills her then tries to bring her back to "life" for some necrophiliac loving. Padded out with some dreadful lounge singing, a gratuitously graphic autopsy scene and a few bare breasts, this never really delivers the zombie goods. The ghouls float about in the eponymous swamp (which is actually inhabited by big black buzzards, not ravens) but don't do much else – although in one scene a disembodied zombie hand strangles a man who tries to blackmail the doc. It's easy to see why this title has slipped into obscurity. Still, it would make a decent double bill with Rollin's *Zombie Lake*.

SWAMP ZOMBIES
2005, USA
Dir: Len Kabasinski. Prod: Lisa McQuiston. Sc: Len Kabasinski
Cast: Brian Heffron, Jasmin St Claire, Pamela Sutch, Shannon Solo, Len Kabasinski

Amateurish, SOV zombie movie shot in the woods around Lake Erie, Pennsylvania. High school kids on a field trip are attacked by the reanimated dead

produced by a local hospital's illegal experiments. Totally worthless and mind-numbingly dull, *Swamp Zombies* can't even muster any decent zombie make-up. Porn star Jasmin St Claire has a supporting role – and gets naked for an obligatory shower scene. Some of her XXX movies have better production values than this hunk of junk.

TALES FROM THE CRYPT
1972, UK
Dir: Freddie Francis. Prod: Max J. Rosenberg, Milton Subotsky. Sc: Milton Subotsky
Cast: Ralph Richardson, Joan Collins, Ian Hendry, Peter Cushing, Nigel Patrick

Living dead fans will need to skip the first, second and fifth tales in this portmanteau collection (though they're actually good fun, especially Joan Collins's nightmare before Christmas) and head along to Cushing's appearance as a bullied neighbour who turns into a ghoul in the third segment. The fourth entry features a man being brought back from the dead over and over again as his wife keeps fluffing her three wishes. Framing the collection is the ghoulish crypt keeper himself, nicely played by Richardson.

TEENAGE ZOMBIES
1957, USA
Dir: Jerry Warren. Prod: Jerry Warren. Sc: Jacques Lecotier [Jerry Warren]
Cast: Don Sullivan, Katherine Victor, Steve Conte, J.L.D. Morrison, Bri [Brianne] Murphy

During a waterskiing trip, a gang of fresh-faced American kids stumble across a secret island inhabited by a Russian scientist (Katherine Victor), who's planning to introduce a biological agent into the water supply that will turn the population of the United States into mindless slaves. The kids have to battle the mad doctor and her zombified henchman to save America from the Reds.

TERROR-CREATURES FROM THE GRAVE
1965, ITALY/USA
Original title: Cinque tombe per un medium
Alternative title: Cemetery of the Living Dead
Dir: Massimo Pupillo. Prod: Frank Merle, Ralph Zucker. Sc: Robert Nathan [Roberto Natale], Robin McLorin [Romano Migliorini]

Cast: Barbara Steele, Walter Brandt [Brandi], Marilyn Mitchell [Mirella Maravidi], Alfred Rice [Alfredo Rizzo], Richard Garrett [Riccardo Garrone]

Horror favourite Barbara Steele headlines this tale about a dead medium named Jeronimus Hauff who calls plague victims up from their graves underneath his castle to avenge himself on his wife. Lots of brooding Italian Gothic atmosphere and some envelope-pushing gore scenes make this a notable but not very exciting genre entry. The terror creatures themselves are the plague-ridden corpses who come to life at the end of the film and take revenge for the dead medium. It's so cheap it limits its zombies to outstretched hands shot in shadow, inching their way along walls, before killing them off with rainwater!

THE TERROR EXPERIMENT
2010, USA
Dir: George Menduluk. Prod: Henry Boger, Justin Jones, Stan Spry. Sc: D. Todd Deeken
Cast: Jason London, C. Thomas Howell, Alicia Leigh William, Lochlyn Munro, Alexander Medeluk

"We have to take back this country. I don't want to die. But if that makes you see the truth, so be it." When a rightwing domestic terrorist unleashes a nerve gas in a crowded federal building, civilians are turned into furious ghouls and filmmaker George Mendeluk taps into post-9/11 anxieties. Trapped by the government-created gas is an IT expert (Jason London) and assorted hangers-on, while outside, C. Thomas Howard's police chief tries to keep the situation under control. The nerve agent acts by over-stimulating the adrenal glands – something this dead-on-arrival B-movie could never be accused of doing.

THEY CAME BACK
2004, FRANCE
Original title: Les revenants
Dir: Robin Campillo. Prod: Caroline Benjo, Carole Scotta. Sc: Robin Campillo, Brigitte Tijou
Cast: Géraldine Pailhas, Jonathan Zaccaï, Frédéric Pierrot, Victor Garrivier, Catherine Samie

The ghouls in this arthouse oddity are different from most. Director Robin Campillo – who co-wrote Laurent Cantet's masterful drama *Time Out*

about the soulessness of the modern corporate office – makes his zombies a metaphor for various social problems. As the dead return to life and head home, they try to reintegrate into society, but it's not that easy. Relatives react in different ways and the government puts them up in emergency housing, struggling to decide what to do with the sudden return of so many ex-citizens. An intelligently leftfield take on the usual zombie apocalypses, this is an ambitiously probing film about grief, social exclusion and the socio-economics of living death. It later spawned a French TV series *The Returned* (*Les revenants* 2012–).

THRILLER
1983, USA
Dir: John Landis. Prod: George Folsey Jr., Michael Jackson, John Landis. Sc: John Landis, Michael Jackson
Cast: Michael Jackson, Ola Ray, Michael Peters, John Command, the voice of Vincent Price

A landmark 1980s music video from superstar Jackson, this ropes in horror maestro John Landis to cook up some suitable scares as Jackson and his girlfriend find their smooching disturbed by ghouls. Notable for reviving the zombie's flagging fortunes and for launching a 1,001 dancing-zombie skits.

TOKYO ZOMBIE
2005, JAPAN
Original title: Tôkyô zonbi
Dir: Sakichi Satô. Prod: Yusaku Toyoshima, Haruo Umekawa. Sc: Sakichi Satô
Cast: Tadanobu Asano, Sho Aikawa, Erika Okuda, Arata Furuta, Hina Matsuoka

After careless Tokyo residents create a towering pile of rubbish dubbed "Black Fuji", the toxic garbage resurrects the dead. Trying to escape the z-apocalypse are slacker garage workers Fujio (Tadanobu Asano) and Mitsuo (Sho Aikawa), whose ju-jitsu skills keep the ambling zombies at bay. Much languid comedy follows. Then, halfway through the proceedings, we're fast-forwarded five years into the future. Tokyo's rich have built a Fiddler's Green-style enclave where living gladiators fight zombie opponents and our heroes' ju-jitsu skills come into play. Cheap, slow-paced and deadpan, *Tokyo Zombie* is a real curio. Writer-director Sato Sakichi previously scripted another, more energetic, manga adaptation, *Ichi the Killer*.

TOMBS OF THE BLIND DEAD
1971, SPAIN/PORTUGAL
Original titles: La noche del terror ciego, A noite do terror cego
Alternative titles: The Blind Dead, Crypt of the Blind Dead, La noche de la muerta ciega, Le tombe dei resuscitati ciechi, Tombs of the Blind Zombies
Dir: Amando de Ossorio. Prod: José Antonio Pérez Giner. Sc: Amando de Ossorio
Cast: Lone Fleming, César Burner, Helen Harp [María Elena Arpón], Joseph Thelman [José Telman], María Silva

The first of de Ossorio's Blind Dead movies set the precedent for all that would follow, with skeletal, sightless zombies pursuing a couple of good-looking lasses and occasionally jumping onto zombie steeds for some operatic slow-mo moments.

TOXIC LULLABY
2010, GERMANY
Dir: Ralf Kemper. Prod: Ralf Kemper, Stephan Haberzetti. Sc: Ralf Kemper
Cast: Samantha Richter, Noah Hunter, Eva Marie Balkenhol, Christian Sprecher, Nima Conrad

Opening in the 1970s, this German outing starts off like a riff on *Let's Scare Jessica to Death* (1971) before becoming a drab, futuristic post-apocalyptic story. Eloise (Samantha Richter) drops a tab of LSD with her mates during a road trip in the hippie era, then wakes up in an uncertain future where the world has been overrun by biting, stumbling zombie "sleepers", and gas-masked survivors dream of a promised Green Island. The dreamlike, druggy shifts between sun-tinted past and bleak future promise something more interesting – but the ambition fizzles out as filmmaker Ralf Kemper concentrates on the latter world.

TOXIC ZOMBIES
1979, USA
Alternative titles: Bloodeaters, Forest of Fear
Dir: Charles McCrann. Prod: Charles McCrann.
Sc: Charles McCrann
Cast: Charles Austin, Beverly Shapiro, Dennis Helfend, Kevin Hanlon, Judy Brown, John Amplas

Marijuana gets sprayed with an experimental pesticide and would-be dope heads are turned into slavering bloodeaters in Charles McCrann's redneck schedule filler. Tom Cole (Charles Austin), the forestry department's finest, is stranded in the backwoods with his family as the maniacs stalk the countryside in search of fresh victims. They're not exactly zombies, but the distributors obviously thought that alternative title *Bloodeaters* just wasn't vivid enough.

TREPANATOR
1991, FRANCE
Dir: N. G. Mount [Norbert Moutier]. Prod: Norbert Moutier. Sc: N. G. Mount [Norbert Moutier]
Cast: Michel Finas, Jean Rollin, Eva Sinclair, Michael Raynaud, Gilles Bourgarel

France delivers a very cheap, very gory, very silly take on *Re-Animator*. When a mad scientist experimenting on not-quite-dead cadavers in an underground lair is arrested, his young son Herbert East (haha) ends up in New York. Years later he continues his father's bloody research in a clinic run by his uncle (Jean Rollin). Heads are trepanned with chainsaws, a few ghouls stumble around and a zombie tosses his own head across a room. How do you say "splatstick" in French?

TRUE LOVE ZOMBIE
2011, USA
Dir: Paul Blevins. Prod: Paul Blevins. Sc: Paul Blevins
Cast: Paul Blevins, Rhonda Blevins, Blake McCurdy, Steve Snyder, Lisa Hunter

The Internet revolutionised movie distribution, but sometimes it's hard not to miss the old days when the barrier to entry was set high enough to ensure at least a miniscule amount of quality control. This brainfart of a DIY zom-com from first-time filmmaker Paul Blevins looks like an Ed Wood Jr. movie that Ed would have disowned. It's essentially a love story as a zombified man (Blevins) is "rehabilitated" by his wife (Rhonda Blevins). Silly and messy, it ticks off a series of sub-Troma clichés: a super soldier zombie virus, Iraq references, Adolf Hitler, bad wigs and even worse VFX. It eventually falls apart under the weight of its own ridiculousness. Totally amateur.

UNA DE ZOMBIS
2003, SPAIN
Dir: Miguel Ángel Lamata. Prod: Santiago Segura, Javier Valiño. Sc: Miguel Ángel Lamata, Miguel Ángel Aijon
Cast: Miguel Ángel Aparicio, Mayte Navales, Miguel Ángel Aijon, Nacho Rubio, Salomé Jiménez

"A Film About Zombies", this delivers plenty of ghouls and possesses a breathless, mordant postmodern wit that takes narrative game-playing into realms that would make Quentin Tarantino proud. The plot folds in on itself so may times it's hard to summarise, but it begins with Goth DJ Caspas (Miguel Ángel Aparicio) and his best mate (Miguel Ángel Aijon) setting out to make a film about (you guessed it...) zombies. Then real zombies appear and things go from crazy to insane.

UNCLE SAM
1996, USA
Dir: Wiliam Lustig. Prod: George G. Braunstein. Sc: Larry Cohen
Cast: David "Shark" Fralick, Christopher Ogden, Isaac Hayes, Anne Tremko, Leslie Neale

This under-the-radar B-movie is directed by William Lustig and written by Larry Cohen, two horror veterans who previously collaborated on the zombie-with-a-badge *Maniac Cop* series. Taking its cue from 1970s classic *Deathdream*, it follows Gulf War veteran Sam (David "Shark" Fralick) who returns from the dead to punish the unpatriotic, the feckless and the corrupt. Dressed in an Uncle Sam outfit, this rotting zombie slasher impales victims on flagpoles on the Fourth of July. Nicely subversive, it takes a sly dig at patriotic fervor and turns America's iconic father figure into a vicious and hateful zombie. Had it arrived during the other Bush's presidency, it might have had more impact – especially on a double bill with *Homecoming*.

UNDEAD
2003, AUSTRALIA
Dir: Michael and Peter Spierig. Prod: Michael and Peter Spierig. Sc: Michael and Peter Spierig
Cast: Felicity Mason, Mungo McKay, Rob Jenkins, Lisa Cunningham, Emma Randall

Zombie cinema has always had more than its fair share of DIY filmmakers willing to grab a video camera, round up a few mates and slap some flour on their faces. This no-budget effort from Australia follows in the homemade footsteps of New Zealand's *Bad Taste* as twins Peter and Michael Spierig turn an outback town into an alien-infested zombie wasteland. Riding through the chaos is a shotgun-wielding fisherman (Mungo McKay) and the town's former beauty queen (Felicity Mason). Splatter fans will dig the gut-munching action (including a zombie fish!), but annoyingly hysterical characters, naff CG and relentless steals from other, better movies prove wearing. You know you're in serious trouble when one of those "better" movies includes Stephen King's *Dreamcatcher*. Gulp.

UNDEAD OR ALIVE: A ZOMBEDY
2007, USA
Dir: Glasgow Phillips. Prod: Deborah del Prete, Gigi Pritzker, David Greathouse. Sc: Glasgow Phillips
Cast: Chris Kattan, James Denton, Navi Rawat, Matt Besser, Chris Coppola

In 1886, Geronimo's surrender marked the end of the Indian Wars. But what if the old Apache chief got the last laugh? In *Undead or Alive* Geronimo curses the white race and the dead return to life to feast on the living. Styled as a "zombedy", this knockabout Western features an army deserter (James Denton) teaming up with an unlikely ladies man (Chris Kattan) and Geronomi's niece (Navi Rawat) to fight the dead. Old Western clichés – the bar-room brawl, the corrupt sheriff, the army fort – get thrown together with some walking, talking dead to very little purpose. Someday, someone will make a proper zombie Western.

THE UNKNOWN TERROR
1957, USA
Dir: Charles Marquis Warren. Prod: Robert Stabler. Sc: Kenneth Higgins
Cast: John Howard, Mala Powers, Paul Richards, May Wynn, Gerald Milton

In a cave somewhere "South of the American continent", a fast-growing fungus is turning people into mouldy ghouls. When a team of American explorers arrive to find their missing spelunking friend, they encounter Dr Ramsay (Gerald Milton), an American scientist researching antibiotics and lording it over the natives after curing them of smallpox. It seems the doctor has been throwing a few natives into the "Cave of Death" and pretty soon the visiting Americans are being attacked by mushroom-skinned ghouls who stumble out of the cave to harass Mala Powers while she's in her nightgown (shades of *I Walked with a Zombie*) before the team discover the horrible truth when they venture down below. The spelunking sequences, trapped underground in a cave where soap-sud fungus oozes over the rocky walls and ghouls lope around, are creepily effective.

URBAN SCUMBAGS VS. COUNTRYSIDE ZOMBIES
1992, GERMANY
Dir: Patrick Hollman, Sebastian Panneck. Prod: Patrick Hollman, Sebastian Panneck. Sc: Patrick Hollman, Sebastian Panneck
Cast: Kai Dombrowski, Viola Colditz, Alexander Laurisch, Andreas Tretow, Constanze Abraham

Intriguing title, snooze-worthy movie. This German production was one of the first Teutonic zombie outings, and it's certainly showing its age. A bunch of kids (the urban scumbags) are sent off to a countryside retreat by their parents, who are fed up of their rebellious ways. But instead of being cured by the doctor and the sergeant-major-type tough guy who run the centre, they find themselves caught up in a zombie outbreak after two Middle Eastern terrorists drop a barrel of toxic biochemicals. What follows is pretty dull even by low-budget zombie outings, with only a few laughing ghouls (apparently the extras suffer from the giggles), amputation by chainsaw and a zombie pushing his mate about in a supermarket trolley as distractions.

VALLEY OF THE ZOMBIES
1946, USA
Dir: Philip Ford. Prod: Dorrell and Stuart McGowan. Sc: Dorrell and Stuart McGowan
Cast: Robert Livingston, Adrian Booth, Ian Keith, Thomas Jackson, Charles Trowbridge

"When I need blood I must have it!" Disappointingly, this Poverty Row movie from Republic doesn't feature a single zombie (or, for that matter, the eponymous valley of them). Undertaker Ian Keith

has discovered a secret formula in "a land of voodoo rites and devil potions" that allows him to exist in some halfway state between life and death. Fair enough. Except he needs a steady supply of blood to keep himself going. That makes this more of a vampire movie, despite its groan-inducing closing gag ("I think I need a drink. Let's get… a zombie!")

VAMPIRES VS ZOMBIES
2003, CANADA
Alternative title: Carmilla, The Lesbian Vampire
Dir: Vince D'Amato. Prod: Rob Carpenter, Damien Foisy. Sc: Vince D'Amato
Cast: Bonny Giroux, C.S. Munro, Maritama Carlson, Brinke Stevens, Melanie Crystal

Shot on the backroads of Vancouver, where no one needs a permit, *Vampires Vs Zombies* disappoints by refusing to actually set the undead against the living dead. It also disappoints thanks to its amateurish production values and acting; not to mention its incoherent story about a vampire called Carmilla (Maritama Carlson) and a rabies-like virus that's turning people into drooling ghouls. A mess.

THE VANGUARD
2008, UK
Dir: Matthew Hope. Prod: Steve Dann, Robert Henry Craft, Matthew Hope. Sc: Matthew Hope
Cast: Ray Bullock Jr., Shiv Grewal, Emma Choy, Steve Weston, Jack Bailey

"No oil, 60m people on the verge of starvation, the virtual collapse of society…" In 2015, the Earth has gone to hell in a hand basket after a bloody scramble for global resources. A single corporation controls what is left of the civilised world, but out in the backwoods savage "biosyns" – ape-like, violent zombies created by scientific experiments – roam free. Through this world moves a mute Bear Grylls type (Ray Bullock Jr.) who's resistant to the biosyn plague, and a brainwashed soldier (Bahi Ghubril) who is now rebelling. British director Matthew Hope shoots in the Hertfordshire woods and crafts a handful of sequences that show he obviously knows one end of a camera from the other. But his overly ambitious script waffles through post-apocalyptic existentialism and reams of exposition to no real purpose. The biosyns are memorable: lolloping, leaping primates with thread-veined faces who drag their knuckles on the ground and occasionally attack one another like rejects from the Dawn of Man sequence in *2001: A Space Odyssey*. Unusual enough to be refreshing, but not entertaining enough to be recommended.

THE VEIL
2005, UK
Dir: Richard Chance. Prod: Richard Chance, John Chance, Michael Himsworth. Sc: John Chance, Richard Chance
Cast: Michael Himsworth, Richard Chance, John Chance, Tom Sadler, Martin Dorkins

Made in Britain: three days after a bio-weapon is released over an English town, a squad of SAS soldiers in gas masks are sent in to assess the situation. What they find are splodgy-faced ghouls stumbling around the streets and inside the houses. Running for over two hours (a more sensible shorter cut was later released), *The Veil* makes the most of its intermittently creepy b&w cinematography, but is sorely hampered by a lack of pace. Worse still, the gas-mask wearing leads are so indistinguishable from one another that character development becomes an uphill struggle. "Weston, is that you? I can't see shit in this mask!" complains one soldier as the cut-off teams try to regroup. We sympathise.

VS THE DEAD
2010, CANADA
Dir: Phil Pattison, Jeff Beckman. Prod: Phil Pattison, Jeff Beckman. Sc: Phil Pattison, Jeff Beckman
Cast: Dave Montour, Brett Hawley, Brandon Dean, Phil Fader, Chris Waldick

A barely coherent opening on-screen crawl and an unconvincing Afghanistan-set prologue establish the backstory: during the War on Terror, US military scientists create Round Two, a drug to revive KIA servicemen that ends up creating Taliban zombies (go figure). Cut to Hamilton, Ontario where a tattoo parlour uses the serum as ink and ghouls take over the town. Gloriously potty-mouthed but fundamentally challenged in the entertainment department.

THE VAULT OF HORROR
1973, UK
Alternative title: Further Tales from the Crypt, Tales from the Crypt II.
Dir: Roy Ward Baker. Prod: Max Rosenberg, Milton Subotsky. Sc: Milton Subotsky.
Cast: Tom Baker, Denholm Elliot, Terry Thomas, Dawn Addams, Michael Craig

This lacklustre outing for UK horror house Amicus fails to capitalise on the joys of *Tales from the Crypt* (1972), and marked the death knell of the E.C. Comics adaptations deal that the studio had been hoping to take to a third instalment. The first of the five stories begins as a group of protagonists find themselves trapped in a lift and decide to pass the time by telling each other about their dreams (as you do). None of the stories involve ghouls, though there's a suitably macabre tale of premature burial. The framing storyline comes into its own in the final moments of the film as the characters discover that they've got more to worry about than just a broken lift. Cue a memorable scene of zombies shuffling towards oblivion.

VENGEANCE OF THE ZOMBIES
1972, SPAIN
Original title: La rebelión de las muertas.
Alternative titles:, Rebellion of the Dead Women, Revolt of the Dead Ones, Der Totenchor der Knochenmänner, La vendetta dei morti viventi, Walk of the Dead
Dir: Léon Klimovsky. Prod: José Antonio Pérez Giner.
Sc: Jacinto Molina
Cast: Paul Naschy [Jacinto Molina], Rommy, Mirta Miller, Vic Winner [Victor Alcazar], María Kosti

The ubiquitous Naschy plays a double lead role here, first as an Indian guru and then as his crazed brother who's turning the daughters of ex-Indian colonials into zombies using voodoo (eh?). He wants vengeance for their attempt to burn him to death years earlier, and he's turning the girls into an army of zombie chicks dressed in black robes. Not content with two lead roles, Naschy also slaps on some horns to play the Devil in a voodoo ceremony where a chicken gets beheaded. Dated Spanish pap.

VERSUS
2000, JAPAN

Dir: Ryuhei Kitamura. Prod: Shin Keishiro. Sc: Ryuhei Kitamura
Cast: Tak Sakaguchi, Hideo Sakaki, Chieko Misaka, Kenji Matsuda, Yuichiro Arai

In essence this could be *Junk* all over again as a couple of escaped convicts meet up with some yakuza types and a kidnapped beauty in a forest just as a horde of living dead are unleashed. That's about as far as the comparison goes, though, as *Versus* spins off to take in inter-dimensional portals, *Highlander*-style swordfights and some outrageously kinetic camera moves. It unspools at a terrific rate, with enough verve and style to make it a bona fide cult classic. It was preceded by the very similar 45-minute *Down to Hell* (1996), which acted as a proof of concept.

THE VIDEO DEAD
1987, USA

Dir: Robert Scott. Prod: Robert Scott. Sc: Robert Scott
Cast: Rocky Duvall, Roxanna Augesen, Sam David McClelland, Vickie Bastel, Michael St Michaels

Whatever you do, don't go watching *Zombie Blood Nightmare*. It's a film that's so bad it will kill you (other films in this book might feel like that, but this one is the real deal). When a beaten-up old TV set arrives on the doorstep of teenagers Jeff (Rocky Duvall) and Zoe (Roxanna Augesen), they switch it on to discover the aforementioned flick running on a continuous loop. Pretty soon, zombies are clambering out of the screen and getting up to all sorts of nonsense in this black horror-comedy. Wandering through the neighbourhood, the ghouls make a nuisance of themselves, ransacking homes and messing about with the kitchen appliances while dementedly giggling about nothing in particular. Fortunately they can be scared off with mirrors and leave you alone if you pretend not to be afraid of them. An obscure little treat well worth tracking down.

THE VINEYARD
1989, USA

Dir: Bill Rice, James Hong. Prod: Harry Mok. Sc: James Hong, Douglas Kondo
Cast: James Hong, Karen Witter, Michael Wong, Cheryl Lawson, Cheryl Madsen

Something of a vanity project for star, co-director and co-writer James Hong, this attempt to blend Asian and Hollywood horror falls flat on its face. Hong is Po, an evil sorcerer living on an island off the Californian coast. He's renowned for his award-winning wines, yet he harbours a guilty secret: the vineyard is nothing more than a front for his magic dabbling. He's trying to keep his youth by brewing a special wine made from the blood of the beautiful boys and gals that he lures to his hideaway. Suddenly, the zombified remains of his previous victims rise from the vineyard to take their revenge. There's lots of T&A as wrinkly old Hong surrounds himself with nubile flesh half his age. The crappy 1980s vibe is compounded by the zombies themselves – a ragged group of *Thriller* rejects who stumble around a blue-lit vineyard where the mist machines are on permanent overdrive.

A VIRGIN AMONG THE LIVING DEAD
1971, LIECHTENSTEIN/FRANCE/BELGIUM

Original titles: Christina, princess de l'érotisme, Une vierge chez les morts vivants
Alternative titles: Eine Jungfrau in den Krallen von Zombies, Testamento diabolico, Una virgine fra i morti viventi, Zombi 4: A Virgin Among The Living Dead
Dir: Jess [Jesús] Franco. Sc: Jess [Jesús] Franco, Peter Kerut, Henry Brald
Cast: Christina von Blanc, Britt Nichols [Carmen Yazalde], Howard Vernon, Anne Libert, Rose Kienkens, Paul Muller

Is it a dream or is real? Let's hope it's all a dream because this inept shocker really makes no sense whatsoever. Whether that's because it's been butchered somewhere in postproduction, or just because director Franco couldn't be bothered to find a decent story to pad out his wonderful collection of titles, isn't clear. Either way, anyone looking for zombie action will be disappointed since there's very little indeed. Young Christine (von Blanc) visits her uncle's chateau and slips into a weird state somewhere between the real and unreal, life and afterlife. Various characters pop up, vanish and reappear again and there's lots of emphasis on a pond in the chateau grounds. Jean Rollin apparently shot the footage in which Christina dreams zombies are after her. His distinctive touch might have been better suited to this morbid yet annoyingly nonsensical outing.

VOODOO DAWN
1989, USA
Dir: Steven Fierberg. Prod: Steven Mackler. Sc: John Russo, Jeffrey Delman, Thomas Rendon, Evan Dunsky
Cast: Raymond St Jacques, Theresa Merritt, Tony Todd, Gina Gershon, Kirk Baily

Not even the four screenwriters (one of them being *Night of the Living Dead* actor/crew member John Russo) can help this voodoo chiller dig itself out of its hole. Nor can the presence of a young, pre-fame Gina Gershon in the cast (bet she's since taken this off her CV). Tony Todd is a voodoo priest terrorising the Deep South by building a zombie out of various body parts; meanwhile the white American heroes join forces with a wise old herbalist to defeat him before it's too late.

VOODOO ISLAND
1957, USA
Alternative title: Silent Death
Dir: Reginald Le Borg. Prod: Howard W. Koch.
Sc: Richard Landau
Cast: Boris Karloff, Beverly Tyler, Elisha Cook Jr., Rhodes Reason, Jean Engstrom

Karloff's researcher leads an expedition to a South Pacific island where several American engineers have vanished and the only survivor has been turned into a zombie. He thinks the whole story's just a publicity gimmick for the opening of a new hotel on the island, but he soon realises that the zombies are real and that the natives are using voodoo to deter the white invaders. A disposable schedule filler.

VOODOO MAN
1944, USA
Dir: William Beaudine. Prod: Sam Katzman, Jack Dietz. Sc: Robert Charles
Cast: Bela Lugosi, John Carradine, George Zucco, Wanda McKay, Louise Currie

Three of Monogram's best-loved horror stars prop up this creaky tale of a mad doctor who abducts starlets off the highway and experiments on them in an attempt to transfer the soul of his zombified wife into their bodies. The experiments never turn out quite right, leaving the doc with a house full of pretty zombie gals to be guarded by his henchmen.

THE WALKING DEAD
1936, USA
Dir: Michael Curtiz. Prod: Louis F. Edelman. Sc: Ewart Adamson, Peter Milne, Robert D. Andrews, Lillie Harward
Cast: Boris Karloff, Ricardo Cortez, Warren Hull, Edmund Gwenn, Marguerite Churchill

Warner Bros. tried to blend their talent for gangster movies with the Universal horror tradition in this interesting take on the zombie. Karloff is the walking-dead man of the title, who is framed by evil mobsters and sent to the electric chair before two faint-hearted eyewitnesses can find the courage to tell the court that he's actually innocent. Fortunately, they know a scientist who's able to revive him… The results aren't entirely successful, and Karloff's zombie ends up moping around, playing the piano and tracking down and killing the men who set him up like some lumbering angel of death.

THE WALKING DEAD
2010– , USA
Dir: Frank Darabont. Prod: Denise Huth, Tom Luse.
Sc: Frank Darabont
Cast: Andrew Lincoln, Jon Bernthal, Norman Reedus, Sarah Wayne Callies, Steven Yeun

Based on the long-running comic series, AMC's primetime TV show took zombies to a mass audience. Breaking viewing records and winning multiple awards, it keeps its zombies true to the Romero template where questions of morality loom large.

WARM BODIES
2013, USA
Dir: Jonathan Levine. Prod: David Hoberman, Todd Lieberman, Bruna Papandrea. Sc: Jonathan Levine
Cast: Nicholas Hoult, Teresa Palmer, Analeigh Tipton, Rob Corddry, Dave Franco

Zombies get their answer to *Twilight* in this teen-friendly tale of star-crossed lovers, one alive and one dead. It's a PG-13 zombie movie totally lacking in bite.

WARNING SIGN
1985, USA
Alternative title: Biohazard
Dir: Hal Barwood. Prod: Jim Bloom. Sc: Hal Barwood, Matthew Robbins
Cast: Sam Waterston, Kathleen Quinlan, Yaphet Kotto, Jeffrey DeMunn

George Lucas and Steven Spielberg's buddy Hal Barwood made his directorial debut on this TV movie. A secret biochemical research centre becomes the site of a zombie outbreak after the employees are exposed to a lethal viral agent. The building is sealed off, but the dead scientists start coming back to life, faces covered in pustules and eyes wild with rage. They take out a platoon of soldiers in clunky biochemical warfare suits but don't get to do a lot else before *Warning Sign* ties up all the loose ends and an antidote is found. The idea of having the platoon film the attacking ghouls with a live-feed camcorder could well have been an influence on James Cameron's later *Aliens*, but that's about all that makes this notable.

WAR OF THE DEAD
2011, USA/LITHUANIA/ITALY
Alternative title: War of the Dead: Stone's War
Dir: Marko Mäkilaakso. Prod: Ramunas Skikas, Barr Porter. Sc: Marko Mäkilaakso, Barr Porter
Cast: Andrew Tiernan, Mikko Leppilampi, Samuel Vauramo, Jouko Ahola, Andreas Wilson

The biggest production ever shot in Lithuania had a troubled history spanning eight years, at least two alternate working titles (*Army of the Dead*, *Stone's War*), an aborted 2006 shoot, and the loss of initially-attached *Dawson's Creek* star James Van Der Beek. It bears all the hallmarks of a production that's been through the meat grinder: shonky characters, lacklustre plotting and a general air of having missed its target. The biggest problem of all, though, is that its zombies are so bland. They may be Hitler's supersoldiers gone wrong, but helmer Marko Mäkilaakso makes them so near-indistinguishable from the living that the movie loses any sense of dread. For a more inspired update of the Nazi zombie cycle, see *Dead Snow* (2009) or the *Outpost* franchise.

WAR OF THE ZOMBIES

1964, ITALY
Original title: Roma contro Roma
Alternative titles: Night Star – Goddess of Electra, Rome Against Rome
Dir: Giuseppe Vari. Prod: Ferruccio De Martino, Massimodo Rita. Sc: Piero Pierotti, Marcello Sartarelli
Cast: Susy Andersen, Ettore Manni, Ida Galli, Mino Doro, John Drew Barrymore

Rome is in revolt as a black-magic sorcerer (John Drew Barrymore) intent on overthrowing the Empire raises an army of dead Roman legionaries to fight his battle for him. Living soldiers are forced to do battle with their dead comrades-in-arms until a centurion named Gaius attacks the effigy of the sorcerer's god and robs him of his power. Although the soldier zombies don't look particularly dead, they get a ghostly flourish thanks to superimposed, ethereal visuals and eerie music that pre-empts the horseriding ghouls of the *Blind Dead* series.

WASTING AWAY
2007, USA
Alternative title: Aaah! Zombies!!
Dir: Matthew Kohnen. Prod: Sean Kohnen.
Sc: Matthew Kohnen, Sean Kohnen
Cast: Matthew Davis, Julianna Robinson, Michael Terry, Betsy Beutler, Colby French

Here's a rarity: a zombie comedy that's both original and funny. When a secret military serum for creating super soldiers ends up in a bowling alley's ice-cream machine (don't you just hate it when that happens?), four college kids are turned into zombies. So far, so conventional. But there's a twist. *Wasting Away* takes the zombies' perspective as the infected kids fail to realise that they've joined the ranks of the living dead and carry on as normal. Flicking between b&w and colour, director Matthew Kohnen gives us two versions of the action: one seen from the zombies' POV where they carry on regardless (give or take their newfound taste for brains), and the other from the living's POV where the kids appear as shuffling, stumbling ghouls. The disconnect in how the zombies perceive themselves and how the world sees them throws up some slyly funny moments, and even though the joke wears thin before it's up, this little flick proves that the term "zombie comedy" doesn't need to be an oxymoron.

WHITE ZOMBIE
1932, USA
Dir: Victor Halperin. Prod: Edward Halperin.
Sc: Garnett Weston
Cast: Bela Lugosi, Madge Bellamy, John Harron,
Joseph Cawthorn, Robert Frazer

The original zombie movie still packs some chills. Two young American visitors to Haiti fall foul of Bela Lugosi's evil voodoo sorcerer, who bewitches Madge Bellamy and turns her into one of his living dead slaves. After her husband storms the sorcerer's castle and battles his gang of thuggish zombies, she is saved from a fate worse than death.

WILD ZERO
1999, JAPAN
Dir: Tetsuro Takeuchi. Prod: Tetsuro Takeuchi.
Sc: Satoshi Takagi
Cast: Masashi Endo, Shitichai Kwancharu, Guitar
Wolf, Bass Wolf, Drum Wolf

Invading aliens turn the Japanese countryside into a zombie-infested wasteland in Tetsuro Takeuchi's Asian answer to a Troma movie. Three rock 'n' roll heroes from the band Guitar Wolf are on hand to help young rocker Ace as he deals with the living dead and has to come to terms with the realization that his new girlfriend is a she who's really a he ("Love has no borders, nationalities or genders!" becomes the film's message). What stands out here is the manic couldn't-give-a-damn energy, the primping and preening leather jacket-clad heroes and the general "anything goes" atmosphere. The zombies are cheap and cheerful creations and everyone has fun blasting their heads off with shotguns. The film ends with Guitar Wolf's front man destroying a UFO as it flies overhead by unsheathing a samurai sword hidden inside his guitar and slicing the space ship in two. Insane.

WITCHDOCTOR OF THE LIVING DEAD
1980S, NIGERIA
Dir/Prod/Sc: Charles Abi Enonchong
Cast: Joe Layode "Garuba", St Mary Enonchong,
Victor Eriabie, Larry Williams

A rare sighting of a SOV Nigerian zombie movie (of which anecdotal evidence suggests there are many, but that few people have actually seen), *Witchdoctor of the Living Dead*'s rarity can't make up for its dearth of cinematic entertainment. The witchdoctor of the title is a Ju-Ju man who's terrorising a rural village by turning into a goat and eating their crops. He's also breeding an army of shuffling zombies to do his bidding. Cursed with production values several leagues behind even the worst that Todd Sheets has to offer, this West African effort ambles through a half-baked storyline in which a big-city detective arrives to counter the zombie menace. Rubber snakes entering and leaving women's orifices add crassness to the proceedings, while the zombies themselves are laughably dozy (a result of both their sheer ineptitude and the lack of ability by the non-RADA cast). Cheap but far from cheerful.

THE WICKEDS
2005, USA
Dir: John Poague. Prod: John Poague. Sc: David Zagorski
Cast: Ron Jeremy, Justin Alvarez, Anna Bridgforth, Kelly
Roth, Bradford Sikes

Stop me if you've heard this one before: a group of teens head out to an infamous haunted house on Halloween. Except: it's daytime because no one can afford to shoot this movie at night. Meanwhile, in a nearby cemetery, a couple of sleazy grave robbers steal a cursed medallion from a corpse who looks like the love child of Dracula and Sid Haig. The theft triggers an outbreak of morts-vivants. Channelling *Children Shouldn't Play with Dead Things* (1972), this unabashedly cheesy slice of lo-fi exploitation offers up a smattering of T&A and a catalogue of star ghouls – brides, naked dead girls, baseball players, bankers – who stumble-march on the house. "What would Bruce Campbell do?" wonders one of the kids in a rare moment of wit. *Duh*, he'd watch a different movie.

WISEGUYS VS ZOMBIES
2003, USA
Dir: Adam Minarovich. Prod: Kevin Woods. Sc: Adam
Minarovich
Cast: Adam Minarovich, William Palko, Catherine
Brissey, Jason Martin, Matthew Pierce

"Bada-Bing, Bada-Doom!" proclaims the DVD

cover of this anaemic Troma effort, but Tony Soprano would not approve. When New York hitmen en route to Miami accidentally unleash a stolen US Army bio-weapon, they turn the supporting cast into zombies. What follows is a very dull amateur hour in which guys wearing too much hair gel and wife-beater vests battle zombies using shotguns, homemade bombs and chainsaws. Troma president Lloyd Kaufman claimed the movie was part of his Dogpile 95 digital filmmaking initiative, a belated riposte to Lars von Trier, announced at Cannes in 2002. "Long before Dogme 95 was born, Troma was making movies with poor lighting, amateur acting and crappy sound. However we haven't been able to rise to the level of boredom that the Dogme 95 films have attained…" Give me *Festen* any day.

WORLD OF THE DEAD, THE ZOMBIE DIARIES
2011, UK
Dir: Kevin Gates, Michael Bartlett. Prod: Rob Weston. Sc: Kevin Gates, Michael Bartlett
Cast: Philip Brodie, Alex Wilton Regan, Rob Oldfield, Vicky Araico, Tobias Bowman

A bigger budget and more confident air pervade this sequel to *The Zombie Diaries*. Four months after the UK has been overrun by ghouls from a mutated bird flu virus, a group of Territorial Army soldiers led by gruff survivor Maddox (Philip Brodie) head out from their overrun compound in search of an infection-free zone. But as they travel cross country, they find themselves in conflict with a group of murderous survivors who are more dangerous than the ghouls.

WORLD WAR Z
2013, USA
Dir: Marc Forster. Prod: Brad Pitt, Dede Gardner, Jeremy Kleiner, Ian Bryce. Sc: Matthew Michael Carnahan, Drew Goddard, Damon Lindelof
Cast: Brad Pitt, Mireille Enos, James Badge Dale, Daniella Kertesz, Matthew Fox

Brad Pitt saves the world from a global zombie pandemic in this blockbuster adaptation of Max Brooks's novel. A turning point in the zombie's on-screen evolution.

WOMANEATER

1957, UK
Dir: Charles Saunders. Prod: Guido Coen. Sc: Brandon Fleming
Cast: George Coulouris, Vera Day, Joy Webster, Peter Wayn, Jimmy Vaughan

A mad scientist is toying with carnivorous plant life in the hope of finding a serum that can resurrect the dead. Despite being schooled by an Amazonian witchdoctor, he soon realises that his plan doesn't really work: the body of his dead maid comes back to life as a rather cantankerous zombie. This low-budget British chiller is notable mainly for its shaggy Amazonian plant – actually a prop man in a rubber suit – that will only secrete a reanimating serum if it gets to munch on beautiful women.

WORKING STIFFS
1989, USA
Dir: Michael Legge. Prod: Jay Washburn, David Lowell, Maury Doyle. Sc: Michael Legge
Cast: Beverly Epstein, Bruce Harding, Tony Ferreira, Alan Kennedy, Michael McInnis

"Work doesn't have to be a four-letter word…" This cheapo SOV production is so threadbare you can hear the camera whirring during most scenes. At employment agency Consolidated Temps – aka "ConTemps" (haha!) – the bosses have a new angle: they're murdering new hires and resurrecting them as zombie slaves using Haitian voodoo. It's like *White Zombie* crossed with *Office Space* – and it's great to see a zombie movie that riffs on Haitian myth (if these enslaved workers eat salt, it's game over). On the case is suspicious temp Lacey (Beverly Epstein) who wonders why the agency's workers have fixed perma-grins and such a dedicated work ethic. Poverty-stricken and badly paced, this over-stretched satire squeezes a few gags out of the difference between working to live and living to work, but doesn't really go anywhere.

YESTERDAY
2010, CANADA
Dir: Rob Grant. Prod: Scott Mainwood. Sc: Rob Grant
Cast: Mike Fenske, Jesse Wheeler, Justin Sproule, Scott Wallis, Mike Kovac

"Is ethical value absolute or relative?" asks a college professor of his students, not long after a drug addict has taken a chunk out of his arm on the way to class. Uh-oh, you can see where this is going can't you? After a viral outbreak turns citizens into zombies with bleeding eyes, a bunch of survivors head out into the British Columbia woods and inevitably split into bickering factions. A competent if modest addition to the living-are-more-dangerous-than-the-dead cycle.

YOROI: SAMURAI ZOMBIE
2008, JAPAN

Original title: Yoroi: Samurai zonbi
Dir: Tak Sakaguchi. Prod: Motoi Hiraiwa, Akihiko Isogai. Sc: Ryûhei Kitamura
Cast: Mitsuru Fukikoshi, Issei Ishida, Tak Sakaguchi, Airi Nakajima, Shintarô Matsubara

No prizes for guessing that the main zombie in this Japanese outing is a towering samurai wearing bushido armour. Resurrected from his grave in a cursed village, he stumbles after a holidaying family, a couple of punkish bank robbers and two bumbling cops – slicing anyone who doesn't run fast enough to escape his razor-sharp katana. Less wacky than most "J-ombie" movies, this benefits from having three distinctive, unstoppable ghouls. Tellingly, though, the samurai zombie concept works better in *Dead Mine* (2011) thanks to a more contained, claustrophobic setting. Screenwriter Ryûhei Kitamura was director of *Versus* and *Battlefield Baseball*, which starred Tak Sakaguchi, who's on directing duties here.

Z108
2012, TAIWAN

Alternative title: Zombie 108
Dir: Joe Chien. Prod: Morris Rong. Sc: Joe Chien
Cast: Morris Rong, Yvonne Yao, Jack Kao, Sona Eyambe, Josh Wilson

Ghouls are on the streets of Taipei in Taiwan's first zombie movie, a demented but troubling and misogynous mash-up of *The Raid*-style action, torture porn nastiness and jerky ghouls created by a genetics experiment gone wrong. Filmmaker Joe Chien delivers all the right B-movie ingredients, but lingers so long on scenes of living-on-living sexual violence that the zombies seem like cuddly teddy bears in comparison. Meanwhile, the restless editing jumbles it into near total incoherence.

Z: A ZOMBIE MUSICAL
2006, USA

Dir: John McLean. Prod: John McLean, Dan Eggleston. Sc: John McLean
Cast: Hanna Hardin, Hallie Martin, Tiffany Janssen, Rob Faubion, Joe "King" Carrasco

Zombies may run nowadays, but they really shouldn't sing. This off-the-wall, so-loopy-it-hurts musical continues in the charmless vein of *Song of the Dead* (2005). Three nude singing nuns are bitten by a zombie pug and end up in Zomburbia, a utopian haven for the living (singing) dead. Except one of the nuns isn't so sure about becoming one of the sex-obsessed, incessantly chatting blue-veined ghouls, and wants to be "reversed". Thrown together on a limited budget, this is a scrappy and crappy addition to the Z musical cycle, with lyrics that are more painful than memorable.

ZEDER (VOICES FROM THE BEYOND)
1983, ITALY

Alternative titles: Revenge of the Dead, Zeder
Dir: Pupi Avati. Prod: Gianni Minervini, Antonio Avati. Sc: Pupi Avati, Maurizio Costanzo, Antonio Avati
Cast: Gabriele Lavia, Anne Canovas, Paolo Tanziani, Cesare Barbetti, Bob Tonelli

Quite unique among Italian zombie movies, Pupi Avati's sublimely creepy *Zeder* dispenses with the usual sub-Romero gore and living dead invasions in favour of a plot that involves folds in the space–time continuum, an ancient typewriter and oblique references to the Holocaust. In 1980s Italy, a writer discovers a bizarre tale imprinted on the ribbon of an old typewriter. Piecing together the words, he learns about "K-Zones" – strange locations in which the laws of time and space don't apply and in which the dead can be brought back to life. The authorities already know about these places and are experimenting with them, which leads to a series of zombie attacks. Deeply mysterious, Avati's chiller eschews everything that defines the Italian cycle in favour of a moody, arthouse atmosphere. Gorehounds will be quite disappointed, but those looking for a unique take on the zombie mythology will be pleasantly surprised by this occult conspiracy thriller.

ZIBAHKHANA

2007, PAKISTAN
Alternative title: Hell's Ground
Dir: Omar Ali Khan. Prod: Omar Ali Khan, Andy Starke, Pete Tombs. Sc: Omar Ali Khan, Pete Tombs
Cast: Kunwar Ali Roshan, Rooshanie Ejaz, Rubya Chaudhry, Haider Raza, Osman Khalid Butt

Billed as Pakistan's first zombie movie, this retro grindhouse outing is surprisingly well made. City kids on their way to a rock concert get chased by stumbling ghouls in saris and a slasher wearing a burka. Good fun.

ZOMBEAK
2007, USA
Dir: Sam Drog. Prod: S.C. Caruso, Wes Campbell. Sc: Sam Drog
Cast: Melissa K. Gilbert, Tracy Yarkoni, Daryl Wilcher, Jason Vin Stein, Adam Morris

"No rednecks, chickens or Satanists were harmed during the making of this movie." When a band of half-arsed devil worshippers kidnap a busty waitress (Melissa K. Gilbert) from Cooters's fast food chicken joint, their plan to summon Satan goes awry. Poor planning leaves the Dark Lord trapped in the body of a sacrificial hen! As the stuffed bird goes on the rampage, its victims are turned into possessed zombies. The DV in this micro-budget feature looks ugly, but Gilbert's spirited, trailer trash performance gives it a spark of life ("C'mon, you Kentucky Fried piece of shit!"). The zombie-Satanic hen is certainly a first – though *Poultrygeist* (2007) does the "Chicken Dead" idea much better.

ZOMBEX
2013, USA
Dir: Jesse Dayton. Prod: Marissa Garrison, Karma Montagne, Jesse Dayton. Sc: Jesse Dayton
Cast: Lew Temple, Malcolm McDowell, David Christopher, Sid Haig, Corey Feldman

In post-Katrina New Orleans a pharma company is handing out experimental antidepressants to help citizens cope with the aftermath of the hurricane. Turns out, though, that the pills are turning them into zombies – a flood of raging ghouls that no levee can hold back. "There isn't enough brain function here for these poor bastards to even tie their shoelaces!" explains Malcolm McDowell's corporate scientist as the city goes to hell (again) and a crusading radio DJ (Lew Temple) tries to find a serum. Confused, ADHD editing and a strangely unapocalyptic apocalypse don't do this film many favours. Corey Feldman and Sid Haig make brief appearances for no discernible reason other than to use their names on the DVD case.

ZOMBI 3
1988, ITALY
Alternative titles: Zombie Flesh Eaters 2
Dir: Lucio Fulci. Prod: Franco Gaudenzi. Sc: Claudio Fragasso
Cast: Deran Sarafian, Beatrice Ring, Richard Raymond [Ottaviano Dell'Acqua], Alex McBride [Massimo Vanni], Ulli Reinthaler

Fulci steps back into the fray with his "official" sequel to *Zombi 2*. The results are bad enough to make one wish all concerned had simply given the franchise the last rites instead. Shot in the Philippines, where celluloid is cheap and extras are even cheaper, this kicks off with a biological weapon triggering a zombie outbreak. If you manage to get past the atrocious direction, costumes and acting that assault you in the first ten minutes, it only gets much, much worse. Fulci apparently left the production before shooting finished, handing over the reins to the uncredited Bruno Mattei. Who can blame him?

ZOMBIBI
2012, NETHERLANDS
Alternative title: Kill Zombie!
Dir: Martijn Smits, Erwin van den Eshof. Prod: Wilco Wolfers, Coen Michielsen, Bob De Lange, Frank Groenveld, René Huybrechtse. Sc: Tijs van Marle
Cast: Yahya Gaier, Gigi Ravelli, Mimoun Ouled Radi, Sergio Hasselbaink, Uriah Arnhen

The Netherlands's multicultural answer to *Shaun of the Dead*: when a space station crashes to Earth oozing green slime, Amsterdam becomes zombie central. A Moroccan office worker (Yahya Gaier) battles to save his girlfriend, accompanied by his waster brother, a badass police woman and two African immigrant thugs. Cartoonish and hyper-kinetic, *Zombibi* is the kind of movie that doesn't take itself too seriously – and it's notable chiefly as a rare example of a Dutch zombie movie.

ZOMBIE 4: AFTER DEATH
1988, ITALY
Original title: After Death (Oltre la morte)
Alternative titles: Return of the Living Dead Part 3,
Zombi Flesh Eaters 3
Dir: Claudio Fragasso. Prod: Franco Gaudenzi.
Sc: Rossella Drudi
Cast: Chuck Peyton, Candice Daly, Alex McBride
[Massimo Vanni], Don Wilson, Jim Gaines

Zombies run wild on a desert island in Claudio Fragasso's late entry in the Italian cycle. Adventurers inadvertently unleash the walking corpses after reading from the *Book of the Dead* (tut). Fending off the zombie hordes with automatic weapons, our heroes work through a turgid movie of tiresome action sequences before the zombies get bored and pick up the guns themselves. Dreadful stuff, which gains trivia points because lead actor Chuck Peyton is actually legendary gay porn star Jeff Stryker.

ZOMBIE 90: EXTREME PESTILENCE
1990, GERMANY
Dir: Andreas Schnaas. Prod: Ralf Hess, Matthias Kerl.
Sc: Andreas Schnaas
Cast: Matthias Kerl, Ralf Hess, Mathias Abbes, Marc
Trinkhaus, Christian Biallas

A crashed airplane spills an AIDS cure that turns people into zombies in this living dead outing from German filmmaker, and *Violent Shit* auteur, Andreas Schnaas. A doctor and his assistant attempt to stop the catastrophe, but most of the film centres on a never-ending stream of micro-budget gore. A baby is pulled from its pram and ripped to pieces (just as well it's only a doll), a man regrets letting a zombie woman go down on him and a chainsaw is wielded with gleeful abandon.

ZOMBIE ABOMINATION: THE ITALIAN ZOMBIE MOVIE – PART 1
2008, USA
Dir: Thomas Berdinski. Prod: Thomas Berdinski.
Sc: Thomas Berdinski
Cast: Jeff Bromley, Laurie Beckeman, LaShelle Mikesell,
Daniel Grams, Keith Zahn

Copyright protected by the Michigan Militia ("Make a copy, we DARE YOU!") this micro-budget spaghetti gore homage begins with a zombie ghoul impaling a man's eyeball on a nail (hello Lucio Fulci) and goes downhill from there. It's barely coherent, runs for over three hours when accompanied by its companion piece *Zombie Atrocity 2: The Italian Zombie Movie, Part 2* (2009), and features zombies, splatter, feminist gas station attendants, aliens and characters named after Italian horror directors. It's a movie for gore fans made by a gore fan. Somehow, though, I don't think the Michigan Militia will be too busy...

ZOMBIE APOCALYPSE
1985, MEXICO
Original title: Cementerio del terror
Alternative title: Le cimetière da la terreur
Dir: Rubén Galindo Jr. Prod: Raúl Galindo. Sc: Rubén
Galindo Jr.
Cast: Hugo Stiglitz, Usi Velasco, Erika Buenfil, Edna
Bolkan

Long after El Santo hung up his mask for the last time, Mexican zombies kept on stumbling along. In cheesy *Zombie Apocalypse*, a bunch of horny teens steal a corspe from the morgue as a Halloween prank and accidentally resurrect it using a book of Satanic magic. It turns out the body is that of a serial killer, Devlon (José Gómez Parcero), who's eager to get back to work – killing the kids and terrorising a bunch of pre-teens who stumble into the murder scene. Director Rubén Galindo Jr. treats it like a slasher movie until the final reel, when Devlon calls up zombies from the cemetery. The rotting ghouls emerge from graves and red-lit tombs like rejects from *Thriller* (one of the kids even has a Michael Jackson jacket on). *Nightmare City* star Hugo Stiglitz plays the Dr Loomis style shrink on the killer's trail and gets to fend off zombies with a giant cross, which he wields like a bazooka. Eat your heart out El Santo.

ZOMBIE A-HOLE
2011, USA
Dir. Dustin Mills. Prod: Dustin Mills. Sc: Dustin Mills
Cast: Brandon Salkil, Josh Eal, Jessica Cook, Elizabeth
Aweiker, Melissa Blair

"There's a good-for-nothing bastard out there with

a face like hell and a smell to match." Ohio auteur Dustin Mills made this "blood and boobs B-movie" between his debut *Puppet Monster Massacre* and the delirious *Bath Salt Zombies*. It's grungy and rough around the edges, yet shot through with fun bad taste and inventive verve. In other words, it's a fantastic antidote to the deluge of brainless micro-budget ghoul flicks that simply cannibalise Romero. Frank Fulci (Josh Eal) and a mysterious one-eyed, one-handed woman named Mercy (Jessica Daniels) are on the trail of the eponymous pinstripe-suited ghoul who's slaughtering twin sisters – usually when they're buck naked. Riffing on 1970s exploitation flicks, Mills delivers a punk DIY treat. High points include miniature Haitian voodoo puppets, slithering intestines, energy-beam welders and a triple role for the wonderful Brandon Salkil (star of the later *Bath Salt Zombies*). The auteur himself has a bit part as Voodoo Bob, a hawker of magic artefacts with terrible negotiation skills.

ZOMBIE APOCALYPSE: REDEMPTION
2008, USA
Dir: Ryan Thompson. Prod: Ryan Thompson. Sc: Adam Goron, Ryan Thompson, Kenny James
Cast: Michael Empson, Kenny James, Michael Harthen, Kelly Knoll, Scott Watson

"The mortality rate is rising, friends, and you have no idea what's coming…" So growls a leather-jacketed Tom Savini lookalike (Kenny James) in this cheapo indie as he helps a couple of college dorks survive the impending z-apocalypse – an outbreak he's secretly connected to. Not to be confused with *2012: Zombie Apocalypse*, the Asylum movie starring Ving Rhames.

THE ZOMBIE ARMY
1991, USA
Dir: Betty Stapleford. Prod: John Kalinowski. Sc: Roger Scearce
Cast: Eileen Saddow, John Kalinowski, Steven Roberts, Jody Amato, Patrick Houtman

Two insane asylum inmates attack a platoon of American soldiers in this lame backyard epic. As they kill the soldiers, the pair reanimate them using electroshock treatment and set them on anyone else who's still living. Utter corn with a few ketchup-bottle gore effects thrown in whenever the interest flags… which is pretty often. The VHS box cover art shows a green-faced ghoul in Uncle Sam stars and stripes proclaiming "I want you for the zombie army" in a parody of the traditional recruitment posters. Memo to Betty Stapleford: zombie cinema does NOT want you!

ZOMBIE ASS: THE TOILET OF THE DEAD
2011, JAPAN
Original title: Zonbi asu
Dir: Noboru Iguchi. Prod: Masahiro Miyata, Naoya Narita, Mikihiko Hirata. Sc: Ao Murata, Jun Tsugita, Noboru Iguchi
Cast: Mayu Sugano, Asana Mamoru, Yuki, Danny, Kentaro Kishi

Tapeworms cause an outbreak of "shit zombies" in this Sushi Typhoon style "J-ombie" outing. Four friends led by Megumi (Arisa Nakamura) are trapped in the rural backwoods as the creatures – created by a renegade scientist Dr Tanaka (Kentaro Shimazu) – run amok. The tapeworms crawl out of the infected's rears, flailing around and occasionally attacking the living in sequences that owe a debt to Japan's tentacle-porn obsessions. It's ugly, gratuitous and so-bad-it's-good. A gold-plated turd.

ZOMBIE BABIES
2011, USA
Dir: Eamon Hardiman. Prod: Jackson Simpkins.
Sc: Eamon Hardiman
Cast: Kaylee Williams, Ruby Larocca, Ford Austin, Shawn C. Phillips, Missy Dawn

Volume is the key to success, believes backwoods abortionist Dr Burt (Brian Gunnoe). His annual abort-a-thons aim to bring in the big bucks from hard-up, up-the-duff patrons. Pity that his unhygienic storage of the aborted remains leads to an outbreak of mutant zombie foetuses… Made on a shoestring budget, this tasteless shock-horror comedy is a total abortion of a movie: terrible acting, shoddy CG and puppets so poorly animated you can literally see the hand behind them. It's cinematic moonshine: homemade, unrefined and lethal.

ZOMBIE BLOODBATH
1993, USA

Dir: Todd Sheets. Prod: Todd Sheets. Sc: Todd Sheets, Jerry Angell, Roger Williams
Cast: Chris Harris, Auggi Alvarez, Frank Dunlay, Jerry Angell, Cathy Metz

"This sounds like a trashy zombie flick to me… not reality!" Kansas backyard filmmaker Todd Sheets and his mates arm themselves with another camcorder for some more heavy-metal zombie action. This time a leak at a nuclear power plant causes the dead to walk. While a bunch of Homer Simpsons in hardhats sit around a boardroom shouting at each other about whether or not they should call Washington, Sheets wastes no time in getting to the action – the zombies are rampaging within the first minute! People's heads "melt" (translation: are drizzled in yoghurt and ketchup) and Kansas residents with bad mullets and big waistlines run, scream and barricade themselves in their homes as the zombies stumble around looking for flesh. There's no doubting Sheets's passion – it's just his ability that's lacking. Best bit: when our heroes stumble into a church looking for help and the congregation leap out of the pews – but they're already ghouls. Do zombies pray? Who knows?

ZOMBIE BLOODBATH 2: RAGE OF THE UNDEAD
1994, USA
Dir: Todd Sheets. Prod: Todd Sheets. Sc: Todd Sheets, Dwen Daggett
Cast: Dave Miller, Kathleen McSweeney, Gena Fischer, Nick Stodden, Jody Rovick

To misquote the great Oscar Wilde: to make one bad movie is a misfortune; to make a whole string of them is nothing short of careless. Todd Sheets returns from the SOV graveyard yet again for another zombie rampage. This time zombies, Satanists and a bunch of gun-toting escaped convicts are terrorising suburban Kansas, trapping a group of screaming locals in a deli as zombies put everyone on the menu. (Oh the irony. Stop! Stop!) Lots of amateur gore shots, mass zombie horde scenes scored by throbbing heavy metal, a bunch of zombie kids and plot development that barely gets beyond people shouting, abusing and killing one another for 90 minutes.

ZOMBIE BLOODBATH 3: UNDEAD ARMAGEDDON
2000, USA

Dir: Todd Sheets. Prod: Todd Sheets. Sc: Todd Sheets, Brian Eklund
Cast: Abe Dyer, Curtis Spencer, Blake Washer, Jolene Durrill, Jen Davis

"It's like *The Breakfast Club* meets Fulci's *Zombie*!!!" was Sheets's own modest assessment of his final film in the *Zombie Bloodbath* trilogy. This time around a bunch of kids stuck in detention are attacked by zombies from the future who come through a time warp. Apparently the corpses were reanimated by the US government to fight an alien invasion in the year 2017 – then dispatched into space when they proved too difficult to control. But we're not in space anymore, Toto. We're in Kansas… Sheets gives us cartoon CG space shuttles, robo-zombies and more character development than usual in what is, relatively speaking, a step up from his earlier efforts. Judging by the end credit outtakes, though, these movies are more fun to make than they are to watch.

ZOMBIE BRIGADE
1988, AUSTRALIA
Alternative title: Night Crawl, Zombie Commando
Dir: Carmelo Musca, Barrie Pattison. Prod: Carmelo Musca, Barrie Pattison. Sc: Carmelo Musca, Barrie Pattison
Cast: John Moore, Khym Lam, Geoff Gibbs, Leslie Wright, Bob Faggetter

In the Outback town of Lizard Gulley, an unscrupulous Mayor Ransom (Geoff Gibbs) bulldozes a Vietnam memorial to make way for a Japanese-funded theme park. In revenge, a druggy squad of vampire Aussie 'Nam vets in green fatigues and joke-store fangs crawl out of the rubble (apparently they were victims of a primitive Viet Cong bio-weapon during the war). As the town is quarantined, an Aboriginal witchdoctor (Michael Fuller) raises an army of much more orderly WWI and WWII zombie veterans to fight back. Scrappily shot on what looks like a budget barely big enough to keep the crew in Fosters for a weekend, this Ozploitation effort struggles to pinpoint its message among much small town bigotry and some very confused-looking monsters.

ZOMBIE CAMPOUT
2002, USA

Dir: Joshua D. Smith. Prod: Joshua D. Smith. Sc: Joshua D. Smith
Cast: Misty Orman, Tiffany Black, John M. Davis, Jeremy Schwab, Alecia Peterman

Despite being obsessed with boobs 'n' beer, this inoffensively goofy SOV movie from Dallas, Texas has a certain innocence about it – like a porno made by virgins. A bunch of kids on a lakeside campout watch as a meteor shower (rendered in hilariously rubbish CG) raise the dead from their graves to lumber around in classic fashion while moaning incessantly. A bunch of white-faced ghoul teens with panda eyes pluck a kid off a swing and devour her, then later snack on a Labrador ("Don't eat my dog, you Satanic bastards!"). Girls in Stars 'n' Stripes bikinis scream a lot, and a character with a copy of the script checks the page numbers and realises they're going to die. Ho, ho. It's all over in 90 lame and cheesy minutes.

ZOMBIE CHEERLEADING CAMP
2008, USA
Dir: Jon Fabris. Prod: Jon Fabris. Sc: Jon Fabris
Cast: Jamie Anne Browne, Chris White, Nicole Lewis, Greene, Brandy Blackmon

This amateurish zombie comedy begins with a poor-taste pictorial prologue set in Dachau, where Nazis experiment with a zombie serum called Vivo Victum. After the US military later dumps barrels of the serum in a cave in North Carolina, a zombified squirrel spreads the infection to a group of dumb hunters and a nearby cheerleading camp. Amateur dramatics, ugly production design and an array of stereotypes (the camp cheerleading teacher, the peeping-tom caretaker) make this far from memorable. Give me a C, give me an R, give me an A, give me a P. What have you got? Exactly.

ZOMBIE CHRONICLES
2001, USA
Dir: Brad Sykes. Prod: David S. Sterling. Sc: Garrett Clancy
Cast: Garrett Clancy, Emmy Smith, Beverly Lynn, Joseph Haggerty

Billed as being "in the tradition of *Tales from the Crypt* and *Dawn of the Dead*", director Brad Sykes's portmanteau *Zombie Chronicles* is really just another example of SOV filmmakers with too much time – and not enough talent – on their hands. Two ghoulish tales are linked by the wraparound story of a reporter investigating a series of bizarre rural legends. In the first tale, a Vietnam-era army sergeant is menaced by a recruit he killed in drill practice; in the second, a group of campers are plagued by some Wild West ghouls. Then the reporter discovers that she's about to become zombie chow… "Being dead rots" according to the DVD sleeve. It can't be as bad as watching this.

ZOMBIE COP
1991, USA
Dir: J.R. Bookwalter. Prod: Scott P. Plummer, J.R. Bookwalter. Sc: Matthew Jason Walsh
Cast: Michael Kemper, Ken Jarosz, James R. Black Jr., Bill Morrison, James Black

A policeman is killed on duty by a voodoo priest, but manages to shoot him just before he carks it. Both cop and priest come back from the dead to continue chasing each other through the streets for another 55 minutes before the credits (thankfully) roll. Bookwalter's follow-up to *The Dead Next Door* merely proves what most zombie fans already guessed: his limitless enthusiasm can't disguise his lack of technical competence.

ZOMBIE COMMANDO
2006, GERMANY
Dir: The Outtake Team [Michael Donner, Marco Goldhofer]. Prod: Melanie Bayersdorfer, Michael Donner, Marco Goldhofer, Alexander Goldhofer. Sc: The Outtake Team [Michael Donner, Marco Goldhofer]
Cast: Christian Ferschl, Thomas Werling, Marco Goldhofer, Michael Donner, Christian Sebesy

In Siberia ("Fucking cold" an on-screen subtitle helpfully informs us) a Z-virus is stolen from a secret laboratory and is soon turning everyone into ghouls. On the case is former commando Ash (co-director Michael Donner, who looks more like a campus bartender than a grizzled special-forces veteran). He's called out of retirement to track down the container holding the virus before it hits the black market and creates a global catastrophe. His team end up in some woods where a bunch of

Goth punks are also heading to a secret party. Another entry in the micro-budget Teutonic zombie tradition, *Zombie Commando* boasts a high splatter content (tree branch in the eye!) and loud death metal. The production values, though, are woeful. If you go down to the woods today... you might meet some talentless kids with a video camera.

ZOMBIE CREEPING FLESH
1980, ITALY/SPAIN

Original titles: Virus, Apocalipsis caníbal
Alternative titles: De Apocalyps der Levende Doden, L'apocalypse des morts vivants, Cannibal Apocalypsy, Hell of the Living Dead, Hell of the Living Death, L'inferno dei morti viventi, Night of the Zombies
Dir: Vincent Dawn [Bruno Mattei]. Prod: Sergio Cortona. Sc: Claudio Fragasso, José María Cunilles
Cast: Margit Evelyn Newton, Frank Garfield [Franco Garofalo], Selan Karay [Selhattin Karadag], Robert O'Neil [José Gras], José Luis Fonoll

The First World's plan to make the Third World eat itself doesn't quite succeed in this spaghetti gorefest. Instead of reducing the world's population, Operation Sweet Death produces cannibal zombies willing to eat anything that moves (particularly evil whitey) after an accident at one of its key facilities. Meanwhile, a SWAT team caught up in the New Guinea-set action is joined by a pair of roving reporters who are trying to get to safety. Shamelessly recycling archive jungle footage nicked from wildlife documentaries and the instantly recognisable *Dawn of the Dead* soundtrack, this is the Italian cycle at its most atrocious. It's a terrible, terrible movie. But that's all part of its... well, charmless charm.

ZOMBIE CULT MASSACRE
1997, USA

Dir: Jeff Dunn. Prod: Steve Losey, Jeff Dunn. Sc: Jeff Dunn
Cast: Bob Elkins, Lonzo Jones, Mike Botouchis, Lani Ford, Randy Rupp

The great redneck movie critic Joe Bob Briggs once described this little movie as "George Romero meets the Branch Davidians in Sturgis, South Dakota". It's as accurate a description as any. Zombies are caught between crazed bikers and Waco-style Jesus freaks in this ambitious amateur outing set in a backwater Midwest town. It's a promising set-up, and one that Dunn does his best to make the most of, throwing everything he can think of at the screen: big-breasted women having their latex cleavages chomped, characters getting mashed on hallucinogenic drugs, bikers zooming around on their crotch rockets and religious zealots muttering about the coming kingdom of Christ. All in all, it's an above-average redneck trashfest. Pass the moonshine.

ZOMBIE DEATH HOUSE
1988, USA

Dir: John Saxon. Prod: Nick Marino. Sc: William Selby, David S. Freeman, Kate Wittcomb
Cast: Dennis Cole, John Saxon, Michael Pataki, Ron O'Neal, Howard George

"This stuff makes the bubonic plague look like the common cold!" When an army scientist (John Saxon) uses a maximum security prison to test out his new super soldier virus, the inmates are turned into zombie-like raging maniacs. Caught up in the chaos is new fish Derek Keelor (Dennis Cole) who's been framed for his girlfriend's murder by a vicious mobster. Prolific genre actor Saxon directs – his first and only helming credit – but doesn't manage to do much with a limited budget and some ugly-looking production design. The zombies aren't dead, but they are angry and adrenalin-charged and rip people's heads off. It's chiefly notable for its on-the-nose AIDS panic as scenes of anal rape give way to nosebleeds (the first sign of infection) and viral contagion.

THE ZOMBIE DIARIES
2007, UK

Dir: Kevin Gates, Michael Bartlett. Prod: Kevin Gates, Michael Bartlett. Sc: Kevin Gates
Cast: Russell Jones, Craig Stovin, Jonnie Hurn, James Fisher, Anna Blades

"Watch the devastation unfold through the eyes of those who were there" is the sell for this, the first found footage zombie movie. Shot on camcorders in true low-budget style, this British effort gets kudos for preceding bigger, better takes on the same idea (notably George Romero's *Diary of the Dead* and Spanish franchise-starter *[REC]*. The film itself is pretty scrappy, shot over the course of several weekends by two journeymen filmmakers (Gates had worked as a freelance cameraman for ITV) and covering the outbreak of a bird flu-like pandemic that ends up turning the population of the UK into zombies. Following three different groups of survivors, beginning with a TV documentary crew who witness the first outbreak of the pandemic in the UK, it's a film of fits and starts. The digital video shoot uses lots of handheld "shakicam" to paper over the production's cracks, but the under-par screenplay isn't as impressive as the on-the-cheap special effects by Scott Orr.

ZOMBIE DOOMSDAY
2010, CANADA
Dir: Tom Townsend. Prod: Nick Bailey, Tom Townsend, Jonathan Ruckman, Lenny Goldsmith. Sc: Nick Bailey, Tom Townsend
Cast: Ron Bush, Johnny Alonso, Richard Cutting, Gary Ugarek, Tracy Teague

One of several found footage zombie movies to emerge post-*Diary of the Dead* (2008), *Zombie Doomsday* begins as a reality TV show following a washed up, big mouthed movie star Chad Worthington (Ron Bush) returning to his home town. The fractious visit turns sour: first he's caught in a restaurant with the film crew during a stick up, then, after a meteor hits, zombies trap him and the rest of the patrons inside. Apparently the actors didn't know about the zombie twist – which may explain why the more scripted first half of the movie works well, while the arrival of the zombies triggers a descent into mass shouting. The ghouls do very little – they can't even be bothered to break into the restaurant – which neuters the threat rather considerably. It comes with a standalone "making of" called *Another Zombie Movie*, which promises to teach aspiring filmmakers how it's done.

ZOMBIE DRIFTWOOD
2010, UK
Dir: Bob Carruthers. Prod: Bob Carruthers. Sc: Phil Eckstein
Cast: Brian Braggs, Peter Kosa, Rita Estevanovich, Karen Bridle, Colin G. Wilson

Why has no one ever done a zombies-on-a-cruise-ship movie? *Zombie Driftwood*'s DVD cover promises that much, with a shot of a run-aground cruise liner on a tropical shore. Sadly, the entirety of this bargain basement zom-com is actually shot in an isolated beach bar on Cayman. Four metalheads attending a concert by real-life British post-punk band October File are caught up in the mayhem as a cruise ship full of zombified tourists sinks off the coast. Since this is a post-pub zombie comedy, the ghouls crawl out of the sea to drink beer, cook up severed hands on the BBQ and wave around dollars ("They're tourists, sell them T-shirts!"). They even take over the island's TV station, leading to a stream of (allegedly) comic zombie TV skits. What could have been a B-movie answer to videogame *Dead Island* proves as washed up as its title suggests.

ZOMBIE DRILLER KILLER
2010, NORWAY
Original title: Mørke sjeler
Alternative title: Dark Souls
Dir: Mathieu Peteul, Cesar Ducasse. Prod: Cesar Ducasse, Mathieu Peteul, Maria Hvig-Gjelseth. Sc: Mathieu Peteul, Cesar Ducasse
Cast: Morten Rudå, Kyree Haugen Sydness, Isa Elise Broch, Karl Sundby, Johanna Gustavsson

Both the English-language title and the high-concept pitch for *Zombie Driller Killer* make it sound like a grindhouse reject: in Norway, a man in an orange boiler suit kills women with a power drill. A few hours later they come back from the dead as black goo spewing "zombies", their central nervous systems infected with some kind of pathogen. So far, so lurid. Except this bleak and wintry horror isn't a gory zombie apocalypse, but a Scandinavian oddity that mixes together *The X-Files* and *Driller Killer* with a soupçon of *The Stuff*, a dash of *Night of the Living Dead* and the tone of *The Girl with the Dragon Tattoo*. With the police uninterested, the father of one of the victims (Morten Rudå) takes matters into his own hands and uncovers a vast conspiracy with ties to Norway's oil industry. Forget what you expect from a film called *Zombie Driller Killer* – this strange, head-scratching movie is something else.

ZOMBIE ED
2013, USA

Dir: Ren Blood. Prod: Alionso Mercado, Stuart Page.
Sc: Ren Blood
Cast: William Cutting, Kelly Petering, Myles McLane,
Trista Robinson, Pedro Mendoza

Ed (William Cutting) has a beat-up car, a crappy
job, a shitty apartment and no hope of ever, ever
getting laid. What could be worse? Becoming a
zombie…? Made for pocket change, this unfunny
zom-com follows Ed as he joins the living dead
underclass. Zombie celebrity, equal-rights
demonstrations ("Zombies were human once
too!") and some veggie cookery fill in the gaps
where the gags should be. Maybe purple-haired,
panda-eyed Ed could just join the zombie support
group in *Last Rites of the Dead* and put us out of
our misery?

ZOMBIE EXS
2012, USA
Dir: George Smith. Prod: George Smith, Paul
Manoogian. Sc: Jean Cohen, George Smith
Cast: Alex Hammel-Shaver, Madison Hart, Scott
Keebler, Kendall Valerio, Brandy Bryant

Hapi Water is the latest bottled H_2O on the market,
infused with "a proprietary blend of herbs".
Problem is, it turns people into zombies. When
Zach (Alex Hammel-Shaver), a loser in love with a
string of "psycho exs", ends up on a TV dating
show sponsored by the manufacturers, he gets
more than he bargained for. In a cruel twist of fate,
the contestants on the show are all his ex girlfriends
– even crueller, they've been turned into decidedly
un-Hapi zombies. This zom-rom-com wears its
Simon Pegg and Edgar Wright influences right on
its sleeve – Videogames! *Shaun of the Dead*! Beer!
Scott Pilgrim! Nick Frost's American cousin! – but
lacks the polish or the heart. A ghoul girl on ghoul
girl interlude, some zombie crowdsurfing and the
ever-present whiff of unreconstructed masculinity
(check out the gun-store conversation) don't do it
many favours.

ZOMBIE FARM
2007, USA
Dir: B. Luciano Barsuglia. Prod: Barry Barsuglia, Hans
Hernke, Shawn Ness. Sc: B. Luciano Barsuglia
Cast: Bobby Field, Kimberly Fisher, Danielle De Luca,
Javier Morga, Christine Cowden

Execrable backyard nonsense as "Taliban
terrorists" put something nasty in the water in a
Californian town. Cannibal rednecks, mental FBI
agents, grumbling zombies and no-budget
production values add up to very little. "Don't
drink the water!" Try the Kool-Aid, instead.

THE ZOMBIE FARM
2010, USA
Dir: Ricardo Island. Prod: Frederico Lapenda, Blaine
McManus. Sc: Ricardo Islas
Cast: Adriana Cataño, Nadia Rowinsky, Khotan,
Monika Muñoz, Roberto Montesinos

When an abused wife consults "Mama Luna"
(Nadia Rowinsky) for advice on how to deal with
her violent husband, she's given a magic potion
that turns him into a zombie – who continues to
terrorise her (hmm, that didn't work well…).
Investigating the wild claims of dead men walking
are a quack psychic (Roberto Montesinos) and a
documentary filmmaker (Adriana Cataño). They
discover that Mama Luna has a farm of living dead
slaves working in the corn fields – the zombie
version of illegal migrants. Likeable, if undercooked,
this Mexican-American production is a rare
example of a zombie movie that returns to the
genre's roots in slavery and voodoo. But its
scattershot screenplay – covering domestic abuse,
comedy psychics, Latino identity and illegal
migrants – isn't helped by the decision to shoot on
location in Lafayette, Louisiana, of all places, nor
its wild shifts between drama and comedy. Not to
be confused with *The Zombie Farm* (2007).

ZOMBIE FLESH-EATERS
1979, ITALY
Original title: Zombi 2
Alternative titles: L'enfer des zombies, The Island of the
Living Dead, Sanguelia, Woodoo: Die Schreckensinsel
der Zombies, Zombie, Zombie 2
Dir: Lucio Fulci. Prod: Ugo Tucci, Fabrizio De Angelis.
Sc: Elisa Briganti
Cast: Tisa Farrow, Ian McCulloch, Richard Johnson, Al
Cliver [Pier Luigi Conti], Auretta Gay [Gregone]

On the Caribbean island of Matul, white doctor
David Menard (Richard Johnson) is trying to stem
the tide of cannibal zombies that are returning
from the dead. Arriving on the island are Anne and

reporter Peter West (Tisa Farrow and Ian McCulloch) who are looking for Anne's missing father. The pair soon find themselves under attack from the zombies. They eventually escape in a sailboat, only to discover that the zombie plague has spread across the globe. A genre classic that features a now legendary shark vs zombie fight.

ZOMBIEGEDDON
2003, USA
Dir: Chris Watson. Prod: Chris Watson, Andrew J. Rausch. Sc: Chris Watson
Cast: Brinke Stevens, Tom Savini, William Smith, Edwin Neal, Robert Z'Dar

Uwe Böll pops up at the start of this Troma movie to warn us that it is "a piece of shit". He's not wrong. With lashings of gore, gratuitous nudity and appearances from Tom Savini as Jesus Christ and Troma head honcho Lloyd Kaufman as a homophobic janitor, it's clear that seriousness isn't high on the agenda. Here Satan unleashes "decayed human beings" that eat the president and then go on the rampage. It's Troma, you know the drill.

ZOMBIE GENOCIDE
1993, IRELAND
Dir: Andrew Harrison. Prod: Andrew Harrison. Sc: Darryl Sloan
Cast: Andrew Harrison, Khris Carville, Darryl Sloan, Phil Topping

Having the distinction of being Ireland's first homemade zombie movie, Andrew Harrison's microbudget outing is an inoffensive but unremarkable trawl through the usual SOV archetypes that was shot over a couple of years and apparently edited "in-camera" using the stop and record buttons on the VCR. Kids return from a camping trip in Portadown to find that zombies have overrun the country. Having missed the evacuation, our heroes are stuck in the suburbs as the army prepares to detonate a nuclear bomb.

ZOMBIE HIGH
1987, USA
Alternative title: The School That Ate My Brain
Dir: Ron Link. Prod: Aziz Ghazal, Marc Toberoff. Sc: Tim Doyle, Aziz Ghazal, Elizabeth Passarelli
Cast: Virginia Madsen, Richard Cox, Kay Kuter, James

Wilder, Sherilynn Fenn

School's so boring the kids are being turned into zombies! Nope, that's sadly not the plot of this po-faced teen horror movie about a school where the vampire teachers turn students into zombie-like automatons so that they can feed off them. The zombies get straight As, dress in identical suits and ties and always turn up to class on time. That's enough to make new student Andrea (Virginia Madsen) smell a rat and start investigating. Disposable filler, but you've gotta love that alternative title.

ZOMBIE HOLOCAUST
1980, ITALY
Original title: Zombi Holocaust
Alternative titles: Doctor Butcher M.D., La terreur des zombies, Zombi holocausto, Zombies unter Kannibalen
Dir: Frank Martin [Marino Girolami]. Prod: Gianfranco Couyoumdjian, Fabrizio De Angelis. Sc: Romano Scandariato
Cast: Ian McCulloch, Alexandra Cole [Alexandra Delli Colli], Sherry Buchanan, Peter O'Neal, Donald O'Brien

Strange goings on at a New York hospital involving missing body parts prompt police detective Peter Chandler (Ian McCulloch) to investigate. Tracking the mystery out to Southeast Asia, he discovers a shocking secret about a mad scientist who's experimenting with brain surgery in the hope of increasing longevity. The experiments aren't going too well, though, which is why the island is awash with mindless zombie corpses who are almost as troubling as the indigenous cannibal savages.

ZOMBIE HONEYMOON
2004, USA
Dir: David Gebroe. Prod: David Gebroe, Christina Reilly. Sc: David Gebroe
Cast: Tracy Coogan, Graham Sibley, Tonya Cornelisse, David M. Wallace, Neal Jones

"In sickness and in health, remember?" A young couple's honeymoon is rudely interrupted when a zombie wanders out of the sea and vomits up some black stuff on the bridegroom, Danny (Graham Sibley). Before he can say "I don't" Danny's been turned into a walking corpse with a taste for human flesh that rapidly becomes uncontrollable.

Will his new wife Denise (Tracy Coogan) accept his sudden transformation into a ghoul and escape on their dream trip to Portugal? Or will his desire to eat everyone he meets lead to an instant divorce? This leftfield, committed indie charts what happens as Denise attempts to stand by her zombie as Danny becomes increasingly unstable. As a horror movie it lacks scares. But it works well as an allegory of love under duress – with zombiedom standing in for a terminal illness – powered by Coogan's engaging performance.

ZOMBIEHOOD
2013, UK

Dir: Steve Best. Prod: Susan Hayes. Sc: Steve Best
Cast: Andy Calderwood, Annabel Pidduck, Aston Fisher, Charlotte Handley, Craig Newson

No-budget British zombies rampage through town and countryside in this Nottingham-set horror that chugs along through the usual bickering survivor clichés as white-collar Dermott (Edward Nudd) and gun-carrying chav Sam (Tom Murton) lock horns about the best strategy to survive. Sticking to its proud British roots, the best set-piece involves cocky Sam swaggering into a pub full of corpses while the survivors load up on crisps – only to run for their lives when the corpses wake up and try to reclaim the packets of Ready Salted.

ZOMBIE HUNTER
2013, USA

Dir: Kevin King. Prod: K. King, Jenniger Kirkham, Chris Le. Sc: Kevin King, Kurt Knight
Cast: Martin Copping, Danny Trejo, Clare Niederpruem, Terry Guthrie, Jake Suazo

After a bright pink street drug called Natas (read it backwards) turns the world into ghouls, Hunter (Martin Copping) drives through a *Mad Max*-style desert wasteland to kill these "brainless globs of walking matter". On the road he meets a Catholic priest called Jesus (Danny Trejo) who's leading a band of refugees in search of safety. Director Kevin King clearly thinks he's the new Robert Rodriguez, and that *Mad Max* might have been better with zombies. He's wrong on both counts.

ZOMBIE HUNTERS
2008, CANADA

Alternative title: Hunting Grounds
Dir: Eric Bilodeau. Prod: Eric Bilodeau. Sc: Jonathan Gagne, Eric Bilodeau
Cast: Patrice Leblanc, Patric Baby, Marie-Eve Lemire, Luc Rivard, Emilie Gilbert-Gagnon

Eric Bilodeau's name is plastered all over this crappy French Canadian sci-fi epic – around nine credits including directing, writing, art direction and editing – so the buck stops with him. Set in a green-screened future that looks like it's been lifted from a mid-1990s videogame, *Zombie Hunters* follows a bunch of Quebec City citizens who escape their walled metropolis and head into the woods to illegally commune with nature. Meanwhile, at a secret military lab regenerative medical research accidentally reanimates the dead. Dodgy VFX and green-screen work, an amateurish script and a trite "reality vs the virtual" theme don't add much.

ZOMBIE ISLAND MASSACRE
1984, USA

Dir: John N. Carter. Prod: David Broadnax.
Sc: William Stoddard, Logan O'Neill
Cast: David Broadnax, Rita Jenrette, Tom Cantrell, Diane Clayre Holub, Ian McMillan

This cheap little effort is dishonest at best as it lures eager audiences into thinking that the reason why a bunch of unlikeable American tourists are getting stalked 'n' slashed in the Caribbean is because they're being pursued by a zombie. Actually, all they've really fallen foul of are some nasty Colombian drug dealers. There's only one zombie in the film, who makes the briefest of appearances in a voodoo ceremony. Pure drivel.

THE ZOMBIEJÄGER
2005, SWEDEN

Dir: Jonas Wolcher. Prod: Jonas Wolcher, Magnus Hedqvist. Sc: Petter Hörberg
Cast: Martin Brisshäll, Nick Holmquist, Christian van Caine, Margareta Strand, Erich Silva

Sweden's first zombie movie stumbles out of the gate like an extended music video for a thrash electronica band. It's pretty plotless – a trio of mercs are hired to help contain a zombie outbreak in Gothenberg. Most of the film is a series of dialogue-free action sequences on the city's streets in which ghouls are shot in the head and used as target practise for shuriken throwing stars. The "less cool than they think they are" heroes eventually track down the skull-faced necromancer bringing the dead back to life. Silly, grim and totally witless, it looks like it was conceived down the pub and shot during the next day's hangover. The fact that this DIY effort found international distribution is either a damning indictment of the Swedish film industry… or a sign that distributors will buy anyting with zombies in it.

ZOMBIE LAKE
1980, FRANCE/SPAIN
Original titles: El lago de los muertos vivientes, Le lac des morts vivants
Alternative title: Zombies Lake
Dir: J.A. Laser [Julián de Lesoeur & Jean Rollin].
Prod: Daniel Lesoeur. Sc: A. L. Mariaux [Marius Lesoeur]
Cast: Howard Vernon, Pierre Escourrou, Robert Foster [Antonio Mayans]

More Nazi zombies in this Eurociné trashfest as a bunch of German soldiers – executed by the resistance and dumped in a lake – come back to life to prey on nude female bathers and the odd Frenchman. Rollin directs this as though it's one of his sensuous vampire tales, trailing off into misty-eye nonsense as a German zombie officer pays a visit to his daughter in the town. Thankfully the director rallies himself for the finale in which the ghouls are napalmed to a crisp.

THE ZOMBIE KING
2012, UK
Dir: Aidan Belizaire. Prod: Rebecca-Clare Evans, Jennifer Chippendale. Sc: Rebecca-Clare Evans, Jennifer Chippendale, George McCluskey
Cast: Edward Furlong, Corey Feldman, George McCluskey, David McClelland, Michael Gamarano

The Zombie King opens with a postman, a milkman and a parking warden fleeing zombies. So far, so quintessentially British. But in a triumph of totally random casting it then ropes in Edward Furlong (troubled, former child star of *Terminator 2*) and Corey Feldman (troubled, former child star of *The Lost Boys*). The down-on-their-luck US

actors look like they're shooting another movie that's been artlessly spliced into this otherwise pointless tale of zombies overrunning the British countryside. Furlong is a grieving widower who turns to black magic to bring back his dead wife and sparks a zombie apocalypse; Feldman is the voodoo god in bondage dress who talks in doggerel ("Seven souls for the seventh day, just a few hours and you'll have your way"). Both of them look more like ravaged, wasted zombies than any of the walking dead extras – and neither has enough star wattage to save this from the DVD bargain bin.

ZOMBIELAND
2009, USA
Dir: Ruben Fleischer. Prod: Gavin Polone. Sc: Rhett Reese, Paul Wernick
Cast: Woody Harrelson, Jesse Eisenberg, Emma Stone, Abigail Breslin, Amber Heard

The first smash-hit zombie comedy, *Zombieland* assaulted the box office with a wanton trail of destruction and a Bill Murray cameo. It earned a mint and arguably paved the way for a very different zombie blockbuster… *World War Z*.

ZOMBIE MASSACRE
2012, ITALY
Alternative title: Apocalypse Z
Dir: Marco Ristori, Luca Boni. Prod: Uwe Böll.
Sc: Marco Ristori, Luca Boni
Cast: Christian Boeving, Mike Mitchell, Ivy Marshall Corbin, Jon Campling, Tara Cardinal

"There is no hope" claims the poster, right above the words: "Uwe Böll presents *Zombie Massacre*". A subliminal warning? After acting as distributor on *Eaters: Rise of the Dead* (2010), Böll teams up with Italian filmmakers Marco Ristori and Luca Boni for a second time – and the results are patchy to say the least. When the US accidentally releases a zombie-creating bio-weapon in Eastern Europe, the White House decides to send in a group of specialists led by Jack Stone (Christian Boeving) to blow up a nuclear power plant and cover their tracks. Böll makes a cameo as the president of the United States. Yes, seriously.

ZOMBIE NATION
2005, USA

Dir: Ulli Lommel. Prod: Nola Roeper, Ulli Lommel.
Sc: Ulli Lommel
Cast: Gunter Ziegler, Brandon Dean, Axel
Montgomery, Phil Lander, Martina Bottesch

A maniac cop abducts and kills women who are driving irresponsibly in this bargain basement outing from director Ulli Lommel, auteur behind such gutter trash as *Prozzie* and *D.C. Sniper*. It's so bad it's beyond words. A bunch of Haitian voodoo priestesses inexplicably manage to make the poor girls come back from the dead in the final third, thanks to a strange ritual that seems to involve one woman being sexually assaulted by a tarantula (maybe I just misunderstood the shot). Meanwhile, the cop has demented flashbacks to his tortured upbringing in an insane asylum. The zombies are barely worthy of the name – the only sign the girls are dead is that their mascara seems to have run. Maybe it's not Maybelline.

ZOMBIE NIGHT
2004, CANADA
Dir: David J. Francis. Prod: David J. Francis, Amber L. Francis. Sc: David J. Francis
Cast: Danny Ticknovich, Dwayne Moniz, Steve Curtis, Sandra Segovic, Andrea Ramolo

"Hey, we don't need any internal fighting here! You two need to start getting along." What would a micro-budget zombie movie be without infighting? You certainly couldn't expect the subpar ghouls in this subpar horror to carry the movie. Beginning with Pakistan and India nuking each other and a wave of blood-spewing zombies stumbling across the Earth, this Canadian indie never even tries to be more than an exercise in box ticking. Bickering survivors? Check. Rednecks tormenting zombies? Check. Attempted rape? Check. The living more dangerous than the dead? Check, check, check. David J. Francis went on to make *Awakening: Zombie Night 2* (2006).

ZOMBIE NIGHTMARE
1987, USA
Dir: Jack Bravman. Prod: Pierre Grisé. Sc: David Wellington
Cast: Jon Mikl Thor, Adam West, Tia Carrere, Manuska Rigaud, Shawn Levy

A carload of teenagers run down and kill a high school baseball player, show no remorse to his mother, and eventually end up suffering at his zombified hands when a voodoo priestess brings him back from the grave. Jon Mikl Thor, one-time front man for imaginatively titled rock band Thor, is the stiff who takes revenge while a police captain played by Adam "Batman" West tries to work out what the hell is going on. The scene in which the loudly moaning ghoul chases a scantily-clad blond through a deserted gymnasium then batters her to death with a baseball bat says it all really – despite the fact that he's so beaten up that his feet don't even point the right way, she's still too dumb to be able to outrun him. Some people are just asking to be killed by zombies.

ZOMBIE NINJA GANGBANGERS
1998, USA
Alternative titles: Bangers, Zombie Ninja Bangers
Dir: Jeff Centauri. Prod: Ross Marshall. Sc: Daryl Carstensen
Cast: Kitten Natividad, Stephanie Beaton, Jeff Centauri, Michael Haboush, Ross Marshall

The first but sadly not the last zombie rape movie (hello, *Deadgirl*), this disturbingly misogynistic film tries to masquerade as cheesy nonsense. The basic premise is that stripper Stephanie Beaton is attacked by randy gangbanging zombies and enlists the help of a friendly bar owner (former Miss Nude Universe Kitten Natividad) and a mad scientist to create a zombie ninja to protect herself. What's so troubling about this film is the gleeful delight that the filmmakers take in it excesses. Bare breasts, gyrating strippers and pole dancers obviously appeal to the usual exploitation market, but the interminable zombie rape scenes in which Beaton is shamelessly abused are completely indefensible.

ZOMBIE RAMPAGE
1991, USA
Dir: Todd Sheets. Prod: Louis Garrett. Sc: Todd Sheets, Erin Kehr
Cast: Dave Byerly, Erin Kehr, Stanna Bippus, Beth Belanti, Ed Dill

Kansas City backyard auteur Todd Sheets has gamely admitted that some of his movies are "unwatchable piece of trashola". That's certainly a fitting tagline for this interminably atrocious outing in which he tries out as many camera tricks as he can think of (like shooting an argument between two characters from underneath them – did he really think seeing up their noses would add tension?). The plot is rudimentary: a suited Kansas City gang leader (Dave Byerly) raises the dead from their graves with the help of some voodoo magic he gets out of a paperback. Sheets and his crew cook up some graphic, and mostly unconvincing, DIY gore shots: the funniest scene has zombies attacking a mom with a pushchair and ripping the "baby", a plastic toy doll, out of its seat. Overall, this is ugly, technically incompetent and totally depressing.

ZOMBIE SELF-DEFENSE FORCE
2005, JAPAN
Original title: Zonbi jieitai
Dir: Naoyuki Tomomatsu. Prod: Masami Teranishi.
Sc: Naoyuki Tomomatsu, Chisato Oogawara
Cast: Miyû Watase, Mihiro Taniguchi, Kenji Arai, Yû Machimura, Masayuki Hase

A UFO crashes in woodland near Mount Fuji, making the dead walk. Trapped soldiers, yakuza gangbangers and a J-pop singer (Mihiro Taniguchi) shelter in a rural house. There they fend off shuffling ghouls and a zombie newborn with big teeth, red ghoul-vision and a cunning habit of luring in its victims by sitting in a corner and sobbing. Later, a fascist general with a rising-sun headband returns to life as a ghoul to spout rightwing, anti-American rhetoric – something that's undercut by just how inept the Japanese military prove to be during the zombie outbreak (with the exception of one female, rather special, soldier). Scrappily made and frenetically paced, this is the first part of a loose "Nihombie" trilogy that includes *Attack Girls Swim Team Vs The Undead* (2007) and *Rika: The Zombie Killer* (2008). The title is a reference to the JSDF – the Japan Self Defense Force established after WWII. As a parody of Japanese nationalism, it's all a bit odd.

ZOMBIE STRIPPERS
2007, USA
Dir: Jay Lee. Prod: Angela Lee, Andrew Golov, Larry

Schapiro. Sc: Jay Lee
Cast: Jenna Jameson, Robert Englund, Roxy Saint, Penny Drake, Whitney Anderson

They're zombies. They're strippers. They're played by porn stars. Why did no one think of this before? Snort too much coke before your Friday afternoon marketing meeting and you could end up with this: a movie designed simply to lift money from the pockets of horny horror fans. The military zombie virus MacGuffin turns the gals into skillful pole dancers with a taste for flesh and the men into mindless zombies. Sadly, writer-director Jay Lee tries to convince us he's not mindless and is actually above it all by shoehorning in some yakking about existential philosophy. Proof that adding Nietzsche to your T&A movie doesn't really add very much at all. Its only moment of wit is blaming the entire outbreak on George W. Bush's (fictional) fourth term.

ZOMBIE: THE RESURRECTION
1997, GERMANY
Dir: Holger Breiner, Torsten Lakomy. Prod: Holger Breiner, Torsten Lakomy Sc: Holger Breiner
Cast: Oliver van Balen, Franz Horn, Tanja Reitter, Sandra Wendt, Holger Breiner

More German zombie splatter. Men old enough to know better don babygro chem suits and fight zombies in an abandoned building while Euro Rave thuds on the soundtrack. Every death scene lasts three times longer than it should, while fake blood is pumped out of hoses badly hidden under zombie extras' T-shirts. And that's just the 15-minute opening credits sequence. Soon we're in the year 2017, where zombies are running amok after WWIII unleashed bio-weapons that rose the dead (or something). This backyard SOV horror comes without subtlety and runs for 60 very, very boring minutes. There's little plot to speak of, just a lot of laughable amateur gore effects – though even more cringeworthy are the inappropriate music choices, the skinny-dipping heroine (Tanja Reitter) and the orgasmic thrill the badly directed zombie extras seem to get from eating flesh.

ZOMBIE TOWN
2006, USA
Alternative title: Night of the Creeps 2: Zombie Town

Dir: Damon LeMay. Prod: Zorinah Juan, Mary Beth French. Sc: Damon LeMay

Cast: Adam Hose, Brynn Lucas, Dennis Lemoine, Philip Burke, Steve Nasuta

Slithering parasites turn the inhabitants of a Vermont town into cannibal ghouls. Shot on a shoestring like a modern day Ed Wood movie, this pretty innocuous, pretty pointless flick has a car mechanic (Adam Hose) leading his redneck town mates against the zombies. Practical effects squirt ketchup bottles with abandon, while Dennis Lemoine's cynical Randy nabs the few vaguely funny lines: "It's like a Goddamn Grandma massacre in here!" Also known as *Night of the Creeps 2: Zombie Town* – a comparison which does *Zombie Town* no favours at all.

ZOMBIE TOXIN
1998, UK
Alternative title: Homebrew
Dir: Tom J. Moose. Prod: Tom J. Moose. Sc: Tom J. Moose, Adrian Ottiwell, Robert Taylor
Cast: Robert Taylor, Adrian Ottiwell, Tom J. Moose, Lee Simpson

"*Monty Python* meets *Dawn of the Dead*" is the woefully inaccurate promise adorning the video sleeve art of this no-budget British effort. Talk about being cheated. It's actually more like "Roy Chubby Brown vs the Zombies" – a stream of scatological gags with a few ghouls thrown in for good measure. It starts with a fishing hook pulling out an eyeball, then proceeds to Hitler and his buddy "Gerbils" (aka Goebbels) plotting to use the toxin of the title to turn wine drinkers into zombies. Be prepared for the close-up of a spotty bum squirting out "zombie diarrhoea" into a ghoul's mouth. Think *Bad Taste* without the wit.

ZOMBIE UNDEAD
2010, UK
Dir: Rhys Davies. Prod: Rhys Davies. Screenplay: Kris Tearse
Cast: Ruth King, Kris Tearse, Barry Thomas, Rod Duncan, Christopher J. Herbert

Zombies feel no pain, which must be a blessing considering how many crappy movies they're roped into. Z-clichés get box-ticked after a terrorist bomb turns Leicester into *corps cadavres* central, trapping survivors in a local hospital. Smothered in ketchup, the non-professional cast stumble around much like their living dead adversaries. Pity no one had the nous to make the two ghouls in Burberry caps the stars. Chavs Vs Zombies? Now that's a movie…

ZOMBIE VS. NINJA
1987, HONG KONG
Alternative title: Zombie Revival: The Super Master
Dir: Charles Lee [Godfrey Ho Jeung Keung]. Prod: Joseph Lai, Betty Chan. Sc: Benny Ho
Cast: Pierre Kirby, Edowan Bersmea, Dewey Bosworth, Thomas Hartham, Patrick Frbezar

"That kid's useless! He can't even beat a zombie!" What better way to learn martial arts than practicing against a never-ending stream of zombies? The Mexican wrestling movie meets Eastern kung fu in this laborious tale of an undertaker's assistant who wants to avenge the death of his father at the hands of a gang of thieves. Prolific Hong Kong filmmaker Godfrey Ho delivers an incoherent chopsocky flick that appears to contain interspliced footage from two, or maybe more, different productions. In the slapstick martial arts section, Ethan (Elton Chong) gets trained in the way of kung fu by his buck-toothed peasant master, who magically resurrects a few stiff-limbed, robotic zombies as sparring partners for his protégé before he faces the villain he must kill. In the other footage, a bunch of Caucasian guys wearing garish pyjamas and headbands emblazoned with the word "NINJA" talk about some stolen gold and occasionally fight each other with swords. Don't expect to see any fight scenes of zombies vs. ninjas. Pah.

ZOMBIE WARS
2007, USA
Alternate titles: War of the Dead, War of the Living Dead
Dir: David A. Prior. Prod: James Brinkley, Bill Ferrell, David A. Prior, Ted Prior. Sc: David A. Prior
Cast: Adam Stuart, Alissa Koenig, Jim Marlow, Kristi Renee Pearce, Jonathon Badeen

Opening with a risible special-effects shot of the Earth from space that could be straight out of

Captain Kirk-era *Star Trek*, *Zombie Wars* possesses an ambition that its quick 'n' cheap, no-frills production can't keep up with. Fifty years after the world has been overrun with zombies, a few isolated bands of self-styled soldiers – including two wisecracking brothers (Adam Stuart, Jim Marlow) – lead the resistance from ramshackle scout camps. In a nod to *Planet of the Apes*, it turns out the zombies have learnt how to communicate with one another and are breeding mute human slaves for food. Could it be that the zombies are getting... *smart*? If they are, they're on their own in this dumb outing from one-man clag factory David A. Prior – best-known for churning out straight-to-video 1980s action movies like *Deadly Prey*, *Mankillers* and *Operation Warzone*.

ZOMBIE WOMEN OF SATAN
2009, UK
Dir: Warren Speed, Steve O'Brien. Prod: Warren Speed, Steve O'Brien. Sc: Warren Speed
Cast: Victoria Hopkins, Warren Speed, Christian Steel, Seymour Mace, Pete Bonner

Shot in England's northeast, this (s)crappy low-budget horror overdoses on kinky carnival trappings. It follows a burlesque circus troupe called Fleshorama – a kind of crap Cirque du Soleil – who end up on a remote farm. There a mad doctor is experimenting on scantily clad female cult members, turning them into zombies with a serum that makes them bleed from their nipples. If there was a joke here, it would have worn thin after the first five minutes.

ZOMBIES
2006, USA
Alternate title: Wicked Little Things
Dir: J.S. Cardone. Prod: J.S. Cardone, Boaz Davidson, Anton Hoeger, Danny Lerner, David Varod. Sc: Ben Nedivi
Cast: Lori Heuring, Scout Taylor-Compton, Chloë Grace Moretz, Geoffrey Lewis, Ben Cross

Originally lined up for Tobe Hooper to direct, this ghostly zombie movie ended up in the hands of J.S. Cardone – the unambitious, if prolific, screenwriter behind *The Scare Hole* and the *8MM2* remake. In retrospect, Hooper might have been the better choice, since a lot of *Zombies* is reminiscent of the family-in-peril creepiness of *Poltergeist*. It certainly isn't much of a zombie movie: a widow (Lori Heuring) and her two daughters move to the Pennsylvania woods (actually Bulgaria) and find that their new house is built over an old mine where kiddie miners were buried alive circa 1913. Pretty soon the white-faced, black-eyed "zombie miner geeks" are queuing up en masse to attack the living with pickaxes and munch on their entrails. Indebted more to *The Ring* and *The Grudge* than Romero, it's a zombie movie in name only.

ZOMBIES GONE WILD
2007, USA
Dir: G.R. Prod: Heidi Meier. Sc: Gary Robert
Cast: Giselle Lopez, Dave Competello, Chris Saphire, Dominique Rochelle, Summer Morgan

Great title – amateur hour movie. Three guys are on Spring Break looking for hot girls but instead end up trapped in 100+ minutes of improvised "comedy" and production values so bad the whole thing looks as if it's been shot by a bunch of five-year olds on a Fisher Price camcorder. One of the actors later wrote a review on IMDb.com warning the public not to buy it and giving some insight into the true horror of working in Z-cinema.

ZOMBIES OF MASS DESTRUCTION
2008, USA
Alternative title: ZMD: Zombies of Mass Destruction
Dir: Kevin Hamedani. Prod: John Sinno. Sc: Ramon Isao, Kevin Hamedani
Cast: Janette Armand, Doug Fahl, Cooper Hopkins, Bill Johns, Russell Hodgkinson

Filmmaker Kevin Hamedani, an Iranian-American, based this satirical comedy on his own experience of being treated with suspicion by his neighbours after the 9/11 attacks. When a zombie outbreak hits Port Gamble, WA – a small town in the Pacific Northwest – the inhabitants find old prejudices coming to the fore. Iranian-American Frida (Janette Armand) is mistaken for both an Iraqi and a terrorist – and her neighbours tie her up and hammer nails into her feet to stop her escaping. Meanwhile, a gay couple (Doug Fahl and Cooper Hopkins) take shelter in an evangelical church, only to be accused of doing the devil's work by the pastor. Copious OTT gore buffers the over-talky drama and lack of guffaws, but no amount of decapitations or eyeball-swallowing can detract from the leaden liberal pontificating

ZOMBIES OF MORA TAU
1957, USA

Alternative title: The Dead That Walk
Dir: Edward Cahn. Prod: Sam Katzman. Sc: Raymond T. Marcus [Bernard Gordon]
Cast: Gregg Palmer, Allison Hayes, Autumn Russell, Joel Ashley, Morris Ankrum

An expedition of treasure hunters head out to West Africa in search of a 19th-century ship called the *Susan B*, which sank off the coast. The ship is rumoured to contain diamonds stolen from the local native tribes. Unfortunately, the zombified remains of the original crew guard the wreck. They rise from the watery depths and attack the American adventurers until the gems are thrown back into the sea.

ZOMBIES OF THE STRATOSPHERE
1952, USA

Alternative title: Satan's Satellites
Dir: Fred C. Brannon. Prod: Franklin Adreon.
Sc: Ronald Davidson
Cast: Judd Holdren, Aline Towne, Wilson Wood, Lane Bradford, Stanley Waxman

Don't be fooled by the title: there aren't any zombies in this old Republic serial, which was stitched together into a feature-length movie and renamed *Satan's Satellites* in 1958. Dastardly Martians are planning to knock the Earth out of its orbit so the red planet can take its place closer to the sun. Can our intrepid heroes – aided by Leonard Nimoy's turncoat alien – defuse the situation in time? You betcha.

ZOMBIES OF WAR
2006, USA

Alternative title: Horrors of War
Dir: Peter John Ross, John Whitney. Prod: Peter John Ross, Sean Reid, Philip R. Garrett. Sc: Peter John Ross, John Whitney, Philip R. Garrett
Cast: Jon Osbeck, Joe Lorenzo, Daniel Alan Kiely, C. Alec Rossel, Chip Kocel

American soldiers in WWII encounter dog-like human zombies created by Nazi science. Shot in Ohio for little money, *Zombies of War* is surprisingly ambitious, and the non-horror war scenes benefit from a range of authentic military vehicles and artillery pieces to deliver a *Band of Brothers* vibe. Elsewhere, though, directors Peter John Ross and John Whitney push the VFX budget to breaking point: CG planes crash unconvincingly and the film's ghouls – zombie/werewolf hybrids and red-skinned, eyeless stormtroopers – are rather laughable. A triumph of logistics over storytelling.

ZOMBIES ON BROADWAY
1945, USA

Alternative titles: Loonies on Broadway
Dir: Gordon Douglas. Prod: Ben Stoloff. Sc: Lawrence Kimble
Cast: Wally Brown, Alan Carney, Bela Lugosi, Anne Jeffreys, Sheldon Leonard

PR agents Wally Brown and Alan Carney are instructed by their gangster boss to find a real walking corpse for his nightclub The Zombie Hut. Taking a trip out to San Sebastian, they encounter Bela Lugosi's mad scientist who has created a zombie serum. Mayhem ensues, allegedly. About as funny as cholera.

ZOMBIES: THE BEGINNING
2007, ITALY

Alternative title: Zombi: La creazione
Dir: Bruno Mattei. Prod: Gianni Paolucci. Sc: Antonio Tentori, Gianni Paolucci
Cast: Yvette Yzon, Alvin Anson, Paul Holme, James Gregory Paolleli, Robert B. Johnson

The second part of Bruno Mattei's filmmaking swansong sees a welcome return for the director's typically ragged ghouls. Make no mistake: it's a terrible piece of schlock, but no one does gut-muncher schlock like the Italians of Mattei's generation. Having survived *Island of the Living Dead* (2006), Sharon (Yvette Yzon) is forced to return to sea by an evil corporation when contact is lost with a nearby island. Before you can shout "*Aliens* ripoff!" she's running around with a bunch of special forces soldiers while zombies emerge from the shadows. She eventually discovers a weird zombie queen lair where a brain in a vat is doing terrible things to pregnant women and ghoul kids with conical heads stumble around. It's stupid, cheap and totally bonkers. Mattei died during production, and as legacies go, this is pretty fitting. As the end credits put it: "Ciao Bruno".

ZOMBIES VS STRIPPERS
2012, USA
Dir. Alex Nicolaou. Prod. Charles Band, Rick Short, John Hackert. Sc. Kent Roudebush, Alex Nicolaou, Nick Francomano
Cast: Circus-Szalewski, Eve Mauro, Victoria Levine, Adriana Sephora, Nihilist Gelo

At the Tough Titty, a sleazy dive of a strip club in LA, standards are falling faster than G-strings. Sleazy owner Spider (Circus-Szalewski) is about to sell up. His strippers are antsy about missing out on a promised trip to the tanning salon, and his bouncer is about as tough as jello. Just when things couldn't get any worse, zombies take over the city. As survivors take shelter in the bar ("the best titties in the city") Spider hikes his cover charge, but he can't keep the living dead from taking a bite out of his business. Low-budget and low-brow, this offering from Full Moon Productions follows their standard MO for cheap 'n' cheerful horror. Lots of strippers jiggle their jiggly bits and a stoner tries to stop a zombie by offering him a toke on joint. Stupid? Yep, that sums this up.

ZOMBIES! ZOMBIES! ZOMBIES!
2007, USA
Alternative title: Strippers Vs Zombies
Dir: Jason Matthew Murphy. Prod: Tony Giordano, Jason Matthew Murphy. Sc: Tony Giordano
Cast: Lyanna Tumaneng, Jessica Barton, Hollie Winnard, Anthony Headen, Juliet Reeves

Put this on a double bill with *Zombie Strippers*… Or even on a triple bill with *Zombies Vs Strippers*… When a bunch of top-heavy exotic dancers find themselves trapped in a zombie apocalypse caused by contaminated crack rocks, they take shelter in their strip club, the Grindhouse. Among the dead are the strippers' mortal enemies the local hookers, who are quickly turned into vomiting, ravenous monsters. As misleading exploitation movie titles go, it's criminally short on both stripping and convincing zombie action, papering over the cracks with a series of lame gags. Worst offenders are the scenes featuring pimp Johnny "Backhand" Vegas (Anthony Headen) who does a bad Samuel L. Jackson impersonation, shouting, "I'm tired of these motherfucking zombies in this motherfucking strip club."

ZOMBIETHON
1986, USA
Dir/Prod/Sc: Ken Dixon
Cast: K. [Karrene] Janyl Caudle, Tracy Burton, Paula Singleton, Janelle Lewis

When they're not eating people, what kind of movies do the living dead like to watch? Zombie flicks of course! In this lame compilation reel of snippets from other movies, director Ken Dixon shoves a group of ghouls in a cinema and lets them watch scenes from *Zombie Lake*, *The Astro-Zombies* and *Oasis of the Zombies*. You almost feel sorry for the poor creatures.

ZOMBIEZ
2004, USA
Dir: ZWS. Prod: ZWS. Sc: ZWS
Cast: Jenicia Garcia, Jakeem Sellers, Randy Clark, Raymond Spencer, Gladimir Georges

Zombiez. See what they did therez? That's about the limit of innovation in this no-budget slice of modern blaxploitation as Josephine (Jenicia Garcia) suddenly meets meat-cleaver-wielding zombies loping about the streets of the 'hood in broad daylight. Apparently they're the living dead footsoldiers of the Doctor (Jakeem Sellers), a shady businessman with a meat packing business, or something. It's hard to say because the movie is about as coherent as a drunk on the third day of a four-day bender. The ghouls act more like gangbangers than zombies, Josephine breaks her ankle then forgets she's wounded, on-screen title cards define esoteric words like "Fear" and "Despair" and the Doctor fires his gun at a man dressed in a chicken outfit just, y'know, for fun. A movie so bad it could put you in a coma… Zombiezzzzzzzzz.

ZOMBI KAMPUNG PISANG!
2007, MALAYSIA
Alternative title: Zombies of Banana Village
Dir: Mamat Khalid. Prod: n/a. Sc: n/a

Cast: Awie, A.C. Mizal, Que Haidar, Sofi Jikan, Ezlynn

The English-language title – *Zombies of Banana Village* – gives a good sense of the zaniness of this Malaysian zom-com. Our heroes are a bunch of slackers whose village is overrun by porridge-faced, talking zombie ghouls in sarongs and headbands. Atmospherically set at night in a jungle village surrounded by smoke machines, it sees our heroes picking up burning torches to fend off the sentient ghouls as they form a political, living dead collective. There's a lot of broad comedy: a chubby kid blasting zombies with a shotgun, a rock band turning up in the middle of the chaos and the ghouls mimicking Michael Jackson. It apparently did gangbuster business at the Malaysian box office, presumably thanks to its satirical digs at the government (I can't comment on that since I couldn't find a version with English subtitles!).

ZOMBIO
1999, BRAZIL

Dir: Petter Baiestorf. Prod: Cesar Souza. Sc: Petter Baiestorf
Cast: Cesar Souza, Denise V., Coffin Souza, Rose De Andrade, Claudia De Sord

Shot on video, scored by death metal and running for only 45 minutes, *Zombio* was Brazil's first foray into the zombie genre. As far as I know it doesn't exist in a print with English subtitles, but its gloopy gore speaks every horror fan's language. When an amorous couple travel out to an isolated spot for some intimacy, they're attacked by zombies summoned by a scantily clad witch. She feeds the ghouls with milky fluid from her veins, then transforms into a tentacled creature that would give H.P. Lovecraft nightmares. Less interested in plotting than body trauma, this goes overboard on cheap gore: a severed head is used to showcase some Pelé footballing skills, and, more disturbingly, the heroine stabs a long-dead walking corpse with an empty beer bottle and watches it fill up with brown grue, only to have it poured on her face a few minutes later. There probably aren't enough antibiotics in the world to save her…

ZOMBREX: DEAD RISING SUN
2010, JAPAN

Dir: Keiji Inafune. Prod: Yusaku Toyoshima. Sc: William Winckler
Cast: Taiki Yoshida, Hiroshi Yazaki, Sei Ando, Shohei Suzuki, Michi Nishijima

Produced by Japanese videogame giant Capcom and released in eight parts on Xbox Live, this was a promotional tie-in for the games series *Dead Rising*. It follows wheelchair-bound George (Taiki Yoshida) and his brother (Hiroshi Yazaki) as they shelter in a warehouse from the ghouls outside. Although they're harassed by street thugs, they also discover that there's a new drug – "Zombrex" – that can stop the infection spreading. Directed by Capcom exec and game maker Keiji Inafune (creator of *Mega Man*), this looks cheap and nasty. Awful dubbing and the decision to shoot most of the film from George's sitting-down perspective don't help much – although his wheelchair power-up is in a class of its own.

BIBLIOGRAPHY

Abbott, Elizabeth. *Haiti: The Duvaliers and Their Legacy*. London: Robert Hale, 1988.

Accomando, Beth. "*Pontypool* Interview with Bruce McDonald," KPBS.org (23 June, 2009). Online at <http://www.kpbs.org/news/2009/jun/23/pontypool/>.

Alexander, Chris. "*Pontypool* Speaking of Zombies," *Fangoria* 283 (May, 2009), 62–65.

Alicoate, Jack. *The 1933 Film Daily Year Book of Motion Pictures*. New York: Wid's Films and Film Folk, 1933.

Bacal, Simon. "Night of the Living Dead: An Interview with John Vulich and Everett Burrell." *Starburst* 19 Monster Special (April, 1994): 64–66.

Badley, Linda. *Film, Horror and the Body Fantastic*. Westport CT and London: Greenwood Press, 1995.

Bai, Meijidai. "Gothic Monster and Chinese Cultural Identity: Analysis of The Note of Ghoul." In Balaji, ed., pp. 105–125.

Balaji, Murali, ed. *Thinking Dead: What the Zombie Apocalypse Means*. Plymouth and Lanham, MA: Lexingham Books, 2013.

Balbo, Lucas and Peter Blumenstock, eds. *Obsession: The Films of Jess Franco*. Berlin: Selbstverlag Frank Trebbin, 1993.

Bald, Wambly. *On the Left Bank: 1929–1933*. Edited by Benjamin Franklin. Athens, Ohio: Ohio University Press, 1987.

Balun, Chris. "Re-Animator." *Fangoria* 234 (July, 2004): 31.

Bansak, Edmund G. *Fearing The Dark: The Val Lewton Career*. Jefferson, NC and London: McFarland and Co., 1995.

Barker, A.D. "Interview: Marc Price – Director of *Colin*," LiveForFilms.com (June, 2010). Online at <http://www.liveforfilms.com/2011/01/29/interview-marc-price-director-of-colin/>.

Barnes and Noble. "Interview: George A. Romero." (8 August, 2000). Published online at <www.barnesandnoble.com/search/interview.asp?ctr=643332>. [link defunct]

BBC News, "Govan zombies taste film success," BBCNews.co.uk (16 April, 2008). Online at <http://news.bbc.co.uk/1/hi/scotland/glasgow_and_west/7351019.stm>.

Beale, Lewis. "The Zombies Brought Him: George Romero Is Back." *New York Times* (3 November, 2004).

Bell, Nelson B. "Thoughts on the Horror Era." The Washington Post (21 February, 1932).

Berger, Howard. "The Prince of Italian Terror." Fangoria 154 (July, 1996): 62–67, 82.

Bernardin, Marc. "Star Trek's Damon Lindelof on Brad Pitt, Having Power as a Writer and His Agony Over *Lost*," The Hollywood Reporter (13 June, 2013). Online at <http://www.hollywoodreporter.com/news/star-trek-into-darkness-world-war-z-520992>.

Billson, Anne. "*World War Z*: The Great Zombie Sell-Out," *Telegraph* (21 June, 2013). Online at <http://www.telegraph.co.uk/culture/film/10110866/World-War-Z-the-great-zombie-sell-out.html>.

Billson, Anne. "The Great Zombie Sell-Out Some Thoughts About *World War Z*," Multiglom: The Anne Billson Blog (22 June, 2013). Online at <http://multiglom.wordpress.com/2013/06/22/zombies-ahoy/>.

Bishop, Kyle William. *American Zombie Gothic: The Rise and Fall (and Rise) of the Walking Dead in Popular Culture*. Jefferson, NC: McFarland and Company, 2010.

Blackburn, Olly. "Bring Out Your Undead," The *Observer* (2 April, 2006). Online at <http://www.guardian.co.uk/film/2006/apr/02/features.review>.

Blaney, Martin. "International Production Case Study: Resident Evil Ground Zero." *Screen International* (5 October, 2001): 18.

Blumenstock, Peter. "Jean Rollin Has Risen from the Grave!" *Video Watchdog* 31 (1995): 36–57.

Blumenstock, Peter. "Michele Soavi: Gravely Speaking." *Fangoria* 149 (January, 1996): 52–55, 77.

Bogle, Donald. *Toms, Coons, Mulattoes, Mammies and Bucks: An Interpretative History of Blacks in American Film*. New York and London: Continuum, 1989.

Bosch, Torie. "First, Eat All The Lawyers," Slate.com (25 October, 2011). Online at <http://www.slate.com/articles/arts/culturebox/2011/10/zombies_the_the_zombie_boom_is_inspired_by_the_economy_.html>.

Botting, Jo. "Catalonian Creeps: An Interview with Jorge Grau." *Shivers* 79 (July, 2000): 22–27.

Boyle, Kirk. "Children of Men and I Am Legend: The Disaster-Capitalism Complex Hits Hollywood," *Jump Cut: A Review of Contemporary Media* 51 (Spring, 2009). Online at <http://www.ejumpcut.org/archive/jc51.2009/ChildrenMenLegend/text.html>.

Brodesser-Akner, Taffy. "Max Brooks Is Not Kidding about the Zombie Apocalypse," *New York Times* (21 June, 2013). Online at <http://www.nytimes.com/2013/06/23/magazine/max-brooks-is-not-kidding-about-the-zombie-apocalypse.html?_r=0>.

Brooks, Max. *The Zombie Survival Guide: Complete*

Protection from the Living Dead. New York: Three Rivers Press, 2003.

Brooks, Max. *World War Z*. New York: Crown, 2006.

Bryan, Peter. "Zombie! Original Synopsis." Reprinted in *Dark Terrors* 16 (December, 1998): 36–37.

Bryce, Allan, ed. *Zombie*. Liskeard, Cornwall: Stray Cat Publishing, 2000.

Burrell, Nigel J. *Knights of Terror: The Blind Dead Films of Amando de Ossorio*. Upton, Cambridgeshire: Midnight Media Publishing, 1995.

Campbell, Andy. "Zombie Apocalypse: CDC Denies Existence Of Zombies Despite Cannibal Incidents," The Huffington Post.com (1 June, 2012). Online at <http://www. huffingtonpost.com/2012/06/01/cdc-denies-zombies-existence_n_1562141.html>.

Cantor, Paul A. "The Apocalyptic Strain in Popular Culture: The American Nightmare Becomes the American Dream," *The Hedgehog Review* 15.2 (Summer 2013). Online at <http://www.iasc-culture.org/THR/THR_article_2013_ Summer_Cantor.php>.

Carroll, Larry. "Zombieland Writers Tell The Hilarious Story Behind Bill Murray's Bizarre Cameo," MTV Movies Blog (5 February, 2010). Online at <http://moviesblog.mtv. com/2010/02/05/zombieland-writers-tell-the-hilarious-story-behind-bill-murrays-bizarre-cameo/>.

Case, Sue Ellen. "Tracking the Vampire." In Gelder, ed. *The Horror Reader*. London and New York: Routledge, 2000, pp. 198–209.

Clarens, Carlos. *An Illustrated History of the Horror Film*. London: Secker and Warburg, 1968.

Compton, Michael. "*Night of the Living Dead: Reanimated*: New Life for the Undead." Fangoria.com (4 April, 2010). Online at <http://www.fangoria.com/index.php/moviestv/ fearful-features/447-night-of-the-living-dead-reanimated-new-life-for-the-undead>. [link defunct]

Crawford, Travis. "*Wild Zero*: Brain-Dead and Loving It." Fangoria 203 (June, 2001): 44–47.

Crawford, Travis. "Director Versus Everybody." *Fangoria* 213 (June, 2002): 50–54.

Davis, Harold Palmer. *Black Democracy: The Story of Haiti*. London: George Allen and Unwin, 1929.

Davis, Wade. *Passage of Darkness: The Ethnobiology of the Haitian Zombie*. London and Chapel Hill: University of North Carolina Press, 1988.

Davis, Wade. *The Serpent and the Rainbow*. London: Collins, 1986.

Deadline Team. "EMMYS: *Walking Dead*'s Frank Darabont," Deadline.com (23 June, 2011). Online at <http://www. deadline.com/2011/06/emmys-the-walking-deads-frank-darabont/>.

Dendle, Peter. *The Zombie Movie Encyclopedia*. Jefferson, NC and London: McFarland and Co., 2001.

Dendle, Peter. *The Zombie Movie Encyclopedia*, Volume 2: 2000–2010. Jefferson, NC and London: McFarland and Co., 2010.

Dionne, Zach. "Amazon's *Zombieland* Show Got 'Hated Out of Existence,' Sad Writer Reports," Vulture.com (17 May, 2013). Online at <http://www.vulture.com/2013/05/ amazon-zombieland-dead.html>.

Donato, Matt. "Interview with Douglas Schulze on Mimesis," WeGotThisCovered.com (18 February, 2013). Online at<http://wegotthiscovered.com/movies/interview-douglas-schulze-mimesis/>.

D'Onofrio, Roberto E. "Jaume Balagueró talks *[REC]* 4: Apocalypse," Fangoria.com (15 November, 2011). Online at <http://www.fangoria.com/index.php/home/all-news/1-latest-news/6058-jaume-balaguero-talks-rec-4-apocalypse>. [link defunct]

Dunbar, William. "Lament for the Makers." In John Burrow, ed. *English Verse 1300–1500*. London and New York: Longman, 1977, pp. 364–369.

Ebert, Roger. "Just Another Horror Movie – Or Is It?" *Reader's Digest* (June, 1969): 128.

Ebert, Roger. "Review of Dawn of the Dead." *Chicago Sun-Times* (20 April, 1979).

Edwards, Phil and Alan Jones. "*The Evil Dead* Speak: An Interview with Sam Raimi and Robert Tapert." *Starburst* 57 (May, 1983): 24–29.

England, Norman. "Who Made This Junk?" *Fangoria* 222 (May, 2003): 40–45.

Entertainment Film Distribution. "UK Publicity Press Notes for *Dawn of the Dead*." (2004).

Fawcett, Neil. "Dusk of the Dead." Published online at <http:// www.homepageofthedead.com>.

Ferrante, Anthony C. "Return of the Living Dead Director." *Fangoria* 171 (April, 1998): 20–22.

Flint, David. *Zombie Holocaust: How The Living Dead Devoured Pop Culture*. London: Plexus Publishing, 2009.

Foundas, Scott. "Dead Men Talking: The Resurrection of the Zombie Godfather George A. Romero." *The Village Voice* (28 June, 2005): 12.

Frasher, Michael. "*Night of the Living Dead*: Remaking George Romero's Horror Classic." *Cinefantastique* 21/3 (December, 1990): 16–17, 19, 20, 22.

Freud, Sigmund. "The 'Uncanny'" (1919). In *On Creativity and the Unconscious* (New York: Harper and Row, 1958), pp. 140–155.

Freud, Sigmund. *The Standard Edition of the Complete Psychological Works of Sigmund Freud*. Trans. James Strachey. London: Hogarth Press, 1986.

Freud, Sigmund. *Totem and Taboo: Some Points of Agreement Between the Mental Lives of Savages and Neurotics*. Trans. James Strachey. New York: Norton, 1950.

Fujiwara, Chris. *Jacques Tourneur: The Cinema of Nightfall*. Jefferson, NC and London: McFarland and Co., 1998.

Gagne, Paul. *The Zombies That Ate Pittsburgh: The Films of George Romero*. New York: Dodd, Mead and Co., 1987.

Gallagher, Brian. "Jay Lee Reveals All in Zombie Strippers," Movieweb.com (23 October, 2008). Online at <http://www.movieweb.com/news/exclusive-jay-lee-reveals-all-in-zombie-strippers>.

Gelder, Ken, ed. *The Horror Reader*. London and New York: Routledge, 2000.

Gelder, Ken. "Introduction to Part Three." In Gelder, ed. pp. 81–83.

Gilchrist, Todd. "*Land of the Dead* on DVD," IGN.com (27 June, 2005). <http://uk.ign.com/articles/2005/06/27/land-of-the-dead-on-dvd>.

Gingold, Mike. "This LAND is Gore Land." Fangoria.com. Published online at <http://www.fangoria.com/fearful_feature.php?id=2675>. [link defunct]

Gingold, Michael. "Gay Zombie Film Banned in Australia," Fangoria.com (20 July, 2010). Online at <http://www.fangoria.com/index.php/home/all-news/1-latest-news/1503-gay-zombie-film-banned-in-australia>. [link defunct]

Goode, Erica and Nate Schweber. "Case Already Tried in Social Media Heads to Court," *New York Times* (12 March, 2013). Online at <http://www.nytimes.com/2013/03/13/us/steubenville-rape-case-heads-to-trial.html>.

Grant, Barry Keith, ed. *The Dread of Difference: Gender and the Horror Film*. Austin: University of Texas Press, 1996.

Grant, Barry Keith. "Taking Back the Night of the Living Dead: George Romero, Feminism, and the Horror Film." In Grant, ed. pp. 200–212.

Grayson, Steve. "On-Set Report: Resident Evil." *Empire* 145 (July, 2001): 50.

Greenfield, Susan. "Facebook Home Could Change Our Brains," *Telegraph* (6 April, 2013). Online at <http://www.telegraph.co.uk/technology/facebook/9975118/Facebook-Home-could-change-our-brains.html>.

Gruben, Adrienne. "Nut Up or Shut Up: Touring through Zombieland with screenwriters Rhett Reese & Paul Wernick," Examiner.com (1 October, 2009). Online at <http://www.examiner.com/article/nut-up-or-shut-up-touring-through-zombieland-with-screenwriters-rhett-reese-paul-wernick>.

Gudino, Rod. "The Dead Walk… Again!: A George A. Romero Retrospective." *Rue Morgue* (July/August, 2003): 14–21.

Haining, Peter, ed. *Zombie! Stories of the Walking Dead*. London: W.H. Allen, 1985.

Halberstam, Judith. *Skin Shows: Gothic Horror and the Technology of Monsters*. Durham, NC: Duke University Press, 1995.

Halfyard, Kurt. "An Interview with Tony Burgess," Twitch.com (29 September 2008). Online at <http://twitchfilm.com/2008/09/an-interview-with-pontypool-author-tony-burgess.html>.

Hanners, John and Harry Kloman. "'The McDonaldization of America': An Interview with George A. Romero." *Film Criticism* 7/1 (Fall, 1982): 69–81.

Hardt, Michael and Antonio Negri. *Empire* (London and Cambridge, MA: Harvard University Press, 2000).

Hart, Hugh. "Industry Buzz," SFGate.com (13 April, 2008). Online at <http://www.sfgate.com/entertainment/article/INDUSTRY-BUZZ-3219754.php>.

Hearn, Lafcadio. "The Country of the Comers-Back." Reprinted in Peter Haining, ed., pp. 54–70.

Heinl, Robert and Nancy Gordon Heinl. *Written in Blood: The Story of the Haitian People 1492–1995*. Lanham, New York and London: University Press of America, 1996.

Hodges, Mike. "Amando de Ossorio: Farewell to Spain's Knight of Horror." *Shivers* 88 (April, 2001): 18–21.

Hutchings, Peter. *Terence Fisher*. Manchester and New York: Manchester University Press, 2001.

Itzkoff, Dave. "Screening of Gay Zombie Film leads to Police Raid in Australia," *New York Times* (15 November, 2010). Online at <http://artsbeat.blogs.nytimes.com/2010/11/15/screening-of-gay-zombie-film-leads-to-police-raid-in-australia/>.

Jancovich, Mark. *Rational Fears: American Horror in the 1950s*. Manchester and New York: Manchester University Press, 1996.

Jettisoundz. "Scooter MacCrae: The Shatter Boy." Jettisoundz.co.uk. Published online at <http://jettisoundz.co.uk/archive/99/mccrae.htm>.

Jones, Alan. "Dellamorte Dellamore." *Cinefantastique* 25/5 (October, 1994): 52–55.

Jones, Alan. "George Romero Interview." *Starburst* 4/12 (August, 1982): 34–38.

Jones, Alan. "Morti Viventi: Zombies Italian-Style." In Bryce ed., pp. 12–27.

Jones, Alan. "Nervous [REC]," *Fangoria* 276 (September, 2008), 32–36.

Jones, Alan. *Profondo Argento: The Man, the Myths and the Magic*. Guildford, Surrey: FAB Press, 2004.

Jones, Alan. "Resident Evil." *Cinefantastique* 34/2 (April, 2002): 10–13.

Kay, Glenn. *Zombie Movies: The Ultimate Guide*. Chicago:

Chicago Review Press, 2012.

King, Richard. "J.R. Bookwalter: A Career in B-Movies and Beyond." *Darkstar* 14/15. Reprinted online at <http://www.darkstarorg.demon.co.uk/intv2.htm>. [link defunct]

King, Stephen. "The Horrors of '79." *Rolling Stone* (27 December, 1979–10 January 1980): 17, 19, 20.

Kipp, Jeremiah. "American Zombie: Mockumentary of the Dead," *Fangoria* 272 (April, 2008), 12.

Kirkman, Robert. *The Walking Dead: Days Gone By*. Orange, California: Image Comics, 2004.

Kristeva, Julia. *Powers of Horror: An Essay on Abjection*. Trans. Leon S. Roudiez. New York: Columbia University Press, 1982.

L.N., "Review of *White Zombie*." *New York Times* (29 July, 1932): 18, 2.

Levy, Frederic. "The Rue Morgue: Looking for French Zombies with Jean Rollin." *Starburst* 4/12 (August, 1982): 26.

Lewis, Joseph. "A Bloody Laugh." *The Point* (26 February, 1970): 14.

Lim, Dennis. "Dante's Inferno," *The Village Voice* (22 November, 2005). Online at <http://www.villagevoice.com/2005-11-22/film/dante-s-inferno/>.

Lucas, Tim. "Versions and Vampires: Jean Rollin on Home Video." *Video Watchdog* 31 (1995): 28–35.

Mandell, Andrea. "Pitt breaks silence on battle to make *World War Z*," USA Today.com (21 June, 2013). Online at <http://www.usatoday.com/story/life/people/2013/06/20/brad-pitt-world-war-z/2433349/>.

Mantle, Burns, ed. *The Best Plays of 1931–1932 and the Year Book of Drama in America*. New York: Dodd, Mead and Co., 1932.

Manzoor, Sarfraz. "My £45 Hit Film: Marc Price on his Zombie Movie *Colin*," *Guardian* (30 July, 2009). Online at <http://www.guardian.co.uk/film/2009/jul/30/marc-price-zombie-film-colin>.

Marks, John. *The Search for the "Manchurian Candidate": The CIA and Mind Control, The Secret History of the Behavioural Sciences*. New York and London: W.W. Norton, 1979.

Marsh, James. "Talking Shit: Discussing Zombie Ass with director Noboru Iguchi & stars Arisa Nakamura & Demo Tanaka," Twitch.com (8 March, 2012). Online at <http://twitchfilm.com/2012/03/yubari-2012-zombie-ass-interview-noboru-iguchi.html>.

Martinez, Bryan. "Foreign Horror: An Interview with John Cairns," *Film Deviant* (18 August, 2013). Online at <www.filmdeviant.com/2013/08/foreign-horror-interview-with-john.html>.

Maslin, Janet. "Review of Night of the Living Dead." *New York Times* (20 April, 1979): 5.

McBride, Joseph. "Val Lewton, Director's Producer." *Action* 11 (January–February, 1976): 10–16.

McCarty, John. *Splatter Movies: Breaking the Last Taboo of the Screen*. New York: St Martin's Press, 1984.

McDonagh, Maitland. "Sometimes They Come Back... Again: The Making of the *Return of the Living Dead* Trilogy." In Bryce, ed. pp. 57–63.

McDonagh, Maitland. "The Living Dead at the Miskatonic Morgue: *Re-Animator* and *Bride of Re-Animator*." In Bryce, ed. pp. 49–55.

McLarty, Lianne. "'Beyond the Veil of the Flesh': Cronenberg and the Disembodiment of Horror." In Grant, ed. pp. 231–252.

Meslow, Scott. "The Post-Apocalyptic Morality of *The Walking Dead*," *The Atlantic* (5 March, 2012). Online at <http://www.theatlantic.com/entertainment/archive/2012/03/the-post-apocalyptic-morality-of-the-walking-dead/253986>

Mondello, Bob. "I Am Legend: A One-Man American Metaphor," NPR.com (14 December, 2007). Online at <http://www.npr.org/templates/story/story.php?storyId=17260869>.

Monthly Film Bulletin. "Review of King of the Zombies." *Monthly Film Bulletin* 8/93 (September, 1941): 116–117.

Morrison, Alan. "Rage Against the Machine." *Empire* 161 (November, 2002): 98–105.

Motion Picture Herald. "Review of *I Walked with a Zombie*." *Motion Picture Herald* 150/12 (20 March, 1943): 1214.

Newman, Kim. "Review of Bad Taste." *The Monthly Film Bulletin* 56/668 (September, 1989), 267–268.

Newman, Kim. *Nightmare Movies: A Critical History of the Horror Movie From 1968–1988*. London: Bloomsbury, 1988.

Newman, Kim. *Nightmare Movies: Horror on Screen Since the 1960s*. London: Bloomsbury Publishing. 2011.

Nietzsche, Friedrich. *Beyond Good and Evil: Prelude to a Philosophy of the Future*. Trans. R.J. Hollingdale 1886. London: Penguin, 1990.

Nugent, Frank S. "Review of Revolt of the Zombies." *New York Times* (5 June, 1936).

Palmerini, Luca M. and Gaetano Mistretta. *Spaghetti Nightmares: Italian Fantasy Horrors as Seen Through the Eyes of their Protagonists*. Key West, Florida: Fantasma Books, 1996.

Peters, Jon. "Exit Humanity's Director Talks Civil War Zombies," KillerFilm.com (21 July, 2011). Online at <http://www.killerfilm.com/spotlight/read/exclusive-exit-humanitys-director-talks-civil-war-zombies-80362>.

Plante, Mike. "Chomp! Bruce LaBruce's Otto," *Filmmaker*

(Fall, 2008), 58–59, 125.

Plummer, Brenda Gale. *Haiti and the United States: The Psychological Moment*. Athens and London, University of Georgia Press, 1992.

Pomerantz, Dorothy. "Attack of the Mockbuster Movie: Hobbits, Zombies and 2-Headed Sharks," *Forbes* (22 October, 2012). Online at <http://www.forbes.com/sites/dorothypomerantz/2012/10/03/attack-of-the-mockbustser-movie-hobbits-zombies-and-2-headed-sharks/>.

Poole, Steven. *Trigger Happy: The Inner Life of Videogames*. London: Fourth Estate, 2000.

Rainville, Keith J. *Zombi Mexicano*. Los Angeles: From Parts Unknown Publications, 2012.

Ray, Man. *Self Portrait*. Boston: Little, Brown and Company, 1963.

Rhodes, Gary D. *White Zombie: Anatomy of a Horror Film*. Jefferson, NC and London: McFarland and Co, 2001.

Rodley, Chris, ed. *Cronenberg on Cronenberg*. London: Faber and Faber, 1992.

Romero, George. "Syndicated Q&A" (4 March, 2008). Reprinted online at <http://www.eatmybrains.com/showfeature.php?id=77>.

Rowe, Michael. "Gunn to the Head." *Fangoria* 231 (April, 2003): 27–28, 30–31.

Rowe, Michael. "Land of the Dead: Home of the Grave." Fangoria 244 (June, 2005): 50–55, 97.

Rowe, Michael. "New 'Dawn' Rising." *Fangoria* 227 (October, 2003): 45.

Salisbury, Mark. "Dead Residents: On the Set of *Resident Evil*." *Total Film* 55 (August, 2001): 8.

Salisbury, Mark. "To Make the Blood Boyle." *Fangoria* 224 (July, 2003): 20–23, 82.

Sandhu, Sukhdev. "*Zibahkhana*: Beware Zombies Wearing Saris," *Telegraph* (11 August, 2007). Online at <http://www.telegraph.co.uk/culture/film/starsandstories/3667146/Zibahkhana-beware-zombies-wearing-saris.html>.

Sartre, Jean Paul. *No Exit: A Play in One Act*. Trans. by Paul Bowles. New York: Samuel French, 1958.

Schaefer, Eric. *Bold! Daring! Shocking! True!: A History of Exploitation Films, 1919–1959*. Durham and London: Duke University Press, 1999.

Schlockoff, Robert. "Lucio Fulci." *Starburst* 4/12 (August, 1982): 51–55.

Schmidt, Hans. *The United States Occupation of Haiti, 1915–1934*. New Brunswick, NJ: Rutgers University Press, 1971.

Screen Edge. "Scooter McCrae: The Shatter Boy." Published online at <http://www.screenedge.com/archive/99/mccrae/htm>. [link defunct]

Seabrook, William. *The Magic Island*. London: George Harrap and Co., 1929.

Seitz, Matt Zoller. "Braaaains! The 10 Essential Zombie Films," Salon.com (30 May 2010). Online at <http://www.salon.com/2010/05/30/essential_zombie_films_slide_show/>.

Senn, Bryan. *Drums of Terror: Voodoo in the Cinema*. Baltimore, MD: Midnight Marquee Press, 1998.

Senn, Bryan. *Golden Horrors: An Illustrated Critical Filmography of Terror Cinema 1931–1939*. Jefferson, NC and London: McFarland and Co., 1996.

SFX Magazine. "Soundbite: Danny Boyle Interview." *SFX* 104 (May, 2003): 85.

Sheets, Todd. "The Extreme Entertainment Mission Statement." Published online at <www.zombiebloodbath.com/mission.html>.

Siegel, Joel E. *Val Lewton: The Reality of Terror*. London: Secker and Warburg, 1972.

Simpson, M.J. "Dead Creatures: Parkinson's Disease," *Fangoria* 206 (September, 2001): 64–67.

Skal, David J. *The Monster Show: A Cultural History of Horror*. London: Plexus, 1994.

Southey, Robert. *History of Brazil*. London: Longman, 1810–1819.

Speyer, Ariana. "Up with Bruce LaBruce," *Interview* (February 13, 2009). Online at <http://www.interviewmagazine.com/film/otto-bruce-labruce#_>.

St. John, Spencer. *Hayti, or The Black Republic*. London: Elder Smith, 1884.

Students' British Board of Film Classification. "Case Study: *The Evil Dead*," BBFC.com. Online at <http://www.bbfc.co.uk/case-studies/evil-dead>.

Thakur, Charu. "Rise of the Zombie: No Threat from *Go Goa Gone* says Luke Kenny," IBN Live (5 April, 2013). Online at <http://ibnlive.in.com/news/rise-of-the-zombies-no-threat-from-go-goa-gone-says-luke-kenny/383091-8-66.html>.

THR Staff, "Oscar Nominee Brad Pitt On The Unmentionables: Marriage, Politics and Religion," *The Hollywood Reporter* (25 January, 2012). Online at <http://www.hollywoodreporter.com/news/brad-pitt-angelina-jolie-oscars-moneyball-tree-of-life-284533/>.

Thrower, Stephen. *Beyond Terror: The Films of Lucio Fulci*. Guildford, Surrey: FAB Press, 1999.

Todorov, Tzvetan. *The Fantastic: A Structural Approach to a Literary Genre*. Trans. Richard Howard. Ithaca, NY: Cornell University Press, 1975.

Tohill, Cathal and Pete Tombs. *Immoral Tales: European Sex and Horror Movies 1956–1985*. 1994. Reprinted New York: St Martin's Griffin, 1994.

Totaro, Donato. "The Italian Zombie Movie: From Derivation to Reinvention." In Schneider, Steven, ed. *Fear without*

Frontiers. Guildford, Surrey: FAB Press, 2003.

Twitchell, James B. *Dreadful Pleasures: An Anatomy of Modern Horror.* Oxford and New York: Oxford University Press, 1985.

US Department for Health and Human Services, Centers for Disease Control and Prevention, *Disaster Preparedness 101: Zombie Pandemic* (October 2011). Online at <http://www.cdc.gov/phpr/zombies.htm>.

Van de Water, F. "Review of *The Magic Island*," *New York Evening Post* (12 January, 1929).

Variety. "Review of *Dawn of the Dead.*" *Variety* (18 April, 1979): 4

Variety. "Review of *Night of the Living Dead.*" *Variety* (16 October, 1968): 5.

Variety. "Review of *White Zombie.*" *Variety* (2 August, 1932): 6.

Wallace, Inez. "I Walked with a Zombie." Reprinted in Haining, ed. pp. 95–102.

Waller, Gregory. *The Living and the Undead: From Stoker's Dracula to Romero's Night of the Living Dead.* Urbana and Chicago: University of Illinois Press, 1986.

Warner, Marina. "The Devil Inside." *Guardian* (2 November, 2002). Online at <http://www.theguardian.com/books/2002/nov/02/film.society>.

Warner, Marina. *Phantasmagoria: Spirits, Visions, Metaphors and Media into the Twenty First Century.* Oxford and New York: Oxford University Press, 2006.

Watt, Mike. "Night of the Living Dead '90." *Cinefantastique* 34 3/4 (June, 2002): 116–119.

Weaver, Tom. *It Came From Weaver Five: Interviews with Moviemakers in the SF and Horror Traditions of the Thirties, Forties, Fifties and Sixties.* Jefferson, NC and London: MacFarland and Co., 1996.

Weaver, Tom. *Poverty Row HORRORS!: Monogram, PRC and Republic Horror Films of the Forties.* Jefferson, NC and London: McFarland and Co, 1993.

Weinstein, Harvey M. *Psychiatry and the CIA: Victims of Mind Control.* London and Washington: American Psychiatric Press, 1990.

Whittington, James. "Exclusive Interview With Keith Wright Director Of *Harold's Going Stiff*," HorrorChannel.com (30 April, 2013). Online at <http://www.horrorchannel.co.uk/articles.php?feature=8194&category=5>.

Whyte, William. *The Organization Man.* New York: Simon Schuster, 1956.

Williams, Tony. "*White Zombie* Haitian Horror," *Jump Cut: A Review of Contemporary Media* 28 (April, 1983). Online at <http://www.ejumpcut.org/archive/onlinessays/JC28folder/WhiteZombie.html>.

Williams, Tony. *The Cinema of George A. Romero: Knight of the Living Dead.* London and New York: Wallflower Press, 2003.

Wloszczyna, Susan. "Romero's *Diary* Breathes New Life into the Dead," USA Today (4 September, 2007). Online at <http://usatoday30.usatoday.com/life/movies/news/2007-09-04-romero-main_N.htm>.

Woerner, Meredith. "First Footage From The *Evil Dead* Reboot. What Does It Mean?" i09.com (16 October, 2012). Online at <http://io9.com/5952201/first-footage-from-the-evil-dead-reboot-what-does-it-mean>.

Woerner, Meredith. "Why George Romero Rejected *The Walking Dead* to make The Zombie Autopsies," io9.com (19 October, 2011). Online at <http://io9.com/5851502/why-george-romero-rejected-the-walking-dead-to-make-the-zombie-autopsies>.

Wood, Robin and Richard Lippe, eds. *American Nightmare: Essays on the Horror Film.* Toronto: Festival of Festivals, 1979.

Wood, Robin. "Apocalypse Now: Notes on the Living Dead." In Wood and Lippe, eds. pp. 91–97.

Wood, Robin. "An Introduction to the American Horror Film." In Wood and Lippe, eds. pp. 7–28.

Wood, Robin. "The Shadow Worlds of Jacques Tourneur." *Film Comment* 8/2 (1972): 64–70.

Worthington, Marjorie. *The Strange World of Willie Seabrook.* New York: Harcourt, Brace & World, 1966.

Yakis, Dan. "Mourning Becomes Romero." *Film Comment* 15 (May–June, 1979): 60–65.

Yi, Ho. "Movie Review: *Zombie 108*" Taipei Times (13 April, 2012). Online at <http://www.taipeitimes.com/News/feat/archives/2012/04/13/2003530202>.

Zimmerman, Samuel. "Zombies Of Mass Destruction," *Fangoria* 290 (February, 2010), 14.

ENDNOTES

1 James B. Twitchell, *Dreadful Pleasures: An Anatomy of Modern Horror* (Oxford and New York: Oxford University Press, 1985), p. 261 and p. 266.

2 Problems of availability have meant that I haven't been able to make reference to the large number of African films that feature zombies. The living dead have apparently made frequent appearances in the home-grown video markets of countries like Nigeria, yet getting hold of this material (which is often shot and distributed quickly, cheaply and with little or no record of production details) has proved difficult. It seems important to recognise their existence, though, if only to highlight the predominant American-European focus of this book. Similarly, the vast literature surrounding the living dead – from EC comic books to pulp novels – and the hundreds of short films featuring zombies, are beyond the scope of this study.

3 Judith Halberstam, *Skin Shows: Gothic Horror and the Technology of Monsters* (Durham, NC: Duke University Press, 1995), p. 21.

4 Ken Gelder, "Introduction to Part Three", in Gelder ed., *The Horror Reader* (London and New York: Routledge, 2000), p. 81.

5 According to the *Oxford English Dictionary*, the first use of the word "zombie" in the English language occurred in 1819 in Robert Southey's *History of Brazil* (London: Longman, 1810–1819). In that book, Southey claims that a "zombie" is synonymous with the Devil. The edition of this book held in the British Library formerly belonged to Samuel Taylor Coleridge – Southey's brother-in-law – who made several pencil annotations in the margins of the text, including one that argues that this definition of the zombie is incorrect. Sadly, the poet doesn't elaborate on why he believes that is so. See Marina Warner, "The Devil Inside", *Guardian* (2 November, 2002). Online at <http://www.theguardian.com/books/2002/nov/02/film.society>.

6 Lafcadio Hearn, "The Country of the Comers-Back", *Harpers Magazine*, 1889. Reprinted in Peter Haining ed., *Zombie! Stories of the Walking Dead* (London: W.H. Allen, 1985), pp. 54–70.

7 White Europeans disparagingly dubbed Haiti "The Black Republic" after the island won its independence in the 18th century. It was also the title of a book on the island by Spencer St John: *Hayti, Or The Black Republic* (London: Elder Smith, 1884).

8 Man Ray, *Self Portrait* (Boston: Little, Brown and Company, 1963), pp. 191–193.

9 Seabrook's comments about the taste of human flesh can be found in Wambly Bald, *On the Left Bank 1929–1933*, ed. Benjamin Franklin (Athens, Ohio: Ohio University Press, 1987), p. 80. For the full story of Seabrook's culinary adventure see Marjorie Worthington, *The Strange World of Willie Seabrook* (New York: Harcourt, Brace & World, 1966), pp. 54–57. Worthington was Seabrook's second wife.

10 Wade Davis, *The Serpent and the Rainbow* (London: Collins, 1986), p. 138.

11 William Seabrook, *The Magic Island* (London: George Harrap and Co., 1929), p. 94.

12 Ibid., p. 94.

13 Ibid., p. 95.

14 Ibid., p. 101.

15 Ibid., p. 102.

16 Ibid., p. 103.

17 F. Van de Water, "Review of The Magic Island", New York Evening Post (12 January, 1929).

18 Seabrook, p. 7.

19 Ibid, p. 7.

20 Robert Heinl and Nancy Gordon Heinl, *Written in Blood: The Story of the Haitian People 1492–1995* (Lanham, New York and London: University Press of America, 1996), p. 41.

21 Harold Palmer Davis, *Black Democracy: The Story of Haiti* (London: George Allen and Unwin, 1929), p. 167.

22 One of the most fascinating films about the occupation and the history of Haiti's ongoing struggle to free itself from American influence is the documentary *Canne Amère* (Bitter Cane, 1983), which was clandestinely filmed over the course of six years during the Duvalier regime.

23 Harold Palmer Davis, p. 171.

24 Hans Schmidt, *The United States Occupation of Haiti, 1915–1934* (New Brunswick, NJ: Rutgers University Press, 1971), p. 68.

25 Ibid., p. 146.

26 Elizabeth Abbott, *Haiti: The Duvaliers and Their Legacy* (London: Robert Hale, 1988), p. 39. Even Seabrook himself was somewhat equivocal about the American occupation of the island. "The presence of the Americans has put an end to revolution, mob violence, and many other deplorable conditions which the entire reasonable world agrees should be put an end to. It has also put an end, or if not an end, a period, to more than a century of national freedom of a peculiar sort, which has existed

nowhere else on earth save in Liberia – the freedom of a Negro people to govern or misgovern themselves and to stand forth as human beings like any others without cringing or asking leave of any white man." Seabrook, p. 269. Such doubts didn't stop him from playing up the island's "savagery" for the sake of a good read, though.

27 Abbott, p. 40.

28 Wade Davis, *Passage of Darkness: The Ethnobiology of the Haitian Zombie* (London and Chapel Hill: University of North Carolina Press, 1988), p. 73.

29 Ibid, p. 73.

30 The details of *Zombie* are taken from *The Best Plays of 1931–1932 and the Year Book of the Drama in America* ed. Burns Mantle (New York: Dodd, Mead and Co, 1932), p. 476.

31 This review is cited by Gary D. Rhodes, *White Zombie: Anatomy of a Horror Film* (Jefferson, NC and London: MacFarland and Co, 2001), p. 85.

32 Bryan Senn, *Drums of Terror: Voodoo in the Cinema* (Baltimore, MD: Midnight Marquee Press, 1998), p. 25.

33 The critical response to *White Zombie* was predominantly negative, with the *New York Times* claiming that there was "no reason" for the film to exist whatsoever. *Variety* was far more generous, however: "in the main the atmosphere of horror is well sustained and sensitive picture goers will get a full quota of thrills". See reviews in the *New York Times* (31 July, 1932) and *Variety* (2 August, 1932) respectively.

34 Bryan Senn, *Golden Horrors: An Illustrated Critical Filmography of Terror Cinema 1931–1939* (Jefferson, NC and London: McFarland and Co., 1996), p. 88.

35 Jack Alicoate, *The 1933 Film Daily Year Book of Motion Pictures* (New York: Wid's Films and Film Folk, 1933), p. 101.

36 Nelson B. Bell, "Thoughts on the Horror Era", *Washington Post* (21 February, 1932).

37 David J. Skal, *The Monster Show: A Cultural History of Horror* (London: Plexus, 1994), p. 169.

38 See Tony Williams, "White Zombie Haitian Horror", *Jump Cut: A Review of Contemporary Media* 28 (April, 1983). Online at <http://www.ejumpcut.org/archive/onlinessays/JC28folder/WhiteZombie.html>.

39 Ibid.

40 These selections from the British press book for *White Zombie* are reprinted in Rhodes, p. 276.

41 Ibid., p. 276.

42 Senn, *Drums of Terror*, p. 39.

43 L. N., "Review of White Zombie", *New York Times* (29 July, 1932).

44 *Ouanga* was originally released by Paramount's British distribution arm in order to sidestep the UK's strict quotas on American film imports. Although the cast and crew were American, the film wasn't actually released in the US until 1942, when it was reissued in a slightly shortened cut as *The Love Wanga*. Given the film's American genesis, it is obviously closely tied to the American interest in the Caribbean, even if the majority of American cinemagoers didn't see it until the occupation was long over. See Senn, *Drums of Terror*, p. 38.

45 One reason why the Hollywood establishment stopped making films about Haiti during the mid-1930s was because the island's troubled politics had begun to attract the interest of the African-American writers of the Harlem Renaissance. Plays like Eugene O'Neil's *The Emperor Jones* (later made into a film) and the so-called "Voodoo Macbeth" adaptation of Shakespeare's play (which relocated the action to Haiti with an all-black Harlem cast under the direction of a young Orson Welles) alerted Hollywood to the fact that the racial and political stakes of the Haitian occupation had, by this point in time, been raised considerably higher than anyone in white America had ever expected.

46 Frank S. Nugent, "Review of Revolt of the Zombies", *New York Times* (5 June, 1936).

47 The nearest Universal ever came to producing a zombie film during the period was the underrated horror movie *The Mad Ghoul* (1943), in which a scientist played by George Zucco discovers an ancient Mayan nerve gas that turns his student into one of the living dead. Significantly, the studio chose "ghoul" rather than "zombie" to describe this state, perhaps because they were unwilling to associate their production with any low-rent zombie movies or the monster's Caribbean heritage.

48 In his cultural history of early exploitation films, Eric Schaefer convincingly argues that Poverty Row movies and exploitation films ought to be regarded as distinct from one another. While both kinds of films boasted terribly cheap production values, exploitation films dealt with subjects that were generally considered forbidden (some combination of sex, drugs and the exotic). In comparison, Poverty Row features aped mainstream Hollywood in everything except quality. Since the 1960s, the label "exploitation" has changed its meaning. During the years between 1919 and 1959, "exploitation" referred to the sensational advertising or promotional techniques that accompanied these films. From the 1960s onwards, "exploitation" was used to describe those films that exploited their subject matter – "sexploitation" or "blaxploitation". The kinds of films each label refers to are very distinct, with the zombie films of the 1960s onwards

falling into the latter category as they exploit their audience's desire for violent, gory horror. See Schaefer, *Bold! Daring! Shocking! True!: A History of Exploitation Films, 1919–1959* (Durham and London: Duke University Press, 1999).

49 Tom Weaver, *Poverty Row Horrors!: Monogram, PRC and Republic Horror Films of the Forties* (Jefferson, NC and London: McFarland and Co, 1993), p. xiii.

50 Ibid., p. xii.

51 Another Monogram zombie contender is *The Face of Marble* (1946). Its status as a zombie movie has always been somewhat in doubt since its ghouls not only act like vampires (drinking blood) but also seem to be ghostly (they can dematerialise and walk through walls). As ever with Monogram's films, such inconsistencies seem to be a result of nothing more than bad writing. John Carradine stars as brain surgeon Professor Randolph, who resurrects the corpse of a drowned fisherman using some new-fangled electro-chemical process he's designed with his assistant, Dr David Cochran (Robert Shayne). The corpse returns to life with a "face of marble". To add further confusion to the proceedings, the scientist's Haitian servants are dabbling in some non-zombie-related voodoo, and the professor's Great Dane is killed and brought back to life as a ghost dog that terrorises the local livestock! Though the marble-faced zombie make-up is quite distinctive, the film barely qualifies as a tale of the walking dead since its ghouls eventually turn into ghosts.

52 Denis Gifford, *A Pictorial History of Horror Movies* (London: Hamlyn, 1973, revised edition 1983), p. 151.

53 Donald Bogle, *Toms, Coons, Mulattoes, Mammies and Bucks: An Interpretative History of Blacks in American Film* (New York and London; Continuum, 1989), p. 36.

54 Ibid., p. 74.

55 Cited by Weaver, p. 36.

56 *Monthly Film Bulletin* Vol. 8, No. 93 (September, 1941).

57 Weaver, p. 130.

58 Peter Dendle, *The Zombie Movie Encyclopedia* (Jefferson, NC and London: McFarland and Co.), 2000, p. 186.

59 Weaver, p. 139.

60 Joseph McBride "Val Lewton, Director's Producer", *Action* 11 (Jan–Feb, 1976), 12.

61 Edmund G. Bansak, *Fearing The Dark: The Val Lewton Career* (Jefferson, NC and London: McFarland and Co., 1995), p. 143.

62 Inez Wallace, "I Walked with a Zombie", *American Weekly* (1940). Reprinted in Haining, pp. 95-102. My emphasis.

63 Joel E. Siegel, *Val Lewton: The Reality of Terror* (London: Secker and Warburg, 1972), p. 41.

64 *Motion Picture Herald*, 150/12 (20 March, 1943).

65 Robin Wood, "The Shadow Worlds of Jacques Tourneur", *Film Comment* 8/2 (1972), 70.

66 Chris Fujiwara, *Jacques Tourneur: The Cinema of Nightfall* (Jefferson, NJ and London: McFarland and Co., 1998), p. 86.

67 Tzvetan Todorov, *The Fantastic: A Structural Approach to a Literary Genre*, trans. Richard Howard (Ithaca, NY: Cornell University Press, 1975).

68 Following *I Walked with a Zombie*, Lewton returned again to the land of the living dead, though with far less success. In the Boris Karloff vehicle *Isle of the Dead* (1945), zombies were replaced with a Poe-like story about a woman who is prematurely buried alive. She goes insane and starts stalking and killing a group of tourists stranded on a Greek island during a plague outbreak. Lewton was generally dismissive of the film, claiming: "It started out as a rather poetic and quite beautiful story of how people, fleeing from the battles of the Greek War of 1912, are caught on this island by plague and through their suffering, come to an acceptance of death as being good […] It ended up as a hodge-podge of horror… This has been a horrible and unfortunate film from the beginning." Lewton also faced interference from his RKO bosses. During pre-production he was warned, "Remember, no messages". To which he politely, but firmly, replied: "I'm sorry but we do have a message and our message is that death is good." Unfortunately, the film was not. See Siegel, pp. 74, 71.

69 The plot of *Valley of the Zombies* is rather similar to Vincent Sherman's *The Return of Dr X* (1939), a film about a mad scientist experimenting with synthetic blood, which starred a young Humphrey Bogart in his debut horror movie appearance. Bogart was sufficiently unimpressed with the low-budget production – which he'd apparently been assigned to as punishment for some unspecified misdemeanour at Warner Bros. – that he branded it a "stinking movie" and completely avoided the horror genre for the rest of his career.

70 Mark Jancovich, *Rational Fears: American Horror in the 1950s* (Manchester and New York: Manchester University Press, 1996), p. 2.

71 Ibid., p. 2.

72 Aubrey Schenck quoted by Tom Weaver in *It Came From Weaver Five: Interviews with Moviemakers in the SF and Horror Traditions of the Thirties, Forties, Fifties and Sixties* (Jefferson, NC and London: MacFarland and Co, 1996), p. 279.

73 Carlos Clarens, *An Illustrated History of the Horror Film* (London: Secker and Warburg, 1968), p. 134.

74 Jancovich, p. 22.

75 William Whyte, *The Organization Man* (New York: Simon Schuster, 1956), p. 397.

76 Harvey M. Weinstein, *Psychiatry and the CIA: Victims of Mind Control* (London and Washington: American Psychiatric Press, 1990), p. 129. For a more detailed history of the American intelligence services' interest in mind control see John Marks, *The Search for the "Manchurian Candidate": The CIA and Mind Control, The Secret History of the Behavioural Sciences* (New York and London: W.W. Norton, 1979).

77 Lianne McLarty, "'Beyond the Veil of Flesh': Cronenberg and the Disembodiment of Horror", in Barry Keith Grant, ed. *The Dread of Difference: Gender and the Horror Film* (Austin: University of Texas Press, 1996), p. 233.

78 Ibid., p. 233.

79 Sigmund Freud, *Totem and Taboo: Some Points of Agreement Between the Mental Lives of Savages and Neurotics*, trans. James Strachey (New York: Norton, 1950), pp. 63–64. I am indebted to Gregory Waller's insightful discussion of Freud in *The Living and the Undead: From Stoker's Dracula to Romero's Night of the Living Dead* (Urbana and Chicago: University of Illinois Press, 1986), pp. 276–77.

80 Freud, "The Uncanny" (1919) in *On Creativity and the Unconscious* (New York: Harper and Row, 1958), p. 150.

81 Peter Hutchings, *Terence Fisher* (Manchester and New York: Manchester University Press, 2001), p. 127.

82 The full details of this treatment can be found in Peter Bryan, "*Zombie!* Original Synopsis", *Dark Terrors* 16 (December, 1998), pp. 36–37. Interestingly, the filmed version of the story keeps the Haitian servants but reduces them to incidental characters – it's the squire and his young hooligan friends who act as the voodoo priests, the black servants merely adding some local "colour".

83 Keith J. Rainville, *Zombi Mexicano* (Los Angeles: From Parts Unknown, 2012), p. 12. Produced in a boutique limited edition run, Rainville's passionate and beautifully designed book is a treat for anyone who wants to know more about the momias cycle of Mexican movies – complete with rare stills, posters and lobby cards. I confess to falling into the semantic trap he talks about; I dismissed the momias movies in the first edition of this book on the assumption that they didn't feature zombies, just Aztec mummies. Ironically, I moved out to Oaxaca, Mexico, just as *Book of the Dead* was published, and made the pilgrimage to Guanajuato to visit the famed museum. The petrified corpses, encased in over-lit glass display cases, were spectacularly creepy – not least of all the way in which death seemed to bequeath each one a frozen, silent scream. But they were also clearly not what I had assumed – at which point I started muttering "mea culpa".

84 The version of the film I saw didn't have a scene where the zombies use hot irons on their victims, but Rainville discusses this moment and even has a still from the movie showing a ghoul armed with such a weapon. Like their Italian and Spanish counterparts of this period, Mexican momias movies often circulated in a variety of prints – some of which were more complete than others. See Rainville, p. 33.

85 Given the film's play on the difference between Them/Us and Self/Other, it seems significant that a later adaptation of Matheson's novel – director Boris Sagal's *The Omega Man* (1971), starring Charlton Heston in the lead role – turned the scenario into a commentary on American race relations. This adaptation styled its ghouls as a group of albino mutants who clearly owed more to radical 1960s groups like the Black Panthers than the vampires of the novel. In this later film, the ghouls are emphatically not supposed to be seen as zombies.

86 "Review of *Night of the Living Dead*", *Variety* (16 October, 1968), 6.

87 Roger Ebert, "Just Another Horror Movie – Or Is It?" *Reader's Digest* (June, 1969), 128. This article was an edited version of a piece that appeared in Ebert's film column in the *Chicago-Sun Times* newspaper.

88 Waller, p. 289.

89 Ibid., p. 275.

90 Dan Yakis, "Mourning Becomes Romero", *Film Comment* 15 (May–June 1979), 62.

91 Waller, p. 274.

92 Linda Badley, *Film, Horror and the Body Fantastic* (Westport CT and London: Greenwood Press, 1995), p. 74.

93 Robin Wood, "An Introduction to the American Horror Film" in Wood and Richard Lippe eds., *American Nightmare: Essays on the Horror Film* (Toronto: Festival of Festivals, 1979), p. 10.

94 Joseph Lewis, "A Bloody Laugh", *The Point* (26 February, 1970), 14.

95 A sign of *Night of the Living Dead*'s success is the number of spoofs it has produced over the years. Two of the weirdest are *Night of the Living Bread* (1990) an eight-minute short in which characters are attacked by slices of white bread, and the breathlessly titled *Night of the Day of the Dawn of the Son of the Bride of the Return of the Revenge of the Terror of the Attack of the Evil Mutant Hellbound Flesh-Eating Subhumanoid Living Dead, Part II* (1992), which replays the original movie in full but with a (supposedly) jokey dubbing track.

96 Spoofing *Night of the Living Dead* was an obvious choice,

if only because the zombies were cheap monsters. Ormsby's duties included preparing the zombie make-up (credited as Alan Omark). It was something he was also responsible for on *Deathdream*, with a young Tom Savini as his assistant, and on the later *Shock Waves* (1976). Ormsby's stories about the *Children* shoot prove that not even the lowest-budgeted film can always rely on the living dead as a cheap casting option – the extras playing the zombies reportedly went on strike after they discovered that the meatball sandwiches being laid on by their employers were far from fresh (they'd been salvaged from the trash at a local Mr. Meatball restaurant). The shooting schedule was delayed for a couple of days until alternative catering arrangements were made. See Alan Ormsby's interview on the UK Exploited Video release of *Children Shouldn't Play with Dead Things*.

97 Prisons and zombies have a long history – a cell block being the best or the worst place to be during a zombie outbreak, depending on how you look at it. For more zombies behind bars see: the climactic battle in a deserted prison in *Raiders of the Living Dead* (1985), the LA prison of *Zombie Death House* (1988), the medieval witches prison in *Prison of the Dead* (2000), the zombie chain gang in *Route 666* (2001), Dr West's experiments in *Beyond Re-Animator* (2003), the breeze block cells in cheapo *Living Dead Lock Up* (2005), the zombie riot in *Dead Men Walking* (2005), the women's prison of *Shadow: Dead Riot* (2005), the prison that becomes a fortress in the second season of *The Walking Dead* (2010–) and the ingenious decision to hide out on Alcatraz in *Rise of the Zombies* (2012)… if only the ghouls couldn't swim!

98 Jean Paul Sartre, *No Exit: A Play in One Act*, trans. Paul Bowles (New York: Samuel French, 1958).

99 Chris Rodley ed., *Cronenberg on Cronenberg* (London: Faber and Faber, 1992), p. 43. *Shivers* isn't the only film by Cronenberg to feature monsters similar to zombies. In *Rabid* (1977) porn star Marilyn Chambers heads the cast as a woman with a penile appendage hidden in her armpit and a thirst for blood after a skin-graft operation goes wrong. Her victims turn into zombified blood drinkers who slowly infect the whole of Canada, prompting the panicking authorities to declare a state of emergency reminiscent of that in Romero's *The Crazies* (here the authorities become as "rabid" as the infected citizens). Judging by these two films, Cronenberg obviously enjoys engaging with the apocalypse – and shares Romero's distaste for the oppressive, consumerist order dominating Canada and the US in the 1970s.

100 Paul Gagne, *The Zombies That Ate Pittsburgh: The Films of George Romero* (New York: Dodd, Mead and

Company), p. 55. Gagne's book is by far the best resource for anyone interested in Romero's life and career.

101 Ten years later, Romero put the zombie to similar use in his own portmanteau horror movie, *Creepshow* (1982), which was also conceived as a homage to the EC comics of the 1950s. In the "Father's Day" segment, a mean old patriarch (Jon Lormer) returns as a zombie and kills his daughter, who murdered him on Father's Day after his cranky demands for cake became too much for her. When daddy comes back from the grave, he turns her decapitated head into the very cake he'd been denied, complete with icing sugar and candles. In "Something To Tide You Over", Leslie Nielsen buries his cheating wife (Gaylen Ross) and her lover (Ted Danson) up to their necks in sand on the beach and watches as the tide comes in. Later that night, the adulterous pair return as seaweed-covered corpses – reminiscent of the living dead in *Zombies of Mora Tau* – and subject him to the same fate. The segment ends with Nielsen dementedly screeching, "I can hold my breath a loooooong time!" It's worth noting that portmanteau horror anthologies often rely on the zombie for some cheap and effective storyline padding – although the results can sometimes be dire. The two walking-dead tales in the lamentable collection *Gallery of Horror* (1966) are a suitably egregious example of just that.

102 *Night of the Zombies* (director Joel M. Reed) has several alternative tiles, including *Gamma 693*, *Night of the Wehrmacht Zombies* and even *Night of the Zombies II*. It was released on video in the UK as *The Chilling*, which meant it was often confused with *The Chilling* (director Jack A. Sunseri and Deland Nuse, 1989). The two films are completely different: the first follows a group of Nazi zombies, the second a group of cryogenically frozen corpses who are reanimated by a freak lightning bolt. The only thing they have in common is their total dearth of entertainment value or technical skill. Just to complicate matters, it's worth noting that Reed's *Night of the Zombies* shouldn't be mistaken for Bruno Mattei's *Zombie Creeping Flesh* (1980) – which is also sometimes known as *Night of the Zombies*. Such is the confused and confusing world of living dead cinema.

103 See Peter Blumenstock, "Jean Rollin Has Risen from the Grave!" *Video Watchdog* 31 (1995), 53. According to Pete Tombs and Cathal Tohill, "even by the low-budget standards of Eurociné the film was ultra cheap. At one point technical problems meant that the camera was running slowly, making the filmed action appear speeded up. There was no possibility of getting it fixed and time was precious, so Rollin had to teach the cast to act in slow motion to compensate." See Pete Tohill and Cathal Tombs,

Immoral Tales: European Sex and Horror Movies 1956–1985 (1994. Reprinted New York: St Martin's Griffin, 1994), p. 155. Pete Tombs would later produce and co-write Pakistan's first gore movie *Zibahkhana* (aka *Hell's Ground*, 2007).

104 There seems to be some disagreement over whether the opening sequence is set in London or Manchester. In interview, Grau talks about shooting the opening section in Manchester – his original plan was to shoot in Glasgow because it was a city where "everything was black", but this proved too expensive to justify. However, in the English-language version of the film, a local farmer comments on George being "up from London" (no doubt because of the dub's overripe, cockney accent!). See Jo Botting, "Catalonian Creeps: An Interview with Jorge Grau", *Shivers* 79 (July, 2000), 25. Bizarrely, for a film that has such a strong sense of place, it was later remade in South Korea as *Goeshi* (aka *Strange Dead Bodies*, 1981).

105 Grau claimed that Galbo's terrific performance was partly motivated by the death of her husband a few days before shooting started: "In some ways I took advantage of her state of mind and let her express her real horror of death." See Botting, 25.

106 Ibid., 25.

107 See Frederic Levy, "The Rue Morgue: Looking for French Zombies with Jean Rollin", *Starburst* 4/12 (August 1982), 26.

108 Ibid., 26.

109 See Blumenstock, 52.

110 See Tim Lucas, "Versions and Vampires: Jean Rollin on Home Video", *Video Watchdog* 31 (1995), 28–35.

111 During the course of de Ossorio's quartet, the story occasionally changes: for instance, angry locals burn out the Templars' eyes in *Return of the Blind Dead*.

112 Amando de Ossorio, quoted by Mike Hodges in his obituary "Amando de Ossorio: Farewell to Spain's Knight of Horror", *Shivers* 88 (April, 2001), 19.

113 Ibid, 20.

114 Tohill and Tombs, p. 5.

115 Ibid., p. 53.

116 Nigel J. Burrell, *Knights of Terror: The Blind Dead Films of Amando de Ossorio* (Upton, Cambridgeshire: Midnight Media Publishing, 1995), p. 5.

117 In Jess Franco's unabashed rip off of the *Blind Dead* series, *Mansion of the Living Dead* (orig. *La mansión de los muertos vivientes*, 1982) he indulges in much the same catalogue of sex and death but is much more explicit. Here a group of topless waitresses on a dream holiday to the Canaries find themselves in a deserted hotel with nothing to do but have sex with one another. As punishment for their sins, they are tried, tortured and gang-raped by a group of cowled zombie monks who are apparently damned members of the Spanish Inquisition.

118 Gagne, p. 83.

119 Ibid., p. 97.

120 Gagne, p. 87.

121 Stephen King "The Horrors of '79" *Rolling Stone* (27 December 1979–10 January 1980), 19.

122 Zombies and bikers make strange, but surprisingly common, bedfellows. The British cult horror movie *Psychomania* first introduced the theme in 1972 with its story of a gang of Hell's Angels aptly called The Living Dead, who are brought back from the grave and go on the rampage in the sleepy English countryside. A worthy successor to this was Antony Balch's dementedly camp movie *Horror Hospital* (1973), which featured homoerotic leather-clad biker boys, a gymnasium full of lobotomised zombies and an unlikely starring role for Robin Askwith. In addition to *Dawn of the Dead*, several other American zombie movies have also mixed bikers and zombies: *Kiss Daddy Goodbye* (aka Revenge of the Zombie, 1981), *Chopper Chicks in Zombietown* (1989), *Zombie Cult Massacre* (1997), *Hot Wax Zombies on Wheels* (1999) and *Biker Zombies from Detroit* (2001). Later examples include *Motocross Zombies from Hell* (2007) and the climax of *Dead Moon Rising* (2007).

123 Barry Keith Grant, "Taking Back the Night of the Living Dead: George Romero, Feminism, and the Horror Film", in Grant ed., p. 202.

124 Robin Wood, "Apocalypse Now: Notes on the Living Dead" in Wood and Richard Lippe eds, *American Nightmare: Essays on the Horror Film* (Toronto: Festival of Festivals, 1979), p. 95.

125 Gagne, p. 89.

126 Romero is generally credited with coining the term "splatter" to describe the post-*Night of the Living Dead* horror movie's emphasis on gory special effects that show the human body in various states of decay and rupture. According to horror-movie historian John McCarty, splatter movies offer audiences the chance to see the impact of physical violence "in every minute, blood spurting, bony, sinewy, muscle-exposing detail". The aim is not to scare audiences, "but to *mortify* them with scenes of explicit gore". See McCarty, *Splatter Movies: Breaking the Last Taboo of the Screen* (New York: St Martin's Press, 1984), p. 1.

127 Gagne, p. 100.

128 Roger Ebert, "Review of *Dawn of the Dead*", *Chicago Sun-Times* (20 April, 1979).

129 "Review of *Dawn of the Dead*", *Variety* (18 April, 1979),

22.

130 Janet Maslin, "Review of *Dawn of the Dead*", New York Times (20 April, 1979).

131 Wood, "An Introduction to the American Horror Film", p. 17.

132 Wood, "Apocalypse Now: Notes on the Living Dead", p. 95.

133 Gagne, p. 91.

134 Alan Jones, "Morti Viventi: Zombies Italian-Style", in Allan Bryce ed., *Zombie* (Liskeard, Cornwall: Stray Cat Publishing, 2000), p. 19.

135 Stephen Thrower, *Beyond Terror: The Films of Lucio Fulci* (Guildford, Surrey: FAB Press, 1999), p. 23.

136 The over-eagerness of various producers to set up their product as sequels to Fulci's own unofficial sequel caused quite a few inconsistencies as various films were touted as "Zombie 3" and "Zombie 4" etc., often with little regard for each other or the niceties of chronological order. The video market's habit of retitling these low-rent films to maximise their appeal didn't help, producing a stream of "unofficial" sequels. By the time Fulci eventually got around to making his own sequel, *Zombi 3* (1988), the market was already saturated. Worse still, Fulci's long-awaited follow-up was a terrible disappointment, a truly execrable piece of incompetence that combined inept performances with a ridiculous storyline about a stolen viral agent that turns the infected into zombie-like monsters. The project might have sunk Fulci's already troubled reputation if it were not for rumours that ill health prevented him from actually taking part in much of the shoot – Bruno Mattei apparently replaced him.

137 One filmmaker who has managed to take this combination of sex and horror beyond the merely silly is Canada's David Cronenberg, whose films frequently focus on a form of pornography that's born out of disgust rather than arousal. While Cronenberg is a ferociously intelligent and talented filmmaker whose work bears little resemblance to the technical ineptitude and hopelessly confused narratives that characterise the Italian movies of the period, the thematic similarities between his work and that of the Italian horror's interest in sexual horror are readily apparent. Giving oneself up to the body's pleasures is, in Cronenberg's *Shivers*, the same as becoming a zombie (as the body revolts and overthrows the head). As Cronenberg explains with typical insight: "There's a Latin quote that goes 'Timor mortis conturbat me', which, roughly translated, means, 'The fear of death disturbs me'. Death is the basis of all horror, and for me death is a very specific thing. It's very physical. That's where I become Cartesian. Descartes was obsessed with the schism between mind and body, and how one relates to the other... My films are very body-conscious. They're very conscious of physical existence as a living organism." See Rodley ed., p. 58.

138 Kristeva's theory of abjection is the basis of her seminal work *Powers of Horror: An Essay on Abjection*, trans. Leon S. Roudiez (New York: Columbia University Press, 1982).

139 Ibid., p. 3.

140 Ibid., pp. 3–4.

141 Thrower, p. 163.

142 Robert Schlockoff, "Lucio Fulci", *Starburst* 4/12 (August, 1982), 54.

143 Thrower, pp. 163–64.

144 See Howard Berger, "The Prince of Italian Terror", *Fangoria* 154 (July, 1996), 65, and Luca M. Palmerini and Gaetano Mistretta, *Spaghetti Nightmares: Italian Fantasy Horrors as Seen Through the Eyes of Their Protagonists* (Key West, Florida: Fantasma Books, 1996), p. 54.

145 Thrower, p. 176.

146 Thrower, p. 60.

147 Perhaps one indication of Fulci's iconoclastic treatment of the afterlife is to be found in David Warbeck's anecdote about shooting the Sea of Darkness scenes of *The Beyond*. According to the actor, the bodies that populate the Sea of Darkness were local winos who were drafted in from outside the studio in Rome with the lure of alcohol. "The only way to get them to lie down was to give them booze." See Thrower, p. 160.

148 Plans for a follow-up to *The Beyond* were briefly considered after the original film's success. The provisional title of *The Beyond 2 – Beyond the Beyond* was suggested. The story was set to pick up after Liza and John's disappearance into The Beyond, although given the fact that Fulci envisioned that realm as one of infinite nothingness, it's hard to see what anyone could have come up with in the way of a storyline! The idea for a sequel was finally shelved after Fulci and Warbeck's deaths in 1996 and 1997 respectively.

149 Schlockoff, 54.

150 Ibid., 54.

151 Ibid., 54.

152 Friedrich Nietzsche, *Beyond Good and Evil: Prelude to a Philosophy of the Future*, trans. R.J. Hollingdale (1886. London: Penguin, 1990), p. 102.

153 Thrower, p. 19.

154 Palmerini and Mistretta, p. 59.

155 The fact that *Day of the Dead* takes place in Florida seems significant, the proximity between America's Sunshine State and the Caribbean being particularly

important.

156 Sue Ellen Case, "Tracking the Vampire", in Gelder ed., *The Horror Reader* (London and New York: Routledge, 2000), p. 209.

157 Gagne, p. 155.

158 *Day of the Dead* was originally conceived as a much bigger picture and one that would have required a hefty $16 million budget to realise on screen (far more than anyone was willing to stump up for a picture that was unlikely to receive an MPAA certificate). According to Gagne, the original treatment was to take the zombie revolution "to a point where the living dead have basically replaced humanity and have gained enough of a rudimentary knowledge to be able to perform a few basic tasks. At the same time, an elite, dictatorial politburo of humans has found that the zombies can be trained, and are exploiting them as slaves." The close links between such a scenario and the zombie's Caribbean origins are pretty obvious. See Gagne, p. 147.

159 Brenda Gale Plummer, *Haiti and the United States: The Psychological Moment* (Athens and London, University of Georgia Press, 1992), p. 217.

160 Davis, *The Serpent and the Rainbow*, p. 123.

161 Ibid., p. 130.

162 Gagne, p. 167.

163 Maitland McDonagh, "Sometimes They Come Back… Again: The Making of the *Return of the Living Dead* Trilogy" in Bryce ed., p. 59.

164 One less well-known director who attempted this particular balancing act of horror, comedy and zombies was Robert Scott. His debut *The Video Dead* (1987) concerns a group of zombies who emerge from a cursed black & white TV set. The only thing the TV ever plays is a movie called *Zombie Blood Nightmare* and, if watched for long enough, the zombies eventually crawl out of the screen into the world of the living. Generally hated by the majority of horror fans – some of whom have frequently described it as one of the worst films of the 1980s – it may well be one of the most underrated films of the genre. It's a fun little movie with enough invention to take on the whole *Return of the Living Dead* franchise put together. While most zombie movies take place in houses where the characters are sheltering from the zombies outside, *The Video Dead* begins with the monsters already indoors. Domesticating its zombies with hilarious results (they sit around the kitchen table, muck about with the blender and generally get in the way), *The Video Dead* neatly lampoons the genre. Several very funny sequences pop up among the creepy tension – in one the young hero chases a zombie bride into the woods, tracking her by the sound of the whirling chainsaw she's carrying. Sadly, this writer seems to be the only horror fan who thinks the movie is any good. Filmmaker Scott hasn't done anything since apart from lots of second-unit and assistant-director TV work. Clearly there's no accounting for taste.

165 Students' British Board of Film Classification, "Case Study: *The Evil Dead*", BBFC.com. Online at <http://www.bbfc.co.uk/case-studies/evil-dead>.

166 Meredith Woerner, "First Footage From *The Evil Dead* Reboot. What Does It Mean?" i09.com (16 October 2012). Online at <io9.com/5952201/first-footage-from-the-evil-dead-reboot-what-does-it-mean>.

167 Phil Edwards and Alan Jones, "*The Evil Dead* Speak: An Interview with Sam Raimi and Robert Tapert", *Starburst* 57 (May, 1983), 29.

168 Chas Balun, "*Re-Animator*" *Fangoria* 234 (July, 2004), 31.

169 Maitland McDonagh, "*Re-Animator* and *Bride of Re-Animator*", in Bryce ed., p. 52. Unsurprisingly, the only time the *Return of the Living Dead* franchise ran into serious trouble with the MPAA was when Brian Yuzna took the reins of the third film in the series in 1993.

170 Kim Newman, "Review of *Bad Taste*", *Monthly Film Bulletin* 56/668 (September, 1989), 267–268.

171 Romero's comments to *The Wall Street Journal* are quoted in Michael Frasher, "*Night of the Living Dead*: Remaking George Romero's Horror Classic", *Cinefantastique* 21/3 (December, 1990), 17.

172 Ibid., 17.

173 See Simon Bacal "*Night of the Living Dead*: An Interview with John Vulich and Everett Burrell", *Starburst* 19 Monster Special (April, 1994), 64-66.

174 Mike Watt, "*Night of the Living Dead* 1990", *Cinefantastique* 34 3/4 (June, 2002), 116.

175 Ibid., 117.

176 Barry Keith Grant, "Taking Back the *Night of the Living Dead*: George Romero, Feminism, and the Horror Film" in Grant ed., p. 202.

177 Ibid., p. 208.

178 Neil Fawcett, "Dusk of the Dead" on Home Page of the Dead.com. Online at <www.homepageofthedead.com>.

179 Barnes and Noble, "Interview: George A. Romero" on Barnes&Noble.com (8 August, 2000). Online at <http://video.barnesandnoble.com/search/interview.asp?ctr=> [link defunct].

180 One could argue that serial killer Jason Voorhees is a kind of zombie. Inexplicably resurrected from the lake where he drowned as a child at the end of *Friday the 13th* (1980), Jason went on to terrorise teens through various sequels. In the sixth film, *Friday the 13th Part VI: Jason Lives*

(1986), he was resurrected from the dead again – this time by a freak lightning bolt. Hovering somewhere between serial killer, zombie and Frankenstein's monster, he's certainly far from alive in any conventional sense.

181 Richard King, "J.R. Bookwalter: A Career in B-Movies and Beyond" *Darkstar* 14/15, reprinted online at <http://www.dso.co.uk/intv2.htm>.

182 Sheets, "The Extreme Entertainment Mission Statement" published online at <www.zombiebloodbath.com/mission.html>.

183 Ibid.

184 Jettisoundz, "Scooter MacCrae: The Shatter Boy", Jettisoundz.co.uk. Published online at <http://jettisoundz.co.uk/archive/99/mccrae.htm>.

185 See the sleeve notes to *I, Zombie*'s VHS release on the Screen Edge label.

186 M.J. Simpson, "*Dead Creatures*: Parkinson's Disease", *Fangoria* 206 (September, 2001), 67.

187 Peter Blumenstock, "Michele Soavi: Gravely Speaking", *Fangoria* 149 (January, 1996), 54.

188 Alan Jones, "Dellamorte dellamore", *Cinefantastique* 25/5 (October, 1994), 53.

189 Ibid., 55.

190 Ibid., 55.

191 Kiyoshi Kurosawa's Suito Homu (*Sweet Home*, 1989) was a Poltergeist-style haunted-house movie with special make-up effects by the legendary Dick Smith. Its Nintendo adaptation was a success in Japan, but it was never released internationally. The nearest gaming equivalent was the *Alone in the Dark* series, which began in 1993.

192 Shinji Mikami, "Preface" in *Resident Evil: The Book* (Capcom, 1996), p. 1. Reprinted by Survivhor.com. Online at <www.survivhor.com>.

193 Ibid., p. 2.

194 Shinji Mikami in a 1996 *GamePro* magazine interview reprinted by *Survivor's Guide Network: Total Coverage of Resident Evil*. Online at <www.planetdreamcast.com/residentevil/sections/interviews/ shinji96.htm>. [link defunct]

195 Steven Poole, *Trigger Happy: The Inner Life of Videogames* (London: Fourth Estate, 2000), p. 79.

196 For a thorough dissection of the *jiangshi* see Meijadai Bai, "Chinese Monster and Cultural Identity: Analysis of The Note of Ghoul", in Murali Balaji ed. *Thinking Dead: What the Zombie Apocalypse Means* (Lanham, MA and Plymouth: Lexingham Books, 2013), pp. 105–125.

197 Norman England, "Who Made This Junk?" *Fangoria* 222 (May, 2003), 40.

198 Travis Crawford, "*Wild Zero*: Brain-Dead and Loving It", *Fangoria* 203 (June, 2001), 44.

199 Crawford, "Director Versus Everybody", *Fangoria* 213 (June, 2002),50.

200 The most comprehensive breakdown of the *Resident Evil* movie's development is an excellent timeline written by Rob McGregor and published on Biohaze.com. Online at <http://www.biohaze.com/specials/removie.html>.

201 See McGregor's timeline. Romero's website is now defunct.

202 Romero's distrust of the American studio system is a frequent topic of his conversation in interviews. "Economically, you can't make money on a small scale with a movie in this country", he told *Film Criticism* in 1982. "The small distributors have gone belly up; there's just no competition any more. You can't get screens. It's part of the McDonaldization of America, unfortunately." See John Hanners and Harry Kloman, "'The McDonaldization of America': An Interview with George A. Romero" in *Film Criticism* 7/1 (Fall, 1982), 74.

203 Letter from an anonymous reader, *Fangoria* 203 (June, 2001), 6.

204 Incredibly, Romero was offered the opportunity to direct *Scream*. He turned it down, saying that he couldn't understand "whether it was supposed to be funny or scary". See Anthony C. Ferrante, "Return of the Living Dead Director", *Fangoria* 171 (April, 1998), 22. One wonders what might have been.

205 The chronology of *Resident Evil*'s production can be found in Martin Blaney's article "International Production Case Study: Resident Evil Ground Zero", *Screen International* (5 October, 2001), 18.

206 Paul W.S. Anderson interviewed by Alan Jones in "Resident Evil" *Cinefantastique* 34/2 (April, 2002), 11. As if to emphasise the change in temperament from previous zombie outings, lead actress Milla Jovovich claimed that the reason why she was drawn to the film was because of her younger brother: "Me and my little brother played this game, like, non-stop last summer, and he thinks I'm God for doing this movie." It was a sure sign that the demographic for *Resident Evil* encompassed children and teenagers rather than adult horror fans – and only by keeping the gore to a bare minimum could the film secure a suitable certificate for such an audience. See Steve Grayson "On-Set Report: Resident Evil", *Empire* 145 (July, 2001), 50.

207 In the US, *Resident Evil* was trimmed to avoid the much-stigmatised NC-17 rating (no one under 17 allowed), which is generally considered to be commercial suicide. The film was released with an R-Restricted rating, which allows anyone under 17 to attend as long as an adult accompanies them (in reality cinemas rarely enforce this

with much strictness). In the UK, the film was granted a 15 certificate without further cuts – a sure sign in Britain's current climate of censorship that its "horror" content was relatively mild.

208 Mark Salisbury, "Dead Residents: On the Set of *Resident Evil*", *Total Film* 55 (August, 2001), 8.

209 Mark Salisbury, "To Make the Blood Boyle", *Fangoria* 224 (July, 2003), 21.

210 Danny Boyle, "Soundbite", *SFX* 104 (May, 2003), 85.

211 Alan Morrison, "Rage Against the Machine", *Empire* 161 (November, 2002), 100.

212 Boyle, 85.

213 Andrew Osmond, "In The Hot Zone", *Cinefantastique* 35/3 (Jun/Jul 2003), 39.

214 Simon Pegg, *Shaun of the Dead* Press Conference (London, 29 March 2004).

215 Edgar Wright, *Shaun of the Dead* Press Conference (London, 29 March 2004).

216 Pegg, Press Conference.

217 Ibid.

218 Ibid.

219 Many thanks to Daniel Etherington for sharing this unpublished section of his interview transcript of his one-on-one conversations with Pegg and Wright on 29 March 2004. Etherington's entertaining chat with them about zombies and videogames can be found online at <http://www.bbc.co.uk/dna/collective/A2499744>.

220 Rod Gudino, "The Dead Walk… Again!: A George A. Romero Retrospective", *Rue Morgue* (July/August, 2003), 16.

221 Antony Timpone "Elegy: Controversy Dawns", *Fangoria* 231 (April, 2004).

222 Michael Rowe, "Gunn to the Head", *Fangoria* 231 (April, 2003), 28.

223 Michael Rowe, "New Dawn Rising", *Fangoria* 227 (October, 2003), 45.

224 Entertainment Film Distribution, "UK Publicity Press Notes for *Dawn of the Dead*" (2004).

225 Michael Rowe, "Gunn to the Head", 28.

226 Zombie comics were, of course, nothing new. The 1990s had its fair share of titles including several series based on movies like *Night of the Living Dead*, *Re-Animator* and *Army of Darkness*. There were also other titles including *Dead King*, *Dead in the West* and *Zombie World*.

227 *Land of the Dead* is also the first film in Romero's series to refer to its walking corpses as "zombies", the earlier films pointedly avoided any definition of them as such.

228 Michael Rowe, "*Land of the Dead*: Home of the Grave", *Fangoria* 244 (June, 2005), 53.

229 Todd Gilchrist "*Land of the Dead* on DVD", IGN.com (27 June, 2005). Online at <http://dvd.ign.com/articles/629/629341p1.html>.

230 Rowe, "*Land of the Dead*: Home of the Grave", 54.

231 Mike Gingold, "This LAND is Gore Land", Fangoria. com. Published online at <http://www.fangoria.com/fearful_feature.php?id=2675>.

232 "Fiddler's Green" is also the title of a 19th-century sailor's song about a mythical realm where seafarers who die on land are destined to spend eternity. It was said to be a place of unlimited mirth, tobacco and rum.

233 Rowe, "*Land of the Dead*: Home of the Grave", 51.

234 Ibid., 54.

235 Ibid., 55.

236 Lewis Beale, "The Zombies Brought Him: George Romero Is Back", *The New York Times* (3 November, 2004).

237 Scott Foundas, "Dead Man Talking: The Resurrection of Zombie Godfather George A. Romero", *The Village Voice* (28th June, 2005), 12.

238 Alan Jones, "George of the Dead", *Shivers* 121 (June, 2005), 13.

239 Pegg, Press Conference.

240 Dennis Lim, "Dante's Inferno", *The Village Voice* (22 November, 2005). Online at <http://www.villagevoice.com/2005-11-22/film/dante-s-inferno/>.

241 Joe Dante talking in "Behind the Scenes: The Making of Homecoming", *Masters of Horror: Homecoming* (Anchor Bay, 2006).

242 Olly Blackburn, "Bring Out Your Undead", *The Observer* (2 April, 2006). Online at <http://www.guardian.co.uk/film/2006/apr/02/features.review>.

243 Breck Eisner, Interview with the author (13 November, 2008).

244 Eisner, Interview with the author (13 November, 2008)

245 See "Transcript of President Bush's Speech", *CNN.com* (September 21, 2001). Online at <http://edition.cnn.com/2001/US/09/20/gen.bush.transcript/>.

246 Samuel Zimmerman, "Zombies Of Mass Destruction", *Fangoria* 290 (February, 2010), 14.

247 Matt Zoller Seitz, "Braaaains! The 10 Essential Zombie Films", *Salon.com* 30 May, 2010. Online at <http://www.salon.com/2010/05/30/essential_zombie_films_slide_show/>.

248 Andy Campbell, "Zombie Apocalypse: CDC Denies Existence Of Zombies Despite Cannibal Incidents", The HuffingtonPost.com (1 June, 2012). Online at <http://www.huffingtonpost.com/2012/06/01/cdc-denies-zombies-existence_n_1562141.html>.

249 See US Department for Health and Human Services, Centers for Disease Control and Prevention, *Preparedness*

101: Zombie Pandemic (October 2011). The CDC's graphic novella reassures readers that, in an outbreak of zombies, the authorities would respond in timely fashion. Apparently the gears of big government are so well oiled and efficient that not a single drop of blood would be spilt – and citizens would be saved with a variation on the flu jab! It's available online at <http://www.cdc.gov/phpr/zombies.htm>.

250 Susan Wloszczyna, "Romero's *Diary* Breathes New Life into the Dead", *USA Today* (4 September, 2007). Online at <http://usatoday30.usatoday.com/life/movies/news/2007-09-04-romero-main_N.htm>.

251 The aftermath of Hurricane Katrina in 2005 looked – to a casual viewer watching the TV news from safety, at least – like a zombie movie without zombies. Inevitably, Katrina eventually inspired a few zombie movies including *Storm of the Dead* (2006) and *Zombex* (2013).

252 George Romero, "Syndicated Q&A" (4 March, 2008). Reprinted online at <http://www.eatmybrains.com/showfeature.php?id=77>.

253 Herner Klenthur, "Exclusive George Romero Interview", *Horror Movies.Ca* (no date). Online at <http://www.horror-movies.ca/george-romero-interview/>.

254 Wloszczyna.

255 Alan Jones, "Nervous *[REC]*", *Fangoria* 276 (September, 2008), 36.

256 Roberto E. D'Onofrio, "Jaume Balagueró talks *[REC] 4: Apocalypse*", Fangoria.com (15 November, 2011). Online at <http://www.fangoria.com/index.php/home/all-news/1-latest-news/6058-jaume-balaguero-talks-rec-4-apocalypse>.

257 Jones, 36.

258 Jeremiah Kipp, "*American Zombie*: Mockumentary of the Dead", *Fangoria* 272 (April, 2008), 12.

259 James Whittington, "Exclusive Interview With Keith Wright Director Of *Harold's Going Stiff*", HorrorChannel.com (30 April, 2013). Online at <http://www.horrorchannel.co.uk/articles.php?feature=8194&category=5>.

260 Erica Goode and Nate Schweber, "Case Already Tried in Social Media Heads to Court", *New York Times* (12 March, 2013). Online at <http://www.nytimes.com/2013/03/13/us/steubenville-rape-case-heads-to-trial.html>.

261 Hugh Hart, "Industry Buzz", SFGate.com (13 April, 2008). Online at <http://www.sfgate.com/entertainment/article/INDUSTRY-BUZZ-3219754.php>.

262 Brian Gallagher, "Jay Lee Reveals All in *Zombie Strippers*", Movieweb.com (23 October, 2008). Online at <http://www.movieweb.com/news/exclusive-jay-lee-reveals-all-in-zombie-strippers>.

263 Ibid.

264 Mike Plante, "Chomp!" *Filmmaker* (Fall, 2008), 59.

265 Ariana Speyer, "Up with Bruce LaBruce", *Interview* (February 13, 2009). Online at <http://www.interviewmagazine.com/film/otto-bruce-labruce#_>.

266 Ibid.

267 Dave Itzkoff, "Screening of Gay Zombie Film leads to Police Raid in Australia", *New York Times* (15 November, 2010). Online at <http://artsbeat.blogs.nytimes.com/2010/11/15/screening-of-gay-zombie-film-leads-to-police-raid-in-australia/>.

268 For a full account of *LA Zombie*'s Australian nightmare see Michael Gingold, "Gay Zombie Film Banned in Australia", Fangoria.com (20 July, 2010). Online at <http://www.fangoria.com/index.php/home/all-news/1-latest-news/1503-gay-zombie-film-banned-in-australia>.

269 Plante, 58.

270 Ho Yi. "Movie Review: *Zombie 108*", *Taipei Times* (13 April, 2012). Online at <http://www.taipeitimes.com/News/feat/archives/2012/04/13/2003530202>.

271 Alex Billington, "Exclusive Interview with *Fido* Director Andrew Currie", *FirstShowing.net* (14 June, 2007). Online at <http://www.firstshowing.net/2007/exclusive-interview-with-fido-director-andrew-currie/>.

272 In Malaysian horror comedy *Zombi Kampung Pisang* (2007) the ghoul outbreak begins after a village elder returning from attending evening prayers at the mosque scolds a bunch of wayward kids. He promptly drops down dead. So much for religious authority. Then the head of the village also keels over and, a little later, the resulting horde of talking zombies start forming a collective against the living. A veiled comment on Malaysia's ruling elite, perhaps?

273 Sukhdev Sandhu, "*Zibahkhana*: Beware Zombies Wearing Saris", *Telegraph* (11 August, 2007). Online at <http://www.telegraph.co.uk/culture/film/starsandstories/3667146/Zibahkhana-beware-zombies-wearing-saris.html>.

274 Charu Thakur, "*Rise of the Zombie*: No Threat from *Go Goa Gone* says Luke Kenny", *IBN Live* (5 April, 2013). Online at <http://ibnlive.in.com/news/rise-of-the-zombies-no-threat-from-go-goa-gone-says-luke-kenny/383091-8-66.html>.

275 The horror anthology *V/H/S 2* (2013) took this idea and ran with it. In the segment "A Ride in the Park" by Eduardo Sánchez (co-director of *The Blair Witch Project*), a cyclist is attacked by zombies and becomes one of the walking dead and attacks a little girl's birthday party. The footage is shot almost entirely via his helmet-cam.

276 Sarfraz Manzoor, "My £45 Hit Film: Marc Price on his

Zombie Movie *Colin*", *Guardian* (30 July, 2009). Online at <http://www.guardian.co.uk/film/2009/jul/30/marc-price-zombie-film-colin>.

277 A. D. Barker, "Interview: Marc Price – Director of *Colin*", LiveForFilms.com (June, 2010). Online at <http://www.liveforfilms.com/2011/01/29/interview-marc-price-director-of-colin/>.

278 Christmas themed zombie movies have a rather unedifying history and include: a mismatched threesome hiding out from Santa-dressed ghouls in *Silent Night, Zombie Night* (2009), *A Cadaver Christmas* (2011) in which a janitor fights ghouls on Christmas Eve and *Stalled* (2012), which also has a janitor but inventively restricts the action to an office bathroom during the Christmas party. Worst of the festive bunch is the atrocious *Santa Claus Vs the Zombies* (2010), a DIY effort that's easily one of the most unwatchable films in this book – which is saying something.

279 James Marsh, "Talking Shit: Discussing *Zombie Ass* with director Noboru Iguchi & stars Arisa Nakamura & Demo Tanaka", Twitch.com (8 March, 2012). Online at <http://twitchfilm.com/2012/03/yubari-2012-zombie-ass-interview-noboru-iguchi.html>.

280 Bryan Martinez, "Foreign Horror: An Interview with John Cairns", *Film Deviant* (18 August, 2013). Online at <www.filmdeviant.com/2013/08/foreign-horror-interview-with-john.html>.

281 See Dorothy Pomerantz, "Attack of the Mockbuster Movie: Hobbits, Zombies and 2-Headed Sharks", *Forbes* (22 October, 2012). Online at <http://www.forbes.com/sites/dorothypomerantz/2012/10/03/attack-of-the-mockbustser-movie-hobbits-zombies-and-2-headed-sharks/>.

282 Beth Accomando, "*Pontypool* Interview with Bruce McDonald", KPBS.org (23 June, 2009). Online at <http://www.kpbs.org/news/2009/jun/23/pontypool/>.

283 Ibid.

284 Kurt Halfyard, "An Interview with Tony Burgess", Twitch.com (29 September 2008). Online at <http://twitchfilm.com/2008/09/an-interview-with-pontypool-author-tony-burgess.html>.

285 Chris Alexander "*Pontypool* Speaking of Zombies", *Fangoria* 283 (May, 2009), 62.

286 Anne Billson, "The Great Zombie Sell-Out Some Thoughts About *World War Z*", *Multiglom: The Anne Billson Blog* (22 June, 2013). Online at <http://multiglom.wordpress.com/2013/06/22/zombies-ahoy/>.

287 I was rather taken aback to see that the zombie girl was called "Fresh Slut Zombie" in the credits. On Googling, I came across an angry blog post from a feminist writer who called out the filmmakers for "slut shaming" and objectifying their female zombie even in death. "We have a woman without a bra or wearing short-shorts, or just a woman in general, and we have the male gaze seeing her and sexualizing her—*EVEN IN HER STATE OF DECAY*—and yet *she* is the slut. *She*, in her natural state, who just *happened* to die while bra-less, is the slut. Not the ridiculously disgusting dude in the station wagon who sees decomposing boobs and feels obliged to masturbate to them. Her. The woman who, so sorry, didn't stop and say 'Oh, before I turn into a zombie I better put on some longer shorts and a bra', is the slut. *This* is misogyny. Even in death, women are subject to the whims of patriarchy and rape culture. I wish she had eaten him." It was a smart, spot-on post. But what was even more interesting was the comments that followed it – including input from the filmmakers who had stumbled across the site and felt compelled to explain themselves. Gardner agreed with the author but revealed that the "Fresh Slut Zombie" name had been quickly added to the credits by director of photography Christian Stella – and the actress's husband – who sounded rather mortified by the feedback. See Olivia A. Cole, "*The Battery*: Even Zombies Can Be Sluts", oliviaacolewordpress.com (13 June, 2013). Online at <http://oliviaacole.wordpress.com/2013/06/13/the-battery-even-zombies-can-be-sluts/>.

288 Dudelson had earlier made *Museum of the Dead* (2003), a painfully threadbare zombie horror set on Halloween with a couple of girls trapped in an unconvincing museum set.

289 Michael Compton, "*Night of the Living Dead: Reanimated:* New Life for the Undead." Fangoria.com (4 April, 2010). Online at <http://www.fangoria.com/index.php/moviestv/fearful-features/447-night-of-the-living-dead-reanimated-new-life-for-the-undead>.

290 Matt Donato, "Interview with Douglas Schulze on *Mimesis*",WeGotThisCovered.com (18 February, 2013). Online at <http://wegotthiscovered.com/movies/interview-douglas-schulze-mimesis/>.

291 Marc Bernardin, "*Star Trek*'s Damon Lindelof on Brad Pitt, Having Power as a Writer and His Agony Over *Lost*", *The Hollywood Reporter* (13 June, 2013). Online at <http://www.hollywoodreporter.com/news/star-trek-into-darkness-world-war-z-520992>.

292 See Lev Grossman, "Zombies are the New Vampires", *TIME* magazine (9 April, 2009).

293 Torie Bosch, "First, Eat All The Lawyers", Slate.com (25 October, 2011). Online at <http://www.slate.com/articles/arts/culturebox/2011/10/zombies_the_the_zombie_boom_is_inspired_by_the_economy_.html>.

294 Very few films in this period returned to the idea of the zombie as a living dead worker. *Office of the Dead* (2009) made a broad link between zombies and the economy. *Z108* had a throwaway scene where the movie's pervert villain keeps a gang of chained zombies in his basement to power a sugar mill-esque generator – a nod to *White Zombie*.

295 Michael Hardt and Antonio Negri, *Empire* (London and Cambridge, MA: Harvard University Press, 2000), p. 136.

296 Kirk Boyle, "*Children of Men* and *I Am Legend*: the Disaster-Capitalism Complex Hits Hollywood", *Jump Cut: A Review of Contemporary Media* 51 (Spring, 2009). Online at <http://www.ejumpcut.org/archive/jc51.2009/ChildrenMenLegend/text.html>.

297 Bob Mondello, "*I Am Legend*: A One-Man American Metaphor", NPR.com (14 December, 2007). Online at <http://www.npr.org/templates/story/story.php?storyId=17260869>.

298 Boyle, "*Children of Men* and *I Am Legend*".

299 *Zombieland*'s estimated production budget is taken from BoxOfficeMojo.com.

300 Adrienne Gruben, "Nut Up or Shut Up: Touring through *Zombieland* with screenwriters Rhett Reese & Paul Wernick", Examiner.com (1 October, 2009). Online at <http://www.examiner.com/article/nut-up-or-shut-up-touring-through-zombieland-with-screenwriters-rhett-reese-paul-wernick>.

301 *Zombieland*'s estimated box office is taken from BoxOfficeMojo.com. A belated attempt to turn *Zombieland* into an Amazon-funded web series flopped after it was, in the words of writer Reese, "hated out of existence" by fans. Zach Dionne, "Amazon's *Zombieland* Show Got 'Hated Out of Existence,' Sad Writer Reports", Vulture.com (17 May, 2013). Online at <http://www.vulture.com/2013/05/amazon-zombieland-dead.html>.

302 Meredith Woerner, "Why George Romero Rejected *The Walking Dead* to make *The Zombie Autopsies*", io9.com (19 October, 2011). Online at <http://io9.com/5851502/why-george-romero-rejected-the-walking-dead-to-make-the-zombie-autopsies>.

303 The Deadline Team, "EMMYS: *Walking Dead*'s Frank Darabont", Deadline.com (23 June, 2011). Online at <http://www.deadline.com/2011/06/emmys-the-walking-deads-frank-darabont/>.

304 The choice of material is noted in Scott Meslow's thought-provoking article, "The Post-Apocalyptic Morality of *The Walking Dead*", *Atlantic* (5 March, 2012). Online at <http://www.theatlantic.com/entertainment/archive/2012/03/the-post-apocalyptic-morality-of-the-walking-dead/253986/>. Interestingly the episodic videogame based on the comic produced by TellTale Games – *The Walking Dead*, 2012 – focussed on this idea of making moral decisions and asked players to consider why they chose the options they chose. It proved a smash hit.

305 Paul A. Cantor, "The Apocalyptic Strain in Popular Culture: The American Nightmare Becomes the American Dream", *The Hedgehog Review* 15.2 (Summer 2013). Online at <http://www.iasc-culture.org/THR/THR_article_2013_Summer_Cantor.php>.

306 Bosch, "First, Eat All the Lawyers".

307 Taffy Brodesser-Akner, "Max Brooks Is Not Kidding about the Zombie Apocalypse", *New York Times* (21 June, 2013). Online at <http://www.nytimes.com/2013/06/23/magazine/max-brooks-is-not-kidding-about-the-zombie-apocalypse.html?_r=0>.

308 THR Staff, "Oscar Nominee Brad Pitt On The Unmentionables: Marriage, Politics and Religion", *Hollywood Reporter* (25 January, 2012). Online at <http://www.hollywoodreporter.com/news/brad-pitt-angelina-jolie-oscars-moneyball-tree-of-life-284533>.

309 Andrea Mandell, "Pitt Breaks Silence on Battle to Make *World War Z*", USA Today.com (21 June, 2013). Online at <http://www.usatoday.com/story/life/people/2013/06/20/brad-pitt-world-war-z/2433349/>.

310 *World War Z* figures from BoxOfficeMojo.com.

311 Peter Hall, "Here's How *World War Z* Originally Ended Before the Reshoots", Movies.com (22 June, 2013). Online at <http://www.movies.com/movie-news/world-war-z-original-ending/12638>.

312 Jon C. Ogg, "Zombies Worth Over $5 Billion to Economy", 247WallStreet.com (25 October, 2011). Online at <http://247wallst.com/investing/2011/10/25/zombies-worth-over-5-billion-to-economy/>.

313 Anne Billson, "*World War Z*: The Great Zombie Sell-Out", *Telegraph* (21 June, 2013). Online at <http://www.telegraph.co.uk/culture/film/10110866/World-War-Z-the-great-zombie-sell-out.html>.

314 This interview was conducted on 20 July, 2009.